Lecture Notes in Computer Science 3670

Commenced Publication in 1973
Founding and Former Series Editors:
Gerhard Goos, Juris Hartmanis, and Jan van Le

Mario Bravetti Leïla Kloul
Gianluigi Zavattaro (Eds.)

Formal Techniques for Computer Systems and Business Processes

European Performance Engineering Workshop, EPEW 2005
and International Workshop on Web Services
and Formal Methods, WS-FM 2005
Versailles, France, September 1-3, 2005
Proceedings

Volume Editors

Mario Bravetti
Università di Bologna
Corso di laurea in Scienze dell'Informazione
Via Sacchi 3, 47023 Cesena (FC), Italy
E-mail: bravetti@cs.unibo.it

Leïla Kloul
Université de Versailles
Laboratoire PRiSM
45 Avenue des Etats-Unis, 78000 Versailles, France
E-mail: kle@prism.uvsq.fr

Gianluigi Zavattaro
Universitá di Bologna
Dipartimento di Scienze dell'Informazione
Mura A. Zamboni, 7, 40127 Bologna, Italy
E-mail: zavattar@cs.unibo.it

Library of Congress Control Number: 2005931522

CR Subject Classification (1998): D.2.4, C.2.4, F.3, D.4, C.4, K.4.4, C.2

ISSN 0302-9743
ISBN-10 3-540-28701-9 Springer Berlin Heidelberg New York
ISBN-13 978-3-540-28701-8 Springer Berlin Heidelberg New York

Springer is a part of Springer Science+Business Media

springeronline.com

Printed in Germany

Typesetting: Camera-ready by author, data conversion by Scientific Publishing Services, Chennai, India
Printed on acid-free paper SPIN: 11549970 06/3142 5 4 3 2 1 0

Preface

This volume contains the proceedings of two international workshops EPEW and WS-FM held at the Université de Versailles Saint-Quentin-en-Yvelines, Versailles, France, 1–3 September 2005.

EPEW (European Performance Engineering Workshop) and WS-FM (International Workshop on Web Services and Formal Methods) were colocated to gather the researchers working across the spectrum of techniques for modelling, specification, analysis and verification of the behavior of computer systems and business processes.

This proceedings contains a selection of 20 research contributions, out of 59 submissions, which went through a rigorous review process by international reviewers. We therefore owe special thanks to all members of both program committees of EPEW and WS-FM and their sub-referees for the excellent work they did in the short time they had.

Additionally, this proceedings includes four invited papers, by Gianfranco Ciardo (University of California at Riverside), Peter G. Harrison (Imperial College London), Cosimo Laneve (University of Bologna) and Wil van der Aalst (Eindhoven University of Technology). These contributions brought an additional dimension to the technical and the scientific merit of these workshops.

Finally, our thanks go to the University of Versailles Saint-Quentin-en-Yvelines, its Laboratoire PRiSM and the CNRS for hosting the workshops and providing technical and financial support.

September 2005

Mario Bravetti
Leïla Kloul
Gianluigi Zavattaro

EPEW

The European Performance Engineering Workshop aims to bring together researchers working on all aspects of performance modelling and analysis of computer and telecommunication systems. Of the 32 regular papers submitted to EPEW 2005, after a rigorous review process, only 10 were accepted for presentation. We are very pleased with the quality of these papers and hope that you will find them interesting. The topics of this workshop are various and include queueing theory, bounding techniques, stochastic model checking, communication schemes analysis for high-speed LAN, QoS analysis in wireless ad hoc networks and optical networks analysis.

Workshop Chair

Leïla Kloul	Université de Versailles, France

Program Committee

Jeremy Bradley	Imperial College London (UK)
Mario Bravetti	University of Bologna (Italy)
Tadeusz Czachórski	IITiS PAN, Gliwice (Poland)
Jean-Michel Fourneau	Université de Versailles (France)
Stephen Gilmore	University of Edinburgh (UK)
Holger Hermanns	University of the Saarland (Germany)
Alain Jean-Marie	Université de Montpellier and INRIA (France)
Helen Karatza	Aristotle University of Thessaloniki (Greece)
Leïla Kloul	Université de Versailles (France)
Kim G. Larsen	University of Aalborg (Denmark)
Fernando López Pelayo	Universidad Castilla-La Mancha (Spain)
Raymond Marie	Université de Rennes and IRISA (France)
Andrew Miner	Iowa State University (USA)
Manuel Núñez	Universidad Complutense de Madrid (Spain)
Brigitte Plateau	ID-IMAG, Grenoble (France)
Ramon Puigjaner	Universidad Illes Balears (Spain)
Marina Ribaudo	University of Genoa (Italy)
Mark Squillante	IBM T.J. Watson Research Center, NY (USA)
Nigel Thomas	University of Newcastle (UK)
Fabrice Valois	CITI, INSA Lyon (France)
Katinka Wolter	Humboldt-Universität zu Berlin (Germany)
Wlodek M. Zuberek	Memorial University (Canada)

Additional Referees

D. Barth
D. Cazorla
G. Chiola
F. Cuartero
J.L. Ferrer-Gomila
S. Galmés
C. Guerrero Tomé
U. Harder
P. Harrison
S. Johr
J.P. Katoen
A. Langville
D. Lime
N. López
G. Massone
M.G. Merayo
N. Mezzetti
N. Pekergin
R. Pulungan
I. Rodríguez
P.P. Sancho
I. Sbeity
W.J. Stewart

Local Arrangements Committee

A. Baffert
C. Ducoin
L. Kloul
C. Lequere
A. Mokhtari

Sponsoring Institutions

CNRS
Laboratoire PRiSM
Université de Versailles Saint-Quentin-en-Yvelines

WS-FM

The International Workshop on Web Services and Formal Methods aims to bring together researchers working on Web Services and formal methods in order to activate a fruitful collaboration in this direction of research. This, potentially, could also have a great impact on the current standardization phase of Web Services technologies. This second edition of the workshop (WS-FM 2005) featured 10 papers selected among 27 submissions after a rigorous review process. The main topics of the conference include: protocols and standards for WS (SOAP, WSDL, UDDI, etc.); languages and descripion methodologies for choreography/orchestration/workflow (BPML, XLANG and BizTalk, WSFL, WS-BPEL, etc.); coordination techniques for WS (transactions, agreement, coordination services, etc.); semantics-based dynamic WS discovery services (based on Semantic Web/Ontology techniques or other semantic theories); security, performance evaluation and quality of service of WS; semi-structured data and XML related technologies; and comparisons with different related technologies/approaches.

Workshop Co-chairs

Mario Bravetti	University of Bologna (Italy)
Gianluigi Zavattaro	University of Bologna (Italy)

Program Committee

Marco Aiello	University of Trento (Italy)
Jean-Pierre Banatre	University of Rennes 1 and INRIA (France)
Boualem Benatallah	University of New South Wales (Australia)
Karthik Bhargavan	Microsoft Research, Cambridge (UK)
Manfred Broy	Technische Universität Munchen (Germany)
Roberto Bruni	University of Pisa (Italy)
Michael Butler	University of Southampton (UK)
Fabio Casati	HP Labs (USA)
Rocco De Nicola	University of Florence (Italy)
Schahram Dustdar	Wien University of Technology (Austria)
Gianluigi Ferrari	University of Pisa (Italy)
Jose Luiz Fiadeiro	University of Leicester (UK)
Peter Furniss	Choreology Ltd. (UK)
Stephanie Gnesi	CNR Pisa (Italy)
Reiko Heckel	University of Leicester (UK)
Nickolas Kavantzas	Oracle Co. (USA)

Leïla Kloul	Université de Versailles (France)
Mark Little	Arjuna Technologies Ltd. (UK)
Natalia López	University Complutense of Madrid (Spain)
Roberto Lucchi	University of Bologna (Italy)
Jeff Magee	Imperial College London (UK)
Fabio Martinelli	CNR Pisa (Italy)
Shin Nakajima	National Institute of Informatics and JST (Japan)
Manuel Nunez	University Complutense of Madrid (Spain)
Fernando Pelayo	University of Castilla-La Mancha, Albacete (Spain)
Marco Pistore	University of Trento (Italy)
Wolfgang Reisig	Humboldt University, Berlin (Germany)
Vladimiro Sassone	University of Sussex (UK)
Frank Van Breugel	York University, Toronto (Canada)
Friedrich Vogt	Technical University of Hamburg-Harburg (Germany)

Additional Referees

M. ter Beek
N. Diernhofer
G. Frankova
C. Guidi
W. Knottenbelt
J.C. Laclaustra
A. Lazovik
P. Massuthe
M. Mazzara
H. Melgratti
M.G. Merayo
T. Priol
S. Ripon
B.A. Schmit
E. Tuosto
G. Wimmel

Organizing Committee

M. Bravetti
L. Kloul
R. Lucchi
G. Zavattaro

Sponsoring Institutions

CNRS
Laboratoire PRiSM
Université de Versailles Saint-Quentin-en-Yvelines

Table of Contents

Invited Speakers

EPEW

WS-FM

Performance Engineering and Stochastic Modelling

Peter Harrison

Imperial College London, South Kensington Campus, London SW7 2AZ, UK
pgh@doc.ic.ac.uk

Abstract. Performance engineering has become a central plank in the design of complex, time-critical systems. It is supported by stochastic modelling, a brief history of which is given, going back to Erlang as long ago as 1909. This in turn developed according to successive new generations of communication and computer architectures and other operational systems. Its evolution through queues and networks is reviewed, culminating in the unification of many specification and solution techniques in a common formalism, stochastic process algebra. Recent results are given on the automatic computation of separable solutions for the equilibrium state probabilities in systems specified in such a formalism. A performance engineering support environment is proposed to integrate these methods with others such as response time analysis and fluid models, which are better suited to large scale aggregation of similar components in a continuous space.

1 Introduction

Performance engineering is about the development of efficient computer and communication systems by providing crucial performance analysis during the design phase. For several decades, computer and communication system design was left to 'experienced engineers' who used their knowledge and experience to successfully construct and 'optimise' both hardware and software architectures. These systems grew from simple stand-alone computers, through mainframes with virtual storage management and multi-access, to client-server systems organised as networks of clusters. More recently still we have distributed internet applications and the Grid. Increasingly from the late nineteen eighties/early nineties, the traditional ad hoc approach has been found inadequate in view of the complexity and sheer size of modern systems. This is hardly surprising in view of other engineering disciplines where the construction of an artefact is invariably preceded by the construction of a *model*, usually a mathematical model, upon which design decisions and parameterisations are based. In fact, the moves to 'structured programming', beginning in the 1970s, specialised programming languages and 'formal methods' defined the basis of software engineering which mirrors the conventional engineering paradigm.

The tools of performance engineering are *quantitative models* that predict metrics which reflect a view of performance. This view depends on who's interested. For the user it is some form of quality of service (QoS), often response

M. Bravetti et al. (Eds.): EPEW 2005 and WS-FM 2005, LNCS 3670, pp. 1–14, 2005.

time, reliability or availability. For the owner of a business that sells Grid resources, it is revenue, based more on the number of customers processed per day. Whatever the metric, the whole system needs to be modelled at an appropriate level of detail. There are several modelling techniques, each playing a vital role in different circumstances. An evolving, dynamic system can be considered as passing through a sequence of states that change upon the occurrence of events. Thus, discrete event simulation is the most natural and general modelling formalism since it is possible to mimic in an abstract model the dynamic behaviour of almost any system. The main issues in simulation are reliable interpretation of the simulation outputs, which are essentially sample paths of an underlying stochastic process, and run-time, which may be prohibitively long in detailed simulations and increase rapidly as tighter confidence bands are imposed.

Hence, where possible, analytical models are preferred, based on a mathematical analysis of the stochastic process that precisely describes the dynamics of the system being modelled. The trouble now is that further approximating assumptions must be made to achieve mathematical and numerical tractability. As a rule, the more tractable the model needs to be, the more approximations are necessary. Hence, when using approximate analytical models, validation must be done, often initially mutual validation between the analytical and simulation models. It is typical for an analytical model to be validated against simulation in simple scenarios, resulting in confidence in both models. Then either model can be used to make predictions in more complex cases. As complexity increases, one of the models will ultimately cease to be numerically tractable, but after validation, confidence is high in the surviving model. Indeed, it may be that it is best to validate a simulation in simple cases against an *exact* analytical model and then use that simulation to validate an approximate analytical model, which is the one intended for practical use.

Although analytical models produce precise predictions with respect to their assumptions and approximations, it is not always easy to interpret their output due to subtle properties like interdependence between, and even existence of, model components. Beware of such subtleties! For example, consider the following gamble. Two boxes are placed in front of you with a piece of gold in each. You can keep the gold from either box (your choice) and you have been told there is exactly double the amount of gold in one box than in the other, but you don't know which is which. You are allowed to open one box, look in and then decide which box's contents you want to keep. What should you do? If you find an amount x of gold in the box you open, you know there is either $2x$ or $x/2$ in the other, with equal probability by the symmetry of your random choice of box. So the average amount in the other box is

$$\frac{2x + \frac{x}{2}}{2} = 1.25x$$

Clearly, then, the best strategy is to choose a box at random, open it, and take the gold from the other box! What's wrong with that?

This paper is organised as follows. In section 2, a brief history is given of stochastic modelling, with a somewhat personal view. This begins with the early work of A.K. Erlang and progresses through queues and queueing networks of various kinds up to the present day, not forgetting the underpinnings of A.A. Markov. In section 3, relatively recent advances in the field of stochastic process algebra (SPA) are reviewed and it is shown how these combine many previous, apparently diverse, Markov models into a unified framework. The use of SPA is then argued as a basis for future performance engineering support environments, ideally to be integrated into software engineering support environments. The paper closes in section 6.

2 A Brief History

The origins of stochastic modelling, as applied to communication systems and operations research, is widely credited to A.K. Erlang, who was the first person to consider the problem of telephone networks quantitatively. By studying a village telephone exchange, he worked out a formula, now known as Erlang's formula, to calculate the fraction of callers attempting to call someone outside the village that must wait because all of the lines are in use. Although Erlang's model is a simple one, the mathematics underlying today's complex communication networks is still based on it in many ways. Erlang continued to investigate these problems and published perhaps his best known work "Solution of some Problems in the Theory of Probabilities of Significance in Automatic Telephone Exchanges" in 1917. Meanwhile, the theory underlying many of today's models, including those considered here, was being developed by A.A. Markov, the well known Russian mathematician, who began publishing in the area shortly after the turn of the 20th century; an interesting review of Markov's life and contributions is [1].

More recently, the focus of attention became Markovian networks of queues, with the famous product-form solutions of Jackson (open and closed networks) in 1963 and Gordon & Newell (closed networks) in 1967 [23,15]. These were generalised to multiple classes of customers, with class-dependent service and routing, and queueing disciplines other than first come first served by Baskett et. al. in 1974 and by Kelly at about the same time. Kelly used a different approach based on so-called *quasi-reversibility*, which is defined in terms of the reversed process of a stationary continuous time Markov chain (CTMC) and actually leads to further generalisations, for example to symmetric queues [24]. Interestingly, the reversed process is key to the unified methodology discussed later in this paper.

Various minor extensions were produced in the 1980s, more sophisticated individual queues were analysed and the focus shifted somewhat to approximate methods that required much less restrictive assumptions and so applied to more realistic scenarios. However, at the end of the 1980s, Gelenbe introduced the concept of the *negative customer*, which removes a customer (said to 'kill' one) from a queue rather than adds to it. This model was motivated by inhibitor signals in biological neural networks – these appear discrete in nature rather than continuously varying potentials. Surprisingly, the resulting Markovian network had a product-form solution, with non-linear traffic equations; the traffic equations hitherto had always been linear in product-form solutions. G-networks were considered something of a major departure from previous product-form analyses since the property of 'local balance' [2] no longer held—apart from the traffic equations being non-linear (or perhaps implying this). Prior to the advent of G-networks, many believed that local balance was a necessary condition for a product-form. Subsequently in [14], Gelenbe showed that his traffic equations had unique solutions – the non-linearity made this a problematic claim, in contrast to the previous linear equations. Subsequently, many variations of G-networks were introduced which preserved the product-form. These included triggers, which allow customers to be transferred from one queue to another and resets which allow jumps from a queue's empty state to an 'equilibrium state' in some sense [11,13].

3 Stochastic Process Algebra

Stochastic process algebra (SPA) is an extension of classical process algebra with time delays and probabilities, aimed at providing performance descriptions of concurrent systems. The inherent compositional structure separates the model of a system into successively more fundamental components and, through the interactions among the components, performance characteristics of complex systems can be assessed. In the last decade or so, a number of SPA modelling formalisms have been developed, such as Timed Processes and Performance Evaluation (TIPP) [20], the first process algebra used for performance modelling, and Performance Evaluation Process Algebra (PEPA) [21], which are both Markovian. A generalised, more expressive language, Extended Markovian Process Algebra (EMPA) [4] incorporated immediate actions, chosen probabilistically through *weights*. PEPA is the simplest language, having the fewest combinators, and deals with *agents*, which are syntactic entities denoting *processes*, and *states* in an underlying continuous time Markov chain (CTMC) that constitutes the semantic model. We will refer to both agents together with the *actions* between them and processes, referring respectively to PEPA syntax and CTMC semantics, describing the *transitions* between states.

The Reversed Compound Agent Theorem (RCAT) is a compositional result that uses Markovian process algebra (MPA) to derive the reversed process of certain cooperations between two continuous time Markov chains at equilibrium [16]. From a reversed process, together with the given, forward process, the joint state probabilities follow as a product of ratios of rates in these two processes, yielding a product-form when one exists. RCAT thereby provides an alternative methodology, with syntactically checkable conditions, which unifies many product-forms, far beyond those for queueing networks. As we have already noted, at the time, the original study of G-networks was revolutionary, with no local balance and non-linear traffic equations. In contrast, the RCAT-based approach goes through unchanged—the only difference is that there are now cooperations between two types of departure transitions at different queues, as well as between departure transitions and arrival transitions, as in conventional queueing networks [18].

3.1 Multi-agent Cooperations

In an extension of PEPA, consider now a multiple agent, pairwise cooperation $\underset{L}{\overset{n}{\underset{k=1}{\bowtie}}} P_k$ $(n \geq 2)$, where $L = \bigcup_{k=1}^{n} L_k$ and L_k is the set of synchronising action types that occur in agent P_k. Every action in each of the n agents cooperates with (at most) one other, such that one instance of the action type is active and the other is passive. The semantics of multi-agent cooperation is given in terms of PEPA's dyadic cooperation combinator:

$$\underset{L}{\overset{n}{\underset{k=1}{\bowtie}}} P_k = (\ldots((P_1 \underset{M_2}{\bowtie} P_2) \underset{M_3}{\bowtie} P_3) \underset{M_4}{\bowtie} \ldots \underset{M_{n-1}}{\bowtie} P_{n-1}) \underset{M_n}{\bowtie} P_n$$

where $M_k = L_k \cap \left(\bigcup_{j=1}^{k-1} L_j \right)$.

Notation

$\mathcal{P}_k$: the set of *passive* action types in P_k;
$\mathcal{A}_k$: the set of *active* action types in P_k;
$\mathcal{P}_k^{i\rightarrow}$: the set of action types in L_k that are *passive* in P_k and correspond to transitions *out of* state i in the Markov process of P_k;
$\mathcal{P}_k^{i\leftarrow}$: the set of action types in L_k that are *passive* in P_k and correspond to transitions *into* state i in the Markov process of P_k;
$\mathcal{A}_k^{i\rightarrow}$: the set of action types in L_k that are *active* in P_k and correspond to transitions *out of* state i in the Markov process of P_k;
$\mathcal{A}_k^{i\leftarrow}$: the set of action types in L_k that are *active* in P_k and correspond to transitions *into* state i in the Markov process of P_k;
$\mathcal{P}^{\underline{i}\rightarrow}$: the set of action types in $L = \bigcup_{k=1}^{n} L_k$ that are *passive* and correspond to transitions *out of* state $\underline{i} = (i_1, i_2, \ldots, i_n)$ in the Markov process of $\underset{L}{\overset{n}{\underset{k=1}{\bowtie}}} P_k$;
$\mathcal{P}^{\underline{i}\leftarrow}$: the set of action types in L that are *passive* and correspond to transitions *into* state $\underline{i}$ in the Markov process of $\underset{L}{\overset{n}{\underset{k=1}{\bowtie}}} P_k$;
$\mathcal{A}^{\underline{i}\rightarrow}$: the set of action types in L that are *active* and correspond to transitions *out of* state $\underline{i}$ in the Markov process of $\underset{L}{\overset{n}{\underset{k=1}{\bowtie}}} P_k$;
$\mathcal{A}^{\underline{i}\leftarrow}$: the set of action types in L that are *active* and correspond to transitions *into* state $\underline{i}$ in the Markov process of $\underset{L}{\overset{n}{\underset{k=1}{\bowtie}}} P_k$;
$\alpha_a^{\underline{i}}$: the instantaneous transition rate *out of* state $\underline{i}$ in the Markov process of $\underset{L}{\overset{n}{\underset{k=1}{\bowtie}}} P_k$ corresponding to *active* action type $a \in L$;

$\top_a$: the unspecified rate associated with the action type a in the action $(a, \top_a)$;
$\boldsymbol{x}$: the vector $(x_{a_1}, \ldots, x_{a_m})$ of positive real variables x_{a_i} when $L = \{a_1, \ldots, a_m\}$;
$\overline{\beta_{\overline{a}}^{\underline{i}}(\boldsymbol{x})}$: the instantaneous transition rate *out of* state $\underline{i}$ in the reversed Markov process of $\bowtie_{k=1, L}^{n} P_k\{\top_a \leftarrow x_a \mid a \in L\}$ corresponding to *passive* action type $a \in L$; note that a is *incoming* to state $\underline{i}$ in the forwards process. We also write $\overline{\beta_{k;a}^{i_k}(\boldsymbol{x})} \equiv \overline{\beta_{\overline{a}}^{\underline{i}}(\boldsymbol{x})}$ where P_k is the component in which a is passive (incoming to state i_k).

The Multiple Agent Reversed Compound Agent Theorem (MARCAT) defines the reversed agent of an n-way cooperation under appropriate conditions, together with a product-form solution for its steady state probabilities, when equilibrium exists.

Theorem 1. *(MARCAT)*
Suppose that the cooperation $\bowtie_{k=1, L}^{n} P_k$ *of agents* P_k*, denoting stationary Markov processes, has a derivation graph*[1] *with an irreducible subgraph* G*. Given that*

(a) every instance of a reversed action, type $\overline{a}$*, of an* active *action type* $a \in \mathcal{A}_k$ *has the same rate* $\overline{p_a}$ *in* $\overline{P_k}$ $(1 \le k \le n)$*,*

(b)

$$\sum_{a \in \mathcal{P}^{\underline{i}\rightarrow}} x_a - \sum_{a \in \mathcal{A}^{\underline{i}\leftarrow}} x_a = \sum_{a \in \mathcal{P}^{\underline{i}\leftarrow} \setminus \mathcal{A}^{\underline{i}\leftarrow}} \overline{\beta_{\overline{a}}^{\underline{i}}(\boldsymbol{x})} - \sum_{a \in \mathcal{A}^{\underline{i}\rightarrow} \setminus \mathcal{P}^{\underline{i}\rightarrow}} \alpha_{\overline{a}}^{\underline{i}} \tag{1}$$

the reversed agent $\overline{\bowtie_{k=1, L}^{n} P_k}$*, with derivation graph containing the reversed subgraph* $\overline{G}$*, is*

$$\bowtie_{k=1, L}^{n} \overline{R_k}\{(\overline{a}, \top) \mid a \in \mathcal{A}_k\}$$

where

$$R_k = P_k\{\top_a \leftarrow x_a \mid a \in \mathcal{P}_k\} \qquad k = 1, \ldots, n$$

$\{x_a\}$ *are the unique solutions (for* $\{\top_a\}$*) of the* rate equations

$$\{\top_a = \overline{p_a} \mid a \in \mathcal{A}_k, 1 \le k \le n\} \tag{2}$$

and $\overline{p_a}$ *is the symbolic rate of action type* $\overline{a}$ *in* $\overline{P_k}$*.*

Furthermore, assuming the cooperation set L *is finite, the cooperation has product-form solution* $\pi(\underline{i}) \propto \prod_{k=1}^{n} \pi_k(i_k)$ *for the equilibrium probability of state* $\underline{i} = (i_1, \ldots, i_n)$*, where* $\pi_k(i_k)$ *is proportional to the equilibrium probability of state* i_k *in* R_k*.*

The proof verifies Kolmogorov's criteria for reversed processes (as for the original RCAT and its extension [16,19]) and is given in full in [17].

[1] As defined in PEPA's semantics [21].

3.2 Conditions of the Theorem

In its most general form, equation 1 of theorem 1 is a complex condition to check—prohibitively so in large (and especially infinite) state spaces. This is because it must hold in every joint state of the cooperation. However, in important special cases checking is straightforward or trivial—for example when the passive actions are 'invisible', leading from a state to itself, whereupon the term $\overline{\beta_{\underline{a}}^{\underline{i}}(\boldsymbol{x})} = x_a$ [19]. More generally, it is typical for equation 1 to hold for all values of the rates $\boldsymbol{x}$; we will require this property when we consider the existence of solutions to the rate equations in section 3.3.

Most importantly, in applications of the original RCAT of [16], extended to multiple cooperations, all passive actions are outgoing from every joint state of the cooperation and all active actions are incoming to every joint state. The condition is then satisfied trivially since the terms on the left hand side cancel and those on the right are both empty sums. This is only to be expected since we could have generalised RCAT directly without introducing new constraints. In particular, MARCAT applies to all of the standard queueing networks, including G-networks and their extensions.

A sufficient set of n conditions to replace equation 1 is, for each k, $1 \leq k \leq n$:

$$\sum_{a \in L_k \cap \mathcal{P}^{\underline{i}\rightarrow}} x_a - \sum_{a \in L_k \cap \mathcal{A}^{\underline{i}\leftarrow}} x_a = \sum_{a \in L_k \cap (\mathcal{P}^{\underline{i}\leftarrow} \setminus \mathcal{A}^{\underline{i}\leftarrow})} \overline{\beta_{\underline{a}}^{\underline{i}}(\boldsymbol{x})} - \sum_{a \in L_k \cap (\mathcal{A}^{\underline{i}\rightarrow} \setminus \mathcal{P}^{\underline{i}\rightarrow})} \alpha_{\underline{a}}^{\underline{i}} \tag{3}$$

for all valid joint states $(i_1, \ldots, i_n)$ in the irreducible chain G of theorem 1. Summing equation 4 over k yields precisely double equation 1 since synchronisations are pairwise: every action type appears in exactly two of the sets L_k $(1 \leq k \leq n)$. In simpler form, this equation can be written:

$$\begin{aligned}\sum_{a \in \mathcal{P}_k^{i_k\rightarrow}} x_a + \sum_{a \in \mathcal{P}_{k^a}^{i_k\rightarrow}} x_a - \sum_{a \in \mathcal{A}_k^{i_k\leftarrow}} x_a - \sum_{a \in \mathcal{A}_{k^a}^{i_k\leftarrow}} x_a = \\ \sum_{a \in \mathcal{P}_k^{i_k\leftarrow} \setminus \mathcal{A}_{k^a}^{i_k\leftarrow}} \overline{\beta_{k;a}^{i_k}}(\boldsymbol{x}) + \sum_{a \in \mathcal{P}_{k^a}^{i_k\leftarrow} \setminus \mathcal{A}_k^{i_k\leftarrow}} \overline{\beta_{k;a}^{i_k}}(\boldsymbol{x}) \\ - \sum_{a \in \mathcal{A}_k^{i_k\rightarrow} \setminus \mathcal{P}_{k^a}^{i_k\rightarrow}} \alpha_{\underline{a}}^{\underline{i}} - \sum_{a \in \mathcal{A}_{k^a}^{i_k\rightarrow} \setminus \mathcal{P}_k^{i_k\rightarrow}} \alpha_{\underline{a}}^{\underline{i}}\end{aligned} \tag{4}$$

where P_{k^a} is the component agent that synchronises with the action a in P_k. Thus, even the worst case requires only checking actions component-wise—the number of checks is of the order of the product of the numbers of local states in each component process, not combinatorial in these numbers. Moreover, the states of a component process will usually be parameterised in the process algebraic specification, e.g. a queue of positive length corresponds to the PEPA agent P_{n+1} and the empty queue to P_0, giving just two parameterised states. The actual number of checks required is the product of the numbers of *parameterised* states.

3.3 Existence and Uniqueness of a Solution

Under quite mild conditions, MARCAT's rate equations have a solution, which is unique (when it can be normalised) by the uniqueness of the equilibrium probabilities of Markov chains. In particular, it is easy to verify that most queueing networks, certainly all variants of G-networks and BCMP networks, have solutions since they possess a certain strongness property, referred to below.

Theorem 2. *In the cooperation* $\underset{L}{\overset{n}{\underset{k=1}{\bowtie}}} P_k$ *of stationary Markov processes* P_k*, defined in theorem 1, the equations for* x_a*,* $a \in \mathcal{A}_k(L_k), 1 \leq k \leq n$*,*

$$x_a = \overline{p_a}\{\top_b \leftarrow x_b \mid b \in L\}$$

where $\overline{p_a}$ *is the reversed rate of* a*, have a unique solution if for each* k*,* $1 \leq k \leq n$ *:*

$$\begin{aligned}\sum_{a \in L_k \cap \mathcal{P}^{\underline{i}\rightarrow}} x_a - \sum_{a \in L_k \cap \mathcal{A}^{\underline{i}\leftarrow}} x_a \\ = \sum_{a \in L_k \cap (\mathcal{P}^{\underline{i}\leftarrow} \setminus \mathcal{A}^{\underline{i}\leftarrow})} \overline{\beta_a^{\underline{i}}(\boldsymbol{y})} - \sum_{a \in L_k \cap (\mathcal{A}^{\underline{i}\rightarrow} \setminus \mathcal{P}^{\underline{i}\rightarrow})} \alpha_a^{\underline{i}}\end{aligned}$$

for all positive vectors $\boldsymbol{y}$ *and provided that at least one active action* $o \in \mathcal{A}^{\underline{i}\leftarrow}$ *is strongly split for all states* $\underline{i}$*.*

Notice that the first condition automatically satisfies the condition of theorem 1 (at $\boldsymbol{y} = \boldsymbol{x}$) and that the second condition is checkable by the hypothesis that the reversed agents of the components P_k are known. The term 'strongly split' is a technical device, essentially meaning that a split action does not become vanishingly small for large $\boldsymbol{y}$; see [17].

3.4 Automation and Implementation

The implementation takes as input the description of a top-level cooperation of MARCAT-compliant processes and executes several rounds to produce the stationary probabilities, $\boldsymbol{\pi}$. Notice that the current implementation is recursive, using nested pairs of cooperating agents rather than applying MARCAT directly. Although somewhat slower for large, non-hierarchical networks, the approach is more general, handling models organised as nested clusters, typical of contemporary architecture design. Extension to reflect MARCAT directly is relatively straightforward and is viewed as an optimisation.

The phases in the algorithm are as follows:

Parsing. We convert the textual description of the processes into an associative array of process descriptors, their outbound transitions and their destination process-names.

The input format is an augmented version of the plain PEPA format where we have also allowed a process descriptor to have subscripts $\boldsymbol{i}, \boldsymbol{j}, \boldsymbol{k}$, which may be referred to as subscripts in the successor process (derivative). i, j, k are assumed to range from zero upwards and in the successor may only be incremented or decremented by a constant integer. This enables us to specify many useful processes with infinite, regular state spaces, while keeping the definition relatively simple.

We store the processes as a keyed, associative array. This ensures that in the later stages we only ever need to walk a structure the size of the description, never the size of the state-space. This is especially important since we are not necessarily working with a finite state-space.

Testing Conditions. The tool performs basic checking that the processes used are well-formed (that successor states are defined) and that they satisfy the conditions for MARCAT – exactly as specified in theorem 1 (with $n = 2$ components) and section 3.2. In the current version, we require that actions of a given type used in pairwise cooperations are all-passive in one half of their cooperation and all-active in the other; this is analogous to the original RCAT of [16].

Forming the Reverse Process. Taking the two-component cooperation, $P_1 \underset{L}{\bowtie} P_2$, for example, we form the reversed process as $\overline{R_1} \underset{L}{\bowtie} \overline{R_2}$, where

$$R_i = P_i\{\top_a \leftarrow x_a \mid a \in \mathcal{P}_i\}$$

for $i = 1, 2$, as per theorem 1. We insert these x_a as unknowns in the definition of the reversed process and construct the rate equations. These equations are known to have a solution by theorem 2 (under its given conditions) but it is not always known symbolically. In the case of standard queueing networks, the rate equations are linear (traffic equations) and an explicit solution can be found in simple cases. However, since a unique solution is known to exist, it makes more sense to leave the x_a as symbolic variables, which can be substituted by particular values by a numerical rate equation solver in particular numerical applications.

By holding the definition of the forward process as a list of tuples, forming the reversed process is cheap — proportional to the number of individual component definitions, not the number of component states, or any combination of the components.

Deriving Stationary Occupation Probabilities. Finally, the generators of the individual, reparameterized component-processes, $\overline{R_k}$, are computed, leading to their own (local) equilibrium state probabilities, as detailed in theorem 1. These yield the factors in the product-form solution for the (unnormalised) stationary probabilities of the joint process.

4 Illustrative Example

Consider an M-node G-network [12], with respective positive/negative external arrival rates $\lambda_1, \ldots, \lambda_M / \Lambda_1, \ldots, \Lambda_M$, service rates $\mu_1, \ldots, \mu_M$, and positive/negative routing probabilities p_{ij} / n_{ij} from node i to node j ($1 \leq i \neq j \leq M$), where $p_{ii} = n_{ii} = 0, \sum_{j=1}^{M} p_{ij} + \sum_{j=1}^{M} n_{ij} \leq 1$. Tasks leave the network from node i with probability $p_{i0} = 1 - \sum_{j=1}^{M}(p_{ij} + n_{ij})$. We do not consider departures from a node back to itself as this is considered part of the definition of the component process for that node. Such departures can be included easily with more complex components.

This network can be described by the PEPA expression $\underset{L}{\overset{M}{\underset{k=1}{\bowtie}}} P_{k,0}$ (starting with an empty network), where, for $1 \leq k \leq M$:

$$
\begin{array}{ll}
P_{k,n} = (e_k, \lambda_k).P_{k,n+1} & n \geq 0 \\
P_{k,n} = (f_k, \Lambda_k).P_{k,n-1} & n > 0 \\
P_{k,n} = (a_{jk}, \top_{jk}).P_{k,n+1} & n \geq 0, 1 \leq j \neq k \leq M \\
P_{k,n} = (b_{jk}, \top_{jk}).P_{k,n-1} & n > 0, 1 \leq j \neq k \leq M \\
P_{k,n} = (d_k, p_{k0}\mu_k).P_{k,n-1} & n > 0 \\
P_{k,n} = (a_{kj}, p_{kj}\mu_k).P_{k,n-1} & n > 0, 1 \leq j \neq k \leq M \\
P_{k,n} = (b_{kj}, n_{kj}\mu_k).P_{k,n-1} & n > 0, 1 \leq j \neq k \leq M
\end{array}
$$

with $L_k = \{a_{jk}, b_{jk} \mid j \neq k\}$. The action types e_k, f_k represent external arrivals (positive and negative, respectively), and a_{jk}, b_{jk} represent customers passing from node j to node k after a service completion at node j (positive and negative, respectively). In the sequel, we use the abbreviations $\top_{ij}$ for $\top_{a_{ij}}$, $\top'_{ij}$ for $\top_{b_{ij}}$, x_{ij} for $x_{a_{ij}}$ and x'_{ij} for $x_{b_{ij}}$, $1 \leq i \neq j \leq M$. It would have been just as easy in principle to define a much more complex G-network with resets, triggers and batches, as considered in two-node networks in [18] for example, but the PEPA definition would have been much longer and, perhaps, obscure. The correct traffic equations would emerge via the rate equations in exactly the same way, however.

In this example, we add 'invisible transitions' to ensure negative arrivals have no effect on an empty queue. These are given by $P_{k,0} = (b_{jk}, \top_{jk}).P_{k,0}$ for $1 \leq j \neq k \leq M$ and have no effect on the semantics of the queue. Thus $\mathcal{P}^{i\rightarrow} = \mathcal{A}^{i\leftarrow} = \bigcup_{k=1}^{M} L_k$ satisfying condition (b) of theorem 1 trivially (this is, of course, an application of the multi-agent version of the original, two-component RCAT [16]). Every instance of the reversed action of an active action with type $a_{ij} \in \mathcal{A}_i$ ($1 \leq i \neq j \leq M$) has (symbolic) rate which is a constant fraction $p_{ij}\mu_i/(\mu_i + \Lambda_i + \sum_k \top'_{ki})$ of the net arrival rate at the M/M/1 queue represented by component i since every active action represents a departure from some queue. Hence, considering the symbols $\top_{ki}, \top'_{ki}$ as variables denoting real rates in preparation for an application of MARCAT,

$$\overline{p_{a_{ij}}} = \frac{p_{ij}\mu_i\left(\lambda_i + \sum_k \top_{ki}\right)}{\mu_i + \Lambda_i + \sum_k \top'_{ki}}$$

at all instances of a_{ij} since λ_i is state-independent. Similarly,

$$\overline{p_{b_{ij}}} = \frac{n_{ij}\mu_i\left(\lambda_i + \sum_k \top_{ki}\right)}{\mu_i + \Lambda_i + \sum_k \top'_{ki}}$$

We can therefore apply MARCAT and obtain the following equations in the variables x_{ij}, x'_{ij} :

$$x_{ij} = \frac{p_{ij}\mu_i\left(\lambda_i + \sum_k x_{ki}\right)}{\mu_i + \Lambda_i + \sum_k x'_{ki}}$$
$$x'_{ij} = \frac{n_{ij}\mu_i\left(\lambda_i + \sum_k x_{ki}\right)}{\mu_i + \Lambda_i + \sum_k x'_{ki}}$$

These equations have a solution by theorem 2. Now let $v_i = \lambda_i + \sum_{k=1}^{M} x_{ki}$ and $v'_i = \Lambda_i + \sum_{k=1}^{M} x'_{ki}$ for $1 \leq i \leq M$. (Recall there are no actions a_{ii} or b_{ii}.) Then these equations reduce to

$$x_{ij} = \frac{p_{ij}\mu_i v_i}{\mu_i + v'_i}$$
$$x'_{ij} = \frac{n_{ij}\mu_i v_i}{\mu_i + v'_i}$$

i.e. after summing over i

$$v_j - \lambda_j = \sum_i \frac{p_{ij}\mu_i v_i}{\mu_i + v'_i}$$
$$v'_j - \Lambda_j = \sum_i \frac{n_{ij}\mu_i v_i}{\mu_i + v'_i}$$

These are precisely the non-linear traffic equations obtained for G-networks by Gelenbe in [10]. Skipping the calculation of the reversed process itself for brevity, the agents R_k of theorem 1 are immediately seen to be $M/M/1$ queues, with arrivals corresponding to any actions that increment the state and service completions corresponding to any actions that decrement it. Thus the total arrival rate is $\lambda_k + \sum_{j=1}^{M} x_{jk} = v_k$ and total service rate is $\mu_k + \Lambda_k + \sum_{j=1}^{M} x'_{jk} = \mu_k + v'_k$. Hence an unnormalised equilibrium probability for state i_k in the process denoted by R_k is

$$\left(\frac{v_k}{\mu_k + v'_k}\right)^{i_k}$$

Gelenbe's theorem then follows directly, for either an open or a closed network, i.e. the equilibrium probability for state $\underline{i}$ in the network is proportional to

$$\prod_{k=1}^{M} \left(\frac{v_k}{\mu_k + v'_k}\right)^{i_k}$$

Notice how, in complex networks with non-linear rate equations, it is easy to check that a solution exists using theorem 2, rather than by using a customised analysis.

5 Environments for Performance Engineering

The preceding section attempted to motivate the use of Stochastic Process Algebra (SPA) as a formalism for specifying performance models, because it has great expressive power yet loses little in terms of being unable to recognise known model structures, missing efficient, established solutions. Hitherto, this had been a major criticism of the idea. Nevertheless, the MPA subset considered is clearly not enough for a general performance specification language. Moreover, the world does not need more specification languages. What is needed is a unified formalism that can describe both qualitative (functional) properties and quantitative (performance) properties. The level of abstraction should be as high as possible, compatible with high level programming languages or, better, higher level program specification languages. One prime candidate is UML which is now widely used in industry. Many attempts have been made to decorate UML with a quantitative description facility, for example by Woodside, Pooley and others [3,25,26]. Our suggestion is to follow this trend and to use an SPA, with the PEPA-based Markovian subset used here, as an intermediate formalism, an 'abstract machine' in compiler terminology.

The correctness of a system could be established by analysing the functional behaviour of the formal specification, either by transforming out its stochastic components and using classical verification techniques, or by direct analysis. Both analytical and simulation models could be generated by suitable compilation of the SPA intermediate specification; this might involve the extraction and subsequent analysis of a Generalised Semi-Markov Process for the latter. The proposed approach obviates the need for separate frameworks for quantitative and qualitative analysis and, by construction, ensures that all analysis is consistent with respect to the single high-level specification.

There are many other mathematical methods used in stochastic modelling not touched on here. Some of these can be incorporated under the SPA umbrella, for example the computation of moments and quantiles of time delay probability distributions; response times are perhaps the most important QoS metric and quantiles are frequently specified, for example in hospital A&E units as well as in the TPC OLTP-benchmarks. Considerable research has also been done on continuous state models, for example fluid flow, Brownian motion and diffusion approximations. To accommodate this, it is proposed to develop a fluid-MPA. In this, the evolution of a component's (real number) state is given by its derivative with respect to time, defined by a sum of *rate* terms, analogous to conventional action-rates in PEPA. Fluid models operate in a Markov environment, defining fluctuating rate-functions, and interact through internal rates that depend on the current state of other components. Known techniques for solving the corresponding systems of differential equations could be applied, involving basic dynamical systems theory. This will lead, in the simplest case, to linear systems, which can be solved by standard spectral techniques when homogeneous. One objective here is to find a compositional solution akin to MARCAT. Otherwise, the main issues are to determine stability, perhaps by identifying Liapunov functions using the fluid-MPA, and to develop (parallel) numerical solution algorithms. It is also important to investigate second-order models, cf. Brownian motion, so that the random fluctuations characterising diffusion can be accounted for.

6 Conclusion

The case has been made for performance engineering environments supported by stochastic modelling, akin to and to be integrated into software engineering environments supported by formal methods in theoretical computer science. It was also suggested that SPA was a natural unifying formalism for many stochastic modelling methodologies, a claim supported by the use of a PEPA-based MPA to find many classes of product-form solutions through the Multiple Agents Reversed Compound Agent Theorem (MARCAT). This methodology has been automated, to a large extent, to facilitate the uniform derivation of many diverse separable solutions—not all pure product-form. These applications range from multi-class queueing networks, through the numerous variants of G-networks, to networks with mutual exclusion and blocking in critical sections [5]. The automated solution is currently restricted to actions that can cooperate in only two agents at a time, e.g. representing departures from one queue passing to another. The method of [18] will be applied to handle multiple, instantaneous transitions in chains of components, but in addition, ongoing research is investigating the possibility that one active action can cooperate with several passive actions simultaneously. This would not only induce an alternate approach to triggers but could also account for other types of simultaneous movement of customers in queueing networks, as in [7] for example.

References

1. G.P. Basharin, A.N. Langville and V.A. Naumov. The life and work of A.A. Markov. *J. Linear Algebra and its Applications*, 386:3-26, July 2004.
2. F. Baskett, K. M. Chandy, R. R. Muntz and F. Palacios, Open, Closed and Mixed Networks of Queues with Different classes of Customers, J. ACM, 22(2):248-260, 1975.
3. A.J. Bennett, A.J. Field and C. M. Woodside. Experimental Evaluation of the UML Profile for Schedulability, Performance and Time. In proc UML 2004, Lisbon, Springer-Verlag Lecture Notes in Computer Science (LNCS 3273):143-157, 2004.
4. M. Bernardo, L. Donatiello and R. Gorrieri. Integrating performance and functional analysis of concurrent systems with EMPA, Proc. of the 1st Workshop on Distributed Systems: Algorithms, Architectures and Languages, pp. 5-6, Levico (Italy), June 1996.
5. R.J. Boucherie. A Characterisation of Independence for Competing Markov Chains with Applications to Stochastic Petri Nets. IEEE Transactions on Software Engineering, 20(7):536–544, July 1994.

6. E. Brockmeyer, H.L. Halstrom and Arns Jensen. *The life and works of A.K. Erlang.* The Copenhagen Telephone Company, 1948.
7. X. Chao, M. Miyazawa and M. Pinedo. *Queueing networks: customers, signals and product form solutions.* Wiley, 1999
8. A.K. Erlang. The Theory of Probabilities and Telephone Conversations. Nyt Tidsskrift for Matematik B, 20, 1909.
9. A.K. Erlang. Solution of some Problems in the Theory of Probabilities of Significance in Automatic Telephone Exchanges. Elektrotkeknikeren, 13, 1917.
10. E. Gelenbe. Random neural networks with positive and negative signals and product form solution. *Neural Computation*, 1(4):502–510, 1989.
11. E. Gelenbe. G-networks with triggered customer movement. *Journal of Applied Probability*, 30:742–748, 1993.
12. E. Gelenbe, The first decade of G-networks, European Journal of Operational Research, 126(2): 231-232, October 2000.
13. E. Gelenbe and J.-M. Fourneau. G-networks with resets. In *Proceedings of PERFORMANCE '02*, Rome, 2002, *Performance Evaluation*, 49:179–191, 2002.
14. E. Gelenbe and R. Schassberger. Stability of product form G-networks. *Probability in the Engineering and Informational Sciences*, 6:271–276, 1992.
15. William J. Gordon and Gordon F. Newell, Closed Queueing Systems with Exponential Servers, Operations Research, 15(2): 254-265, Mar-Apr 1967.
16. P.G. Harrison. Turning Back Time in Markovian Process Algebra. Theoretical Computer Science, 290(3):1947-1986, January 2003.
17. P.G. Harrison. Separable equilibrium state probabilities via time reversal in Markovian process algebra. Theoretical Computer Science, 2005, under review.
18. P.G. Harrison. Compositional reversed Markov processes, with applications to G-networks. *Performance Evaluation*, 57(3):379-408, July 2004.
19. P.G. Harrison. Reversed processes, product forms and a non-product form. *J. Linear Algebra and its Applications*, 386:359-382, July 2004.
20. H. Hermanns, M. Rettelbach, and T. Wei. Formal Characterisation of Immediate Actions in SPA with Nondeterministic Branching. The Computer Journal, 38(7):530-541, 1995.
21. Jane Hillston. A Compositional Approach to Performance Modelling. PhD thesis, University of Edinburgh, 1994.
22. J. Hillston and N. Thomas. Product form solution for a class of PEPA models. *Performance Evaluation*, 35:171–192, 1999.
23. J. R. Jackson. Jobshop-like queueing systems. Management Science, 10(1):131-142, 1963.
24. F.P. Kelly. Reversibility and Stochastic Networks. John Wiley & Sons Ltd, 1979.
25. P.J. B. King and R. Pooley. Derivation of Petri Net Performance Models from UML Specifications of Communications Software. Tools and Techniques for Computer Performance Evaluation (TOOLS 2000), Chicago, pp262-276, 2000.
26. Dorin B. Petriu and Murray Woodside. A Metamodel for Generating Performance Models from UML Designs. In proc UML 2004, Lisbon, Springer-Verlag Lecture Notes in Computer Science (LNCS 3273):143-157, 2004.

Implicit Representations and Algorithms for the Logic and Stochastic Analysis of Discrete–State Systems*

Gianfranco Ciardo

Department of Computer Science and Engineering,
University of California, Riverside,
CA 92521, USA
ciardo@cs.ucr.edu

As discrete–state systems are pervasive in our society, it is essential that we model and analyze them effectively, both prior to putting them in operation and during their useful life. The size of their state space, however, is a huge obstacle in practice. Often, the "easy" way to tackle this problem is to use some type of simulation, but this technique has obvious limitations. For performance analysis, simulation can at best offer only a statistical approximation, i.e., confidence intervals, while, for logic analysis, the situation is even worse, as it can only find errors, not prove correctness. Ultimately, these limitations stem from the same source: simulation only visits a fraction of the reachable states. Indeed, the fraction of the states that can actually be explored in a reasonable amount of time becomes exponentially smaller as the complexity of the system being modeled (measured in number of components, parts, etc.) increases.

One way to attack this problem is to employ *implicit representations* whose memory and time requirements are often much less than linear in the number of states of the system under study. In this context, two techniques emerged in the mid '80s are particularly relevant.

- Since the introduction of *binary–decision diagrams* (BDDs) [1], *symbolic* algorithms have proven themselves very effective for the verification of discrete–state systems, especially digital hardware and protocols. Systems with 10^{20} or more states have become amenable to exact logic analysis, leading to the wide adoption of *model checking* by major hardware and software vendors.
- In an apparently distant area of research, the structure of a Markovian discrete system has been exploited to develop a *Kronecker algebra* representation of the infinitesimal generator matrix of the system [11]. By avoiding the need to store this matrix, which is the largest data structure required for a steady–state or transient analysis of a Markov model, systems with a factor of 10 or more states can be studied than with ordinary sparse–storage methods. While this improvement is not as impressive as that of symbolic model

* Work supported in part by the National Science Foundation under grants CNS-0501747 and CNS-0501748.

M. Bravetti et al. (Eds.): EPEW 2005 and WS-FM 2005, LNCS 3670, pp. 15–17, 2005.

checking, the idea has spurred much research and further advancements in the two decades following its introduction.

BDDs, Kronecker representations, and several other variants that have been introduced in the literature can all be seen as *implicit* representations of vector or matrices, as opposed to *explicit* representations; the fundamental difference between the two being that, when using the latter, the memory, hence time, requirements are always at least proportional to the number of (nonzero) entries in the vector or matrix being stored, while the former is enormously more efficient in many cases.

In this talk, we first survey and organize several types of decision diagrams which can be employed for logic or Markov analysis, and briefly illustrate important algorithms that manipulate them, from fixed–point algorithms used in state–space generation [3,7] and CTL model checking [6] to vector–matrix multiplications [2] needed for the numerical solution of a Markov model: *multiway decision diagrams* (MDDs) [12], *multi–terminal decision diagrams* (MTBDDs, MTMDDs) [8], *additive or multiplicative edge–valued decision diagrams* (EVBDDs, EV^{+}MDDs and EV*MDDs) [9,5], *matrix diagrams* (MxDs) [4,10], and a new variant particularly efficient when storing matrices, *identity–reduced decision diagrams.*

Then, we focus on the need for approximate solutions of Markov models that have been encoded implicitly. This is an important challenge to be tackled, because, while we can analyze the logic behavior and even encode the infinitesimal generator of systems with huge state spaces, the exact numerical solution of the underlying Markov model still requires the storage of an explicit probability vector in practice. We present some known results, and discuss potential research directions.

References

1. R. E. Bryant. Graph-based algorithms for boolean function manipulation. *IEEE Trans. Comp.*, 35(8):677–691, Aug. 1986.
2. P. Buchholz, G. Ciardo, S. Donatelli, and P. Kemper. Complexity of memory-efficient Kronecker operations with applications to the solution of Markov models. *INFORMS J. Comp.*, 12(3):203–222, 2000.
3. G. Ciardo, R. Marmorstein, and R. Siminiceanu. Saturation unbound. In H. Garavel and J. Hatcliff, editors, *Proc. Tools and Algorithms for the Construction and Analysis of Systems (TACAS)*, LNCS 2619, pages 379–393, Warsaw, Poland, Apr. 2003. Springer-Verlag.
4. G. Ciardo and A. S. Miner. A data structure for the efficient Kronecker solution of GSPNs. In P. Buchholz, editor, *Proc. 8th Int. Workshop on Petri Nets and Performance Models (PNPM'99)*, pages 22–31, Zaragoza, Spain, Sept. 1999. IEEE Comp. Soc. Press.
5. G. Ciardo and R. Siminiceanu. Using edge-valued decision diagrams for symbolic generation of shortest paths. In M. D. Aagaard and J. W. O'Leary, editors, *Proc. Fourth International Conference on Formal Methods in Computer-Aided Design (FMCAD)*, LNCS 2517, pages 256–273, Portland, OR, USA, Nov. 2002. Springer-Verlag.

6. G. Ciardo and R. Siminiceanu. Structural symbolic CTL model checking of asynchronous systems. In W. Hunt, Jr. and F. Somenzi, editors, *Computer Aided Verification (CAV'03)*, LNCS 2725, pages 40–53, Boulder, CO, USA, July 2003. Springer-Verlag.
7. G. Ciardo and J. Yu. Saturation-based symbolic reachability analysis using conjunctive and disjunctive partitioning. In *Proc. CHARME*, Saarbrücken, Germany, Oct. 2005. Springer-Verlag. To appear.
8. M. Fujita, P. C. McGeer, , and J. C.-Y. Yang. Multi-terminal binary decision diagrams: an efficient data structure for matrix representation. *Formal Methods in System Design*, 10:149–169, 1997.
9. Y.-T. Lai, M. Pedram, and B. K. Vrudhula. Formal verification using edge-valued binary decision diagrams. *IEEE Trans. Comp.*, 45:247–255, 1996.
10. A. S. Miner. Efficient solution of GSPNs using canonical matrix diagrams. In R. German and B. Haverkort, editors, *Proc. 9th Int. Workshop on Petri Nets and Performance Models (PNPM'01)*, pages 101–110, Aachen, Germany, Sept. 2001. IEEE Comp. Soc. Press.
11. B. Plateau. On the stochastic structure of parallelism and synchronisation models for distributed algorithms. In *Proc. ACM SIGMETRICS*, pages 147–153, Austin, TX, USA, May 1985.
12. A. Srinivasan, T. Kam, S. Malik, and R. K. Brayton. Algorithms for discrete function manipulation. In *Int. Conference on CAD*, pages 92–95. IEEE Comp. Soc. Press, 1990.

PiDuce: A Process Calculus with Native XML Datatypes*

Allen L. Brown Jr.[1], Cosimo Laneve[2], and L. Gregory Meredith[3]

[1] Microsoft Corporation, Redmond, Washington, USA
[2] Department of Computer Science, University of Bologna, Italy
[3] Harvard Medical School, Boston, USA and Djinnisys Corporation, Seattle, USA

Abstract. We develop the static and dynamic semantics of PiDuce, a process calculus with XML values, schemas, and pattern matching. PiDuce values include channel names, therefore the structure of values may not reveal anything about their schemas. This is problematic in the pattern matching algorithm because it requires to verify whether a schema of a channel is a subschema of a pattern. Such a verification has exponential cost, in general. In order to reduce the computational complexity of the pattern matching, channel schemas are constrained to occur in tail positions of sequences and to be labelled-determined.

1 Introduction

The π-calculus has been introduced as a basic formalism for modelling concurrent systems [19]. Its data language is quite simple: only tuples of channel names are admitted. Extensions of the basic model with datatypes, such as integers, booleans, and lists, as well as with polymorphism, have been already explored [18,21]. In this paper we continue this research by investigating an extension of π-calculus with values and datatypes that closely approximates standard values and datatypes of the web: XML documents and XML schemas, respectively.

Our extension of π-calculus, called PiDuce, has values that may contain channels – a role often played by Uniform Resource Identifiers (URIs) in the web –, as in π-calculus and in XML instances. Correspondingly, datatypes, called schemas, may contain types describing collections of channels that carry messages of similar structure. For instance, the following PiDuce fragment

$$\overline{x}[u] \;\mid\; x(v : \langle \texttt{Int} \rangle).\, \overline{v}[5]$$

consists of two processes in parallel: the process on the left outputs the channel u on x, the process on the right receives a channel carrying integers – this is indicated by the schema $\langle$Int$\rangle$ – and outputs 5 on it. If the input and output on x communicate, the value 5 will be emitted on u.

* Aspects of this investigation conducted at the University of Bologna were supported in part by a Microsoft initiative in concurrent computing and web services.

M. Bravetti et al. (Eds.): EPEW 2005 and WS-FM 2005, LNCS 3670, pp. 18–34, 2005.

PiDuce also retains mechanisms for constructing and deconstructing values. Construction is performed by tagging existing values and putting them in sequence. Deconstruction is achieved by patterns and pattern matching. For instance, the fragment

$$\overline{x}[a[\mathtt{5}]\,\mathtt{,}\,b[\mathtt{4}]] \ \mid\ x(a[u:\mathtt{Int}]\,\mathtt{,}\,b[v:\mathtt{Int}]).\,\overline{z}[c[v]\,\mathtt{,}\,d[u]]$$

exchanges the document $a[\mathtt{5}]\,\mathtt{,}\,b[\mathtt{4}]$ during the communication on x, grasps the values 5 and 4 by means of the pattern $a[u : \mathtt{Int}]\,\mathtt{,}\,b[v : \mathtt{Int}]$, and constructs a new value $c[\mathtt{4}]\,\mathtt{,}\,d[\mathtt{5}]$, which is emitted on the channel z.

By combining input choices and patterns it is possible to write sophisticated processes in PiDuce. For instance, the fragment:

$$u(v : S).\,P \ +\ u(v : T).\,Q$$

selects the continuation P or Q according to the received value has schema S or T, respectively. (The choice is nondeterministic if the received value matches with both.) The selection is performed by the pattern matching algorithm that parses the value according to the structure of the pattern. This algorithm has a cost that is proportional to the product of the sizes of the pattern and of the received value, when such a value does not contain channels. When the received value contains a channel, as when it is x, the pattern matching reduces to computing the subschema relation between the schema of x and those of $v : S$ and $v : T$. In turn, this relation calculates a language inclusion and it is decidable because PiDuce schemas define *regular tree languages*.

However the subschema relation has exponential cost in the size of the schemas [17] and this cost may significantly degrade the run-time efficiency of possible implementations since pattern matching is liberally used in PiDuce. To circumvent this problem, channel schemas are restricted to occur in tail position of sequences and to be *labelled-determined*, that is they have a deterministic model as regards labelled transitions (the model is nondeterministic as regards channel transitions). PiDuce labelled-determined schemas admit a subschema relation with a polynomial computational complexity [8].

The subschema relation, which is original to this contribution, uses a "simulation relation" in the style of [3,20]. In particular, we associate handles to schemas and, in order to derive that S is a subschema of T, we verify that the handles of S are (recursively) contained into the handles of T. The containment goes straight to the structure of the handles when schemas are labelled-determined. Otherwise the structure is not powerful enough. To illustrate the problem, let $S = (a + b)[\mathtt{Int} + \mathtt{String}]\,\mathtt{,}\,c[\mathtt{Int}]$ and $T = a[\mathtt{Int}]\,\mathtt{,}\,c[\mathtt{Int}] + a[\mathtt{String}]\,\mathtt{,}\,c[\mathtt{Int}] + b[\mathtt{Int} + \mathtt{String}]\,\mathtt{,}\,c[\mathtt{Int}]$. It turns out that $S <: T$ however, to demonstrate this, one has to pick one addend of T, let it be $T' = a[\mathtt{Int}]\,\mathtt{,}\,c[\mathtt{Int}]$, compute the difference of S and T', and show that this difference is in T. In this case the difference is $a[\mathtt{String}]\,\mathtt{,}\,c[\mathtt{Int}] + b[\mathtt{Int} + \mathtt{String}]\,\mathtt{,}\,c[\mathtt{Int}]$ and it is clearly contained in T.

PiDuce possesses a static semantics ensuring that invalid terms can never be produced. This is achieved by a careful control over the interplay between the schemas of the messages and the schemas declared for the channels carrying them. It is worth noticing that, due to the subschema relation, the static semantics also entails subtyping polymorphism. The static semantics is demonstrated to be sound; this yields a subject reduction property (a well-typed process transits to well typed processes) and a progress property (a well-typed process does not get stuck).

Related Works. `PiDuce` has been strongly influenced by `XDuce`, a functional language for `XML` processing [12]. In `XDuce`, values do not carry channels, and the subschema relation is never needed at run-time. Our paper may also be read as an investigation of the extension of `XDuce` values and schemas with channels.

Several integrations of processes and semistructured data have been studied in recent years. Two similar contributions, that are contemporary and independent to this one, are [10,2]. The schema language in [10] is the one of [5] plus the channel constructors for input, output, and input-output capability. No apparent restriction to reduce the computational complexity of pattern matching is proposed. The schema language of [2] is simpler than the that of `PiDuce`. In particular recursion is omitted and labeled schemas have singleton labels.

Other contributions integrating semistructured data and processes are discussed in order. `TulaFale` [6], a process language with `XML` data, is especially designed to address web services security issues such as vulnerability to `XML` rewriting attacks. The language has no static semantics. The integration of `PiDuce` with the security features of `TulaFale` seems a promising direction of research. X$d\pi$ [11] is a language that supports dynamic web page programming. This language is π-calculus with locations plus the explicit primitives for process migration, for updating data, and for running a script. The emphasis of X$d\pi$ is towards behavioral equivalences and analysis techniques for behavioral properties. A similar contribution to [11] is Active `XML` [1] that uses an underlying model consisting of a set of peer locations with data and services.

Structure of the Paper. We proceed as follows. We introduce `PiDuce` in Section 2, together with a few examples to elucidate the syntactic constructs, and motivate our design choices. We examine the static semantics of `PiDuce` in Section 3, and we discuss the motivations supporting its design. We introduce the dynamic semantics in Section 4 and we demonstrate a soundness theorem in Appendix A. We conclude with Section 5 where we also discuss few current directions of research.

2 PiDuce

The syntax of `PiDuce` includes the categories *labels*, *values*, *schemas*, *patterns*, and *processes* that are defined by the rules in Table 1. Several countably infinite sets are used in the syntax: the set of *tags*, ranged over by $a, b, \cdots$; the set of *variables*, ranged over by $u, x, \cdots$; the set of *schema names*, ranged over by $\mathtt{U}, \mathtt{V}, \cdots$.

Table 1. Syntax of PiDuce

$L ::=$		**label**
	a	(tag)
	~	(wildcard label)
	$L + L$	(union)
	$L \setminus L$	(difference)
$V ::=$		**value**
	$()$	(void)
	u	(variable)
	$a[V]$	(labelled value)
	$a[V],V$	(sequence)
$F ::=$		**pattern**
	S	(schema)
	$u : F$	(variable pattern)
	$L[F]$	(labelled pattern)
	$L[F],F$	(sequence pattern)

$S ::=$		**schema**
	$()$	(void schema)
	$\langle S \rangle$	(channel schema)
	$L[S]$	(labelled schema)
	$L[S],S$	(labelled sequence sch.)
	$S + S$	(union schema)
	$\mathtt{U}$	(schema name)
$P ::=$		**process**
	$\mathbf{0}$	(nil)
	$\overline{u}[V]$	(output)
	$\sum_{i \in I} u_i(F_i).P_i$	(input choice)
	$P \mid P$	(parallel)
	$(u : \langle S \rangle)P$	(new)
	$!P$	(replication)

Labels. Labels specify collections of tags. The semantics of labels is defined by the following function $\widehat{\cdot}$:

$$\widehat{a} = \{a\} \qquad \widehat{\sim} = L \qquad \widehat{L + L'} = \widehat{L} \cup \widehat{L'} \qquad \widehat{L \setminus L'} = \widehat{L} \setminus \widehat{L'}$$

We write $a \in L$ for $a \in \widehat{L}$.

Values. PiDuce values are the set of terms V containing $()$, variables and sequences of elements that are labelled values with the tailing element that may be a labelled value or a variable. For example $a[v],u$ or $a[u],b[()]$ are values, whilst $a[u],()$ or $u,a[()]$ are not values. Variables are either channels or represent placeholders to be instantiated with other values. Channels play an operational role similar to that played by URIs when the latter are used as endpoints for communicating with web services. For example

$$\mathit{message}[\mathit{title}[()], \mathit{chan}[u]]$$

is a value containing an empty title and a channel u. This channel could be used by the receiver, for instance, to send back an acknowledgment. In the following $a[()]$ is always shortened to $a[\,]$.

Schema. Schemas describe sets of values that are structurally similar. The schema $()$ describes the value $()$; $\langle S \rangle$ describes channels that carry messages of schema S; $L[S]$ describes the values $a[V]$ such that $a \in L$ and V is of schema S; $L[S],S'$ describes values $a[V],V'$ where $a[V]$ and V' are of schema $L[S]$ and S', respectively (when S' describes $()$, the schema $L[S],S'$ also includes the values described by $L[S]$); $S + S'$ describes values that are in S or in S'. The schema $\mathtt{U}$ describes the least set of values such that $\mathtt{U} = \mathbb{E}(\mathtt{U})$, where $\mathbb{E}$ maps schema names to schemas and fulfils the following finiteness property. Let *names*(S) be the least set containing the schema names in S and such that if $\mathtt{U} \in names(S)$ then $names(\mathbb{E}(\mathtt{U})) \subseteq names(S)$. A map $\mathbb{E}$ is *finite* if, for every $\mathtt{U} \in \mathtt{dom}(\mathbb{E})$, the set $names(\mathtt{U})$ is finite. We notice that this property implies that PiDuce schemas define *tree regular languages* [17].

For example, the schema that collects booleans is $\mathtt{true}[\mathtt{()}] + \mathtt{false}[\mathtt{()}]$; the schema that collects an emptyset of values is Empty defined by Empty = Empty; the schema that collects any channel, no matter what it can carries, is $\langle\mathtt{Empty}\rangle$; the schema that collects all the values is Any defined by $\mathtt{Any} = \mathtt{()} + \sim[\mathtt{Any}]\mathtt{,Any} + \langle\mathtt{Empty}\rangle$. We observe that $\langle\mathtt{Empty}\rangle$ and $\langle\mathtt{Any}\rangle$ are very different. $\langle\mathtt{Empty}\rangle$ refers to any channels, $\langle\mathtt{Any}\rangle$ refers only to channels that can carry arbitrary data. For instance $\langle a[\mathtt{()}]\rangle$ is an $\langle\mathtt{Empty}\rangle$ but not an $\langle\mathtt{Any}\rangle$. As for values, the schema () in $L[\mathtt{()}]$ will be always omitted.

PiDuce channel schemas $\langle S\rangle$ are such that S is *labelled-determined*, according to the next definition. Let μ range over internal schema representations (), $\langle\rangle(S)$, $L(S\ ;\ T)$ and let $S \downarrow \mu$, read S *has a handle* μ, be the least relation such that:

$\mathtt{()} \downarrow \mathtt{()}$	
$\langle S\rangle \downarrow \langle\rangle(S)$	
$L[S] \downarrow L(S\ ;\ \mathtt{()})$	if $\widehat{L} \neq \emptyset$ and there is μ such that $S \downarrow \mu$
$L[S]\mathtt{,}T \downarrow L(S\ ;\ T)$	if there are μ, μ' such that $L[S] \downarrow \mu$ and $T \downarrow \mu'$
$S + T \downarrow \mu$	if $S \downarrow \mu$ or $T \downarrow \mu$
$\mathtt{U} \downarrow \mu$	if $\mathbb{E}(\mathtt{U}) \downarrow \mu$

We observe that Empty has no handle. The schema $a[\,]\mathtt{,Empty}$ has no handle as well; the reason is that a sequence has an handle provided that every element of the sequence has an handle. We also remark that a channel $\langle S\rangle$ always retains an handle. A schema S is *not-empty* if and only if S has a handle; it is *empty* otherwise.

Definition 1. *The set* ldet *of* labelled-determined schemas *is the least set containing empty schemas and such that:*

1. $\mathtt{()} \in \mathtt{ldet}$;
2. *if* $S \in \mathtt{ldet}$ *then* $\langle S\rangle \in \mathtt{ldet}$ *and* $L[S] \in \mathtt{ldet}$;
3. *if* $S \in \mathtt{ldet}$ *and* $T \in \mathtt{ldet}$ *then* $L[S]\mathtt{,}T \in \mathtt{ldet}$;
4. *if* $S \in \mathtt{ldet}$ *and* $T \in \mathtt{ldet}$ *and, for every* $S \downarrow L(S'\ ;\ S'')$ *and* $T \downarrow L'(T'\ ;\ T'')$, $L \cap L' = \emptyset$ *then* $S + T \in \mathtt{ldet}$;
5. *if* $\mathbb{E}(\mathtt{U}) \in \mathtt{ldet}$ *then* $\mathtt{U} \in \mathtt{ldet}$.

For example, $a[S] + (\sim \setminus a)[T]$ and $\sim[S] + \langle S\rangle + \langle T\rangle$ are labelled-determined schemas. The schemas $a[\,]+(a+b)[\,]$ and $\langle a[\,]+\sim[\,]\rangle$ are not labelled-determined.

We observe that the labelled-determinedness restriction will be applied to channel schemas only. For instance, $a[\,] + \sim[\,]$ is a legal PiDuce schema. We also recall that labelled-determinedness and the syntactic constraint that channel schemas always occur in tail positions of sequences entail a polynomial algorithm for language inclusion of channel schemas [8]. As discussed in the introduction, this is fundamental for an efficient pattern matching algorithm (see also Section 3).

Patterns. Patterns allow the deconstruction of values using matching. The pattern S is matched by values of schema S. A variable $u : F$ can be bound in the course of matching to a value described by the schema represented by F (see below). For example, $u : a[\;] + b[\;]$ may bind values such as $a[\;]$ or $b[\;]$; $u : \langle a[\;]\rangle$ may bind any channel value of schema $\langle a[\;]\rangle$, but it does not bind a channel value of schema $\langle a[\;] + b[\;]\rangle$; the pattern $u : a[v : b[\;]]$ binds two variables at the same time: u to values of schema $a[b[\;]]$ and v to values of schema $b[\;]$. The pattern $L[F]$ is a shorthand for $L[F]\texttt{,}\texttt{()}$; $L[F]\texttt{,}F'$ is matched by values of the form $a[V]\texttt{,}V'$, with $a \in L$ and V and V' match with F and F', respectively. The pattern $L[F]\texttt{,}F'$ is also matched by values $a[V]$ if $a[V]$ matches with $L[F]$ and $\texttt{()}$ matches with F'.

The *schema represented* by a pattern F, in notation $\texttt{schof}(F)$ is defined inductively by

$$\begin{aligned}
\texttt{schof}(S) &= S \\
\texttt{schof}(u : F) &= \texttt{schof}(F) \\
\texttt{schof}(L[F]) &= L[\texttt{schof}(F)] \\
\texttt{schof}(L[F]\texttt{,}F') &= L[\texttt{schof}(F)]\texttt{,}\texttt{schof}(F')
\end{aligned}$$

PiDuce patterns retain the following *well-formedness* properties:

1. *linearity with respect to variables*: variables occurring in a pattern do not clash;
2. *not-emptiness*: patterns F are such that $\texttt{schof}(F)$ is always not-empty. (Patterns such as u : Empty are excluded because they are practically useless and theoretically troublesome (see Proposition 2 and Theorem 1).)

Processes. Processes define the set of computing entities in PiDuce. **0** is the idle process; $\overline{u}[V]$ outputs the value V on the channel u; $\sum_{i \in I} u_i(F_i).P_i$ inputs on the channel u_i a value that matches with F_i yielding a substitution σ and behaves as $P\sigma$. The family I in the input choice is assumed to be finite. The process $(u{:}\langle S\rangle)P$ defines a new channel u and binds it within the continuation P; $!P$ is the process that always spawns copies of P. The channels u in $\overline{u}[V]$ and u_i in $\sum_{i \in I} u_i(F_i).P_i$ are called *subjects* of output and input, respectively.

As it is usual in concurrent calculi, the choice in the process $\sum_{i \in I} u_i(F_i).P_i$ is unordered. For example, the process

$$\begin{aligned}
&\mathit{print}(u : \texttt{File}).\,\overline{\mathit{printbw}}[u] \\
&+ \mathit{print}(u : \texttt{Picture}).\,\overline{\mathit{printc}}[u] \\
&+ \mathit{print}(u : \texttt{Any}).\,\overline{\mathit{error\text{-}handler}}[u]
\end{aligned}$$

takes a value on the channel print, and forwards it either to the black and white printer if it matches with File, or to the color printer if it matches with Picture, or to an error-handler, otherwise (File and Picture are two schema names). However it may be the case that the branch $\mathit{print}(u : \texttt{Any}).\,\overline{\mathit{error\text{-}handler}}[u]$ is picked, even if a file or a picture is received because such values also match with Any. Said otherwise, input choices badly express a standard pattern matching mechanism of programming languages, the first-matching semantics. When

`PiDuce` is turned into a real concurrent programming language it should be extended with a native first-matching mechanism (indeed, this is the case in [9]).

`PiDuce` processes retain the *output capability* property: every channel received in input may be used in the continuation either as subject of outputs, or within values.

Free and Bound Variables. The set $\mathtt{fv}(\cdot)$ is defined for values, patterns, and processes as follows:

$\mathtt{fv}(V)$: is the set of variables occurring in V;

$\mathtt{fv}(F)$: is the set of variables occurring in F;

$\mathtt{fv}(P)$: is the set of variables occurring in P and, recursively, in the bodies of the constant invocations, that are not *bound.* An occurrence of x in P is *bound* in the input $u(F).P$ if $x \in \mathtt{fv}(F)$; an occurrence of u in P is *bound* in $(u\!:\!S)P$. Bound variables are noted $\mathtt{bv}(\cdot)$.

The definitions of α-conversion and substitution for bound variables are standard.

Design Remarks. The design of the `PiDuce` schema and pattern languages, as well as most of the algorithms regarding these features, has been strongly influenced by the `XDuce` [12] and `CDuce` [5] prototypes. The differences are discussed in order.

`PiDuce` schemas omit primitive schemas, such as `integer` and `string`, but these may be added without any difficulty. For simplicity sake, schemas such as $(S+T)$,R are also excluded, while they are admitted by the formalism in [13]: such schemas would have entangled the definition of labelled-determinedness. A major departure with respect to the schema in the above languages (and in `XML` DTDs or in `XML` Schema) is entailed by the channel schemas, which are new. These schemas are used in `PiDuce` to verify the correct use of channels.

In `PiDuce` processes, channels that are received in input can be used in the continuations only with *output capability.* Such output capability means that a process receiving a channel cannot redefine that channel by accepting additional inputs meant for that channel (a reasonable constraint in web services). Output capability plays an important role in the static semantics because it entails subtyping polymorphism in schemas that include channel schemas.

3 The Static Semantics

We begin with the basic notion of subschema; the static semantics of values and of processes are defined afterwards.

Subschema. The semantic definition of subschema in [12] does not adapt well to `PiDuce`. In particular, since values contain channels, in order to verify that a channel u belongs to a schema S, one is reduced to verifying that the schema of

u is a subschema of S. To circumvent this circularity we use an "operational" definition – a *simulation* relation – in the style of [3,20].

The subschema relation uses handles defined in Section 2 to manifest all the branches of the syntax tree of a schema and to get rid of useless () elements. In the following definition we use the intersection operator on labels: $L \cap L' \stackrel{\text{def}}{=} \sim \setminus ((\sim \setminus L) + (\sim \setminus L'))$.

Definition 2. *The* subschema relation <: *is the largest relation on schemas such that S <: T implies:*

1. *if $S \downarrow ()$ then $T \downarrow ()$;*
2. *if $S \downarrow \langle\rangle(S')$ then $T \downarrow \langle\rangle(T')$ and T' <: S';*
3. *if $S \downarrow L(S' \,;\, S'')$ then $T \downarrow L'(T' \,;\, T'')$ with $\widehat{L} \cap \widehat{L'} \neq \emptyset$ and:*
   (a) *either $\widehat{L} \subseteq \widehat{L'}$, S' <: T', and S'' <: T'';*
   (b) *or $(L \setminus L')[S'], S'' + (L \cap L')[R'], S'' + (L \cap L')[S'], R''$ <: T, for some R' and R'' such that S' <: $T' + R'$ and S'' <: $T'' + R''$.*

We notice that, in the definition of S <: T, when $S \downarrow L(S' \,;\, S'')$ and T is labelled-determined, case *3.(b)* reduces to $(L \setminus L')[S'], S''$ <: T. For example it is easy to verify that $a[\,]$ <: $a[\,] + b[\,]$ and $\langle a[\,] + b[\,]\rangle$ <: $\langle a[\,]\rangle$. The definition of subschema allows us to derive that $c[a[\,]+b[\,]], (d[\,]+e[\,])$ is a subschema of $T = c[a[\,]], d[\,] + c[b[\,]], (d[\,]+e[\,]) + c[a[\,]], e[\,]$. In particular, since $T \downarrow c(a[\,] \,;\, d[\,])$, one may reduce the problem to verifying that $c[R'], (d[\,]+e[\,]) + c[a[\,]+b[\,]], R''$ <: T with $R' = b[\,]$ and $R'' = e[\,]$. The relationship $c[b[\,]], (d[\,]+e[\,])$ <: T is immediate because it is the second addend of T. As regards $c[a[\,]+b[\,]], e[\,]$ <: T we observe that $T \downarrow c(b[\,] \,;\, d[\,] + e[\,])$. This reduces to the verification of $c[a[\,]], e[\,]$ <: T, which is true because $c[a[\,]], e[\,]$ is the third addend of T.

A few properties of <: are in order.

Proposition 1. *1.* <: *is reflexive and transitive;*
2. *(Contravariance of $\langle\cdot\rangle$) S <: T if and only if $\langle T\rangle$ <: $\langle S\rangle$;*
3. *For every S,* `Empty` <: S <: `Any` *and* $\langle$`Any`$\rangle$ <: $\langle S\rangle$ <: $\langle$`Empty`$\rangle$.

The computational complexity of the subschema relation. Let $\|S\|$ be the *size* of the schema S, namely the size of the syntax tree of S, plus the sizes of the syntax trees of $\mathbb{E}(\mathtt{U})$ such that $\mathtt{U} \in$ *names*(S). The computational complexity of S <: T is exponential in $\|S\|$ and $\|T\|$ ([17], chapter 1). When S and T are labelled-determined schemas that do not contain channel constructors, there is an algorithm (using tree automata) for computing S <: T whose computational complexity is $O(\|S\| \times \|T\|)$ ([17], chapter 1). But `PiDuce` schemas are not labelled-determined with respect to channel constructors. Nevertheless, the syntactic constraints on `PiDuce` channel schemas (channels may only occur in tail positions of sequences) yields a computational complexity for S <: T of $O((\|S\|+\|T\|)^3)$. The algorithm uses two boolean tables of size $(\|S\|+\|T\|)^2$: the table `testing` stores schemas that are being tested, and the table `test_false` stores schemas that have been tested and the algorithm has failed. At each step, which costs $O(\mathtt{max}(\|S\|, \|T\|))$, the algorithm stores `true` either in `testing` or in `test_false`, and the two tables never store `true` in the same position. Therefore there are at most $(\|S\| + \|T\|)^2$ iterations. A detailed discussion of the required algorithm can be found in [8].

Typing rules for values. An *environment* Γ is a finite partial map from variables to schemas. We write $\mathtt{dom}(\Gamma)$ for the set of variables in Γ; we write $\emptyset$ for the *empty environment*, and $u : S$ for the singleton map. We let $\Gamma + \Gamma'$ be $(\Gamma \setminus \mathtt{dom}(\Gamma')) \cup \Gamma'$, where $\Gamma \setminus X$ removes from Γ all the bindings of names in X. The environments we consider in the following are always well-formed: Γ is *well-formed* if, for every u, $\Gamma(u)$ is not-empty.

The judgment $\Gamma \vdash V : S$ – read V has type S in the environment Γ – is the least relation satisfying the following rules:

$$\text{(EMPTY)}\ \Gamma \vdash () : () \qquad \text{(VAR)}\ \frac{\Gamma(u) = S}{\Gamma \vdash u : S} \qquad \text{(LAB)}\ \frac{\Gamma \vdash V : S}{\Gamma \vdash a[V] : a[S]} \qquad \text{(SEQ)}\ \frac{\Gamma \vdash V : S \quad \Gamma \vdash V' : S'}{\Gamma \vdash a[V]\texttt{,}V' : a[S]\texttt{,}S'}$$

These rules and the well-formedness of environments entail the following properties.

Proposition 2. *1. Let $\Gamma \vdash V : S$ and S <: $\langle T \rangle$, for some T. Then V is a variable and S is a channel schema.*

2. Let Γ be such that, for every $u \in \mathtt{dom}(\Gamma)$, $\Gamma(u)$ is labelled-determined. If $\Gamma \vdash V : S$ then S is labelled-determined.

We observe that Proposition 2.1 would be false if Γ were not well-formed. For instance take $\Gamma = u : \mathtt{Empty}$ and $V = a[u]$; then the hypotheses hold, but the conclusion is false. Proposition 2.2 is relevant because, at run-time, environments map variables to channel schemas. Henceforth communicated values always retain labelled-determined schemas.

Typing Rules for Processes. Let $\mathtt{Env}(F)$ be the following function taking a pattern and giving an environment:

$$\begin{array}{rcl}
\mathtt{Env}(S) & = & \emptyset \\
\mathtt{Env}(u : F) & = & u : \mathtt{schof}(F) + \mathtt{Env}(F) \\
\mathtt{Env}(L[F]) & = & \mathtt{Env}(F) \\
\mathtt{Env}(L[F]\texttt{,}F') & = & \mathtt{Env}(F) + \mathtt{Env}(F')
\end{array}$$

It is worth noticing that, in $u : \mathtt{schof}(F) + \mathtt{Env}(F)$ and $\mathtt{Env}(F) + \mathtt{Env}(F')$, the summands have disjoint domains, due to the linearity constraint on patterns.

The judgment $\Gamma \vdash P$ – read P is well typed in the environment Γ – is the least relation satisfying the following rules:

$$\text{(NIL)}\quad \Gamma \vdash \mathbf{0} \qquad \text{(OUT)}\quad \frac{\Gamma \vdash u : \langle S \rangle \quad \Gamma \vdash V : T \quad T <: S}{\Gamma \vdash \overline{u}[V]}$$

$$\text{(INP)}\quad \frac{\begin{pmatrix} \Gamma \vdash u_i : \langle S_i \rangle & \Gamma + \mathtt{Env}(F_i) \vdash P_i \\ S_i <: \sum_{j \in I,\, u_j = u_i} \mathtt{schof}(F_j) & \end{pmatrix}^{i \in I}}{\Gamma \vdash \sum_{i \in I} u_i(F_i).P_i}$$

$$\text{(PAR)}\quad \frac{\Gamma \vdash P \quad \Gamma \vdash P'}{\Gamma \vdash P \mid P'} \qquad \text{(NEW)}\quad \frac{\Gamma + u : \langle S \rangle \vdash P}{\Gamma \vdash (u : \langle S \rangle)P} \qquad \text{(REP)}\quad \frac{\Gamma \vdash P}{\Gamma \vdash !P}$$

Rules (NIL), (PAR), (NEW), and (REP) are standard. Rule (OUT) types outputs. The premise $T <: S$ entails that the subject of the input is a channel. It is worth noticing that, if $S = \mathtt{Empty}$, then there is no T such that $\Gamma \vdash V : T$ and $T <: \mathtt{Empty}$. Therefore outputs on channels of schema Empty are forbidden. On the contrary, if $S = \mathtt{Any}$, then $\overline{u}[V]$ is always well typed. Rule (INP) types input guarded choices. The second hypothesis is easy to explain: it enforces the typing of the continuation of every summand in the environment Γ plus that defined by the pattern. The third hypothesis may be understood as follows. Assume there are exactly n summands inputting on the same channel u, and let $F_1, \cdots, F_n$ be the corresponding patterns. Let $\langle S \rangle$ be the schema of u. Then the hypothesis establishes that $S <: \mathtt{schof}(F_1) + \cdots + \mathtt{schof}(F_n)$. It is worth recalling that $\mathtt{schof}(F_1) + \cdots + \mathtt{schof}(F_n)$ is in general not labelled-determined. This allows programmers to write processes such as $x(v : a[\mathtt{Int}]).P + x(v : a[\mathtt{String}]).Q$. We also remark that $\Gamma + \mathtt{Env}(F_i)$ is well-formed because of the not-emptiness restriction of patterns.

4 The Operational Semantics

This section defines the semantics of patterns and processes. In order to cope with values that may carry (channel) variables, both the pattern matching and the transition relations take an associated environment into account.

Patterns. Patterns decompose the structure of values and select parts of them. The algorithm, called *pattern-matching*, yields a substitution in case the decomposition succeeds. Let σ and σ' be two substitutions with disjoint domains. We write $\sigma + \sigma'$ to denote the function that is the union of σ and σ'. Every union in the following rules is always well defined because of the linearity constraint placed on patterns.

The *pattern match* of a value V with respect to a pattern F in an environment Γ, written $\Gamma \vdash V \in F \leadsto \sigma$, is the least relation satisfying the following rules:

$$\text{(EMP)}\ \frac{S \downarrow ()}{\Gamma \vdash () \in S \leadsto \emptyset} \qquad \text{(VAR)}\ \frac{u \in \mathtt{dom}(\Gamma) \quad \Gamma(u) <: S}{\Gamma \vdash u \in S \leadsto \emptyset}$$

$$\text{(LABEL-VOID)}\ \frac{S \downarrow L(S' \,;\, S'') \quad a \in L \qquad \Gamma \vdash V \in S' \leadsto \emptyset \quad \Gamma \vdash () \in S'' \leadsto \emptyset}{\Gamma \vdash a[V] \in S \leadsto \emptyset} \qquad \text{(SEQ-VOID)}\ \frac{S \downarrow L(S' \,;\, S'') \quad a \in L \qquad \Gamma \vdash V \in S' \leadsto \emptyset \quad \Gamma \vdash V'' \in S'' \leadsto \emptyset}{\Gamma \vdash a[V]\mathtt{,}V'' \in S \leadsto \emptyset}$$

$$\text{(PAT-VAR)}\ \frac{\Gamma \vdash V \in F \leadsto \sigma}{\Gamma \vdash V \in u : F \leadsto [u \mapsto V] + \sigma}$$

$$\text{(LABEL)}\ \frac{\mathtt{fv}(L[F]\mathtt{,}F') \neq \emptyset \quad a \in L \qquad \Gamma \vdash V \in F \leadsto \sigma \quad \Gamma \vdash () \in F' \leadsto \sigma'}{\Gamma \vdash a[V] \in L[F]\mathtt{,}F' \leadsto \sigma + \sigma'} \qquad \text{(SEQ)}\ \frac{\mathtt{fv}(L[F]\mathtt{,}F') \neq \emptyset \quad a \in L \qquad \Gamma \vdash V \in F \leadsto \sigma \quad \Gamma \vdash V' \in F' \leadsto \sigma'}{\Gamma \vdash a[V]\mathtt{,}V' \in L[F]\mathtt{,}F' \leadsto \sigma + \sigma'}$$

We discuss (VAR), (PAT-VAR), and (SEQ). Rule (VAR) verifies if a variable value matches with a schema S: it reduces to verifying the subschema relation between the schema of the variable and S. Rule (PAT-VAR) defines a substitution of a variable in a pattern. Rule (SEQ) matches a value with a sequence pattern. Since sequence patterns are linear with respect to variables, the substitution $\sigma + \sigma'$ is always well defined. We notice that no rule is defined for the pattern $L[F]$: this pattern is always rewritten into $L[F]\mathtt{,}()$.

When the matched value does not contain variables, the pattern matching algorithm has a cost that is proportional to the product of the size of the value and the size of the pattern. This is because the schema of the pattern is not labelled-determined; if such a schema was labelled-determined then the cost should have been linear with respect to the size of the value. The presence of variables in values reduces the pattern matching to the subschema relation, see the right premise of (VAR), which has an exponential cost, in general. However, if every variable in the environment Γ has a channel schema – that is always the case at run-time, see the following transition relation – then the subschema relation reduces to computing the subschema between labelled-determined schemas, which has a polynomial cost. More precisely, in the premise $\Gamma(u) <: S$ of (VAR), $\Gamma(u) = \langle T \rangle$, for some T. In order to match the pattern, one has to verify that T is greater than one schema in $\{S' \mid \langle S \rangle \downarrow \langle\rangle S'\}$. Then (1) every such check is polynomial because the schemas are labelled-determined, and (2) there are at most $\|S\|$ checks because the cardinality of $\{S' \mid S \downarrow \langle\rangle S'\}$ is smaller.

Proposition 3. *Let $\Gamma \vdash V : S$ and $\Gamma \vdash V \in F \leadsto \sigma$. Then $S <: \mathtt{schof}(F)$.*

Processes. Let $\mu, \nu, \cdots$ range over τ, input $u(F)$, and bound output $(\Gamma)\overline{u}[V]$ such that $\mathtt{dom}(\Gamma) \subseteq \mathtt{fv}(V)$. The bound output $(\Gamma)\overline{u}[V]$ is shortened to $\overline{u}[V]$ when $\Gamma = \emptyset$. We use the following auxiliary functions:

fv: $\mathtt{fv}(\tau) = \emptyset$, $\mathtt{fv}(u(F)) = \{u\}$, and $\mathtt{fv}((\Gamma)\overline{u}[V]) = (\{u\} \cup \mathtt{fv}(V)) \setminus \mathtt{dom}(\Gamma)$.
bv: $\mathtt{bv}((\Gamma)\overline{u}[V]) = \mathtt{dom}(\Gamma)$, $\mathtt{bv}(u(F)) = \mathtt{fv}(F)$, and $\mathtt{bv}(\tau) = \emptyset$.

The *transition relation* of PiDuce, $\xrightarrow{\mu}$, is the least relation satisfying the rules:

$$\Gamma \vdash \overline{u}[V] \xrightarrow{\overline{u}[V]} \mathbf{0} \qquad \Gamma \vdash \textstyle\sum_{i\in I} u_i(F_i).P_i \xrightarrow{u_i(F_i)} P_i$$

$$\frac{\Gamma + u{:}\langle S\rangle \vdash P \xrightarrow{\mu} Q \quad u \notin \mathtt{fv}(\mu) \cup \mathtt{bv}(\mu)}{\Gamma \vdash (u{:}\langle S\rangle)P \xrightarrow{\mu} (u{:}\langle S\rangle)Q} \qquad \frac{\Gamma + v{:}\langle S\rangle \vdash P \xrightarrow{(\Gamma')\overline{u}[V]} Q \quad v \neq u \quad v \in \mathtt{fv}(V) \setminus \mathtt{dom}(\Gamma')}{\Gamma \vdash (v{:}\langle S\rangle)P \xrightarrow{(\Gamma' + v:\langle S\rangle)\overline{u}[V]} Q}$$

$$\frac{\Gamma \vdash P \xrightarrow{\mu} P' \quad \mathtt{bv}(\mu) \cap \mathtt{fv}(Q) = \emptyset}{\Gamma \vdash P \mid Q \xrightarrow{\mu} P' \mid Q}$$

$$\frac{\Gamma \vdash P \xrightarrow{(\Gamma')\overline{u}[V]} P' \quad \Gamma \vdash Q \xrightarrow{u(F)} Q' \quad \mathtt{dom}(\Gamma') \cap \mathtt{fv}(Q) = \emptyset \quad \Gamma + \Gamma' \vdash V \in F \leadsto \sigma}{\Gamma \vdash P \mid Q \xrightarrow{\tau} (\Gamma')(P' \mid Q'\sigma)} \qquad \frac{\Gamma \vdash P \xrightarrow{\mu} Q \quad \mathtt{bv}(\mu) \cap \mathtt{fv}(P) = \emptyset}{\Gamma \vdash !P \xrightarrow{\mu} Q \mid !P}$$

plus the symmetric rules for parallel.

This transition relation is similar to that of the π-calculus [19], except for the environment Γ. This environment is partially supplied by enclosing news and partially by the global environment. In particular, bound outputs gather an environment. This means that a communication between a sender and a receiver also carries information about the schema of the variables in the message. In practice this is the case: a web service URI is always shipped with its WSDL document containing, for instance, the protocol that must be used to invoke the service. In case of PiDuce, this WSDL document also contains the schema of the service. However our semantics does not require that the schema information is sent *together with* the message. For example, a service receiving a message on a generic channel and forwarding it to another service does not need to know the schema of the received message. Hence a lazy implementation of schema requests is plausible. Such an implementation downloads schemas only if they are needed by the pattern matching algorithm in the communication and the invocation rules.

In practice, PiDuce processes have free variables that are channels. Such processes may be typed in environments mapping variables to channel schemas, let us call them *channel environments*. A relevant property of the transition relation is that if $\Gamma \vdash P \xrightarrow{\tau} Q$ and Γ is a channel environment, then the pattern matching in the communication rule – the last but one rule – still uses a channel environment. This is critical for computing the transition relation with a polynomial cost.

We conclude this section by asserting the soundness of the static semantics. Proofs are reported in the Appendix A. The first property states that well-typed processes always transit to well-typed processes.

Theorem 1. *(Subject Reduction) Let $\Gamma \vdash P$. Then*

1. *if $\Gamma \vdash P \stackrel{(\Gamma')\overline{u}[V]}{\longrightarrow} Q$ then (a) $\Gamma + \Gamma' \vdash Q$, and (b) $\Gamma \vdash u : \langle S \rangle$ and $\Gamma + \Gamma' \vdash V : T$ with $T <: S$;*
2. *if $\Gamma \vdash P \stackrel{u(F)}{\longrightarrow} Q$ then $\Gamma + \mathtt{Env}(F) \vdash Q$ and $\Gamma \vdash u : \langle S \rangle$;*
3. *if $\Gamma \vdash P \stackrel{\tau}{\longrightarrow} Q$ then $\Gamma \vdash Q$.*

The second soundness property concerns *progress*, that is, an output on a channel will be consumed if an input on the same channel is available. In order to guarantee progress, it is necessary to restrict (well-formed) environments. To illustrate the problem, consider the following judgment:

$$u : \langle \mathtt{Int} + \mathtt{String} \rangle, v : \mathtt{Int} + \mathtt{String} \vdash \overline{u}[v] \mid (u(x : \mathtt{Int}).\mathbf{0} + u(x : \mathtt{String}).\mathbf{0})$$

The reader may verify that it is derived by our type system, however no interaction may occur because the schema of the value v is neither a subschema of $\mathtt{schof}(x : \mathtt{Int})$ or of $\mathtt{schof}(x : \mathtt{String})$. In fact this circumstance never occurs in practice: if a value is sent, the unique variables it may contain are channels. Under this constraint, progress is always guaranteed. A similar remark may be made for pattern matching. For generic environments Γ it may be the case that $\Gamma \vdash V : S$ and $S <: \mathtt{schof}(F)$ but there is no σ such that $\Gamma \vdash V \in F \rightsquigarrow \sigma$. Consider for instance $\Gamma = u : a[b[\;]]$, $V = u$, and $F = a[v : b[\;]]$.

Let $P \stackrel{\mu}{\longrightarrow}$ be an abbreviation for "there exists Q such that $P \stackrel{\mu}{\longrightarrow} Q$.

Theorem 2. *(Progress) Let Γ be such that, for every $u \in \mathtt{fv}(V)$, $\Gamma(u)$ is a channel schema.*

1. *If $\Gamma \vdash V : S$ and $S <: T + R$ then either $S <: T$ or $S <: R$.*
2. *If $\Gamma \vdash V : S$ and $S <: \mathtt{schof}(F)$ then there is σ such that $\Gamma \vdash V \in F \rightsquigarrow \sigma$.*
3. *If $\Gamma \vdash P$, $P \stackrel{(\Gamma')\overline{u}[V]}{\longrightarrow}$ and $P \stackrel{u(F)}{\longrightarrow}$ then there are F' and σ such that $P \stackrel{u(F')}{\longrightarrow}$ and $\Gamma + \Gamma' \vdash V \in F' \rightsquigarrow \sigma$.*

5 Conclusions and Ongoing Research

`PiDuce` is a process language with native `XML` datatypes and operators for constructing and deconstructing `XML` documents. It has been designed for modeling applications that are intrinsically concurrent, such as web services orchestrations and choreographies.

In this paper we have focussed on the theory of `PiDuce`. In order to reduce the computational complexity of the pattern matching algorithm, channel schemas have been constrained to be labelled-determined and to occur in the tail positions of sequences. These constraints guarantee a polynomial computational complexity of the subschema relation, a mechanism used in the pattern matching.

The PiDuce schema language has been designed with a bias towards simplicity. A number of design choices may be changed without affecting the computational complexity of the subschema relation. A thorough analysis of variants of PiDuce schemas and their expressive power is left to future investigations.

Most of our current efforts are in prototyping a distributed implementation of PiDuce. As a matter of facts, PiDuce appears to be a basic computational model of current orchestration and choreography languages of services in the web, such as BizTalk [22], WSFL [16], WS-CDL [14], and Bpel4ws [4]. The prototype [9], is intended to serve as a distributed virtual machine for a these languages A significant next step will be the extension of PiDuce with a transactional operator, possibly along the lines of [7,15]. Such an extension will be used to compile technologies such as BizTalk or Bpel4ws.

Acknowledgments. The authors thank Samuele Carpineti, David Richter, and Lucian Wischik for the interesting discussions and for having spotted several errors in previous drafts of this paper.

References

1. S. Abiteboul, O. Benjelloun, I. Manolescu, T. Milo, and R. Weber. Active XML: Peer-to-peer data and Web services integration. In *VLDP 2002: Proceedings of the Twenty-Eighth International Conference on Very Large Data Bases, Hong Kong SAR, China*, pages 1087–1090. Morgan Kaufmann Publishers, 2002.
2. L. Acciai and M. Boreale. XPi: a typed process calculus for XML messaging. In *7th Formal Methods for Object-Based Distributed Systems (FMOODS'05)*, volume 3535 of *Lecture Notes in Computer Science*, pages 47 – 66. Springer-Verlag, 2005.
3. R. M. Amadio and L. Cardelli. Subtyping recursive types. *ACM Transactions on Programming Languages and Systems*, 15(4):575–631, 1993.
4. T. Andrews and et.al. Business Process Execution Language for Web Services. Version 1.1. Specification, BEA Systems, IBM Corp., Microsoft Corp., SAP AG, Siebel Systems, 2003.
5. V. Benzaken, G. Castagna, and A. Frisch. CDuce: an XML-centric general-purpose language. In *Proceedings of the 8th ACM SIGPLAN International Conference on Functional Programming (ICFP-03)*, pages 51–63. ACM Press, 2003.
6. K. Bhargavan, C. Fournet, A. Gordon, and R. Pucella. Tulafale: A security tool for web services. In *Formal Methods for Components and Objects (FMCO 2003)*, volume 3188 of *LNCS*, pages 197–222. Springer, 2004.
7. R. Bruni, C. Laneve, and U. Montanari. Orchestrating transactions in join calculus. In *13th International Conference on Concurrency Theory (CONCUR'02)*, volume 2421 of *LNCS*, pages 321–337. Springer, 2002.
8. S. Carpineti and C. Laneve. A rude contract language for web services. Extended Abstract at www.cs.unibo.it/BoPi, 2005.

9. S. Carpineti, C. Laneve, and P. Milazzo. BoPi: a distributed machine for experimenting web services technologies. In *5th International Conference on Application of Concurrency to System Design (ACSD'05)*, pages 202–212. IEEE Press, 2005.
10. G. Castagna, R. D. Nicola, and D. Varacca. Semantic subtyping for the π-calculus. In *20th IEEE Symposium on Logic in Computer Science (LICS'05)*. IEEE Computer Society, 2005.
11. P. Gardner and S. Maffeis. Modelling dynamic web data. In *9th International Workshop on Database Programming Languages (DBPL'03)*, volume 2921 of *Lecture Notes in Computer Science*, pages 130 – 146. Springer-Verlag, 2003.
12. H. Hosoya and B. C. Pierce. XDuce: A statically typed XML processing language. *ACM Transactions on Internet Technology (TOIT)*, 3(2):117–148, 2003.
13. H. Hosoya, J. Vouillon, and B. C. Pierce. Regular expression types for XML. In *Proceedings of the International Conference on Functional Programming (ICFP)*, pages 11–22. ACM Press, 2000.
14. N. Kavantzas, G. Olsson, J. Mischkinsky, and M. Chapman. Web Services Choreography Description Languages. Oracle Corporation, 2003.
15. C. Laneve and G. Zavattaro. Foundations of web transactions. In *Foundations of Software Science and Computation Structures (FOSSACS'05)*, volume 3441 of *LNCS*, pages 282–298. Springer, 2005.
16. F. Leymann. Web Services Flow Language (wsfl 1.0). Technical report, IBM Software Group, 2001.
17. D. Lugiez, F. Jacquemard, H. Comon, M. Tommasi, M. Dauchet, R. Gilleron, and S. Tison. Tree automata techniques and applications. 2002.
18. R. Milner. Functions as processes. *Journal of Mathematical Structures in Computer Science*, 2(2):119–141, 1992.
19. R. Milner, J. Parrow, and D. Walker. A calculus of mobile processes, part I/II. *Journal of Information and Computation*, 100:1–77, Sept. 1992.
20. B. C. Pierce and D. Sangiorgi. Typing and subtyping for mobile processes. *Mathematical Structures in Computer Science*, 6(5), 1996.
21. D. N. Turner. *The Polymorphic Pi-Calculus: Theory and Implementation.* PhD thesis, University of Edinburgh, 1996. ECS-LFCS-96-345.
22. S. Woodgate, S. Mohr, and B. Loesgen. *Microsoft BizTalk Server 2004 Unleashed.* Sams, 2004.

A Soundness of the Static Semantics

The following basic statements are standard preliminary results for the subject reduction theorem.

Lemma 1. *(Weakening) If $\Gamma \vdash P$ and $u \notin \mathtt{fv}(P)$ then $\Gamma + u : S \vdash P$. Similarly for $\Gamma \vdash V : S$.*

Lemma 2. *(Substitution)*

1. *Let $\Gamma + u : S \vdash V : T$ and $\Gamma \vdash V' : S'$ such that $S' <: S$. Then $\Gamma \vdash V\{^{V'}/_{u}\} : T'$ with $T' <: T$.*
2. *Let $\Gamma + u : S \vdash P$ and the free occurrences of u in P are not subjects of inputs. If $\Gamma \vdash V : T$, and $T <: S$ then $\Gamma \vdash P\{^{V}/_{u}\}$.*

Proof. The demonstration is by induction on the structures of the proofs of $\Gamma + u : S \vdash V : T$ and $\Gamma + u : S \vdash P$. We only discuss the case when the last rule is (OUT). Then $P = \overline{w}[V']$ and the premises of the rule are the judgments $\Gamma + u : S \vdash w : \langle R \rangle$ and $\Gamma + u : S \vdash V' : S'$, and the predicate

$$S' <: R \tag{1}$$

We must prove $\Gamma \vdash \overline{w}[V']\{^V/_u\}$. By $\Gamma + u : S \vdash V' : S'$, the hypothesis $\Gamma \vdash V : T$, $T <: S$, and the substitution lemma for values, we obtain

$$\Gamma \vdash V'\{^V/_u\} : T' \tag{2}$$

$$T' <: S' \tag{3}$$

As regards the subject of the output, there are two subcases: (a) $u \neq w$ and (b) $u = w$. Case (a) follows by (1), (3) and transitivity of $<:$. Case (b) implies $S = \langle R \rangle$ and, by Proposition 2, V is a variable and T is a channel schema. Let V be u'. By the substitution lemma for values

$$\Gamma \vdash u' : \langle T'' \rangle \tag{4}$$

and $\langle T'' \rangle <: \langle R \rangle$. Then $\Gamma \vdash \overline{w}[V']\{^V/_u\}$ follows by (2), (4), the relations $\langle T'' \rangle <: \langle R \rangle$, (1), (3), the controvariance of $\langle \cdot \rangle$ and the transitivity of $<:$. □

The soundness of pattern matching is established by the next lemma.

Lemma 3. *(Pattern Matching)*

1. *If $\Gamma \vdash V \in F \rightsquigarrow \sigma$ and $u \notin \mathtt{fv}(V)$ then $\Gamma + u : T \vdash V \in F \rightsquigarrow \sigma$.*
2. *If $\Gamma \vdash V : S$ and $\Gamma \vdash V \in F \rightsquigarrow \sigma$ then, for every $u \in \mathtt{fv}(F)$, $\Gamma \vdash \sigma(u) : T$ and $T <: \mathtt{Env}(F)(u)$.*

The preliminaries are in place for the subject reduction theorem.

Theorem 1. *(Subject Reduction) Let $\Gamma \vdash P$. Then*

1. *if $\Gamma \vdash P \stackrel{(\Gamma')\overline{u}[V]}{\longrightarrow} Q$ then $\Gamma + \Gamma' \vdash Q$, $\Gamma \vdash u : \langle S \rangle$ and $\Gamma + \Gamma' \vdash V : T$ with $T <: S$;*
2. *if $\Gamma \vdash P \stackrel{u(F)}{\longrightarrow} Q$ then $\Gamma + \mathtt{Env}(F) \vdash Q$ and $\Gamma \vdash u : \langle S \rangle$;*
3. *if $\Gamma \vdash P \stackrel{\tau}{\longrightarrow} Q$ then $\Gamma \vdash Q$.*

Proof. The demonstration proceeds by induction on the structure of the proof of $\Gamma \vdash P \stackrel{\mu}{\longrightarrow} Q$ and by cases on the last rule that has been applied. We only detail the case of the communication rule

$$\frac{\Gamma \vdash P \stackrel{(\Gamma')\overline{u}[V]}{\longrightarrow} P' \quad \Gamma \vdash Q \stackrel{u(F)}{\longrightarrow} Q' \quad \mathtt{dom}(\Gamma') \cap \mathtt{fv}(Q) = \emptyset \quad \Gamma + \Gamma' \vdash V \in F \rightsquigarrow \sigma}{\Gamma \vdash P \mid Q \stackrel{\tau}{\longrightarrow} (\Gamma')(P' \mid Q'\sigma)}$$

Since $\Gamma \vdash P \mid Q$, the premises of (PAR) give $\Gamma \vdash P$ and $\Gamma \vdash Q$. By $\mathtt{dom}(\Gamma') \cap \mathtt{fv}(Q) = \emptyset$ and Lemma 1, $\Gamma + \Gamma' \vdash Q'$. By inductive hypotheses on $\Gamma \vdash P \stackrel{(\Gamma')\overline{u}[V]}{\rightarrow} P'$ and $\Gamma \vdash Q \stackrel{u(F)}{\rightarrow} Q'$ we obtain:

$$\Gamma + \Gamma' \vdash P' \tag{5}$$
$$\Gamma + \Gamma' \vdash V : T \tag{6}$$
$$\Gamma \vdash u : S \tag{7}$$
$$\Gamma + \Gamma' + \mathtt{Env}(F) \vdash Q' \tag{8}$$

By Lemma 3(2) applied to $\Gamma + \Gamma' \vdash V \in F \rightsquigarrow \sigma$ and (6) we obtain that, for every $v \in \mathtt{fv}(F)$, $\Gamma + \Gamma' \vdash \sigma(v) : T'$ and $T' <: \mathtt{Env}(F)(v)$. By the substitution lemma applied to this last judgment and (8), we derive $\Gamma + \Gamma' \vdash Q'\sigma$. We conclude with (NEW): $\Gamma \vdash (\Gamma')(P' \mid Q'\sigma)$.

The theorem about progress is discussed below.

Theorem 2. *(Progress) Let Γ be such that, for every $u \in \mathtt{fv}(V)$, $\Gamma(u)$ is a channel schema.*

1. *If $\Gamma \vdash V : S$ and $S <: T + R$ then either $S <: T$ or $S <: R$.*
2. *If $\Gamma \vdash V{:}S$ and $S <: \mathtt{schof}(F)$ then there is σ such that $\Gamma \vdash V \in F \rightsquigarrow \sigma$.*
3. *If $\Gamma \vdash P$, $P \stackrel{(\Gamma')\overline{u}[V]}{\rightarrow}$ and $P \stackrel{u(F)}{\rightarrow}$ then there are F' and σ such that $P \stackrel{u(F')}{\rightarrow}$ and $\Gamma + \Gamma' \vdash V \in F' \rightsquigarrow \sigma$.*

Proof. The proof of items 1 and 2 are simple and therefore omitted. As regards item 3, we consider the proof of $P \stackrel{u(F)}{\rightarrow}$. By Theorem 1(2) applied to $\Gamma \vdash P$ and $P \stackrel{u(F)}{\rightarrow}$ we obtain $\Gamma \vdash u : \langle S \rangle$. Then, we consider the proof tree of $P \stackrel{u(F)}{\rightarrow}$. It must have an axiom (the leaf of the proof tree) whose shape is

$$\sum_{i \in I} u_i(F_i).P_i \stackrel{u(F)}{\rightarrow}$$

Correspondingly, in the proof tree of $\Gamma \vdash P$ there is a judgment $\Gamma + \Gamma'' \vdash \sum_{i \in I} u_i(F_i).P_i$, for some Γ''. This judgment must have been proved with an instance of (INP) that yields $S <: \sum_{j \in I, u_j = u} \mathtt{schof}(F_i)$. By a similar argument applied to $P \stackrel{(\Gamma')\overline{u}[V]}{\rightarrow}$, using (OUT), there are Γ''' and T such that $\Gamma + \Gamma''' + \Gamma' \vdash V{:}T$ and $T <: S$. Therefore, by transitivity of $<:$, $T <: \sum_{j \in I, u_j = u} \mathtt{schof}(F_i)$. By item 1(a), there exists F_k such that $T <: \mathtt{schof}(F_k)$. Additionally, by Lemmas 1 and 2, $\Gamma + \Gamma''' + \Gamma' \vdash V{:}T$ may be simplified into $\Gamma + \Gamma' \vdash V{:}T$. We conclude by item 1(b). $\square$

Life After BPEL?

W.M.P. van der Aalst[1,2], M. Dumas[2], A.H.M. ter Hofstede[2], N. Russell[2], H.M.W. Verbeek[1], and P. Wohed[3]

[1] Eindhoven University of Technology, Eindhoven, The Netherlands
w.m.p.v.d.aalst@tm.tue.nl
[2] Queensland University of Technology, Brisbane, Australia
{m.dumas, a.terhofstede, n.russell}@qut.edu.au
[3] Université Henri Poincaré, Nancy, France
petia.wohed@cran.uhp-nancy.fr

Abstract. The *Business Process Execution Language for Web Services* (BPEL) has emerged as a standard for specifying and executing processes. It is supported by vendors such as IBM and Microsoft and positioned as the "process language of the Internet". This paper provides a critical analysis of BPEL based on the so-called *workflow patterns*. It also discusses the need for languages like BPEL. Finally, the paper addresses several challenges not directly addressed by BPEL but highly relevant to the support of web services.

1 Introduction

Web services, an emerging paradigm for architecting and implementing business collaborations within and across organizational boundaries, are currently of interest to both software vendors and scientists. In this paradigm, the functionality provided by business applications is encapsulated within web services: software components described at a semantic level, which can be invoked by application programs or by other services through a stack of Internet standards including HTTP, XML, SOAP, WSDL and UDDI [3,12]. Once deployed, web services provided by various organizations can be inter-connected in order to implement business collaborations, leading to *composite web services*.

The *Business Process Execution Language for Web Services* (BPEL4WS, or BPEL for short) has emerged as the de-facto standard for implementing processes based on web services [9]. Systems such as Oracle BPEL Process Manager, IBM WebSphere Application Server Enterprise, IBM WebSphere Studio Application Developer Integration Edition, and Microsoft BizTalk Server 2004 support BPEL, thus illustrating the practical relevance of this language. Although intended as a language for connecting web services, its application is not limited to cross-organizational processes. It is expected that in the near future a wide variety of process-aware information systems [13] will be realized using BPEL. Whilst being a powerful language, BPEL is difficult to use. Its XML representation is very verbose and only readable to the trained eye. It offers many constructs and typically things can be implemented in many ways, e.g.,

M. Bravetti et al. (Eds.): EPEW 2005 and WS-FM 2005, LNCS 3670, pp. 35–50, 2005.

using links and the flow construct or using sequences and switches. As a result only experienced users are able to select the right construct. Several vendors offer a graphical interface that generates BPEL code. However, the graphical representations are a direct reflection of the BPEL code and are not intuitive to end-users. Therefore, BPEL is closer to classical programming languages than e.g. the more user-friendly workflow management systems available today.

It is interesting to put BPEL in a historical perspective. In the seventies, people like Skip Ellis [15], Anatol Holt [27], and Michael Zisman [48] were already working on so-called office information systems, which were driven by explicit process models. It is interesting to see that the three pioneers in this area independently used Petri-net variants to model office procedures. In the seventies, organizations were not connected and only few people inside one organization were linked through some kind of network. During the seventies and eighties there was great optimism about the applicability of office information systems. Unfortunately, few applications succeeded. As a result of these experiences, both the application of this technology and research almost stopped for a decade. Consequently, hardly any advances were made in the eighties. In the nineties, once again there was huge interest in these systems. The number of workflow products developed in the past decade and the many papers on workflow technology illustrate the revival of office information systems. Today workflow management systems are readily available [4,33,37] and workflow technology is hidden in many applications, e.g., ERP, CRM, and PDM systems. However, their application is still limited to specific industries such as banking and insurance. Since 2000 there has been a growing interest in web services. This resulted in a stack of Internet standards (HTTP, XML, SOAP, WSDL, and UDDI) which needed to be complemented by a process layer. Several vendors proposed competing languages, e.g., IBM proposed WSFL (Web Services Flow Language) [32] building on FlowMark/MQSeries and Microsoft proposed XLANG (Web Services for Business Process Design) [45] building on Biztalk. BPEL [9] emerged as a compromise between both languages.

The goal of this paper is to critically analyze BPEL. We analyze the language itself using a patterns-based approach [5]. In addition, we discuss the focus of BPEL. In our view organizations do *not* need to agree on a common execution language. We will argue that there are more important issues to be addressed, e.g., having a higher-level language to describe both processes and interactions and being able to monitor running composite web-services/choreographies.

The remainder of this paper is organized as follows. Section 2 briefly introduces the BPEL language and its focus. In Section 3 we discuss existing work on workflow patterns and relate this to BPEL. In Section 4 we question the need for a language like BPEL. Section 5 proposes the real challenges we should focus on in the context of BPEL: (1) generating and analyzing BPEL code (Section 5.1), (2) "real" choreography (Section 5.2), and (3) process mining, conformance testing and mediation (Section 5.3). Section 6 concludes the paper by providing some pointers to the "Petri and Pi" initiative which aims at combining efforts on theory, languages, tools, and applications in the web services domain.

2 BPEL

BPEL [9] supports the modeling of two types of processes: executable and abstract processes. An *abstract*, (not executable) *process* is a business protocol, specifying the message exchange behavior between different parties without revealing the internal behavior for any one of them. This abstract process views the outside world from the perspective of a single organization or (composite) service. An *executable process* views the world in a similar manner, however, things are specified in more detail such that the process becomes executable, i.e., an executable BPEL process specifies the execution order of a number of *activities* constituting the process, the *partners* involved in the process, the *messages* exchanged between these partners, and the *fault* and *exception handling* required in cases of errors and exceptions.

A BPEL process itself is a kind of flow-chart, where each element in the process is called an *activity*. An activity is either a primitive or a structured activity. The set of *primitive activities* contains: `invoke`, invoking an operation on a web service; `receive`, waiting for a message from an external source; `reply`, replying to an external source; `wait`, pausing for a specified time; `assign`, copying data from one place to another; `throw`, indicating errors in the execution; `terminate`, terminating the entire service instance; and `empty`, doing nothing.

To enable the presentation of complex structures the following *structured activities* are defined: `sequence`, for defining an execution order; `switch`, for conditional routing; `while`, for looping; `pick`, for race conditions based on timing or external triggers; `flow`, for parallel routing; and `scope`, for grouping activities to be treated by the same fault-handler. Structured activities can be nested and combined in arbitrary ways. Within activities executed in parallel the execution order can further be controlled by the usage of `links` (sometimes also called control links, or guarded links), which allows the definition of directed graphs. The graphs too can be nested but must be acyclic.

As indicated in the introduction, BPEL builds on IBM's WSFL (Web Services Flow Language) [32] and Microsoft's XLANG (Web Services for Business Process Design) [45] and combines the features of a block structured language inherited from XLANG with those for directed graphs originating from WSFL. As a result simple things can be implemented in two ways. For example a sequence can be realized using the `sequence` or `flow` elements (in the latter case links are used to enforce a particular order on the parallel elements), a choice based on certain data values can be realized using the `switch` or `flow` elements, etc. However, for certain constructs one is forced to use the block structured part of the language, e.g., a *deferred choice* (see next section and [5]) can only be modeled using the `pick` construct. For other constructs one is forced to use the links, i.e., the more graph-oriented part of the language, e.g., two parallel processes with a one-way synchronization require a `link` inside a `flow`. In addition, there are very subtle restrictions on the use of links: "A link MUST NOT cross the boundary of a while activity, a serializable scope, an event handler or a compensation handler... In addition, a link that crosses a fault-handler boundary MUST be outbound, that is, it MUST have its source activity within the fault handler and its target activity within a scope that encloses the scope associated with the fault handler. Finally, a link MUST NOT create a control cycle, that is, the source activity must not have the target activity as a logically preceding activity, where an activity A logically precedes an activity B if the initiation of B semantically requires the completion of A. Therefore, directed graphs created by links are always acyclic." (see page 64 in [9]). All of this makes the language complex for end-users. A detailed or complete description of BPEL is beyond the scope of this paper. For more details, the reader is referred to [9] and various web sites such as the web site of the OASIS technical committee on WS-BPEL: `http://www.oasis-open.org/committees/tc_home.php?wg_abbrev=wsbpel`.

3 Patterns-Based Analysis of BPEL

Based on earlier experiences in the workflow domain, we have evaluated BPEL using the so-called workflow patterns [5]. The initial set of 20 workflow patterns focused exclusively on control-flow aspects. We will briefly discuss our experiences with BPEL based on these patterns. However, before doing so, we would like to emphasize that the patterns initiative (`www.workflowpatterns.com`) is not limited to control-flow. We have developed a comprehensive set of *data patterns* [43]. These patterns describe the different ways of dealing with data in the context of some process-aware information systems [13] (e.g., a workflow management system like Staffware, an ERP system like SAP R/3, or integration middleware like WebSphere). In the context of workflow management, we distinguish four classes of data patterns: *data visibility* (relating to the extent and manner in which data elements can be viewed by various components of a workflow process), *data interaction* (focusing on the manner in which data is communicated between active elements within a workflow), *data transfer* (considering the means by which the actual transfer of data elements occurs between workflow components and describe the various mechanisms by which data elements can be passed across the interface of a workflow component) and *data-based routing* (characterizing the manner in which data elements can influence the operation of other aspects of the workflow, particularly the control flow perspective). We have also developed a comprehensive set of *resource patterns* [42] that capture the various ways in which resources are represented and utilized in workflows. These patterns are also grouped into a number of categories: *creation patterns*, *push patterns*, *pull patterns*, *detour patterns*, *auto-start patterns*, *visibility patterns*, and *multiple resource patterns*. Since they are less relevant in the context of BPEL, we do not elaborate on them in any detail. Other related work includes Colored Petri Net (CPN) patterns [38], Enterprise Application Integration (EAI) patterns [26], and Service Interaction (SI) patterns [10].

For a detailed description and discussion of the patterns and more pointers we refer the reader to `www.workflowpatterns.com` and [5,43]. As an illustration, we describe control-flow pattern WCFP16 (Deferred Choice).

WCFP16 Deferred Choice. A point in a process where one among several alternative branches is chosen based on information which is not necessarily available when this point is reached. This differs from the normal exclusive choice, in that the choice is not made immediately when the point is reached, but instead several alternatives are offered, and the choice between them is delayed until the occurrence of some event.

Example: When a contract is finalized, it has to be reviewed and signed either by the director or by the operations manager, whoever is available first. Both the director and the operations manager would be notified that the contract is to be reviewed: the first one who is available will proceed with the review.

Note that WCFP16 is different from the WCFP 4 (i.e., Exclusive Choice): The choice is not based on a decision or data but on a choice resolved by the environment. BPEL clearly supports this pattern. The `pick` (for race conditions based on timing or external triggers) directly offers the desired functionality.

Table 1. An analysis of BPEL based on the workflow control-flow patterns [47]

pattern	pattern name	BPEL
WCFP1	sequence	+
WCFP2	parallel split	+
WCFP3	synchronization	+
WCFP4	exclusive choice	+
WCFP5	simple merge	+
WCFP6	multi choice	+
WCFP7	synchronizing merge	+
WCFP8	multi merge	–
WCFP9	discriminator	–
WCFP10	arbitrary cycles	–
WCFP11	implicit termination	+
WCFP12	multiple instances no synchronization	+
WCFP13	multiple instances design time knowledge	+
WCFP14	multiple instances runtime knowledge	–
WCFP15	multiple instances without a priori knowledge	–
WCFP16	deferred choice	+
WCFP17	interleave parallel routing	+/–
WCFP18	milestone	–
WCFP19	cancel activity	+
WCFP20	cancel case	+

Tables 1 and 2 summarize the results of our pattern-based evaluation of BPEL. For each control-flow and data pattern, we checked whether it is possible to realize the pattern with BPEL. If BPEL directly supports the pattern through one of its constructs, it is rated +. If the pattern is not *directly* supported, it is rated +/-. Any solution that results in "spaghetti-like constructs" or is not possible at all, is considered as giving no direct support and is rated –. These ratings should be interpreted with care as indicated in [5,43].

We cannot give a detailed explanation of each pattern or of the evaluation of BPEL based on this material (for this we refer to [5,43,47]). However, a general observation that we would like to make is that BPEL is more powerful than

Table 2. An analysis of BPEL based on the workflow data patterns [43]

pattern	pattern name	BPEL
WDP1	task data	+/–
WDP2	block data	–
WDP3	scope data	+
WDP4	folder data	–
WDP5	multiple instance data	–
WDP6	case data	+
WDP7	workflow data	–
WDP8	environment data	+
WDP9	data interaction between tasks	+
WDP10	data interaction – block task to decomposition	–
WDP11	data interaction – decomposition to block task	–
WDP12	data interaction – to multiple instance task	–
WDP13	data interaction – from multiple instance task	–
WDP14	data interaction – case to case	+/–
WDP15	data interaction – task to environment – push-oriented	+
WDP16	data interaction – environment to task – pull-oriented	+
WDP17	data interaction – environment to task – push-oriented	+/–
WDP18	data interaction – task to environment – pull-oriented	+/–
WDP19	data interaction – case to environment – push-oriented	–
WDP20	data interaction – environment to case – pull-oriented	–
WDP21	data interaction – environment to case – push-oriented	–
WDP22	data interaction – case to environment – pull-oriented	–
WDP23	data interaction – workflow to environment – push-oriented	–
WDP24	data interaction – environment to workflow – pull-oriented	–
WDP25	data interaction – environment to workflow – push-oriented	–
WDP26	data interaction – workflow to environment – pull-oriented	–
WDP27	data passing by value – incoming	+
WDP28	data passing by value – outgoing	+
WDP29	data passing – copy in/copy out	–
WDP30	data passing by reference – unlocked	+
WDP31	data passing by reference – locked	+/–
WDP32	data transformation – input	–
WDP33	data transformation – output	–
WDP34	task precondition – data existence	+/–
WDP35	task precondition – data value	+
WDP36	task postcondition – data existence	–
WDP37	task postcondition – data value	–
WDP38	event-based task trigger	+
WDP39	data-based task trigger	+/–
WDP40	data-based routing	+

most traditional process languages. The control-flow part of BPEL inherits almost all constructs of the block structured language XLANG and the directed graphs of WSFL. Therefore, it is no surprise that BPEL indeed supports the union of patterns supported by XLANG and WSFL. BPEL offers direct support for the Multi Choice (WCFP6) and Synchronizing Merge (WCFP7), but not for

Arbitrary Cycles (WCFP10). This is a consequence of the "dead-path elimination" principle inherited from WSFL. BPEL, through the concept of serializable scopes, is one of the few languages to support the Interleaved Parallel Routing pattern (WCFP17), although with some restrictions. BPEL is also one of the few languages that fully supports the notion of scope data elements (WDP3). It provides support for a scope construct which allows related activities, variables and exception handlers to be logically grouped together. The default binding for data elements in BPEL is at case level and they are visible to all of the components in a process. However, variables can be bound to scopes within a process definition which may encompass a number of tasks and there is also the ability for messages to be passed between tasks when control passes from one task to another.

So the overall observation is that BPEL is an expressive language with some limitations. However, BPEL is also a very complicated language with many concepts. This complexity is reflected in the large number of issues that have been raised within the OASIS WS-BPEL standardization committee (217 as of June 2005), and which have delayed the release of the WS-BPEL 2.0 standard specification.

4 Do We Need BPEL?

In the previous section, we concluded that BPEL may be too complex but, compared to other languages, it is also very powerful. In this section, we do not focus on the specific qualities of BPEL. Instead we focus on the question: "Do we need a language like BPEL?".

Although BPEL can be used as a classical workflow language, its development was triggered by the web service paradigm. Therefore, BPEL was intended initially for pure cross-organizational processes in a web services context: "BPEL4WS provides a language for the formal specification of business processes and business interaction protocols. By doing so, it extends the Web Services interaction model and enables it to support business transactions." (see page 1 in [9]). However, it can also be used to support intra-organizational processes. The authors of BPEL [9] envision two possible uses of the language: "Business processes can be described in two ways. Executable business processes model actual behavior of a participant in a business interaction. Business protocols, in contrast, use process descriptions that specify the mutually visible message exchange behavior of each of the parties involved in the protocol, without revealing their internal behavior. The process descriptions for business protocols are called abstract processes. BPEL is meant to be used to model the behavior of *both executable and abstract processes*." In our view, executable and abstract processes should not be supported by a single language. Most attention has been devoted to BPEL as an execution language. In our opinion BPEL failed as a language for modeling abstract processes. Moreover, a BPEL specification is always given from the viewpoint of *one* of the interacting partners. Web Services provided by partners can be used to perform work in a BPEL business process. Invoking an

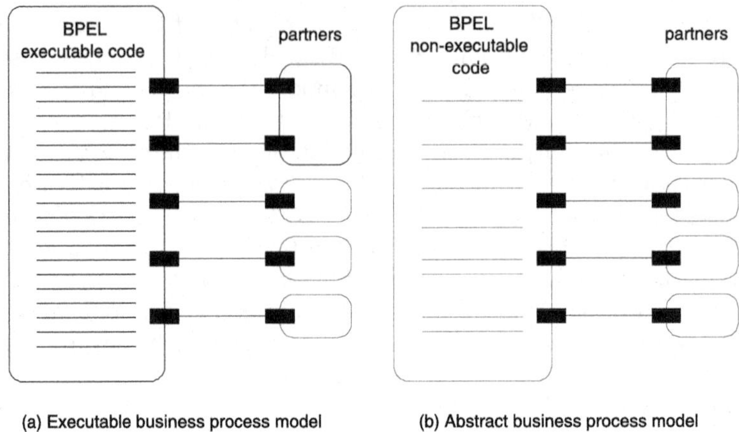

(a) Executable business process model (b) Abstract business process model

Fig. 1. The two ways in which BPEL can be used

operation on such a service is a basic activity that can be specified using BPEL. Figure 1 shows the two possible uses of BPEL. The figure clearly illustrates that in both cases the work is *seen from the perspective of one of the partners*!

Figure 1 raises the question why every partner should standardize on BPEL as a process language. A partner providing a service may implement its underlying processes in any language without the other partner knowing, i.e., *interacting partners do not need to agree on a language like BPEL.* Therefore, the answer to "Do we need a language like BPEL?" is No! Nevertheless, BPEL has become the de-facto standard and may in the future facilitate organizations migrating from one system to another. In addition, BPEL incorporates a number of specialized features for web services development including direct support for XML data definition and manipulation, a dynamic binding mechanism based on explicit manipulation of endpoint references, a declarative mechanism for correlating incoming messages to process instances (which is essential for asynchronous communication), etc. As such, BPEL may be seen as an attractive alternative to conventional (object-oriented) programming languages when it comes to developing web services.

5 Let Us Focus on the Real Challenges!

Although a language like BPEL is not essential for parties to cooperate, its dominance raises the question of how to facilitate the use of BPEL and to identify the missing functionality. In other words: we want to address the "real" challenges in the context of BPEL. This is the reason the title of this paper is "Life after BPEL?". In this section we briefly discuss three challenges: "generating and analyzing BPEL code", "real choreography", and "process mining, conformance testing, and mediation".

5.1 Generating and Analyzing BPEL Code

Since BPEL is increasingly supported by various engines it becomes interesting to link it to other types of models. This is useful for two reasons: (1) BPEL more closely resembles a programming language than a modeling language and (2) BPEL itself does not allow for any form of analysis other than being executable (e.g., no verification, performance analysis, etc.). Therefore, there are two interesting translations: (1) a translation from a "higher-level" notation to BPEL and (2) a translation from BPEL to a model that allows for analysis.

Until now, attention has focused on the second translation. Several attempts have been made to capture the behavior of BPEL in a formal way. Some advocate the use of finite state machines [19,20,21], others process algebras [18,31], and yet others use abstract state machines [16,17] or Petri nets [39,35,44]. A comparative summary of mappings from BPEL to formal languages is given in Table 3. The columns of the table correspond to the following criteria:

- *Tech* indicates the formalization technique used: FSM for finite state machines, PA for Process Algebra, ASM for Abstract State Machines and PN for Petri Nets.
- *SA* indicates whether the mapping covers structured activities fully (+), partially (+/–) or not at all (–). It can be seen that this feature is covered by all proposed mappings.
- *CL* indicates whether the formalization covers control links. Here a +/- rating is given for partial mappings of control links (e.g. not covering join conditions which is a feature associated to control links).
- *EH* indicates whether the formalization covers event and exception handling. Some references cover fault handling, but do not cover compensation and/or event handling, in which case, a +/– rating is assigned.
- *Comm* indicates whether the mapping can be applied to systems of interconnected BPEL processes (+) or if they are restricted to individual processes (–). In the former case, it is possible to use the mapping to detect potential mismatches between two or more BPEL processes which are expected to communicate with each other.
- *TAV* indicates whether a tool for automatic verification is provided. Some authors [19,31] have developed and/or used tools for BPEL verification but only to perform simple syntactic checks such as detecting cyclic dependencies generated by control links, or unnecessary checks such as deadlock-freeness of individual BPEL processes.[1] In these cases a +/– rating is given. This latter rating is also given to proposals where formal analysis is possible but requires significant manual steps. Finally, some authors refer to the possibility of performing formal verification [18,17], but do not develop any automated means of doing so. In this case, a – rating is given.

In industry, various tools and mappings are being developed to generate BPEL code from a graphical representation. Tools such as the IBM WebSphere

[1] Individual BPEL processes are deadlock-free by construction [35].

Table 3. A comparative summary of some of the related work on BPEL formalization and analysis

	Tech	SA	CL	EH	Comm	TAV
[21]	FSM	+	–	–	+	+
[20]	FSM	+	–	–	+	+/–
[19]	FSM	+	–	+/–	–	+/–
[18]	PA	+	–	+	–	–
[31]	PA	+	+	–	–	+/–
[17]	ASM	+	+/–	–	–	–
[35,44]	PN	+	+/–	+	+	+/–
[39]	PN	+	+	+	–	+

Choreographer and the Oracle BPEL Process Manager offer a graphical notation for BPEL. However, this notation directly reflects the code and there is no intelligent mapping. This implies that users have to think in terms of BPEL constructs (e.g., blocks, syntactical restrictions on links, etc.). More interesting is the work of Stephen White that discusses the mapping of BPMN to BPEL [46] and the work by Jana Koehler and Rainer Hauser on removing loops in the context of BPEL [30]. However, none of these publications provides a mapping of some (graphical) process modeling language onto BPEL: [46] merely presents the problem and discusses some issues using examples and [30] focuses on only one piece of the puzzle. This motivated us to develop a mapping from Colored Petri Nets (CPNs) to BPEL [6]. Clearly, both types of mappings are highly relevant. However, the quality of these mappings needs to be improved and there should be more agreement on the precise semantics of BPEL.

5.2 Real Choreography

As indicated in Section 4 interacting partners do not need to agree on a language like BPEL. However, they need to agree on an overall global process. Currently terms like *choreography* and *orchestration* are used to refer to the problem of agreeing on a common process. Some people distinguish between choreography and orchestration, e.g., "In orchestration, there's someone – the conductor – who tells everybody in the orchestra what to do and makes sure they all play in sync. In choreography, every dancer follows a pre-defined plan - everyone independently of the others." We will not make this distinction and simply assume that *choreographies define collaborations between interacting parties*, i.e., the coordination process of interconnected web services all partners need to agree on. Figure 2 illustrates the notion of a choreography.

Within the Web Services Choreography Working Group of the W3C, a working draft defining version 1.0 of the *Web Services Choreography Description Language* (WS-CDL) has been developed [29]. The scope of WS-CDL is defined as follows: "Using the Web Services Choreography specification, a contract containing a global definition of the common ordering conditions and constraints under which messages are exchanged, is produced that describes, from a global

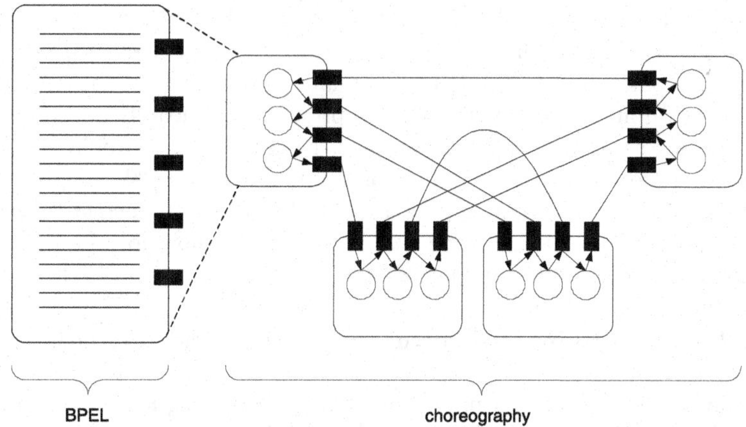

Fig. 2. A choreography defines collaborations between interacting parties

viewpoint, the common and complementary observable behavior of all the parties involved. Each party can then use the global definition to build and test solutions that conform to it. The global specification is in turn realized by a combination of the resulting local systems, on the basis of appropriate infrastructure support. The advantage of a contract based on a global viewpoint as opposed to any one endpoint is that it separates the overall global process being followed by an individual business or system within a domain of control (an endpoint) from the definition of the sequences in which each business or system exchanges information with others. This means that, as long as the observable sequences do not change, the rules and logic followed within a domain of control (endpoint) can change at will and interoperability is therefore guaranteed." [29]. This definition is consistent with the critique in Section 4 and Figure 2. Unfortunately, like most standards in the web services stack, the language is verbose and complex. Somehow the essence as shown in Figure 2 is lost. Moreover, the language again defines concepts such as "sequence", "choice", and "parallel" in some ad-hoc notation with unclear semantics. This suggests that some parts of the language are an alternative to BPEL while they are not. The main problem is that WS-CDL is not declarative. A choreography should allow for the specification of the "what" without having to state the "how". This is similar to the difference between a program and its specification. One can specify what an ordered sequence is without specifying an algorithm to do so!

In [1] we describe a more theoretical approach to the problem. The paper describes the P2P (Public-To-Private) approach which addresses one of the most notorious problems in this domain: How to design an inter-organizational workflow such that there is local autonomy without compromising the consistency of the overall process. The approach uses a notion of inheritance and consists of three steps: (1) create a common understanding of the inter-organizational workflow by specifying the shared public workflow, (2) partition the public workflow over the organizational entities involved, and (3) for each organizational entity: create a private workflow which is a subclass of the relevant part of the public workflow. In [1] it is shown that this approach avoids typical anomalies in business-to-business collaboration (e.g., deadlocks and livelocks) and yields an inter-organizational workflow which is guaranteed to realize the behavior specified in the public workflow. The P2P approach relies heavily on the use of Petri nets and a formal notion of inheritance. Nevertheless, it would be interesting to adopt these ideas in the context of languages such as WS-CDL and BPEL. Another, more declarative, approach could be based on *temporal logic* [34,40]. Languages such as *Linear Temporal Logic* (LTL) allow for the definition and verification of desirable behavior [23,24,25].

5.3 Process Mining, Conformance Testing, and Mediation

Assuming that there is a running process (possibly implemented using BPEL) and a choreography specification (possibly specified in WS-CDL), it is interesting to check whether each partner/web-service is well behaved. Note that partners have no control over each other's services. Moreover, partners will not expose the internal structure and state of their services. The closed and uncontrollable nature of web-services may generate a variety of problems. Fortunately, *process mining* [7] and *conformance testing* [2] techniques may be of assistance. For both we need to assume the existence of an *event log* [7]. For example, one may log the messages exchanged between all parties involved in a choreography (either distributed or through some coordinator). Using this event log, we may use process mining techniques to reconstruct part of the process that actually took place. This way one can "discover" the actual choreography. However, in an ideal situation this choreography is given in terms of a predefined process model. The coexistence of event logs and process models raises the question of conformance. This question may be viewed from two angles. First of all, the model may be assumed to be "correct" because it represents the way partners should work, and the question is whether the events in the log are consistent with the process model. For example, the log may contain "incorrect" event sequences not possible according to the model. This may indicate violations of choreography all parties previously agreed upon. Second, the event log may be assumed to be "correct" because it is what really happened. In the latter case the question is whether the choreography that has been agreed upon is no longer valid and should be modified. To actually measure conformance, we have developed a tool called *Conformance Checker*. This tool has been developed in the context of the *ProM framework*[2]. The ProM framework offers a wide range of tools related to process mining, i.e., extracting information from event logs [7]. At this point in time we are investigating the addition of plug-ins specific for the mining of web services. Some preliminary investigations have been reported in [14,22].

Another prominent issue, complementary to conformance, is that of *mediation*. When it is found (either a priori through model comparison or a posteriori through mining), that the conversation protocol that a given service provides does not match the conversation protocol that it is expected to provide, there

---

[2] Both documentation and software can be downloaded from `www.processmining.org`.

are basically two options: (1) modify the service to suit the new expected conversation protocol; or (2) mediate between the conversation protocol of the service as it is, and the conversation protocol as it should be. The former option is usually not suitable because the same service may interact with other services that rely on the conversation protocol that the service currently provides. In other words, the same service may participate in different collaborations such that in each of these collaborations a different conversation protocol is expected from it. Thus, mediation between the *provided conversation protocol* of a service, and the various conversation protocols that are expected from it (i.e., the *required conversation protocols*), is generally unavoidable. This issue has been widely studied in the area of software components where it is known as *adaptation*. However, most of the work on component adaptation focuses on structural mediation (i.e., mediating different structural interfaces and specifically, between different data types). Since services are expected to participate in collaborations driven by process models, behavioral mediation is a prominent requirement. Some work has been done in this area both in the components and services community [28,11,8], but there is still no overarching framework and supporting tools for behavioral service mediation are missing.

6 Petri and Pi

In discussions, Petri nets [41] and Pi calculus [36] are often mentioned as two possible formal languages that could serve as a basis for languages such as BPEL and WS-CDL. Some vendors claim that their systems are based on Petri nets or Pi calculus and other vendors suggest that they do not need a formal language to base their system on. In essence there are three "camps" in these discussions: the "Petri net camp", the "Pi calculus" (or process algebra) camp, and the "Practitioners camp" (also known as the "No formalism camp"). This was the reason for starting the "Petri nets and Pi calculus for business processes" working group (`http://www.smartgroups.com/groups/petri_and_pi`) in June 2004. Its goal is to have discussions and meetings on the formal foundations of BPM in general and languages like BPEL in particular. The working group was initiated by Robin Milner, Wil van der Aalst, Rob van Glabbeek, Roger Whitehead, and Keith Harrison-Broninski. The first meeting of this working group took place in June 2005 at Eindhoven University of Technology. Interesting elements of the first meeting were the identification of meaningful patterns and the sharing of solutions of common examples using languages such as BPEL, WS-CDL, colored Petri nets, Pi calculus, YAWL, statecharts, CCS, SOS, RAD, etc.

Most of the topics discussed in this paper are relevant to the Petri and Pi working group. In fact, this paper was inspired by the Eindhoven workshop of this group. Interested readers are invited to join this working group by sending an e-mail to `petri_and_pi-owner@smartgroups.com` or one of its members with the request to become a member.

References

1. W.M.P. van der Aalst. Inheritance of Interorganizational Workflows: How to agree to disagree without loosing control? *Information Technology and Management Journal*, 4(4):345–389, 2003.
2. W.M.P. van der Aalst. Business Alignment: Using Process Mining as a Tool for Delta Analysis and Conformance Testing. *Requirements Engineering Journal*, 2005 (to appear).
3. W.M.P. van der Aalst, M. Dumas, and A.H.M. ter Hofstede. Web Service Composition Languages: Old Wine in New Bottles? In *Proceeding of the 29th EUROMICRO Conference: New Waves in System Architecture*, pages 298–305. IEEE Computer Society, Los Alamitos, CA, 2003.
4. W.M.P. van der Aalst and K.M. van Hee. *Workflow Management: Models, Methods, and Systems.* MIT press, Cambridge, MA, 2002.
5. W.M.P. van der Aalst, A.H.M. ter Hofstede, B. Kiepuszewski, and A.P. Barros. Workflow Patterns. *Distributed and Parallel Databases*, 14(1):5–51, 2003.
6. W.M.P. van der Aalst and K.B. Lassen. Translating Workflow Nets to BPEL4WS. BETA Working Paper Series, Eindhoven University of Technology, Eindhoven, 2005.
7. W.M.P. van der Aalst, B.F. van Dongen, J. Herbst, L. Maruster, G. Schimm, and A.J.M.M. Weijters. Workflow Mining: A Survey of Issues and Approaches. *Data and Knowledge Engineering*, 47(2):237–267, 2003.
8. M. Altenhofen, E. Boerger, and J. Lemcke. An execution semantics for mediation patterns. In *Proceedings of the BPM2005 Workshops: Workshop on Choreography and Orchestration for Business Process Managament*, Nancy, France, September 2005.
9. T. Andrews, F. Curbera, H. Dholakia, Y. Goland, J. Klein, F. Leymann, K. Liu, D. Roller, D. Smith, S. Thatte, I. Trickovic, and S. Weerawarana. Business Process Execution Language for Web Services, Version 1.1. Standards proposal by BEA Systems, International Business Machines Corporation, and Microsoft Corporation, 2003.
10. A. Barros, M. Dumas, and A.H.M. ter Hofstede. Service Interaction Patterns: Towards a Reference Framework for Service-based Business Process Interconnection. QUT Technical report, FIT-TR-2005-012, Queensland University of Technology, Brisbane, 2005. (To appear in BPM 2005.)
11. B. Benatallah, F. Casati, D. Grigori, H. Motahari-Nezhad, and F. Toumani. Developing Adapters for Web Services Integration. In *Proceedings of the International Conference on Advanced Information Systems Engineering (CAiSE)*, Porto, Portugal, June 2005. Springer Verlag.
12. E. Christensen, F. Curbera, G. Meredith, and S. Weerawarana. Web Services Description Language (WSDL) 1.1. http://www.w3.org/TR/wsdl, 2001.
13. M. Dumas, W.M.P. van der Aalst, and A.H.M. ter Hofstede. *Process-Aware Information Systems.* Wiley & Sons, 2005.
14. S. Dustdar, R. Gombotz, and K. Baina. Web Services Interaction Mining. Technical Report TUV-1841-2004-16, Information Systems Institute, Vienna University of Technology, Wien, Austria, 2004.
15. C.A. Ellis. Information Control Nets: A Mathematical Model of Office Information Flow. In *Proceedings of the Conference on Simulation, Measurement and Modeling of Computer Systems*, pages 225–240, Boulder, Colorado, 1979. ACM Press.

16. D. Fahland and W. Reisig. ASM-based semantics for BPEL: The negative control flow. In *Proc. 12th International Workshop on Abstract State Machines*, pages 131–151, Paris, France, 2005.
17. R. Farahbod, U. Glässer, and M. Vajihollahi. Specification and validation of the business process execution language for web services. In *Abstract State Machines 2004*, volume 3052 of *Lecture Notes in Computer Science*, pages 79–94, Lutherstadt Wittenberg, Germany, May 2004. Springer-Verlag, Berlin.
18. A. Ferrara. Web services: A process algebra approach. In *Proceedings of the 2nd international conference on Service oriented computing*, pages 242–251, New York, NY, USA, 2004. ACM Press.
19. J.A. Fisteus, L.S. Fernández, and C.D. Kloos. Formal verification of BPEL4WS business collaborations. In *Proceedings of the 5th International Conference on Electronic Commerce and Web Technologies (EC-Web '04)*, volume 3182 of *Lecture Notes in Computer Science*, pages 79–94, Zaragoza, Spain, August 2004. Springer-Verlag, Berlin.
20. H. Foster, S. Uchitel, J. Magee, and J. Kramer. Model-based Verification of Web Service Composition. In *Proceedings of 18th IEEE International Conference on Automated Software Engineering (ASE)*, pages 152–161, Montreal, Canada, October 2003.
21. X. Fu, T. Bultan, and J. Su. Analysis of Interacting BPEL Web Services. In *International World Wide Web Conference: Proceedings of the 13th international conference on World Wide Web*, pages 621–630, New York, NY, USA, 2004. ACM Press.
22. W. Gaaloul, S. Bhiri, and C. Godart. Discovering Workflow Transactional Behavior from Event-Based Log. In *On the Move to Meaningful Internet Systems 2004: CoopIS, DOA, and ODBASE: OTM Confederated International Conferences, CoopIS, DOA, and ODBASE 2004*, volume 3290 of *Lecture Notes in Computer Science*, pages 3–18, 2004.
23. D. Giannakopoulou and K. Havelund. Automata-Based Verification of Temporal Properties on Running Programs. In *Proceedings of the 16th IEEE International Conference on Automated Software Engineering (ASE'01)*, pages 412–416. IEEE Computer Society Press, Providence, 2001.
24. K. Havelund and G. Rosu. Monitoring Programs Using Rewriting. In *Proceedings of the 16th IEEE International Conference on Automated Software Engineering (ASE'01)*, pages 135–143. IEEE Computer Society Press, Providence, 2001.
25. K. Havelund and G. Rosu. Synthesizing Monitors for Safety Properties. In *Proceedings of the 8th International Conference on Tools and Algorithms for the Construction and Analysis of Systems (TACAS 2002)*, volume 2280 of *Lecture Notes in Computer Science*, pages 342–356. Springer-Verlag, Berlin, 2002.
26. G. Hohpe and B. Woolf. *Enterprise Integration Patterns.* Addison-Wesley Professional, Reading, MA, 2003.
27. A. W. Holt. Coordination Technology and Petri Nets. In *Advances in Petri Nets 1985*, volume 222 of *Lecture Notes in Computer Science*, pages 278–296. Springer-Verlag, Berlin, 1985.
28. H.W. Schmidt and R.H. Reussner. Generating adapters for concurrent component protocol synchronisation. In *Proceedings of the Fifth IFIP International Conference on Formal Methods for Open Object-Based Distributed Systems (FMOODS)*, Enschede, The Netherlands, March 2002. Kluwer Academic Publishers.
29. N. Kavantzas, D. Burdett, G. Ritzinger, T. Fletcher, and Y. Lafon. Web Services Choreography Description Language, Version 1.0. W3C Working Draft 17-12-04, 2004.

30. J. Koehler and R. Hauser. Untangling Unstructured Cyclic Flows A Solution Based on Continuations. In *On the Move to Meaningful Internet Systems 2004: CoopIS, DOA, and ODBASE: OTM Confederated International Conferences, CoopIS, DOA, and ODBASE 2004*, volume 3290 of *Lecture Notes in Computer Science*, pages 121–138, 2004.
31. M. Koshkina and F. van Breugel. Verification of Business Processes for Web Services. Technical report CS-2003-11, York University, October 2003. Available from: http://www.cs.yorku.ca/techreports/2003/.
32. F. Leymann. Web Services Flow Language, Version 1.0, 2001.
33. F. Leymann and D. Roller. *Production Workflow: Concepts and Techniques.* Prentice-Hall PTR, Upper Saddle River, New Jersey, USA, 1999.
34. Z. Manna and A. Pnueli. *The Temporal Logic of Reactive and Concurrent Systems: Specification.* Springer-Verlag, New York, 1991.
35. A. Martens. Analyzing Web Service Based Business Processes. In *Proceedings of the 8th International Conference on Fundamental Approaches to Software Engineering (FASE 2005)*, volume 3442 of *Lecture Notes in Computer Science*, pages 19–33. Springer-Verlag, Berlin, 2005.
36. R. Milner. *Communicating and Mobile Systems: The Pi-Calculus.* Cambridge University Press, Cambridge, UK, 1999.
37. M. zur Muehlen. *Workflow-based Process Controlling: Foundation, Design and Application of workflow-driven Process Information Systems.* Logos, Berlin, 2004.
38. N.A. Mulyar and W.M.P. van der Aalst. Patterns in Colored Petri Nets. BETA Working Paper Series, WP 139, Eindhoven University of Technology, Eindhoven, 2005.
39. C. Ouyang, W.M.P. van der Aalst, S. Breutel, M. Dumas, A.H.M. ter Hofstede, and H.M.W. Verbeek. Formal Semantics and Analysis of Control Flow in WS-BPEL. BPM Center Report BPM-05-13, BPMcenter.org, 2005.
40. A. Pnueli. The Temporal Logic of Programs. In *Proceedings of the 18th IEEE Annual Symposium on the Foundations of Computer Science*, pages 46–57. IEEE Computer Society Press, Providence, 1977.
41. W. Reisig and G. Rozenberg, editors. *Lectures on Petri Nets I: Basic Models*, volume 1491 of *Lecture Notes in Computer Science.* Springer-Verlag, Berlin, 1998.
42. N. Russell, W.M.P.van der Aalst, A.H.M. ter Hofstede, and D. Edmond. Workflow Resource Patterns: Identification, Representation and Tool Support. In *Proceedings of the 17th Conference on Advanced Information Systems Engineering (CAiSE'05)*, volume 3520 of *Lecture Notes in Computer Science*, pages 216–232. Springer-Verlag, Berlin, 2005.
43. N. Russell, A.H.M. ter Hofstede, D. Edmond, and W.M.P. van der Aalst. Workflow Data Patterns: Identification, Representation and Tool Support. Accepted for publication in *Proceedings of the 24th International Conference on Conceptual Modeling (ER'2005)*, Springer-Verlag, Berlin, 2005.
44. C. Stahl. Transformation von BPEL4WS in Petrinetze (In German). Master's thesis, Humboldt University, Berlin, Germany, 2004.
45. S. Thatte. XLANG Web Services for Business Process Design, 2001.
46. S. White. Using BPMN to Model a BPEL Process. *BPTrends*, 3(3):1–18, March 2005.
47. P. Wohed, W.M.P. van der Aalst, M. Dumas, and A.H.M. ter Hofstede. Analysis of Web Services Composition Languages: The Case of BPEL4WS. In *22nd International Conference on Conceptual Modeling (ER 2003)*, volume 2813 of *Lecture Notes in Computer Science*, pages 200–215. Springer-Verlag, Berlin, 2003.
48. M.D. Zisman. *Representation, Specification and Automation of Office Procedures.* PhD thesis, University of Pennsylvania, Warton School of Business, 1977.

On Moments of Discrete Phase-Type Distributions

Tuğrul Dayar

Department of Computer Engineering, Bilkent University,
TR-06800 Bilkent, Ankara, Turkey
tugrul@cs.bilkent.edu.tr

Abstract. Recently, an efficient and stable method to compute moments of first passage times from a subset of states classified as safe to the other states in ergodic discrete-time Markov chains (DTMCs) has been proposed. This paper shows that the same method can be used to compute moments of discrete phase-type (DPH) distributions, analyzes its complexity on various acyclic DPH (ADPH) distributions, and presents results on a set of DPH distributions arising in a test suite of DTMCs.

1 Introduction

Discrete and continuous phase-type (PH) distributions have been introduced by Neuts [12,13] more than two decades ago. Although continuous PH distributions have been extensively used over the years in stochastic modeling, discrete PH (DPH) distributions have not been as widely studied, and there seems to be room for research to understand their merits and properties (see, for instance, [1,2,16]). This paper aims at rectifying the situation from a moment computation point of view.

Recently, an efficient and stable method to compute moments of first passage times from a subset of states classified as safe to the other states in ergodic discrete-time Markov chains (DTMCs) has been proposed in [4]. Although a recurrence for the moment vector of first passage times involving a common coefficient matrix and the previous moment vector on the right-hand side for the continuous-time case had been known for some time (see, for instance, [9]), a similar recurrence had not been given for the discrete-time case. The difficulty in the discrete-time case lied in the fact that equations involved factorial moments rather than moments and there was no obvious way to go from factorial moments to moments. The method proposed in [4] reduced the computation of the first k moment vectors of first passage times from a subset of states to the solution of k linear systems with a common coefficient matrix and right-hand sides governed by a novel recurrence involving the binomial coefficients and the first $(k-1)$ moment vectors. The efficiency and stability of the proposed method rest respectively on the smaller linear systems solved with a common coefficient matrix and the particular implementation of the Grassmann-Taksar-Heyman (GTH) method [8] used in factorizing the coefficient matrix.

M. Bravetti et al. (Eds.): EPEW 2005 and WS-FM 2005, LNCS 3670, pp. 51–63, 2005.

Since the first passage time from a given set of states to the other states in an ergodic DTMC is also the absorption time in the other states, it is possible to use the method proposed in [4] to compute moments of DPH distributions. It is our belief that moment matching techniques will benefit from the ability to compute higher moments of DPH distributions without having to resort to generating functions, transform techniques, or factorial moments. Therefore, in this paper we investigate the effects of using the proposed method of computing moments on various DPH distributions by concentrating on complexity issues.

The organization of the paper is as follows. In section 2, we provide a background on DPH distributions and introduce the moment computation method. In section 3, we give two examples of nonacyclic DPH distributions that have been used in stochastic modeling. In section 4, we investigate the computation of moments of acyclic DPH distributions and give an example. In section 5, we present results on moments of DPH distributions obtained from a test suite of DTMCs, and in section 6 we conclude.

2 Discrete Phase-Type Distributions

Let H be the random variable associated with the time to absorption in a finite DTMC, P, of order $(n_\mathcal{S}+1)$ with $n_\mathcal{S}$ transient states and one absorbing state conditioned on an initial probability (row) vector, τ. Then $f_H(h) = \Pr\{H = h\}$ is said to be the probability mass function of a discrete phase-type (DPH) distribution of order $n_\mathcal{S}$.

Let us assume that the transient states are those in $\mathcal{S} = \{0, 1, \ldots, n_\mathcal{S} - 1\}$ and the absorbing state is $n_\mathcal{S}$; otherwise, the states can always be renumbered. In matrix form, we have

$$P = \begin{pmatrix} P_{\mathcal{S},\mathcal{S}} & p_\mathcal{S} \\ 0^T & 1 \end{pmatrix}, \tag{1}$$

where $p_\mathcal{S} = (I - P_{\mathcal{S},\mathcal{S}})e$ and e is the column vector of ones of appropriate length. Now, let $\tau_\mathcal{S} = (\tau_0, \tau_1, \ldots, \tau_{n_\mathcal{S}-1})$, and note that $P_{\mathcal{S},\mathcal{S}}$ and $\tau_\mathcal{S}$ uniquely determine $p_\mathcal{S}$ and $\tau_{n_\mathcal{S}}$, respectively. The pair $(\tau_\mathcal{S}, P_{\mathcal{S},\mathcal{S}})$ is called the representation of the DPH random variable H. When $P_{\mathcal{S},\mathcal{S}}$ (can be symmetrically permuted to or) is in upper-triangular form, the DPH distribution is said to be acyclic [1].

In this paper, for brevity, we consider only those DPH distributions for which $\tau_{n_\mathcal{S}} = 0$ (implying that an absorption time of zero in (1) is not possible), and therefore we have

$$f_H(h) = \Pr\{H = h\} = \tau_\mathcal{S} P_{\mathcal{S},\mathcal{S}}^{h-1} p_\mathcal{S} \quad \text{for} \quad h \geq 1. \tag{2}$$

When a DPH distribution $(\tau_\mathcal{S}, P_{\mathcal{S},\mathcal{S}})$ is used to model a stochastic process which upon absorption starts anew according to the initial probability distribution $\tau_\mathcal{S}$, we say we have a DPH renewal process with interrenewal times that are DPH distributed.

Noticing that H with the probability mass function in (2) is also the random variable associated with time of first passage from the transient states in $\mathcal{S}$ to the absorbing state $n_{\mathcal{S}}$ as in [4], its $(i+1)$st moment is given by

$$E[H^{i+1}] = \sum_{h=0}^{\infty} h^{i+1} f_H(h) = \tau_{\mathcal{S}} m^{(i+1)} \quad \text{for} \quad i \geq 0. \tag{3}$$

Here, $m^{(i+1)}$ is the $(i+1)$st moment vector of time to absorption and satisfies the recurrence

$$(I - P_{\mathcal{S},\mathcal{S}})m^{(i+1)} = \sum_{j=0}^{i} (-1)^{i-j} \binom{i+1}{j} m^{(j)} \quad \text{for} \quad i \geq 0 \quad \text{with} \quad m^{(0)} = e \tag{4}$$

in which

$$\binom{i+1}{j} = \frac{(i+1)!}{j!(i+1-j)!}$$

denotes the binomial coefficient in Pascal's triangle that is read "$(i+1)$ choose j" [7]. The proof of this result appears in the appendix of [4] and follows from various identities involving binomial coefficients and Stirling numbers [7]. In passing, we remark that the coefficient matrix, $(I - P_{\mathcal{S},\mathcal{S}})$, of the linear system in (4) is nonsingular when P is ergodic (due to the irreducibility assumption in its definition).

Using the identity

$$\binom{i+1}{j} = \binom{i}{j-1} + \binom{i}{j}$$

of binomial coefficients [7], the following algorithm to compute the moment vectors, $m^{(i+1)}$, $i \geq 0$, has been given in [4]. Here, we have added one more line to compute the moments, $E[H^{i+1}]$, $i \geq 0$, as well. When a DPH distribution is used to model a stochastic process which upon absorption starts anew according to the given initial probability distribution, Algorithm 1 computes moment vectors and moments associated with DPH distributed interrenewal times.

ALGORITHM 1

Computing the kth moment vector and moment of a DPH distribution.

LU factorize $(I - P_{\mathcal{S},\mathcal{S}})$ using GTH;
$a_0 = 1$; $a_1 = -1$; $m^{(0)} = e$;
Solve for $m^{(1)}$ in $LUm^{(1)} = m^{(0)}$;
For $i = 1$ up to $k-1$ {
  $a_{i+1} = -1$;
  For $j = i$ down to 1
    $a_j = a_{j-1} - a_j$;
  $a_0 = -a_0$;
  Solve for $m^{(i+1)}$ in $LUm^{(i+1)} = \sum_{j=0}^{i} a_j m^{(j)}$;
  $E[H^{i+1}] = \tau_{\mathcal{S}} m^{(i+1)}$;
}

The order, n_S, of the DPH distribution is mostly small, in the order of tens, thereby suggesting the use of a direct method for the solution of (4). The GTH implementation proposed in [4] for the factorization $(I - P_{S,S}) = LU$ at the outset of Algorithm 1 executes on a nonhomogeneous, but consistent linear system with a singular coefficient matrix of order $(n_S + 1)$ in the form of a modified Gaussian elimination. Other than ensuring stability, this implementation turns out to be very efficient since it can be coded completely in row-wise sparse format with delayed row updates [15].

Now, let nz_{LU} denote the sum of the nonzeros in the strictly lower-triangular part of L (since ones along its diagonal are not stored) and U. Also let k denote the order of the highest moment vector to be computed. Then, in addition to the time to sparse factorize $(I - P_{S,S})$ at the outset, which is cubic in n_S in the worst case when the matrix is full, Algorithm 1 takes $(k-1)[2nz_{LU} + n_s(k+3) + k/2]$ floating-point arithmetic operations for a total of $(k-1)$ passes. In terms of space complexity, it requires $(nz_{LU} + (k+2)n_S + (k+1))$ floating-point and $(nz_{LU} + n_S + 1)$ integer storage space. See [4] for details. Here, we have also accounted for the time and space required by the computation of each moment as in the last line of the outer for-loop of Algorithm 1.

In the next section, we give two examples of nonacyclic DPH distributions used as renewal processes.

3 Examples

We provide two DPH distributions that have been used in traffic modeling.

Example 1. The interrupted Bernoulli process (IBP). When the arrival of pack-

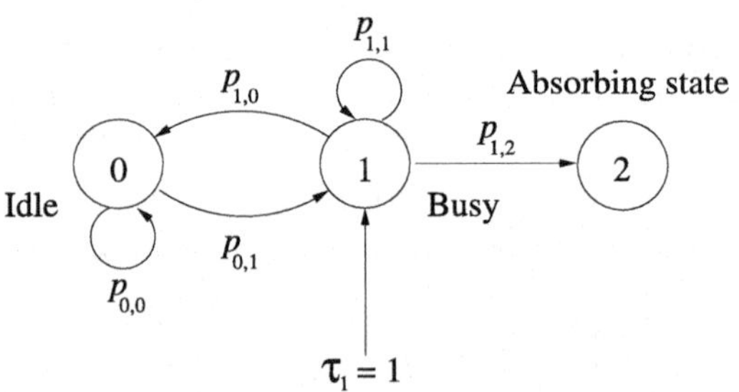

Fig. 1. The IBP interrenewal distribution

ets to a node in a communication network is of bursty nature, one may use the interrupted Bernoulli process (IBP) to model the arrival of packets. This form of arrivals is inspired by the fact that, most of the time packets arrive to a node from several external sources and they happen to be grouped in bursts.

The IBP is a DPH renewal process which is governed by busy and idle periods. Time is thought of as being slotted and state changes may only occur at points that are multiples of a slot duration. The IBP interrenewal distribution in Figure 1 is represented by the DTMC

$$P_{IBP} = \left(\begin{array}{cc|c} p_{0,0} & p_{0,1} & 0 \\ p_{1,0} & p_{1,1} & p_{1,2} \\ \hline 0 & 0 & 1 \end{array}\right), \tag{5}$$

whose (2×2) principal submatrix is nonacyclic, and the initial probability vector $\tau_S = (0, 1)$. After an absorption, the DPH renewal process starts anew so as to remain in the busy period where renewals (that is, arrivals) can take place.

It is also possible to view the transition probabilities in (5) as given by

$$p_{0,1} = \beta, \ p_{1,0} = \alpha, \ \text{and} \ p_{1,2} = (1-\alpha)\lambda,$$

where λ is the probability of a renewal in the particular slot within a busy period [11]. Note that when $\lambda = 1$, the self-loop in state 1 does not exist. This is understandable since then at each slot in the busy period a renewal takes place.

Using the (2×2) principal submatrix of P_{IBP}, we obtain

$$I - P_{S,S} = \begin{pmatrix} 1 - p_{0,0} & -p_{0,1} \\ -p_{1,0} & 1 - p_{1,1} \end{pmatrix}$$

which has the L and U factors

$$L = \begin{pmatrix} 1 & 0 \\ -p_{1,0}/(1-p_{0,0}) & 1 \end{pmatrix}, \ U = \begin{pmatrix} 1 - p_{0,0} & -p_{0,1} \\ 0 & 1 - p_{1,1} + p_{0,1}p_{1,0}/(1-p_{0,0}) \end{pmatrix}.$$

Then the remaining steps of Algorithm 1 can be executed to compute moments of the IBP interrenewal distribution.

Example 2. Markov modulated Bernoulli process (MMBP). Consider a slightly different version of the Markov modulated Bernoulli process (MMBP) that has been proposed to emulate self-similarity in [14] with initial probability vector $\tau_S = (0, 0, \ldots, 0, 1)$ and absorbing DTMC

$$P_{MMBP} = \left(\begin{array}{ccccc|c} \sum_{n_S-1} & 0 & \cdots & 0 & (q/a)^{n_S-1} & 0 \\ 0 & \sum_{n_S-2} & \cdots & 0 & (q/a)^{n_S-2} & 0 \\ \vdots & \vdots & \ddots & \vdots & \vdots & \vdots \\ 0 & 0 & \cdots & \sum_1 & (q/a) & 0 \\ 1/a^{n_S-1} & 1/a^{n_S-2} & \cdots & 1/a & (1-\lambda)\sum_0 & \lambda\sum_0 \\ \hline 0 & 0 & \cdots & 0 & 0 & 1 \end{array}\right), \tag{6}$$

where $0 < q \le a$, $1 < a$, $0 < \lambda \le 1$, $\sum_0 = 1 - \sum_{j=0}^{n_S-1} 1/a^j$ (hence, $0 < \sum_0 < 1$), and $\sum_i = 1 - (q/a)^i$ for $1 \le i \le n_S - 1$. Observe that IBP is a special case of MMBP in which $n_S = 2$, $\alpha = 1/a$, and $\beta = q/a$.

Using the nonacyclic $(n_S \times n_S)$ principal submatrix of P_{MMBP} in (6), we obtain

$$I - P_{S,S} = \begin{pmatrix} 1-\sum_{n_S-1} & 0 & \cdots & 0 & -(q/a)^{n_S-1} \\ 0 & 1-\sum_{n_S-2} & \cdots & 0 & -(q/a)^{n_S-2} \\ \vdots & \vdots & \ddots & \vdots & \vdots \\ 0 & 0 & \cdots & 1-\sum_1 & -(q/a) \\ -1/a^{n_S-1} & -1/a^{n_S-2} & \cdots & -1/a & 1-(1-\lambda)\sum_0 \end{pmatrix}$$

which has the L and U factors

$$L = \begin{pmatrix} 1 & 0 & \cdots & 0 & 0 \\ 0 & 1 & \cdots & 0 & 0 \\ \vdots & \vdots & \ddots & \vdots & \vdots \\ 0 & 0 & \cdots & 1 & 0 \\ \frac{-1}{a^{n_S-1}(1-\sum_{n_S-1})} & \frac{-1}{a^{n_S-2}(1-\sum_{n_S-2})} & \cdots & \frac{-1}{a(1-\sum_1)} & 1 \end{pmatrix},$$

$$U = \begin{pmatrix} 1-\sum_{n_S-1} & 0 & \cdots & 0 & u_{0,n_S-1} \\ 0 & 1-\sum_{n_S-2} & \cdots & 0 & u_{1,n_S-1} \\ \vdots & \vdots & \ddots & \vdots & \vdots \\ 0 & 0 & \cdots & 1-\sum_1 & u_{n_S-2,n_S-1} \\ 0 & 0 & \cdots & 0 & u_{n_S-1,n_S-1} \end{pmatrix},$$

where

$$u_{i,n_S-1} = -(q/a)^i - \sum_{j=0}^{i-1} u_{j,n_S-1}/(a^{n_S-j}(1-\sum_{n_S-j})) \quad \text{for} \quad 0 \le i \le n_S - 2,$$

$$u_{n_S-1,n_S-1} = 1-(1-\lambda)\sum_0 - \sum_{j=0}^{n_S-2} u_{j,n_S-1}/(a^{n_S-j}(1-\sum_{n_S-j})).$$

Then the remaining steps of Algorithm 1 can be executed to compute the moments of the MMBP interrenewal distribution.

See, for instance, section 2.5 of [10] for other examples, and observe that there is a lot of sparsity in $P_{S,S}$ as in Example 2. In fact, no fill-in (i.e., nonzeros in the L and U factors replacing zeros in the coefficient matrix) is introduced during the LU factorization of $(I - P_{S,S})$ since it is a matrix with arrowhead nonzero structure.

Although we were able to give explicitly the LU factorization of $(I-P_{S,S})$ for the examples considered in this section, in general this cannot be done, and the factorization needs to be performed numerically using the GTH implementation discussed in [4]. However, for the class of DPH distributions discussed in the next section, the factorization is available explicitly.

4 Acyclic Discrete Phase-Type Distributions

We consider three types of acyclic discrete phase-type (ADPH) distributions. It is our assumption that the matrix $P_{S,S}$ in the ADPH representation is already in upper-triangular form. This implies that there is no need to LU factorize $(I-P_{S,S})$ at the outset of Algorithm 1. In other words, $L = I$ and $U = (I-P_{S,S})$.

Now, let us define

$$b^{(i+1)} = \sum_{j=0}^{i} a_j m^{(j)} \quad \text{for} \quad i \geq 0 \quad \text{with} \quad m^{(0)} = e.$$

In the general acyclic case, when $(I - P_{S,S})$ is upper-triangular, the last to next step in the outer for-loop of Algorithm 1 can be rewritten as

$$m_k^{(i+1)} = (b_k^{(i+1)} + \sum_{k'=k+1}^{n_S-1} p_{k,k'} m_{k'}^{(i+1)})/(1-p_{k,k}) \quad \text{for} \quad k = n_S - 1 \text{ down to } 0.$$

When $(I - P_{S,S})$ is upper-bidiagonal, the same step can be rewritten as

$$\begin{aligned} m_{n_S}^{(i+1)} &= b_{n_S-1}^{(i+1)}/(1-p_{n_S-1,n_S-1}), \\ m_k^{(i+1)} &= (b_k^{(i+1)} + p_{k,k+1} m_{k+1}^{(i+1)})/(1-p_{k,k}) \quad \text{for} \quad k = n_S - 2 \text{ down to } 0. \end{aligned}$$

Note that this is the case when the ADPH distribution is discrete Erlang (DE) with n_S phases. When S is a diagonal matrix, the last step reduces to

$$m_k^{(i+1)} = b_k^{(i+1)}/(1-p_{k,k}) \quad \text{for} \quad 0 \leq k \leq n_S - 1.$$

Then, for a total of $(k-1)$ passes Algorithm 1 takes $(k-1)[2nz_U + n_s(k+3) + k/2]$ floating-point arithmetic operations, and requires $(nz_U + (k+2)(n_S+1) - 1)$ floating-point and $(nz_U + n_S + 1)$ integer storage space for ADPH distributions of order n_S. Observe that when $(I-P_{S,S})$ is upper-triangular, nz_U can be anywhere between n_S and $n_S(n_S+1)/2$.

Next is an example of an acyclic DPH renewal process.

Example 3. The discrete Erlang process (DEP). Discrete Erlang process (DEP) is a DPH renewal process with $l(= n_S)$ phases and the interrenewal distribution in Figure 2. It is represented by the initial probability vector $\tau_S = (1, 0, \ldots, 0)$ and the order $(l+1)$ DTMC

$$P_{DEP} = \left(\begin{array}{ccccc|c} 1-a & a & & & & \\ & 1-a & a & & & \\ & & 1-a & \ddots & & \\ & & & \ddots & a & \\ & & & & 1-a & a \\ \hline & & & & 0 & 1 \end{array}\right), \quad (7)$$

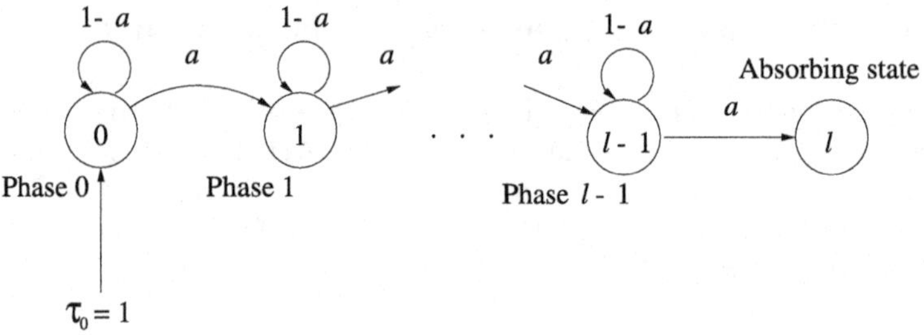

Fig. 2. The DEP interrenewal distribution

whose $(l \times l)$ principal submatrix is acyclic; DEP reduces to the geometric distribution with parameter a when $l = 1$. In the general case, it can be conceived as the convolution of l independent geometric distributions with parameter a.

Using the acyclic $(n_{\mathcal{S}} \times n_{\mathcal{S}})$ principal submatrix of P_{DEP} in (7), we obtain the upper-bidiagonal matrix

$$I - P_{\mathcal{S},\mathcal{S}} = \begin{pmatrix} a & -a & & & \\ & a & -a & & \\ & & a & \ddots & \\ & & & \ddots & -a \\ & & & & a \end{pmatrix}.$$

Then the moments of the DEP interrenewal distribution can be computed by following Algorithm 1 after its first step.

5 Numerical Results

In this section, we present results that illustrate the computation of moments of DPH distributions. We have implemented the proposed method in C using double-precision IEEE floating-point arithmetic [3], performed and timed all experiments under Cygwin 1.5.15-1 on a Pentium IV 3.4 GHz processor and a 1 GB main memory running Windows XP. In each problem, the degree of coupling, $\|p_{\mathcal{S}}\|_\infty$, and the average degree of coupling, $\|p_{\mathcal{S}}\|_1/n_{\mathcal{S}}$ (see (1)), are reported so as to indicate the inherent difficulty associated with computing the moments accurately [4].

We have experimented with two groups of problems. The first group consists of order 10, 20, 30, and 40 versions of MMBP (Example 2) and order 10^1, 10^2, 10^3, 10^4 versions of DEP (Example 3), and the particular initial distributions. The second group consists of order 10^1, 10^2, 10^3, 10^4 principal submatrices of the test suite of twelve DTMCs [6] that have been used in [5] and uniform initial distributions. In all problems, we have computed the first ten moments (whenever possible) in double precision floating-point arithmetic, but report results regarding only the first, second, fifth, and tenth moments in order to save space. The computation of binomial coefficients does not pose problems since the largest entry in the tenth row of Pascal's triangle, 10 choose 5, is equal to, 252. Note that 10^{308} is about the size of the largest positive number in double precision floating-point arithmetic, and any attempt to compute moment vectors with larger values than this will be futile. When we detect overflow in any of the moment vectors, we indicate it with n/a in the tables and do not compute further moment vectors.

All times are reported in seconds of CPU time. In the tables, T_s denotes the time to generate in core the absorbing DTMC in row-wise sparse format, to transform the rows corresponding to $\mathcal{S}$ of the sparse DTMC so that elements of those rows are ordered according to column indices when the matrix is input from a file, and to determine the number of nonzeros in $P_{\mathcal{S},\mathcal{S}}$; T_{LU} denotes the time to perform symbolic LU analysis on $(I - P_{\mathcal{S},\mathcal{S}})$ and its sparse factorization (step 1 of Algorithm 1) as discussed in section 2; and T_m denotes the time to compute the first ten moments using Algorithm 1. Hence, the sum of T_{LU} and T_m is the time it takes Algorithm 1 to execute. In order to improve the confidence in the timing results, we have timed each experiment three times and have reported the average. In the tables, $nz_{\mathcal{S}}$ denotes the number of nonzeros in $(I - P_{\mathcal{S},\mathcal{S}})$, which can be different than that in $P_{\mathcal{S},\mathcal{S}}$ due to zero diagonal elements. We have reported $nz_{\mathcal{S}}$ and nz_{LU} so that the amount of fill-in resulting from the LU factorization can be observed.

In P_{MMBP} and P_{DEP}, $p_{\mathcal{S}}$ has a single nonzero element such that $\|p_{\mathcal{S}}\|_\infty = \lambda \sum_0$ and $\|p_{\mathcal{S}}\|_\infty = a$ (see (6) and (7)), respectively. Hence, $\|p_{\mathcal{S}}\|_1 = \|p_{\mathcal{S}}\|_\infty$ and for these two examples we only report $\|p_{\mathcal{S}}\|_\infty$. Furthermore, since $(I - P_{\mathcal{S},\mathcal{S}})$ has symmetric nonzero structure in both examples and does not yield any fill-in during the factorization, it also turns out to be the case that $nz_{\mathcal{S}} = nz_{LU}$. The CPU timings (T_s, T_{LU}, T_m) in order 10, 20, 30, 40 versions of MMBP are all zero. The CPU timings in order 10^1, 10^2, 10^3 versions of DEP are all zero and the CPU timings in order 10^4 version of DEP are $(T_s, T_{LU}, T_m) = (0, 3, 0)$. Therefore, these timings do not appear in Tables 1 and 2.

Observe that it is more the average degree of coupling than the degree of coupling which determines the value of the first moment in MMBP with $q = 1.0$ and DEP, and hence their other moments. There is a high degree of variability in the MMBP interrenewal distribution even for small orders and that moments exceeding 10^{100} appear for order 30 or larger. On the other hand, the DEP interrenewal distribution approaches the deterministic distribution as the order increases. For $a = 1.0$, $P_{\mathcal{S},\mathcal{S}}$ has only an upper-diagonal resulting in immediate determinism. Recall that it takes only 3 seconds to find the first ten moments of the DEP interrenewal distribution of order 10^4 and that this time is spent in the first step of Algorithm 1.

Regarding the twelve test matrices used in the set of experiments reported in Table 5, we remark that they arise in six applications, namely 2D, pushout, mutex, ncd, qn, telecom, and that (easy, hard, medium), (mutex, mutex_alt1, mutex_alt2), and (ncd, ncd_alt1, ncd_alt2) are respectively three different versions of the pushout, mutex, and ncd problems. Furthermore, all test matrices except those of pushout are uniformized continuous-time MCs. With this second

Table 1. Moments of the MMBP interrenewal distribution

a	q	λ	(n, nz)	n_S	(nz_S, nz_{LU})	$\|ps\|_\infty$	$E[H^1]$	$E[H^2]$	$E[H^5]$	$E[H^{10}]$
2.0	1.0	0.1	(11,30)	10	(28,28)	2.0e-4	5.1e4	5.3e9	4.3e25	4.6e53
		0.5				9.8e-4	1.0e4	2.1e8	1.4e22	5.0e46
		1.0	(11,29)			2.0e-3	5.1e3	5.3e7	4.6e20	5.4e43
	2.0	0.1	(11,21)			2.0e-4	1.0e4	2.1e8	1.3e22	4.6e46
		0.5				9.8e-4	2.0e3	8.4e6	4.3e18	4.7e39
		1.0	(11,20)			2.0e-3	1.0e3	2.1e6	1.3e17	4.6e36
	1.0	0.1	(21,60)	20	(58,58)	1.9e-7	1.0e8	2.2e16	1.5e42	5.9e86
		0.5				9.5e-7	2.1e7	8.8e14	4.9e38	6.1e79
		1.0	(21,59)			1.9e-6	1.0e7	2.2e14	1.6e37	6.1e76
	2.0	0.1	(21,41)			1.9e-7	1.0e7	2.2e14	1.5e37	5.8e76
		0.5				9.5e-7	2.1e6	8.8e12	4.9e33	6.0e69
		1.0	(21,40)			1.9e-6	1.0e6	2.2e12	1.5e32	5.8e66
	1.0	0.1	(31,90)	30	(88,88)	1.9e-10	1.6e11	5.2e22	1.3e58	4.3e118
		0.5				9.3e-10	3.2e10	2.1e21	4.2e54	4.4e111
		1.0	(31,89)			1.9e-9	1.6e10	5.2e20	1.3e53	4.4e108
	2.0	0.1	(31,61)			1.9e-10	1.1e10	2.3e20	1.7e52	7.4e106
		0.5				9.3e-10	2.1e9	9.2e18	5.5e48	7.6e99
		1.0	(31,60)			1.9e-9	1.1e9	2.3e18	1.7e47	7.4e96
	1.0	0.1	(41,120)	40	(118,118)	1.8e-13	2.2e14	9.7e28	6.2e73	9.6e149
		0.5				9.1e-13	4.4e13	3.9e27	2.0e70	9.9e142
		1.0	(41,119)			1.8e-12	2.2e13	9.7e26	6.2e68	9.7e139
	2.0	0.1	(41,81)			1.8e-13	1.1e13	2.4e26	1.9e67	9.4e136
		0.5				9.1e-13	2.2e12	9.7e24	6.2e63	9.6e129
		1.0	(41,80)			1.8e-12	1.1e12	2.4e24	1.9e62	9.4e126

Table 2. Moments of the DEP interrenewal distribution

a	(n, nz)	n_S	(nz_S, nz_{LU})	$\|ps\|_\infty$	$E[H^1]$	$E[H^2]$	$E[H^5]$	$E[H^{10}]$
0.1	(11,21)	10^1	(19,19)	1.0e-1	1.0e2	1.1e4	2.2e10	2.6e21
0.5				5.0e-1	2.0e1	4.2e2	5.2e6	8.7e13
1.0	(11,11)			1.0e0	1.0e1	1.0e2	1.0e5	1.0e10
0.1	(101,201)	10^2	(199,199)	1.0e-1	1.0e3	1.0e6	1.1e15	1.5e30
0.5				5.0e-1	2.0e2	4.0e4	3.4e11	1.3e23
1.0	(101,101)			1.0e0	1.0e2	1.0e4	1.0e10	1.0e20
0.1	(1001,2001)	10^3	(1999,1999)	1.0e-1	1.0e4	1.0e8	1.0e20	1.0e40
0.5				5.0e-1	2.0e3	4.0e6	3.2e16	1.0e33
1.0	(1001,1001)			1.0e0	1.0e3	1.0e6	1.0e15	1.0e30
0.1	(10001,20001)	10^4	(19999,19999)	1.0e-1	1.0e5	1.0e10	1.0e25	1.0e50
0.5				5.0e-1	2.0e4	4.0e8	3.2e21	1.0e43
1.0	(10001,10001)			1.0e0	1.0e4	1.0e8	1.0e20	1.0e40

group of problems, we aim at having an understanding of the kind of moment values that arise in DPH distributions and assessing the performance of Algorithm 1 in computing these moments.

Table 3. Moments of DPH interrenewal distributions arising in twelve test matrices

Problem (n, nz)	n_S	(nz_S, nz_{LU})	$\Vert p_S \Vert_\infty$	$\frac{\Vert p_S \Vert_1}{n_S}$	(T_s, T_{LU}, T_m)	$E[H^1]$	$E[H^2]$	$E[H^5]$	$E[H^{10}]$
2D	10^1	(25,42)	8.9e-1	2.7e-1	(0,0,0)	3.1e0	1.4e1	2.8e3	7.2e7
(16641,	10^2	(352,1746)	9.0e-1	8.9e-2		8.0e0	9.3e1	3.4e5	8.5e11
66049)	10^3	(3843,60340)	9.2e-1	2.8e-2		2.4e1	8.8e2	9.5e7	6.1e16
	10^4	(39588,1662849)	9.4e-1	5.8e-3	(0,5,1)	3.7e2	2.6e5	2.2e14	5.0e29
easy	10^1	(43,50)	9.8e-1	3.9e-1	(0,0,0)	1.9e0	4.5e0	1.0e2	4.5e4
(20301,	10^2	(596,1723)	9.8e-1	1.3e-1		5.5e0	4.2e1	4.3e4	1.0e10
140504)	10^3	(6648,57706)	9.9e-1	4.4e-2		1.6e1	3.6e2	9.9e6	6.5e14
	10^4	(68880,1866042)	9.8e-1	1.4e-2	(1,6,1)	4.9e1	3.5e3	3.1e9	6.3e19
hard	10^1	(43,50)	9.0e-2	3.6e-2	(0,0,0)	5.0e1	5.5e3	5.6e10	9.1e23
(20301,	10^2	(596,1723)	9.4e-2	1.2e-2		6.0e2	9.5e5	3.1e16	3.6e35
140504)	10^3	(6648,57706)	9.8e-2	4.0e-3		5.9e3	1.0e8	4.2e21	7.1e45
	10^4	(68880,1866042)	9.1e-2	1.3e-3	(1,6,1)	5.6e4	9.5e9	4.0e26	6.7e55
medium	10^1	(43,50)	5.0e-2	2.0e-2	(0,0,0)	1.9e3	7.9e6	4.0e18	4.2e39
(20301,	10^2	(596,1723)	6.9e-2	6.9e-3		6.9e12	9.6e25	2.0e66	9.9e134
140504)	10^3	(6648,57706)	9.0e-2	2.3e-3		3.0e41	1.8e83	3.1e209	n/a
	10^4	(68880,1866042)	5.4e-2	7.0e-4	(1,6,2)	1.1e134	2.4e268	n/a	n/a
mutex	10^1	(28,100)	2.2e-2	1.9e-2	(1,0,0)	1.0e2	2.2e4	1.9e12	9.7e26
(39203,	10^2	(464,9398)	2.1e-2	1.6e-2		7.2e2	1.1e6	3.6e16	3.6e35
563491)	10^3	(7296,833658)	2.1e-2	1.2e-2	(1,7,0)	2.8e4	1.7e9	2.7e24	1.9e51
	10^4	(109492,66540178)	1.5e-2	7.2e-3	(2,4415,10)	3.3e7	2.3e15	5.3e39	7.1e81
mutex_alt1	10^1	(28,100)	2.2e-5	1.9e-5	(1,0,0)	2.1e5	8.9e10	5.0e28	6.4e59
(39203,	10^2	(464,9398)	2.1e-5	1.6e-5		2.7e9	1.5e19	1.7e49	7.7e100
563491)	10^3	(7296,833658)	2.1e-5	1.2e-5	(1,7,0)	1.9e16	7.5e32	3.3e83	2.7e169
	10^4	(109492,66540178)	1.5e-5	7.2e-6	(2,4385,10)	2.6e25	1.4e51	1.5e129	5.9e260
mutex_alt2	10^1	(28,100)	2.2e-8	1.9e-8	(1,0,0)	2.1e8	8.9e16	5.1e43	6.5e89
(39203,	10^2	(464,9398)	2.1e-8	1.6e-8		2.7e15	1.5e31	1.8e79	8.1e160
563491)	10^3	(7296,833658)	2.1e-8	1.2e-8	(1,7,0)	1.9e28	7.5e56	3.3e143	2.7e289
	10^4	(109492,66540178)	1.5e-8	7.2e-9	(2,4526,47)	2.6e43	1.4e87	1.5e219	n/a
ncd	10^1	(34,56)	1.7e-2	2.0e-3	(0,0,0)	4.7e3	6.5e7	1.7e21	1.4e45
(23426,	10^2	(508,2662)	9.1e-2	8.8e-3		7.9e3	2.1e8	2.6e22	2.2e47
156026)	10^3	(6040,122706)	3.5e-1	1.7e-2		1.6e4	7.4e8	3.1e23	8.1e48
	10^4	(65444,5615910)	9.9e-1	2.7e-2	(1,33,1)	4.7e4	6.0e9	3.5e25	3.4e52
ncd_alt1	10^1	(34,56)	1.7e-2	2.0e-3	(0,0,0)	3.7e3	4.1e7	5.1e20	9.1e43
(23426,	10^2	(508,2662)	9.1e-2	8.8e-3		7.1e3	1.6e8	7.9e21	7.3e45
156026)	10^3	(6040,122706)	3.5e-1	1.7e-2		1.5e4	6.8e8	2.1e23	2.2e48
	10^4	(65444,5615910)	9.9e-1	2.7e-2	(1,33,1)	4.6e4	5.9e9	3.2e25	2.4e52
ncd_alt2	10^1	(34,56)	1.7e-2	1.9e-3	(0,0,0)	3.6e8	5.8e17	1.8e46	1.7e95
(23426,	10^2	(508,2662)	9.0e-2	8.8e-3		2.1e17	1.5e35	4.7e89	9.9e181
156026)	10^3	(6040,122706)	3.5e-1	1.7e-2		1.0e31	3.6e62	1.2e158	n/a
	10^4	(65444,5615910)	9.9e-1	2.7e-2	(1,33,4)	3.4e53	4.4e107	6.8e270	n/a
qn	10^1	(26,50)	4.4e-1	2.1e-1	(1,0,0)	9.1e0	2.1e2	2.2e7	1.8e17
(104625,	10^2	(388,3837)	6.2e-1	1.6e-1		3.9e1	5.2e3	1.1e11	6.1e24
593115)	10^3	(4688,285709)	6.2e-1	1.1e-1	(1,1,0)	4.2e2	7.0e5	2.6e16	3.4e35
	10^4	(53224,17064913)	6.2e-1	5.6e-2	(1,325,3)	4.3e4	6.0e9	1.2e26	6.0e54
telecom	10^1	(34,48)	4.2e-3	1.1e-3	(0,0,0)	8.3e3	1.6e8	8.8e21	2.3e46
(20491,	10^2	(442,1420)	7.4e-3	5.3e-4		3.1e7	2.0e15	4.0e39	4.3e81
101041)	10^3	(4814,43098)	1.7e-2	3.2e-4		1.6e21	5.4e42	1.5e108	5.5e218
	10^4	(49234,610098)	8.4e-2	2.3e-4	(1,3,1)	4.3e192	n/a	n/a	n/a

Six of the DTMCs (ncd, ncd_alt1, ncd_alt2, mutex, mutex_alt1, mutex_alt2) have symmetric nonzero structure; however, all DPH distributions arising from the twelve test matrices yield some fill-in. For the mutex, mutex_alt1, mutex_alt2, and qn test matrices, nz_{LU} for the order 10^4 DPH distribution is larger than 10^7, thereby making it the most difficult to solve. Otherwise, the first ten moments of all DPH distributions of order 10^3 and smaller can be computed in 8 seconds. If the mutex, mutex_alt1, mutex_alt2, and qn problems are excluded, the first ten moments of DPH distributions of order 10^4 can be computed in 38 seconds. The time spent by Algorithm 1 after its first step in all of these problems is within 4 seconds. Hence, it is again the LU factorization which dominates the computation, and it becomes excessive in the mutex, mutex_alt1, and mutex_alt2 problems with order 10^4 (note that the discrepancy in the T_{LU} timings in this case is less than 5% and is immaterial). But then again, 10^4 is a relatively large order to consider in practice. Furthermore, when overflow is encountered in computing a particular moment, we notice that the computation time for that particular moment in T_m increases considerably. See, for instance, mutex_alt2 with order 10^4. This situation can be attributed to the exceptions generated during the forward and backward solutions with the L and U factors in the body of the outer for-loop of Algorithm 1 when there is overflow.

As in the first set of experiments, we again observe that the smaller the average degree of coupling, the larger the moments become and the more difficult it is to obtain accurate results. However, through the particular DPH distributions arising in the twelve test matrices, we also understand that it is not only the average degree of coupling but also the values of the nonzeros in the L and U factors (and therefore the values in $(I - P_{\mathcal{S},\mathcal{S}})$) that determine how the moments grow. See, for instance, the value of the first moment in telecom with order 10^4, which has an average degree of coupling 2.3×10^{-4}.

6 Conclusion

In this paper, we have presented a recently introduced method to compute higher moments of DPH distributions in row-wise sparse format and have conducted numerical experiments on a test suite of DTMCs with it. The method is based on factorizing a nonsingular matrix as large as the order of the DPH distribution using a form of GTH with delayed row updates and solving as many linear systems with different right-hand sides as the number of moments desired. It has been shown that the factorization is available explicitly up to a symmetric permutation when the DPH distribution is acyclic, and therefore need not be computed. Timing results have been given to indicate the efficiency of the proposed method. First moments much larger than the reciprocal of the average degree of coupling have been reported, especially when the order of the DPH distribution becomes large. When the order is 10^4 or larger, there are cases which show that it will be useful to consider a fill reducing ordering of the coefficient matrix since the amount of fill-in during factorization may become excessive.

References

1. A. Bobbio, A. Horváth, M. Scarpa, and M. Telek. Acyclic discrete phase type distributions: properties and a parameter estimation algorithm. *Performance Evaluation*, 54(1):1–32, Sep 2003.
2. A. Bobbio, A. Horváth, and M. Telek. The scale factor: a new degree of freedom in phase-type approximation. *Performance Evaluation*, 56(1–4):121–144, Mar 2004.
3. T. Dayar. *Software for computing moments of phase type distributions*, 2005. Available from `http://www.cs.bilkent.edu.tr/~tugrul/software.html`.
4. T. Dayar and N. Akar. Computing moments of firt passage times to a subset of states in Markov chains. *SIAM Journal on Matrix Analysis and Applications*, to appear. Also as Technical Report BU-CE-0414, Department of Computer Engineering, Bilkent University, Ankara, Turkey, Dec 2004. Available from `http://www.cs.bilkent.edu.tr/tech-reports/2004/BU-CE-0414.pdf`.
5. T. Dayar and W. J. Stewart. Comparison of partitioning techniques for two-level iterative methods on large, sparse Markov chains. Technical Report BU-CEIS-9805, Department of Computer Engineering and Information Science, Bilkent University, Ankara, Turkey, Apr 1998. Available from `http://www.cs.bilkent.edu.tr/tech-reports/1998/BU-CEIS-9805.ps.gz`.
6. T. Dayar and W. J. Stewart. *A test suite of Markov chains*, 2005. Available from `http://www.cs.bilkent.edu.tr/~tugrul/matrices.html`.
7. R. L. Graham, D. E. Knuth, and O. Patashnik. *Concrete Mathematics: A Foundation for Computer Science*. Addison-Wesley Publishing Company, Reading, Massachusetts, U.S.A., 1989.
8. W. K. Grassmann, M. I. Taksar, and D. P. Heyman. Regenerative analysis and steady state distributions for Markov chains. *Operations Research*, 33(5):1107–1116, Sep–Oct 1985.
9. B. R. Haverkort. *Performance of Computer Communication Systems: A Model-based Approach*. John Wiley & Sons, Chichester, England, 1998.
10. G. Latouche and V. Ramaswami. *Introduction to Matrix Analytic Methods in Stochastic Modeling*. SIAM Press, Philadelphia, Pennslyvania, U.S.A., 1999.
11. S. Nakazawa, K. Kawahara, S. Yamaguchi, and Y. Oie. Performance comparison with layer 3 switches in case of flow- and topology-driven connection setup. In *IEEE Global Telecommunications Conference, Rio de Janeiro, Brazil*, volume 1a of *GLOBECOM'99*, pages 79–86. IEEE Press, New York, U.S.A., Dec 1999.
12. M. F. Neuts. Probability distributions of phase type. In *Liber amicorum Prof. Emeritus H. Florin*, pages 173–206. Department of Mathematics, University of Louvain, Belgium, 1975.
13. M. F. Neuts. *Matrix-Geometric Solutions in Stochastic Models: An Algorithmic Approach*. Johns Hopkins University Press, Baltimore, Maryland, U.S.A., 1981.
14. S. Robert and J.-Y. Le Boudec. New models for pseudo self-similar traffic. *Performance Evaluation*, 30(1–2):57–68, Jul 1997.
15. W. J. Stewart. *Introduction to the Numerical Solution of Markov Chains*. Princeton University Press, Princeton, New Jersey, U.S.A., 1994.
16. M. Telek and A. Heindl. Matching moments for acyclic discrete and continuous phase-type distributions of second order. *International Journal of Simulation: Systems, Science & Technology*, 3(3–4):47–57, Dec 2002.

Zero-Automatic Queues

Thu-Ha Dao-Thi and Jean Mairesse

LIAFA, CNRS-Université Paris 7, France
{daothi, mairesse}@liafa.jussieu.fr

Abstract. We introduce and study a new model: *0-automatic queues.* Roughly, 0-automatic queues are characterized by a special buffering mechanism evolving like a random walk on some infinite group or monoid. The salient result is that all 0-automatic queues are quasi-reversible. When considering the two simplest and extremal cases of 0-automatic queues, we recover the simple $M/M/1$ queue, and Gelenbe's G-queue with positive and negative customers.

Keywords: $M/M/1$ queue, G-queue, quasi-reversibility, product form.

1 Introduction

Here is an informal description of a special type of 0-automatic queue (corresponding to a free product of three finite monoids). Consider a queue with a single server and an infinite capacity buffer. Customers are colored either in Red, Blue, or Green, with a finite set of possible shades within each color: $\Sigma_R, \Sigma_B, \Sigma_G$. In the buffer, two consecutive customers of the same color either cancel each other or merge to give a new customer of the same color. Customers of different colors do not interact. This is illustrated in Figure 1.

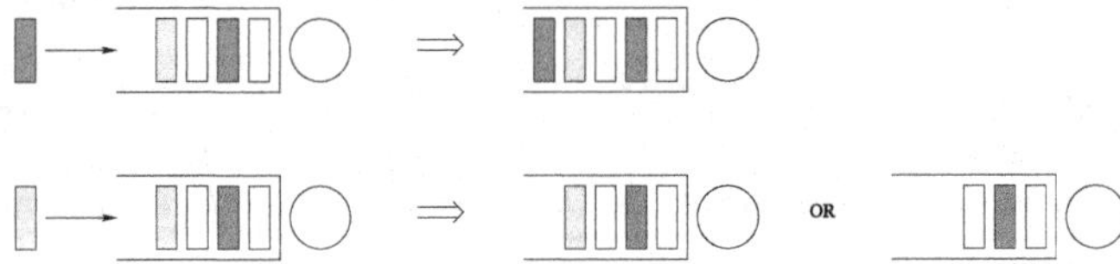

Fig. 1. A 0-automatic queue

The shades get modified in the merging procedure, according to an internal law: $\Sigma_i \times \Sigma_i \rightarrow \Sigma_i \cup \{1\}$, with 1 coding for the cancellation. The only but crucial restriction is that each internal law should be associative.

We now give a more detailed account of the model and results. Zero-automatic queues may be viewed as the synthesis of a simple queue and a random walk on a 0-automatic pair. We first recall these last two models.

The $M/M/1/\infty$ FIFO queue, or simply $M/M/1$ queue, is the Markovian queue with arrivals and services occurring at constant rate, say λ and μ, a single

M. Bravetti et al. (Eds.): EPEW 2005 and WS-FM 2005, LNCS 3670, pp. 64–78, 2005.

server, an infinite capacity buffer, and a First-In-First-Out discipline. This is arguably the simplest and also the most studied model in queueing theory, with at least one book devoted to it [1]. The queue-length process is a continuous time jump Markov process and its infinitesimal generator Q is given by: $\forall n \in \mathbb{N},\ Q(n,n+1) = \lambda,\ Q(n+1,n) = \mu$. Under the stability condition $\lambda < \mu$, the queue-length process is ergodic, and its stationary distribution π is given by:

$$\pi(n) = \left(1 - \frac{\lambda}{\mu}\right)\left(\frac{\lambda}{\mu}\right)^n . \tag{1}$$

Besides, and this constitutes the celebrated Burke Theorem, the departure process in equilibrium has the same law as the arrival process.

Let us introduce the a priori completely unrelated model of random walk on a 0-automatic pair studied in [12,11].

Let X be an infinite group or monoid with a finite set of generators Σ. Let ν be a probability measure on Σ and let $(x_i)_{i\in\mathbb{N}}$ be a sequence of Σ-valued i.i.d. r.v.'s of law ν. Let $(X_n)_n$ be the sequence of X-valued r.v.'s defined by: $X_0 = 1_X,\ X_{n+1} = X_n * x_n = x_0 * x_1 * \cdots * x_n$, where 1_X is the unit element of X and $*$ is the group or monoid law. By definition, $(X_n)_n$ is a realization of the random walk (X, ν).

We now assume that the pair (X, Σ) is *0-automatic*. The definition will be given in Section 2. For the moment, it suffices to say that the elements of X can be set in bijection with a regular language $L(X, \Sigma) \subset \Sigma^*$. The random walk $(X_n)_n$ is viewed as evolving on $L(X, \Sigma)$. If $X_n = ua, a \in \Sigma$, and $x_n = b \in \Sigma$, then

$$X_{n+1} = u \text{ if } a*b = 1_X, \quad X_{n+1} = uc \text{ if } a*b = c \in \Sigma, \quad X_{n+1} = uab \text{ otherwise.} \tag{2}$$

In words, the 0-automatic assumption implies that the multiplication by a generator has a simple and local effect. Now assume that the random walk is transient. Let $\nu^\infty(u\Sigma^{\mathbb{N}})$ be the probability that the random walk goes to infinity in the "direction" u (i.e. $\nu^\infty(u\Sigma^{\mathbb{N}}) = P\{\exists N, \forall n \geq N, X_n \in u\Sigma^*\}$). The following is the main result in [11]:

$$\forall u = u_1 \cdots u_n \in L(X, \Sigma), \quad \nu^\infty(u\Sigma^{\mathbb{N}}) = \widehat{q}(u_1)\cdots\widehat{q}(u_{n-1})\widehat{r}(u_n) , \tag{3}$$

where $\forall a \in \Sigma,\ \widehat{q}(a) \in (0,1), \widehat{r}(a) \in (0,1)$.

The expressions in (1) and (3) share a common "multiplicative" structure. Guided by this analogy, we want to merge the two models together. To that purpose, we make the following elementary observation: if we block the server in an $M/M/1$ queue, the number of waiting customers after n arrivals is $A_n = n$. And $(A_n)_n$ can be viewed as the (not so random) random walk on the 0-automatic pair $((\mathbb{N}, +), \{1\})$ associated with the probability $\nu : \ \nu(1) = 1$.

Now, replace the trivial random walk $(A_n)_n$ by a more complex random walk $(X_n)_n$ on a 0-automatic pair (X, Σ). Hence, the random walk $(X_n)_n$ constitutes the buffering mechanism in a queue with a blocked server. A *0-automatic queue* is the model obtained when unblocking the server. The set Σ is the set of possible *classes* for customers. Upon arrival, a new customer (class b) interacts with the customer presently at the back-end of the buffer (class a) according to (2). At the front-end of the buffer, customers are served at constant rate.

Let $\widehat{\gamma}$ be the drift or rate of escape to infinity of the random walk $(X_n)_n$. The stability condition for the 0-automatic queue associated with $(X_n)_n$ is given in Section 4: $\lambda\widehat{\gamma} < \mu$. Under this condition, in Section 5, we prove that the stationary distribution p for the queue-content process has a "multiplicative" structure:

$$\forall u = u_1 \cdots u_n \in L(X, \Sigma), \quad p(u) = (1-\rho)\rho^n q(u_1) \cdots q(u_{n-1}) r(u_n) , \qquad (4)$$

for some numbers $\rho \in (0,1)$, $\forall a \in \Sigma$, $q(a) \in (0,1), r(a) \in (0,1)$. (These numbers are in general different from their counterparts in (1) and (3).) Furthermore, the departure process from the queue is a Poisson process of rate $\rho\mu$. Thus we have an extension of Burke Theorem to all 0-automatic queues. Using standard terminology, 0-automatic queues are *quasi-reversible.*

To be more precise, given $(X_n)_n$, several variants of 0-automatic queues can be defined depending on the way customers are incorporated in an empty queue (boundary condition). There is precisely *one* choice for which the result in (4) holds. The numbers $\rho, q(\cdot), r(\cdot)$, as well as the right boundary condition, are determined implicitly via the unique solution of a set of algebraic equations, see Theorems 5.1 and 5.2 for a precise statement.

Aside from the free monoid, the next simplest example of a 0-automatic pair is the free group over one generator: $((\mathbb{Z}, +), \{1, -1\})$. The corresponding 0-automatic queues are variations of Gelenbe's G-queues, or queues with positive and negative customers, which were quite extensively studied in the 90's, see [6,5] and the bibliography in [7]. General 0-automatic queues can be viewed as a wide generalization of this setting. This is illustrated in Section 6.

The $M/M/1$ queue is the basic primitive for building Jackson networks, which have the remarkable property of having a "product-form" stationary distribution. More generally, networks made of quasi-reversible nodes tend to have a product form distribution, see for instance [14]. In an ongoing work [2], we prove that it is indeed the case for Jackson-type networks of 0-automatic queues.

Due to lack of space, the proofs are not included. They can be found in the corresponding research report [3], where the relationship between 0-automatic queues and Quasi-Birth-and-Death processes is also detailed.

2 Preliminaries: Random Walks on 0-Automatic pairs

The symbol $\sqcup$ is used for the disjoint union of sets. Given a set T, a vector $x \in \mathbb{R}^T$, and $S \subset T$, set $x(S) = \sum_{u \in S} x(u)$.

We recall the needed material on random walks on 0-automatic pairs. The presentation closely follows [11,12].

Monoids and groups. Given a set Σ, the free monoid generated by Σ is denoted by Σ^*. The unit element is denoted by 1_{Σ^*}. As usual, the elements of

Σ and Σ^* are called *letters* and *words*, respectively. The subsets of Σ^* are called *languages*. The *length* (number of letters) of a word u is denoted by $|u|_\Sigma$.

Let $(X, *)$ be a group or monoid with set of generators Σ. The unit element of X is denoted by 1_X. When X is a group, the inverse of $x \in X$ is denoted by x^{-1}. We always assume that: $1_X \notin \Sigma$, and in the group case that: $x \in \Sigma \implies x^{-1} \in \Sigma$. Denote by $\pi : \Sigma^* \to X$ the monoid homomorphism which associates to a word $a_1 \cdots a_k$ of Σ^* the element $a_1 * \cdots * a_k$ of X. A language L of Σ^* is a *cross-section* of X if the restriction of π to L is a bijection. The inverse map $\Phi : X \to L$ is then called the *normal form* map. The *length* with respect to Σ of an element x of X is : $|x|_\Sigma = \min\{k \mid x = a_1 * \cdots * a_k, a_i \in \Sigma\}$.

The *Cayley graph* $\mathfrak{X}(X, \Sigma)$ of X with respect to Σ is the directed graph with nodes X and arcs $u \to v$ if $\exists a \in \Sigma,\ u * a = v$.

Consider a relation $R \subset \Sigma^* \times \Sigma^*$, and let $\sim_R$ be the least congruence on Σ^* such that $u \sim_R v$ if $(u, v) \in R$. Let X be isomorphic to the quotient monoid $(\Sigma^* / \sim_R)$. We say that $\langle\, \Sigma \mid u = v, (u, v) \in R \,\rangle$ is a *monoid presentation* of X and we write $X = \langle\, \Sigma \mid u = v, (u, v) \in R \,\rangle$.

Given a set S, denote by $\mathbb{F}(S)$ the free group generated by S. Let S^{-1} be the set of inverses of the generators. A monoid presentation of $\mathbb{F}(S)$ is

$$\mathbb{F}(S) = \langle\, S \sqcup S^{-1} \mid aa^{-1} = 1, a^{-1}a = 1,\ \forall a \in S \,\rangle\,. \tag{5}$$

Given two groups or monoids X_1 and X_2, we denote by $X_1 \star X_2$ the *free product* of X_1 and X_2. Roughly, the elements of $X_1 \star X_2$ are the finite alternate sequences of elements of $X_1 \backslash \{1_{X_1}\}$ and $X_2 \backslash \{1_{X_2}\}$, and the law is the concatenation with simplification. More rigorously, the definition is as follows. Set $S = X_1 \sqcup X_2$. The *free product* $X_1 \star X_2$ is defined by the monoid presentation:

$$\langle\ S \mid (\forall u, v \in S^*),\ u1_{X_i}v = uv, \quad (\forall a, b, c \in X_i, \text{ s.t. } c = a * b),\ uabv = ucv\ \rangle\,.$$

If X_1 and X_2 are groups, then $X_1 \star X_2$ is also a group. The free product of more than two groups or monoids is defined analogously.

Zero-automatic pairs. Define the language $L(X, \Sigma) \subset \Sigma^*$ of *locally reduced words* by:

$$L(X, \Sigma) = \{u_1 \cdots u_k \mid \forall i \in \{1, \ldots, k-1\}, u_i * u_{i+1} \notin \Sigma \cup \{1_X\}\}\,. \tag{6}$$

Define the sets: $\forall a \in \Sigma$,

$$\text{Left}(a) = \{b \in \Sigma \mid b * a \notin \Sigma \cup \{1_X\}\}, \quad \text{Right}(a) = \{b \in \Sigma \mid a * b \notin \Sigma \cup \{1_X\}\}\,.$$

Definition 2.1. *Let $(G, *)$ be a group with finite set of generators Σ. We say that the pair (G, Σ) is 0-automatic if $L(G, \Sigma)$ is a cross-section of G.*

The name *0-automatic* comes from [11]. Under other names, the notion had been studied for instance in [15,9]. In these last two references, it is proved that if (G, Σ) is a 0-automatic pair, then G is isomorphic to a *plain group*, i.e. a free product of finitely many finite groups and a finitely generated free group.

However the set Σ may be larger than a "natural" set of generators of the plain group. In [11], a procedure is proposed which computes all the Σ's such that (G, Σ) is 0-automatic, for a given plain group G. Four different characterizations of 0-automatic pairs, completing the one in Definition 2.1, are collected in [11, Theorem 3.6].

Definition 2.2. *Let $(M, *)$ be a monoid with finite set of generators Σ. Assume that $L(M, \Sigma)$ is a cross-section. Let $\Phi : M \to L(M, \Sigma)$ be the corresponding normal form map. Assume that: $\forall u \in M$ s.t $\Phi(u) = u_1 \cdots u_k$, $\forall a \in \Sigma$,*

$$\Phi(a * u) = \begin{cases} u_2 \cdots u_k & \textit{if } a * u_1 = 1_M \\ v u_2 \cdots u_k & \textit{if } a * u_1 = v \in \Sigma \\ a u_1 \cdots u_k & \textit{otherwise} \end{cases}, \tag{7}$$

and assume that the analog holds for $\Phi(u * a)$.

Assume furthermore that : $\forall a, b \in \Sigma$ such that $a * b \in \Sigma$,

$$\mathit{Right}(a * b) = \mathit{Right}(a), \qquad \mathit{Left}(a * b) = \mathit{Left}(b) . \tag{8}$$

Then we say that the pair (M, Σ) is 0-automatic.

In the group case, the conditions (7) and (8) are implied by the fact that the language of locally reduced words is a cross-section.

When (X, Σ) is 0-automatic with X infinite, the Cayley graph $\mathcal{X}(X, \Sigma)$ has a tree-like structure. The removal of any node disconnects the graph. Besides, the number of elementary circuits going through a given node is finite.

Here are some examples of 0-automatic pairs:

- Let X be a finite group or monoid. Then $(X, X \backslash \{1_X\})$ is 0-automatic.
- Let Σ be a finite set. The pairs (Σ^*, Σ) and $(\mathbb{F}(\Sigma), \Sigma \sqcup \Sigma^{-1})$ are 0-automatic.
- Let (X_1, Σ_1) and (X_2, Σ_2) be 0-automatic. Then $(X_1 \star X_2, \Sigma_1 \sqcup \Sigma_2)$ is 0-automatic.

The *graph of successors* $\mathcal{N}\mathrm{ext}(X, \Sigma)$ of a 0-automatic pair (X, Σ) is the directed graph with nodes Σ and arcs $u \to v$ if $v \in \mathrm{Right}(u)$.

When $X = G$ is an infinite group not isomorphic to $\mathbb{Z}$, then $\mathcal{N}\mathrm{ext}(G, \Sigma)$ is strongly connected [11, Lemma 3.13]. Also, when X is the free product of two or more monoids, then $\mathcal{N}\mathrm{ext}(X, \Sigma)$ is clearly strongly connected.

Random walks on monoids and groups. Let $(X, *)$ be a group or monoid with finite set of generators Σ. Let ν be a probability distribution over Σ. Consider the Markov chain on the state space X with one-step transition probabilities given by: $\forall x \in X, \forall a \in \Sigma$, $P_{x, x*a} = \nu(a)$. This Markov chain is called the *(right) random walk* (associated with) (X, ν).

Let $(x_n)_n$ be a sequence of i.i.d. r.v's distributed according to ν. Set

$$X_0 = 1_X, \quad X_{n+1} = X_n * x_n = x_0 * \cdots * x_n . \tag{9}$$

Then $(X_n)_n$ is a realization of the random walk (X, ν). For all $x, y \in X$, we have $|x * y|_\Sigma \leq |x|_\Sigma + |y|_\Sigma$. Applying Kingman's Subadditive Ergodic Theorem yields the following (first noticed by Guivarc'h [8]): there exists $\gamma \in \mathbb{R}_+$ such that

$$\lim_{n\to\infty} \frac{|X_n|_\Sigma}{n} = \gamma \quad \text{a.s and in } L^p, \ \forall 1 \leq p < \infty\,. \tag{10}$$

We call γ the *drift* of the random walk. When $\gamma > 0$, the random walk is transient.

Random walks on 0-automatic pairs. It is convenient to introduce the notion of a 0-automatic triple.

Definition 2.3. *A triple (X, Σ, ν) is said to be* 0-automatic *if: (i) (X, Σ) is a 0-automatic pair with X infinite; (ii) ν is a probability measure whose support is included in Σ and generates X.*

The Traffic Equations play an essential role in the study of the random walk.

Definition 2.4 (Traffic Equations). *The* Traffic Equations (TE) *associated with a 0-automatic triple (X, Σ, ν) are the equations of the variables $(x(a))_{a\in\Sigma} \in \mathbb{R}^\Sigma$ defined by: $\forall a \in \Sigma$,*

$$x(a) = \nu(a)x(Right(a)) + \sum_{u*v=a} \nu(u)x(v) + \sum_{\substack{v\in Left(a)\\ u*v=1_X}} \nu(u)\frac{x(v)}{x(Right(v))}x(a)\,. \tag{11}$$

An admissible solution *is a solution belonging to $\{x \in \mathbb{R}^\Sigma \mid x_i > 0, \ \sum_i x_i = 1\}$.*

Quite often in the paper, we assume the following additional Conditions on the 0-automatic triple (X, Σ, ν):

C1. the graph $\mathcal{N}\mathrm{ext}(X, \Sigma)$ is strongly connected;

C2. the random walk (X, ν) is transient.

As mentioned above, Condition **C1** is always satisfied when X is a group other than $\mathbb{Z}$, or a free product. Condition **C2** is not very restrictive either. There are only two cases in which (X, ν) is not transient: (i) the triple $(\mathbb{Z}, \{-1, 1\}, \{1/2, 1/2\})$; (ii) the triples $(\mathbb{Z}/2\mathbb{Z} \star \mathbb{Z}/2\mathbb{Z}, \{a, b\}, \nu)$, for any ν, where a and b are the respective generators of the two cyclic groups. See [11] for details.

Define:

$$\mathcal{B} = \{x \in \mathbb{R}^\Sigma \mid \forall i, x_i > 0, \sum_i x_i = 1\}, \quad \bar{\mathcal{B}} = \{x \in \mathbb{R}^\Sigma \mid \forall i, x_i \geq 0, \sum_i x_i = 1\}\,. \tag{12}$$

By multiplying both sides of (11) by $\prod_b x(\mathrm{Right}(b))$, we obtain a new set of Equations without denominators. With some abuse, a solution r in $\bar{\mathcal{B}}$ of this last set of Equations is still called a solution of the TE.

Next result can be easily deduced from the proof of [11, Theorem 4.5].

Proposition 2.1. *Let (X, Σ, ν) be a 0-automatic triple. The Traffic Equations TE have at least one solution in $\bar{\mathcal{B}}$. Assume now that the Conditions* **C1-C2** *also hold. The TE have a unique solution in $\bar{\mathcal{B}}$, and this solution belongs to $\mathcal{B}$.*

The interest of Proposition 2.1 is that the harmonic measure and the drift can be expressed in function of the solution to the TE.

Define the set $L^\infty \subset \Sigma^{\mathbb{N}}$ by

$$L^\infty = \{u_0u_1\cdots u_k\cdots \in \Sigma^{\mathbb{N}} \mid \forall i \in \mathbb{N}, u_{i+1} \in \mathrm{Right}(u_i)\} . \tag{13}$$

A word belongs to L^∞ iff all its finite prefixes belong to $L(X,\Sigma)$. The set L^∞ should be viewed as the "boundary" of X.

Let $(X_n)_n$ be a realization of the random walk which is assumed to be transient. The *harmonic measure* of the random walk is the probability measure ν^∞ on L^∞ with finite-dimensional marginals defined by:

$$\forall u_1\cdots u_k \in L(X,\Sigma),\ \nu^\infty(u_1\cdots u_k\Sigma^{\mathbb{N}}) = P\{\exists N, \forall n \geq N,\ \Phi(X_n) \in u_1\cdots u_k\Sigma^*\}.$$

This defines indeed a measure on L^∞ because the random walk is transient, and because $\Phi(X_n)$ and $\Phi(X_{n+1})$ differ by at most one symbol by 0-automaticity. Intuitively, the harmonic measure ν^∞ gives the direction in which $(X_n)_n$ goes to infinity.

For a proof of next result, see [11, Theorem 4.5] and [12, Theorem 3.3]. In the case of the free group, the result appears in [4,13], see also the survey [10].

Theorem 2.1. *Let (X,Σ,ν) be a 0-automatic triple satisfying* **C1-C2**. *Let $\widehat{r} = (\widehat{r}(a))_{a\in\Sigma}$ be the unique admissible solution to the Traffic Equations. Set $\widehat{q}(a) = \widehat{r}(a)/\widehat{r}(Right(a))$, for all $a \in \Sigma$. The harmonic measure ν^∞ and the drift $\widehat{\gamma}$ of the random walk (X,ν) are given by:*

$$\forall u_1\cdots u_k,\quad \nu^\infty(u_1\cdots u_k\Sigma^{\mathbb{N}}) = \widehat{q}(u_1)\cdots\widehat{q}(u_{k-1})\widehat{r}(u_k),$$
$$\widehat{\gamma} = \sum_{a\in\Sigma}\nu(a)\left[\widehat{r}(Right(a)) - \sum_{b\mid a*b=1_X}\widehat{r}(b)\right].$$

3 The Zero-Automatic Queue

The 0-automatic queue is defined informally in Section 1. Now we give a formal definition via the infinitesimal generator of the queue-content process.

Definition 3.1 (Zero-automatic queue). *Let (X,Σ,ν) be a 0-automatic triple. Let $L(X,\Sigma)$ be the set of locally reduced words, defined in (6). Consider $r \in \bar{\mathcal{B}}$, see (12), and $\lambda,\mu \in \mathbb{R}_+^*$. The* 0-automatic queue *of type $(X,\Sigma,\nu,r,\lambda,\mu)$ is defined as follows. The* queue-content *$(M(t))_{t\in\mathbb{R}_+}$ is a continuous time jump Markov process on the state space $L(X,\Sigma)$ with infinitesimal generator Q defined by: $\forall u = u_n\cdots u_1 \in L(X,\Sigma)\setminus\cup_{a\in\Sigma}\{a\}^*$,*

$$\begin{cases} Q(u,bu) = \lambda\nu(b)\ , & \forall b \in Left(u_n) \\ Q(u,bu_{n-1}\cdots u_1) = \lambda\sum_{c\mid c*u_n=b}\nu(c)\ , & \forall b \in \Sigma\setminus\{u_n\},\ \exists c\in\Sigma,\ c*u_n = b \\ Q(u,u_{n-1}\cdots u_1) = \lambda\sum_{c\mid c*u_n=1_X}\nu(c) & \\ Q(u,u_n\cdots u_2) = \mu & \end{cases} \tag{14}$$

and, for all $a \in \Sigma$ such that $a \in Right(a)$, and for all $n \geq 1$,

$$\begin{cases} Q(a^n, ba^n) \quad = \lambda\nu(b) \ , & \forall b \in \mathit{Left}(a) \\ Q(a^n, ba^{n-1}) = \lambda \sum_{c|c*a=b} \nu(c) \ , & \forall b \in \Sigma \setminus \{a\}, \ \exists c \in \Sigma, \ c * a = b \\ Q(a^n, a^{n-1}) \quad = \mu + \lambda \sum_{c|c*a=1_X} \nu(c) \end{cases} \tag{15}$$

and, finally, the boundary condition is,

$$Q(1_{\Sigma^*}, a) \ = \ \lambda\nu(a)r(Right(a)) \ , \quad \forall a \in \Sigma \, . \tag{16}$$

We denote by $M/M/(X, \Sigma)$ any 0-automatic queue of type $(X, \Sigma, \nu, r, \lambda, \mu)$.

In words, the queue $M/M/(X, \Sigma)$ is formed by a single server with FIFO discipline and an infinite capacity buffer in which the buffering occurs according to the random walk (X, ν). It is a multiclass queue (classes Σ) but the class does not influence the way customers get served, only the way they get buffered.

The intuition behind the form of the boundary condition is as follows: the buffer-content is viewed as the visible part of an iceberg consisting of an infinite word of L^∞, see (13). When the buffer is empty, new customers are incorporated depending on the invisible part of the iceberg, whose first marginal is assumed to be r. This last point will find an a-posteriori justification in Theorem 5.1.

The two simplest examples of 0-automatic queues are the ones associated with (i) the free monoid $(\mathbb{N}, +)$ and (ii) the free group $(\mathbb{Z}, +)$. They correspond to well-known objects.

The simple queue. Consider the free monoid $X = \{a\}^* = \{a^k, k \in \mathbb{N}\}$ over the single generator set $\Sigma = \{a\}$. Hence, for any $\lambda, \mu \in \mathbb{R}_+^*$, there is only one possible associated queue: $(X, \Sigma, \nu, r, \lambda, \mu)$, where $\nu(a) = r(a) = 1$. By specializing the infinitesimal generator Q given in Definition 3.1, we get: $\forall n \in \mathbb{N}$,

$$Q(a^n, a^{n+1}) = \lambda, \quad Q(a^{n+1}, a^n) = \mu \, .$$

This is the simple $M/M/1/\infty$ queue with arrival rate λ and service rate μ.

The G-queue. Consider the free group $X = \mathbb{F}(a) = \{a^k, k \in \mathbb{Z}\}$ and the set of generators $\Sigma = \{a, a^{-1}\}$. Let ν be a probability measure on Σ such that $\nu(a) > 0, \nu(a^{-1}) > 0$. Consider $r \in \mathcal{B}$ and $\lambda, \mu \in \mathbb{R}_+^*$. The 0-automatic queue $(\mathbb{F}(a), \Sigma, \nu, r, \lambda, \mu)$ has an infinitesimal generator Q given by: $\forall n \in \mathbb{N}$,

$$\begin{cases} Q(a^n, a^{n+1}) = \lambda\nu(a), & Q(a^{n+1}, a^n) = \mu + \lambda\nu(a^{-1}) \\ Q(a^{-n}, a^{-(n+1)}) = \lambda\nu(a^{-1}), & Q(a^{-(n+1)}, a^{-n}) = \mu + \lambda\nu(a) \\ Q(1_{\Sigma^*}, a) = \lambda\nu(a)r(a), & Q(1_{\Sigma^*}, a^{-1}) = \lambda\nu(a^{-1})r(a^{-1}) \, . \end{cases}$$

This is close to the mechanism of the G-queue, a queue with positive and negative customers introduced in [6,7]. We go back to this model in Section 6.

The definition of 0-automatic queues has the flexibility to allow for many variations and extensions, see Section 6 for a couple of examples.

4 Stability Condition for a Zero-Automatic Queue

Throughout Sections 4 and 5, the model is as follows. Let (X, Σ, ν) be a 0-automatic triple satisfying the Conditions **C1-C2**. Fix λ and μ in $\mathbb{R}_+^*$ and r in $\mathcal{B}$. Consider the 0-automatic queue $(X, \Sigma, \nu, r, \lambda, \mu)$.

Let $M = (M_t)_t$ be the queue-content process. Proposition 4.1 characterizes the stability region of the 0-automatic queue.

Proposition 4.1. *The process M is irreducible. Let $\widehat{\gamma}$ be the drift of the random walk (X, ν). We have:*

$$\begin{aligned}\left[\lambda\widehat{\gamma} < \mu\right] &\iff M \text{ ergodic}\\ \left[\lambda\widehat{\gamma} = \mu\right] &\iff M \text{ null recurrent}\\ \left[\lambda\widehat{\gamma} > \mu\right] &\iff M \text{ transient}\,.\end{aligned}$$

5 Stationary Distribution of a Stable Queue

5.1 The Twisted Traffic Equations

The Traffic Equations, see Def. 2.4, play a central role in studying the random walk. We now introduce equations which play a similar role for the queue.

Definition 5.1 (Twisted Traffic Equations). *The* Twisted Traffic Equations TTE *associated with $(X, \Sigma, \nu, \lambda, \mu)$ are the equations of the variables (η, x), $\eta \in \mathbb{R}_+^*$, $x = (x(a))_{a \in \Sigma} \in \mathbb{R}_+^{\Sigma}$, defined by:*

$$\eta(\lambda+\mu)x(a) = \eta^2 \mu x(a) + \lambda\nu(a)x(Right(a)) + \eta\lambda \sum_{u*v=a} \nu(u)x(v) \qquad (17)$$
$$+\eta^2\lambda \sum_{\substack{v\in Left(a)\\ u*v=1_X}} \nu(u)\frac{x(v)}{x(Right(v))}x(a)\,.$$

According to Proposition 2.1, there is a unique admissible solution to the Traffic Equations, that we denote by $\widehat{r} = (\widehat{r}(a))_{a\in\Sigma}$. We denote by $\widehat{\gamma}$ the drift of the random walk (X, ν).

Let us investigate some properties of the solutions to the TTE. First, if (ρ, r) is a solution to the TTE with $r \in \bar{\mathcal{B}}$, then r belongs to $\mathcal{B}$. This follows directly from the shape of the TTE and from Condition **C1**.

Second, if we set $\eta = 1$ in the Twisted Traffic Equations (17), and perform the obvious simplifications, we obtain the Traffic Equations (11). It implies that $(1, \widehat{r})$ is a solution to the TTE for all λ and μ.

Lemma 5.1. *Let (ρ, r), $\rho \in \mathbb{R}_+^*, r \in \mathcal{B}$, be a solution to the TTE. We have either $(\rho, r) = (1, \widehat{r})$, or*

$$\rho = \frac{\lambda\sum_{a\in\Sigma}\nu(a)r(Right(a))}{\mu + \lambda\sum_{u*v=1_X}\nu(u)r(v)}\,. \qquad (18)$$

The relevant solutions to the TTE will turn out to be the ones satisfying (18). This leads us to the next Definition.

Definition 5.2. *A solution* (ρ, r) *to the TTE is called an* admissible solution *if* $\rho \in \mathbb{R}_+^*, r \in \mathcal{B}$, *and if (18) is satisfied.*

Lemma 5.2. *If* $\lambda\widehat{\gamma} = \mu$, *then* $(1, \widehat{r})$ *is an admissible solution to the TTE. If* $(1, r)$ *is an admissible solution to the TTE, then* $r = \widehat{r}$ *and* $\lambda\widehat{\gamma} = \mu$.

Lemma 5.3. *There always exists an admissible solution to the TTE.*

5.2 The Main Results

Next Lemma begins to establish the link between the Twisted Traffic Equations and the queue $M/M/(X, \Sigma)$. Theorems 5.1-5.2-5.3 are the main results.

Lemma 5.4. *Let* (ρ, r) *be an admissible solution to the TTE. Consider the 0-automatic queue of type* $(X, \Sigma, \nu, r, \lambda, \mu)$. *Let* Q_r *be the infinitesimal generator of the queue-content process. Consider the measure* $p_{\rho,r}$ *on* $L(X, \Sigma)$ *defined by:*

$$\forall a_1 \cdots a_n \in L(X, \Sigma), \quad p_{\rho,r}(a_1 \cdots a_n) = \rho^n \frac{r(a_1)}{r(Right(a_1))} \cdots \frac{r(a_{n-1})}{r(Right(a_{n-1}))} r(a_n). \tag{19}$$

We have $p_{\rho,r} Q_r = 0$. *Conversely, assume there exist* $\rho \in \mathbb{R}_+^*$ *and* $r \in \mathcal{B}$ *such that the measure* $p_{\rho,r}$ *defined by (19) satisfies* $p_{\rho,r} Q_r = 0$. *Then* (ρ, r) *is an admissible solution to the TTE.*

Theorem 5.1. *Let* (X, Σ, ν) *be a 0-automatic triple. The Conditions* **C1-C2** *of page 69 are assumed to hold. Fix* λ *and* μ *in* $\mathbb{R}_+^*$.

Let (ρ, r) *be an admissible solution to the TTE. Consider the 0-automatic queue* $(X, \Sigma, \nu, r, \lambda, \mu)$. *Denote by* $M_r = (M_r(t))_t$ *the queue-content process. We have:*

$$\begin{array}{rcl} [\rho < 1] \iff [\lambda\widehat{\gamma} < \mu] \iff & [M_r \textit{ ergodic}] \\ [\rho = 1] \iff [\lambda\widehat{\gamma} = \mu] \iff & [M_r \textit{ null recurrent}] \\ [\rho > 1] \iff [\lambda\widehat{\gamma} > \mu] \iff & [M_r \textit{ transient}] . \end{array}$$

Assume that $\lambda\widehat{\gamma} < \mu$. *The stationary distribution* $\pi_{\rho,r}$ *of the process* M_r *is given by:* $\forall a_1 \cdots a_n \in L(X, \Sigma)$,

$$\pi_{\rho,r}(a_1 \cdots a_n) = (1-\rho) p_{\rho,r}(a_1 \cdots a_n) = (1-\rho)\rho^n q(a_1) \cdots q(a_{n-1}) r(a_n) , \tag{20}$$

where $q(a) = r(a)/r(Right(a))$ *for all* $a \in \Sigma$.

Assume that $\lambda\widehat{\gamma} = \mu$. It follows immediately from Lemma 5.2 and Theorem 5.1 that $(1, \widehat{r})$ is the unique admissible solution to the TTE. We now have a more interesting result in the same vein.

Theorem 5.2. *Consider the same model as in Theorem 5.1. Assume furthermore that (X, Σ) satisfies at least one of the following two conditions: (i) X is a group; (ii) $X = X_1 \star \cdots \star X_k$, with X_i being finite monoids, and $\Sigma = \sqcup_i (X_i \backslash \{1_{X_i}\})$. Assume that $\lambda\widehat{\gamma} < \mu$. Then the TTE have a unique admissible solution. In particular, there is only one variant of the 0-automatic queue $M/M/(X, \Sigma)$ with a product form distribution.*

In a 0-automatic queue, 'departures' occur both at the front-end and at the back-end of the buffer. Here we consider only the front-end departures, i.e. the ones corresponding to service completions and not to buffer cancellations.

Let $M = (M(t))_t$ be the queue-content process of some 0-automatic queue $M/M/(X, \Sigma)$. A *departure* is an instant of jump of M corresponding to a jump of the type: $u_n \cdots u_1 \to u_n \cdots u_2$ for $u = u_n \cdots u_1 \in L(X, \Sigma) \setminus \{1_{\Sigma^*}\}$. When $u = a^n, a \in \Sigma, n \geq 1$ (the case (15) in Definition 3.1), some special care must be taken. The jumps of type $a^n \to a^{n-1}$ which are *departures* occur at rate μ. The *departure process* is the point process of departures.

Theorem 5.3. *The model is the same as in Theorem 5.1. Assume that $\lambda\widehat{\gamma} < \mu$. Let (ρ, r) be an admissible solution of the TTE. Consider the 0-automatic queue $(X, \Sigma, \nu, r, \lambda, \mu)$. The stationary departure process is a Poisson process of rate $\rho\mu$. Furthermore, for all t, the queue-content at time t is independent of the departure process up to time t.*

When specializing to $(X, \Sigma) = (\{a\}^*, \{a\})$, we recover Burke Theorem.

6 Examples

In this Section, we illustrate the above results. Another purpose is to show the modelling flexibility provided by 0-automatic queues.

Consider the following three "types" of tasks.

- Classical type. Tasks are processed one by one with no simplification occuring in the buffer: $aa = aa$. The corresponding pair is $(\mathbb{N}, \{1\}) \sim (\{a\}^*, \{a\})$.
- Positive/negative type. Tasks are either positive (a) or negative (a^{-1}) and two consecutive tasks of opposite signs cancel each other: $aa^{-1} = a^{-1}a = 1$. The corresponding pair is $(\mathbb{Z}, \{1, -1\}) \sim (\mathbb{F}(a), \{a, a^{-1}\})$. The relevance of this type for applications is discussed in [7].
- "One equals many" type. It takes the same time to process one or several consecutive instances of the same task: $aa = a$. Think for instance of a ticket reservation where the number of requests is only reflected by an integer value in a menu-bar choice. The corresponding pair is $(\mathbb{B}, \{a\})$ where $\mathbb{B}$ is the Boolean monoid $\mathbb{B} = \langle\, a \mid a^2 = a \,\rangle$.

To model a server where several of the above types (and possibly several copies of the same type) can be processed, one just has to perform the free product of the corresponding monoids or groups. A couple of examples follow.

When the model is simple enough, the TTE can be solved explicitly to get closed form formulas as for $\mathbb{N} \star \mathbb{B}$ below. In all cases and like any set of algebraic equations, the TTE can be solved with any prescribed precision.

The free product $\mathbb{N} \star \mathbb{B}$. Consider the 0-automatic triple $(\{a\}^* \star \langle\, b \mid b^2 = b\,\rangle, \Sigma = \{a, b\}, \nu)$, where $\nu(a) = p$, $\nu(b) = 1 - p$, $p \in (0, 1)$. In Figure 2, we illustrate the corresponding buffering mechanism.

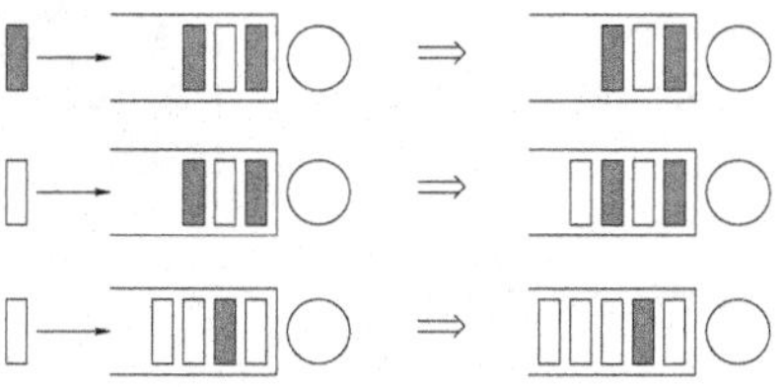

Fig. 2. The queue $M/M/(\mathbb{N} \star \mathbb{B}, \Sigma)$ with a in white and b in dark gray

The Conditions **C1-C2** of page 69 are satisfied. The unique solution $\hat{r}$ of the TE is: $\widehat{r}(c) = p$, $\widehat{r}(b) = 1 - p$. The drift of the random walk is $\widehat{\gamma} = (2 - p)p$.

According to Theorem 5.2, the associated TTE have a unique admissible solution that we denote by (ρ, r). Solving the TTE, we obtain that ρ is a solution of $f(Y) = 0$, where:

$$f(Y) = \mu^2 Y^3 + (\mu^2 + \mu\lambda + \lambda\mu p)Y^2 + (\lambda^2 p + \lambda\mu p)Y - \lambda^2 p^2 + \lambda^2 p\,.$$

The relation between $r(b)$ and ρ is given by: $\rho = [r(b)(1 - p) + p]\lambda/\mu$.

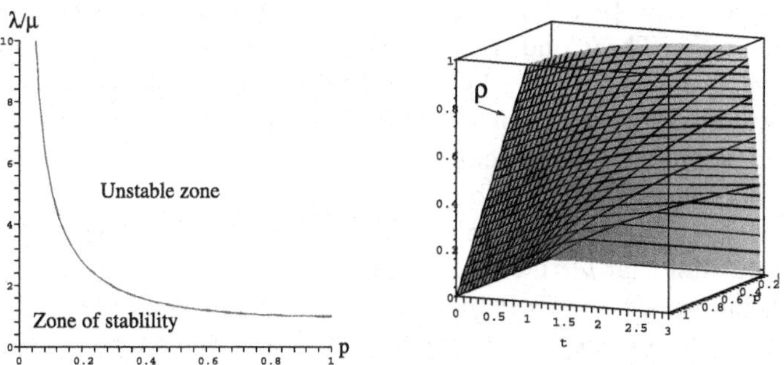

Fig. 3. $\mathbb{N} \star \mathbb{B}$: The stability region (left) and the load ρ (right)

In Figure 3 (left), we show the stability region of the queue. The abcissa is p and the ordinate is λ/μ. In Figure 3 (right), we plot the load ρ as a function of p and $t = \lambda/\mu$, for $p \in (0, 1)$ and $\lambda/\mu \in (0, \min(1/\widehat{\gamma}, 2))$. Hence, ρ is always smaller or equal to 1, see Theorem 5.1.

The free product $\mathbb{N} \star \mathbb{Z} \star \mathbb{B}$. Consider the queue associated with the triple $(\{a\}^* \star \mathbb{F}(b) \star \langle\, c \mid c^2 = c\,\rangle, \Sigma = \{a, b, b^{-1}, c\}, \nu)$ where $\nu(a) = p, \nu(b) = \nu(b^{-1}) = q/2$, and $\nu(c) = 1 - p - q$ with $p, q, p + q \in (0, 1)$.

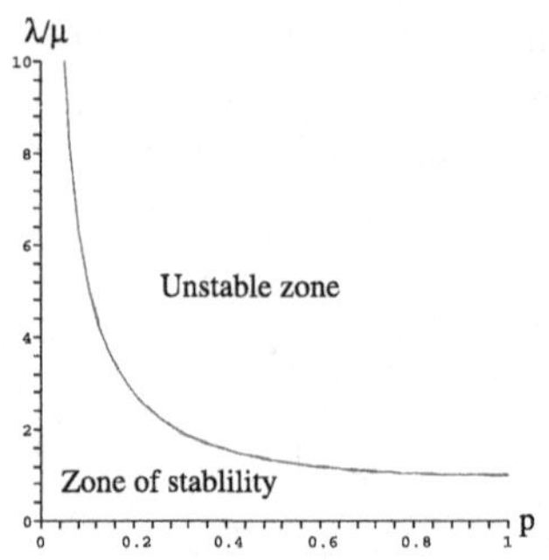

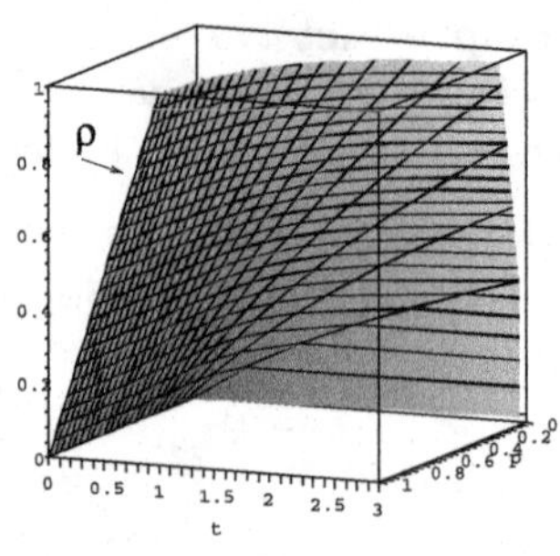

Fig. 4. Stability region of the $M/M/1/(\mathbb{N}\star\mathbb{Z}\star\mathbb{B}, \Sigma)$ queue. The axis are p, q, and λ/μ.

The unique solution $\widehat{r}$ of the associated TE is

$$\widehat{r}(b) = \widehat{r}(b^{-1}) = \frac{1}{2} - \frac{\sqrt{1-q^2}}{2(1+q)}, \ \widehat{r}(a) = \frac{p(1-\widehat{r}(b))}{1-\widehat{r}(b)-q\widehat{r}(b)}, \ \widehat{r}(c) = 1 - \widehat{r}(a) - 2\widehat{r}(b).$$

Applying Theorem 2.1, the drift of the random walk is given by: $\widehat{\gamma} = p + (1 - p - q)(1 - \widehat{r}(c)) + q(1 - 2\widehat{r}(b))$. ¿From there, we obtain Figure 4: the stability region is the region below the surface.

The free group $\mathbb{Z}$ and the free product $\mathbb{N} \star \mathbb{Z}$. Consider the 0-automatic queue $(\mathbb{F}(a), \Sigma = \{a, a^{-1}\}, \nu, r, \lambda, \mu)$, where ν is a non-degenerate probability measure on Σ. The Condition **C1** is not satisfied, and the Condition **C2** is not satisfied when $\nu(a) = \nu(a^{-1}) = 1/2$. (In this last case, the random walk (X, ν) is null recurrent.) Consequently, only part of the results from Section 5 hold, and some new phenomena appear. Below, we give the results without full justification. The details can be found in [3].

The drift of the random walk is easily computed: $\widehat{\gamma} = |\nu(a) - \nu(a^{-1})|$.

Assume first that $\nu(a) = \nu(a^{-1})$. Solving the TTE, we get that $(\lambda/(2\mu+\lambda), r)$ is a solution for all $r \in \bar{\mathcal{B}}$. It means that the queue is stable and has a product form distribution under any boundary condition. This interesting behavior can be traced back to the fact that the random walk (X, ν) is not transient.

Assume now that $\nu(a) \neq \nu(a^{-1})$. There are 2 possible solutions for the TTE:

$$(\rho_1, r_1) = \left(\frac{\lambda\nu(a)}{\mu + \lambda\nu(a^{-1})}; (1,0)\right), \qquad (\rho_2, r_2) = \left(\frac{\lambda\nu(a^{-1})}{\mu + \lambda\nu(a)}; (0,1)\right). \tag{21}$$

The two solutions correspond to extremal values for r, it means that in the buffer, there is only one type of customer with probability 1. Here we recover a model very close to the classical G-queue.

Set $\underline{\rho} = \min\{\rho_1, \rho_2\}$ and $\bar{\rho} = \max\{\rho_1, \rho_2\}$ and define $\underline{r}$ and $\bar{r}$ accordingly. We have:

$$\underline{\rho} < 1, \qquad [\bar{\rho} < 1] \iff [\lambda\widehat{\gamma} < \mu] .$$

The stationary distribution of the 0-automatic queue $(\mathbb{F}(a), \Sigma, \nu, \underline{r}, \lambda, \mu)$ is:

$$\pi_{\underline{r}}(1_{\Sigma^*}) = 1 - \underline{\rho}, \quad \pi_{\underline{r}}(x^n) = (1 - \underline{\rho})\underline{\rho}^n, \ \forall n \geq 1, \tag{22}$$

where $x = a$ if $\nu(a) < \nu(a^{-1})$, and $x = a^{-1}$ if $\nu(a) > \nu(a^{-1})$. When $\lambda\widehat{\gamma} < \mu$, the 0-automatic queue $(\mathbb{F}(a), \Sigma, \nu, \bar{r}, \lambda, \mu)$ also has a product form stationary distribution of the form (22) with $\bar{\rho}$ instead of $\underline{\rho}$.

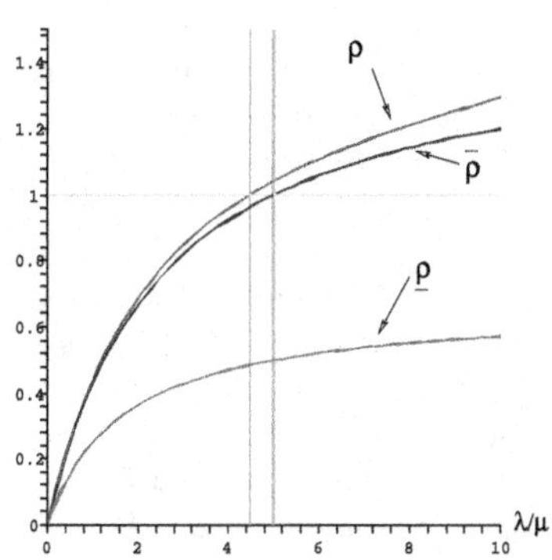

Fig. 5. $\mathbb{F}(a)$ and $\mathbb{F}(a) \star \{c\}^*$: the load as a function of λ/μ

To summarize, when $\lambda\widehat{\gamma} < \mu$, there are two variants of the 0-automatic queue with a product form. We would like to argue that one of the two makes more "physical" sense.

To that purpose, consider the 0-automatic triple $(\mathbb{F}(a) \star \{c\}^*, \{a, a^{-1}, c\}, \nu)$ with $0 < \nu(c) \ll 1$. Here, the Conditions **C1-C2** are satisfied. According to Theorem 5.2, there exists a single variant of the queue with a product form. The question is to determine which one of the two solutions in (21) is recovered when letting $\nu(c)$ go to 0.

Since the TTE are difficult to solve explicitly, we content ourselves with numerical evidence. In Figure 5, we plot ρ, $\bar{\rho}$, and $\underline{\rho}$ as functions of λ/μ. The plots are for $\nu(a) = 3/5$ and $\nu(c) = 0.01$ in the case of ρ. We see that ρ tends to the larger solution $\bar{\rho}$. The two vertical lines have an abcissa equal to the inverse of the drift $\widehat{\gamma}^{-1}$ for the random walk on $\mathbb{F}(a)$ and $\mathbb{F}(a) \star \{c\}^*$ respectively.

References

1. J.W. Cohen. *The single server queue.* North-Holland, Amsterdam, 1982. 2nd edition.
2. T.-H. Dao-Thi and J. Mairesse. Zero-automatic networks. In preparation.
3. T.-H. Dao-Thi and J. Mairesse. Zero-automatic queues. LIAFA reseach report 2005-03, Univ. Paris 7, 2005.
4. E. Dynkin and M. Malyutov. Random walk on groups with a finite number of generators. *Sov. Math. Dokl.*, 2:399–402, 1961.

5. J.-M. Fourneau, E. Gelenbe, and R. Suros. *G*-networks with multiple classes of negative and positive customers. *Theoret. Comput. Sci.*, 155(1):141–156, 1996.
6. E. Gelenbe. Product-form queueing networks with negative and positive customers. *J. Appl. Probab.*, 28(3), 1991.
7. E. Gelenbe and G. Pujolle. *Introduction to queueing networks. 2nd ed.* John Wiley & Sons, Chichester, 1998.
8. Y. Guivarc'h. Sur la loi des grands nombres et le rayon spectral d'une marche aléatoire. *Astérisque*, 74:47–98, 1980.
9. R. Haring-Smith. Groups and simple languages. *Trans. Amer. Math. Soc.*, 279(1):337–356, 1983.
10. F. Ledrappier. Some asymptotic properties of random walks on free groups. In J. Taylor, editor, *Topics in probability and Lie groups: boundary theory*, number 28 in CRM Proc. Lect. Notes, pages 117–152. American Mathematical Society, 2001.
11. J. Mairesse. Random walks on groups and monoids with a Markovian harmonic measure. LIAFA research report 2004-05, Université Paris 7, 2004.
12. J. Mairesse and F. Mathéus. Random walks on free products of cyclic groups and on Artin groups with two generators. LIAFA research report 2004-06, Université Paris 7, 2004.
13. S. Sawyer and T. Steger. The rate of escape for anisotropic random walks in a tree. *Probab. Theory Related Fields*, 76(2):207–230, 1987.
14. R. Serfozo *Introduction to Stochastic Networks.* Springer-Verlag, Berlin, 1999.
15. J. Stallings. A remark about the description of free products of groups. *Proc. Cambridge Philos. Soc.*, 62:129–134, 1966.

A Unified Approach to the Moments Based Distribution Estimation – Unbounded Support

Árpád Tari[1], Miklós Telek[2], and Peter Buchholz[1]

[1] Universität Dortmund, Germany
[2] Budapest University of Technology and Economics, Hungary
arpad@sch.bme.hu, telek@hit.bme.hu, peter.buchholz@cs.uni-dortmund.de

Abstract. The problem of moments has been studied for more than a century. This paper discusses a practical issue related to the problem of moments namely the bounding of a distribution based on a given number of moments. The presented approach is unified in the sense that all measures of interests are provided as a quadratic expression of the same Hankel-matrix.

Application examples indicate the importance of the presented approach.

Keywords: reduced moment problem, moments based distribution bounding, Hankel matrix.

1 Introduction

The aim of making stochastic models of real systems is usually to evaluate some performance parameters of the system. Since the parameters of interest are random variables in stochastic models the goal of the analysis is often to characterize these random variables by their distribution. Real-life problems often require the solution of huge models and/or the evaluation of time demanding numerical procedures. One way of avoiding these problems is to introduce certain simplifications that result in the reduction of the complexity, another way is to approximate the measure. The approach proposed in this paper is along the second line. Instead of calculating the distribution of the measure of interest we calculate some of its first moments and approximate the distribution based on them as it is depicted in Figure 1. The thickness of the arrows indicates the usual complexity of the algorithms available in the literature for the different type calculations. Having a complex stochastic model it is usually faster to calculate the moments of the measure of interest than its distribution and the calculation of an approximation or bounds of the distribution from the moments can be done very efficiently.

The drawback of this approach is that the computation yields only an approximation of the distribution, not its exact values. Fortunately, one can have an idea on the error of this approach because it is also possible to bound the distribution based on known moments. As a consequence, it becomes possible

M. Bravetti et al. (Eds.): EPEW 2005 and WS-FM 2005, LNCS 3670, pp. 79–93, 2005.

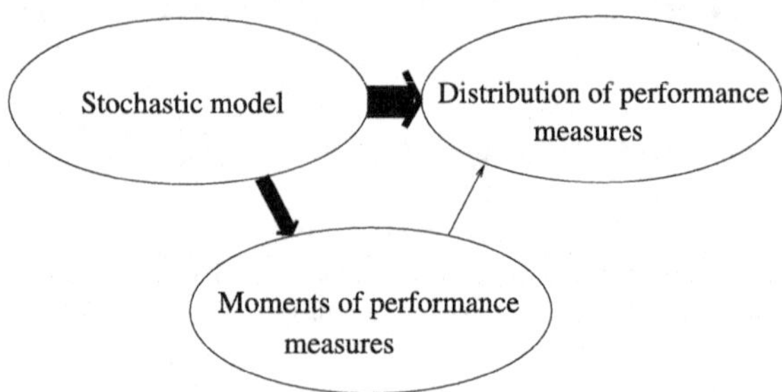

Fig. 1. Using moments to estimate performance measures

to bound performance measures of real systems where moments are also computable, but a direct analysis of the distribution is infeasible.

The task of moments-based distribution estimation can be formulated as follows. We have an unknown distribution function $\sigma(x)$ with support on $[a, b]$ and we know the following quantities:

$$\mu_i = \int_a^b x^i \, \mathrm{d}\sigma(x), \qquad i = 0, 1, 2, \ldots, 2n, \tag{1}$$

where μ_i is called the ith moment of the distribution $\sigma(x)$. We look for a procedure to estimate $\sigma(x)$ at some point $x = C$.

Many algorithms exist that are able to fit certain types of distributions to some given moments. For example, it is usually obvious to fit distributions with one parameter to μ_1 and with two parameters to μ_1 and μ_2. Fitting of $\mu_1 - \mu_3$ with acyclic phase type distribution is presented in [4]. Appie van de Liefvoort provided a method to fit arbitrary number of moments with matrix exponential distribution in [6]. Any of these methods provides a particular $\tilde{\sigma}(C)$ value assuming the considered class of distributions. Unfortunately, the error of this estimate it is not known if the performance measure does not belong to the considered class of distributions.

To overcome this difficulty we look for minimal and maximal estimates of $\sigma(C)$ over the class of all valid distribution functions. In this way we define a lower and an upper limit, which bound all distribution functions in point C having moments $\mu_i, (i = 0, 1, 2, \ldots, 2n)$. No distribution function has smaller and no has larger value at C, than the limits we present. The bounds are strict in the sense that there exist always a distribution that reaches these values.

The problem to determine the distribution based on its moments is called "*the reduced moment problem*" (where the word reduced means that only a finite number of moments is known). The term was introduced by Stieltjes who did the first extensive study on the subject in [14], though Chebyshev solved a particular case of the problem as early as 1873. Markov, Hamburger, Hausdorff, Nevanlinna, M. Riesz, Carleman and Stone wrote the most important articles about the moment problem. One can find a good historical overview in [12]. The case when the limits of the integral in (1) are $(-\infty, \infty)$ is referred to as Hamburger moment problem. It means that the considered set of distributions has a support in the whole $(-\infty, \infty)$ interval (*unbounded support*), which is the most general case.

The mathematical tools involved in the solution of this problem were continued fractions, approximate quadratures of integrals, singular integral equations, orthogonal polynomials and operators in Hilbert space [12]. Our approach is based mainly on matrix operations, though we also rely on the theory of orthogonal polynomials.

The method presented here is basically the same as the one in [9], but with major improvements: we eliminated the moments transformation step of that method and deduced simpler formulas which resulted in notable simplification of the algorithm. In contrast with [9] here we present a unified approach where all related quantities are expressed with quadratic matrix expressions of the same matrix ($\boldsymbol{M}^{-1}$).

We intend to present this paper in a way that is simple and easy to understand and does not require any special mathematical knowledge from the reader and we also provide references to the related mathematical background. Furthermore we present details about our implementation of the procedure, which is not always obvious due to potential numerical problems.

The paper is organized as follows: Section 2 defines the conditions that have to be fulfilled in order to use our estimation algorithm. Sections 3 and 4 summarize the theoretical background and the bounding procedure of the moment based estimation. In Section 5 a step-by-step instruction to evaluate the algorithm can be found. Section 6 provides an overview of the applicability of the proposed approach and gives insights into the numerical issues. An example is analyzed in Section 7 focused on the strengths and applicabilities of our approach. Section 8 concludes the paper.

2 Necessary Conditions

Before calculating an estimate of $\sigma(\cdot)$ based on $\mu_i, (i = 0, 1, 2, \ldots, 2n)$ we need to check if a non-decreasing function exists whose moments are $\mu_i, (i = 0, 1, 2, \ldots, 2n)$. This can be checked using the theorem of Hausdorff [1, p. 30]:

Theorem 1. *[1] Let $\mu_0, \mu_1, \mu_2, \ldots, \mu_{2n}$ be a sequence of real numbers. These numbers can be a moments of a distribution function with support $(-\infty, \infty)$ if and only if*

$$|\boldsymbol{M}_k| \geq 0, \qquad k = 0, 1, \ldots, n, \tag{2}$$

where

$$\boldsymbol{M}_k = \begin{pmatrix} \mu_0 & \mu_1 & \cdots & \mu_k \\ \mu_1 & \mu_2 & \cdots & \mu_{k+1} \\ \vdots & \vdots & \ddots & \vdots \\ \mu_k & \mu_{k+1} & \cdots & \mu_{2k} \end{pmatrix}, \qquad k = 0, 1, \ldots, n \tag{3}$$

is the so-called Hankel-matrix of dimension $(k+1) \times (k+1)$.

Definition 2. *[18] The $n \times n$ real matrix $\boldsymbol{A}$ is called* positive definite, *if*

$$\boldsymbol{\xi}^T \boldsymbol{A} \boldsymbol{\xi} > 0 \tag{4}$$

for any nonzero real vector $\boldsymbol{\xi} \in \mathbb{R}^n$. This is equivalent to the requirement that the determinants associated with all upper-left submatrices of $\boldsymbol{A}$ are positive.

According to this definition the matrix $\boldsymbol{M}$ is positive definite. The following lemma states the same about its inverse.

Lemma 3. *[18] If $\boldsymbol{A}$ is a $n \times n$ positive definite matrix, then $\boldsymbol{A}^{-1}$ is also positive definite.*

It follows from Theorem 1 that we have constraints only on an odd number of moments (including μ_0). Indeed, if $\mu_i, (i = 0, 1, 2, \ldots, 2n)$ is a valid moment sequence then μ_{2n+1} can take any value in $(-\infty, \infty)$ and $\mu_i, (i = 0, 1, 2, \ldots, 2n+1)$ remains to be a valid moments sequence. As a consequence μ_{2n+1} does not carry any information about the possible limits of $\sigma(\cdot)$, hence we simply discard it if μ_{2n+2} is not known.

Theorem 4. *[16] $\sigma(\cdot)$ consists of exactly n distinct points of increase if and only if*

$$|\boldsymbol{M}_0| > 0, |\boldsymbol{M}_1| > 0, \ldots, |\boldsymbol{M}_{n-1}| > 0, |\boldsymbol{M}_n| = 0. \tag{5}$$

In this case $|\boldsymbol{M}_{n+1}| = |\boldsymbol{M}_{n+2}| = \ldots = 0$ and the moment problem is said to be determined.

In the special case when the moment problem is determined there is exactly one discrete distribution (with n points) with the given moments and upper and lower bounds are identical.

From now on we assume non-determined moment problem and denote by $\boldsymbol{M}$ the largest possible Hankel-matrix, that can be formed from the known moments: $\boldsymbol{M} = \boldsymbol{M}_n$.

3 Discrete Reference Distribution

We construct a discrete distribution from the given moments. This distribution has an interesting extremal property: among the distribution functions having the μ_i, $i = 0, 1, \ldots, 2n$ moments it has the largest concentrated mass at point C.

The construction of this discrete distribution can be considered as the solution of a system of equations. We have the μ_i, $i = 0, 1, \ldots, 2n$ moments and point C and we search for a discrete distribution with moments μ_i, $i = 0, 1, \ldots, 2n$ and a maximum mass at C. The following lemma gives some more information about this distribution.

Lemma 5. *[12, p. 42] A distribution function with exactly $n+1$ points of increase is uniquely determined by a single point of them. To each real value C there corresponds one and only one distribution function with $n+1$ or n points of increase, which contains C among its points. The distribution function has $n+1$ points of increase, if C is not a root of the following polynomial:*

$$P(x) = \begin{vmatrix} \mu_0 & \mu_1 & \dots & \mu_n \\ \vdots & \vdots & \ddots & \vdots \\ \mu_{n-1} & \mu_n & \dots & \mu_{2n-1} \\ 1 & x & \dots & x^n \end{vmatrix} \tag{6}$$

and has n points otherwise.

If there is a discrete distribution supported exactly on $n+1$ points (including C), then this discrete distribution can be constructed from the definition of moments:

$$\mu_i = p\,C^i + \sum_{j=1}^{n} p_j\, x_j^i \ . \tag{7}$$

This task can also be formulated as finding the appropriate values of $x_1, x_2, \dots, x_n, p_1, p_2, \dots, p_n, p$ so that

$$\boldsymbol{M} - \boldsymbol{R}\boldsymbol{S}^T = \boldsymbol{0}, \tag{8}$$

where

$$\boldsymbol{R} = \begin{pmatrix} p & p_1 & \dots & p_n \\ pC & p_1 x_1 & \dots & p_n x_n \\ pC^2 & p_1 x_1^2 & \dots & p_n x_n^2 \\ \vdots & \vdots & \ddots & \vdots \\ pC^n & p_1 x_1^n & \dots & p_n x_n^n \end{pmatrix} = (p\,\boldsymbol{c}, p_1\,\boldsymbol{x_1}, \dots, p_n\,\boldsymbol{x_n}) \tag{9}$$

$$\boldsymbol{S} = \begin{pmatrix} 1 & 1 & \dots & 1 \\ C & x_1 & \dots & x_n \\ C^2 & x_1^2 & \dots & x_n^2 \\ \vdots & \vdots & \ddots & \vdots \\ C^n & x_1^n & \dots & x_n^n \end{pmatrix} = (\boldsymbol{c}, \boldsymbol{x_1}, \dots, \boldsymbol{x_n}) \tag{10}$$

and $\boldsymbol{x_i}$ and $\boldsymbol{c}$ are vectors of order n formed by the powers of x_i and C, respectively:

$$\boldsymbol{x_i}^T = \left(1, x_i, x_i^2, \dots, x_i^n\right)^T, \qquad \boldsymbol{c}^T = \left(1, C, C^2, \dots, C^n\right)^T, \tag{11}$$

$\boldsymbol{0}$ is an $(n+1) \times (n+1)$ zero matrix.

Lemma 6. *If $\boldsymbol{A}$ is a $n \times n$ nonsingular matrix, $\boldsymbol{U}$ and $\boldsymbol{V}$ are $n \times n$ nonsingular matrices such that*

$$\boldsymbol{A} - \boldsymbol{U}\boldsymbol{V}^T = \boldsymbol{0}, \tag{12}$$

where $\mathbf{0}$ *is a zero matrix of order* n*, then*

$$\boldsymbol{V}^T \boldsymbol{A}^{-1} \boldsymbol{U} = \boldsymbol{I}, \tag{13}$$

where $\boldsymbol{I}$ *is identity matrix of order* n*.*

Proof. Since $\boldsymbol{U}$ and $\boldsymbol{V}$ are of order n and their inverses exist we have

$$\begin{aligned} \boldsymbol{A} &= \boldsymbol{U}\boldsymbol{V}^T, \\ \boldsymbol{U}^{-1}\boldsymbol{A}\left(\boldsymbol{V}^T\right)^{-1} &= \boldsymbol{I}, \\ \boldsymbol{V}^T\boldsymbol{A}^{-1}\boldsymbol{U} &= \boldsymbol{I}^{-1} = \boldsymbol{I}, \end{aligned}$$

where we took the inverse of both sides in the last step. □

According to Lemma 6 we can write:

$$\boldsymbol{I} = \boldsymbol{S}^T \boldsymbol{M}^{-1} \boldsymbol{R}$$

$$\boldsymbol{I} = \begin{pmatrix} \boldsymbol{c}^T \\ \boldsymbol{x_1}^T \\ \vdots \\ \boldsymbol{x_n}^T \end{pmatrix} \boldsymbol{M}^{-1} \; (p\,\boldsymbol{c}, p_1\,\boldsymbol{x_1}, \ldots, p_n\,\boldsymbol{x_n})$$

$$\begin{pmatrix} 1\,0 \ldots 0 \\ 0\,1 \ldots 0 \\ \vdots\;\vdots\;\ddots\;\vdots \\ 0\,0 \ldots 1 \end{pmatrix} = \begin{pmatrix} p\,\boldsymbol{c}^T\boldsymbol{M}^{-1}\boldsymbol{c} & p_1\,\boldsymbol{c}^T\boldsymbol{M}^{-1}\boldsymbol{x_1} & \ldots & p_n\,\boldsymbol{c}^T\boldsymbol{M}^{-1}\boldsymbol{x_n} \\ p\,\boldsymbol{x_1}^T\boldsymbol{M}^{-1}\boldsymbol{c} & p_1\,\boldsymbol{x_1}^T\boldsymbol{M}^{-1}\boldsymbol{x_1} & \ldots & p_n\,\boldsymbol{x_1}^T\boldsymbol{M}^{-1}\boldsymbol{x_n} \\ \vdots & \vdots & \ddots & \vdots \\ p\,\boldsymbol{x_n}^T\boldsymbol{M}^{-1}\boldsymbol{c} & p_1\,\boldsymbol{x_n}^T\boldsymbol{M}^{-1}\boldsymbol{x_1} & \ldots & p_n\,\boldsymbol{x_n}^T\boldsymbol{M}^{-1}\boldsymbol{x_n} \end{pmatrix} \tag{14}$$

Note that $x_1, \ldots, x_n$ and C must be all different, otherwise $\boldsymbol{S}$ and $\boldsymbol{R}$ are singular.

The element $[1,1]$ of this matrix equation gives:

$$p = \frac{1}{\boldsymbol{c}^T\,\boldsymbol{M}^{-1}\,\boldsymbol{c}} \;. \tag{15}$$

This p has an important extremal property.

Theorem 7. *p is the maximum possible mass at point C that a distribution may have whose first $2n$ moments are $\{\mu_0, \ldots, \mu_{2n}\}$.*

The difference of any 2 distributions ($\sigma_1(x)$ and $\sigma_2(x)$) with first $2n$ moments equal to $\{\mu_0, \ldots, \mu_{2n}\}$ cannot be greater than p:

$$\left| \int_{-\infty}^{C+0} \mathrm{d}\sigma_1(x) - \int_{-\infty}^{C-0} \mathrm{d}\sigma_2(x) \right| \leq p \;. \tag{16}$$

For a proof see Appendix A.

Let us consider the first columns of the matrices in (14) below $[1,1]$:

$$p\,\boldsymbol{x_i}^T\boldsymbol{M}^{-1}\boldsymbol{c} = 0, \qquad i = 1, 2, \ldots, n \;. \tag{17}$$

According to Lemma 3 $\boldsymbol{M}^{-1}$ is a positive definite matrix and it follows that $p > 0$. So the left hand side of (17) equals to 0 if x_i $(i = 1, 2, \ldots, n)$ is the root of the polynomial

$$w(x) = \boldsymbol{x}^T \boldsymbol{M}^{-1} \mathbf{c}, \tag{18}$$

where $\boldsymbol{x}$ is a vector consisting of the powers of the unknown x. This polynomial is of order n, and the roots $x_1, \ldots, x_n$ must be real and different [15], which involves that all the roots of $w(x)$ appear in (14). So the points of the discrete distribution are actually the roots of $w(x)$ and they are real and distinct according to the theory of orthogonal polynomials [15].

The diagonal elements of the matrix equation results the weights of the discrete distribution:

$$p_i = \frac{1}{\boldsymbol{x_i}^T \boldsymbol{M}^{-1} \boldsymbol{x_i}} \qquad i = 1, 2, \ldots, n \ , \tag{19}$$

since $\boldsymbol{M}^{-1}$ is a positive definite matrix, it follows that $\boldsymbol{x_i}^T \boldsymbol{M}^{-1} \boldsymbol{x_i} > 0$.

If C coincides with one of the x_i roots, then the discrete distribution would have only n points which means that we should have $\boldsymbol{M} := \boldsymbol{M}_{n-1}$ as starting point in creating a discrete distribution instead of $\boldsymbol{M}_n$, otherwise all other steps of the process are the same.

$\sigma(x)$ denotes the discrete distribution supported on the $x_1, x_2, \ldots, x_n, C$ points with weights $p_1, p_2, \ldots, p_n, p$.

4 Lower and Upper Limits

The following theorem is the base for finding the minimum and maximum values of all the functions having the same $\{\mu_0, \ldots, \mu_{2n}\}$ moments.

Let $\sigma^*(x)$ be a distribution satisfying (2) whose moments are $\mu_0, \ldots, \mu_{2n}$, but different from $\sigma(x)$.

Theorem 8. *The following relations hold for $\sigma(x)$ and $\sigma^*(x)$:*

$$\int_{-\infty}^{C-0} \mathrm{d}\sigma^*(x) \geq \int_{-\infty}^{C-0} \mathrm{d}\sigma(x), \tag{20}$$

$$\int_{-\infty}^{C+0} \mathrm{d}\sigma^*(x) \leq \int_{-\infty}^{C-0} \mathrm{d}\sigma(x) + p \ . \tag{21}$$

The proof of Theorem 8 is provided in Appendix B.

According to this theorem no function has either smaller and greater value at C than $\sigma(x)|_{x=C-0}$ and $\sigma(x)|_{x=C+0}$ have. $\sigma(x)|_{x=C-0}$ and $\sigma(x)|_{x=C+0}$ can be calculated as

$$\int_{-\infty}^{C-0} \mathrm{d}\sigma(x) = \sum_{i:x_i<C} p_i = L, \qquad \int_{-\infty}^{C+0} \mathrm{d}\sigma(x) = \sum_{i:x_i<C} p_i + p = U \ . \tag{22}$$

The lower limit of the distribution is obtained as the sum of the weights of the points smaller than C, i.e. L, and the upper limit is the sum of the lower limit and the maximum mass at C, i.e. U.

The x_i roots of (18) depend on C, but their location can be characterized by a series independent of C according to the following theorem. Let us denote by $u_1, \ldots, u_n$ the roots of $P(x)$ defined in (6). These roots are also real and different [15].

Theorem 9. *If C is such that $u_{j-1} < C < u_j$ and the $x_1, x_2, \ldots, x_n$ and $u_1, u_2, \ldots, u_n$ roots are increasingly ordered then the $x_1, x_2, \ldots, x_n, C$ and the $u_1, u_2, \ldots, u_n$ numbers are mutually separated as*

$$x_1 < u_1 < x_2 < u_2 < \ldots < u_{j-1} < C < u_j < x_j < u_{j+1} < \ldots < u_n < x_n. \quad (23)$$

The proof is provided in Appendix C.

According to Theorem 9 the number of x_i roots smaller (greater) than C equals to the number of u_i roots smaller (greater) than C. In this way the u_i roots define the number of points in the summation in (22). Based on Theorem 9 it is sufficient to calculate only the x_i roots smaller than C, (or alternatively the x_i roots greater than C).

Another consequence of Theorem 9 is that once the roots of $P(x)$ are calculated (this has to be done only once independent of C), we only need to calculate the roots of $w(x)$ in either the (u_1, C) or the (C, u_n) interval – depending on which contains less u_i roots. In this way we can reduce the number of roots to compute (it is no more than $\lfloor \frac{n}{2} \rfloor$) and we know the intervals where the roots are located, which allows the use of sophisticated numerical algorithms.

5 Steps of the Algorithm

Given: $\mu_0, \mu_1, \ldots, \mu_m$ and a set of C values where we need to bound the distribution.

1. Test if the moments satisfy the

$$|\boldsymbol{M}_k| \geq 0 \qquad k = 0, 1, \ldots n \quad (24)$$

   inequalities. We denote the number of applicable moments (for which the (24) inequalities hold) by $2n+1$ $(\mu_0, \ldots, \mu_{2n})$.
2. Find the roots of the polynomial $P(x)$:

$$P(x) = \begin{vmatrix} \mu_0 & \mu_1 & \cdots & \mu_n \\ \vdots & \vdots & \ddots & \vdots \\ \mu_{k-1} & \mu_k & \cdots & \mu_{2n-1} \\ 1 & x & \ldots & x^k \end{vmatrix} . \quad (25)$$

   The roots are called $u_1 < u_2 < \ldots < u_n$.

3. Do for each C point of interest
   (a) If $C = u_i$ for some i then $\boldsymbol{M} := \boldsymbol{M}_{n-1}$ else $\boldsymbol{M} := \boldsymbol{M}_n$.
   (b) Calculate the largest possible p:

$$p = \frac{1}{\boldsymbol{c}^T \boldsymbol{M}^{-1} \boldsymbol{c}} . \tag{26}$$

   (c) Calculate the points of the reference discrete distribution: if (u_1, C) contains less u_i than (C, u_n), then find all the roots of the following polynomial that are *smaller* than C :

$$\boldsymbol{c} \boldsymbol{M}^{-1} \boldsymbol{x}^T = 0, \tag{27}$$

   where

$$\boldsymbol{x}^T = \left(1, x, x^2, \ldots, x^n\right)^T . \tag{28}$$

   Else find all the roots of the same polynomial that are *greater* than C . The results are the x_i, $i = 1, \ldots, r$ points, where r denotes the number of roots that had to be calculated: $r \leq \left\lfloor \frac{n}{2} \right\rfloor$.
   (d) Calculate the weights of the reference discrete distribution:

$$p_i = \frac{1}{\boldsymbol{x_i}^T \boldsymbol{M}^{-1} \boldsymbol{x_i}}, \qquad i = 1, 2, \ldots, r . \tag{29}$$

   (e) L and U are given by the following formula, if the interval (u_1, C) contains less u_i than (C, u_n):

$$L = \sum_{i: x_i < C} p_i, \qquad U = L + p, \tag{30}$$

   else

$$L = U - p, \qquad U = 1 - \sum_{i: x_i > C} p_i . \tag{31}$$

6 Implementation Notes

The presented algorithm involves tasks which are numerically hard and unstable in general (calculating determinants and matrix inverse, finding the roots of a polynomial), but the matrices and the polynomials we consider have special properties that commonly eliminate these numerical difficulties.

First of all we calculate determinants of symmetric matrices. We use the LU-decomposition [8, p. 43 – 50] for the calculation. We experienced numerical problems with matrices larger than 11 × 11, and this limits the applicability to less than 23 moments using standard floating point numbers.

To invert a positive definite symmetric matrix we use *Cholesky decomposition* with backsubstitution (see [8, p. 96–98]). The Cholesky decomposition is extremely stable numerically and approximately two times faster than the alternative methods for solving linear equations. The algorithm fails only when the matrix is not positive definite.

For finding all the roots of $P(x)$ we use the *Laguerre's method* [8, p. 371 – 374]. In general it is not so easy to find the roots of a polynomial when we know nothing about the location of the roots. But this algorithm works well, if all the roots of a polynomial are real, because then it is theoretically guaranteed that the method converges to a root from any starting point, and fortunately this is the case for $P(x)$. Technically it requires complex arithmetic even while converging to real roots.

Finding the roots of the polynomial $w(x)$ is an easier task (remember that not all of them is needed). According to Theorem 9 a single real root of $w(x)$ lies in (u_{i-1}, u_i) (or in (u_i, u_{i+1}) if $u_i > C$). Finding a root in a bounded interval is much easier, than in the case when we know nothing about the position. For this task we use the *bisection algorithm* [8, p. 350 – 354].

The overall algorithm is neither CPU, nor memory intensive. In order to estimate a distribution in N points we perform

- $\lfloor \frac{n+1}{2} \rfloor$ times – calculation of determinants;
- 1 time – finding n roots of $P(x)$;
- 1 time – inversion of an $(n+1) \times (n+1)$ matrix ;
- N times – findings of max. $\lfloor \frac{n}{2} \rfloor$ roots of $w(x)$;
- $2N$ times – vector-matrix multiplications of size $(n+1) \times (n+1)$;
- $2N$ times – scalar product of vectors of size $(n+1)$.

7 Example of Application

This section presents an example where the two-step performance analysis process (model → moments → measure) presented in Figure 1 has advantage compared to the direct computation of the value of a distribution function (model → measure).

A telecommunication system example was introduced in [3]. The authors considered a bandwidth-sharing strategy on a single link for the following 3 traffic classes:

- *rigid*: always requires peak bandwidth allocation;
- *adaptive*: it has a peak and minimum bandwidth requirement, and the actual transfer rate depends on the link utilization (for example live video transfer or voice conversation, where quality degradation is allowed to a certain degree, but high delay variance is not preferred);
- *elastic*: similar to the adaptive class, but these flows are in the system until a given amount of data is transferred (e.g. ftp-connections, where delay is allowed but data loss is not).

The number of ongoing rigid, adaptive and elastic traffic flows $(n_{\text{rigid}}, n_{\text{adaptive}}, n_{\text{elastic}})$ represents the system state in a given instant due to the applied memoryless assumptions. Figure 2(a) shows the part of the state space, where $n_{\text{rigid}} = 1$. The states, where flows cannot get their maximum bandwidth are filled with grey. The numbers below the state identifier show the actual bandwidth of the adaptive and elastic flows expressed in fraction of the maximum required bandwidth.

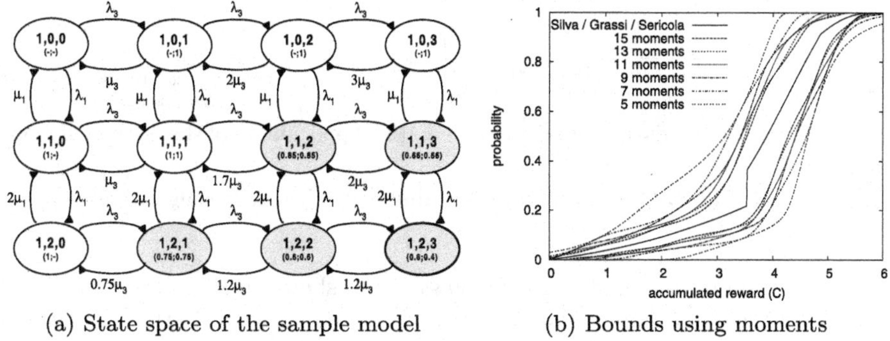

(a) State space of the sample model

(b) Bounds using moments

Fig. 2. Analyzing the sample model

Using this model one can evaluate the call blocking probabilities and average throughput of adaptive and elastic flows, but it is also possible to check the *throughput threshold constraint*, which is a constraint on the probability that the user-perceived throughput during the transfer of a file falls below a certain prescribed level. The calculation of the last measure requires evaluation of the MRM.

We used the MRMSolve 2.0 tool [5] to compare the complexity of the direct and the moments based analysis. The methods of Nabli and Sericola [7], De Souza and Gail [13], Donatiello and Grassi [2] result directly in the distribution and the method of Rácz and Telek [10,17] provides the moments of the performance measure of interest.

[5] compares the different MRM solution methods. Here we only demonstrate their limits of applicability. We used a dual AMD Opteron 248 (2.2 GHz) system with 6 GB of memory running Linux operating system for the calculations. The computation time was determined by the standard Unix `time` command.

Figure 2(b) shows that we get correct bounds applying our estimation method. The more moments we use the tighter the bounds are. The methods of De Souza–Gail, Donatiello–Grassi and Nabli–Sericola result the same values.

Figure 3 is a logarithmic plot of the computation time against the size of the state space. The algorithms of De Souza–Gail and Donatiello–Grassi were terminated after 5 hours with 5,600 states, the method of Nabli and Sericola became unstable (resulting negative values of probabilities) at 7,800 states.

The method of moments (Rácz and Telek) is much faster than the others, which was predictable because it yields less information about the distribution, but its main advantage is its robustness compared to the other methods: it was

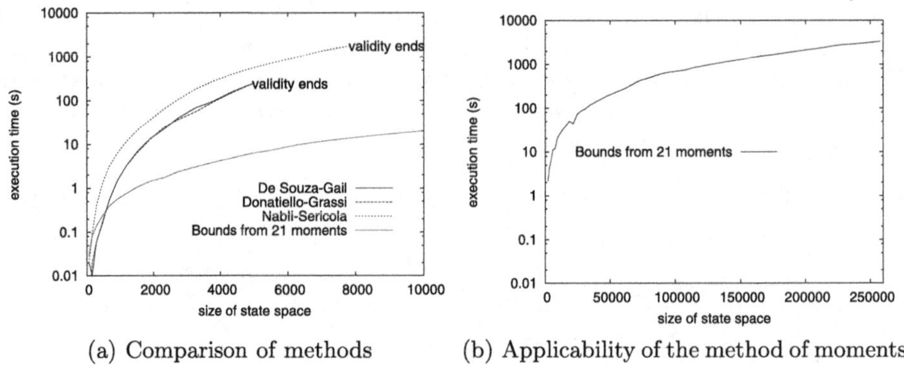

(a) Comparison of methods (b) Applicability of the method of moments

Fig. 3. CPU requirements of different MRM-solver algorithms

able to deal with a model of 260,000 states as shown in Fig. 3(b). Note that the time of the computation is dominated by the moment calculation algorithm; the estimation of the distribution based on the moments in 10,000 points required 1.44 s.

8 Conclusions

This paper presents an algorithm to bound a distribution based on a finite number of its moments. There are elaborated theoretical results about this problem, but the solution proposed here is different from the ones found in the literature, even though it relies on them. We also focused on the implementation and the numerical issues of the problem.

The presented example demonstrates a case when the moments based analysis is the only computationally feasible one among the solutions available in the literature.

Further research is needed to investigate the numerical behaviour of the algorithm with increased arithmetic precision. We also intend to improve the bounds based on additional information about the distribution (e.g., distributions with finite support). This kind of consideration requires refinements in the estimation procedure.

References

1. N. I. Akhiezer. *The classical moment problem and some related questions in analysis.* Hafner publishing company, New York, 1965. (translation of Н. И. Ахиезер: Классическая Проблема Моментов и Некоторые Вопросы Анализа, published by Государственное Издательство Физико-Математической Литературы, Moscow, 1961).
2. L. Donatiello and V. Grassi. On evaluating the cumulative performance distribution of fault-tolerant computer systems. *IEEE Transactions on Computers*, 1991.

3. G. Fodor, S. Rácz, and M. Telek. On providing blocking probability- and throughput guarantees in a multi-service environment. *International Journal of Communication Systems*, 15:4:257–285, May 2002.
4. A. Horváth M. Telek and G. Horváth. Analysis of inhomogeneous Markov reward models. *Linear algebra and its application*, 386:383–405, 2004.
5. G. Horváth, S. Rácz, Á. Tari, and M. Telek. Evaluation of reward analysis methods with MRMSolve 2.0. In *1st International Conference on Quantitative Evaluation of Systems (QEST) 2004*, pages 165–174, Twente, The Netherlands, Sept 2004. IEEE CS Press.
6. A. van de Liefvoort. The moment problem for continuous distributions. Technical report, University of Missouri, WP-CM-1990-02, Kansas City, 1990.
7. H. Nabli and B. Sericola. Performability analysis: a new algorithm. *IEEE Transactions on Computers*, 45:491–494, 1996.
8. W. H. Press, B. P. Flannery, S. A. Teukolsky, and W. T. Vetterling. *Numerical Recipes in C: The Art of Scientific Computing.* Cambridge University Press, 1993. http://lib-www.lanl.gov/numerical/bookcpdf.html.
9. S. Rácz. *Numerical analysis of communication systems through Markov reward models.* PhD thesis, Technical University of Budapest, 2000.
10. S. Rácz and M. Telek. Performability analysis of Markov reward models with rate and impulse reward. In M. Silva B. Plateau, W. Stewart, editor, *Int. Conf. on Numerical solution of Markov chains*, pages 169–187, Zaragoza, Spain, 1999.
11. P. Rózsa. *Lineáris algebra és alkalmazásai.* Tankönyvkiadó, 1991. in Hungarian.
12. J. A. Shohat and D. J. Tamarkin. *The problem of moments.* Americal Mathematical Society, Providence, Rhode Island, 1946. Mathematical surveys.
13. E. de Souza e Silva and H.R. Gail. Calculating cumulative operational time distributions of repairable computer systems. *IEEE Transactions on Computers*, C-35:322–332, 1986.
14. T. Stieltjes. Reserches sur les fractions continues. *Ann. Fac. Sci. Univ. Toulouse*, 2:1–122, 1894. in French.
15. G. Szegö. *Orthogonal polynomials.* American Mathematical Society, Providence, Rhode Island, 1939.
16. Aldo Tagliani. Existence and stability of a discrete probability distribution by maximum entropy approach. *Applied Mathematics and Computation*, 110:105–114, 2000.
17. M. Telek and S. Rácz. Numerical analysis of large Markovian reward models. *Performance Evaluation*, 36&37:95–114, Aug 1999.
18. Eric W. Weisstein. Positive definite matrix.http://mathworld.wolfram.com/PositiveDefiniteMatrix.html.

A Proof of Theorem 7

To prove the theorem we need the following lemma:

Lemma 10. *[11] If $\boldsymbol{A}$ is a nonsingular $n \times n$ matrix, $\boldsymbol{u}$ and $\boldsymbol{v}$ are n dimensional vectors and d is an arbitrary real number, then*

$$\begin{vmatrix} d & \boldsymbol{v}^T \\ \boldsymbol{u} & \boldsymbol{A} \end{vmatrix} = |\boldsymbol{A}| \left(d - \boldsymbol{v}^T \boldsymbol{A}^{-1} \boldsymbol{u} \right) . \tag{32}$$

The maximal mass according to [12, p. 72], can be written as:

$$p_{\max} = -\begin{vmatrix} \mu_0 & \mu_1 & \dots & \mu_n \\ \mu_1 & \mu_2 & \dots & \mu_{n+1} \\ \vdots & \vdots & \ddots & \vdots \\ \mu_n & \mu_{n+1} & \dots & \mu_{2n} \end{vmatrix} \Bigg/ \begin{vmatrix} 0 & 1 & C & \dots & C^n \\ 1 & \mu_0 & \mu_1 & \dots & \mu_n \\ C & \mu_1 & \mu_2 & \dots & \mu_{n+1} \\ \vdots & \vdots & \vdots & \ddots & \vdots \\ C^n & \mu_n & \mu_{n+1} & \dots & \mu_{2n} \end{vmatrix} \tag{33}$$

By Lemma 10 we can write the denominator of the right hand side of (33) as $-|\boldsymbol{M}|\ \boldsymbol{c}^T \boldsymbol{M}^{-1} \boldsymbol{c}$. In addition the numerator is the determinant of $\boldsymbol{M}$, hence

$$p_{\max} = -\frac{|\boldsymbol{M}|}{-|\boldsymbol{M}|\ \boldsymbol{c}^T \boldsymbol{M}^{-1} \boldsymbol{c}} = \frac{1}{\boldsymbol{c}^T \boldsymbol{M}^{-1} \boldsymbol{c}}, \tag{34}$$

which had to be proven. The second statement of the theorem is proved in [1, p. 66].

B Proof of Theorem 8

Using $\sigma_1(x) := \sigma(x)$ and $\sigma_2(x) := \sigma^*(x)$ substitutions by Theorem 7 we have:

$$\left| \int_{-\infty}^{C+0} \mathrm{d}\sigma(x) - \int_{-\infty}^{C-0} \mathrm{d}\sigma^*(x) \right| \le p\ . \tag{35}$$

Resolving the absolute value sign this equals:

$$\int_{-\infty}^{C+0} \mathrm{d}\sigma(x) - p \le \int_{-\infty}^{C-0} \mathrm{d}\sigma^*(x) \le \int_{-\infty}^{C+0} \mathrm{d}\sigma(x) + p. \tag{36}$$

By the construction of $\sigma(x)$ it follows that

$$\int_{-\infty}^{C+0} \mathrm{d}\sigma(x) = \int_{-\infty}^{C-0} \mathrm{d}\sigma(x) + p\ . \tag{37}$$

Substituting it to the leftmost inequality we get:

$$\int_{-\infty}^{C-0} \mathrm{d}\sigma(x) \le \int_{-\infty}^{C-0} \mathrm{d}\sigma^*(x), \tag{38}$$

which is (20). Now using $\sigma_1(x) := \sigma^*(x)$ and $\sigma_2(x) := \sigma(x)$ substitutions Theorem 7 gives

$$\left| \int_{-\infty}^{C+0} \mathrm{d}\sigma^*(x) - \int_{-\infty}^{C-0} \mathrm{d}\sigma(x) \right| \le p. \tag{39}$$

Resolving the absolute value sign we have:

$$\int_{-\infty}^{C-0} \mathrm{d}\sigma(x) - p \le \int_{-\infty}^{C+0} \mathrm{d}\sigma^*(x) \le \int_{-\infty}^{C-0} \mathrm{d}\sigma(x) + p, \tag{40}$$

whose rightmost inequality gives (21).

C Proof of Theorem 9

To prove the theorem we need the following lemma.

Lemma 11. *[1, p. 64]) Assume that the $\{\mu_0, \ldots, \mu_{2n-1}\}$ sequence satisfies (2) and $\tilde{\sigma}(x)$ is a distribution whose first $2n$ moments are $\mu_0, \mu_1, \ldots, \mu_{2n-1}$. In this case, for $i = 1, 2, \ldots, n-1$ we have*

$$\int_{-\infty}^{u_i+0} \mathrm{d}\tilde{\sigma}(u) \leq \rho_{n-1}(u_1) + \rho_{n-1}(u_2) + \ldots + \rho_{n-1}(u_i) \leq \int_{-\infty}^{u_{i+1}-0} \mathrm{d}\tilde{\sigma}(u), \quad (41)$$

where $u_1, \ldots, u_n$ are the roots of $P(x)$,

$$\rho_n(x) = \frac{1}{\sum_{j=0}^{n} |P_j(x)|^2}, \quad (42)$$

$$P_0(x) = 1 \qquad \textit{and} \qquad P_n(x) = \frac{1}{\sqrt{|\boldsymbol{M}_{n-1}|\,|\boldsymbol{M}_n|}} \begin{vmatrix} \mu_0 & \mu_1 & \cdots & \mu_n \\ \mu_1 & \mu_2 & \cdots & \mu_{n-1} \\ \vdots & \vdots & \ddots & \vdots \\ 1 & x & \ldots & x^n \end{vmatrix} . \quad (43)$$

If in addition it is known that $\tilde{\sigma}(x)$ has more than n points of increase, then the $\leq$ signs in (41) can be replaced by $<$ signs and the following inequalities hold:

$$0 < \int_{-\infty}^{u_1-0} \mathrm{d}\tilde{\sigma}(u), \qquad \int_{-\infty}^{u_n+0} \mathrm{d}\tilde{\sigma}(u) < \mu_0 . \quad (44)$$

There are $n+1$ points of increase in $\sigma(\cdot)$ ($x_1, \ldots, x_n$ and C). Applying Lemma 11 for $\tilde{\sigma}(\cdot) = \sigma(\cdot)$ implies that the $\leq$ signs are replaced by $<$ signs in (41), i.e.

$$\int_{-\infty}^{u_i+0} \mathrm{d}\sigma(u) < \int_{-\infty}^{u_{i+1}-0} \mathrm{d}\sigma(u) . \quad (45)$$

This means that in any (u_i, u_{i+1}) $(i = 1, \ldots, n-1)$ interval there must be at least one point of increase of $\sigma(x)$. Furthermore (44) implies that there is at least one point of increase in the $(-\infty, u_1)$ and at least one point of increase in the (u_n, ∞) intervals.

Considering that $\sigma(\cdot)$ has $n+1$ points of increase results the theorem.

Bounds for Point and Steady-State Availability: An Algorithmic Approach Based on Lumpability and Stochastic Ordering*

A. Bušić and J.M. Fourneau

PRiSM, Université de Versailles Saint-Quentin-en-Yvelines,
45, Av. des Etats-Unis 78000 Versailles, France
{abusic, jmf}@prism.uvsq.fr

Abstract. Markov chains and rewards have been widely used to evaluate performance, dependability and performability characteristics of computer systems and networks. Despite considerable works, the numerical analysis of Markov chains to obtain transient or steady-state distribution is still a difficult problem when the chain is large or the eigenvalues badly distributed. Thus bounding techniques have been proposed for long to analyze steady-state distribution.

Here, we show how to bound some dependability characteristics such as steady-state and point availability using an algorithmic approach. The bound is based on stochastic comparison of Markov chains but it does not use sample-path arguments. The algorithm builds a lumped Markov chain whose steady-state or transient distributions are upper bounds in the strong stochastic sense of the exact distributions. In this paper, the implementation of algorithm is detailed and we show some numerical results. We also show how we can avoid the generation of the state space and the transition matrix to model chains with more than 10^{10} states.

1 Introduction

The use of Markov chains to model complex system reliability and availability is becoming increasingly common. The definition and generation of large-scale Markov models from high level specifications is relatively easy and efficient in both time and memory requirements. The remaining difficulty is that of actually solving the Markov chain and deriving useful performance characteristics from it.

Consider an irreducible finite continuous-time Markov chain X whose stochastic transition rate matrix is given by Q. Then there exists the steady-state distribution π of the Markov chain X which is the unique solution to the system of equations $\pi Q = 0$. An availability measure is defined by separating the states into two classes, UP states and DOWN states. A state is said to be UP if the system is operational for that state; otherwise it is DOWN. Let U denote the set of

* This work is supported by ACI Sécurité, project Sure-Paths.

M. Bravetti et al. (Eds.): EPEW 2005 and WS-FM 2005, LNCS 3670, pp. 94–108, 2005.

UP states. The reliability at time t is defined as the probability that the system has always been in the UP states between 0 and t:

$$R(t) = Pr(X_s \in U, \forall \ s \ \in \ [0, t[).$$

The point availability is the probability that the system is operational at time t:

$$PAV(t) = Pr(X_t \in U)$$

and the steady-state availability is the limit, if it exists, of this probability. It can also be defined as the expectation of a reward on the steady state distribution of X: $A = \sum_{i|i \text{ is UP}} \pi(i)$. The usual way to compute these quantities is based on the uniformization method. Let δ be an arbitrary positive value and $\lambda = \max_i\{-Q(i,i)\}+\delta$. Let us build the uniformized version of Q by: $P = (Id-Q/\lambda)$. P is a discrete time Markov chain. Let us denote by P_U the block of P associated to transitions between UP states and let π_0 be the initial distribution of X. Using uniformization, we can compute $R(t)$ by:

$$R(t) = \sum_{n=0}^{\infty} e^{-\lambda t} \frac{(\lambda t)^n}{n!} \pi_0 P_U^n 1$$

and, because of the properties of the exponential function, the summation can be truncated. We first compute $N(t, \epsilon)$ which is the minimal value of n such that $\sum_{n=0}^{n} e^{-\lambda t} \frac{(\lambda t)^n}{n!}$ is larger than $1 - \epsilon$, and we finally obtain an approximation of $R(t)$ which is a lower bound of the exact value:

$$R(t) \approx \sum_{n=0}^{N(t,\epsilon)} e^{-\lambda t} \frac{(\lambda t)^n}{n!} \pi_0 P_U^n 1.$$

Let 1_U be the indicator function of set U. We get $PAV(t)$ after a similar construction based on uniformization:

$$PAV(t) \approx \sum_{n=0}^{N(t,\epsilon)} e^{-\lambda t} \frac{(\lambda t)^n}{n!} \pi_0 P^n 1_U.$$

As P and Q have the same steady-state distribution, we can use P to compute or bound the availability. Thus, we must compute transient and steady state probability distribution for matrix P. But for many problems these matrices are so huge that this is not even possible to build them or to solve the steady-state or the transient distribution. Thus we must use methods which provide a guarantee on these reliability measures and which are not limited by the size of the state space. Note that we are interested in bounding continuous time CTMC, however, due to the uniformization process, we consider discrete time Markov chain (DTMC).

Bounding methods have always received considerable attention in performance or reliability evaluation. Indeed, the problems we have to solve are often too complex to be analyzed exactly. For instance, the numerical computation of the steady-state distribution of Markov chains is difficult when the chain is large or the eigenvalues badly distributed. The main approach for bounding steady-state availability has been proposed by Muntz and his co-authors [11,9]. The method has been improved by Carrasco [1], Rubino and Mahevas [10]. The theoretical background is based on Courtois's polyhedral results on steady-state equation [3]. However this method only works for bounding steady-state rewards.

Here we present a new method which allows to obtain bounds for transient and steady-state rewards. Our approach is based on stochastic comparison of Markov chains and lumpability. The stochastic comparison provides the guarantee for both transient and steady-state measures while lumpability allows to consider smaller chains which are easier to solve. The theory is based on an algorithmic derivation for sample-path comparison of Markov Chains based on necessary conditions on the transition matrix. This approach restricted on steady-state distribution and rewards has recently been surveyed [6], LIMSUB an algorithm based on lumpability has been proved [8] and a tool has been demonstrated [7]. Here we show how we can extend this theory for transient rewards as point availability and reliability. As the theoretical background is not based on Courtois's results on steady state, the requirements of our method are distinct from the assumptions needed by Muntz's algorithm and its generalizations.

The comparison of Markov chains requires an order on the state space because the order on random variables is defined by means of the set of non-decreasing functions. Thus, we order the states such that the UP states have indices that are smaller than the indices of the DOWN states, then we can define A as: $A = \sum_i \pi(i)r(i)$ where the reward $r(i)$ is a non-increasing function which is equal to 1 for the first states of the chain (the UP states) and 0 for all the other states. We wish to compute a lower bound for A. We shall let this lower bound be denoted by B. Notice that we may restate the problem by computing an upper bound for $1 - A$. This upper bound will be given by $1 - B$. In this case, the reward function is now a non-decreasing function on the state indices already defined. This property is an important requirement of the strong stochastic ordering as we will see in section 2.

Here we consider the modeling of highly available multicomponent systems such as the example studied by Muntz [11] and Carrasco [1]. A typical system consists of several disks, CPUs and controllers. We have two types of failures: soft and hard. The failures may occur in batches and all the failed items compete to be repaired. The system is operational if there is enough CPU, disks and controllers. Clearly, if the number of components is large, the state space is huge and the UP states are relatively rare. Furthermore, if the system is highly available, the UP states concentrate most of the probability distribution. For instance, the system depicted in Fig. 1 has more than $9.0\ 10^{10}$ states and 10^{12} transitions. This is even not possible to generate and store the state space and the transition matrix. Thus we show how we can operate in two phases: the first step consists in designing an ad-hoc algorithm (called LL, Lumpable and Larger) which builds from the specification a lumpable matrix which is larger in the stochastic sense. Of course, we store the lumped matrix instead of the original one. Then, during the second phase, we can apply the new bounding algorithm LMSUB to obtain the final matrix which can be numerically analyzed. As the chain is huge we must derive very efficient algorithms. So we report in section 4 some details about an efficient implementation of our new algorithm LMSUB (Lumpable Monotone Stochastic Upper Bound). As LMSUB is strongly related to LIMSUB these details can also be used to program a more efficient version of LIMSUB than the description in [8]. LMSUB algorithm is devoted to the study of problems with reducible chains while LIMSUB has several instructions to build an irreducible chain. This is the main difference between these algorithms. LMSUB has been specially developed to study reliability issues which imply chains with absorbing states.

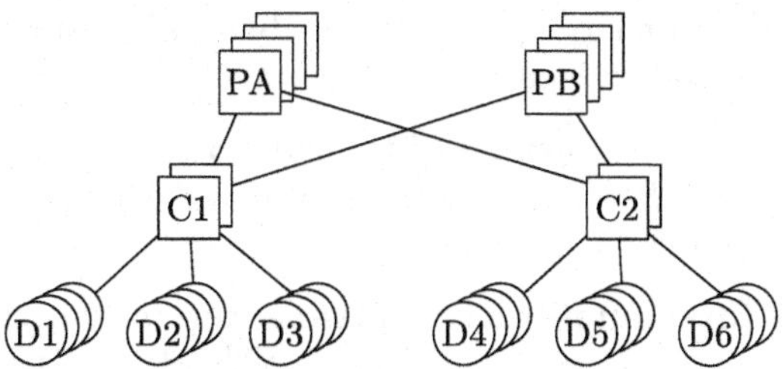

Fig. 1. System studied by Muntz and Carrasco

The paper is organized as follows. In section 2 we present the basic results we need about stochastic bounds, lumpability and algorithmic comparison of Markov chains. Section 3 is devoted to the theoretical aspects of bounding transient rewards. In section 4 we show how we can improve the algorithms to deal with extremely huge state space. Finally, we present some numerical results in section 5 for some typical problems introduced by Muntz and his colleagues [11].

2 Stochastic Bounds and Lumpability

We restrict ourselves to discrete time Markov chains (DTMC) with finite state space $E = \{1, 2, \ldots, n\}$. The strong stochastic ordering ("st-ordering" for short) has been defined by Stoyan[14] by means of the set of non-decreasing functions. For discrete random variables, we use the following algebraic equivalent formulation which is much more convenient:

Definition 1. *If X and Y are random variables taking values on a finite state space $\{1, 2, \ldots, n\}$ and respectively having p and q as probability distribution vectors, then X is said to be less than Y in the strong stochastic sense, that is, $X \preceq_{st} Y$ iff $\sum_{j=k}^{n} p_j \leq \sum_{j=k}^{n} q_j$ for $k = 1, 2, \ldots, n$.*

Bounds on the distribution imply bounds on performance measures that are non-decreasing functions of the state indices. Observe that performance measures such as average population size, tail probabilities and so on are non-decreasing functions. In our context, the reward that we wish to bound (i.e., $1-A$) is a non-decreasing function once the state space has been correctly ordered. Let us now illustrate definition 1 by an example:

Example 1. Let $\alpha = (0.1, 0.3, 0.4, 0.2)$ and $\beta = (0.1, 0.1, 0.5, 0.3)$. It follows then that $\alpha \preceq_{st} \beta$ since:

$$\begin{bmatrix} 0.2 & \leq 0.3 \\ 0.2+0.4 & \leq 0.3+0.5 \\ 0.2+0.4+0.3 & \leq 0.3+0.5+0.1 \end{bmatrix}$$

It has been known for some time that monotonicity [6] and comparability of transition probability matrices yield sufficient conditions for the stochastic comparison of Markov chains and their transient and steady-state distributions. Furthermore, st-monotonicity and st-comparability of matrices may be completely characterized by linear algebraic constraints [6].

Definition 2 (St-comparison of transition matrices). *Let P and R be two transition matrices. P is st-smaller than R if and only if $\sum_{k=j}^{n} P_{i,k} \leq \sum_{k=j}^{n} R_{i,k}$ for all k and i between 1 and n.*

Definition 3 (St-monotonicity of transition matrix). *Let P be a transition matrix. P is st-monotone if and only if $\sum_{k=j}^{n} P_{i-1,k} \leq \sum_{k=j}^{n} P_{i,k}$, for all k between 1 and n and for all i between 2 and n.*

We present now the relevant theorem for the stochastic comparison of Markov chains [14]. The statement below assumes that P, the original matrix we want to bound, is not monotone and that we want to obtain an upper bound.

Theorem 1. *Let $X(t)$ and $Y(t)$ be two DTMC and P and R be their respective stochastic matrices. If*

- $X(0) \preceq_{st} Y(0)$,
- *R is st-monotone,*
- $P \preceq_{st} R$,

then $X(t) \preceq_{st} Y(t)$, for all $t > 0$. If X and Y have steady-state distributions π_X and π_Y, then $\pi_X \preceq_{st} \pi_Y$.

Using this theorem and assuming that we want to compute an upper bound for P, which is the transition matrix of the problem we have to solve, we must find R such that:

$$\begin{cases} \sum_{k=j}^{n} P_{i,k} \leq \sum_{k=j}^{n} R_{i,k}, & \forall\, i, j, \\ \sum_{k=j}^{n} R_{i,k} \leq \sum_{k=j}^{n} R_{i+1,k}, & \forall\, i < n, j. \end{cases} \tag{1}$$

The first set of inequalities states that P is stochastically smaller than R while the second set shows that R is st-monotone. But these two sets of constraints do not help for the numerical resolution for transient or steady-state expected rewards. Thus we also impose additional restrictions on the structure of R in order to facilitate the computation of the bounds. Specifically, we shall insist here that the matrix R be ordinary lumpable.

Definition 4. (Ordinary lumpability). *Let P be the transition probability matrix of an irreducible finite DTMC and let C_k, $k = 1, 2, \ldots, M$ be a partition defined on the states of this Markov chain. Thus, each state of the Markov chain belongs to one and only one of the so-called* macro-states C_k. *The chain is said to be* ordinary lumpable *with respect to the partition C_k if and only if, for all states e and f belonging to the same arbitrary macro state C_k, we have*

$$\sum_{j \in C_i} p_{e,j} = \sum_{j \in C_i} p_{f,j}, \quad \text{for all macro states} \quad C_i, \quad i = 1, 2, \ldots, M. \tag{2}$$

Fourneau et al.[8] have shown that ordinary lumpability constraints are consistent with the relations specified by equation (1). Furthermore, they have designed and implemented an algorithm, called LIMSUB, which constructs a matrix R that possesses all these properties. The lumped matrix is much much smaller than the original matrix. This lumped matrix is readily solved and the bounds obtained from it may be applied to the original Markov chain.

We will now show how Theorem 1 and a slightly modified version of this algorithm establish a common methodology for computing both transient and steady-state bounds.

3 Bounds for Reliability: Extending the Theory

Our new LMSUB algorithm is based on LIMSUB [8] algorithm. Unfolding relations (1), and satisfing relations (2) for the bounding matrix and a given partition, we obtain a lumpable, st-monotone upper bound. The proof of this new algorithm is almost identical to the proof of LIMSUB algorithm so we refer the reader to [8]. LMSUB algorithm, hovever, does not care about irreducibility and can be, therefore, used to compute bounds of reducible matrices.

We will illustrate this algorithm on the following example. Assume that the chain has 5 states and the state-space is partitioned into two macro-states: $(1, 2)$ and $(3, 4, 5)$. Clearly, relations (1) allow that we compute the lumped matrix column by column. And we must perform some additional computations at the boundaries of the blocks to insure that the matrix is lumpable. In relations (1) we replace inequalities by equalities during the first step. The relations are unrolled and the equalities are arranged in increasing order for i and in decreasing order for j. During the second step, we must modify the first column of the block to insure that each block has a constant row sum in order to satisfy relations (2). The matrices below show the initial matrix (on the left), then the matrix after the computation of three columns using step 1, the modification of these elements due to the second step, and finally the lumped matrix (on the right). The values modified during the second step are boxed.

$$\begin{bmatrix} 0.2 & 0.2 & 0.1 & 0.3 & 0.2 \\ 0.1 & 0.2 & 0.1 & 0.5 & 0.1 \\ 0.0 & 0.3 & 0.5 & 0.1 & 0.1 \\ 0.1 & 0.2 & 0.4 & 0.3 & 0.0 \\ 0.0 & 0.1 & 0.0 & 0.9 & 0.0 \end{bmatrix} \quad \left[\begin{array}{cc|ccc} & & 0.1 & 0.3 & 0.2 \\ & & 0.1 & 0.4 & 0.2 \\ \hline & & 0.1 & 0.4 & 0.2 \\ & & 0.1 & 0.4 & 0.2 \\ & & 0.0 & 0.7 & 0.2 \end{array}\right] \quad \left[\begin{array}{cc|ccc} & & \boxed{0.2} & 0.3 & 0.2 \\ & & 0.1 & 0.4 & 0.2 \\ \hline & & \boxed{0.3} & 0.4 & 0.2 \\ & & \boxed{0.3} & 0.4 & 0.2 \\ & & 0.0 & 0.7 & 0.2 \end{array}\right] \quad \begin{bmatrix} 0.3 & 0.7 \\ 0.1 & 0.9 \end{bmatrix}$$

In Fourneau et al.[8], only the comparison of steady-state distributions was considered. However, theorem 1 states that the sample-paths are ordered. Thus the comparison of distributions is also true for transient distributions and rewards. And it is even not necessary that the chains are irreducible. It is possible to use this theorem to compare probability of reaching an absorbing state. This is particularly useful when we want to bound the reliability $R(t)$ because we only consider the restriction of the initial matrix to the UP states and one absorbing DOWN state.

We know that "st"-bounds are associated with non-decreasing rewards. Then, if $X(t) \preceq_{st} Y(t)$ at time t and $r(i)$ is a non-decreasing reward function, it follows that

$$\sum_i r(i)Prob(X(t) = i) \leq \sum_i r(i)Prob(Y(t) = i).$$

Now suppose that we use any algorithm which builds a lumpable upper bound. Let C_p be an arbitrary macro-state of the partition we have used to build the bound. Let us now design a new reward function $s(p)$ as the maximum of $r(i)$ for states i in C_p. Clearly, we have two important properties:

Property 1. *$s(p)$ is non-decreasing because the states are initially ordered according to the macro-state and $r(i)$ is non-decreasing.*

Property 2. *At each time step t, the probability of being in macro state C_p multiplied by the reward $s(p)$ is greater than the sum of the individual rewards multiplied by the probabilities of all the states in macro state C_p:*

$$s(p)Prob(Y(t) \in C_p) \geq \sum_{i \in C_p} r(i)Prob(Y(t) = i).$$

As the stochastic matrix associated with Y is lumpable, the left hand-side of the former inequality can be computed using the *lumped* chain Z. Combining both inequalities we get, for all t,

$$\sum_i r(i)Prob(X(t) = i) \leq \sum_p s(p)Prob(Z(t) = p).$$

Putting everything together we obtain the following more general result concerning our algorithms.

Theorem 2. *Let X be a finite aperiodic DTMC and let $r()$ be non-decreasing rewards defined on the states of X. Consider an arbitrary partition of the state space such that states which belong to the same macro-state are contiguous.*

Let Y be the finite DTMC obtained by LMSUB. Y is lumpable and let Z be the lumped version of Y. Assume that $X_0 \preceq_{st} Y_0$. We define the rewards $s()$ at the macro-state level as the maximal reward for the individual states. Then:

- *For any instant t, the expected reward at time t $E_X(r)(t)$ is upper bounded by the expected reward $E_Z(s)(t)$.*
- *The steady-state reward $E_X(r)$ is upper bounded by $E_Z(s)$.*

And both computations $E_Z(r)(t)$ and $E_Z(r)$ require working on matrix Z which is much smaller.

Let us now turn back to the reliability and point availability problem. Clearly, we have two values for the reward: 0 and 1. So we suggest the following for the partition and the corollary it clearly implies:

Rule 1. *Do not group in the same macro-state* UP *and* DOWN *states.*

Corollary 1. *Using this rule, it is not even necessary to compute the maximum and we bound directly the point availability, the reliability and steady-state availability of X by the same values computed on lumped matrix Z.*

3.1 Avoiding the Generation of the Whole State Space

The fundamental requirement is the existence of the transition matrix on the Markov chain on disk. But for some problem of reliability of multicomponent systems, this is even not possible to generate and store the state space and the transition matrix. For instance, the system studied by Muntz [11] and Carrasco [1] has more than $9.0\ 10^{10}$ states and 10^{12} transitions. Thus the matrix stored in sparse format represents more than one terabyte. Clearly, alternative description based on tensor product [12] or MTMDD [2] may be useful for the transition matrix. But in our problem even the state space is too large.

So, instead of generating the initial matrix using the visit of reachable states from an initial one with a BFS (Breadth First Search) algorithm, we design a new algorithm (called LL for Lumpable, and Larger) to build a matrix which is larger in the stochastic sense and which is lumpable. Of course, we only build and store the lumped matrix. We obtain a transition probability matrix as we also perform the uniformization process during the generation. It is worthy to remark that this matrix is not monotone in general. This matrix will be the input of LMSUB algorithm in the next step. So we perform two aggregations of the chain before the analysis.

A careful inspection of this state space shows that most of the states are DOWN states. So we use the following rules to design the first step macro-states:

Rule 2. *Do not aggregate the* UP *states during the first step.*

Rule 3. *During the first step aggregate the* DOWN *states which have the same total number of faults.*

Now we have to find the transition probabilities within this new chain. Here, we assume that the description of the model is based on events: an event has a rate and when we apply an event to a state, we obtain the resulting state. The rate does not depend on the states. These assumptions are used to explain how we group transitions. They are not necessary and the same work can be done with other formalisms as well. For the sake of concision, it is not possible to give a proved version of the algorithm here. Algorithm LL is based on the following ideas to obtain a lumpable larger bound:

- Do not change the transition probabilities between simple states.
- The transition from a simple state x to an aggregated state C_p is the sum of the transition probabilities from x to y, for all y in C_p.
- For transitions leaving an aggregated state C_p to an aggregated state C_q (if C_q is a single state, just modify step 4).
  1. label all transitions with the events,
  2. group the transitions and the events according to the number of failures (for instance, a "+1" transition models a new fault),
  3. if an event is associated to two (or more) numbers of failures, then modify the transitions as follows: all the transitions labeled with this event must now join the largest state reached by this event from a state in macro-state C_p.
     For instance, if event u is associated to one or two new faults, then modify the transitions such that now event u is always two new faults.
  4. Then do the summation for all the states in C_q.

Finally we perform the uniformization. Clearly, this algorithm is problem dependent. However, from this specification, we can clearly state that the matrix is larger in the stochastic sense (we move transitions to upper states) and lumpable.

Finally, the total comparison process does not depend of the algorithm used to obtain a lumpable stochastically larger matrix. And clearly the bound obtained by LMSUB or LIMSUB of the matrix we obtain is also a bound of the original matrix we are not able to store.

4 Improving the Algorithms

Even if LIMSUB algorithm described in [8] and our new algorithm are closely related, there are several points concerning the implementation which differ considerably. In this section we present the main modifications that speed up the algorithm, especially in case of a transition matrix with relatively few non-zero elements per state, compared to the size of the state space. It also allows the computation of a bound of a reducible transition matrix which is necessary in our approach to bound the reliability of repairable systems.

4.1 LMSUB, LIMSUB and the Irreducibility Issue

In [8] only the irreducible transition matrices with some additional properties (see [8], Theorem 3) have been considered. To ensure that the irreducibility property is maintained by LIMSUB algorithm the authors in [8] avoid deleting transitions and, if necessary, add small sub-diagonal transitions.

When computing the bounds for transient distributions, we might want to compute the bounds even for the reducible matrices. In order to obtain the reliability bounds using our approach, for instance, we need to compute an st-monotone upper bound of a matrix having one absorbing state (corresponding to the DOWN states of the model). In our implementation of this algorithm we leave the choice to the user if the bound to be computed needs to be irreducible or not.

4.2 Avoiding Computations

The algorithm computes the bounding matrix column per column beginning with the last column. It is clear that it is necessary to store only one column of the matrix P at a time. Only after the first step (Algorithm 1) we know how to modify the first column of the block to obtain a constant row sum. Furthermore due to st-monotonicity, we know that the maximal row sum is obtained with the last row of the block.

```
        for bloc=M to 1 do
step1:      for column=last(block) to first(block) do
                computeCol(column);
            end
step2:      endBlock();
        end
```

Algorithm 1: LIMSUB algorithm [8]

We keep the first step as described in [8]. For the second step, however, there is no need to recompute the first column of a block as all the information needed to compute the next column is only the vector of partial sums $ps_Q^{(j)} = (\sum_{k=j}^{n} q_{i,k})_{i=1}^{n}$ of the lumpable bound Q for the current column j. As the lumpability imposes that this sum is constant for all the rows of a block and, due to the st-monotonicity constraints, we know that the maximal value is obtained for the last row of a block, we need only to store one single value per block. This value is already known at the end of step 1 of the algorithm, so the second step can be completely avoided.

4.3 Sparse Matrix Implementation

The repairable system models have often a huge state space but relatively few transitions per state, which makes interesting to use the sparse representation of transition matrices. Our implementation of LMSUB algorithm exploits this representation and uses the adapted data structures to reduce further the computations. For instance, for the vector $ps_Q^{(j)}$ of partial sums for the current column j of the lumpable bound Q, we store only the index and the value for the rows this sum strictly increases (the elements of $ps_Q^{(j)}$ are increasing because of the st-monotonicity constraints), i.e we store $(i, ps_Q^{(j)})$ if and only if $\sum_{k=j}^{n} q_{i,k} - \sum_{k=j}^{n} q_{i-1,k} > 0$ (with $\sum_{k=j}^{n} q_{-1,k} = 0$). Notice that it is necessary to use only one such structure (a list for example) during the whole computation process as the elements of $ps_Q^{(j)}$ are computed in increasing order, so the old elements, corresponding to the column $j-1$ with indices smaller than the current position, are no longer needed. This allows us to compute only the elements of $ps_Q^{(j)}$ whose value is different from $ps_Q^{(j+1)}$.

Furthermore, we know that those changes are due to the non-zero elements in the column j of the original matrix P (st-comparison between P and Q).

Between the two non-zero elements of P at the positions denoted by i_1 et i_2, it is only necessary to update the list containing the information on $ps_Q^{(j)}$ vector, i.e. to erase some elements if they are smaller or equal to the last computed element (at position i_1).

We illustrate this on the example below. On the left is the initial matrix and on the right the bound obtained by LMSUB algorithm. In the table in the middle the first column represents the current column, the second the number of computations performed for that column and the last one the sparse-vector $ps_Q^{(j)}$ throughout the computation process. One can notice that the number of computations performed is sometimes even smaller (column 2) than the number of non-zero elements in the corresponding column of the initial matrix. This is the consequence of the fact that, once the partial sum of value 1 is encountered, the computation of the current column is finished. Note that the "lump" steps do not require computation following the previous remarks.

$$\left[\begin{array}{cc|ccc|cc} 0.3 & 0.6 & 0 & 0 & 0.1 & 0 & 0 \\ 0.4 & 0 & 0.5 & 0 & 0 & 0.1 & 0 \\ \hline 0.1 & 0 & 0.3 & 0.4 & 0 & 0 & 0.2 \\ 0 & 0.7 & 0 & 0 & 0.3 & 0 & 0 \\ 0.1 & 0 & 0.5 & 0 & 0 & 0.4 & 0 \\ \hline 0 & 0 & 0 & 0.8 & 0 & 0.2 & 0 \\ 0 & 0.5 & 0 & 0 & 0.1 & 0.3 & 0.1 \end{array}\right]$$

col.	comp.	sparse vector $ps_Q^{(j)}$
7	2	$\{(3, 0.2)\}$
6	4	$\{(2, 0.1), (3, 0.2), (5, 0.4)\}$
lump:	0	$\{(1, 0.1), (3, 0.4)\}$
5	3	$\{(1, 0.1), (3, 0.4), (7, 0.5)\}$
4	2	$\{(1, 0.1), (3, 0.6), (6, 1)\}$
3	3	$\{(1, 0.1), (2, 0.6), (3, 0.9), (6, 1)\}$
lump:	0	$\{(1, 0.6), (3, 0.9), (6, 1)\}$
2	2	$\{(1, 0.7), (3, 0.9), (4, 1)\}$
1	0	$\{(1, 1)\}$
lump:	0	$\{(1, 1)\}$

$$\begin{bmatrix} 0.4 & 0.5 & 0.1 \\ 0.1 & 0.5 & 0.4 \\ 0 & 0.6 & 0.4 \end{bmatrix}$$

5 Numerical Results

In this section we give some numerical results for two examples of repairable systems [1,11]. The first example is rather small and it is presented here in order to illustrate the quality of our bounds as it is possible to solve the transient and steady-state distributions of the original system. We use LMSUB and LIMSUB but LL is useless. The second example has more than 9×10^{10} states with the number of transitions of order of 10^{12}. So we are not even able to generate the whole transition rate matrix. Yet it is still possible to provide the bounds both for transient and steady-state rewards using our approach.

In the first example we have a system composed of: a front-end (FE), a database (DB), and two processing subsystems having each a switch (S), a memory (M) and two processors (P). The system is operational if it is possible to access the database i.e. if front-end, database and at least one processing subsystem are operational. A processing subsystem is operational if the corresponding switch, memory and at least one processor are operational. The failures and reparations of components are modeled by exponential distributions. The failure rates are $1/120h^{-1}$ for processors and $1/2400h^{-1}$ for other components and repair rates are $1h^{-1}$ for all the components. A processor failure contaminates

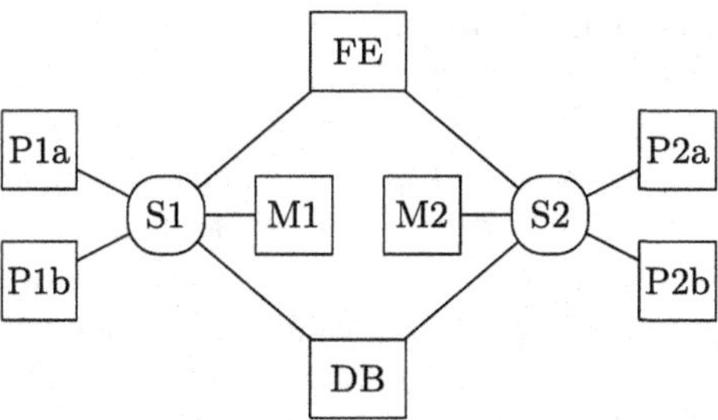

Fig. 2. First example

the database with probability 0.01. Once the system is down the components do not fail. The components are repaired by a single repairman with the priority given to front-end and database, followed by switches and memories, and then the processors. Within the same priority group the components are chosen at random. We consider the preemptive policy.

The original model has 142 states from which 32 are operational. The maximal number of failed components is 7. Notice that for our approach the order of states is important as all the UP states must precede the DOWN states. Furthermore, we take into account the fact that the LMSUB algorithm yields better bounds for the initial matrix which is almost st-monotone. The choice of partition is also very important as the lumpability step of the algorithm performs much better if the states within the same block have similar properties.

Within the same class of states (UP or DOWN) we ordered the states according to the number of failed components. We chose the following partition : all the states of the same class with the same number of failed components form a block, except the states with only one failure which are left as single-state blocks. This gives 17 blocks, 9 of them composed of UP states.

Solving the original model we obtained steady-state availability $A = 0.998835$. The lower bound obtained by our method is 0.998667. In figure 3 we present the

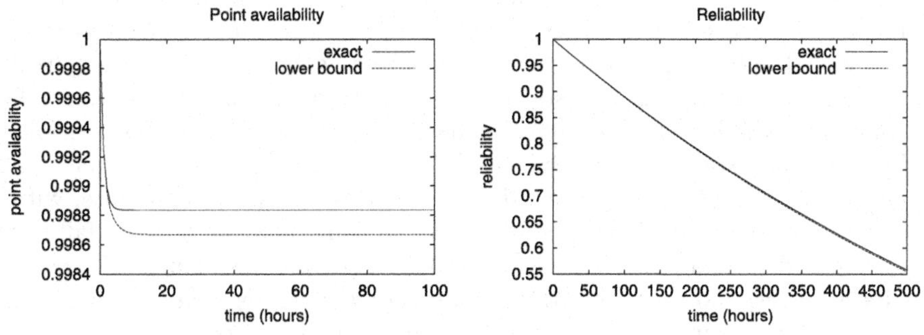

Fig. 3. The exact point availability (left) and reliability (right), and their lower bounds for the first example

transient bounds for point availability and reliability for this example. We can notice that both results are really close to the exact values.

The second example is presented in figure 1. The system is operational if at least one of processor PA or PB is operational, at least one controller of each type and at least three out of four disks of each of the six clusters are operational. Only one processor of each type is active and only the active processors can fail. A failure of active processor PA is propagated to the active processor PB with probability 0.1. The failures and reparations of components are exponentially distributed. The failure rates are given in table 1. There are two failure modes (soft and hard) which occur with equal probability. When the system is operational the repair rates are $0.1h^{-1}$ in the soft mode and $0.05h^{-1}$ in the hard mode. When the system is down, the rates are 10 times larger as the consequence of the additional precautions to be taken when the system is operational. There is only one repairman who chooses the component to be repaired at random from the set of failed components.

Table 1. Failure rates (h^{-1}) for the second example

Component	PA, PB and C1	C2	D1	D2	D3	D4	D5	D6
Failure Rate	1/2000	1/4000	1/6000	1/8000	1/10000	1/12000	1/14000	1/16000

The model has only 36 components of 10 different types yet the state-space is of order of 9.0 10^{10}. We used the technique described in section 3.1 to reduce the state space. All the UP states are generated and the DOWN states are aggregated according to the number of failed components. This gives a new model with 1312235 states (1312200 UP and 35 DOWN macro-states) and 25754089 transitions.

First let us consider the ordering of the states and the edge between UP states and DOWN states. We have chosen the UP state with the maximal number (15) of simultaneous failures for the system to still be operational, in which all the failures are hard failures and the only operational processor is PB, to be the last UP ($last_{UP}$) state. Let D_k denote the DOWN macro-state with k failures. Then for all $D_k, k \geq 3$ there is a transition (D_k, D_{k-1}) and the only transition from DOWN macro states to UP states is the transition $(D_2, last_{UP})$. Also, there are transitions $(D_k, D_{k+1}), \forall k < 36$ and $(D_k, D_{k+2}), \forall k < 35$, so the new transition matrix is irreducible. It is also aperiodic due to the uniformization constant $\lambda > \max_i\{-Q_{i,i}\}$, so we can use the optimized version of LIMSUB algorithm.

In the second step the UP states are reordered increasingly in number of failed components followed by number of hard failures. The UP states are followed by the DOWN states ordered increasingly in number of failed components. The partition contains 172 subsets: all the UP states, except $last_{UP}$ state, with the same number of failed components and the same number of hard failures are aggregated forming 136 blocks followed by $last_{UP}$ state then by 35 one-state blocks corresponding to the DOWN states, already aggregated in the first step.

The lower bound for steady-state availability of the second system obtained by this method is 0.999132158 (upper bound for unavailability is 0.000867842). The lower bounds for point availability are given in figure 4 (left).

In table 2 we give computational times for all three steps. For the third step we also report the time needed by LIMSUB [8] algorithm (on the same machine). We can notice that on this example our algorithm is approximately twice faster. This is a consequence of the improvement made during the normalization part of the algorithm as well as the better utilization of the matrix sparse structure.

When we bound the reliability, we are only interested in UP states. We are computing the lower bound for reliability with the st-monotone upper bound of the chain. We obtain this bound by aggregating all the DOWN states into one absorbing state. We ordered UP states and regrouped them into blocks according to the number of failed components followed by the number of hard failures. This gives us a partition into 137 blocks: 136 corresponding to UP states and 1 to the absorbing DOWN state. The lower bounds for reliability for the second system are reported in figure 4 (right).

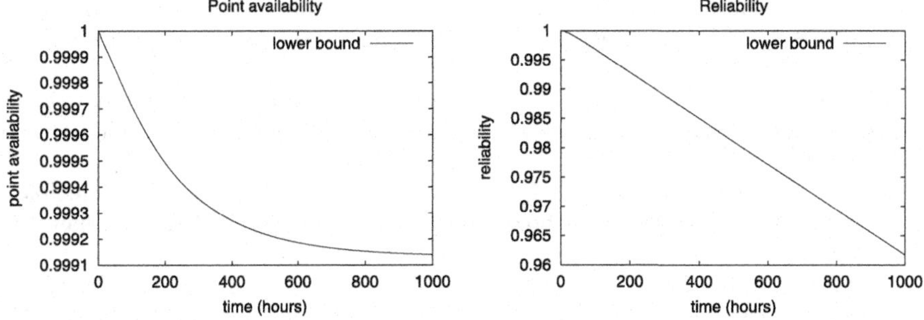

Fig. 4. Lower bounds for point availability and reliability for the second example

Table 2. CPU times in seconds on a PC (CPU 3.20GHz, 896MB of RAM) to compute the point availability for the second example

generation	reordering	LMSUB (ird)	LIMSUB [8]
182.0	95.52	56.54	107.3

6 Conclusion

In this paper we have extended the theory of algorithmic bounds to reliability and availability problems. The theory now includes transient and steady-state analysis and the Markov chains may be irreducible or have an absorbing state. We have also improved the algorithms to be more efficient as the chains are very large. We have also suggested that high level formalisms may be used to build lumpable matrices which are larger in the stochastic sense. Of course, only the lumped matrix is generated and stored. A version of this algorithm based on Stochastic Automata Network is currently under development.

References

1. J.A. Carrasco, "Bounding steady-state availability models with group repair and phase type repair distributions", Performance Evaluation, V35 (1999), 193–204.
2. G. Ciardo and A.S. Miner. "Storage alternatives for larger structured state spaces." In R. Marie, B. Plateau, M.Calzarossa, and G. Rubino, editors, Proc. 9th Int. Conf. on Modelling Techniques and Tools for Computer Performance Evaluation, LNCS 1245, pages 44-57, St. Malo, France, June 1997. Springer-Verlag.
3. P.J. Courtois, P. Semal, "Bounds for the positive eigenvectors of nonnegative matrices and their approximations", J. ACM, V31 (4) (1984), 804–825.
4. T. Dayar, J.M. Fourneau, N. Pekergin, "Transforming stochastic matrices for stochastic comparison with the st-order", RAIRO-RO, V37 (2003), 85–97.
5. T. Dayar, N. Pekergin: "Stochastic comparison, reorderings, and nearly completely decomposable Markov chains." In: Proceedings of the International Conference on the Numerical Solution of Markov Chains (NSMC'99), (Ed. Plateau, B. Stewart, W.), Prensas universitarias de Zaragoza. (1999) 228-246.
6. J.M. Fourneau, N. Pekergin. "An algorithmic approach to stochastic bounds", LNCS 2459, Performance evaluation of complex systems: Techniques and Tools, pp 64–88, 2002.
7. J.M. Fourneau, M. Lecoz, N. Pekergin and F. Quessette, "An open tool to compute stochastic bounds on steady-state distributiuon and rewards", IEEE Mascots 2003, Orlando, USA.
8. J.M. Fourneau, M. Lecoz, F. Quessette, "Algorithms for an irreducible and lumpable strong stochastic bound", Numerical Solution of Markov Chains, 2003, USA.
9. J.C.S. Lui, R. Muntz, "Computing bounds on steady state availability of repairable computer systems", J. ACM, V41 (4) (1994), 676–707.
10. S. Mahevas, G. Rubino, "Bounding asymptotic dependability and performance measures", Second IEEE International Performance and Dependability Symposium, USA, 1996, 176–186.
11. R. Muntz, E. de Souza e Silva, A. Goyal, "Bounding availability of repairable computer systems", IEEE Trans. on Computers, V38 (12) (1989), 1714–1723.
12. B. Plateau, "On the stochastic structure of parallelism and synchronization models for distributed algorithms", Proc. of the SIGMETRICS Conference, Texas, 1985, 147–154.
13. W.J. Stewart, "Introduction to the Numerical Solution of Markov Chains", Princeton University Press, 1994.
14. D. Stoyan, "Comparison Methods for Queues and Other Stochastic Models", Wiley, 1983.

Stochastic Model Checking with Stochastic Comparison*

Nihal Pekergin[1,2] and Sana Younès[1]

[1] PRiSM, Université de Versailles Saint-Quentin en Yvelines,
45 Av. des Etats Unis, 78000 Versailles, France
[2] Centre Marin Mersenne, Université Paris 1, 75013 Paris, France
{nih, sayo}@prism.uvsq.fr

Abstract. This paper presents a stochastic comparison based method to check state formulas defined over Discrete Time Markov Reward Models. High-level specifications like stochastic Petri nets, Stochastic Automata Networks, Stochastic Process Algebras have been developed to construct large Markov models. However computation of transient and steady-state distributions are limited to relatively small parameter sizes because of the state space explosion problem. Stochastic comparison technique by which both transient and steady-state bounding distributions can be computed, lets to overcome this problem. On the other hand, bounding techniques are useful in Model Checking, since we check generally formulas to see if they meet some bounds or not. We propose to apply stochastic bounding algorithms to construct bounding distributions and to check formulas through these distributions.

1 Introduction

Model checking has been introduced as an automated technique to verify functional properties of systems expressed in a formal logic like Computational Tree Logic (CTL) [6]. This formalism has been extended with some probabilistic operators to Probabilistic CTL and Continuous Stochastic Logic (CSL)[3]. Stochastic Model Checking is typically based on discrete time or continuous time Markov chains or Markov decision processes. For performance and/or dependability applications, stochastic model checking has been extended to models with some rewards on states and/or transitions in which logic formalisms PRCTL(Probabilistic Reward Computational Tree Logic)[2] and CSRL (Stochastic Reward Logic)[13] are used.

We propose to check the reward based formulas of stochastic models by applying stochastic comparison approach. Indeed, to check these formulas transient or steady-state distribution of the underlying Markov chain must be computed. However the numerical computation of these distributions may be very complex or intractable because of the state space explosion. The stochastic comparison has been shown to be an efficient method to overcome this problem [10]. This

* This work is partially supported by ACI Sécurité SurePath

M. Bravetti et al. (Eds.): EPEW 2005 and WS-FM 2005, LNCS 3670, pp. 109–123, 2005.

method consists in computing bounding distributions rather than the exact distributions by analysing "simpler" bounding chains. Simple bounding models can be constructed by reducing state space size or by imposing some specific structures on bounding chains which let to apply some specific methods like matrix-geometric, product form solution, etc.

The stochastic comparison has been largely used in different areas of applied probability as well as in reliability, performance evaluation, dependability applications [16,18]. There are different stochastic ordering relations and the most known is the strong stochastic ordering ($\leq_{st}$) which yields the comparison of the underlying distributions. Comparison in the sense of this ordering can be established by coupling constructions, by sample-path comparisons or by some analytical methods. However these are generally model oriented techniques. We apply here algorithmic stochastic bounding techniques to construct bounding models in a fully automated manner. Therefore the proposed methodology can be easily integrated to model checkers.

Let us explain the proposed methodology: We are interested in formulas defined as rewards on distributions of a time-homogeneous Discrete Time Markov Chain (DTMC). Thus we need to compute a transient or steady-state distribution. We construct bounding chains by aggregating the states of the original one by means of the algorithm given in [11] which based on the stochastic monotonicity and the comparison of stochastic matrices and the lumpability of Markov chains. The rewards are evaluated through bounding distributions. The state space size may be drastically reduced by aggregation, that will reduce the numerical complexity to compute distributions of the bounding chains. Therefore it is possible to apply numerical methods to compute efficiently the bounding distributions. Obviously, there are some constraints to construct aggregated state space and to order macro-states because of the stochastic ordering constraints and the underlying formula. These issues are discussed in section 4.

The bounding techniques can be applied to efficiently check stochastic models since exact values are not always necessary, and it suffices to show that the underlying formulas meet some bounds. In [7], the bounds on state reachability probabilities of Markov decision processes are computed by abstraction of the underlying model defined on smaller state spaces. If the verification of the considered property cannot be concluded, the abstract model is refined until a verdict to the property can be deduced from the computations. For reward based model checking, generally used rewards such as average population, loss rates, blocking probabilities are defined as non decreasing functions of the transient or steady-state distributions. Thus the stochastic comparison in the sense of the $\leq_{st}$ ordering which is associated to the non decreasing functions can be applied to bound such rewards.

The remaining of the paper is organised as follows: in section 2, we provide a brief introduction of stochastic comparison. In section 3, we present reward based stochastic model checking formalism given in [2]. Section 4 is devoted to the proposed methodology to improve the stochastic reward based model checking. Finally, in section 5, we give some numerical examples to illustrate the proposed methodology.

2 Stochastic Comparison

In this section, we present some preliminaries on the stochastic comparison method and we refer to the books [16,18] for the theoretical issues and different applications of this method.

Definition 1. *Let X and Y be random variables taking values on a totally ordered space S. Then X is said to be less than Y in the strong stochastic sense, ($X \leq_{st} Y$) if and only if $E[f(X)] \leq E[f(Y)]$ for all non decreasing functions $f : S \to R$, whenever the expectations exist.*

Indeed $\leq_{st}$ ordering gives the comparison of the underlying probability distribution functions: $X \leq_{st} Y \leftrightarrow Prob(X > a) \leq Prob(Y > a) \quad \forall a \in S$. Thus it is more probable for Y to take larger values than for X. Since the $\leq_{st}$ ordering yields the comparison of sample-paths, it is also known as sample-path ordering.

We give in the next proposition the $\leq_{st}$ comparison in the case of finite state space $S = \{1, 2, \cdots, n\}$.

Property 1. Let X, Y be random variables taking values on $S = \{1, 2, \cdots, n\}$ and p, q be probability vectors which are respectively denoting distributions of X and Y.

$X \leq_{st} Y \leftrightarrow \sum_i^n p[i] \leq \sum_i^n q[i] \quad \forall i = \{n, n-1, \cdots, 1\}$

The stochastic comparison of random variables has been extended to the comparison of Markov chains.

Definition 2. *Let $\{X(t),\ t > 0\}$ and $\{Y(t),\ t \geq 0\}$ be two DTMC taking values in S. $\{X(t),\ t \geq 0\}$ is said to be less than $\{Y(t),\ t \geq 0\}$ in the strong stochastic sense, that is, $\{X(t),\ t \geq 0\} \leq_{st} \{Y(t),\ t \geq 0\}$ iff $X(t) \leq_{st} Y(t) \ \ \forall t$.*

The comparison of Markov chains yields the comparison of transient distributions at each time, and if the limit distributions exist, we have also the comparison of the steady-state distributions. It is shown that monotonicity and comparability of time-homogeneous DTMC yield sufficient conditions for their stochastic comparison [16].

Theorem 1. *Let $\{X(t), t \geq 0\}$ and $\{Y(t), t \geq 0\}$ be two time-homogeneous DTMC and P and Q be their respective probability transition matrices. $P[i,*]$ indicates row i of matrix P. Then $\{X(t), t > 0\} \leq_{st} \{Y(t), t > 0\}$, if*

- *$X(0) \leq_{st} Y(0)$,*
- *st-monotonicity of at least one of the matrices holds, that is,*

$$\textit{either } P[i,*] \leq_{st} P[i+1,*] \quad \textit{or} \quad Q[i,*] \leq_{st} Q[i+1,*]$$

- *st-comparability of the matrices holds, that is, $P[i,*] \leq_{st} Q[i,*] \ \ \forall i$.*

In [1] an algorithm based on this theorem is given to construct an optimal st-monotone upper bounding Markov chain. This algorithms takes an irreducible stochastic matrix P as input and returns as output a st-monotone upper bounding matrix, Q, such that, $P \leq_{st} Q$. Indeed, the monotonicity and comparability constraints can be given as in equation 1. Note that inequalities are replaced by equalities to construct optimal bounds.

$$\begin{cases} \sum_{k=j}^{n} Q[1,k] = \sum_{k=j}^{n} P[1,k] \\ \sum_{k=j}^{n} Q[i+1,k] = max(\sum_{k=j}^{n} Q[i,k], \sum_{k=j}^{n} P[i+1,k]) \end{cases} \quad (1)$$

In this algorithm that will be called Vincent's algorithm, the construction is done from the last column to the first column and within a column from the first row to the last row. This idea has been extended to devise algorithms to construct st-monotone, bounding stochastic matrices having some specific structures to simplify their numerical analysis [10]. In [5,11] it is shown that ordinary lumpability constraints given in the following Property 2 are consistent with the st-monotonicity. Thus for a given P, it is possible to construct a st-monotone, lumpable, bounding matrix. Let us give the lumpability constraints for discrete time Markov chains.

Property 2. Let Q be the probability transition matrix of an irreducible finite time-homogeneous DTMC, $\mathcal{A} = \{A_1, A_2, \cdots, A_n\}$ be a partition of states. The chain is ordinary lumpable according to partition $\mathcal{A}$, if and only if for all states e and f in the same arbitrary macro state A_i, we have:

$$\sum_{j \in A_k} Q[e,j] = \sum_{j \in A_k} Q[f,j] \quad \forall \; macro-state \;\; A_k \in \mathcal{A}$$

The algorithm given in [11] (LIMSUB Algorithm) constructs for a given irreducible, time-homogeneous stochastic matrix P, and partition of states, $\mathcal{A} = \{A_1, \cdots, A_m\}$, a total order relation on $\mathcal{A}$: $A_1 \leq A_2 \leq \cdots \leq A_m$, a st-monotone, lumpable according to $\mathcal{A}$, irreducible upper bounding matrix Q. There are two steps in this algorithm. The first step is based on Vincent's algorithm to satisfy the stochastic monotonicity and comparison constraints (see equations 1) while the second step is to satisfy the lumpability constraints. We explain this algorithm through the following example. Let P be the input matrix and state space be divided into two partitions $A_1 = \{1,2\}$ and $A_2 = \{3,4\}$. Q is the matrix computed from Vincent's algorithm in the first step. Thus Q is $\leq_{st}$ monotone and upper bounding matrix of P. The modified entries are given bolded and superscripts indicate if the probabilities are increased or decreased. In the second step, the sum of probabilities in each macro-state is adjusted to make Q lumpable. Hence Q_{sup} computed from Q is lumpable.

$$P = \left[\begin{array}{cc|cc} 0.2 & 0.2 & 0.2 & 0.4 \\ 0.2 & 0.1 & 0.4 & 0.3 \\ \hline 0.1 & 0.4 & 0.2 & 0.3 \\ 0.1 & 0.1 & 0.4 & 0.4 \end{array}\right] \quad Q = \left[\begin{array}{cc|cc} 0.2 & 0.2 & 0.2 & 0.4 \\ 0.2 & 0.1 & \mathbf{0.3}^{-} & \mathbf{0.4}^{+} \\ \hline 0.1 & \mathbf{0.2}^{-} & \mathbf{0.3}^{+} & \mathbf{0.4}^{+} \\ 0.1 & 0.1 & 0.4 & 0.4 \end{array}\right]$$

$$Q_{sup} = \left[\begin{array}{cc|cc} 0.2 & \mathbf{0.1}^- & \mathbf{0.3}^+ & 0.4 \\ 0.2 & 0.1 & 0.3 & 0.4 \\ \hline 0.1 & \mathbf{0.1}^- & \mathbf{0.4}^+ & 0.4 \\ 0.1 & 0.1 & 0.4 & 0.4 \end{array}\right] \qquad Q_{sup} = \left[\begin{array}{cc} 0.3 & 0.7 \\ 0.2 & 0.8 \end{array}\right]$$

It is also possible to derive lower bounds from the following algorithm by reversing the order of states and then running algorithm LIMSUB on the permuted P. By permuting again the computed upper bounding matrix, we obtain the st-monotone, lower bounding matrix, Q_{inf}. In the sequel, the upper bounding matrix will be denoted by Q_{sup}.

The stochastic comparison approach consists in analysing the bounding matrices Q_{inf} and Q_{sup} to provide bounds on transient distributions and the steady-state distribution of P. Obviously the numerical analysis of the lumpable bounding matrices is much easier than that of P due to the state space reduction.

3 Model Checking with Discrete Time Reward Markov Chains

The underlying system is modelled by a labelled, finite, ergodic (irreducible, aperiodic, positive recurrent) discrete time Markov chain $\mathcal{D} = (S, P, L)$ where S is a finite set of states, $P : S \times S \rightarrow [0, 1]$ is the transition matrix and $L : S \rightarrow 2^{AP}$ is the labelling function which assigns to each state s, the set $L(s)$ of atomic propositions valid in s. AP denotes the finite set of atomic propositions.

For Markov chains, there are two types of state probabilities: transient probabilities where the system is considered at time n. Let $\pi(s, s', n)$ be the probability that the system is in state s' within n steps given the system starts in state s. The steady-state probabilities are the long-run probabilities where the system reaches an equilibrium: $\pi(s, s') = lim_{n\rightarrow\infty}\pi(s, s', n)$ is the steady-state probability of state s'. For ergodic DTMC, $\pi(s, s')$ exists and is independent of the initial state s and that will be noted by $\pi(s')$.

We are interested in the Probabilistic Reward CTL (PRCTL) logic given in [2]. It is indeed the extension of the Probabilistic CTL (PCTL) logic [12] to specify performability measure over Discrete Time Markov Reward Models. In these models a reward (cost) is associated to each state s. Let $\rho : S \rightarrow \mathbf{R}_{\geq 0}$ be the reward assignment function. Every time the system enters (leaves) state s, it incurs reward $\rho(s)$ which can be a constant or a random variable [14]. We give briefly the syntax of the PCTL logic.

Let $n \in \mathbf{N} \cup \{\infty\}$ and I be an interval of real numbers, namely $I \subseteq \mathbf{R}_{\geq 0}$, $p \in [0, 1]$, and $\triangleleft$ a binary comparison operator. The syntax of PRCTL:

$$\phi ::= true \mid a \mid \phi \vee \phi \mid \neg\phi \mid \mathcal{P}_{\triangleleft p}(\phi\, \mathcal{U}_I^J\, \phi) \mid \mathcal{L}_{\triangleleft p}(\phi)$$

$$\mathcal{I}_I^n(\phi) \mid \mathcal{C}_I^n(\phi) \mid \mathcal{E}_I^n(\phi) \mid \mathcal{E}_I(\phi)$$

The first four operators are classical logic operators, while the fifth and the sixth ones are from the PCTL logic. The path formula $\mathcal{P}_{\triangleleft p}(\phi\, \mathcal{U}_I^J\, \phi)$ asserts that the probability for paths starting in s and satisfying $\phi\,\mathcal{U}_I^J\,\phi$ meets the bound $\triangleleft p$. The state formula $\mathcal{L}_{\triangleleft p}(\phi)$ asserts that the steady-state probability to be in ϕ states meets the bound $\triangleleft p$.

The last four formulas are inspired from performance measures of DTMC with rewards [14] and included in the PRCTL logic [2]. These are all state formulas and defined from transient or steady-state distribution of the underlying Markov chain.

The formula $\mathcal{I}_I^n(\phi)$ is satisfied, if the instantaneous expected reward in ϕ-states (states which satisfy formula ϕ) at the n-th step, starting in state s, meets the bounds of I:

$$\mathcal{I}_I^n(\phi) \text{ is satisfied iff } \sum_{s' \models \phi} \pi(s, s', n)\rho(s') \in I \tag{2}$$

The formula $\mathcal{C}_I^n(\phi)$ is satisfied, if the expected accumulated reward in ϕ-states up to the n-th transition meets the bound of I:

$$\mathcal{C}_I^n(\phi) \text{ is satisfied iff } \sum_{i=0}^{n-1} \sum_{s' \models \phi} \pi(s, s', i)\rho(s') \in I \tag{3}$$

The formula $\mathcal{E}_I^n(\phi)$ is satisfied if the expected reward per unit time in ϕ-states up to the n-th transition meets the bound of I:

$$\mathcal{E}_I^n(\phi) \text{ is satisfied iff } \frac{1}{n} \sum_{i=0}^{n-1} \sum_{s' \models \phi} \pi(s, s', i)\rho(s') \in I \tag{4}$$

The formula $\mathcal{E}_I(\phi)$ is the long-run expected reward per unit-time (reward rate) for ϕ-states which is the limiting case of $\mathcal{E}_I^n(\phi)$. ($\mathcal{E}_I(\phi)$=$\lim_{n\to\infty} \mathcal{E}_I^n(\phi)$). If the steady-state exists, $\mathcal{E}_I(\phi)$ is satisfied if:

$$\mathcal{E}_I(\phi) \text{ is satisfied iff } \sum_{s' \models \phi} \pi(s')\rho(s') \in I \tag{5}$$

The other state operator of the PCTL logic, $\mathcal{L}_{\triangleleft p}(\phi)$ can be also defined by means of the steady-state distribution and it is satisfied if:

$$\mathcal{L}_{\triangleleft p}(\phi) \text{ is satisfied iff } \sum_{s' \models \phi} \pi(s') \triangleleft p \tag{6}$$

4 Model Checking by Stochastic Comparison

In this section we explain the proposed methodology to check reward based stochastic models by applying stochastic comparison method. This methodology is composed of three main steps and the treatment in each step depends on the considered formula ϕ that will be checked:

1. Partition of the state space and ordering of macro-states.
2. Construction of the bounding chains through algorithm LIMSUB (see section 2) and computing transient or steady-state distribution as a function of the the considered formula (see section 3).
3. Checking the underlying formula.

4.1 State Space Partition

We divide state space S into two subset S_{no} and S_{yes} such that S_{yes} contains ϕ-states ie. $S_{yes} = \{s \in S \mid s \models \phi\}$ and S_{no} contains states which do not verify ϕ ie. $S_{no} = \{s \in S \mid s \not\models \phi\}$.

We order state space to have S_{no} followed by S_{yes}. We are especially interested in S_{yes} since the rewards are computed over these states. In performance and dependability applications the size of S_{yes} is small compared to the size of S_{no}. In general the states of S_{no} are aggregated into macro-states to reduce the state space size. However there is no constraint on the ordering of these macro-states and on the rewards assigned to them. But if states of S_{yes} are aggregated, because of the $\leq_{st}$ stochastic ordering, some constraints on the macro-state ordering and on the rewards must be satisfied (figure 1).

Suppose that S_{yes} is divided into k macro-states: $S_{yes} = \{A_1, A_2, \ldots, A_k\}$. The rewards for macro-states are defined as follows:

- to compute upper bounds, $\rho_{sup}(A_i) = \max\{\rho(s), s \in A_i\}$.
- to compute lower bounds, $\rho_{min}(A_i) = \min\{\rho(s), s \in A_i\}$.

Since $\leq_{st}$ stochastic ordering is associated to increasing reward functions (see definition 1), macro-states are ordered according to the increasing rewards. Let us remark that the macro-state ordering may be different for the upper and the lower bounding computations. For the sake of simplicity, we suppose in the sequel that macro-states are ordered as follows: $\rho(A_1) \leq \rho(A_2) \leq \cdots \leq \rho(A_k)$ $\rho \in \{\rho_{sup}, \rho_{inf}\}$.

The atomic propositions of macro-states must be also updated: for each macro-state A_i, $L(A_i) = \cap_{s \in A_i} L(s)$. Let us emphasise that the accuracy of the bounds depends on the aggregation procedure: if the number of macro-states is small, bounds will be less accurate. By increasing the number of macro-states the accuracy can be improved with detriment of the numerical complexity. Thus a trade-off between the accuracy of results and the computation efficiency must be found.

4.2 Construction and Computing of Bounding Chains

Once the state space is partitioned, the bounding chains are constructed through algorithm LIMSUB given in section 2. Recall that the input parameters are the stochastic matrix of the underlying model, P and the partition $\mathcal{A}$=$\{A_1, A_2 \cdots A_m\}$. The upper bounding matrix Q_{sup} is returned as the output of algorithm LIMSUB. The lower bounding matrix Q_{inf} can be constructed by reversing the

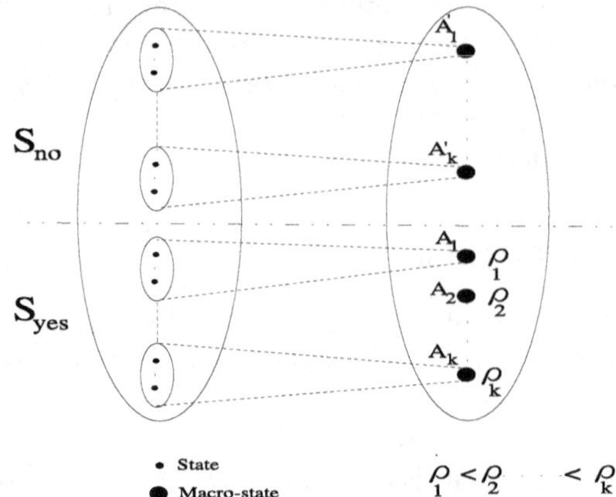

Fig. 1. Partition and ordering of state space

order of macro-states. In this case the inputs of algorithm LIMSUB are P, and the partition $\mathcal{A} = \{A_m, A_{m-1} \cdots A_1\}$. By permutating the output matrix, we obtain the lower bounding matrix, Q_{inf}.

Transient and steady-state distributions of the bounding chains Q_{inf} and Q_{sup} can be efficiently computed by applying conventional numerical methods. We refer to Stewart's book [19] for numerical methods to compute distributions of Markov chains.

We can derive the inequalities on state probabilities. By construction, Q_{sup} and Q_{inf} are st-monotone and $Q_{inf} \leq_{st} P \leq_{st} Q_{sup}$. Thus it follows from theorem 1 that transient distributions (and the steady-state distribution if it exists) of the underlying Markov chains are $\leq_{st}$ comparable. Let $\pi_{bound}(s, A_j, n)$ be the probability that the bounding Markov chain is in macro-state A_j at step n beginning in state s at time 0 and $\pi_{bound}(A_j)$ be the probability that the bounding Markov chain is in macro-state A_j at the steady-state. The following inequalities follow from property 1 of the $\leq_{st}$ ordering.

Property 3. – *Transient state probability bounds:*

$$\sum_{j=i}^{m} \pi_{inf}(s, A_j, n) \leq \sum_{j=i}^{m} \sum_{s' \in A_j} \pi(s, s', n) \leq \sum_{j=i}^{m} \pi_{sup}(s, A_j, n) \quad \forall i \in \{m, m-1, \cdots 1\} \tag{7}$$

– *Steady-state state probability bounds:*

$$\sum_{j=i}^{m} \pi_{inf}(A_j) \leq \sum_{j=i}^{m} \sum_{s' \in A_j} \pi(s') \leq \sum_{j=i}^{m} \pi_{sup}(A_j) \quad \forall i \in \{m, m-1, \cdots 1\} \tag{8}$$

4.3 Checking of State Formulas

In this section, we show how state formulas of the PRCTL logic can be checked through the bounding distributions. Remember that for a given state formula ϕ, the state space is partitioned and ordered such that the states satisfying ϕ, S_{yes} are greater (after) than that of S_{no}. Let suppose that $\mathcal{A} = \{A_1, \cdots, A_{k-1}, A_k, A_{k+1} \cdots A_m\}$ and $S_{yes} = \{A_k, A_{k+1}, \cdots A_m\}$. Thus by taking $i = k$ in equations 7 and 8, we have the following probability bounds for ϕ states:

$$\sum_{A_i \in S_{yes}} \pi_{inf}(s, A_i, n) \leq \sum_{s' \models \phi} \pi(s, s', n) \leq \sum_{A_i \in S_{yes}} \pi_{sup}(s, A_i, n) \tag{9}$$

$$\sum_{A_i \in S_{yes}} \pi_{inf}(A_i) \leq \sum_{s' \models \phi} \pi(s') \leq \sum_{A_i \in S_{yes}} \pi_{sup}(A_i) \tag{10}$$

In the following proposition, we provide transient and steady-state reward bounds. Recall that rewards of macro-states are defined as follows: $\rho_{sup}(A_i) = max\{\rho(s), s \in A_i\}$ and $\rho_{inf}(A_i) = min\{\rho(s), s \in A_i\}$. And macro-states of S_{yes} are ordered according to increasing rewards: $\rho(A_k) \leq \rho(A_{k+1}) \cdots \leq \rho(A_m)$, $\rho \in \{\rho_{inf}, \rho_{sup}\}$. As it has been stated before, the macro-state ordering may be different for the upper and the lower bounding computations. Without loss of generality we take the same ordering in both cases. In fact ϕ is satisfied in all macro-states of S_{yes}, so rewards are computed for all macro-states of S_{yes}.

Proposition 1. *We have the following inequalities on rewards:*

– Transient reward bounds:

$$\sum_{A_i \in S_{yes}} \pi_{inf}(s, A_i, n)\rho_{inf}(A_i) \leq \sum_{s' \models \phi} \pi(s, s', n)\rho(s') \leq \sum_{A_i \in S_{yes}} \pi_{sup}(s, A_i, n)\rho_{sup}(A_i) \tag{11}$$

– Steady-state reward bounds:

$$\sum_{A_i \in S_{yes}} \pi_{inf}(A_i)\rho_{inf}(A_i) \leq \sum_{s' \models \phi} \pi(s')\rho(s') \leq \sum_{A_i \in S_{yes}} \pi_{sup}(A_i)\rho_{sup}(A_i) \tag{12}$$

Proof. By construction, the distributions are $\leq_{st}$ comparable (equations 7, 8). Therefore we have the inequalities between the increasing functionals of these distributions (see definition 1). In fact inequalities 11, 12 are the increasing functionals on these distributions. Reward function of S_{no} states is zero and in the upper bound some rewards are replaced by greater values while they are replaced by smaller values in the lower bound. □

For a given reward formula $R(\phi)$, let $R_{sup}(\phi)$ (resp. $R_{inf}(\phi)$) be the reward on the macro-states of S_{yes} computed through the upper (resp. lower) bounding distribution. The following proposition gives how we can check formula $R(\phi)$ to see if it meets the bound of $I \in [r_{min}, r_{max}]$.

Proposition 2. *1. if $R_{inf}(\phi) \geq r_{min}$ and $R_{sup}(\phi) \leq r_{max}$ then we can conclude that $R(\phi)$ is true*

2. if $R_{inf}(\phi) \geq r_{max}$ or $R_{sup}(\phi) \leq r_{min}$ then we can conclude that $R(\phi)$ is false

3. *otherwise, we cannot conclude if $R(\phi)$ is true or not, through these bounding distributions. We can either modify the aggregation scheme (partition of states) or try to compute exact rewards.*

Proof. We give here the proof by specifying $R(\phi)$ for the sake of simplicity. Let us consider $\mathcal{E}_I(\phi)$ which is satisfied, if $\sum_{s' \models \phi} \pi(s')\rho(s') \in I$. It follows from equation 12 that

$$R_{inf}(\phi) \leq \mathcal{E}_I(\phi) \leq R_{sup}(\phi)$$

Thus, case 1 allows us to conclude that $\mathcal{E}_I(\phi)$ is satisfied:

$$r_{min} \leq R_{inf}(\phi) \leq \mathcal{E}_I(\phi) \leq R_{sup}(\phi) \leq r_{max}$$

Similarly, case 2 lets us to conclude that $\mathcal{E}_I(\phi)$ is not satisfied. Otherwise the rewards computed on bounding distributions do not let us to check $\mathcal{E}_I(\phi)$.

Let us remark that the case of transient reward formulas follows from equation 11. In the same manner formula $\mathcal{L}_{\lhd p}(\phi)$ can be checked by means of equation 10. □

5 Numerical Examples

In this section, we present numerical results computed from the proposed methodology. We consider four finite buffers in tandem where each buffer is a D/D/1/B queue (figure 2). The external arrivals and the services in all stages are independently, identically distributed batch processes with maximum size G. Let p_{ik} be the probability that k packets are served during a slot in stage $i, 1 \leq i \leq 4$ and $0 \leq k \leq G$. Indeed the service in stage i constitutes the arrivals to stage $i+1$. External arrivals are denoted by p_{0k}. At the end of a slot, it is assumed that first the end of services takes place and then the arrived packets are accepted. The packet acceptance mechanism is the rejection: a packet which arrives to a full buffer is lost.

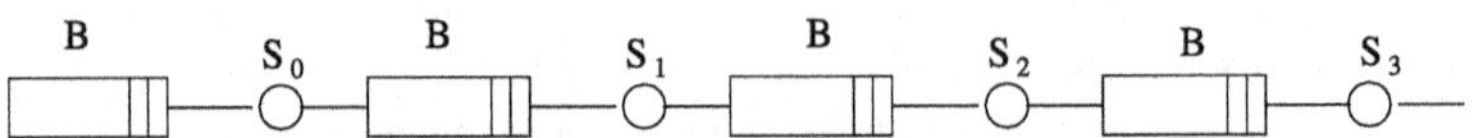

Fig. 2. A tandem queue with four buffers

Let $N_i(t), \quad 1 \leq i \leq 4$ be the number of packets at time t in buffer i. Thus $\{(N_4(t), N_3(t), N_2(t), N_1(t)),\ t \geq 0\}$ is a Discrete Time Markov chain of size $(B+1)^4$. In the sequel, we denote by $s = (n_4, n_3, n_2, n_1)$ a state of this Markov chain. We are interested in packet loss characteristics in buffer 4. Since all earlier stages must be taken into account to compute packet losses in this buffer, we must consider whole Markov chain of $(B+1)^4$ size. Thus the numerical complexity to solve the underlying model increases rapidly with B.

We define the following atomic propositions related to buffer 4:

- *frth-full* is valid if the fourth buffer is full. $S_{yes} = \{s \mid n_4 = B\}$
- *frth-loss* is valid if a packet loss may occur. $S_{yes} = \{s \mid n_4 > B - G\}$

Based on these atomic propositions, we check the following state formulas:

Steady-state formulas:

- $\mathcal{E}_{[0,10^{-7}]}(frth\text{-}loss)$ to check whether the long-run loss rate in buffer 4 is lower than 10^{-7} or not.
- $\mathcal{L}_{\leq 10^{-9}}(frth\text{-}full)$ to check whether the probability that buffer 4 is full in steady-state is less than 10^{-9} or not.

Transient formulas: For all these formulas we suppose that at the beginning all buffers are empty.

- $\mathcal{I}^{n}_{[0,10^{-9}]}(frth\text{-}loss)$ to check whether the expected packet loss at time n, $n \in \{40, 50\}$, meets the bound of I or not.
- $\mathcal{C}^{n}_{[0,10^{-9}]}(frth\text{-}loss)$ to check whether the expected cumulated packet loss up to time n, $n \in \{40, 50\}$, meets the bound or not.
- $\mathcal{E}^{n}_{[0,10^{-9}]}(frth\text{-}loss)$ to check whether the expected packet loss per unit time up to time n, $n \in \{40, 50\}$, meets the bound or not.

We now give the rewards assigned to states to compute these formulas related to packet losses in buffer 4. For a given state $s = (n_4, n_3, n_2, n_1)$,

$$\rho(s) = \sum_{j=0}^{G}\sum_{k=0}^{G} p_{3j} \cdot p_{4k} \cdot (\max(0, n_4 + \min(n_3, j) - k - B)) \tag{13}$$

To check these state formulas, we must compute transient or steady-state distribution of the underlying Markov chain. We check these formulas by solving upper bounding aggregated Markov chains to overcome state-space explosion. First we construct the exact Markov chain by means of evolution equations of the system [9]. In fact we begin by a state and generate all transitions (states) by taking into account the events which can occur in the system and their probabilities.

The second step is to aggregate states to define macro-states. We define macro states regarding to the number of customers in buffer 3 and 4 without considering the number of packets in the first two stages. Thus a macro-state (n_4, n_3) contains all states (n_4, n_3, i, j) $\forall i, j \in [0, B]$. Due to this aggregation procedure, the state space size will be reduced to $(B + 1)^2$. We reorder states using the lexicographic ordering to put together states of macro-states before running LIMSUB algorithm. Moreover states of S_{yes} must be after states of S_{no} and they must be ordered according to increasing rewards because of the $\leq_{st}$ ordering. In the considered example the reward function is largely compatible with the lexicographic ordering, we must reorder only a little number of states (equation 13).

The last step is to solve the upper bounding aggregated Markov chain (Q_{sup}) to compute the bounding distributions. Since it is defined on a reduced state

Table 1. Arrival process

Probabilities		External arrivals	First stage service	Second stage service	Third stage service	Fourth stage service
$\mathcal{PROC}_1$	p_0	0.7	0.3	0.4	0.6	0.2
	p_1	0.2	0.5	0.3	0.2	0.4
	p_2	0.1	0.2	0.3	0.2	0.4
$\mathcal{PROC}_2$	p_0	0.7	0.3	0.4	0.5	0.3
	p_1	0.2	0.5	0.3	0.3	0.3
	p_2	0.1	0.2	0.3	0.4	0.4

Table 2. Results obtained with the arrival process $\mathcal{PROC}_1$

Formulas	B	Exact	Bound	Valid?
$\mathcal{E}_{[0,10^{-9}]}(frth\text{-}loss)$	25	5.9610^{-16}	3.4910^{-11}	yes
	30	-	1.1310^{-10}	yes
$\mathcal{I}^{40}_{[0,10^{-9}]}(frth\text{-}loss)$	25	2.910^{-20}	1.7610^{-11}	yes
	30	-	$5.68\ 10^{-11}$	yes
$\mathcal{I}^{50}_{[0,10^{-9}]}(frth\text{-}loss)$	25	10^{-18}	$2.81\ 10^{-11}$	yes
	30	-	$1.09\ 10^{-10}$	yes
$\mathcal{C}^{40}_{[0,10^{-9}]}(frth\text{-}loss)$	25	6.8910^{-20}	1.310^{-10}	yes
	30	-	$3.67\ 10^{-10}$	yes
$\mathcal{C}^{50}_{[0,10^{-9}]}(frth\text{-}loss)$	25	3.7710^{-18}	3.710^{-10}	yes
	30	-	$1.26\ 10^{-9}$	unknown
$\mathcal{E}^{40}_{[0,10^{-9}]}(frth\text{-}loss)$	25	1.7210^{-21}	3.2710^{-12}	yes
	30	-	$9.17\ 10^{-12}$	yes
$\mathcal{E}^{50}_{[0,10^{-9}]}(frth\text{-}loss)$	25	$7.55\ 10^{-18}$	7.4110^{-12}	yes
	30	-	$2.52\ 10^{-11}$	yes
$\mathcal{L}_{\leq 10^{-9}}(frth\text{-}full)$	25	2.3510^{-15}	1.2310^{-10}	yes
	30	-	1.2110^{-12}	yes

space, this can be done efficiently. We have applied an indirect method (Gauss-Seidel) [19] to compute bounding distributions.

We fix the maximum size of batches, $G = 2$ and consider two different arrival processes, $\mathcal{PROC}_1$ and $\mathcal{PROC}_2$. The probabilities of having i batches, p_i $0 \leq i \leq 2$ for external arrivals and for services in each stage are given in the following table.

In table 2, we give the results computed for arrival process $\mathcal{PROC}_1$. For each formula we give results for $B = 25$ and $B = 30$. However, we could not solve the

Table 3. Results obtained with the arrival process $\mathcal{PROC}_2$

Formulas	B	Exact	Bound	Valid?
$\mathcal{E}_{[0,10^{-7}]}(frth\text{-}loss)$	25	7.09 10^{-14}	1.04 10^{-7}	unknown
	30	-	1.79 10^{-8}	yes
$\mathcal{I}^{40}_{[0,10^{-7}]}(frth\text{-}loss)$	25	3.4 10^{-17}	1.8 10^{-8}	yes
	30	-	3.37 10^{-11}	yes
$\mathcal{I}^{50}_{[0,10^{-7}]}(frth\text{-}loss)$	25	7.910^{-16}	4.410^{-8}	yes
	30	-	1.5510^{-10}	yes
$\mathcal{C}^{40}_{[0,10^{-7}]}(frth\text{-}loss)$	25	8.54 10^{-17}	1.08 10^{-7}	unknown
	30	-	1.4210^{-10}	yes
$\mathcal{C}^{50}_{[0,10^{-7}]}(frth\text{-}loss)$	25	3.3 10^{-15}	4.31 10^{-7}	unknown
	30	-	1.0610^{-9}	yes
$\mathcal{E}^{40}_{[0,10^{-7}]}(frth\text{-}loss)$	25	2.1310^{-18}	2.710^{-9}	yes
	30	-	3.56 10^{-12}	yes
$\mathcal{E}^{50}_{[0,10^{-7}]}(frth\text{-}loss)$	25	6.610^{-17}	8.6 10^{-9}	yes
	30	-	2.13 10^{-11}	yes
$\mathcal{L}_{\leq 10^{-7}}(frth\text{-}full)$	25	2.22 10^{-13}	2.95 10^{-7}	unknown
	30	-	5.0410^{-8}	yes

chain with $B = 30$ because of its size (see table 4). In the last column we give if the formula can be checked through these bounding distributions or not. For this arrival process, most of the formulas can be checked through these bounding distributions. In the last column, *unknown* indicates that we cannot conclude whether the formula is satisfied or not through these bounding distributions.

In table 3, we give the results under arrival process $\mathcal{PROC}_2$. For this arrival process, some formulas cannot be checked through these bounding distributions. We can change the aggregation procedure to have more detailed representation of the underlying system.

The numerical results are computed in an Intel Pentium 4 with CPU 2.8 GHz and 1.5GBytes memory. Let us give computation times for different steps for exact and bounding Markov chains (see table 4). We give in columns *Size*

Table 4. Comparison of original and bounding model sizes

	Exact Markov chain				Bounding Markov chain			
B	Size	Entries	Generation	Resolution	Size	Entries	Generation	Resolution
25	456 976	77 970 677	9 min	16 min	676	13 397	6 min	0.001s
30	923 521	163 169 007	10 min	-	961	19 242	12 min	0.13 s

the state space size, and in columns *Entries* the number of non null entries of the chain. For the exact chain, *Generation* time corresponds to the time for generating the underlying Markov chain, while it corresponds to the reordering of states and the execution of LIMSUB algorithm for the bounding chain.

We can see that the resolution times are drastically reduced for bounding chains due to the state space size reduction. Therefore it will be possible to check large models through bounding distributions. Actually, the underlying matrix is stored in the memory during the computation of the bounding model. However the bounding chain is constructed column by column so it is possible to avoid the storage of whole matrix using Kronecker or MTBDD structures. These issues are under work to be able to check very large models.

6 Conclusions

In this paper we show how algorithmic stochastic bounding techniques can be applied to check state formulas in the PRCTL logic. Indeed we must compute a transient or the steady-state distribution of the underlying DTMC to check state formulas. However the computation of these distributions has high numerical complexity or is intractable because of the well-known state space explosion problem. On the other hand we do not need in general exact values to check these formulas. Therefore bounding techniques are useful in stochastic model checking. We proposed to apply stochastic bounding algorithms to overcome the state space explosion problem. Since bounding models can be constructed in a fully automated manner by means of the bounding algorithms, the proposed methodology can be easily integrated to model checkers.

In this work we are interested only on state formulas, but this approach can be also extended to path formulas. In fact we apply the $\leq_{st}$ stochastic ordering, which is also called as sample-path ordering. Intuitively this means that if two chains are comparable in this stochastic ordering sense, their sample-paths are comparable. We are working on the application of $\leq_{st}$ stochastic ordering to check path formulas.

Acknowledgements. The authors thank Jean-Michel Fourneau for fruitful discussions.

References

1. Abu-Amsha, O., Vincent, J.M.: An algorithm to bound functionals of Markov chains with large state space. In: *4th INFORMS Conference on Telecommunications*, Boca Raton, Florida, (1998)
2. Andova, S., Hermanns, H., Katoen, J.P.: Disrete-time rewards model-checked. In Formal Modelling and Analysis of Timed Systems (FORMATS 2003), Marseille France.
3. Aziz, A., Sanwal, K., Singhal,V. and Brayton R.: Model checking continuous time Markov chains. *ACM Trans. on Comp. Logic*, 1(1), p. 162-170, 2000.

4. Baier, C., Haverkort, B., Hermanns, H., Katoen, J.P.: Automated performance and dependability evaluation using Model Checking. *LNCS 2459, Performance evaluation of complex systems: Techniques and Tools*, pp 64-88, 2002.
5. Benmammoun, M., Fourneau, J.M., Pekergin, N., Troubnikoff, A.: An algorithmic and numerical approach to bound the performance of high speed networks. In IEEE MASCOTS 2002, Fort Worth, USA, pp. 375-382.
6. Clarke, E.M., Emerson,A., Sistla, A. P.: Automatic verification of finite-state concurrent systems using temporal logic specifications. *ACM Trans. on Programming Languages and Systems* 8(2):244–263, 1986.
7. D'Argenio, P.R. Jeannet, B., Jensen, H.E. and Larsen, K.G. Reduction and Refinement Strategies for Probabilistic Analysis. In Proc *Process Algebra and Probabilistic Methods Performance Modeling and Verification*, Springer-Verlag, 2001.
8. Fourneau, J.M., Pekergin, N., Younès, S.:Improving Stochastic Model Checking with Stochastic Bounds. In SAINT Modelling and Performance Evaluation in Next Generation Internet Workshop, 2005.
9. Fourneau, J.M., Lecoz, M., Pekergin, N., Quessette, F.: An open tool to compute stochastic bounds on steady-state distributions and rewards. In IEEE MASCOTS 2003, pp. 219-225.
10. Fourneau,J.M., Pekergin, N.: An algorithmic approach to stochastic bounds. *LNCS 2459, Performance evaluation of complex systems: Techniques and Tools*, pp 64-88, 2002.
11. Fourneau, J.M., Lecoz, M. and Quessette, F.: Algorithms for irreducible and lumpable strong stochastic bound. *Linear Algebra and its Applications* 386(2004) 167-185, 2004.
12. Hansson,H. and Jonsson B.: A logic for reasoning about time and reliability. In *Form. Asp. of Comp.* **6**: 512-535, 1994.
13. Haverkort, B., Cloth, L., Hermanns, H., Katoen, J.P. and E C. Baier: Model Checking Performability Properties In Proc. *Dependability Systems and NETWORKS (DSN) 2002, IEEE CS Press*, 2002.
14. Kulkarni, V.G.: *M*odeling and Analysis of Stochastic Systems.Chapman& Hall, 1995.
15. Kwiatkowska, M., Norman, G., Parker D.: PRISM: Probabilistic Symbolic Model Checker. In Proc.*TOOLS 2002, volume 2324 of LNCS*, p. 200-204, Springer-Verlag April 2002.
16. Muller, A. and Stoyan, D.: *Comparison Methods for Stochastic Models and Risks*, Wiley , New York,2002.
17. Pekergin N.:Stochastic performance bounds by state space reduction. *Performance Evaluation*, 36-37, pages 1-17, 1999.
18. Shaked, M. and Shantikumar, J.G.: *Stochastic Orders and Their Applications*, Academic Press, San Diago, 1994.
19. Stewart W. J: *Introduction to the Numerical Solution of Markov Chains.* Princeton University Press, (1994)

Delay Analysis of the Go-Back-N ARQ Protocol over a Time-Varying Channel

Koen De Turck and Sabine Wittevrongel

SMACS*Research Group,
Department of Telecommunications and Information Processing,
Ghent University, Sint-Pietersnieuwstraat 41, B-9000 Gent, Belgium
{kdeturck, sw}@telin.UGent.be

Abstract. In this paper we present an analytical technique, based on the use of probability generating functions, to analyze the throughput performance and the transmitter buffer behavior of a Go-Back-N ARQ system, with the notable complication that the errors in the channel are correlated in time. We model the transmitter buffer as a discrete-time queue with infinite storage capacity and independent and identically distributed packet arrivals. Arriving packets are stored in the queue until they are successfully transmitted over the channel. The probability of an erroneous transmission is modulated by a general Markov chain with M states, rather than assuming stationary channel errors.

We find explicit expressions for the probability generating functions of the buffer content and packet delay. From these functions moments and tail probabilities can be derived. Numerical results illustrate the impact of the error process on the system performance.

1 Introduction

When packets need to be transmitted from point A (the *transmitter*) to point B (the *receiver*) over an error-prone channel, such as contemporary wireless channels, special measures have to be taken to provide a more reliable transmission. A popular method to ensure this is to use an Automatic Repeat reQuest (ARQ) protocol ([1]).

There are many different types of ARQ protocols, but they have all two things in common. First, there must be some way for the receiver to check whether a packet has been received correctly or not. So usually, the transmitter adds an *error checking code* to each packet so the receiver can detect the most commonly occurring errors. Secondly, the channel must be *bi-directional.* When a packet is received, the receiver must send a message to the transmitter to notify the transmitter of the condition of that packet, i.e., an acknowledgement (ACK) if it is intact or a negative acknowledgement (NAK) if an error occurred. Since not all arriving packets can be sent immediately, one needs to implement a queue at the transmitter side.

* SMACS: Stochastic Modeling and Analysis of Communication Systems

M. Bravetti et al. (Eds.): EPEW 2005 and WS-FM 2005, LNCS 3670, pp. 124–138, 2005.

In the present paper, we study the Go-Back-N ARQ (GBN-ARQ) protocol. In GBN-ARQ, the transmitter keeps sending packets available in its queue, until a NAK is received. In that case, the incorrectly received packet is sent again, as well as every following packet (for which no feedback message has been received yet). This is illustrated in Fig. 1 for a feedback delay $s = 2$.

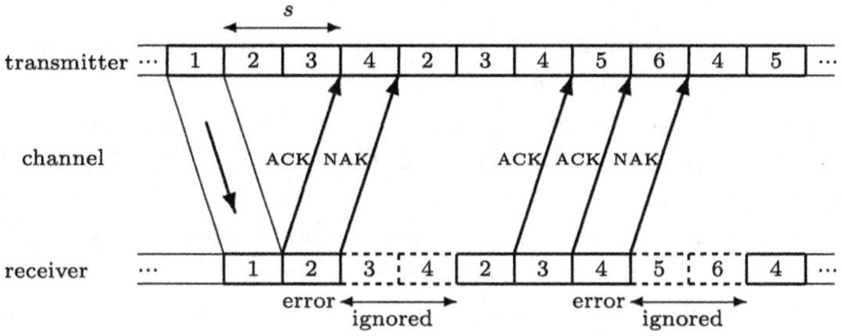

Fig. 1. Go-Back-N protocol ($s = 2$)

There has been research on the queueing analysis of the GBN-ARQ protocol. However, the majority of research has been under the assumption of random independent transmission errors, see e.g. [2]-[4]. The model we propose in this paper is different from previous studies in that we allow the errors occurring in the channel to be *correlated in time.* This assumption is necessary when dynamical, time-varying channels are studied. Specifically, the channel state process is modeled by means of a Markov chain with M states and with a fixed error probability in every state.

Some previous work on the buffer analysis of ARQ protocols over a time-varying channel exists. For example, in [5] the GBN-ARQ protocol has been considered, but only the throughput and the buffer content have been analyzed, whereas in this paper, we also provide a full analysis of the packet delay. In [6], the queueing performance of stop-and-wait ARQ over a dynamic channel has been studied in case the number of states $M = 2$. The selective-repeat protocol with correlated errors has been investigated in [7], but the model is basically a so-called *ideal* ARQ system. This means that there is no feedback delay: acknowledgements are received instantly, which simplifies the analysis. In this paper we present a full queueing analysis in terms of both buffer content and delay of the GBN-ARQ protocol for nonindependent channel errors.

The outline of the paper is as follows. The mathematical model of the GBN-ARQ transmitter queue is introduced in Sect. 2, along with some specific assumptions. In Sect. 3, we identify a sufficient description of the state of the system at an arbitrary slot and provide the main equations that govern its behavior. We obtain a closed-form expression for the probability generating function (pgf) of the buffer content. Section 4 provides a simple derivation of the throughput efficiency. In Sect. 5 we provide a full analysis of the packet delay. We calculate the pgf of the packet delay and also derive moments and the tail distribution. Then, in Sect. 6 we consider the special case of a two-state Markov model, also known as a Gilbert-Elliott model ([8]). Section 7 provides some illustrative numerical examples. Finally, conclusions are drawn in Sect. 8.

2 Model Description

In this paper we investigate the throughput efficiency and the transmitter buffer behavior of a system working under a GBN-ARQ protocol.

The general modeling assumptions are as follows. The data to be transmitted are divided into blocks of fixed length. The time needed to transmit one block is called a slot. Synchronous transmission is used, i.e., the time axis is divided into slots and transmission always starts at the beginning of a slot. After a constant period of s slots, an acknowledgement signal from the receiver containing information on whether the block was correctly received or not arrives at the transmitter. This interval of s slots is called the feedback delay of the channel. It is assumed that no errors occur in the acknowledgement messages.

During each slot j, a random number of packets a_j arrive at the transmitter. The a_js are assumed to be independent and identically distributed (iid) random variables with mean α and pgf $A(z)$. The packets are stored in an infinite discrete-time queue until they are successfully transmitted over the channel. Note that due to the synchronous transmission mode, a packet arriving in an empty queue is not transmitted until the next slot.

We model the error process in the channel by a general Markov chain with M states. The transition probabilities are given by

$$q_{ij} = \text{Prob[state in next slot is } j| \text{ state in current slot is } i],$$

which can also be written as a transition probability matrix $\mathbf{q}$. State i has an error probability of e_i. When there is an error, the packet sent during that slot will be incorrectly received, and the sender will receive a NAK message s slots later. We define the matrix $\mathbf{e}$ as the diagonal matrix with elements $e_1, \ldots, e_M$. We also introduce the notation $\bar{x} \triangleq 1 - x$. Likewise, $\bar{\mathbf{e}}$ is a diagonal matrix with elements $\bar{e}_1, \ldots, \bar{e}_M$.

3 Analysis of the Buffer Content

We simplify the analysis by considering a modified system (first introduced in [2]) in which the sender can 'look into the future'. This means that directly after a packet is sent, the sender knows if, s slots later, it will receive an ACK or a NAK message. On a future ACK, the packet can leave the buffer immediately, since the sender knows it will not be needed again. On the other hand, when a NAK is expected, the sender halts for s slots, for the receiver would discard any newly transmitted packet anyway. We say that the system during these s slots is in 'recovery mode', which can be divided into s stages, numbered $1, \ldots, s$. In every other slot the system is in 'send mode'.

This modified system is closely related to the real system. In fact, from a performance point of view, the only difference is that every packet stays exactly s slots longer in the real system than it would in the modified system. For an iid arrival process we can derive the following relation between the pgf $U_{\text{real}}(z)$ of the buffer occupancy in the real system and the corresponding pgf $U_{\text{modified}}(z)$ in the modified system:

$$U_{\text{real}}(z) = A(z)^s U_{\text{modified}}(z). \tag{1}$$

Indeed, since every packet stays s slots longer in the system, we must add the arrivals during s slots to get the real system content.

In what follows, we will first derive an expression for the partial pgf of the buffer occupancy when the system is in send mode. Next, the partial pgf of the buffer occupancy in recovery mode is calculated. The pgf of the buffer occupancy is then found by adding the partial pgfs for each mode.

Let slot k be the ith slot the system is in send mode. Let σ be a mapping function such that $\sigma(i) = k$. Let us define v_k be the buffer content at the beginning of this slot in send mode and let s_k be the channel state during slot k; the random variable a_k denotes the number of packets arriving during slot k. Then we can write the following system equations:

(a) when $v_k = 0$:

$$(v_{\sigma(i+1)}, s_{\sigma(i+1)}) = (a_k, \tilde{s}_k);$$

(b) when $v_k > 0$:

$$(v_{\sigma(i+1)}, s_{\sigma(i+1)}) = \begin{cases} (v_k - 1 + a_k, \tilde{s}_k), & \text{with probability } \bar{e}_{s_k}, \\ (v_k + \sum_{i=0}^{s} a_{k+i}, \hat{s}_k), & \text{with probability } e_{s_k}, \end{cases}$$

where $\tilde{s}_k$ is the state of the Markov chain during slot $k+1$, and $\hat{s}_k$ is the state during slot $k+s+1$. Let us define $V_{j,k}(z)$ as the partial pgf of the buffer content at the beginning of slot k when the channel is in state j, i.e.,

$$\begin{aligned} V_{j,k}(z) &= \sum_{n=0}^{\infty} \text{Prob}[v_k = n, s_k = j] z^n \\ &= \text{Prob}[s_k = j] \text{E}[z^{v_k} | s_k = j]. \end{aligned} \tag{2}$$

In equilibrium (for $k \to \infty$) $V_{j,k}(z)$ will become independent of k and converge to a limiting partial pgf $V_j(z)$. By means of the above system equations, we can establish a relation between the partial pgfs $V_j(z), 1 \leq j \leq m$, as follows:

$$
\begin{aligned}
V_j(z) = \lim_{k\to\infty} \Bigg\{ & \sum_{l=1}^{M} \text{Prob}[v_k = 0, s_k = l] \\
& \times \sum_{n=0}^{\infty} \text{Prob}[a_k = n, \tilde{s}_k = j | v_k = 0, s_k = l] z^n \\
& + \sum_{m=1}^{\infty} \sum_{l=1}^{M} \text{Prob}[v_k = m, s_k = l] \\
& \times \sum_{n=0}^{\infty} \Big(\bar{e}_l \text{Prob}[v_k - 1 + a_k = n, \tilde{s}_k = j | v_k = m, s_k = l] z^n \\
& \qquad + e_l \text{Prob}[v_k + \sum_{i=0}^{s} a_{k+i} = n, \hat{s}_k = j | v_k = m, s_k = l] z^n \Big) \Bigg\} \\
= & \sum_{l=1}^{M} V_l(0) A(z) q_{lj} \\
& + \sum_{l=1}^{M} [V_l(z) - V_l(0)] \left(\frac{A(z)}{z} \bar{e}_l q_{lj} + A(z)^{s+1} e_l (\mathbf{q}^{s+1})_{lj} \right). \qquad (3)
\end{aligned}
$$

In this equation, the matrix $\mathbf{q}^{s+1}$ denotes the $(s+1)$-step transition probability matrix of the channel process. Let us introduce the following vector notation: $\mathbf{V}(z) = (V_1(z), \ldots, V_M(z))$. Then the above relation can be rewritten as

$$
\mathbf{V}(z) = A(z)\mathbf{V}(0)\mathbf{q} + (\mathbf{V}(z) - \mathbf{V}(0))[\frac{A(z)}{z}\bar{\mathbf{e}}\mathbf{q} + A(z)^{s+1}\mathbf{e}\mathbf{q}^{s+1}].
$$

Solving this equation for $\mathbf{V}(z)$, we get

$$
\mathbf{V}(z) = \mathbf{V}(0)\,[zA(z)\mathbf{q} - \mathbf{d}(z)]\,[z\mathbf{I} - \mathbf{d}(z)]^{-1}, \qquad (4)
$$

where

$$
\mathbf{d}(z) = A(z)\,\bar{\mathbf{e}}\mathbf{q} + zA(z)^{s+1}\,\mathbf{e}\mathbf{q}^{s+1} \qquad (5)
$$

and $\mathbf{I}$ denotes the $M \times M$ identity matrix.

In a similar way, we now derive an expression for the partial pgf of the buffer content during recovery mode. It follows that the vector of partial pgfs of the buffer length in stage 1 of the recovery mode $\mathbf{W}_1(z)$ is related to $\mathbf{V}(z)$ by the following equation:

$$
\mathbf{W}_1(z) = (\mathbf{V}(z) - \mathbf{V}(0))\mathbf{e}\mathbf{q}\,A(z). \qquad (6)
$$

This equation expresses that to get into recovery mode, the buffer must be non-empty and there must be an error during this slot.

The vector of partial pgfs of the buffer content in other states of the recovery mode can be found using the following recursive relation:

$$
\mathbf{W}_i(z) = A(z)\mathbf{W}_{i-1}(z)\mathbf{q}.
$$

Successive application of this relation leads to

$$\mathbf{W}_i(z) = \mathbf{W}_1(z)\mathbf{q}^{i-1}A(z)^{i-1}. \tag{7}$$

Combination of (6) and (7) finally allows us to write every $\mathbf{W}_i(z)$ in terms of $\mathbf{V}(z)$ as

$$\mathbf{W}_i(z) = (\mathbf{V}(z) - \mathbf{V}(0))\mathbf{e}\mathbf{q}^i A(z)^i, \quad 1 \leq i \leq s.$$

The distribution of the buffer content with the system being in any recovery stage is given by $\mathbf{W}_{\text{tot}}(z)$:

$$\begin{aligned}\mathbf{W}_{\text{tot}}(z) &= \sum_{i=1}^{s} \mathbf{W}_i(z) \\ &= (\mathbf{V}(z) - \mathbf{V}(0))\mathbf{e}\mathbf{q}A(z)(\mathbf{I} - \mathbf{q}^s A(z)^s)(\mathbf{I} - \mathbf{q}A(z))^{-1}. \end{aligned} \tag{8}$$

So we have found formulas for the buffer content in every mode of the system. We can also obtain the pgf of the buffer content in equilibrium. In particular, we have (with $\mathbf{1}$ an $M \times 1$ vector with all elements 1)

$$U_{\text{modified}}(z) = (\mathbf{V}(z) + \mathbf{W}_{\text{tot}}(z))\mathbf{1}. \tag{9}$$

The only remaining unknown in all these formulas is the vector $\mathbf{V}(0)$. This vector can be found by expressing that $\mathbf{V}(z)$ cannot have any singularities inside the unit circle. The factor $(z\mathbf{I} - \mathbf{d}(z))^{-1}$ can be written as

$$(z\mathbf{I} - \mathbf{d}(z))^{-1} = \frac{1}{\det(z\mathbf{I} - \mathbf{d}(z))}\mathrm{Adj}(z\mathbf{I} - \mathbf{d}(z)).$$

Now it can be proven that only the determinant will introduce singularities inside the unit circle (and not the Adj(.) expression). Since $\mathbf{V}(z)$ is a pgf, the singularities must be removable. With techniques shown in [9], it can be proven that $\det(z\mathbf{I} - \mathbf{d}(z))$ has a zero in 1, and $M-1$ zeros inside the unit circle. Let $\zeta_i, i = 1, \ldots, M-1$ be these zeros inside the unit circle. Expressing that the ζ_is are removable singularities leads to the following set of equations:

$$0 = \mathbf{V}(0)[\zeta_i A(\zeta_i)\mathbf{q} - \mathbf{d}(\zeta_i)]\mathrm{Adj}[\zeta_i\mathbf{I} - \mathbf{d}(\zeta_i)]\mathbf{1}, \quad \text{for all } i.$$

By applying the normalization condition $U_{\text{modified}}(1) = 1$, a last equation is found. Thus the vector $\mathbf{V}(0)$ can be calculated.

4 Throughput Efficiency

The throughput η is defined as the expected number of packets that can be transmitted per slot when there are always packets available (heavy traffic assumption). Hence, η is a measure for the maximum output rate at which the system can transmit incoming packets.

To find an expression for the throughput, we observe the system at send instants. Or equivalently, to use the terminology of Sect. 3, we observe the system in send mode. As there are always packets available, the next send instant is either one slot away when the current packet is correctly transmitted or $s+1$ slots when it is not. So the channel state during send instants is modulated by the modified Markov chain $\mathbf{q}' \triangleq \bar{\mathbf{e}}\mathbf{q} + \mathbf{e}\mathbf{q}^{s+1}$. Note that it follows from (5) that $\mathbf{q}' = \mathbf{d}(1)$. Moreover $\mathbf{q}'$ is a stochastic matrix. So according to the Perron-Frobenius Theorem ([10]), one of its eigenvalues is 1. The corresponding left eigenvector (let us call it $\boldsymbol{\pi}$) is the steady-state probability vector $\boldsymbol{\pi}$ of the modified Markov process. Using the steady-state probabilities π_i, the throughput η can be written as

$$\eta = \frac{\sum_{i=1}^{M} \pi_i \bar{e}_i}{\sum_{i=1}^{M} \pi_i (1 + e_i s)}. \tag{10}$$

5 Analysis of the Packet Delay

In this section we derive an expression for the pgf of the packet delay in the case that the error process is modulated by an M-state Markov chain. We first derive an expression for the probability generating matrix (pgm) of the service time $\mathbf{S}(z)$, and then we can find the pgf of the packet delay in terms of $\mathbf{S}(z)$. Finally, we point out how to find moments and the tail distribution of the delay.

5.1 Distribution of the Service Time

We define the service time of a packet as the time interval (expressed in slots) that starts with the slot (in send mode) where the packet is transmitted for the first time and ends with the slot where the packet leaves the system. We consider again the modified system, so packets leave the buffer at the end of the slot where they are correctly transmitted.

Service times in the studied model are not iid, unlike the situation with uncorrelated errors, because the exact distribution of the service time depends on the channel state in the slot during which the service of the packet starts.

Using a similar approach as in [6], we introduce a pgm $\mathbf{S}(z)$ (with dimension $M \times M$) of a service time. Specifically, the element $[\mathbf{S}(z)]_{ii'}$ is the (partial) pgf of the service time that starts in channel state i and is followed by a slot with channel state i'. This approach has the advantage that we can express the pgm of the length of n subsequent service times simply as $\mathbf{S}(z)^n$. We can derive the pgm $\mathbf{S}(z)$ rather elegantly by stating the following recursive relation:

$$\mathbf{S}(z) = \bar{\mathbf{e}}\mathbf{q}z + \mathbf{e}\mathbf{q}^{s+1}z^{s+1}\mathbf{S}(z).$$

Indeed, a service lasts exactly one slot when the packet is immediately correctly transmitted. When it is not, the service lasts $s+1$ slots *plus* a remaining service time, which also has pgm $\mathbf{S}(z)$. We must not forget to multiply by the right transition probabilities of the channel state ($\mathbf{q}$ and $\mathbf{q}^{s+1}$). From the above relation, we can derive $\mathbf{S}(z)$ as

$$\mathbf{S}(z) = (\mathbf{I} - \mathbf{e}\mathbf{q}^{s+1}z^{s+1})^{-1}\bar{\mathbf{e}}\mathbf{q}z. \tag{11}$$

Note that this distribution holds for the modified system, where service times do not overlap. Service times in the real system are s slots longer, but may overlap. Let us now denote by $\boldsymbol{\sigma}$ the steady-state probability vector of $\mathbf{S}(1)$. Stated otherwise, $\boldsymbol{\sigma}$ is the steady-state probability vector of the channel state in the first slot of a service time. Another expression for the throughput can then be found as

$$\eta^{-1} = \boldsymbol{\sigma}\mathbf{S}'(1)\mathbf{1}. \tag{12}$$

It has been shown that expressions (10) and (12) are the same.

5.2 Pgf of the Packet Delay for an M-State Channel Model

Now that we have obtained an expression for $\mathbf{S}(z)$, we can proceed with the calculation of the pgf of the packet delay. Again, we first consider the modified system, and then convert the thus found pgf to the real system, where packets have to stay in the buffer until an ACK has arrived at the transmitter.

We consider an arbitrary packet $\mathcal{P}$ that arrives during some slot $\mathcal{I}$. Let k be the channel state during slot $\mathcal{I}$, and u the buffer content at the beginning of slot $\mathcal{I}$ (also for the modified system of course). The delay of packet $\mathcal{P}$ starts at the beginning of slot $\mathcal{I}+1$ and stops at the end of the slot where packet $\mathcal{P}$ is correctly transmitted and leaves the buffer.

Let ℓ be the number of packets arriving in the buffer in slot $\mathcal{I}$ that will be served no later than (but including) $\mathcal{P}$. We also introduce the notation $\ell_k = \text{Prob}[\ell = k]$. In [11] it was proven that the pgf $L(z)$ of ℓ is given by

$$L(z) = \frac{z(1 - A(z))}{\alpha(1 - z)}, \tag{13}$$

with α the mean number of arrivals per slot; $\alpha = A'(1)$.

In order to derive the pgf $D_{\text{modified}}(z)$ of the delay of $\mathcal{P}$ in the modified system, we will first condition on the state of the system in slot $\mathcal{I}$. We first consider the case where the system is in send mode during slot $\mathcal{I}$ and the buffer is empty. In that case, exactly ℓ packets must be transmitted before packet $\mathcal{P}$ can leave the system and the transmission of the first can immediately start in the next slot. So the packet delay consists of ℓ subsequent service times. Let $D_{e,k}(z)$ be the partial pgf of the packet delay when the system is in send mode, the buffer is empty and the channel state is k. Then we can write

$$\begin{aligned} D_{e,k}(z) &= V_k(0) \sum_{j=1}^{\infty} \ell_j \boldsymbol{\epsilon}_k \mathbf{q} \mathbf{S}(z)^j \mathbf{1} \\ &\triangleq V_k(0) \boldsymbol{\epsilon}_k \mathbf{q} L(\mathbf{S}(z)) \mathbf{1}, \end{aligned} \tag{14}$$

where $\boldsymbol{\epsilon}_k$ is the kth unit vector, and $V_k(0)$ is, according to the notation introduced in Sect. 3, the probability of having an empty buffer in send mode when the channel state is k. In the above equation, we have introduced the convenient shorthand notation $L(\mathbf{S}(z))$ to denote a matrix that is a power series in the pgm $\mathbf{S}(z)$ with the same coefficients as the power series expansion in z of $L(z)$. Similar notations will be used frequently in the remainder of this Section.

Secondly, we will consider the case where the system is in send mode during slot $\mathcal{I}$ and the buffer is non-empty. In this case, the system is busy serving another packet when $\mathcal{P}$ arrives. The delay of packet $\mathcal{P}$ will end when $u + \ell$ packets have been served. However, we must be careful: the system is already serving one of these $u + \ell$ packets in slot $\mathcal{I}$, and we only begin to count the delay at the beginning of the next slot. The pgm of the remaining service time of the packet in service during slot $\mathcal{I}$ is therefore not $\mathbf{S}(z)$, but rather $\frac{\mathbf{S}(z)}{z}$. These observations lead to the following expression for the partial pgf $D_{s,k}(z)$ of the packet delay when the system is in send mode, the buffer is non-empty and the channel state is k:

$$D_{s,k}(z) = \frac{1}{z}\epsilon_k(V_k(\mathbf{S}(z)) - V_k(0))L(\mathbf{S}(z))\mathbf{1}. \tag{15}$$

The last case we must consider is when the packet $\mathcal{P}$ arrives during a slot where the system is in recovery mode, say for example in stage j. Again, we have to determine how long it takes to serve $u+\ell$ packets. Since the system is in recovery mode, the sender must wait $s - j$ slots before it can retransmit the packet that was already in service before the recovery period. Note that after the recovery period, the remaining service time of the packet the system was serving is given by $\mathbf{S}(z)$ and the pgf of u is in this case given by $W_{j,k}(z)$. Hence, the partial pgf $D_{r,j,k}(z)$ of the delay when the system is in stage j of recovery mode and the channel state is k, is obtained as

$$D_{r,j,k}(z) = \epsilon_k \mathbf{q}^{s-j+1} z^{s-j} W_{j,k}(\mathbf{S}(z))L(\mathbf{S}(z))\mathbf{1}. \tag{16}$$

The pgf $D_{\text{modified}}(z)$ of the packet delay in the modified system is the sum of all partial pgfs:

$$D_{\text{modified}}(z) = \sum_{k=1}^{M} D_{e,k}(z) + \sum_{k=1}^{M} D_{s,k}(z) + \sum_{k=1}^{M}\sum_{j=1}^{s} D_{r,j,k}(z). \tag{17}$$

Finally, since in reality a packet has to stay in the buffer until the transmitter knows it has been transmitted correctly through the arrival of an ACK s slots after the packet's transmission, packets stay exactly s slots longer in the real system than in the modified system and the pgf $D_{\text{real}}(z)$ of the packet delay in the real system is therefore given by

$$D_{\text{real}}(z) = z^s D_{\text{modified}}(z). \tag{18}$$

In order to write $D_{\text{modified}}(z)$ in an explicit form, a spectral decomposition of $\mathbf{S}(z)$ is needed. To derive the spectral decomposition of an $M \times M$ matrix parametrized in some variable z, the characteristic equation must be solved, which is a polynomial equation of the Mth order. As was proven by Abel, a general solution only exists for $M \leq 4$.

5.3 Moments of the Packet Delay

It is possible to extract the moments of the packet delay from $D_{\text{real}}(z)$ by using the moment-generating property of pgfs. In particular, the mean packet delay can be found by evaluation of the first-order derivative of $D_{\text{real}}(z)$ with respect to z at $z = 1$, i.e., $\mathrm{E}[d_{\text{real}}] = D_{\text{real}}'(1)$. The variance of the packet delay can be expressed as

$$var[d_{\text{real}}] = D_{\text{real}}''(1) + D_{\text{real}}'(1) - [D_{\text{real}}'(1)]^2,$$

where $D_{\text{real}}''(1)$ is the second-order derivative of $D_{\text{real}}(z)$ in $z = 1$.

5.4 Tail Distribution

In this Section we derive the tail distribution of the packet delay, i.e., the probability that the delay equals a given value n, for a sufficiently large value of n. In principle, we can determine the tail distribution of a discrete random variable by applying the inversion formula for z-transforms and Cauchy's residue theorem from complex analysis ([12]) on its probability generating function and keeping only the contribution of the pole of the pgf with the smallest modulus outside the unit disk, as explained e.g. in [13]. From the expression (18) for $D_{\text{real}}(z)$, we find that the pole of $D_{\text{real}}(z)$ with the smallest modulus is given by

$$z_d = A(z_u),$$

where z_u is the dominant pole of the pgf $U_{\text{real}}(z)$ of the buffer content, i.e., the zero of $\det(z\mathbf{I}-\mathbf{S}(A(z)))$ outside the unit disk with the smallest modulus. Indeed, it is possible to show that $A(z_u)$ is the zero with minimal modulus outside the unit disk of the factor $\det(z_u\mathbf{I} - \mathbf{S}(z))$ in the denominator of $D_{\text{real}}(z)$. Taking into account the contribution of the dominant pole z_d and keeping in mind that $\mathrm{Prob}[d_{\text{real}} = n]$ is the coefficient of z^n in the series expansion of $D_{\text{real}}(z)$, we obtain the following expression for $\mathrm{Prob}[d_{\text{real}} = n]$ for sufficiently large n:

$$\mathrm{Prob}[d_{\text{real}} = n] \approx -\frac{C_d}{z_d} z_d^{-n},$$

where C_d is the residue of $D_{\text{real}}(z)$ in the point $z = z_d$.

6 Special Case: Gilbert-Elliott Model

In this Section we will study the specific case of a Gilbert-Elliott model ([8]), which is a Markov chain with only 2 states, which are labelled 0 and 1, or 'GOOD' and 'BAD' (see Fig. 2). The parameters e_0 and e_1 are the error probabilities of the channel in resp. state 0 and 1. Of course, the designations GOOD and BAD make only sense when $e_0 < e_1$, but this is not a requirement for the analysis.

The Gilbert-Elliott model is completely defined by 2 parameters q_0 and q_1, where

$$q_i = \mathrm{Prob}[\text{state in next slot is } i|\text{ state in current slot is } i].$$

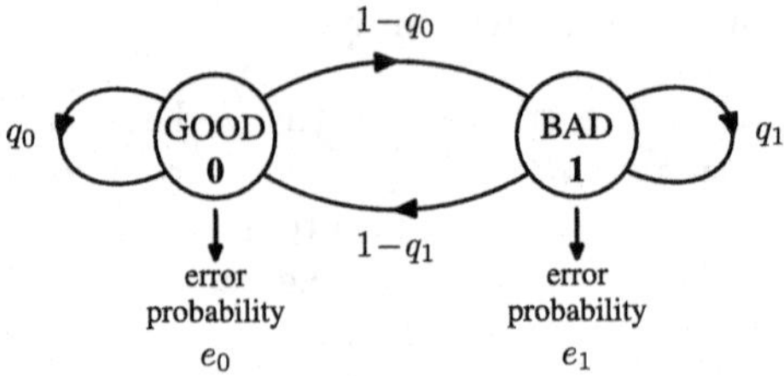

Fig. 2. Gilbert-Elliott model

Rather than using q_0 and q_1, we define the parameters

$$\sigma = \frac{1 - q_0}{2 - q_0 - q_1} \text{ and } K = \frac{1}{2 - q_0 - q_1} \tag{19}$$

to be understood as follows: σ is the fraction of the time that the system is in state 1, while the parameter K can be seen as a measure for the mean lengths of 0- and 1-periods. Specifically, the mean length of a 1-period is K/σ, of a 0-period it is $K/\bar{\sigma}$. Therefore, the factor K can be seen as a measure for the *absolute* lengths of the 0-periods and 1-periods, while σ characterizes their *relative* lengths.

6.1 Throughput

Using the general method outlined in Sect. 4, we find an explicit formula of the throughput

$$\eta = \frac{\psi_0(K)\sigma\bar{e}_0 + \psi_1(K)\bar{\sigma}\bar{e}_1}{\psi_0(K)\sigma(1 + se_0) + \psi_1(K)\bar{\sigma}(1 + se_1)} \tag{20}$$

with $\psi_0(K) \triangleq 1 - \phi\bar{e}_1 - \phi^{s+1}e_1$ and $\psi_1(K) \triangleq 1 - \phi\bar{e}_0 - \phi^{s+1}e_0$ (where $\phi = 1 - \frac{1}{K}$).

In previous papers e.g. [6] it was shown that for stop-and-wait protocols operating over a Gilbert-Elliott channel, the throughput is independent of K. This is not the case for Go-Back-N ARQ protocols. An interesting fact is that the throughput of the protocol actually gets better for larger K, but we shall see that correlation does have a negative effect on the mean packet delay. When $K \to \infty$ the throughput reaches a maximum

$$\eta_{\max} = \sigma\frac{\bar{e}_0}{1 + se_0} + \bar{\sigma}\frac{\bar{e}_1}{1 + se_1}.$$

In case of an uncorrelated error channel ($K = 1$) we find with $e = \sigma e_0 + \bar{\sigma}e_1$:

$$\eta_{\text{static}} = \frac{\bar{e}}{1 + se}.$$

6.2 Pgf of the Packet Delay

The pgf of the delay $D_{\text{real}}(z)$ consists of a number of terms of the following form:

$$\begin{aligned} D^*(z) &= z^{n_*}\mathbf{r}F(\mathbf{S}(z))\mathbf{1} \\ &= z^{n_*}\mathbf{r}\sum_{k=0}^{\infty} f_k\mathbf{S}(z)^k\mathbf{1}, \end{aligned} \tag{21}$$

where $\mathbf{r}$ is a certain row vector, $F(z)$ is a pgf and $\mathbf{S}(z)$ is the pgm of the service time. In order to get an explicit formula for $D^*(z)$, we need to write $\mathbf{S}(z)^k$ in a form which we can actually evaluate. To do this we derive the spectral decomposition ([10]) of $\mathbf{S}(z)$. This pgm has dimension 2×2, so its characteristic equation $(\det(\lambda(z)\mathbf{I}-\mathbf{S}(z)) = 0)$ is quadratic. Let $\lambda_1(z), \lambda_2(z)$ be the roots of this equation. Now we introduce two matrices $\mathbf{B}_1(z)$ and $\mathbf{B}_2(z)$, called *constituents* which can be found by using following formulas:

$$\mathbf{B}_1(z) = \frac{\mathbf{S}(z) - \lambda_2(z)\mathbf{I}}{\lambda_1(z) - \lambda_2(z)}$$

and

$$\mathbf{B}_2(z) = \frac{\mathbf{S}(z) - \lambda_1(z)\mathbf{I}}{\lambda_2(z) - \lambda_1(z)}.$$

Now it can be shown that $\mathbf{S}(z)^k$ can be written as

$$\mathbf{S}(z)^k = \sum_i \lambda_i(z)^k\mathbf{B}_i(z). \tag{22}$$

Finally, by combining (21) and (22) we get:

$$\begin{aligned} D^*(z) &= z^{n_*}\mathbf{r}\sum_{k=0}^{\infty} f_k \sum_i \lambda_i(z)^k\mathbf{B}_i(z)\mathbf{1} \\ &= z^{n_*}\mathbf{r}\sum_i F(\lambda_i(z))\mathbf{B}_i(z)\mathbf{1} \\ &= z^{n_*}\sum_i b_i(z)F(\lambda_i(z)), \end{aligned}$$

where $b_i(z) = \mathbf{r}\mathbf{B}_i(z)\mathbf{1}$. We can do this for each term of $D_{\text{real}}(z)$, and in this manner obtain its explicit expression.

7 Numerical Examples

In this Section we provide some numerical examples. In all our examples we use a Gilbert-Elliott model for the channel. We assume geometrically distributed arrivals with mean $\alpha = 0.3$.

In Fig. 3 we illustrate the influence of the error correlation on the throughput performance. Specifically, in this figure we have plotted the throughput η as a

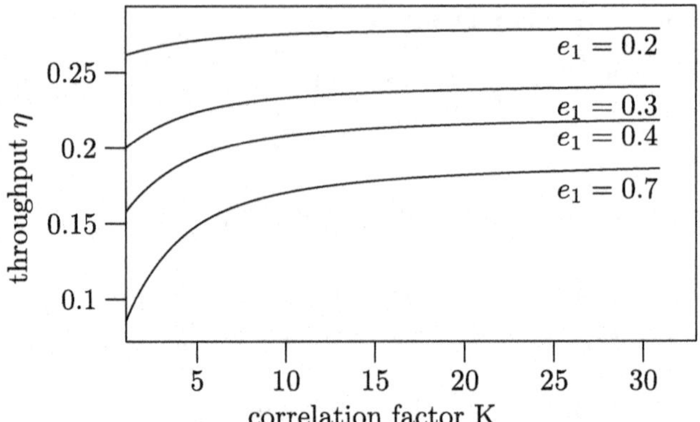

Fig. 3. Throughput η versus the correlation factor K, for $s = 15$, $\sigma = 0.5$, $e_0 = 0.1$, and $e_1 = 0.2, 0.3, 0.4, 0.7$

function of the correlation factor K, for a feedback delay $s = 15$, $\sigma = 0.5$, $e_0 = 0.1$ and various values of e_1. We only consider positively correlated channels (thus $K > 1$), as only these are of practical interest. We observe that the throughput increases when K gets larger, growing towards an asymptotical maximum, as was already noted in Sect. 6. We also see that the throughput gets worse as e_1 increases, i.e., when the condition of the BAD state deteriorates.

Figure 4 shows the mean packet delay $\mathrm{E}[d_{\mathrm{real}}]$ as a function of the correlation factor K, for $s = 2, \sigma = 0.5, e_0 = 0.1$ and various values of e_1. It is clear from this figure that the mean delay also increases as K gets larger. We also note that

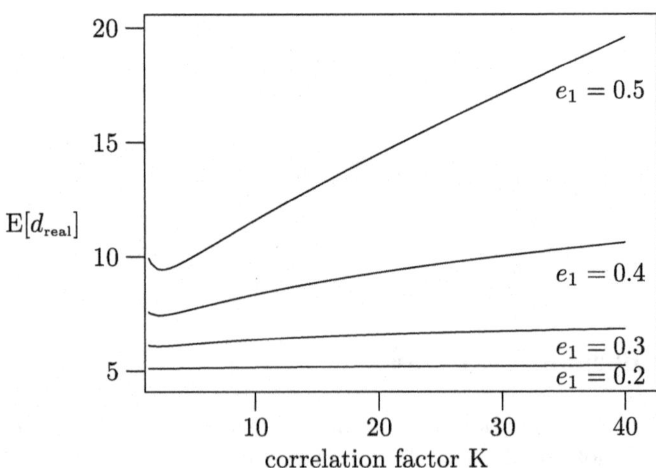

Fig. 4. The mean packet delay $\mathrm{E}[d_{\mathrm{real}}]$ versus the correlation factor K, for $s = 2$, $\sigma = 0.5$, $e_0 = 0.1$, and $e_1 = 0.2, 0.3, 0.4, 0.5$

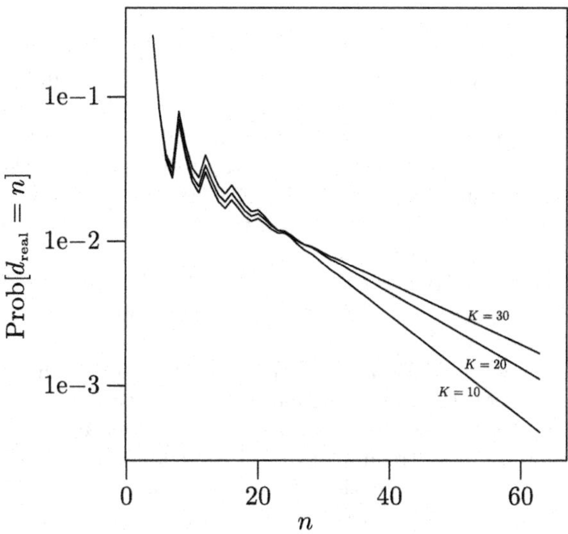

Fig. 5. Logarithmic plot of Prob[$d_{real} = n$] versus n, for $s = 2, \sigma = 0.5, e_0 = 0.1, e_1 = 0.4$, and $K = 10, 20, 30$

for lower values of the error probability in the BAD state e_1, the mean delay reaches an asymptotical limit, but when e_1 gets higher than a certain value, the mean delay keeps on increasing linearly.

Finally, in Fig. 5 we have plotted the probability Prob[$d_{real} = n$] of having a packet delay of n slots versus the value of n, for $s = 2, \sigma = 0.5, e_0 = 0.1, e_1 = 0.4$ and various values of K. These curves have been obtained by inversion of the pgf $D_{real}(z)$ by means of a method explained in [14]. We see that the packet delay over a more correlated channel has a heavier tail, which again shows that correlation of the channel has an important influence on the performance of the system.

8 Conclusions

We have studied a Go-Back-N ARQ protocol over a time-varying channel. We analyzed the steady-state distributions of the buffer content and of the packet delay. By using the spectral decomposition of the pgm of the service time, we were able to find the pgf of the packet delay in explicit form when the channel has two states. Additionally, we were able to express a simple relation between the tail distributions of the packet delay and buffer content. Finally, by means of some examples we have discussed the influence of the model parameters on the queue performance.

Acknowledgement

This work has been supported by the Interuniversity Attraction Poles Programme - Belgian Science Policy.

References

1. Bhunia, C.T.: ARQ - Review and modifications. IETE Technical Review **18** (2001) 381–401
2. Towsley, D., Wolf, J.K.: On the statistical analysis of queue lengths and waiting times for statistical multiplexers with ARQ retransmission schemes. IEEE Transactions on Communications **25** (1979) 693–703
3. Konheim, A.G.: A queueing analysis of two ARQ protocols. IEEE Transactions on Communications **28** (1980) 1004–1014
4. De Munnynck, M., Wittevrongel, S., Lootens, A., Bruneel, H.: Queueing analysis of some continuous ARQ strategies with repeated transmissions. Electronics Letters **38** (2002) 1295 – 1297
5. Towsley, D.: A statistical analysis of ARQ protocols operating in a non-independent error environment. IEEE Transactions on Communications **27** (1981) 971–981
6. De Vuyst, S., Wittevrongel, S., Bruneel, H.: Delay analysis of the Stop-and-Wait ARQ scheme under correlated errors. Proceedings of HET-NETs 2004, Performance Modelling and Evaluation of Heterogenous Networks (26-28 July 2004, Ilkley, West Yorkshire, UK), p. 21/1–21/11
7. Kim, J.G., Krunz, M.: Delay analysis of selective repeat ARQ for transporting Markovian sources over a wireless channel. IEEE Transactions on Vehicular Technology **49** (2000) 1968–1981
8. Gilbert, E.N.: Capacity of a burst noise channel. The Bell System Technical Journal **39** (1960) 1253–1265
9. Gail, H. R., Hantler, S. L., Taylor, B. A.: Spectral analysis of $M/G/1$ and $G/M/1$ type Markov chains. Adv. Appl. Prob. **28** (1996) 114–165
10. Gantmacher, F. R.: The Theory of Matrices, Volume 1. AMS Chelsea Publishing, Providence, Rhode Island (1959)
11. Bruneel, H.: Buffers with stochastic output interruptions. Electronics Letters **19** (1983) 735–737
12. Kleinrock, L.: Queueing Systems, Volume I: Theory. Wiley, New York (1975)
13. Bruneel, H., Kim, B.G.: Discrete-time models for communication systems including ATM. Kluwer Academic Publishers, Boston (1993) (ISBN: 0-7923-9292-2)
14. Abate, J., Whitt, W.: Numerical inversion of probability generating functions. Operations Research Letters **12** (1992) 245–251

Performance Tuning of Failure Detectors in Wireless Ad-hoc Networks: Modelling and Experiments

Corine Marchand and Jean-Marc Vincent*

Laboratoire ID - IMAG, MESCAL project (CNRS - INRIA - INPG - UJF),
ZIRST 51, Avenue Jean Kuntzmann, 38330 Montbonnot Saint Martin, France
{Corine.Marchand, Jean-Marc.Vincent}@imag.fr

Abstract. We consider wireless ad-hoc networks and implement failure detections mechanisms. These failure detectors provide elementary information for high level distributed algorithms such as consensus, election or agreement. The aim is to guarantee a quality of service for these mechanisms. Stochastic models for tuning failure detectors are proposed based on frequency analysis and contention modelling. Tuning methods are suggested for setting time-out delays. The theoretical results were validated experimentally on a wireless platform, based on a statistical analysis of the measurements.

1 Introduction

Technological advances in wireless devices such as laptop computers, personal digital assistants (PDAs), or mobile phones, bring significance to new wireless technologies. Progress in wireless communication protocols, e.g. Bluetooth, WIFI, allow the use of new ad-hoc networking schemes. It follows that new challenges arise from the communication variability in wireless networks and the unpredictable disconnections of those heterogeneous devices, creating very dynamic topologies called ad-hoc wireless networks.

In this context, the distributed environment we consider is composed of heterogeneous devices which form a dynamic group. This environment is completely distributed (no predefined memory or stable server in our case). In addition, this environment is also unstable: due to unpredictable disconnections of devices and the variability of communication latencies, failures can occur.

In this unreliable environment, the main goal is that each device should offer its local resources and services to one another, and could benefit from services provided by other devices. So, to manage services and resource sharing and to maintain the consistency of the group regarding newcomers and devices that voluntarily disconnect themselves, we have developed middleware modules in order to be able to make some decisions. Accordingly, our previous works [11,5] focus on distributed agreement problems in unreliable environments, and more specifically on consensus protocols.

To solve the agreement problem, several algorithms have been proposed. In particular Chandra & Toueg [2] establish that the consensus problem could be solved in an asynchronous context with unreliable failure detectors. These detectors provide local

* This work was partially supported by FT R&D CRE MIRRA and DECORE-IMAG project.

M. Bravetti et al. (Eds.): EPEW 2005 and WS-FM 2005, LNCS 3670, pp. 139–154, 2005.

estimation of the state of entities on the network. Thus a detector either suspects an other site, or not. The estimation of the detector is clearly unreliable, but if the information is asymptotically correct, the agreement is eventually obtained.

From an implementation point of view, failure detectors on each site communicate with each others. The estimates of the failure detector about the status of all other devices are delivered to an upper layer in form of a list containing the suspected devices. These failure detectors implement a function that, according to some information, make the decision to suspect or not. A typical function is a time-out delay : if the failure detector has not heard from a site since some time-out period, then it suspects the remote site.

The objective of this paper is to analyze the quality of service of such failure detector and apply the modelling approach to a wireless ad-hoc architecture. The infrastructure have been implemented and tested in an industrial context (CRE MIRRA with France-Télécom R&D) and in the RNRT SIDRAH project. Configurations with heterogeneous devices (PC, Laptop, PDA) have been used. Experiments shows that parameter tuning should be set according to the type of device and the global load of the network. Stochastic analysis of the system is then confirmed.

The paper is organized as follows. Section 2 introduces the failure detectors. Then, Section 3, stochastic models are derived and quality of service factors computed. The last part is devoted to experimental results and analysis.

2 Failure Detectors

2.1 Theoretical Concept

The working principle of failure detectors is to provide, at a given time and for a given process, a list of suspected devices. As failure detectors are considered unreliable, this list can contain wrong information about remote devices (suspicion of a device correctly present or no suspicion of a failed device).

Each device e_i included in the system has its own failure detector module. So, with this module, each device can obtain information, periodically or on demand, concerning the global state of the system.

However, information provided by a local failure detector does not necessarily indicate the real state of the system. The failure detector only suspects that some devices have crashed or are disconnected. Note that failure detectors are inherently unreliable because the information they provide may be incorrect.

Chandra & Toueg [2] characterize failure detectors with two properties: the *accuracy* property, which restricts false suspicions that failure detectors can make, and the *completeness* property, which requires that failure detectors eventually suspect every failed devices. In this paper, we focus on the $\Diamond S$ class of failure detectors, called *Eventually Strong* [2].

2.2 Failure Detector Implementation

From among the several strategies that have been proposed to implement failure detectors, e.g., heartbeat or query (pinging), we choose to use the classical heartbeat detection model.

The heartbeat technique is based on the periodic emission of messages from each failure detector to everyone. In our implementation we divide the failure detector into two modules. We distinguish between the spreading information, which is included in the failure detector export module, and the gathering information, which is treated by the failure detector import module.

As a consequence, every export module periodically broadcasts a message (see figure 1) to inform other devices of its reachable state.

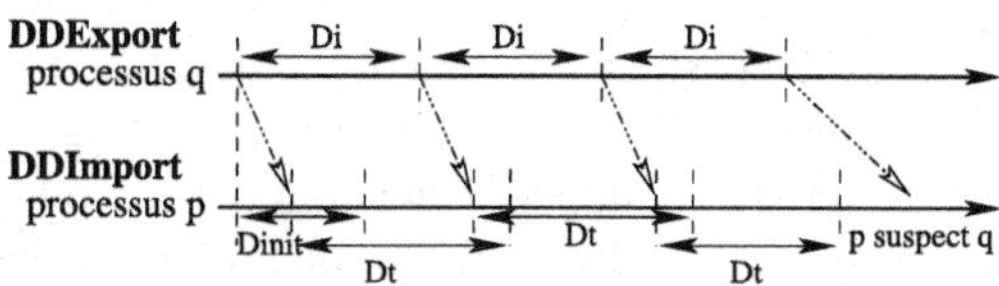

Fig. 1. Heartbeat principle

When an failure detector import module of an entity $e1$ receives a message from another device $e2$, it invokes its suspicion estimation function. This function in the simplest case works by arming a timeout. This mechanism is repeated until every one received a message from $e2$. Otherwise, if the import module of $e1$ does not receive a new message from $e2$ after the expiration of the timeout, it adds $e2$ to its list of suspected devices. The device $e2$ will be remove from this list when $e1$ receives a new message from $e2$.

This implementation technique introduces two parameters: the heartbeat period and the timeout delay. The heartbeat period is the time between two successive emissions in the failure detector export module of each device. The timeout delay is used in the import module. This parameter is the waiting period after which the failure detector of a device $e1$ starts to suspect a device $e2$ of having failed.

2.3 Quality of Service of Failure Detectors

Intuitively, the failure detectors' quality of service can be defined by: (1) the failure detector reactivity, which should be the fastest possible and (2) the failure detector should avoid false suspicions. Thus, the quality of a failure detector depends on its reactivity against external events and on its capacity to provide correct information. This quality of service notion was introduced and developed in [3] [9].

At run-time the failure detector is influenced by the two parameters [13] : D_i, the time period between two emissions of device i, and $\theta_j(i)$, the timeout delay for device i in the failure detector import module of device j. Therefore, the failure detector quality of service closely depends on the tuning of these parameters.

To define the quality of service of failure detectors, we have to address several tradeoffs. First, there is a tradeoff between the failure detector's reactivity and the number of sent messages over the network. Indeed, a decrease in heartbeat emission time period D_i allows for a better reactivity, thus limiting the duration of time devices are under false suspicion. However, this is at the cost of increased network utilization, which in turn may degrade overall system performance.

The desired properties of a failure detector are to 1) avoid suspecting devices that are available and 2) suspect devices that are not available as fast as possible. As the reactivity is related to the value of the time period, the failure detector's reliability depends on the timeout tuning. Thus, one has to balance the existing tradeoff between failure detector reliability and reactivity.

3 Stochastic Models

In this section we present stochastic modelling of failure detector mechanisms based on heartbeat. The goal is to provide a model that allows for tuning of the failure suspicion function. In fact, according to a set of parameter values, the model establishes the quality of service offered by the failure detector. This quality of service can be tuned by the user to fit the needs of the application.

The two quality of service criteria studied in this section are the reactivity of the failure detector and the quality of information given by the detector. The difficulty is to establish the tradeoffs between these two properties. The reactivity is the delay needed by a failure detector to detect the crash of the process. It is directly related to time-out and heartbeat period. The quality of information given by the detector is estimated by a false suspicion rate and the probability that the failure detector is in a state of suspicion. The reactivity is a decreasing function of the time-out value, as is the suspicion rate, that is also decreasing.

3.1 False Detection Probability

The difficulty for modelling such systems is the complexity of latency estimations. Figure 2 shows that the reception delay between two heartbeats send by the same failure detector depends on (1) the time taken by the beat in the communication stack of the sender, (2) the latency on the network taking losses into account, (3) the time spent in the communication stack of the receiver (4) and finally the time needed by the receiver failure detector process to access the information.

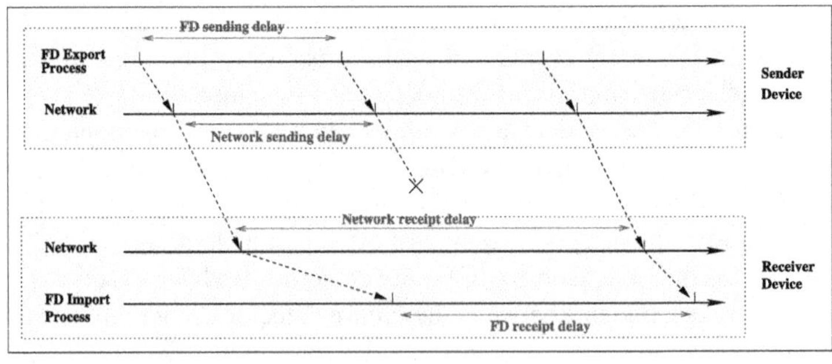

Fig. 2. Running principle between two failure detectors

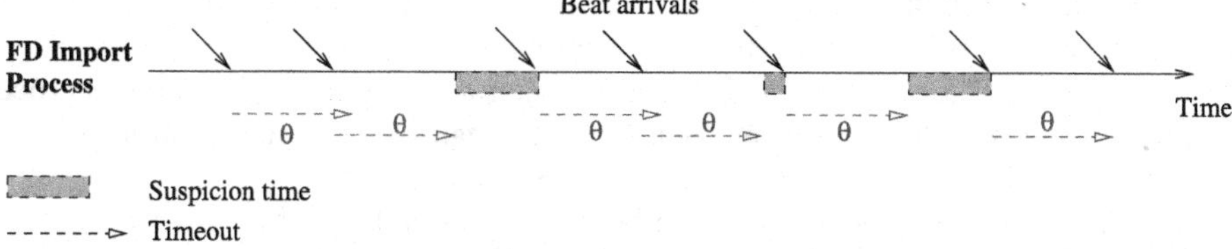

Fig. 3. Receptions and Suspicions

In the failure detector, suspicion occurs when the reception module has not received a beat during some fixed time-out period. In this paper, the time-out θ is supposed to be constant in all experiments.

The false suspicion rate $\phi_I(\theta)$ is defined by the asymptotic ratio of the suspecting period (grey blocks on figure 3) to the observation period.

Denote by λ_0 the emission beat rate and λ the reception rate. The mean inter-arrival time of beats is $\frac{1}{\lambda}$ and $\lambda = \lambda_0.(1-p)$ with p the loss rate of messages on the network. Let $\{X_n\}_{n\in\mathrm{N}}$ be the sequence of inter-arrivals of beats on the receiver. So

$$\lim_{n\to+\infty} \frac{1}{n}\sum_{i=1}^{n} X_i = \frac{1}{\lambda}.$$

With this notation, it is possible to give an asymptotic expression for $\phi_I(\theta)$.

$$\phi_I(\theta) = \lim_{n\to+\infty} \frac{\sum_{i=1}^{n}(X_i-\theta)^+}{\sum_{i=1}^{n} X_i} = \lambda \lim_{n\to+\infty} \frac{1}{n}\sum_{i=1}^{n}(X_i-\theta)^+, \tag{1}$$

with x^+ the positive part of x.

To analyze the behavior of the failure detector and estimate $\phi_I(\theta)$, the system will be considered to be time homogeneous. Then parameters are constant on a sufficiently large period to ensure stationarity of the random process.

In a first model, we suppose that the heartbeat receiving process may be considered as a renewal process and the impact of variability of the inter-arrivals of beats on suspicion rate is established. A second model focuses on the impact of the latency in the receiver stack on the suspicion rate.

3.2 Variable Sending Delay

An current implementation of the heartbeat sender is a simple loop of waiting periods.

```
loop forever
      wait(period)
      send(heartbeat)
end loop
```

When this algorithm is perturbated by the operating system or access to the network, variability occurs and heartbeats are not periodic.

In a first approximation, we consider the inter-arrival process as a renewal process. It corresponds to strategies when the receiver estimates the distribution of inter-arrivals and tries to fix the time-out according to some histogram.

Then, because the inter-arrivals of beats are independent with the same probability law, the failure suspicion rate is just

$$\phi_I(\theta) = \lambda \mathbb{E}\left[X - \theta\right]^+ . \tag{2}$$

This kind of formula is of high interest because it rapidly gives the order of Φ_I when the shape of the distribution of inter-arrivals distribution of beats is known.

Exponential Model. In the case when the inter-arrivals are exponentially distributed with rate λ. The arrival process is a Poisson process and

$$\phi_I(\theta) = \lambda \int_0^{+\infty} (x-\theta)^+ \lambda e^{-\lambda x} dx = e^{-\lambda\theta} \tag{3}$$

In figure 4, the first curve shows exponential decreasing of $\phi_I(\theta)$ depending on time-out. As an example, to achieve a false suspicion rate of 10^{-3} the adequate time-out should be seven times the mean inter-arrival period.

In fact, when the inter-arrival X exhibits an *new better than used in expectation property (NBUE)*, the quantity $\Phi_I(\theta)$ is bounded from above by the exponential model and so

$$\phi_I(\theta) \leq e^{-\lambda\theta}.$$

Moreover, if we need to decrease the false suspicion rate by an adaptative scheme, an additive increment strategy will be sufficient.

Low Variance Model. In many cases the exponential model overestimates the false suspicion rate, typically when the variance of inter-arrivals is small. To obtain finer results, Erlang distributions with parameters $(k, k\lambda)$ and density

$$f_X(x) = \frac{(k\lambda)^k x^{k-1} e^{-k\lambda x}}{(k-1)!},$$

with mean $\frac{1}{\lambda}$ and variance $\frac{1}{k\lambda^2}$. Then

$$\phi_I(\theta) = \lambda \int_0^{+\infty} \frac{(k\lambda)^k x^{k-1} e^{-k\lambda x}}{(k-1)!} (x-\theta)^+ dx \tag{4}$$

It may be shown that

$$\Phi_I(\theta) = e^{-k\lambda\theta} P_k(\lambda\theta),$$

where P_k is a polynomial of degree $k-1$. For small values of k, figure 4 shows the suspicion probability for a mean inter-arrivals of beats equal to 1 and a variance of $\frac{1}{k}$.

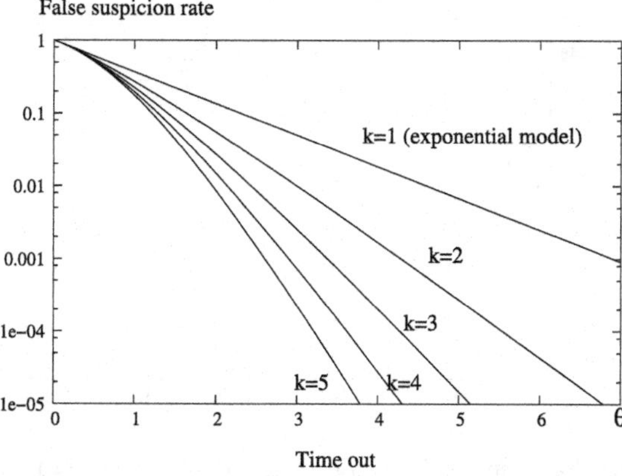

Fig. 4. Suspicion probability related to reactivity for the low variance model

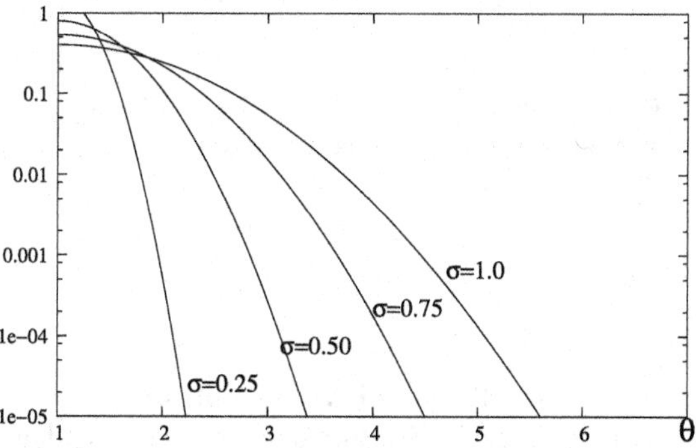

Fig. 5. Suspicion probability related to reactivity for the normal model

For example, with a variance $\frac{1}{5\lambda^2}$, a time-out of three times the inter-arrivals of beats is sufficient to ensure a false suspicion rate of 10^{-3}.

In the case when the inter-arrival could be modelled by a normal distribution with mean $\frac{1}{\lambda}$ and standard deviation σ, we can bound the false suspicion rate by

$$\phi_I(\theta) \leq \frac{\sigma}{\sqrt{2\pi}} e^{-\frac{(\theta-\frac{1}{\lambda})^2}{2\sigma^2}} \tag{5}$$

In this case, figure 5 indicates the false suspicion rate. Naturally, these curves decrease more rapidly than the Erlang model. For a standard deviation of 0.5, taking a time-out of 3 times the period is sufficient to guarantee a false suspicion rate of 10^{-3}.

High Variance Model. Unfortunately, the observed distribution could exhibit large values and when tail of the distribution is not of a negative exponential form. Then Pareto distribution functions ($\alpha > 2$) could be used

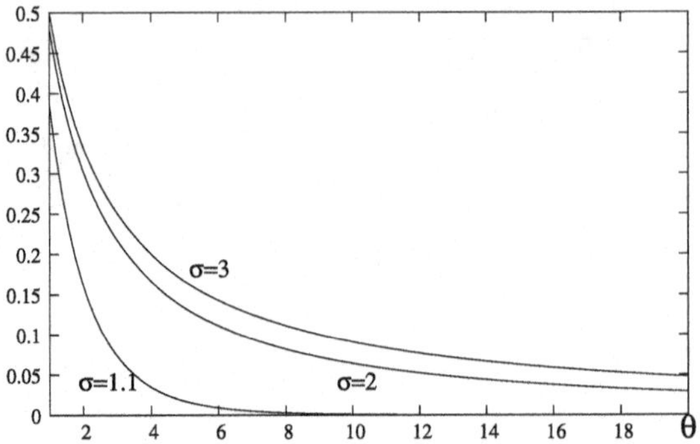

Fig. 6. Suspicion probability related to reactivity for the Pareto model

$$f_X(x) = \frac{\alpha - 1}{\alpha - 2} \frac{1}{(1 + \frac{x}{\alpha-2})^\alpha}. \tag{6}$$

For these parameters, the mean has been fixed to 1 and the variance, for $\alpha > 3$, is $\frac{\alpha-1}{\alpha-3}$. The false suspicion rate could easily be computed by

$$\Phi_I(\theta) = \frac{1}{(1 + \frac{\theta}{a-2})^{a-2}}.$$

In this situation, it is clear that the high variability of inter-arrivals of beats produces a very poor quality of service of the failure detector . Even with a standard deviation of 1.1 the time out period should be more then ten times the heartbeat period to achieve a suspicion rate of 10^{-3}.

Synthesis. In this table the inter-arrivals of beats is 1 and the time-out function gives the quality of service for false suspicions.

Distribution shape	Properties	Time-out function
Exponential	Most mixed distribution, bound for *New Better than Used in Expectation* distribution	$e^{-\theta}$
Erlang(k, k)	Exponential tail, low coefficient of variation	$P_k(\theta)e^{-k\theta}$
Gauss(1, σ^2)	White noise model around a deterministic value	$\leq \frac{\sigma}{\sqrt{2\pi}} e^{-\frac{(\theta-1)^2}{2\sigma^2}}$
Pareto(α)	Heavy tail distribution	$\frac{1}{(1+\frac{\theta}{a-2})^{a-2}}$ if $\alpha > 3$

3.3 Queueing of Heartbeat Messages

General Model. During experimentations, we observe that the delay between heartbeats mainly depends on the nature of the receiver: laptop or PDA. This suggests that the capability of the receiver introduces variability of inter-beats periods. Moreover, inter-arrivals appear to be correlated and the correlation could be important. Observing the phenomena at the network level by a non-intrusive "sniffer" we establish that heart-beats are emitted as specified (e.g., periodically). The problem is due to the time spent by the receiver module to get the heartbeat from its own network buffer. Consequently, we have to take into account the contention of heartbeats on the receiver and variability appear when the heartbeat is delivered from the network layer to the heartbeat module at the middleware layer. A queueing model (figure 7) is used to describe the system.

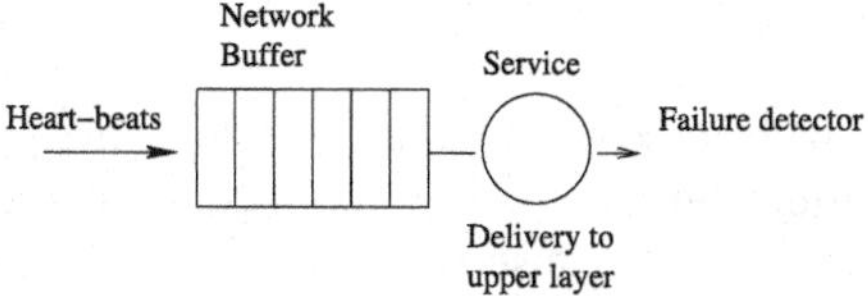

Fig. 7. Model for beats delivery

In such a queueing model denote the arrival process of beats by $\{A_n\}_{n\in\mathbb{N}}$ and the sequence of service delays for delivering the beats by $\{S_n\}_{n\in\mathbb{N}}$.

The interesting process for dimensioning is the inter-output process denoted by $\{Z_n\}_{n\in\mathbb{N}}$. The aim of this section is to compute the stationary distribution of this process. Following the evolution equation approach [1] the process $\{Z_n\}$ satisfies

$$Z_{n+1} = S_{n+1} + [A_{n+1} - R_n]^+ , \tag{7}$$

where R_n is the residual service time of clients in the queue just after the nth arrival. This expression is obtained by the study of two cases :
- the server is busy at the arrival of client $n+1$, it begins its service at the end of the preceding client and the inter-output corresponds to the service time of client $n+1$;
- the queue is empty, $A_{n+1} - R_n$ is positive and represent the elapsed time between the last client output and the arrival of client $n+1$.

Provided that arrival and service processes are stationary ergodic, the queueing system is stable if $\mathbb{E}S < \mathbb{E}A$. Thus, the embedded process $\{R_n\}$ is also stationary and consequently, the process $\{Z_n\}$ converges to a stationary distribution denoted by Z.

The $GI/M/1$ Case. We suppose now that the inter-arrivals are independent with the distribution density $f_A(.)$. The services are considered exponentially distributed with rate μ and independent. The system is modelled by a $GI/M/1$ queue, this queue is stable iff $\frac{1}{\mu\mathbb{E}A} < 1$. The embedded process (number of clients in the queue) at arrival times is a homogeneous Markov chain and the stationary distribution is geometrically distributed with parameter β defined as the unique fixed point of the equation

$$\beta = \mathcal{L}_A(\mu(1-\beta)),$$

where $\mathcal{L}_A(.)$ is the Laplace transform of the inter-arrivals density f_A [10].

Moreover, because of the memoryless property of service time, the residual service time R is exponentially distributed with rate $\mu(1-\beta)$. The residual service time is a geometric sum of i.i.d. exponentially distributed random variables.

Given an inter-arrival distribution, it is possible to numerically compute the distribution of

$$Z = S + [A - R]^+ ;$$

and to deduce the false suspicion probability given a reactivity θ as

$$\mathbb{P}(Z > \theta) = \mathbb{P}\left(S + [A - R]^+ > \theta\right). \tag{8}$$

The $D/M/1$ Case. In the case when failure detectors have periodic heartbeats (period $A = \frac{1}{\lambda}$), the formulation above could be simplified. First, we compute the rate of the exponential distribution of R. Because $\mathcal{L}_A(t) = e^{-At}$, β is the unique solution of

$$\beta = e^{-A\mu(1-\beta)}.$$

Then we compute the distribution of $[A - R]^+$:

$$\mathbb{P}\{(A-R)^+ \leq x\} = \begin{cases} 0 & if\, x < 0; \\ e^{-\mu(1-\beta)A} & if\, x = 0; \\ e^{-\mu(1-\beta)(A-x)} & if\, 0 \leq x \leq A; \\ 1 & if\, x \geq A. \end{cases} \tag{9}$$

Then we form the convolution of the service time distribution and the distribution of $(A - R)^+$:

$$\begin{aligned} \mathbb{P}\{Z \leq x\} &= \mathbb{P}\{(A-T)^+ + S \leq x\} \\ &= \int_0^x \mathbb{P}\{(A-T)^+ \leq x - s\}\mu e^{-\mu s} ds \\ &= \int_0^x P\{(A-T)^+ \leq t\}\mu e^{-\mu(x-t)} dt \end{aligned}$$

$$\mathbb{P}\{Z \leq x\} = \begin{cases} \frac{1}{2-\beta}(e^{-\mu(1-\beta)(A-x)} - e^{-\mu((1-\beta)A+x)}) & if\, x \leq A; \\ 1 - \frac{e^{-\mu x}}{2-\beta}(e^{-\mu(1-\beta)A} + (1-\beta)e^{\mu A}) & if\, x \geq A. \end{cases} \tag{10}$$

The density is obtained by differentiation

$$fz(x) = \begin{cases} \frac{\mu}{2-\beta} e^{-\mu(1-\beta)A}((1-\beta)e^{\mu(1-\beta)x} + e^{-\mu x}) & if\, x < A; \\ \frac{\mu}{2-\beta} e^{-\mu x}(e^{-\mu(1-\beta)A} + (1-\beta)e^{\mu A}) & if\, x \geq A. \end{cases} \tag{11}$$

For a given θ, the false suspicion rate is

$$\phi_I(\theta) = \frac{1}{A}\mathbb{E}\,[Z-\theta]^+ = \int_0^\infty (x-\theta)^+ f_Z(x)\,dx.$$

After some computation, for $\theta > A$, we obtain

$$\mathbb{E}\,[X-\theta]^+ = \frac{1}{(2-\beta)\mu} e^{-\mu\theta}(e^{-\mu(1-\beta)A} + (1-\beta)e^{\mu A}) \qquad \theta \geq A, \tag{12}$$

and we deduce

$$\phi_I(\theta) = \frac{1}{A(2-\beta)\mu} e^{-\mu\theta}(e^{-\mu(1-\beta)A} + (1-\beta)e^{\mu A}) \qquad \theta \geq A. \tag{13}$$

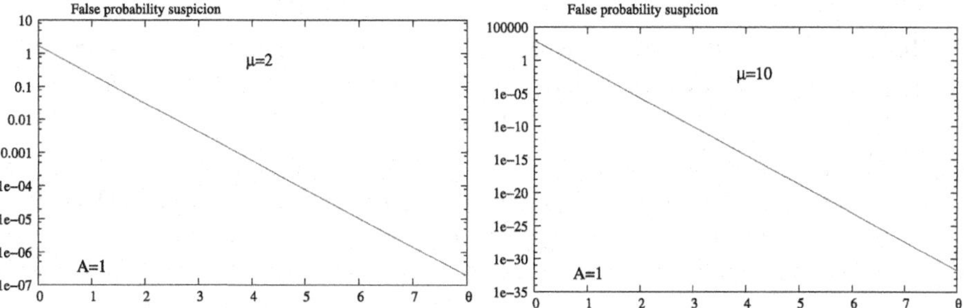

Fig. 8. False suspicion probability, $D/M/1$ model $A = 1$

When the system is loaded, the impact on false suspicion probability is important. For example, if the time to retrieve the heartbeat on the network is about half of the heartbeat period ($\mu = 2\lambda$), we should fix a time-out of four times the inter-arrival period to get a quality of service less than 10^{-3}.

From a practical point of view, this model permits us to adapt the suspicion policy of the failure detector to the architecture of the device. Moreover we may deduce the impact of the size of the network on the queueing system by considering μ as a function of the number of devices in the network.

However, these results are obtained for a deterministic arrival process on the receiver. This hypothesis could be weakened by modifying the arrival law. Using a Poisson process arrival, the queue is a $M/M/1$ and the output process is a Poisson process. In this case, we apply results from the previous section. Moreover, stochastic ordering techniques provides results on arrival processes that could compare with deterministic and Poisson process. This gives stochastic bounds for the dimensioning.

4 Experimentation

In this section we will use a real system to illustrate the relationship between the timeout value and the quality of information provided by the failure detectors.

4.1 First Approach

Experimental Design: This first study utilized 2 laptop devices (Linux 800 Mhz) and 2 personal digital assistants (Linux 200 Mhz). The interconnections were based on a 802.11b wireless ad-hoc network. The failure detector modules developed were installed in each device (import module and export module). Thus, each device has an unreliable view of the global system based on the information in its own failure detector's import module. The parameter settings used for the import modules were 100 ms for the heartbeat time period, the timeout value was not fixed (infinite value). During the experiment which lasted approximately 15 minutes, about 10,000 measures were obtained. The system appeared to be stressed. In the experiment, the system's reactivity was of the order of 1 second. Since the experiment was conducted in a dedicated environment, i.e., no other applications were running, it is to be expected that in a system under standard application load the delay will likely increase.

Results: These graphic representations illustrate the various behaviors existing between a PDA and a laptop. Note that, in all these experiments, the environment was "stressed", the heartbeat losses could be significant (loss rate was around 50% when the receiver was a PDA).

As we can see in the graphics, if the timeout value had been fixed at 200 ms ($\theta = 2*$ the heartbeat emission time period), it would have been a too small value for some of the devices and would have generated a lot of false suspicions. Indeed, when the sending and receiver device are laptops (see figure 12), the distribution of heartbeat receipt delays is centered around the emission duration mean value (100 ms). Most of these durations are included between 50 ms and 150 ms. Therefore, a timeout value fixed at 200 ms seems to be appropriate in spite of false suspicions engendered, since the system reactivity is preserved.

On the other hand, when the receiver is a PDA (figures 9 and 11), the distribution curves show that a timeout value equal to 200 ms is not adapted because it generates too many false suspicions.

Thus, this experiment points out the importance of good parameter setting. According to the kind of devices, a same parameter configuration does not imply a same quality of information:

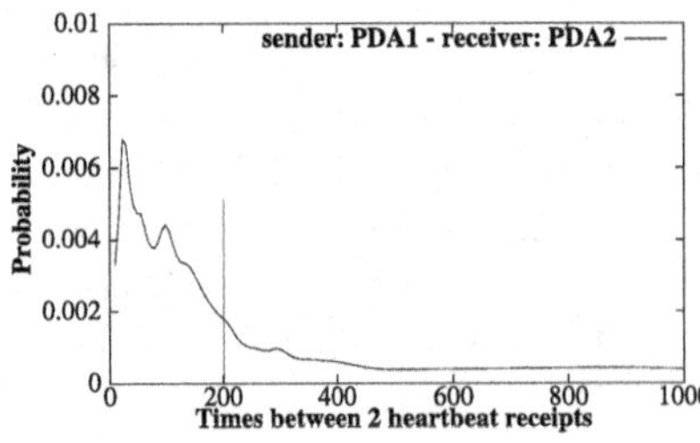

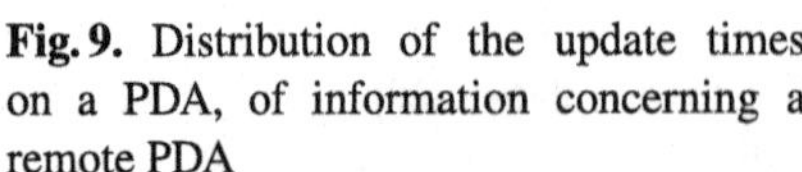

Fig. 9. Distribution of the update times on a PDA, of information concerning a remote PDA

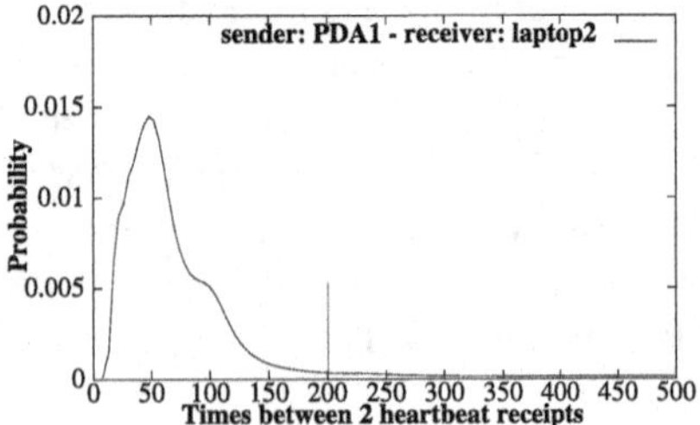

Fig. 10. Distribution of the update times on a laptop concerning information of a remote PDA

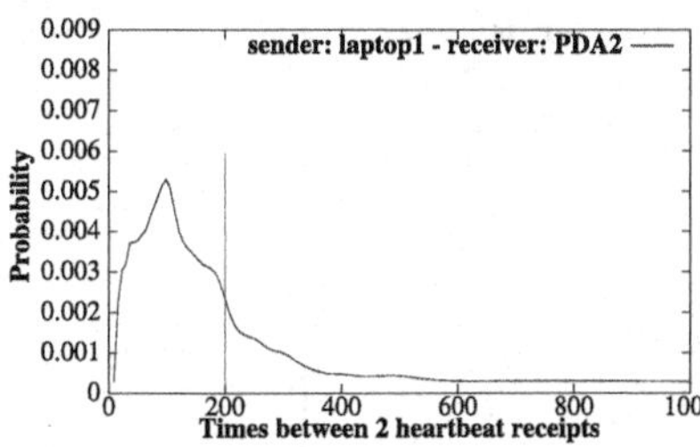

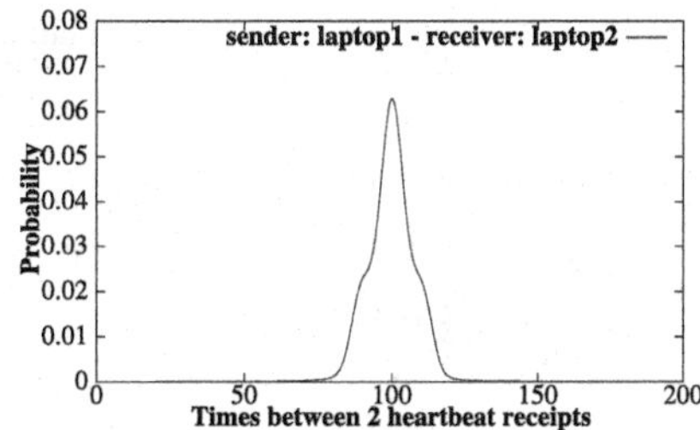

Fig. 11. Distribution of the update times, on a PDA of information concerning a remote laptop

Fig. 12. Distribution of the update times, on a laptop concerning information of a remote laptop

- A laptop will not wrongly suspect another laptop (figure 12)
- A PDA often stands a good chance of suspecting a laptop which is present in the system (figure 11)

4.2 An "Ideal Setting" Experimentation

Experimental Design: The high loss rate observed in the previous experiment denotes that the heartbeat emission frequency is not adequate and it disrupts the system network. Then, the goal of this next experimentation is to obtain a sample of measures which will be used as a reference for the models. The parameters may be adjusted so that the network works correctly, which means there is no voluntary stress or overload.

In this experiment, the system was composed with 6 devices: 3 PDAs (ipaq linux 200 Mhz), 2 laptops (linux 800 Mhz) and 1 laptop device which is used as a network sensor (linux 800 Mhz). The sensor role is to capture network traffic and record all heartbeat packets. This sensor will allow us to get an exterior view of the system behavior during the experimentation. Parameters setting:

- Heartbeat emission period time: 500 ms
- Timeout : none
- Experimental duration: around 15 minutes

Losses: With this parameter setting, the heartbeat mechanism do not overload the system studied. Essentially due to external disturbances in wireless environment, heartbeat message losses are then limited (approximately 2 out of 1000 messages).

Heartbeat Reception Analysis: Figure 13 represents the distribution of elapsed time between two receipts of messages from the same device. Note that the distributions are slightly different according to the type of emitter/receiver devices.

If the timeout value is fixed at $2 * (heartbeat\ period\ time)$, then the wrong suspicion rate is of the order of 10^{-3} when the receiver devices are laptops, and of 10^{-2} when receivers are PDAs.

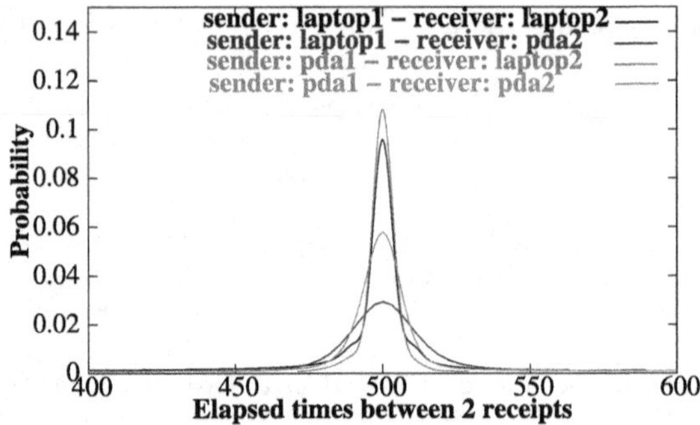

Fig. 13. Distributions of the update times

4.3 Experimentation in a Disrupted Environment

Experimental Design: For this experiment, the platform configuration is like the previous one. However, contrary to the previous experiment, here we introduced a voluntary disruption. To do this, a laptop is used to generate a data transfer (ping with 4 KB/20ms packets) to an external device during the experiment.

Losses: To compare with the previous experiment, the loss rate is more important in this case (around 15% of the messages are lost). Whereas the loss rate is between approximatively 6% and 9% for all other devices, it is approximatively 44% for the device which generate the network overload.

Heartbeat Reception Analysis: As in the previous section, figure 14 illustrates the elapsed time between two heartbeat messages from a same remote device received by each device.

In this context, it is possible to get durations between two successive receipts which could be more than six times the average of heartbeat emission delays. As we can see

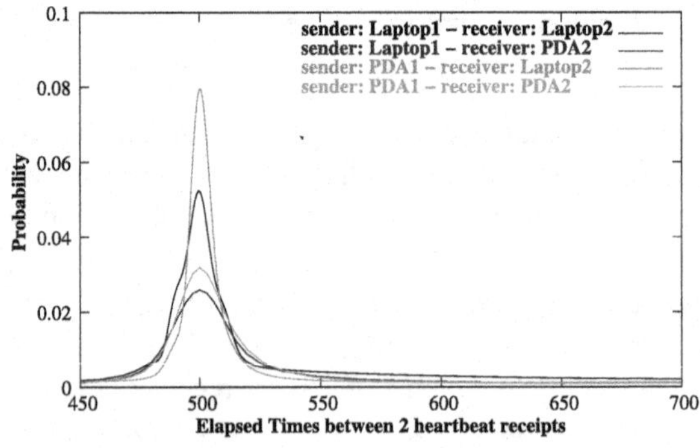

Fig. 14. Distributions of the update times

in figure 14, there are many long receipt durations when the receiver is a PDA. Moreover, some delays between heartbeat receipts are very small. This phenomenon may be explained by the fact that after a long waiting time (before receiving the next heartbeat message), because of the heartbeat messages are regularly sent, several messages could arrive closely together.

Thus, it seems that a correlation exists between successive waiting times of two heartbeat receipts and should be used in further modelling.

5 Conclusion

Tuning failure detectors is of great importance for the efficient control of distributed systems. However, the tradeoff between the quality of information and the reactivity of failure detectors should be established clearly. In this paper we demonstrated that stochastic models, taking into account the architecture, can be useful for setting specific time-out delays.

This study should now be extended to a finer analysis of correlation. Auto-regressive approaches could follow the evolution of the network, especially since network delays depend on the load on the network. Another approach could be a finer description of the spatial organization of the network. Distances between devices could affect the reliability of communications. In this case, stochastic geometry techniques could be efficiently used to model the knowledge an entity could built of the whole system.

References

1. F. Baccelli and P. Brémaud. *Elements of Queuing Theory*. Springer-Verlag, 1994.
2. Chandra, T. and Toueg, S. Unreliable Failure Detectors for Reliable Distributed Systems. *Journal of the ACM*, 43(2):225–267, March 1996.
3. Chen, W. and Toueg, S. and Aguilera, M. On the Quality of Service of Failure Detectors. In *International Conference on Dependable Systems and Networks (DSN 2000)*, New York, 2000. IEEE Computer Society Press.
4. Coccoli, A. and Urbán, P. and Bondavalli, A. and Schiper, A. Performance Analysis of a Consensus Algorithm Combining Stochastic Activity Networks and Measurements. In *Proc. Int'l Conf. on Dependable Systems and Networks (DSN)*, pages 551–560, Washington, DC, USA, June 2002.
5. Durand, Y. and Perret, S. and Vincent, J-M. and Marchand, C. and Ottogalli, F-G. and Olive, V. and Martin, S. and Dumant, B. and Chambon, S. SIDRAH: A software infrastructure for a resilient community of wireless devices. In *smart Objects conference*, pages 134–137, 2003.
6. Fischer, M. and Lynch, N. and Paterson, M. Impossibility of Distributed Consensus with One Faulty. *Journal of the ACM*, 32(2):374–382, 1985.
7. Fortier, P. and Michel, H. *Computer Systems Performance Evaluation and Prediction*. Digital Press, 2003.
8. Haverkort, B. *Performance of Computer Communication Systems*. John Wiley & Sons, 1998.
9. Hurfin, M. and Raynal, M. A Simple and Fast Asynchronous Consensus Protocol Based on a Weak Failure Detector. *Distributed Computing*, 12(4):209–223, 1999.
10. L. Kleinrock. *Queuing systems : theory*, volume 1. J. Wiley & Sons, 1975.
11. C. Marchand. *Mise au point d'algorithmes répartis dans un environnement fortement variable, et expérimentation dans le contexte des pico-réseaux*. PhD thesis, Institut National Polytechnique de Grenoble, 2004.

12. Nelson, R. *Probability, Stochastic Processes, and Queueing Theory: The Mathematics of Computer Performance Modeling*. Springer-Verlag, 1995.
13. Sergent, N. and Défago, X. and Schiper, A. Impact of a Failure Detection Mechanism on the Performance of Consensus. In *Proc. IEEE Pacific Rim Symp. on Dependable Computing (PRDC)*, Seoul, Korea, December 2001.
14. Wolff, R. *Stochastic Modeling and the Theory of Queues*. Prentice-Hall International Editions, 1989.

Hypergraph Partitioning for Faster Parallel PageRank Computation

Jeremy T. Bradley, Douglas V. de Jager,
William J. Knottenbelt, and Aleksandar Trifunović

Department of Computing, Imperial College London,
180 Queen's Gate, London SW7 2BZ, United Kingdom
{jb, dvd03, wjk, at701}@doc.ic.ac.uk

Abstract. The PageRank algorithm is used by search engines such as Google to order web pages. It uses an iterative numerical method to compute the maximal eigenvector of a transition matrix derived from the web's hyperlink structure and a user-centred model of web-surfing behaviour. As the web has expanded and as demand for user-tailored web page ordering metrics has grown, scalable parallel computation of PageRank has become a focus of considerable research effort.

In this paper, we seek a scalable problem decomposition for parallel PageRank computation, through the use of state-of-the-art hypergraph-based partitioning schemes. These have not been previously applied in this context. We consider both one and two-dimensional hypergraph decomposition models. Exploiting the recent availability of the Par*k*way 2.1 parallel hypergraph partitioner, we present empirical results on a gigabit PC cluster for three publicly available web graphs. Our results show that hypergraph-based partitioning substantially reduces communication volume over conventional partitioning schemes (by up to three orders of magnitude), while still maintaining computational load balance. They also show a halving of the per-iteration runtime cost when compared to the most effective alternative approach used to date.

1 Introduction

The PageRank metric is a widely-used hyperlink-based estimate of the relative importance of web pages [1]. The standard algorithm for determining PageRank uses power method iterations that converge to the maximal eigenvector of a transition matrix. This matrix is derived from a web graph that reflects the hyperlink structure of the web and a user-centred model of web-surfing behaviour.

The sheer size and high growth rate of the web necessitates a scalable parallel/distributed approach to PageRank computation. In turn, the scalability of such an approach demands detailed scrutiny of computation and communication overheads induced by problem decomposition over available processors. A poor decomposition results in excessive communication overhead and/or a poor computational load balance with correspondingly poor run times.

In addition to size considerations, web search engines are recognising the need to tailor search results to different classes of users (or individual users),

M. Bravetti et al. (Eds.): EPEW 2005 and WS-FM 2005, LNCS 3670, pp. 155–171, 2005.

and other contextual information [2]. This is achieved in practice by performing distinct PageRank computations (using distinct personalisation vectors) for each class of user or search context. Since these repeated calculations have the same structure (in terms of matrix sparsity pattern), it is often worthwhile investing considerable effort in finding a high-quality decomposition that can be reused for every PageRank calculation.

A promising state-of-the-art approach for producing high-quality decompositions (that has been used in many contexts, ranging from VLSI circuit layout to distributed database design), is hypergraph partitioning [3,4,5]. Hypergraphs are extensions of graph data structures, in which (hyper)edges connect arbitrary sets of vertices. Like graphs, hypergraphs can represent the structure of many sparse, irregular problems, and may be partitioned such that a cut metric is minimised subject to a load balancing constraint. However, hypergraph cut metrics provide a more expressive and accurate model than their graph counterparts. For example, in the decomposition of a sparse matrix for parallel matrix–vector multiplication, hypergraph models quantify communication volume exactly, whereas graph models can only provide an approximation [4].

This paper considers, for the first time, the application of hypergraph-based decomposition techniques to the parallel PageRank computation problem. We show how this problem can be mapped onto a hypergraph partitioning problem, for both one- and two-dimensional decompositions. The partitioning of hypergraphs of large scale has only recently become a practical proposition with the development of parallel hypergraph partitioning tools such as Par*k*way [6] and the forthcoming Zoltan implementation [7]. Exploiting the Par*k*way tool as part of a parallel PageRank computation pipeline, we present experimental results using a gigabit PC cluster on three public-domain web graphs, ranging in size from a university-domain to a national-level crawl. The results show a substantial reduction in per-iteration communication volume, yielding a runtime reduction of up to 70% over the most effective current alternative.

The remainder of this paper is organised as follows. Section 2 presents technical details of the PageRank algorithm. Section 3 describes the application of hypergraph partitioning to parallel PageRank computation. Section 4 discusses our results. Finally, Section 5 concludes and presents ideas for future work.

2 PageRank Algorithm

The PageRank computation for ranking hypertext-linked web pages was originally outlined by Page and Brin [1]. Later Kamvar *et al.* [8] presented a more rigorous formulation of PageRank and its computation. In fact, the latter description differs from the original; however, apart from the respective treatment of so-called *cul de sac* pages (web pages with no out-links, sometimes called dead-end pages), the difference is largely superficial [9]. A good discussion of the issues involved along with analysis of other variations in the PageRank algorithm can be found in Langville *et al.* [10]. We shall concern ourselves here with the Kamvar *et al.* formulation.

Two intuitive explanations are offered for PageRank [8]. The first presents PageRank as an analogue of citation theory: that is, an out-link from a web page w to a web page w' is an indication that w' may be "important" to the author of w. Many such links into w', especially from pages that are themselves "important", should raise the importance of w' relative to other web pages. More specifically, the importance that is propagated from w to w' should be proportional to the importance of w and inversely proportional to the number of out-links from w. This account of PageRank is still incomplete as it does not take into account any form of user *personalisation*, or how to deal with *cul de sac* pages.

The second conceptual model of PageRank is called the *random surfer* model. Consider a surfer who starts at a web page and picks one of the links on that page at random. On loading the next page, this process is repeated. If a *cul de sac* page is encountered, then the surfer chooses to visit a random page. During normal browsing, the user may also decide, with a fixed probability, not to choose a link from the current page, but instead to jump at random to another page. In the latter case, to support both unbiased and personalised surfing behaviour, the model allows for the specification of a probability distribution of target pages.

The PageRank of a page is considered to be the (steady-state) probability that the surfer is visiting a particular page after a large number of click-throughs. Calculating the steady-state probability vector corresponds to finding a maximal eigenvalue of the modified web-graph transition matrix. As shown in Section 2 below, this can be done via an iterative numerical method based on sparse matrix–vector multiply operations.

Random Surfer Model. In the random surfer model, the web is represented by a graph $G = (V, E)$, with web pages as the vertices, V, and the links between web pages as the edges, E. If a link exists from page u to page v then $(u \rightarrow v) \in E$.

To represent the following of hyperlinks, we construct a transition matrix $\mathbf{P}$ from the web graph, setting:

$$p_{ij} = \begin{cases} \frac{1}{\deg(u_i)} & : \text{if } (u_i \rightarrow u_j) \in E \\ 0 & : \text{otherwise} \end{cases}$$

where $\deg(u)$ is the out-degree of vertex u, i.e. the number of outbound links from page u. From this definition, we see that if a page has no out-links, then this corresponds to a zero row in the matrix $\mathbf{P}$.

To represent the surfer's jumping from *cul de sac* pages, we construct a second matrix $\mathbf{D} = \mathbf{d}\mathbf{p}^T$, where $\mathbf{d}$ and $\mathbf{p}$ are both column vectors and:

$$d_i = \begin{cases} 1 : \text{if } \deg(u_i) = 0 \\ 0 : \text{otherwise} \end{cases}$$

and $\mathbf{p}$ is the personalisation vector representing the probability distribution of destination pages when a random jump is made. Typically, this distribution is taken to be uniform, i.e. $p_i = 1/n$ for an n-page graph $(1 \leq i \leq n)$. However, it need not be as many distinct personalisation vectors may be used to represent different classes of user with different web browsing patterns. This flexibility comes at a cost, though, as each distinct personalisation vector requires an additional PageRank calculation.

Putting together the surfer's following of hyperlinks and his/her random jumping from *cul de sac* pages yields the stochastic matrix $\mathbf{P}' = \mathbf{P} + \mathbf{D}$, where $\mathbf{P}'$ is a transition matrix of a discrete-time Markov chain (DTMC).

To represent the surfer's decision not to follow any of the current page links, but to instead jump to a random web page, we construct a *teleportation* matrix $\mathbf{E}$, where $e_{ij} = p_j$ for all i, i.e. this random jump is also dictated by the personalisation vector.

Incorporating this matrix into the model gives:

$$\mathbf{A} = c\mathbf{P}' + (1 - c)\mathbf{E} \tag{1}$$

where $0 < c < 1$, and c represents the probability that the user chooses to follow one of the links on the current page, i.e. there is a probability of $(1 - c)$ that the surfer randomly jumps to another page instead of following links on the current page.

This definition of $\mathbf{A}$ avoids two potential problems. The first is that $\mathbf{P}'$, although a valid DTMC transition matrix, is not necessarily irreducible (i.e. it might have more than one strongly connected subset of states) and aperiodic. Taken together, these are a sufficient condition for the existence of a unique steady-state distribution. Now, provided $p_i > 0$ for all $1 \leq i \leq n$, irreducibility and aperiodicity are trivially guaranteed.

The second problem relates to the rate of convergence of power method iterations used to compute the steady-state distribution. This rate depends on the reciprocal of the modulus of the subdominant eigenvalue (λ_2). For a general $\mathbf{P}'$, $|\lambda_2|$ may be very close to 1, resulting in a very poor rate of convergence. However, it has been shown in [11] that in the case of matrix $\mathbf{A}$, $|\lambda_2| \leq c$, thus guaranteeing a good rate of convergence for the widely taken value of $c = 0.85$.

Given the matrix $\mathbf{A}$, we can now define the unique PageRank vector, π, to be the steady-state vector or the maximal eigenvector that satisfies:

$$\pi\mathbf{A} = \pi \tag{2}$$

Power Method Solution. Having constructed $\mathbf{A}$ we might naïvely attempt to find the PageRank vector of Eq. (2) by using a direct power method approach:

$$\mathbf{x}^{(k+1)} = \mathbf{x}^{(k)}\mathbf{A} \tag{3}$$

where $\mathbf{x}^{(k)}$ is the kth iterate towards the PageRank vector, π. However looking at the current size of the web and its rate of growth since 1997 (currently 8 billion indexed pages [12]), it is clear that this is not a practical approach for realistic web graphs. The reason for this is that $\mathbf{A}$ is a (completely) dense matrix. Accordingly, the PageRank algorithm, as cited in for instance Kamvar *et al.* [13], reduces Eq. (3) to a series of sparse vector–matrix operations on the original $\mathbf{P}$ matrix.

1. $\mathbf{x}^{(0)} := \mathbf{p}^T$
2. $\mathbf{y} := c\mathbf{x}^{(k)}\mathbf{P}$
3. $\omega := \|\mathbf{x}^{(k)}\|_1 - \|\mathbf{y}\|_1$
4. $\mathbf{x}^{(k+1)} := \mathbf{y} + \omega\mathbf{p}^T$
5. Repeat from 2. until $\|\mathbf{x}^{(k+1)} - \mathbf{x}^{(k)}\|_1 < \epsilon$

Fig. 1. Pseudocode description of the PageRank algorithm

In particular, transforming Eq. (3) gives:

$$\begin{aligned}\mathbf{x}^{(k+1)} &= \mathbf{x}^{(k)}\mathbf{A} \\ &= c\mathbf{x}^{(k)}\mathbf{P}' + (1-c)\mathbf{x}^{(k)}\mathbf{E} \\ &= c\mathbf{x}^{(k)}\mathbf{P} + c\mathbf{x}^{(k)}\mathbf{D} + (1-c)\mathbf{x}^{(k)}(\mathbf{1}\mathbf{p}^T)\end{aligned} \tag{4}$$

Now $\mathbf{x}^{(k)}\mathbf{D} = (\|\mathbf{x}^{(k)}\|_1 - \|\mathbf{x}^{(k)}\mathbf{P}\|_1)\mathbf{p}^T$, where $\|\mathbf{a}\|_1 = \sum_i |a_i|$ is the 1-norm of $\mathbf{a}$ and further $\|\mathbf{a}\|_1 = \mathbf{1}^T\mathbf{a}$ if $a_i \geq 0$ for all i. It can be shown inductively that $\|\mathbf{x}^{(k)}\|_1 = 1$ for all k, so:

$$\begin{aligned}\mathbf{x}^{(k+1)} &= c\mathbf{x}^{(k)}\mathbf{P} + c(1 - \|\mathbf{x}^{(k)}\mathbf{P}\|_1)\mathbf{p}^T + (1-c)(\mathbf{x}^{(k)}\mathbf{1})\mathbf{p}^T \\ &= c\mathbf{x}^{(k)}\mathbf{P} + (1 - c\|\mathbf{x}^{(k)}\mathbf{P}\|_1)\mathbf{p}^T\end{aligned} \tag{5}$$

This leads to the algorithm shown in Fig. 1. When distributing this algorithm, it is important to distribute the sparse matrix–vector calculation of $\mathbf{x}^{(k)}\mathbf{P}$ in such a way so as to balance computational load as evenly as possible across the processors and minimise communication overhead between processors. This latter optimisation is where we introduce hypergraph partitioning for $\mathbf{P}$.

Later, in Section 4, we refine the coarse notion of communication overhead to distinguish between number of messages sent, total communication volume (in terms of number of floating point elements sent), as well as maximum number of messages sent by a processor.

3 Parallel PageRank Computation

We consider the parallel formulation of the PageRank algorithm from Section 2 for which the kernel operation is parallel sparse matrix–vector multiplication. Note that, although our discussion is presented in the context of power method solution, there is nothing to prevent the application of our technique to other iterative linear system solvers with a sparse matrix–vector multiplication kernel, such as the Krylov subspace methods proposed in [14]. Furthermore, our approach does not preclude the application of power method acceleration techniques, for example those proposed in [8].

Efficient Parallel Sparse Matrix–Vector Multiplication. Let $\mathbf{Ax} = \mathbf{b}$ be the sparse matrix–vector product to be computed in parallel on p distributed processors that are connected by a network. The general form of a parallel algorithm for sparse matrix–vector multiplication with an arbitrary non-overlapping distribution of the matrix and the vectors across the processors is given in [5]:

1. Each processor sends its components x_j to those processors that possess a non-zero a_{ij} in column j.
2. Each processor computes the products $a_{ij}x_j$ for its non-zeros a_{ij} and adds the results for the same row index i. This yields a set of contributions b_{is}, where s is the processor identifier $0 \leq s < p$.
3. Each processor sends its non-zero contributions b_{is} to the processor that is assigned vector element b_i.
4. Each processor adds the contributions received for its components b_i, giving $b_i = \sum_{s=0}^{p-1} b_{is}$.

Efficient parallel sparse matrix–vector multiplication requires intelligent *a priori* partitioning of the sparse matrix non-zeros across the processors. This ensures that interprocessor communication during stages 1 and 3 is minimised and computational load balance is achieved across the processors. We note that the computational requirement of step 2 dominates that of step 4. Henceforth, we assume that the computational load of the entire algorithm is represented by step 2.

Recently, a number of hypergraph-based models for parallel sparse matrix–vector multiplication that correctly model total communication volume and per-processor computational load have been proposed [4,15,16,5]. These have addressed the shortcomings implicit in traditional graph models [17]. In [4], a hypergraph-based model for 1-dimensional decomposition of the sparse matrix is proposed. A 1-dimensional decomposition implies that processors either store entire rows or entire columns of the matrix. Note that, in the case of row-wise decomposition, this has the effect of making the communication step 3 in the parallel sparse matrix–vector multiplication pipeline redundant; in the case of column-wise decomposition, step 1 is redundant. The hypergraph-based models in [15,16,5] are 2-dimensional, which means to say that they model a general distribution of matrix non-zeros to processors (not necessarily assigning entire rows or columns of the matrix to processors). Although here both steps 1 and 3 may incur communication overhead, the overall communication volume should be at least as low as that of the 1-dimensional decomposition (at least for optimal partitions, since the 1-dimensional decomposition is a special case of the 2-dimensional decomposition).

In previous work on efficient parallel PageRank implementation, only naïve 1-dimensional matrix decompositions have been considered. In [14], the authors reject traditional graph partitioning models as a plausible approach, on account of the apparent power-law distribution of the number of non-zeros in the rows of web graph transition matrices. Instead, they use a relatively simple load balancing scheme that assigns consecutive rows of the matrix to each processor. Our work here demonstrates that this power-law distribution does not appear to be a significant obstacle in the context of a hypergraph-based approach.

In this paper, we consider both 1-dimensional decomposition, based on the hypergraph model presented in [4], and 2-dimensional decomposition, based on the models presented in [15,5]. Since the output vector **b** of the parallel sparse matrix–vector product is reused as the input vector **x** in the subsequent iteration, we note that the processor that is assigned the vector component b_i should also be assigned the vector component x_i (resulting in a *symmetric* decomposition of the vector elements).

Description of the Hypergraph Models. A hypergraph is a set system $(V, \mathcal{E})$ on a set V, here denoted $H(V, \mathcal{E})$, such that $\mathcal{E} \subset \mathcal{P}(V)$, where $\mathcal{P}(V)$ is the power set of V. The elements of the set V are called the *vertices* of the hypergraph and $\mathcal{E}$ the set of *hyperedges*, where each hyperedge $e \in \mathcal{E}$ is a subset of the set V. When $\mathcal{E} \subset V^{(2)}$, each hyperedge has cardinality two and the resulting set system is known as a *graph*. A hypergraph $H(V, \mathcal{E})$ is said to be hyperedge-weighted if each hyperedge $e \in \mathcal{E}$ has an associated integer weight. Correspondingly, in a vertex-weighted hypergraph $H(V, \mathcal{E})$, each vertex $v \in V$ has an integer weight.

Given a hypergraph $H(V, \mathcal{E})$, with $V = \{v_1, \ldots, v_n\}$ and $\mathcal{E} = \{e_1, \ldots, e_n\}$, the corresponding *incidence matrix* $\mathbf{A} = (a_{ij})$ is the $n \times n$ matrix with entries

$$a_{ij} = \begin{cases} 1 \text{ if } v_i \in e_j \\ 0 \text{ otherwise} \end{cases} \tag{6}$$

A k-way *partition* Π $(k > 1)$ of the set V is a finite collection $\Pi = \{P_1, \ldots, P_k\}$, of subsets of V (or parts), such that $P_i \cap P_j = \emptyset$ for all $1 \leq i < j \leq k$ and $\bigcup_{i=1}^{k} P_i = V$. A hyperedge is said to be cut by a partition if it spans (i.e. has a vertex in) at least two parts of a partition. The goal of the hypergraph partitioning problem is to find a k-way partition $\Pi = \{P_1, \ldots, P_k\}$, with corresponding part weights W_i, $1 \leq i \leq k$, such that an objective function $f_o : (\Pi, \mathcal{E}) \rightarrow \mathbb{Z}$ is optimised, while a balance constraint over the part weights is maintained. That is, for some ϵ $(0 < \epsilon \ll 1)$:

$$W_i < (1 + \epsilon) W_{avg} \tag{7}$$

for all $1 \leq i \leq k$. The part weights W_i are computed as the sum of the constituent vertex weights. Here we consider the objective function known as the $k-1$ metric, shown in Eq. (8), where λ_i represents the number of parts spanned by hyperedge e_i and $w(e_i)$ is the weight of hyperedge e_i.

$$f_o(\Pi, \mathcal{E}) = \sum_{i=1}^{n} (\lambda_i - 1) w(e_i) \tag{8}$$

As the hypergraph partitioning problem is NP-hard [18], in practice a good sub-optimal partition is sought in low-order polynomial time using heuristic multilevel algorithms.

1-Dimensional Sparse Matrix Decomposition. Without loss of generality, we describe the hypergraph model for 1-dimensional row-wise sparse matrix decomposition, i.e. where all non-zeros in a row of the matrix are allocated to the same processor. A similar column-wise model follows from considering the allocation of all non-zeros in a column of the matrix to the same processor. These 1-dimensional hypergraph-based models were first proposed in [4].

The hypergraph model $H(V, \mathcal{E})$ for the decomposition of a sparse matrix $\mathbf{A}$ is constructed as follows. The rows of the matrix $\mathbf{A}$ form the set of vertices V in the hypergraph $H(V, \mathcal{E})$ and the columns form the set of hyperedges $\mathcal{E}$. That is, if $a_{ij} \neq 0$, then hyperedge $e_j \in \mathcal{E}$, defined by column j of the matrix $\mathbf{A}$, contains vertex $v_i \in V$. The weight of vertex $v_i \in V$ is given by the number of non-zero elements in row i of the matrix $\mathbf{A}$, representing the computational load induced by assigning row i to a processor. The weights of each hyperedge are set to unity.

The allocation of the rows of the matrix $\mathbf{A}$ to p processors for parallel sparse matrix–vector multiplication corresponds to a p-way partition Π of the above hypergraph $H(V, \mathcal{E})$. Ignoring the negligible impact of stage 4, as mentioned earlier, the computational load on each processor i is given by the number of scalar multiplications performed on that processor during stage 2 of the general parallel sparse matrix–vector multiplication pipeline. This quantity is given by the number of non-zeros of the matrix $\mathbf{A}$ allocated to that processor, which is in turn given by the weight of part P_i.

The vector elements x_i and b_i are allocated to the processor that is allocated row i of the matrix $\mathbf{A}$. There remains one further condition that the hypergraph model must satisfy to ensure that the k-1 metric on partition Π exactly represents the total communication volume incurred during a single parallel sparse matrix–vector multiplication (in this case stage 1 only). We require that for all $1 \leq i \leq n$, $v_i \in e_i$ holds. If this is not the case for some $1 \leq i' \leq n$, then we add $v_{i'}$ to hyperedge $e_{i'}$. The weight of $v_{i'}$ is not modified.

Thus, finding a partition that minimises the k-1 metric over the hypergraph while maintaining the balance constraint in Eq. (7) directly corresponds to minimising communication volume during parallel sparse matrix–vector multiplication while maintaining a computational load balance.

2-Dimensional Sparse Matrix Decomposition. The 2-dimensional sparse matrix decomposition takes a more general approach, no longer imposing the restriction of allocating entire rows (or columns) of the matrix $\mathbf{A}$ to the same processor, as in 1-dimensional decomposition. Instead, a general distribution of matrix non-zeros to processors is considered. This may introduce additional communication operations during stage 3 in the general parallel sparse matrix–vector multiplication pipeline, but the aim is to reduce the overall communication volume. Here we describe the hypergraph model $H(V, \mathcal{E})$ introduced in [15,5]. Each non-zero $a_{ij} \neq 0$ is modelled by a vertex $v \in V$ so that a p-way partition Π of the hypergraph $H(V, \mathcal{E})$ will correspond to an assignment of matrix non-zeros across p processors.

In order to define the hyperedges of the hypergraph model, consider the cause of communication between processors in stages 1 and 3 of the parallel sparse matrix–vector multiplication pipeline. In stage 1, the processor with non-zero a_{ij} requires vector element x_j for computation during stage 2. This results in a communication of x_j to the processor assigned a_{ij} if x_j is assigned to a different processor to a_{ij}. The dependence between non-zeros in column j of matrix $\mathbf{A}$ and vector element x_j can be modelled by a hyperedge, whose constituent vertices are the non-zeros of column j of the matrix $\mathbf{A}$. So that the communication volume associated with communicating vector element x_j is given by $\lambda_j - 1$, where λ_j denotes the number of parts spanned by the column j hyperedge, we require that the column j hyperedge contains the vertex corresponding to non-zero a_{jj}. If a_{jj} is zero in the matrix $\mathbf{A}$, we can add a "dummy" vertex with zero weight corresponding to a_{jj}. The fact that this vertex has weight zero means that its allocation to a processor will have no bearing on the processor's computational load, while the exact communication volume during stage 1 is modelled correctly.

In stage 3, the processor assigned vector element b_i requires the value of the inner product of row i of the matrix $\mathbf{A}$ with the vector $\mathbf{x}$. Thus, a communication between processors is induced if matrix non-zero a_{ij} is assigned to a different processor from vector entry b_i. The dependence between non-zeros in row i of matrix $\mathbf{A}$ and vector element b_i can be modelled by a hyperedge, whose constituent vertices are the non-zeros of row i of the matrix $\mathbf{A}$. This is analogous to modelling the communication of stage 1 with column hyperedges and likewise, "dummy" vertices corresponding to a_{ii} are added to row hyperedge i if the value of a_{ii} in matrix $\mathbf{A}$ is zero.

The hypergraph model $H(V, \mathcal{E})$ is then partitioned into p parts such that the k-1 metric is minimised, subject to the balance constraint of Eq. (7) (thus maintaining computational load balance during stage 2). In our implementation, this is done using a parallel multilevel partitioning algorithm [19,6].

Note that, except for restricting vector elements x_i and b_i to the same processor, we have not explicitly allocated vector entries to processors. The overall communication volume during the parallel sparse matrix–vector multiplication will be correctly modelled by the 2-dimensional hypergraph model, provided that we allocate the vector elements to processors in the following fashion. For the vector element with index i:

1. If both the row i hyperedge and the column i hyperedge are not cut, then assign vector elements x_i and b_i to the processor assigned vertices from row i and column i hyperedges.
2. If the row i hyperedge is cut and the column i hyperedge is not cut, then assign vector elements x_i and b_i to the processor assigned vertices from column i hyperedge.
3. If the row i hyperedge is not cut and the column i hyperedge is cut, then assign vector elements x_i and b_i to the processor assigned vertices from row i hyperedge.
4. If both the row i hyperedge and the column i hyperedge are cut, then let R_i denote the set of processors that contain row i hyperedge elements and let C_i denote the set of processors that contain column i hyperedge elements. Since either $a_{ii} \neq 0$ or there exists a "dummy" vertex in the row i and column i hyperedges corresponding to a_{ii}, the set $T_i = R_i \cap C_i$ is non-empty and vector elements x_i and b_i may be assigned to any of the processors in T_i.

With the additional freedom in the assignment of vector elements to processors given by case 4 above, it may be possible to further decrease the *maximum* number of messages sent or received by an individual processor while keeping the overall communication volume constant. In our implementation of stage 4 above, the vector elements x_i and b_i are allocated to the first part in T_i encountered during traversal of matrix $\mathbf{A}$.

4 Experimental Results

In this section, we apply four decomposition strategies to calculate PageRanks for three publicly available web graphs. Each web graph was generated from a crawl of a particular domain or combination of domains; we represent them by a sparse matrix $\mathbf{A}$ with non-zero a_{ij} whenever there exists a link from page i to page j. The Stanford and Stanford_Berkeley web graphs were obtained from the University of Florida Sparse Matrix Collection [20] and represent lexically ordered crawls of the Stanford and combined Stanford/Berkeley domains respectively. The India-2004 web graph represents a breadth-first crawl of the `.in` domain conducted in 2004, obtained from the UbiCrawler public data set [21]. The main characteristics of the corresponding matrices are given in Table 1.

The two hypergraph decomposition methods of Section 3 were tested against two naïve load balancing methods. In the cyclic row-striping matrix decomposition, the non-zeros of the matrix $\mathbf{A}$ in row with index i are assigned to the processor $i \bmod p$. Vector elements x_i and b_i are also allocated to processor $i \bmod p$. This ensures that each processor is allocated the same number (± 1) of rows of matrix $\mathbf{A}$ and vector elements of $\mathbf{x}$ and $\mathbf{b}$. However, this scheme does not take into account the distribution of the non-zeros within the rows.

The load balancing scheme presented in [14], hereafter referred to as the GleZhu scheme, attempts to balance the number of non-zeros across the processors, while assigning consecutive rows of the matrix $\mathbf{A}$ to each processor. A threshold value $\tau_p = (w_n n + w_\eta \eta)/p$ is computed, where n is the number of rows and η the number of non–zeros in the matrix. The parameters w_n and w_η were both set to unity in [14]. Starting with row index zero and $i = 0$, the load–balancing algorithm then assigns consecutive rows of matrix $\mathbf{A}$ and consecutive elements of vectors $\mathbf{x}$ and $\mathbf{b}$ to each processor i, maintaining the value of $\tau_i = w_n n_i + w_\eta \eta_i$, where n_i is the number of rows and η_i the number of non–zeros assigned thus far to processor i. When τ_i exceeds τ_p, the algorithm begins to assign subsequent rows to processor $i + 1$.

Table 1. Characteristics of the test hypergraphs

WebGraph	#rows	#columns	#non-zeros
Stanford	281 903	281 903	2 594 228
Stanford_Berkeley	683 446	683 446	8 262 087
India-2004	1 382 908	1 382 908	16 917 053

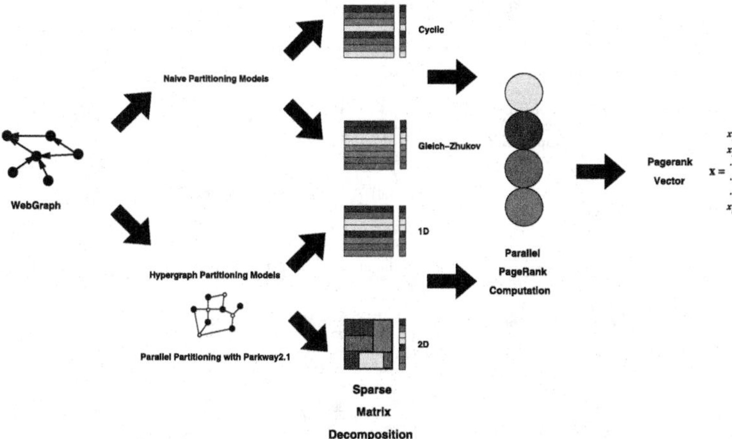

Fig. 2. Parallel PageRank Calculation Pipeline

Experimental Setup. Our parallel PageRank computation pipeline is shown in Fig. 2. Taking the web graph matrix **A** as input, a decomposition of this matrix across p processors is performed using either one of the hypergraph partitioning-based models (i.e. 1D or 2D) or one of the load balancing row-wise decomposition methods (i.e. cyclic or GleZhu).

The hypergraph partitioning-based schemes compute a p-way partition of the hypergraph representation of the sparse web matrix using the parallel hypergraph partitioning tool Par*k*way2.1 [6]. In our experiments, we have used a 5% balance constraint for hypergraph partitioning, meaning that the weight of each part in the partition of the hypergraph must not exceed the average part weight by more than 5% ($\epsilon = 0.05$ in Eq. (7)). The computed hypergraph partition is then used to allocate the rows (in the case of 1D partitioning) or the non-zeros (in the case of 2D partitioning) of the web matrix to the processors.

Finally, the algorithm described in Section 2 is used to compute the PageRank vector for the matrix, with all matrix–vector and vector operations performed in parallel. The criterion of convergence for the PageRank calculation was taken to be 10^{-8} and convergence was computed using the L_1 norm.

The architecture used in all the experiments consisted of a Beowulf Linux Cluster with 8 dual processor nodes. Each node has two Intel Pentium 4 3.0GHz processors and 2GB of RAM. The nodes are connected by a gigabit Ethernet network. The algorithms were implemented in C++ using the Message Passing Interface (MPI) standard.

Results. For each matrix decomposition method, we observed the following measures of communication cost during each parallel PageRank iteration: total communication volume (the total volume of all messages sent); number of

Table 2. Stanford Web graph Results

$p = 4$	Cyclic	GleZhu	1D hypergraph	2D hypergraph
decomposition time(s)	Neg.	Neg.	15.2	1 181
#iterations	83	83	85	88
per iteration time(s)	0.2153	0.1681	0.0699	0.0762
$\mathbf{Ax} = \mathbf{b}$ time(s)	0.2028	0.1621	0.0583	0.0657
$\mathbf{Ax} = \mathbf{b}$ comp. time(s)	0.0607	0.0390	0.0551	0.0599
$\mathbf{Ax} = \mathbf{b}$ comm. time(s)	0.1427	0.1237	0.0035	0.0058
#messages	12	12	12	19
max non-zeros per proc.	614 346	583 653	607 030	601 362
max vector elems per proc.	70 476	73 611	90 601	87 253
max per proc. comm. vol.	304 442	267 683	12 344	1 318
total comm. vol.	601 964	530 420	13 849	1 399
$p = 8$	Cyclic	GleZhu	1D hypergraph	2D hypergraph
decomposition time(s)	Neg.	Neg.	13.2	1 061
#iterations	79	79	83	86
per iteration time(s)	0.1854	0.1473	0.0443	0.0465
$\mathbf{Ax} = \mathbf{b}$ time(s)	0.1716	0.1415	0.0318	0.0365
$\mathbf{Ax} = \mathbf{b}$ comp. time(s)	0.0425	0.0169	0.0269	0.0309
$\mathbf{Ax} = \mathbf{b}$ comm. time(s)	0.1299	0.1253	0.0055	0.0056
#messages	56	56	44	64
max non-zeros per proc.	326 891	297 854	303 515	299 503
max vector elems per proc.	35 238	38 962	49 443	55 398
max per proc. comm. vol.	255 053	231 233	31 564	1 660
total comm. vol.	989 071	894 098	34 221	2 285
$p = 16$	Cyclic	GleZhu	1D hypergraph	2D hypergraph
decomposition time(s)	Neg.	Neg.	18.3	543.1
#iterations	75	76	79	81
per iteration time(s)	0.1810	0.1446	0.0515	0.0513
$\mathbf{Ax} = \mathbf{b}$ time(s)	0.1614	0.1377	0.0347	0.0353
$\mathbf{Ax} = \mathbf{b}$ comp. time(s)	0.0532	0.0182	0.0242	0.0277
$\mathbf{Ax} = \mathbf{b}$ comm. time(s)	0.1094	0.1203	0.0116	0.0076
#messages	240	240	147	207
max non-zeros per proc.	192 857	155 898	151 757	151 236
max vector elems per proc.	17 619	21 208	31 215	28 221
max per proc. comm. vol.	186 331	173 525	39 820	2 214
total comm. vol.	1 364 285	1 325 808	74 137	4 307

messages sent; the maximum total communication volume of messages sent and received by a single processor during stage 1, in the case of row-wise decomposition, and the maximum total communication volume of messages sent and received by a single processor during stages 1 and 3, in the case of 2D decomposition.

The purely load balancing matrix decomposition approaches do not attempt to minimise the metrics above. The 1D and 2D hypergraph-based methods aim to minimise the overall communication volume. In row-wise decomposition methods, the number of messages sent during parallel sparse matrix–vector multiplication is at most $p(p-1)$. In the 2D method, the number of messages is at most $2p(p-1)$.

Tables 2, 3 and 4 present results of our experiments on the Stanford, Stanford_Berkeley and india-2004 web graphs, respectively. The following statistics are also recorded, for the combination of different web graph models being run on 4, 8 and 16 processor clusters using the 4 distinct partitioning algorithms: decomposition time (time taken to prepare the partition for each of the different partitioning algorithms); number of iterations (number of iterations to convergence of the distributed PageRank algorithm); per iteration times (average time for a single PageRank iteration); $\mathbf{Ax} = \mathbf{b}$ time (average time to perform a single $\mathbf{Ax} = \mathbf{b}$ iteration); $\mathbf{Ax} = \mathbf{b}$ comp. time (time taken to complete the local computation of an $\mathbf{Ax} = \mathbf{b}$ iteration); $\mathbf{Ax} = \mathbf{b}$ comm. time (time taken to complete the interprocessor communication of an $\mathbf{Ax} = \mathbf{b}$ iteration); Max non-zeros per proc. (maximum number of non-zeros allocated per processor); Max vector elems

Table 3. Stanford Berkeley Web graph results

$p = 4$	Cyclic	GleZhu	1D hypergraph	2D hypergraph
decomposition time(s)	Neg.	Neg.	22.9	5 169
#iterations	84	87	89	89
per iteration time(s)	0.4596	0.0618	0.0353	0.0377
$\mathbf{Ax} = \mathbf{b}$ time(s)	0.4341	0.0527	0.0253	0.0264
$\mathbf{Ax} = \mathbf{b}$ comp. time(s)	0.0632	0.0237	0.0239	0.0244
$\mathbf{Ax} = \mathbf{b}$ comm. time(s)	0.3714	0.0293	0.0018	0.0019
#messages	12	12	12	20
max non-zeros per proc.	1 977 527	1 906 240	1 990 554	1 989 151
max vector elems per proc.	170 862	188 568	204 129	243 758
max per proc. comm. vol.	810 530	112 101	6 432	2 023
total comm. vol.	1 605 286	165 765	6 648	2 081
$p = 8$	Cyclic	GleZhu	1D hypergraph	2D hypergraph
decomposition time(s)	Neg.	Neg.	18.4	3 304
#iterations	80	85	85	84
per iteration time(s)	0.4616	0.0458	0.0285	0.0246
$\mathbf{Ax} = \mathbf{b}$ time(s)	0.4376	0.0395	0.0202	0.0167
$\mathbf{Ax} = \mathbf{b}$ comp. time(s)	0.0774	0.0123	0.0136	0.0130
$\mathbf{Ax} = \mathbf{b}$ comm. time(s)	0.3578	0.0276	0.0071	0.0038
#messages	56	56	42	62
max non-zeros per proc.	1 063 001	961 340	994 257	994 592
max vector elems per proc.	85 431	115 805	131 713	142 253
max per proc. comm. vol.	727 768	129 977	35 117	2 620
total comm. vol.	2 744 682	269 095	45 132	3 479
$p = 16$	Cyclic	GleZhu	1D hypergraph	2D hypergraph
decomposition time(s)	Neg.	Neg.	18.8	1 842
#iterations	76	85	85	83
per iteration time(s)	0.5955	0.0518	0.0351	0.0238
$\mathbf{Ax} = \mathbf{b}$ time(s)	0.5549	0.0443	0.0271	0.0150
$\mathbf{Ax} = \mathbf{b}$ comp. time(s)	0.1435	0.0110	0.0101	0.0102
$\mathbf{Ax} = \mathbf{b}$ comm. time(s)	0.4132	0.0340	0.0169	0.0048
#messages	240	178	129	165
max non-zeros per proc.	627 253	510 616	497 659	497 055
max vector elems per proc.	42 716	73 665	78 873	69 754
max per proc. comm. vol.	548 922	120 589	80 112	3 242
total comm. vol.	4 002 962	478 162	147 590	7 302

per proc. (maximum number of vector elements allocated per processor); Max per proc. comm vol. (maximum communication volume sent and received by a processor); Total comm. vol. (total communication volume of number of floating point elements sent in a single PageRank iteration).

Note that, due to numerical errors (truncation and roundoff), the number of iterations is not constant across the different methods. We observe that the application of hypergraph partitioning attracts a significantly lower overall communication overhead. 2D partitioning is the most effective at reducing overall communication volume, although this does not always translate into a lower PageRank per-iteration time, on account of the higher number of messages sent, and the relatively high message start-up cost on our gigabit PC cluster.

Fig. 3 displays the total per-iteration communication volume for each partitioning algorithm. It shows that the GleZhu technique has a lower communication overhead than the naïve cyclic partitioning, as might be expected. We also see that, when compared to the GleZhu method, hypergraph partitioning reduces communication volume by an order of magnitude for 1D hypergraph partitioning and by 2 orders of magnitude for 2D hypergraph partitioning.

Fig. 4 shows the overall PageRank iteration time for GleZhu, 1D and 2D hypergraph partitions of the Stanford_Berkeley web matrix on the 16-processor cluster. The *computation* label refers to the time taken to compute a single $\mathbf{Ax} = \mathbf{b}$ iteration. The *communication* label represents the time taken in com-

Table 4. India Web graph Results

$p = 4$	Cyclic	GleZhu	1D hypergraph	2D hypergraph
decomposition time(s)	Neg.	Neg.	557.5	13 480
#iterations	81	84	84	85
per iteration time(s)	0.7577	0.1142	0.0762	0.0781
$\mathbf{Ax} = \mathbf{b}$ time(s)	0.7094	0.0972	0.0537	0.0528
$\mathbf{Ax} = \mathbf{b}$ comp. time(s)	0.1243	0.0501	0.0526	0.0506
$\mathbf{Ax} = \mathbf{b}$ comm. time(s)	0.5856	0.0475	0.0015	0.0022
#messages	12	12	11	24
max non-zeros per proc.	4 346 286	4 319 031	4 431 469	4 264 282
max vector elems per proc.	345 727	381 623	501 669	557 602
max per proc. comm. vol.	1 326 626	147 078	2 110	1 901
total comm. vol.	2 646 280	223 467	2 428	3 018
$p = 8$	Cyclic	GleZhu	1D hypergraph	2D hypergraph
decomposition time(s)	Neg.	Neg.	280.9	11 360
#iterations	77	81	83	81
per iteration time(s)	0.8489	0.0756	0.0458	0.0444
$\mathbf{Ax} = \mathbf{b}$ time(s)	0.7985	0.0641	0.0290	0.0292
$\mathbf{Ax} = \mathbf{b}$ comp. time(s)	0.1455	0.0251	0.0276	0.0263
$\mathbf{Ax} = \mathbf{b}$ comm. time(s)	0.6537	0.0395	0.0024	0.0028
#messages	56	56	46	105
max non-zeros per proc.	2 196 083	2 165 349	2 218 547	2 185 533
max vector elems per proc.	172 864	204 069	335 547	309 293
max per proc. comm. vol.	1 214 716	105 491	3 248	2 996
total comm. vol.	4 800 997	266 447	4 758	5 867
$p = 16$	Cyclic	GleZhu	1D hypergraph	2D hypergraph
decomposition time(s)	Neg.	Neg.	157.3	7 857
#iterations	74	81	79	80
per iteration time(s)	0.9548	0.0577	0.0396	0.0405
$\mathbf{Ax} = \mathbf{b}$ time(s)	0.8755	0.0455	0.0229	0.0255
$\mathbf{Ax} = \mathbf{b}$ comp. time(s)	0.2797	0.0207	0.0194	0.0198
$\mathbf{Ax} = \mathbf{b}$ comm. time(s)	0.5987	0.0257	0.0045	0.0055
#messages	240	240	154	306
max non-zeros per proc.	1 124 363	1 126 092	1 110 174	1 091 597
max vector elems per proc.	86 432	122 143	182 236	198 703
max per proc. comm. vol.	928 783	88 210	4 486	3 896
total comm. vol.	7 237 257	313 198	14 433	11 684

munication when performing a single $\mathbf{Ax} = \mathbf{b}$ iteration. The results for the cyclic technique are not shown as they are orders of magnitude larger and our main interest here is in comparing the GleZhu method (as the best currently used alternative) with the hypergraph versions. We see that the overall PageRank iteration time is dictated by the communication overhead incurred in performing the distributed $\mathbf{Ax} = \mathbf{b}$ calculation. As might be expected, the computation element and the residual of the PageRank computation (those calculations not involving the distributed matrix–vector multiplication) of the algorithm contribute an (approximately) fixed cost to the overall iteration time. We observe that 1D and 2D hypergraph partitioning successfully reduce the communication overhead by factors of 2 and 6 respectively. This reduction results in a decrease in the overall PageRank iteration time by 50% in the 2D case.

We note that, contrary to intuition, in some cases computation times do vary significantly depending on decomposition method used. We conjecture that this occurred because we did not make any attempt to optimise the caching behaviour of our parallel PageRank solver. As a consequence the GleZhu method (which assigned consecutive vector elements to processors) has a good cache hit rate; conversely the cyclic method (which assigned vector elements on a striped basis) suffers a poor cache hit rate.

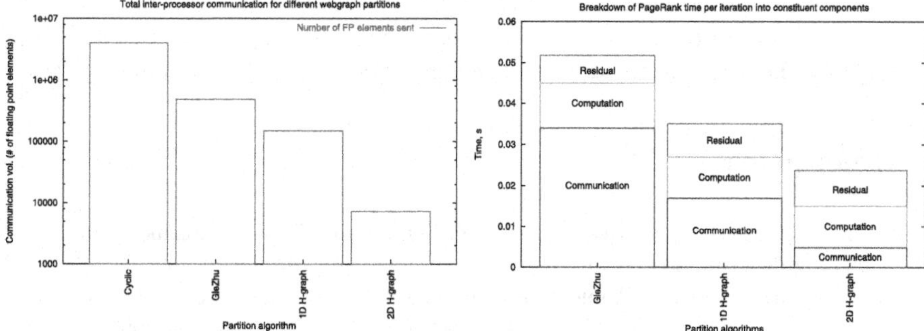

Fig. 3. Total per-iteration communication volume for 16-processor Stanford_Berkeley PageRank computation

Fig. 4. Per-iteration execution time for 16-processor Stanford_Berkeley PageRank computation

5 Conclusion and Future Work

In this paper, we have sought to speed up the execution of parallel PageRank computation through the use of hypergraph partitioning-based decomposition techniques. We have investigated the application of both one- and two-dimensional hypergraph models, and compared them to conventional load balancing decomposition methods. Our experiments on a gigabit PC cluster have shown that hypergraph-based models consistently and substantially decrease distributed per-iteration communication overhead, resulting in the halving of per-iteration run-time when compared to the best available currently-used alternative.

Because of the initial partitioning overhead, the proposed technique is particularly applicable when performing PageRank calculations with multiple personalisation vectors, since the same partition can be reused at no additional cost. We observed that the partitioning overhead was relatively low for the 1D hypergraph decomposition when compared to the 2D hypergraph decomposition. We have some observations to make about this. Firstly, the 2D hypergraph decomposition is a harder problem to solve, since the more sophisticated layout requires the solution of a much larger hypergraph partitioning problem instance with unique characteristics. Secondly, the parallel partitioning tool used (i.e. Par*k*way 2.1) is constantly evolving and has not yet been optimised for 2D decomposition. Furthermore, other emerging hypergraph partitioning tools (e.g. Zoltan [7]) promise potentially much faster parallel execution times, for both 1D and 2D decomposition.

In terms of future work, the current decomposition models aim to minimise total communication volume only. However, depending on the characteristics of the interconnection network used, performance may also be significantly affected by factors such as the number of messages sent or the maximum communication volume passing through a processor. To this end, we aim to develop hypergraph models which incorporate message and communication volume balancing constraints. Secondly, the 2D hypergraph-based decomposition gives rise to a hypergraph where each vertex is incident on exactly two hyperedges. Faster parallel partitioning algorithms may be developed, exploiting this favourable structure.

References

1. L. Page, S. Brin, R. Motwani, and T. Winograd, "The PageRank citation ranking: Bringing order to the web," Tech. Rep. 1999–66, Stanford Univ., November 1999.
2. T. H. Haveliwala, "Topic sensitive PageRank: A context-sensitive ranking algorithm for web search," Tech. Rep., Stanford University, March 2003.
3. C. Alpert, J.-H. Huang, and A. Kahng, "Recent Directions in Netlist Partitioning," *Integration, the VLSI Journal*, vol. 19, no. 1–2, pp. 1–81, 1995.
4. U. V. Catalyurek and C. Aykanat, "Hypergraph-partitioning-based decomposition for parallel sparse matrix–vector multiplication," *IEEE Transactions on Parallel and Distributed Systems*, vol. 10, no. 7, pp. 673–693, 1999.
5. B. Vastenhouw and R. H. Bisseling, "A Two-Dimensional Data Distribution Method for Parallel Sparse Matrix-Vector Multiplication," *SIAM Review*, vol. 47, no. 1, pp. 67–95, 2005.
6. A. Trifunovic and W. J. Knottenbelt, "Par*k*way2.0: A Parallel Multilevel Hypergraph Partitioning Tool," in *Proc. 19th International Symposium on Computer and Information Sciences* (C. Aykanat, T. Dayar, and I. Korpeoglu, eds.), vol. 3280 of *Lecture Notes in Computer Science*, pp. 789–800, Springer, 2004.
7. E. Boman, K. Devine, R. Heaphy, U. Catalyurek, and R. Bisseling, "Parallel hypergraph partitioning for scientific computing," Tech. Rep. SAND05–2796C, Sandia National Laboratories, Albuquerque, NM, April 2005.
8. S. D. Kamvar, T. H. Haveliwala, C. D. Manning, and G. H. Golub, "Extrapolation methods for accelerating PageRank computations," in *Twelfth International World Wide Web Conference*, (Budapest, Hungary), pp. 261–270, ACM, May 2003.
9. D. de Jager, "PageRank: Three distributed algorithms," M.Sc. thesis, Department of Computing, Imperial College London, London SW7 2BZ, UK, September 2004.
10. A. N. Langville and C. D. Meyer, "Deeper inside PageRank," *Internet Mathematics*, vol. 1, no. 3, pp. 335–400, 2004.
11. T. H. Haveliwala and S. D. Kamvar, "The second eigenvalue of the google matrix," Tech. Rep., Computational Mathematics, Stanford University, March 2003.
12. "Google." `http://www.google.com/`. 20th June 2005.
13. S. D. Kamvar, T. H. Haveliwala, C. D. Manning, and G. H. Golub, "Exploiting the block structure of the web for computing PageRank," Stanford database group tech. rep., Computational Mathematics, Stanford University, March 2003.
14. D. Gleich, L. Zhukov, and P. Berkhin, "Fast parallel PageRank: A linear system approach," Tech. Rep., Institute for Computation and Mathematical Engineering, Stanford University, 2004.
15. U. V. Catalyurek and C. Aykanat, "A Fine-Grain Hypergraph Model for 2D Decomposition of Sparse Matrices," in *Proc. 8th International Workshop on Solving Irregularly Structured Problems in Parallel*, (San Francisco, USA), April 2001.
16. B. Ucar and C. Aykanat, "Encapsulating Multiple Communication-Cost Metrics in Partitioning Sparse Rectangular Matrices for Parallel Matrix-Vector Multiples," *SIAM Journal of Scientific Computing*, vol. 25, no. 6, pp. 1837–1859, 2004.

17. B. A. Hendrickson, "Graph partitioning and parallel solvers: Has the Emperor no clothes," in *Proc. Irregular'98*, vol. 1457 of *LNCS*, pp. 218–225, Springer, 1998.
18. M. R. Garey and D. S. Johnson, *Computers and Intractability: A Guide to the Theory of NP-Completeness.* W.H. Freeman and Co., 1979.
19. A. Trifunovic and W. Knottenbelt, "A Parallel Algorithm for Multilevel k-way Hypergraph Partitioning," in *Proc. 3rd International Symposium on Parallel and Distributed Computing*, (University College Cork, Ireland), pp. 114–121, July 2004.
20. T. Davis, "University of Florida Sparse Matrix Collection," March 2005. http://www.cise.ufl.edu/research/sparse/matrices.
21. "UbiCrawler project." `http://webgraph-data.dsi.unimi.it/`.

Prediction of Communication Latency over Complex Network Behaviors on SMP Clusters*

Maxime Martinasso[1,2,**] and Jean-François Méhaut[1]

[1] Laboratoire ID-IMAG, ZIRST 51 avenue Jean Kuntzmann, 38330 MontBonnot Saint-Martin, France
[2] BULL SA, 1 rue de Provence, BP 208 38432 ECHIROLLES Cedex, France
{maxime.martinasso, jean-francois.mehaut}@imag.fr

Abstract. Using MPI as communication interface, one or several applications may introduce complex communication behaviors over the network of a cluster. This effect is increased when nodes of the cluster are multi-processors, and where communications can income or outgo from the same node with a common interval time. Our interest is to understand the effects of complex communication schemes over a network of SMP nodes, and then to identify different network conflicts. Network conflicts stand for a network component (links, NIC, or MPI stack, etc.) shared between communications. This paper describes a set of experiments generating network conflicts and their analysis, in order to accurately predict communication latencies. This analysis is based on cluster of bi-processor with a Myrinet network, using as communication interface a LAM MPI-2 implementation over GM protocol.

Keywords: Performance evaluation, communication model, Myrinet, wormhole network, cluster of SMP, communication latency.

1 Introduction

Many parallel applications, communicating through a network, used MPI [12] to spread relevant data for their computations. Within MPI, an application is divided in MPI tasks, which contain call of the communication primitives. MPI tasks may be distributed over a cluster.

Clusters are becoming more efficient and sophisticated. A cluster of SMP nodes, linked by a high performance network, is an example of efficient cluster. Our experiments were performed over a bi-processor cluster connected by a Myrinet network.

The communication complexity created by several applications executed in the same time, over efficient clusters, likely generates complicated network behaviors. In opposition of common LAN network (as ethernet), high performance networks reduce communication control and so handle communications in an

* This work was supported by BULL SA and INRIA.

** To whom correspondence should be addressed.

M. Bravetti et al. (Eds.): EPEW 2005 and WS-FM 2005, LNCS 3670, pp. 172–186, 2005.

easiest way to understand communication behaviors. Nevertheless, these communication behaviors bring up difficulty to accurately estimate communication delay of applications over a cluster. Complex communication behaviors generate contention or conflict on network resources. Contention is an overexploitation of the network resource, creating communication delay as commented in [10]. Conflict occurs when several communications share the same network resources.

This paper introduces an analysis of network conflicts induced by complex communication behaviors. After a description of Myrinet network characteristics and an exposition of several existing communication models, section 4 will describe our analysis of network conflicts, which leads to our communication model in section 5. Our model accuracy is discussed in section 6, and finally, the paper ends with a conclusion.

2 Overview of Myrinet and GM Protocol

Myrinet is a high-speed local-area network or system-area network for computer systems. A Myrinet network is composed of point-to-point links that connects hosts and switches. The network link can deliver 2 Gbits/sec bandwith in each direction. Myrinet is based on packet-switching technology where the packets are wormhole-routed through a network consisting of switching elements and network interface cards (NIC). Each NIC, attached to the host's I/O bus, contains a programmable processor (Lanai) and onboard memory that is used to store the control program and communication buffers. This programmability provides flexibility in designing communication software. Several low-level communication protocols have been designed for Myrinet networks, from research teams (Fast Message [13], BIP [4]) or from Myricom (GM and MX). These protocols tried to exploit the specificities of parallel computing on clusters in order to propose more efficient and dedicated systems. In this paper, we have used the GM protocol from Myricom.

To increase the data transfer rate, the NIC adaptor is equipped with three DMA engines. Two DMA engines are associated with the packet interface: one for receiving packets and one for sending packets. The third DMA engine is used for data transfer between the NIC memory and the host memory through the host interface. This third DMA engine is a potential bottleneck for simultaneous sending and receiving operations.

Like most systems that support DMA, the onboard memory can be mapped into user space and is this accessible directly to user processes. The memory mapping technique is commonly known as "memory pinning". In order to support zero-copy API, the DMA operations can be performed with arbitrary byte counts and byte alignments.

GM is a user-level communication protocols that runs over the Myrinet and provides a reliable ordered delivery of packets with low latency and high bandwidth. The basic send/receive operations of GM works as follows:

To send a message, a user application generates a send descriptor, referred to as a send event in GM, to the NIC. The NIC translates the event to a send token and appends it to the send queue for the desired destination. With outstanding send tokens to multiple destinations, the NIC processes the tokens to different destinations in a round-robin manner. To send a message for a token, the NIC has also to wait for the availability of a send packet, i.e.. the send buffer to accommodate the data. The data is read from the host memory with a DMA into a send packet and injected into the network. The NIC keeps a send record of the sequence number and the time for each packet it has sent. If the acknowledges is not received within the timeout period, the sender will retransmit the packet. When all the send records are acknowledged, the NIC will pass the send token to the LAM MPI library.

To receive a message, the host provides some registered memory as the receive buffer by preposting a receiving descriptor. A posted receive descriptor is translated into a receive token by the NIC. When the NIC receives a packet, it checks the sequence number. An unexpected packet is dropped immediately. For an expected packet, the NIC locates a receive token, writes the packet data in the host memory with DMA, and then acknowledges the sender. When all the packets for the message have arrived, the NIC will also generate a receive event to the host process for it to detect the arrived message. In our case, this event will be caught by the LAM-MPI library.

3 Network Communication Models

Network communication can use MPI primitives to send and receive messages. MPI performance was investigated in [9] for high performance networks such as Myrinet. The authors shown the impact of buffer reuse, intra-node communication latency, and memory usage against the communication performance of several MPI primitives. If we focus on cluster of SMP nodes, more MPI performance studies were presented in [7], for different kind of platform.

A popular communication model developed is the LogP model [5] and is version LogGP model [3] for long messages. Both models use a linear model characterized by 4 parameters: L (as delay), o (as overhead), g (as bandwidth) and P (as number of processors). LogGP model introduce a new parameter G (as gap per byte). Impacts of each parameters was analyzed in [11], with methods to measure model parameters. Like these two models, and if we focus on wormhole model, a basic approach to predict communication delays is to used a linear model featured by an overhead cost and a communication rate factor (applied to message length and network path). In network based on wormhole communications, this kind of models is sufficient in case of each communication is independent and does not share any network resource. Although, as one or several MPI applications, composed by several MPI tasks, can spread messages through overlapped communication time, these linear models poorly predict communication delays.

A first approach of communication sharing effects was introduce by [8]. The authors predict communication delay with a linear model taking into account the path sharing over a Myrinet network of workstation. Their study was based on the protocols GM and BIP but without MPI as user interface. Their model gives a first approach of sharing network resource. Communications are modeling by a piece-wise linear equation, and in case of sharing path, this equation is multiplied by the maximum number of communications within the sharing conflict. They evaluate their model against two communication schemes with synchronous sends. Their model gives good results for some communications of their schemes, but the authors do not provide more insight about communication influences and so for communication delays predicted with low accuracy. This paper enhances the understanding of network conflicts, and presents conflicts of communication between SMP nodes using MPI as user communication interface.

4 Conflict Analysis

Our approach, to understand communication behaviors over Myrinet, is to measure communication time following different communication schemes. The analysis focus on a set of particular schemes suitable to enclose most of the communication behaviors. Communications in these schemes can be of two types: external communication, going through the Myrinet links and switch, or internal, between two tasks on two processors of the same SMP node. These communication schemes must be relevant of network communication conflicts. A network conflict is produce when simultaneous communications access the same network component. We study three kinds of network conflicts:

– sharing resource system of node in full-duplex communication
– sharing one part of a full-duplex link
– conflict between internal communication and external communication

4.1 Testbed

The platform used to take these communication time measures is the INRIA's icluster2 [1] composed by 104 bi-Itamium2 nodes. Its Myrinet network includes one 128-port switch (reference M3-E128) connected to Myrinet interconnect cards (reference M3F-PCI64C-2). Measured latency is equal to $13.9\mu s$. The Myrinet protocol is a GM protocol version 2.1.9 accessed by a LAM 7.1.1 MPI 2 implementation [6]. In LAM small messages have a length lower than 64Kb. We keep this delimitation between small and long messages. MPI tasks will be mapped as one task per processors, meaning that a node can have at maximum two MPI tasks. Linux kernel is on version 2.4.21.

4.2 Communication Method and Measurements

Several way of implementing communication between MPI tasks can lead to different network performance. As consequence, it is interesting to introduce in this paragraph our communication method of the different benchmarks used to analyze network behavior.

Sending is done through blocking send defined by the standard *MPI_Send* primitive. To synchronize MPI tasks between them, we used a MPI synchronization barrier, we highlight to the reader that using synchronization barrier gives implicitly an order for the tasks to continue their executions.

Cache effects can also influence measurements. To avoid cache effects, we executed several not-measured communication before each benchmark. A side effect of this cache avoidance method is to set the Myrinet switch and so to not take into account the time to create the different wormholes between nodes. As a Myrinet switch per-hop delay is about $0.5\mu s$, this side effect of cache avoidance can be consider as insignificant.

Measured time is done at the source task, starting before the MPI send and ending when the MPI send method terminates. Message length corresponds to the length specified in the *MPI_Send* primitive, and does not correspond to the effective length send over the network (MPI implementation add a small envelope to the message). Thus, effective message length are always greater than specified length and a 0-specified length is not meaningless. If one MPI task has to receive two messages from two others tasks, we used the MPI flag *MPI_ANY_SOURCE* in the receive function, to avoid a fixed order of receive.

4.3 Communication Schemes

Communication schemes are necessary to test communication behaviors. A communication scheme is a set of communications between MPI tasks.

Therefore, a communication scheme is characterized by its MPI task distributions over the nodes and by its communications parameters, such as number of communications, message length, starting time, etc. To help in understanding, communication schemes will be identified by the string "$c/n - p_1p_2..p_c$" where c is the number of communications, n the number of nodes and the remaining sequence of pairs represents the communicating nodes. As an example, consider a two-communication scheme over three nodes identified by 2/3-0121 in which both node 0 and node 2 send messages to node 1. To graphically view the communication scheme identification, the reader can refer to Fig. 1.

4.4 Communication Conflicts Analysis

Conflicts appear when tasks send messages through complex communication schemes. We associate communication schemes into several set used to express the three network conflicts mentioned above, plus one start case used as reference of communication time. We test these schemes with homogeneous communications (same start time and same messages length for each communication) and heterogeneous communications. For each schemes, we evaluate the average communication time and standard deviation of each communication. These calculations is done over a sample size of 10000 experiments.

Experiments. In our investigation of network conflict, we had made a large number of experiments. We present in this section only relevant cases. The curves, presented in next section, are calculated with schemes set to homogeneous communications.

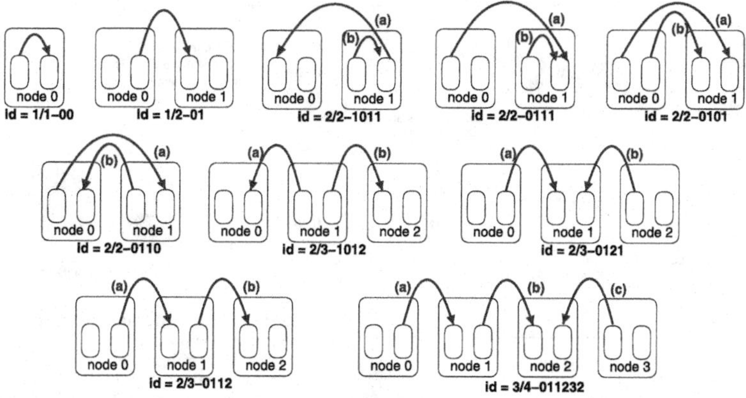

Fig. 1. Identification of communication schemes

Reference Cases: 1/1-00 ***and*** 1/2-01**.** Schemes with only one communication will serve us as reference to compare network conflicts. Scheme 1/1-00 determines reference time for internal communication and scheme 1/2-01 for external communication. Fig. 2 shows different average and standard deviation values for these schemes in function of message length (in Bytes). To evaluate the Lam MPI time overhead we add the same curve with only the GM protocol, calculated with the tool *gm_allsize* provided with the GM library. We remind the fact that the GM curves do not include the MPI envelope length, which has significant effects for small messages.

One first analysis, comparing this two schemes show that the average communication time is regular for both communications (small standard deviation). More precisely for long messages, the time is linear ($y = \alpha.x + \beta$) in function of the message length. If we go further in this direction with more experiments, we can calculate the linear coefficients α and β. In case of external communication $\alpha_{ext} = 0.004193$ $[\mu s.Byte^{-1}]$ and $\beta_{ext} = 78.125[\mu s]$ for internal communication $\alpha_{int} = 0.004301$ $[\mu s.Byte^{-1}]$ and $\beta_{int} = 59.59[\mu s]$.

If we look at internal communication with small messages, as sender and receiver share the same system resources and the same system load, we have a higher variability (higher standard deviation) as their communication delays are low and close to system resource sharing latency. The stair shape for small messages comes from the GM protocol version 2.1, which fragments long messages into packets of most 4KB [2]. If we compare both internal and external communication, it appears that for messages greater than 256KB, internal communication consumes more time than external communication, probably caused by the same reason of system resource sharing delay.

Sharing Resource System on Full-Duplex Link: 2/2-0110, 2/3-0112**.** Both scheme 2/2-0110 and 2/3-0112 test the sharing resource system accessed, on full-duplex link, by both send and receive methods in the same time. Figure 3 presents the delays of scheme 2/2-0110, the delay values of scheme 2/3-0112 are similar.For

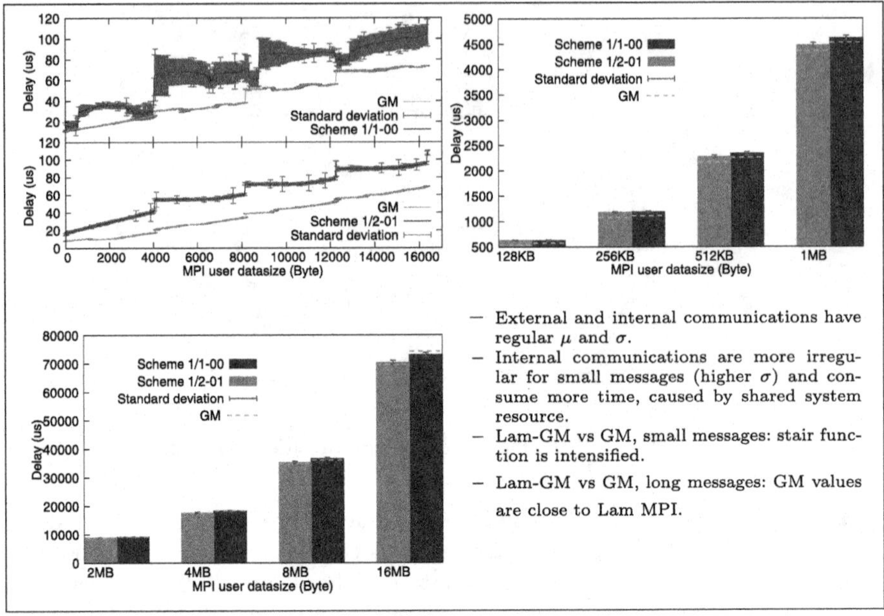

Fig. 2. 1/1-00 and 1/2-01 schemes comparison, μ and σ values

small messages, as we test sharing resources is difficult to well interpret the delay with high standard deviation. Nevertheless communication (a) appears to follow a stair function (as scheme 1/2-01).Communication (b) is more chaotic. We remind that MPI synchronization barrier involves an implicit order, and in our case communication (a) starts before communication (b), explaining the more chaotic aspect of communication (b). For long messages, both (a) and (b) have the same communication time, with a small standard deviation. Still, the comparison with scheme 1/2-01 shows a delay caused by system resource sharing.

To estimate the rate of this delay, we used heterogeneous communication. Considering a linear equation as $y = \alpha_o.x + \beta_o$, we can measure the sharing overhead rate $\alpha_o = 0.004663\ [\mu s.Byte^{-1}]$ and $\beta_o = 102.33[\mu s]$. This overhead is explained by the Myrinet NIC architecture, which includes a DMA engine shared for data transfer (sending/receiving) between the NIC memory and the host memory.

Sharing One Part of the Full-Duplex Link: 2/2-0101, 2/3-0121, 2/3-1012. The three schemes 2/2-0101, 2/3-0121 and 2/3-1012 test the half-part sharing of full-duplex link, following combinations of sending and receiving. The scheme 2/3-0121 delays are presented in Fig. 4, but these three schemes reveal the same communication behavior. Small message delays are regular following a stair case function.

Long messages indicate an interesting behavior. The delay for both communication (a) and (b) of the three schemes are two times the delay of the

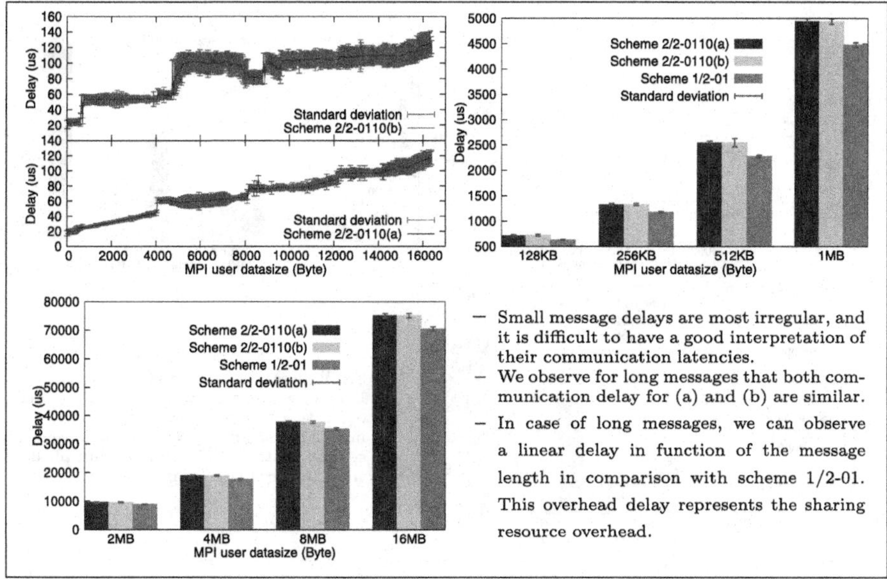

Fig. 3. 2/2-0110 and 1/2-01 schemes comparison, μ and σ values

reference scheme. This particularity was already shown in [8]. In their Myrinet model of communication, in case of simultaneous communications, they multiply their equation of communication delay by the maximum number of messages concurrently using links on the path.

Indeed, this communication behavior is more complicated, if we test it in heterogeneous case with different start time and message lengths. Within this case, for one message, communication delay will be augmented by the intersection time of all the others communications with the same destination node (and so in case of same message lengths and same start time, the delay will be multiplied by the number of communications). We can explain this effect by the fact that the GM protocol fragments packets enabling the interlacing of the communications over the shared part of the network path.

External Versus Internal Communication: 2/2-0111, 2/2-1011. In that paragraph we evaluate external and internal communication together. Figure 5 presents the behavior of scheme 2/2-0111, (scheme 2/2-1011 has an equivalent behavior).

For small messages we get again a stair function for both schemes. For long messages we notice that the outgoing external communication is greater than the internal communication, but in case of incoming external communication it is the contrary. Mixing message lengths, communications are serialized meaning that one communication starts after the other ends (and its delay is the sum of both delays). More specifically, the high standard deviation of both schemes reveals an order between communications. This order is not always identical

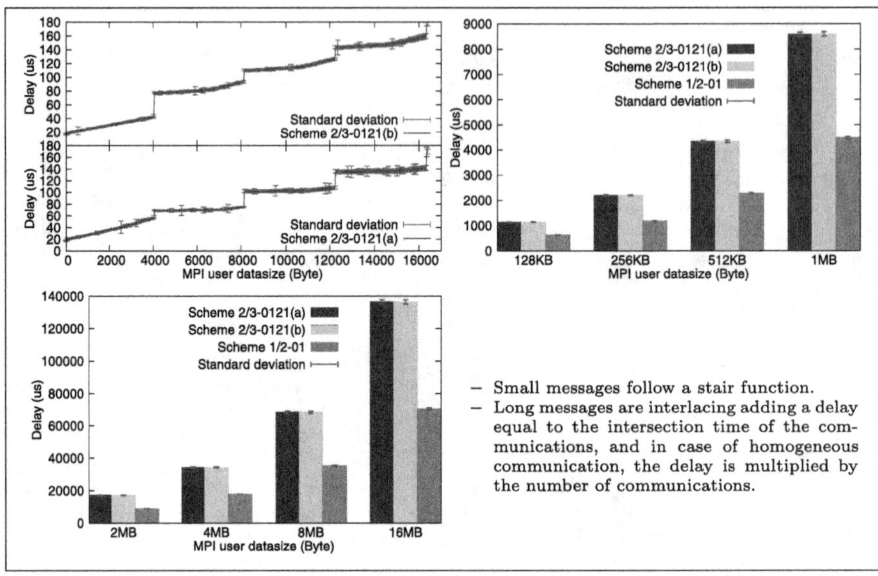

Fig. 4. 2/3-0121 and 1/2-01 schemes comparison, μ and σ values

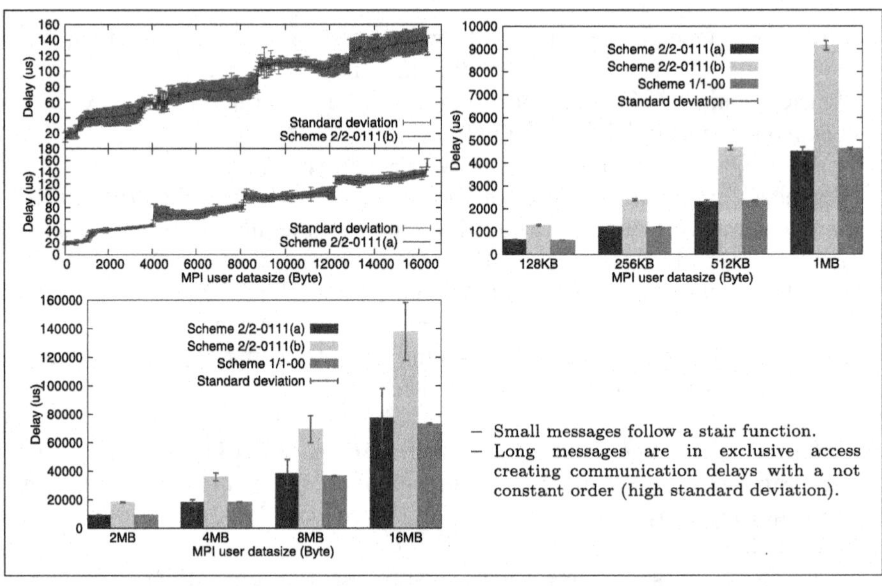

Fig. 5. 2/2-0111 and 1/1-00 schemes comparison, μ and σ values

among the 10000 experiments. In other words, during a set of experiments, in some experiments external communication waits for internal communication, and in some other experiments it is inverted, and this whatever the scheme.

Probably, the main reason for this effect is the serialization of the *MPI_Recv* method call in the source code of the benchmark. Effectively, as a task MPI need to receive two messages from two different sources, we used two calls of *MPI_Recv* with the *MPI_ANY_SOURCE* flag. This flag avoid a fixed order, but we cannot remove the order.

As we test only with bi-processor SMP nodes, we cannot really understand this conflict, as we cannot set simultaneously external and internal communication (a common interval time between communications leads to ordered communications on bi-processor nodes).

5 Myrinet Communication Model over SMP Cluster

The previous section described experiments over communication conflicts of Myrinet communications through MPI. This section will present a model of communication over Myrinet and MPI taking into account these communication conflicts. We chose to only study long messages, as consequence of the strong standard deviation of small message delays that does not permit to have a good insight of network conflicts and can lead to wrongly identify the model accuracy. Furthermore, our tests (on bi-processors) do not provide us a good comprehension of external/internal conflict and so to present a model of it.

We model sharing resources conflict and conflict of sharing an half part of full-duplex links by two functions over communications. Communications are represented by vectors of four elements: source node, destination node, start time, and message length. Communications are written like $s \overset{st,m}{\frown} d$ where a message of length m is send at time st from s to d.

We are interested in the computation of the communication delay δ. In case of no conflict, a communication delay is calculated by the linear function *delay* defined as:

$$delay(m, \alpha, \beta) = \begin{cases} 0, & m = 0 \\ \alpha * m + \beta, & otherwise \end{cases}$$

where α and β are measured and m is the message length.

Sharing Resource Conflict. Sharing resource conflict occurs only when a node shares sending communications and receiving communications with a common interval time.

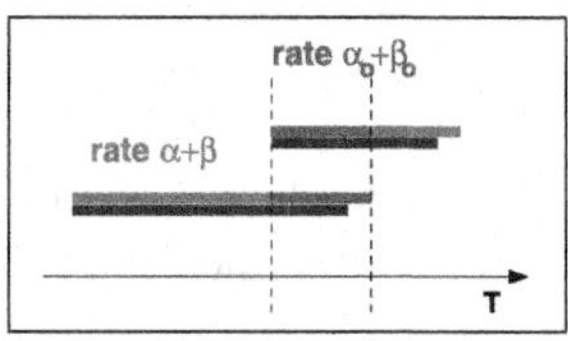

Fig. 6. Sharing rate

Thus, the function used to model sharing resource conflict is only defined over communications where for a set C of N communications $\nexists i \in C, j \in C \,|\, src_i \neq dest_j$ or $src_j \neq dest_i$ and $\bigcap_{k=1}^{N} [st_k; st_k + delay(m_k, \alpha, \beta)] \neq \emptyset$.

The model is described as follow: let two communications within this conflict, their delays will be composed by a communication delay with rate (α_o, β_o) applied to the intersection length of both messages and a communication delay with rate (α, β) applied to the rest of the message length.

We define the function *Share*, which calculates the communication delays δ_1 and δ_2 of two communications, $C_1 = i \overset{st_1, m_1}{\curvearrowright} j$ and $C_2 = j \overset{st_2, m_2}{\curvearrowright} k$ with $st_1 \leq st_2$, on sharing resource conflict:

$$Share(C_1, C_2) = \begin{cases} \text{if } st_1 + delay(m_1, \alpha, \beta) \leq st_2 + delay(m_2, \alpha, \beta) \\ \begin{cases} \delta_1 = delay(m_1 - \gamma, \alpha, \beta) + delay(\gamma, \alpha_o, \beta_o) \\ \delta_2 = delay(m_2 - \gamma, \alpha_o, \beta_o) + delay(\gamma, \alpha_o, \beta_o) \end{cases} \\ \text{otherwise} \\ \begin{cases} \delta_1 = delay(m_1 - m_2, \alpha, \beta) + delay(m_2, \alpha_o, \beta_o) \\ \delta_2 = delay(m_2, \alpha_o, \beta_o) \end{cases} \end{cases}$$

with $\gamma = m_1 - \frac{st_2 - st_1}{\alpha}$.

Sharing an Half Part of Full-Duplex Links: Interlacing. Sharing an half part of full-duplex links appears when communications on a same node and with a common interval time are sending or receiving messages. This conflict creates an interlacing effect. As the precedent case, the function used to model this conflict is only defined over communications where for a set C of N communications, $\nexists i \in C, j \in C \,|\, src_i \neq src_j$ or $dest_j \neq dest_i$ and $\bigcap_{k=1}^{N} [st_k; st_k + delay(m_k, \alpha, \beta)] \neq \emptyset$.

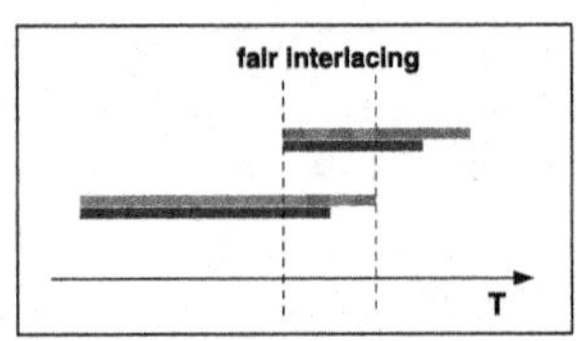

Fig. 7. Fair interlacing

In this model, we add for each communication message length, the communication intersection length. Then, we compute the communication latency like in there were any conflict. In that way we consider a fair interlacing of messages fragmented by the protocol GM.

We define the function *Inter*, which calculates the communication delays δ_1 and δ_2 of two communications, $C_1 = i \overset{st_1, m_1}{\curvearrowright} j$ and $C_2 = i \overset{st_2, m_2}{\curvearrowright} k$ with $st_1 \leq st_2$, on sharing half part of full-duplex link, as:

$$Inter(C_1, C_2) = \begin{cases} \text{if } st_1 + delay(m_1, \alpha, \beta) \leq st_2 + delay(m_2, \alpha, \beta) \\ \begin{cases} \delta_1 = delay(m_1 + \gamma, \alpha, \beta) \\ \delta_2 = delay(m_2 + \gamma, \alpha, \beta) \end{cases} \\ \text{otherwise} \\ \begin{cases} \delta_1 = delay(m_1 + m_2, \alpha, \beta) \\ \delta_2 = delay(2 * m_2, \alpha, \beta) \end{cases} \end{cases}$$

with $\gamma = m_1 - \frac{st_2 - st_1}{\alpha}$.

Mixing Conflicts. Complex communication schemes can lead to have in the same time both conflicts. Let's take an example, consider communications: $C_1 = i \overset{st_1, m_1}{\curvearrowright} j$, $C_2 = j \overset{st_2, m_2}{\curvearrowright} k$, and $C_3 = l \overset{st_3, m_3}{\curvearrowright} k$.

Communication delays are calculated like in previous cases separating conflicts, even if communication in distinct conflicts have a common interval time.

From the example, we get: $Share(C_1, C_2)=(\delta_1, \delta_2')$ and $Inter(C_2, C_3) = (\delta_2'', \delta_3)$, even if C_1 and C_3 have a common interval. Communication delay of C_2 is calculated as $\delta_2 = max(\delta_2', \delta_2'')$. We generalized the example, for all combination of *Share* and *Inter*, taking the maximum calculated delay of communication in both conflicts.

6 Model Accuracy

In this last section we evaluate the accuracy of our model against observed delays. Observed delays were calculated over a sample length of 10000 experiments. The value of the function parameters are $\alpha = 0.004193$, $\beta = 78.125$, $\alpha_o = 0.004663$ and $\beta_o = 102.33$. We confront our model to different schemes with communications having different start time (Δ as start time delay) and message lengths. One issue we met, is to make an interval delay about few *ms* between communication start time. We used the function *usleep* with a setting parameter creating the expected interval delay. We present for each conflict some relevant results among the large number of experiments we did.

Table 1 displays communication time for reference scheme (without conflict). The modeling values match quite perfectly the average observed values, as the parameters of the function *delay* were determined from these values.

Tables 2 and 3 display results for scheme 2/2-0110, representing the sharing resource conflict. Our communication time prediction is close to observed values for homogeneous and heterogeneous communications, validating the model using two different communication rates.

Tables 4 and 5 display results for scheme 2/3-0121, and confront our model against the conflict of sharing an half part of full-duplex links. We suggested a

Table 1. Communication time (μs) for scheme 1/2-01, using the function *delay*

	256 KB	2 MB	4 MB	8 MB
obs	1177 ± 13	8872 ± 89	17663 ± 176	35250 ± 352
mod	1177	8771	17664	35251

Table 2. Communications delay (μs) for scheme 2/2-0110

			$\Delta = 0$		$\Delta \simeq 1000$		$\Delta \simeq 4000$		$\Delta \simeq 8000$
obs	256 KB	(a)	1321 ± 21	(a)	1244 ± 40	(a)	x	(a)	x
	256 KB	(b)	1329 ± 42	(b)	1232 ± 40	(b)	x	(b)	x
mod	256 KB	(a)	1324	(a)	1290	(a)	x	(a)	x
	256 KB	(b)	1324	(b)	1290	(b)	x	(b)	x
obs	4 MB	(a)	19026 ± 73	(a)	18979 ± 205	(a)	18885 ± 136	(a)	18672 ± 46
	4 MB	(b)	19081 ± 202	(b)	19000 ± 155	(b)	18839 ± 67	(b)	18650 ± 192
mod	4 MB	(a)	19660	(a)	19626	(a)	19290	(a)	18841
	4 MB	(b)	19660	(b)	19626	(b)	19290	(b)	18841

Table 3. Communications delay (μs) for scheme 2/2-0110

		$\Delta = 0$	$\Delta \simeq 1000$	$\Delta \simeq 10000$	$\Delta \simeq 30000$
obs	256 KB	(a) 1468 ± 53	(a) 1231 ± 62	(a) x	(a) x
	4 MB	(b) 17889 ± 117	(b) 17796 ± 158	(b) x	(b) x
mod	256 KB	(a) 1324	(a) 1324	(a) x	(a) x
	4 MB	(b) 17890	(b) 17890	(b) x	(b) x
obs	2 MB	(a) 9810 ± 63	(a) 9678 ± 74	(a) 10041 ± 61	(a) 9657 ± 42
	8 MB	(b) 36055 ± 200	(b) 36085 ± 191	(b) 35926 ± 192	(b) 35953 ± 207
mod	2 MB	(a) 9881	(a) 9881	(a) 9881	(a) 9553
	8 MB	(b) 36339	(b) 36339	(b) 36339	(b) 35933

Table 4. Communications delay (μs) for scheme 2/3-0121

		$\Delta = 0$	$\Delta \simeq 1000$	$\Delta \simeq 4000$	$\Delta \simeq 8000$
obs	256 KB	(a) 2138 ± 33	(a) 1339 ± 183	(a) x	(a) x
	256 KB	(b) 2198 ± 10	(b) 1339 ± 189	(b) x	(b) x
mod	256 KB	(a) 2276	(a) 1276	(a) x	(a) x
	256 KB	(b) 2276	(b) 1276	(b) x	(b) x
obs	4 MB	(a) 32232 ± 109	(a) 31637 ± 262	(a) 32240 ± 114	(a) 27694 ± 275
	4 MB	(b) 34215 ± 43	(b) 33561 ± 274	(b) 34219 ± 63	(b) 29129 ± 350
mod	4 MB	(a) 35251	(a) 34251	(a) 31252	(a) 27251
	4 MB	(b) 35251	(b) 34251	(b) 31252	(b) 27251

Table 5. Communications delay (μs) for scheme 2/3-0121

		$\Delta = 0$	$\Delta \simeq 1000$	$\Delta \simeq 10000$	$\Delta \simeq 30000$
obs	256 KB	(a) 2046 ± 27	(a) 1231 ± 62	(a) x	(a) x
	4 MB	(b) 18634 ± 88	(b) 17796 ± 158	(b) x	(b) x
mod	256 KB	(a) 2276	(a) 1276	(a) x	(a) x
	4 MB	(b) 18764	(b) 17764	(b) x	(b) x
obs	2 MB	(a) 16075 ± 72	(a) 15074 ± 250	(a) 16218 ± 85	(a) 15053 ± 285
	8 MB	(b) 43428 ± 116	(b) 42289 ± 290	(b) 43541 ± 105	(b) 42326 ± 388
mod	2 MB	(a) 17664	(a) 17664	(a) 17664	(a) 14044
	8 MB	(b) 44044	(b) 44044	(b) 44044	(b) 40424

model with a fair interlacing communications. Results validate this choice, but in case of different communication start time, the communication starting first seems to be faster than the second one, and thus creating a interlacing favoring the first communication. Nevertheless this favored-first interlacing effect seems to be really difficult to quantify, and a fair interlacing predict accurately this conflict.

Mixing conflict is the most difficult behavior to model. The model gives good results, Table 6, but seems to reduce its accuracy if communications in different

Table 6. Communications delay (μs) for scheme 3/4-011232

	$\Delta_{ab} = \Delta_{bc} = 0$	$\Delta_{ab} \simeq 1000, \Delta_{bc} \simeq 2000$	$\Delta_{ab} \simeq 1000, \Delta_{bc} \simeq 6000$
obs 1 MB	(a) 6071 ± 158	(a) 5672 ± 144	(a) 5088 ± 68
obs 2 MB	(b) 16831 ± 138	(b) 15511 ± 456	(b) 11635 ± 337
obs 4 MB	(c) 25873 ± 17	(c) 24261 ± 450	(c) 19882 ± 287
mod 1 MB	(a) 4991	(a) 4657	(a) 4657
mod 2 MB	(b) 17664	(b) 15664	(b) 11664
mod 4 MB	(c) 26458	(c) 24458	(c) 20458

conflicts are overlapped. In that case more complex phenomenon appears making in relation communications in different conflicts.

7 Conclusion

The main interest of this paper was to study and understand the behavior of communication conflicts over a cluster of SMP nodes. We used complex communication schemes to exhibit three main classes of conflict and to study their behaviors. Our analysis was based on Lam-MPI as communication interface, over a bi-processor cluster with a Myrinet network.

From this analysis we accurately model two conflicts and their combinations, and we validated it against several communication schemes. Two conflicts were identified: sharing system resource conflict and sharing half part of a full-duplex link conflict. To understand plainly the third conflict between internal and external communications, the presented analysis was limited by the used of bi-processor nodes.

In future works, we envisage to achieve the same study over different high performance networks and protocols, such as Quadrics or Infiny Band, and with cluster of multi-processor nodes greater than bi-processor as aim to extend the communication model.

References

1. Icluster2, 2004. http://i-cluster2.inrialpes.fr/.
2. GM Performance Measurements, 2005. http://www.myricom.com/myrinet/performance/index.html.
3. Alexandrov A., Ionescu M., Schauser K. and Scheiman C. LogGP: Incorporating Long Messages into the LogP model - One step closer towards a realistic model for parallel computation. *7th Annual Symposium on Parallel Algorithms and Architectures*, July 1995.
4. B. Tourancheau. High Speed Networks for Clusters, the BIP-Myrinet Experience. In *Proceedings of the 7th European PVM/MPI Users' Group Meeting on Recent Advances in Parallel Virtual Machine and Message Passing Interface*, page 9, 2000.
5. Culler D., Karp R., Patterson D., Sahay A., Santos E., Schauser K., Subramonian R. and von Eicken T. LogP: a practical model of parallel computation. *Commun. ACM*, 39(11):78–85, 1996.

6. G. Burns, R. Daoud and J. Vaigl. LAM: An Open Cluster Environment for MPI. In *Proceedings of Supercomputing Symposium*, pages 379–386, 1994.
7. K. Al-Tawil and C. A. Mortiz. Performance modeling and evaluation of MPI. *J. Parallel Distrib. Comput.*, 61(2):202–223, 2001.
8. Kim S. C. and Lee S. Measurement and Prediction of Communication Delays in Myrinet Networks. *J. Parallel Distrib. Comput.*, 61(11):1692–1704, 2001.
9. Liu J., Chandrasekaran B., Wu J., Jiang W., Kini S., YU W., Buntinas D., Wyckoff P. and D K. Panda. Performance Comparison of MPI Implementations over InfiniBand, Myrinet and Quadrics. In *SC '03: Proceedings of the 2003 ACM/IEEE conference on Supercomputing*, page 58, 2003.
10. M. Martinasso. Étude et modélisation de la congestion réseau sur des architectures de grappes modulaires. In *16ème Rencontres Francophones du Parallélisme - RENPAR'05*, April 2005.
11. Martin R., Vahdat A., Culler D. and Anderson T. Effects of communication latency, overhead, and bandwidth in a cluster architecture. *Proceedings of the 24th annual international symposium on Computer architecture*, pages 85–97, 1997.
12. Message Passing Interface Forum. MPI: A message-passing interface standard. *International Journal of Supercomputer Applications*, pages 165–414, 1994.
13. S. Pakin, M. Lauria and A. Chien. High performance messaging on workstations: Illinois Fast Messages (FM) for Myrinet. 1995.

A Diffusion Approximation Model of an Electronic-Optical Node

Tadeusz Czachórski[1] and Ferhan Pekergin[2]

[1] IITiS, Polish Academy of Sciences,
ul. Bałtycka 5, 44-100 Gliwice, Poland
tadek@iitis.gliwice.pl

[2] LIPN, CNRS UMR 7030 Université Paris-Nord,
99, avenue Jean-Baptiste Clément,
93430 Villetaneuse, France
pekergin@lipn.univ-paris13.fr

Abstract. The article presents a diffusion approximation model applied to investigate the process of filling a large optical packet by smaller and coming irregularly electronical packets. The use of diffusion approximation enables us to include the general distributions of interarrival times, also the self-similarity of the input process, as well as to investigate transient states. We propose a novel diffusion process with jumps representing the end of the filling the buffer due to arrival of too large packet and we give the transient solution to this process. The model allows us to study the distribution of interdeparture times and the distribution of the space occupied in the optical packet.

1 Introduction

Designing of smart edge routers and shaping the self-similar traffic in optical switched networks arise recently a lot of interest. Here, we propose an analytical approach which we consider useful in modelling and dimensioning of buffers in the edge routers between electronic and optical networks. We study a single buffer where packets of various sizes, classified by the class of service and the destination, are stored to build an optical packet of a fixed size. We already studied this problem with the use of simulation model, remarking that self-similar traffic at the entrance of such a buffer remains self-similar when leaving it. Now we are building analytical model based on diffusion approximation. In section 2 we summarize the diffusion approximation and our previous contributions to this approach, i.e. a method to solve transient diffusion models, in section 3 we present the new model to analyse the process of buffer filling, in section 4 a numerical example proves that this approach may give reasonable results in relatively short (compared to simulation, especially simulation of transient states) time.

M. Bravetti et al. (Eds.): EPEW 2005 and WS-FM 2005, LNCS 3670, pp. 187–199, 2005.

2 The Principles of Diffusion Approximation: G/G/1/N Model

Let $A(x)$, $B(x)$ denote the interarrival and service time distributions at a service station. The distributions are general, it is assumed that their two first moments are known: $E[A] = 1/\lambda$, $E[B] = 1/\mu$, $\mathrm{Var}[A] = \sigma_A^2$, $\mathrm{Var}[B] = \sigma_B^2$. Denote also the squared coefficients of variation $C_A^2 = \sigma_A^2\lambda^2$, $C_B^2 = \sigma_B^2\mu^2$. Let $N(t)$ be the number of customers present in the system at time t. For a single class FIFO queue, the changes $N(t+\Delta t) - N(t)$ have approximately normal distribution with mean $(\lambda-\mu)\Delta t$ and variance $(\sigma_A^2\lambda^3 + \sigma_B^2\mu^3)\Delta t$, provided that the time Δt is sufficiently long and the station is working without interruption, e.g. [K1]. Diffusion approximation, e.g. [G1] replaces the process $N(t)$ by a continuous diffusion process $X(t)$ whose incremental changes $dX(t) = X(t+dt) - X(t)$ are normally distributed with the mean βdt and variance αdt, where β, α are the coefficients of the diffusion equation

$$\frac{\partial f(x,t;x_0)}{\partial t} = \frac{\alpha}{2}\frac{\partial^2 f(x,t;x_0)}{\partial x^2} - \beta\frac{\partial f(x,t;x_0)}{\partial x} \tag{1}$$

which defines the conditional pdf $f(x,t;x_0)dx = P[x \le X(t) < x+dx \mid X(0) = x_0]$ of $X(t)$. Hence, both processes $X(t)$ and $N(t)$ have normally distributed changes; the choice $\beta = \lambda - \mu$, $\alpha = \sigma_A^2\lambda^3 + \sigma_B^2\mu^3 = C_A^2\lambda + C_B^2\mu$ ensures the same ratio of time-growth of mean and variance of these distributions. Function $f(n,t;n_0)$ approximates the distribution $p(n,t;n_0)$ of customers of all classes present in the queue.

Formal justification of diffusion approximation is in limit theorems for $G/G/1$ system given by Iglehart [I1]. If $\hat{N}_n$ is a series of random variables derived from $N(t)$:

$$\hat{N}_n = \frac{N(nt) - (\lambda-\mu)nt}{(\sigma_A^2\lambda^3 + \sigma_B^2\mu^3)\sqrt{n}},$$

then the series is weakly convergent (in the sense of distribution) to ξ where $\xi(t)$ is a standard Wiener process (diffusion process with $\beta = 0$ i $\alpha = 1$) provided that $\varrho > 1$, i.e. if the system is unstable. In the case of $\varrho = 1$ the series $\hat{N}_n$ is convergent to ξ_R. The $\xi_R(t)$ process is $\xi(t)$ process limited to half-axis $x > 0:$ $\xi_R(t) = \xi(t) - \inf\,[\xi(u),\ \ 0 \le u \le t]$. There is no similar theorems for service stations in equilibrium ($\varrho < 1$) and we should rely on heuristic confirmation of the utility of this approximation.

If the input stream λ is composed of K classes of customers having intensities $\lambda^{(k)}$, with total intensity $\lambda = \sum_{k=1}^{K}\lambda^{(k)}$ and service parameters for a class k are $E[B^{(k)}] = 1/\mu^k$, $\mathrm{Var}[B^{(k)}] = {\sigma_B^{(k)}}^2$, then the PDF $B(x)$ of joint for all classes service time distribution is expressed as

$$B(x) = \sum_{k=1}^{K}\frac{\lambda^{(k)}}{\lambda}B^{(k)}(x),$$

and

$$\frac{1}{\mu} = \sum_{k=1}^{K} \frac{\lambda^{(k)}}{\lambda} \frac{1}{\mu^{(k)}} ,$$

$$C_B^2 = \mu^2 \sum_{k=1}^{K} \frac{\lambda_{(k)}}{\lambda} \frac{1}{\mu^{(k)2}} ({C_B^{(k)}}^2 + 1) - 1 . \quad (2)$$

If we assume that the input streams are independent, the global number of arrived during Δt customers is normally distributed with variance $\lambda C_A^2 \Delta t = \sum_{k=1}^{K} \lambda^{(k)} {C_A^{(k)}}^2 \Delta t$, hence

$$C_A^2 = \sum_{k=1}^{K} \frac{\lambda^{(k)}}{\lambda} {C_A^{(k)}}^2 . \quad (3)$$

The above equations yield α, β of the diffusion equation.

Boundary conditions for Eq. (1) should be also defined. In [G1] diffusion approximation of a $G/G/1/N$ station was studied as a process $X(t)$ which is defined on the closed interval $x \in [0, N]$. When the process comes to $x = 0$, it remains there for a time exponentially distributed with the parameter λ and then it returns to $x = 1$; when it comes to $x = N$, it remains there for a time which is exponentially distributed with the parameter μ and then it starts at $x = N - 1$. The use of barriers with jumps (instantaneous returns) gives better results than the use of reflecting barriers applied earlier [N1] where probability of the process being at the barriers was neglected. With barriers with jumps, the diffusion equation is supplemented by the balance equations for $p_0(t) = P[X(t) = 0]$, $p_N(t) = P[X(t) = N]$ and becomes

$$\begin{aligned}
\frac{\partial f(x,t;x_0)}{\partial t} &= \frac{\alpha}{2} \frac{\partial^2 f(x,t;x_0)}{\partial x^2} - \beta \frac{\partial f(x,t;x_0)}{\partial x} + \\
&\quad + \lambda p_0(t) \delta(x-1) \\
&\quad + \mu p_N(t) \delta(x - N + 1) , \\
\frac{dp_0(t)}{dt} &= \lim_{x \to 0} [\frac{\alpha}{2} \frac{\partial f(x,t;x_0)}{\partial x} - \beta f(x,t;x_0)] \\
&\quad - \lambda p_0(t) , \\
\frac{dp_N(t)}{dt} &= - \lim_{x \to N} [\frac{\alpha}{2} \frac{\partial f(x,t;x_0)}{\partial x} - \beta f(x,t;x_0)] \\
&\quad - \mu p_N(t) .
\end{aligned} \quad (4)$$

In original works only the steady-state solution of Eq. (4) is given. Our approach, proposed in [C1], is first to solve the diffusion equation with absorbing barriers (the process ends when it comes to a barrier) placed at $x = 0$ and $x = N$ with the use of standard analytical methods (the method of mirrors) and obtain the pdf $\phi(x, t; x_0)$ of this process, then to express the pdf $f(x, t; x_0)$ of the diffusion with instantaneous returns from the barriers as a superposition of functions $\phi(x, t; x_0)$:

$$f(x, t; \psi) = \phi(x, t; \psi) + \int_0^t g_1(\tau)\phi(x, t-\tau; 1)d\tau + \int_0^t g_{N-1}(\tau)\phi(x, t-\tau; N-1)d\tau \quad (5)$$

where for $t = 0$, $\phi(x, t; x_0) = \delta(x - x_0)$ and for $t > 0$

$$\phi(x, t; x_0) = \frac{1}{\sqrt{2\Pi\alpha t}} \sum_{n=-\infty}^{\infty} \Big\{ \exp\left[\frac{\beta x'_n}{\alpha} - \frac{(x - x_0 - x'_n - \beta t)^2}{2\alpha t}\right] - \exp\left[\frac{\beta x''_n}{\alpha} - \frac{(x - x_0 - x''_n - \beta t)^2}{2\alpha t}\right]\Big\} \quad (6)$$

$x'_n = 2nN$, $x''_n = -2x_0 - x'_n$, and ψ is the initial condition and $\phi(x, t; \psi) = \int_0^N \phi(x, t; \xi)\psi(\xi)d\xi$. Functions $g_1(\tau)$, $g_{N-1}(\tau)$ are the densities of starting new processes (after a jump from the barrier) at points $x = 1$ and $x = N - 1$. These densities are given by a system of balance equations (7), (9) for probability flows coming *in* and *out* of the barriers; the equations make use of first passage times from starting points to the barriers and of the densities of sojourn times in the barriers (the assumption on exponentially distributed times spent in barriers is not now needed).

Densities $\gamma_0(t)$, $\gamma_N(t)$ of probability that at time t the process enters $x = 0$ or $x = N$ are

$$\begin{aligned}\gamma_0(t) &= p_0(0)\delta(t) + [1 - p_0(0) - p_N(0)]\gamma_{\psi,0}(t) + \int_0^t g_1(\tau)\gamma_{1,0}(t-\tau)d\tau \\ &\quad + \int_0^t g_{N-1}(\tau)\gamma_{N-1,0}(t-\tau)d\tau\ , \\ \gamma_N(t) &= p_N(0)\delta(t) + [1 - p_0(0) - p_N(0)]\gamma_{\psi,N}(t) + \int_0^t g_1(\tau)\gamma_{1,N}(t-\tau)d\tau \\ &\quad + \int_0^t g_{N-1}(\tau)\gamma_{N-1,N}(t-\tau)d\tau\ ,\end{aligned} \quad (7)$$

where $\gamma_{1,0}(t)$, $\gamma_{1,N}(t)$, $\gamma_{N-1,0}(t)$, $\gamma_{N-1,N}(t)$ are densities of the first passage times between corresponding points, e.g.

$$\gamma_{1,0}(t) = \lim_{x\to 0}\Big[\frac{\alpha}{2}\frac{\partial\phi(x, t; 1)}{\partial x} - \beta\phi(x, t; 1)\Big]\ . \quad (8)$$

For absorbing barriers

$$\lim_{x\to 0} \phi(x,t;x_0) = \lim_{x\to N} \phi(x,t;x_0) = 0 \,,$$

hence $\gamma_{1,0}(t) = \lim_{x\to 0} \frac{\alpha}{2} \frac{\partial \phi(x,t;1)}{\partial x}$. The density function of first passage time from $x = x_0$ to $x = 0$ is

$$\begin{aligned} \gamma_{x_0,0}(t) &= \lim_{x\to 0} [\frac{\alpha}{2} \frac{\partial}{\partial x} \phi(x,t;x_0) - \beta \phi(x,t;x_0)] \\ &= \frac{x_0}{\sqrt{2\Pi \alpha t^3}} e^{-\frac{(\beta t+1)^2}{2\alpha t}} \,. \end{aligned}$$

The functions $\gamma_{\psi,0}(t)$, $\gamma_{\psi,N}(t)$ denote densities of probabilities that the initial process, started at $t = 0$ at the point ξ with density $\psi(\xi)$ will end at time t by entering respectively $x = 0$ or $x = N$.

Densities $g_1(t)$ and $g_N(t)$ may be expressed with the use of functions $\gamma_0(t)$ and $\gamma_N(t)$:

$$\begin{aligned} g_1(\tau) &= \int_0^\tau \gamma_0(t) l_0(\tau - t) dt \,, \\ g_{N-1}(\tau) &= \int_0^\tau \gamma_N(t) l_N(\tau - t) dt \,, \end{aligned} \tag{9}$$

where $l_0(x)$, $l_N(x)$ are the densities of sojourn times in $x = 0$ and $x = N$; the distributions of these times are not restricted to exponential ones as it is in Eq. (4). The integrals in Eq. (5) are in fact convolutions of functions and we may rewrite this equation as

$$\begin{aligned} f(x,t;\psi) = \phi(x,t;\psi) + g_1(t) * \phi(x,t;1) d\tau + \\ g_{N-1}(t) * \phi(x,t;N-1) \end{aligned} \tag{10}$$

where $*$ denotes the convolution, or, transforming it with the use of Laplace transform, as

$$\begin{aligned} \bar{f}(x,s;\psi) = \bar{\phi}(x,s;\psi) + \bar{g}_1(s)\, \bar{\phi}(x,s;1) \\ + \bar{g}_{N-1}(s)\, \bar{\phi}(x,s;N-1) \,. \end{aligned} \tag{11}$$

Laplace transforms of Eqs. (7), (9) give $\bar{g}_1(s)$ and $\bar{g}_{N-1}(s)$, hence the Laplace transform $\bar{f}(x,s;\psi)$ of the density function $f(x,t;\psi)$ is obtained and supplemented by transforms of probabilities that at the moment t the process is in a barrier

$$\begin{aligned} \bar{p}_0(s) &= \frac{1}{s} \left[\bar{\gamma}_0(s) - \bar{g}_1(s) \right] , \\ \bar{p}_N(s) &= \frac{1}{s} \left[\bar{\gamma}_N(s) - \bar{g}_{N-1}(s) \right] . \end{aligned} \tag{12}$$

Expressions (11), (12) are inverted numerically, e.g. with the use of Stehfest algorithm.

This transient solution is obtained for constant parameters. To introduce $\alpha(t)$, $\beta(t)$ reflecting evolution of input streams, the time axis is divided into small intervals during which parameters are kept constant and the solution at the end of one interval gives the initial conditions to the diffusion equation in the next interval and with new parameters. Sometimes we need diffusion parameters $\alpha(x,t)$, $\beta(x,t)$ depending also on the value of the process – this is a way to reflect control mechanisms reacting on the queue size or to model parallel servers. In this case, the diffusion interval $x \in [0,N]$ is divided into subintervals of appropriate (e.g. unitary) length and the parameters are kept constant within these subintervals. The equations for space-intervals are solved together with balance equations for probability flows between neighboring intervals. For each time- and space-subinterval with constant parameters, transient solution is obtained. As previously, the Laplace transforms of density functions are inverted numerically.

This method was implemented in a software package and is able to solve large queueing network models: we analyzed already transient states at a network of 37 stations of G/G/20/20 type representing a part of wireless cellular network. It was also used to model dynamics of flows subject to some traffic control mechanisms encountered in communication networks:

— control mechanisms at the entrance of a network: leaky bucket, also in presence of correlated (self-similar) input, jumping window, and sliding window;

— space-priority queues at a network switch: a queue with threshold and with push-out algorithm;

— the traffic dynamics along a virtual path composed of a certain number of nodes, and a feed-back algorithm of traffic control between nodes and sources.

3 The Buffer Model

Basing on the solution developped in the previous section and using similar notation, we build a diffusion model for the assembly buffer at electronic-optical (E/O) node. We assume that the size of incoming electronic packets is between 1 and M blocks, without precising the size of block, i.e. the granularity of the input stream. The input stream in the model is composed of M independent streams and a stream m, $m = 1, \ldots M$ represents packets of the size of m blocks. The parameters of this stream are λ_m, C^2_{Am}. As the diffusion proces represents the number of blocks, we should determine the mean value and variance of the number of blocks arriving during a time-unit. Assuming that once for m times we have an arrival of a block following specified pattern and then $(m-1)$ immediate arrivals correlated with the first one, we obtain the parameters for the block interarrival time distribution

$$\lambda_{mb} = m\lambda_m, \quad C^2_{Amb} = mC^2_{Am} + m - 1 \tag{13}$$

The parameters of the total input stream being a sum of M streams are computed using (3) and (13). We study the accumulation of blocks in the buffer, therefore the diffusion parameters are defined only by input process,there is no service time,

$$\beta = \sum_{m=1}^{M} \lambda_{mb} \quad \alpha = \sum_{m=1}^{M} \lambda_{mb} C^2_{Amb}. \tag{14}$$

We assume the asynchronous work of the node: when an incoming packet is too large to be put into the buffer (the number of blocks in this packet is greater than the place still available in the buffer), the content of the buffer is sent as optical packet and the last packet that did not match the left buffer space is put to the empty buffer – the process of building a new packet is being started. We assume also the time-out T after which the packet is sent regardless its content.

The goal of the model is to obtain the distribution of interdeparture times and the distribution of the number of blocks occupied in the optical packet leaving the node.

Let N be the size of optical buffer expressed in blocks. The value of the diffusion process $X(t)$ at time t represents the current number of blocks already occupied inside the buffer. We consider diffusion process on the interval $x \in (0, N-1)$. Within this interval we distinguish M subintervals: subinterval no.1 $(0, N-M)$, and $M-1$ subintervals of unitary length: subinterval no. 2 is $x \in (N-M, N-M+1)$, ..., subinterval no. M is $x \in (N-2, N-1)$. Between subintervals, i.e. at the points $x = N-M, N-M+1, \ldots, N-2$ and $x = N-1$ we place imaginary barriers that allow us to make a balance of probability flows and to represent interactions among subintervals. The barriers are introduced only to manipulate the probability density flows. These flows represent the probability densities corresponding to the events that the incoming packet is too large to be placed at the buffer, hence the optical packet is sent and the filling of a new packet is started. E.g. the flow from the barrier placed at $x = N-M$ going to $x = M$ corresponds to the arrival of a packet of M blocks when in the buffer there is only the place for $M-1$ blocks. An optical packet lacking $M-1$ blocks is sent and M blocks are put to the empty buffer starting the filling of a new packet. The barriers are absorbing ones, as at previous section, hence we may use for each subinterval the solution for the process density $f(x,t;x_0)$ similar to the obtained above in Eq. (10) giving only proper starting points and starting intensities. The flows absorbed by the barriers reappear on their other side at the distance ε.

Let $\gamma_i^L(t)$ represent the flow coming to the barrier placed at $x = i$ from its left side and $\gamma_i^R(t)$ be the flow coming to this barrier from its right side. The flows start diffusion processes at both sides of the barrier, at points $x = i-\varepsilon$ and $x = i+\varepsilon$ with intensities $g_i^L(t)$ and $g_i^R(t)$. The whole flow $\gamma_i^R(t)$ is transmitted to $x = i - \varepsilon$

$$g^L_{N-i}(t) = \gamma^R_{N-i}(t)$$

but only a part of the flow $g_i^L(t)$ enters $x = i+\varepsilon$. The flow $g_i^L(t)$ is divided in the following way. The part of this probability flow which corresponds to the arrivals of packets which are smaller than $M-i$ blocks and may be put into the buffer reappears immediately at $x=i+\varepsilon$ as $g_i^R(t)$. The part of $\gamma_i^L(t)$ which represents the arrivals of packets having exactly the size of $M-i$ blocks still available at the buffer is directed to the barrier at $x=0$ (the optical packet is sent full, with maximal number of blocks occupied). The part of $\gamma_i^L(t)$ representing the flow of packets of size $k > N-i$ which are too large to be stocked in the current optical packet is directed to the points $x=k$ at the first interval. The barrier at $x=N-1$ injects flows to $x=0$ (the arrivals of one-block packets completing the buffer) and to $x=2,\ldots,M$.

The barrier at $x=0$ acts similarly as in $G/G/1/N$ model, the sojourn time in this barrier corresponds to the time when the buffer is empty, then the jumps are performed to points $x=1,\ldots M$ as to the empty buffer the packets of the size $1,\ldots,M$ may arrive.

Having all this in mind we determine the intensity $g_{0,k}(t)$ of jumps (i.e the density of starting a new diffusion process at a corresponding point) from the barrier at $x=0$ to a point $x=k$:

$$g_{0,k}(\tau) = \int_0^\tau \frac{k\lambda_k}{\sum_{l=1}^M l\lambda_l} \gamma_0(t) l_0(\tau - t)dt \ ,$$

where $l_0(t)$ is the soujourn time density and the input flow $\gamma_0(t)$ contains all flows directed to the barrier from other barriers as well as flows coming to if from starting points inside the first interval:

$$\begin{aligned}\gamma_0(t) = \gamma_{\psi_1,0}(t) + \\ &\sum_{l=1}^M g_l(t) * \gamma_{l,0}(t) + g_{N-M}^L(t) * \gamma_{N-M-\varepsilon}(t) + \\ &\sum_{l=1}^M \gamma_{N-l}^L(t) \Lambda_l \end{aligned} \qquad (15)$$

The first term corresponds to the flow coming from initial distribution of the probability mass (function $\psi_1(x)$ inside first interval), the second line represents flows coming from starting points inside first interval ($x=1,2,\ldots,M$ and $x=N-M-\varepsilon$), and the last sum gathers flows from barriers. We denote:

$$\Lambda_i = \frac{i\lambda_i}{\sum_{l=1}^M l\lambda_l}, \qquad \Omega_k = \frac{\sum_{l=1}^k \Lambda_l}{\sum_{l=1}^M \Lambda_l}$$

Let us note that

$$g_{N-i}^R(t) = \Omega_{i-1} \gamma_{N-i}^L(t)$$

and

$$g_i(t) = \Lambda_i \gamma_0(t) * l_0(t)$$

The solution for the first subinterval $0 < x \leq N - M$

$$f_1(x,t;\psi_1) = \phi(x,t;\psi_1) + \sum_{i=1}^{M} g_i(t) * \phi(x,t;i) + g^L_{N-M}(t) * \phi(x,t;N-M-\varepsilon), \tag{16}$$

for an interval $i = 2, \ldots M - 1$

$$f_i(x,t;\psi_i) = \phi(x,t;\psi_i) + g^R_{N-M+i-2}(t) * \phi(x,t;N-M+i-2+\varepsilon)(t) + g^L_{N-M+i-1}(t) * \phi(x,t;N-M+i-1-\varepsilon), \tag{17}$$

and

$$f_M(x,t;\psi_M) = \phi(x,t;\psi_i) + g^R_{N-2}(t) * \phi(x,t;N-2+\varepsilon)(t) \tag{18}$$

We obtain steady-state solution finding

$$\lim_{s\to 0} s\bar{f}(x,s;\psi_i) = \lim_{t\to\infty} f(x,t;\psi_i).$$

The density of the packet interdeparture times $d(t)$ is obtained by summing all densities that end the buffer filling, namely all probability flows from barriers at $x = N - M, \ldots N - 1$ to points $x = 0, 1, \ldots, M$ computed in the model where these flows are not reinjected into the diffusion interval but accumulated in a supplementary state "departure of the packet".

To incorporate in the model the timeout T, the probability mass which at time $t = T$ is still inside the interval $(0, N - 1)$ (have not yet gone to the supplementary state) is at this moment moved immediately to the supplementary state. The distribution of the number of blocs inside the dispatched packet is obtained using probability of all possible events: probability mass accumulted at the supplementary state through the jumps from barriers to $x = 0$ represents probability that the packet leavs with all blocks occupied. Probability mass accumulated in the supplementary state coming through jumps to $x = 1$ represents probability that the packet leaves with one block empty, etc.

4 Numerical Example

In numerical example below we take $N = 50, 100, 150, 200, 250$, $M = 20$, $p_m = 1/M$ (the traffic intensity for each stream is $\lambda_m = 0.01$), $m = 1, \ldots 20$, i.e. the size of optical packet is $N = 50, 100, 150, 200, 250$ blocks, the electronic packets are of size $1, \ldots, 20$ blocks, and all these packets are equiprobable. The streams are Poisson, hence $C^2_{Am} = 1$, $m = 1, \ldots 20$. Naturally, we may easily insert any value of λ_m, p_m, C^2_{Am}.

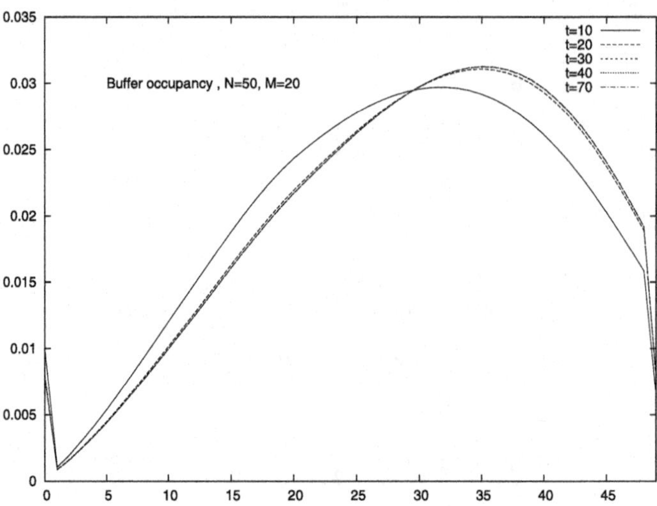

Fig. 1. Distribution $f(x, t; 0)$ of the number of blocks in the buffer as a function of time, $N = 50$

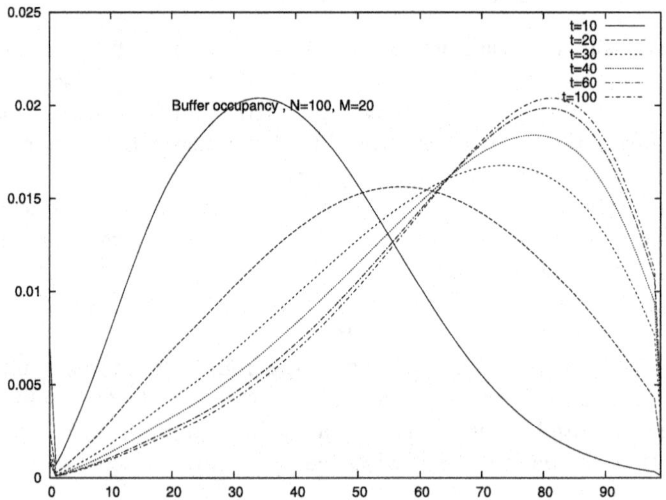

Fig. 2. Distribution $f(x, t; 0)$ of the number of blocks in the buffer as a function of time, $N = 100$

Figs. 1-5 show the solution $f(x, t; 0)$ of diffusion equations, that means the functions $f_1(x, t; 0), \ldots, f_M(x, t; 0)$ given by eqs. (16), (17), (18). They present the buffer filling as a function of time. We have chosen the case $x_0 = 0$: the initial buffer is empty. Numerical inversion of Laplace transforms was done with

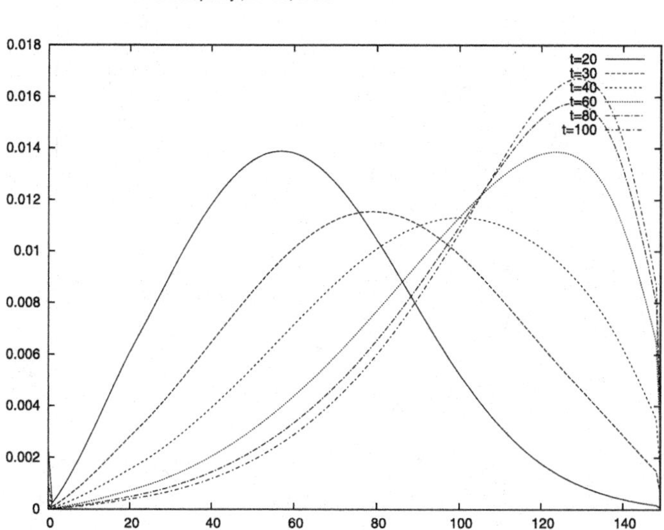

Fig. 3. Distribution $f(x,t;0)$ of the number of blocks in the buffer as a function of time, $N = 150$

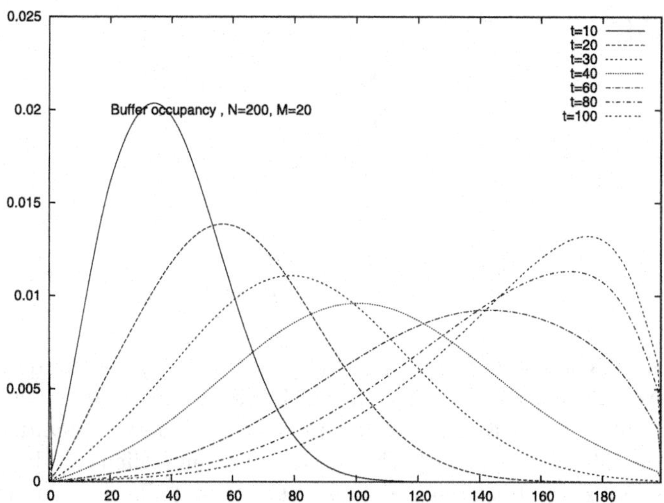

Fig. 4. Distribution $f(x,t;0)$ of the number of blocks in the buffer as a function of time, $N = 200$.

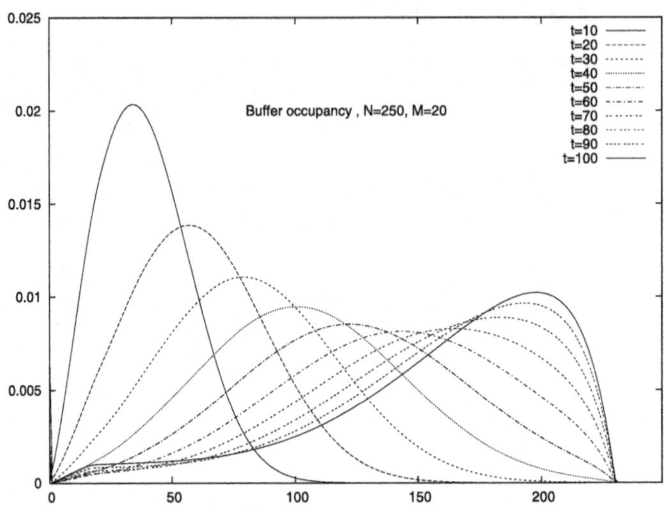

Fig. 5. Distribution $f(x, t; 0)$ of the number of blocks in the buffer as a function of time, $N = 250$

the use of Stehfest algorithm. In this algorithm a function $f(t)$ is obtained from its transform $\bar{f}(s)$ for any fixed argument t as

$$f(t) = \frac{\ln 2}{2} \sum_{i=1}^{N} V_i \, \bar{f}\left(\frac{\ln 2}{t} i\right) , \tag{19}$$

where

$$V_i = (-1)^{H/2+i} \times \tag{20}$$

$$\times \sum_{k=\lfloor \frac{i+1}{2} \rfloor}^{\min(i,H/2)} \frac{k^{H/2+1}(2k)!}{(H/2-k)!k!(k-1)!(i-k)!(2k-i)!} .$$

H is an even integer end depends on a computer precision; we used $H = 14$.

The figures illustrate the ease with which transient solutions may be studied for different sets of parameters and prove the numerical soundness of the procedure: the introduction of 20 subintervals with multiplicity of flows between barriers does not disturb the results. Some other results, such as interdeparture time distribution or the distribution of the number of blocks inside optical packets, having clue importance for the quality of service at the optical side of the network may be obtained on their basis.

5 Conclusions

Presented model may be useful to investigate the transient states and the dynamics of flows on the edge between electronic and optical networks. They may include self-similar input rates and investigate the influence of the node on the characteristics of the traffic. We do not present here any real validation of the model, but a comparison with simulation results presented in [D1] as well as long-term experience with other diffusion models, and their validation via simulations, prove that such models give in general reasonable estimations. However, the programming effort needed to obtain them is not negligable.

Acknowledgment

This work has been supported by the CNRS-PAN project *Diffusion approximation in transient analysis and evaluation of networks with integrated services* and the EuroNGI Network of Excellence.

References

[C1] Czachórski, T.: A method to solve diffusion equation with instantaneous return processes acting as boundary conditions. Bulletin of Polish Academy of Sciences, Technical Sciences, **41**, no. 4, pp. 417-451, 1993.

[D1] Domańska, J., Kotuliak, I., Atmaca, T., and Czachórski, T.: Optical packet filling. Proc. of 10th Polish Teletraffic Symposium, 2003.

[G1] Gelenbe, E. On Approximate Computer Systems Models. Journal of ACM, **22** (1975), no. 2.

[I1] Iglehart, D.: Weak Convergence in Queueing Theory. Advances in Applied Probability **5** (1973), no. 5, 570-594.

[K1] Kleinrock, L.: Queueing Systems, vol. II. Wiley, New York, 1976.

[N1] Newell, G. F.: Applications of Queueing Theory. Chapman and Hall, London, 1971.

Choreographing Security and Performance Analysis for Web Services

Stephen Gilmore[1], Valentin Haenel[1], Leïla Kloul[2], and Monika Maidl[3]

[1] Laboratory for Foundations of Computer Science, The University of Edinburgh, Scotland
[2] PRiSM, Université de Versailles, 45, avenue des Etats-Unis, 78000 Versailles, France
[3] Siemens AG, CT IC3, Otto-Hahn-Ring 6, 81739 München, Germany

Abstract. We describe a UML-based method which supports model-driven development of service-oriented architectures including those used in Web services. Analysable content is extracted from the UML models in the form of process calculus descriptions. These are analysed to provide strong guarantees of satisfactory security and performance. The results are reflected back in the form of a modified version of the UML model which highlights points of the design which can give rise to operational difficulties. A design platform supporting the methodology, *Choreographer*, interoperates with state-of-the-art UML modelling tools such as Poseidon. We illustrate the approach on an example.

1 Introduction

Web services must deliver secure services to users in order that financial and other confidential transactions can be conducted without interference. Off-the-shelf solutions are not available. Web services need to build end-to-end security from the point-to-point security afforded by standard network protocols. Even if a secure system can be created, scaling up to large user populations provides a steep challenge. The availability of many different forms of assistance (caching, stateless session beans, process isolation and others) means that the challenge of building scalable systems is complicated further by difficult-to-quantify approaches to system performance tuning.

We have developed a design platform, *Choreographer*, which seeks to assist with the development of secure systems with quantified levels of performance. To provide an accessible entry point for practising Web service developers the methodology which we support uses the UML. This is a novel feature of our work: we use a modelling language where a specification language or process calculus might more often be used to initiate the analysis. Many UML designs are not analysed either qualitatively or quantitatively. Here we provide support for both types of analysis, and illustrate the value of the analysis via an example.

We use a range of UML diagram types to express the security and performance considerations of the system. As a principle, we use standard UML notation: there are no notational extensions or additional diagram types. This decision has two beneficial consequences. First, a UML modeller using this methodology does not need to learn any supplementary notation. Second, we are able to use standard UML tools such as Poseidon [1] to edit the UML diagrams which we use.

M. Bravetti et al. (Eds.): EPEW 2005 and WS-FM 2005, LNCS 3670, pp. 200–214, 2005.

We use class diagrams, collaboration diagrams, sequence diagrams and state diagrams to describe the system under study in UML terms. Additional diagram types may be used in the UML project which is accepted as an input to Choreographer. These can be used for other purposes in model-driven development, such as automatic code generation, and will not interfere with the analysis process. Our aim is to disrupt existing model-driven development approaches as little as possible while adding value to the UML modelling work which would be going on in any case.

Different models can be used for different purposes in the design of an application and so the methodology supported by our design platform allows modellers to either do a security analysis alone, or a performance analysis, or both. That is, the annotated versions of models which result from one run can be used again as inputs to Choreographer to perform a different type of analysis. The consequence of this is that a modeller using an established operational procedure to determine satisfactory levels of security (resp. performance) can use our design platform to do performance (resp. security) analysis alone. They are not forced to adopt both of the kinds of analysis which we offer if they do not need both, or already have a preferred way to do one of them.

The original contribution of this paper is to present a UML-based methodology for integrated security and performance analysis. The method is supported by a well-engineered tool and set on the formal foundation of dedicated process calculi with custom analysers. We describe the UML-based methodology which Choreographer supports and discuss the implementation of the Choreographer platform itself. We describe its use on a typical Web service creation problem: a Web-based micro-business. We believe that the Choreographer software tool could also be used for high-level analysis of other service-oriented architecture questions such as the assessment of service discovery protocols but we do not demonstrate this in the present paper.

Structure of This Paper: The paper is structured as follows: the Choreographer analysis tool is presented in Section 2. The example application is a web-based micro business, described in Section 3. This is followed by a UML model and its associated performance and security models in Sections 4, 5 and 6. Related work and conclusions follow.

2 Choreographer

One feature of the methodology which we support with the Choreographer design platform tool is that modellers are able to express the models which are input to Choreographer in standard UML. The analysis process is initiated by invoking Choreographer on a UML project archive. The formal content of the UML model is stored in such an archive in an XML-based interchange representation (XMI). Software connectors termed *extractors* process the XMI representation of the input model and derive an analysable form of the model expressed in a process calculus. We use different process calculi for security and performance analysis: LySa [2] for the former and PEPA [3] for the latter.

Another key feature of the method is that the results of the analysis are reflected back as a modified version of the original UML model. The *reflectors* which do this are also available as software components which take the original UML project and the results of the analysers as inputs and write their results as complete UML projects in which the results of the analysis have been incorporated. The purpose of this is to ensure that the interpretation of the analysis results can be undertaken at the UML level and that the UML is not being used only as a model description language from which a process calculus representation is generated.

The Choreographer platform is designed to support UML-centered development but is flexible enough to accommodate other modes of use in addition. These might simply be preferred by designers or developers who are using the platform or they might be needed to support a style of development favoured by the institution or software house which commissioned the development. Thus, a guiding principle of the design of Choreographer is that the processing of UML models should be made visible to the developer in order that the mapping between UML diagram elements and constructs of the process calculi beneath is transparent. This principle ensures that modellers have access to the representations which are needed to understand how their diagram elements are interpreted in the analysis process.

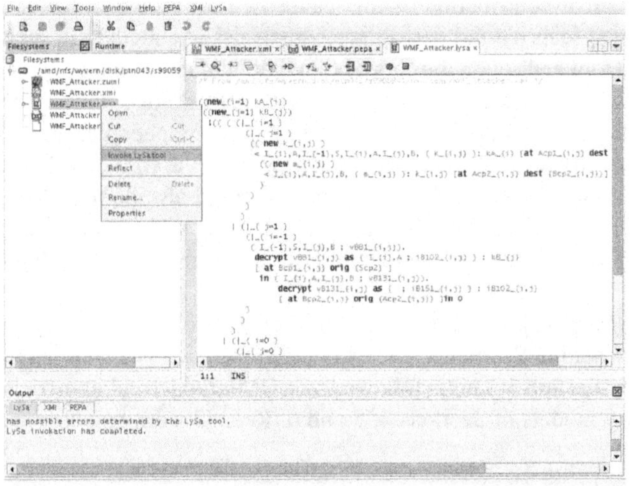

Fig. 1. The Choreographer user interface

In terms of its appearance, the Choreographer platform follows the conventional design of an IDE, as seen in Figure 1. The main design area divides into an explorer on the left, an editor on the right, and a message console beneath these. The explorer provides a view onto the local file system which is structured in order to group related documents into logical projects. The editor is language-aware with contextual modes: we have implemented editors for the process calculi which we use in the security and performance analysis process. The console is used to feed back to the user information about the progress of commands or analyses which have been launched from the application menus. Concise summaries of the analyses are printed into the console to allow information about the outcome to be obtained without having to initiate the reflection process and render the results in the Poseidon UML modelling tool.

3 The Web-Based Business System

The case study provided by our industrial partner is a business-to-business Web service to enable e-business based on a peer-to-peer authentication and communication paradigm. The objective of this system is to provide support to micro web-based businesses which do not themselves have the capability to develop proprietary solutions for e-business.

The service is accessible through both wired Internet connections and mobile devices using standard protocols such as the wireless application protocol. The system will present the various services offered by the service providers according to a coherent layout and will provide an interface for service access. While users should be able to process their transactions on a peer-to-peer basis, it is necessary to provide a central portal at which users register and can search for services. Registration and searching for services can be handled by UDDI.

The system naturally decomposes into three parts: the portal, service providers and customers (Figure 2). The upper part of Figure 2 describes that part of the functionality which involves the portal. The lower part concerns the peer-to-peer functionality.

The Portal. The portal enables remote data search and service navigation. Moreover it constitutes the interface between the customers and the service providers during the on-line business transactions. The e-business data management provides access to distributed products and services catalogues. The portal supports a significant number of concurrent sessions while providing end-to-end security of the transactions.

The Service Provider. A new service provider joining the system first must register at the portal. A registered service provider can publish its services onto the portal dynamically. The list of its services can be accessed by any customer through the portal. Each provider will be able to modify its published services list by adding a new product; changing the characteristics of an existing one; or removing a service from the list. At any moment, a service provider can quit the system by unregistering from the portal. The service provider can also handle transactions directly with customers who have registered at the service provider.

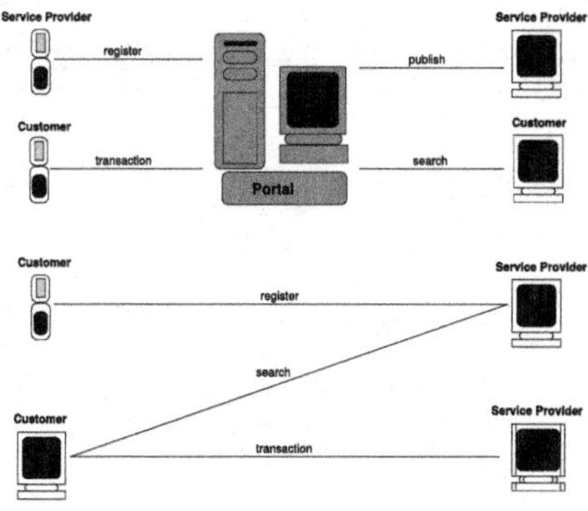

Fig. 2. Architecture of the web-based business system

The customer. Like the service providers, new customers have to register at the portal before being able to use its services. The registered customers are informed by the portal about available services, the newly published services, and the modified or removed ones. The user may perform on-line transactions via the portal to buy products he is interested in by selecting them from the list. The customers' order requests are then routed by the portal to the appropriate service provider. Alternatively, a customer can choose to communicate peer-to-peer with a chosen service provider after registering directly with this service provider.

4 UML Model of the System

We turn now to our model of the above system. The performance model of the system consists of a collaboration between sequential object instances which undertake timed activities either individually, or in collaboration with other objects. Thus the UML diagram types which are used to describe this model are class diagrams (identifying the kinds of the objects in the system), state diagrams (detailing the behaviour of the objects) and collaboration diagrams (introducing an operational configuration of the system with named object instances collaborating on sets of activities).

Performance analysis of the system is conducted via the generation and solution of a continuous-time Markov chain (CTMC) representation of the system, thus the durations of all of the activities in the system are quantified by providing the parameter to a negative exponential distribution.

The state diagram which represents a buyer in the system is shown in Figure 3.

Other components in the model are not much more complex than that of the buyers. Figure 4 shows that the model of the service providers in the system have common synchronisation points with the buyers (reflecting exchanges which are not routed through the central portal in the system, for reasons of scalability). Where these synchronisation points occur, one of the interacting components specifies the rate of occurrence of the activity and the other passively co-operates with these activities.

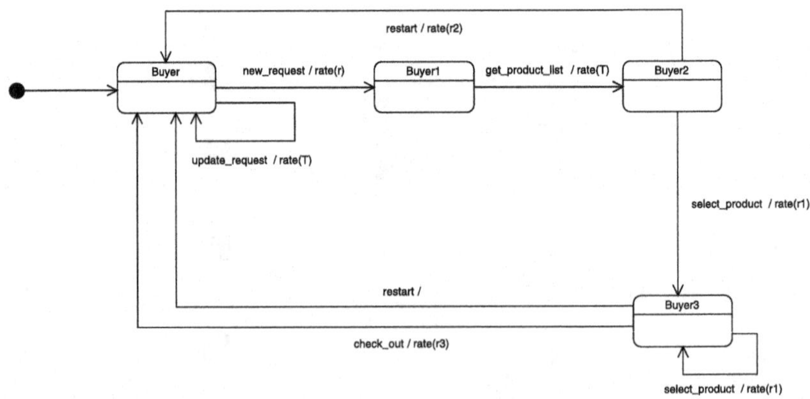

Fig. 3. State diagram of the Buyer in the Web-based micro-business model

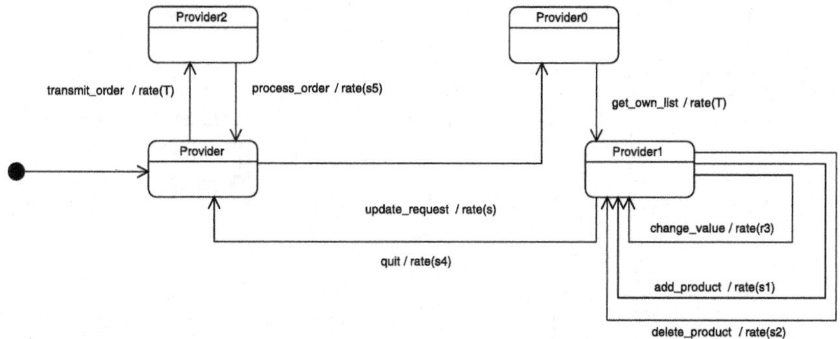

Fig. 4. State diagram of the Provider in the Web-based micro-business model

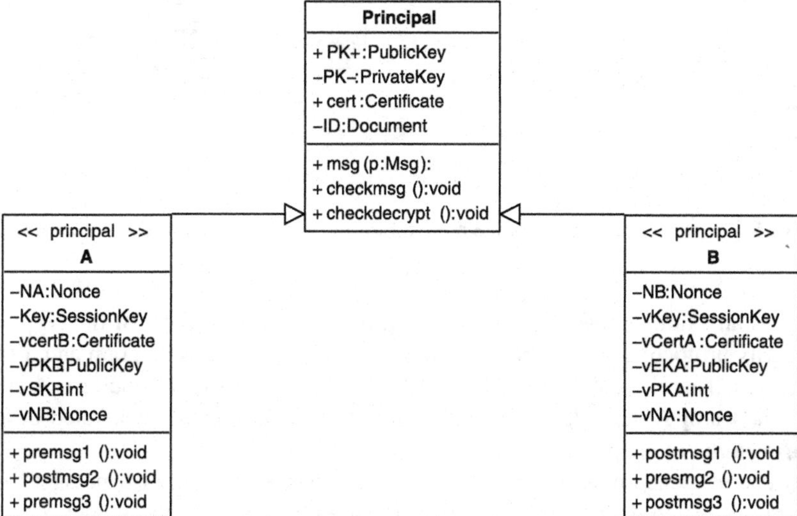

Fig. 5. The class diagram for the principals involved in secure transactions

In the UML design, security relevant information is specified by the ForLySa profile [4], which provides the means to annotate class diagrams and sequence diagrams with security-specific data. More precisely, ForLysa allows us to specify cryptographic security protocols with two participants (A and B) who typically exchange a new session key. Such protocols use cryptographic concepts like cryptographic keys and nonces, which are provided by two classes in the ForLysa profile: the class *Msg* for messages and the class *Principal* for participants of the protocol. The class *Msg* has attributes holding the sender and receiver of the message and the encrypted and unencrypted payloads of the message; the latter are objects of appropriate classes, and these classes contain methods for encrypting and decrypting data. The class *Principal* contains attributes for the private/public keys or symmetric keys associated with a principal, and specifies methods for sending and checking of messages.

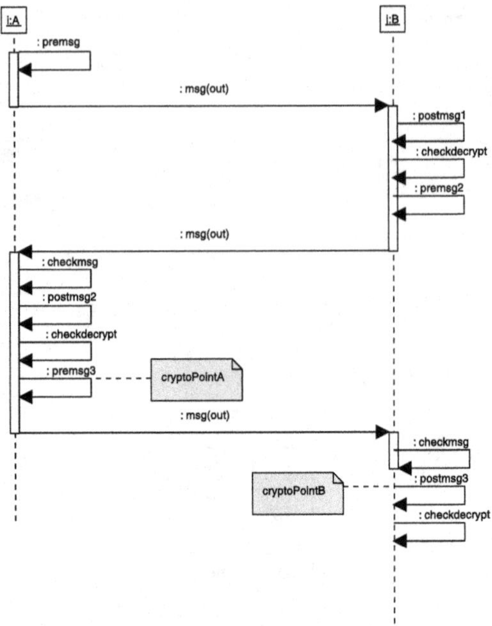

Fig. 6. The sequence diagram of the protocol for the principals involved in secure transactions

As an example, we show the UML design in Choreographer of the cryptographic security protocol described in Section 6, consisting of a class diagram and a sequence diagram. The class diagram, shown in Figure 5, specifies two principals A and B, as subclasses of *Principal*, which have attributes to hold the data generated or acquired during a run of the protocol.

The sequence diagram in Figure 6 describes the exchange of messages between A and B which defines the protocol. For each message, first the sender prepares and encrypts the content in method *premsg* by providing values for the attributes of a variable *out* of class *Msg*. When receiving a message, the recipient checks its contents (eg. correct addresses) with method *checkmsg*, then decrypts the encrypted parts with method *postmsg*. This assigns a value to the attribute which holds the decrypted content of the message. The decrypted part is then analysed in *checkdecrypt* where the receiver checks that the content has the required format. Figure 5 shows the call sequence for these methods, while the body of each method is specified by constraints which are not visible in the diagram.

5 Performance Analysis

The performance analysis of the above UML project proceeds by extracting a performance model in Hillston's Performance Evaluation Process Algebra (PEPA) [3]. This extraction is performed automatically by the Choreographer design platform.

5.1 The PEPA Model

The objects whose behaviour is specified by state diagrams in the UML model give rise to PEPA components in the process algebra model. The first component, *Portal*, models the behaviour of the interface between the service providers and the customers. The second component, *Provider*, models any provider registered in the system. The last component, *Buyer*, is used to model the behaviour of a customer. Note that in this model, we assume that both buyers and providers are already known to the system: they have already registered.

Component *Buyer.* In an on-line transaction, the system user starts by sending a request to the portal about a specific product he is interested in—for example, books. This can be done by a simple click on the icon titled "Books" in the main pages of available products provided by the portal. This is modelled by action type *new_request*. The response of the portal is to send to the customer the catalogue or list of books available with all characteristics. We model this using action type *get_product_list*. Once the customer has the targeted list, he can select all the items he wants (action *select_product*) and then go to the check out (action *check_out*). This last step allows the buyer to place an order for selected items. At any moment the customer can change his mind and stop the process. This is modelled using action type *restart*. Note that action type *get_product_list* has an unspecified rate in component *Buyer* because the rate is defined by the portal which will send the list of products at his rhythm.

$$
\begin{aligned}
Buyer &\stackrel{\text{def}}{=} (new\_request, r).Buyer_1 + (update\_request, \top).Buyer \\
Buyer_1 &\stackrel{\text{def}}{=} (get\_product\_list, \top).Buyer_2 \\
Buyer_2 &\stackrel{\text{def}}{=} (select\_product, r_1).Buyer_3 + (restart, r_2).Buyer \\
Buyer_3 &\stackrel{\text{def}}{=} (select\_product, r_1).Buyer_3 + (restart, r_2).Buyer \\
&\quad + (check\_out, r_3).Buyer
\end{aligned}
$$

Component *Provider.* Once a service provider is registered, he may either send a request to the system to update the list of products or services he has published or receive an order from the portal. The former is modelled using action type *update_request* and the latter using action type *transmit_order*. In the first case, he will receive the list of services he owns (action *get_own_list*) and can then make all of the changes which he wants to using action types *add_product*, *delete_product* and *change_values*. Once he is finished with the updates he can leave the system (action type *quit*). In the second case, he will consider the customer order and do what is necessary to satisfy the request. This is modelled using action type *process_order*.

$$
\begin{aligned}
Provider &\stackrel{\text{def}}{=} (update\_request, s).Provider_0 + (transmit\_order, \top).Provider_2 \\
Provider_0 &\stackrel{\text{def}}{=} (get\_own\_list, \top).Provider_1 \\
Provider_1 &\stackrel{\text{def}}{=} (add\_product, s_1).Provider_1 + (delete\_product, s_2).Provider_1 \\
&\quad + (change\_values, s_3).Provider_1 + (quit, s_4).Provider \\
Provider_2 &\stackrel{\text{def}}{=} (process\_order, s_5).Provider
\end{aligned}
$$

Component *Portal.* The portal manages both the buyers and the providers. All activities of component *Portal* are synchronizing activities, either with the buyers or the providers.

$$
\begin{aligned}
Portal &\stackrel{\text{def}}{=} (new\_request, \top).Portal_1 + (update\_request, \top).Portal_3 \\
&+ (select\_product, \top).Portal_1 + (restart, \top).Portal \\
&+ (check\_out, \top).Portal_2 + (get\_product\_list, v_1).Portal_1 \\
Portal_1 &\stackrel{\text{def}}{=} (get\_product\_list, v_1).Portal_1 + (select\_product, \top).Portal_1 \\
&+ (restart, \top).Portal + (check\_out, \top).Portal_2 \\
&+ (new\_request, \top).Portal_1 \\
Portal_2 &\stackrel{\text{def}}{=} (transmit\_order, v).Portal + (select\_product, \top).Portal_2 \\
&+ (restart, \top).Portal_2 + (check\_out, \top).Portal_2 \\
&+ (new\_request, \top).Portal_2 + (get\_product\_list, v_1).Portal_2 \\
Portal_3 &\stackrel{\text{def}}{=} (get\_list, v_2).Portal_3 + (add\_product, \top).Portal_3 \\
&+ (delete\_product, \top).Portal_3 + (change\_values, \top).Portal_3 \\
&+ (quit, \top).Portal
\end{aligned}
$$

The Complete System: The behaviour of the actors of the online system and their interactions between each other are captured by component $Web\_Business$ which is defined as follows:

$$
\begin{aligned}
&Web\_Business \stackrel{\text{def}}{=} \\
&\quad (Buyer \underset{K}{\bowtie} \dots \underset{K}{\bowtie} Buyer) \underset{L}{\bowtie} ((Provider || \dots || Provider) \underset{M}{\bowtie} Portal)
\end{aligned}
$$

where the synchronising sets are defined as follows:

$$
\begin{aligned}
K &= \{update\_request\} \\
L &= \{new\_request, get\_product\_list, select\_product, restart, check\_out, \\
&\quad update\_request\} \\
M &= \{update\_request, get\_own\_list, transmit\_order, add\_product, \\
&\quad delete\_product, change\_values, quit\}
\end{aligned}
$$

Remark: The use of action *update_request* in component *Buyer* ensures that during the updates of a product list by its owner, the buyers do not have access to this list. As all components of the model must synchronise on *update_request*, it will not be enabled unless all occurrences of component *Buyer* are in their initial state.

5.2 Numerical Results

In this section we give an idea of the performance measures which we can compute in the context of such an application. We are mainly interested in the throughput of the portal. We consider a system composed of five buyers and one provider. This simple system allows us to retain intellectual control of the behaviour of the throughput in a system with a portal based architecture. All curves are plotted as a function of the arrival rate r of the requests of one buyer.

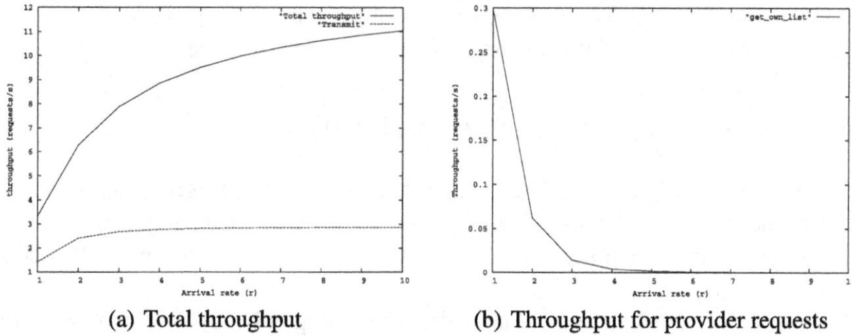

(a) Total throughput

(b) Throughput for provider requests

Fig. 7. Throughput computation

- Figure 7(a) depicts the total throughput of the portal in terms of buyer's requests to get a product list and to select a product from a list, and the provider's requests to get its own list. This figure also gives the throughput part related to the transmission of the orders to the provider. As we can see, the transmission of the buyer's orders is a very small part of the throughput of the system. This may be explained by the fact that the buyers spend the greater part of their time selecting products. Moreover, once an item is selected, a buyer may decide to abandon or restart. Thus not all buyers end up checking out with purchases.
- Figure 7(b) shows the behaviour of the part of the portal throughput related to the provider requests (*get_own_list*). Unlike what we have seen in Figure 7(a), this throughput decreases as the arrival rate increases. As we have more requests from the buyers, the portal spends more time dealing with these requests, and thus less time with the provider requests.

6 Security Analysis

The security of a networked service depends heavily on the ability of users to send confidential messages via wireless or Internet connections, and to confirm the identity of the partner in their message exchange. Cryptographic techniques are usually used both to ensure the confidentiality of messages and for authentication.

But cryptography is not a magic wand to make everything all right. The main issue is that sending encrypted messages is only safe if only the authorized parties have the corresponding key. So data security becomes a key management problem [5], and the main task consists of designing an appropriate protocol for *authenticated key exchange*. Such a protocol allows two or more participants to exchange a cryptographic session key in such a way that the participants are assured that only the intended parties obtain the session key. Confidentiality and integrity of data is then guaranteed by encrypting all data with the session key. The main tool for providing proper authentication in such a key-exchange protocol is again cryptography, and hence an analysis tool must be able to deal with cryptographic concepts. Before describing the LySatool [2] used by Choreographer, we first discuss the security requirements of the web-based business system, and show the key exchange protocol chosen for the project. The protocol can be realised by the use of WS-Security, which provides all of the necessary mechanisms.

6.1 Security Analysis for the Web-Based Business System

In the case study, all communication should be encrypted to guarantee data confidentiality and integrity. This means that before starting a data exchange, a service provider and a customer or the portal and a user have to use a protocol for authenticated session key exchange.

For this protocol, there is a choice between using either symmetric cryptography or public key cryptography in a protocol for authenticated key exchange. When using symmetric key cryptography, the communication has to be conducted via a central server, and all users have to share initial symmetric keys with the server. The design goal of the project of providing peer-to-peer communication between service providers and customers would be violated if communication between users necessarily involved a central server. Moreover, initial distribution of secret symmetric keys is difficult to achieve in a practical way. Hence a protocol based on public key cryptography is used. In order to link a user identity U to a public key, it is essential to use certificates $cert_U$, e.g. X.509 certificates, which are signed by some trusted certification authority.

(1) A $\rightarrow$ B: A, $cert_A$
(2) B $\rightarrow$ A: {B, NB}:K_A^+, $cert_B$
(3) A $\rightarrow$ B: {A, NB, K_{AB}}:K_B^+

The aim of the protocol is to provide authenticated key exchange between A and B, i.e. after the exchange both A and B are assured that only they know the new session key K_{AB}. More precisely, correct authentication is achieved by the protocol if A can be sure that message (3) can only be decrypted by B, while B knows that message (3) can only be sent by A.

6.2 LySa Model of the Protocol

The informal notation of the protocol used above leaves implicit a number of assumptions and does not completely describe actions such as decrypting with a certain key, comparing nonces, and checking certificates. Moreover it is crucial to specify the environment in which the protocol is executed, i.e. the actions which potential attackers can perform.

For a formal analysis, these assumptions have to be specified. LySa provides a format for this, which is essentially a process algebra, enriched by cryptographic notions such as encryption and decryption, symmetric keys, public and private keys, allowing it to model authenticated key exchange protocols. More precisely, LySa is based on the π-calculus. The main difference from the π-calculus and the Spi-calculus is that there are no channels: messages can be arbitrarily intercepted and redirected. Moreover, pattern matching is used to check that a message contains expected values (such as nonces), and to bind values to free variables. Each participant in the protocol (in our case A and B) is modelled by a separate process. Each message of the protocol corresponds to two actions: one performed by the sender who encrypts and sends the message, and one performed by the receiver who decrypts the message, checks the content, and might store parts of it.

As an example, consider message (3), sent from A to B. Sending of messages is denoted by $\langle \ldots \rangle$.

$$(\text{new}K_{AB})\langle A, B, \{|A, vNB, K_{AB}|\} : \mathrm{K}_B^+\rangle$$

The first argument in the $\langle \ldots \rangle$ expression denotes the sender (A), the second the recipient (B), and the rest is the content of the message. The content in this case consists of only one, encrypted, part. The terms are either names such as A, B, and K_{AB}, or variables such as vNB which has been bound to the value of NB when A received message (2). Sending message (3) is preceded by generating a new session key K_{AB} which nobody except A knows. This is modelled by restriction with the 'new' operator.

Input of a message is denoted by $(\ldots)$. We show the receiving action associated with (3), which is performed by process B:

$$(A, B; x).\text{decrypt } x \text{ as } \{|A, NB; vK|\} : \mathrm{K}_B^-$$

An incoming message is matched with an output, whereby the terms before the semicolon have to match while the variables after the semicolon are bound to values after successful matching. Accordingly, the first term denotes the sender and the second term denotes the recipient of the message. Encrypted terms are bound to a free variable and decrypted in the next step. Pattern matching is again applied to the content of an encrypted message. In the example, B only accepts the message if the first argument is A, and the second is the nonce NB which B has chosen for message (2). Note that B has to decide with which key to decrypt the message. For message (3), this is the private key K_B^-.

As described, the protocol consists of two classes of processes: the process for A and the process for B. In the LySa model every participant can act either as A or B. Moreover, the replication operator ! indicates that any pair of participants perform an unlimited number of possibly concurrent sessions. The attacker built into the LySa model has the usual powers of the standard Dolev-Yao attacker [6], i.e. they can use all of the information obtained from messages sent between participants to compose messages which can be sent to any participant.

6.3 Security Analysis with LySa

The analysis performed by the LySatool is to ask whether for multiple runs of the protocols between a number of participants, and in the presence of a standard (Dolev-Yao) network attacker, correct authentication is guranteed. The underlying technique is static analysis, more specifically the Succinct Solver Suite [7] provides the implementation of the solution procedures which are deployed to effect the analysis. LySa has been designed to verify correct authentication, and can also check confidentiality of data. The analysis of correct authentication is based on the use of assertions, which annotate the points in the protocol at which encryption and decryption takes place ('cryptopoints'). At an encryption point these assertions specify the destinations where it is believed that the complementary decryption can occur. At a decryption point the assertions specify the points where it is believed that the complementary encryption occurred.

For the key exchange protocol of the web-based business system, the LySa assertions specify that message (3) is correctly authenticated. More precisely, sending of message (3) is annotated with [at $a3$ dest $b3$] while receiving of message (3) has annotation [at $b3$ orig $a3$].

Hence, the assertions state correct (mutual) authentication of the communicating parties. The LySa tool checks whether an attacker is able to impersonate a legitimate participant and hence violate correct authentication. If the analysis shows that all assertions are correct in the presence of an attacker, we learn that the protocol guarantees correct authentication.

We have analysed the key exchange protocol for the web-based business system with LySa and shown that it provides authenticated key exchange. Moreover, we experimented with variants of the protocol and showed that omitting data from messages in the protocol makes it insecure. As an example, we show an attack which is possible when omitting the name A in message (3):

(1) A $\rightarrow$ B: A, $cert_A$
(2) B $\rightarrow$ A: {B, NB}:K_A^+, $cert_B$
(3) A $\rightarrow$ B: { NB, K_{AB}}:K_B^+

After A has started a regular session with B, the attacker I starts a parallel session with B, and afterwards sends the response of B instead of the second message in the first session. Then the intruder intercepts the response of A in the first session and misuses it as message (3) in the second session.

(1) A $\rightarrow$ B: A, $cert_A$
(1') I $\rightarrow$ B: I, $cert_I$
(2') B $\rightarrow$ I: {B, NB' }:K_I^+
(2) I_B $\rightarrow$ A: {B, NB' }:K_A^+
(3) A $\rightarrow$ I_B: { NB', K }:K_B^+
(3') I $\rightarrow$ B: { NB', K}:K_B^+

The result is that K is the new session key for the session A thinks she is conducting with B as well as for the session between B and I. This means that I can intercept messages encrypted by A with the key K_{AB} and make B believe that the message comes from I.

7 Related Work

With regard to the performance analysis of UML models there are a range of significant prior works which have similarities with the performance-related part of our work. In many cases, these map UML diagrams of various kinds to other analysable representations including stochastic Petri nets [8, 9], layered queueing networks [10], generalised semi-Markov processes [11] and others. Some works are particularly noteworthy for their careful consideration of the role of the UML metamodel in the performance analysis process [12]. Our work has some similarities with the above, and many differences (different diagram types, different performance analysis technology). Two things are unique to our work here: an integrated technology for security analysis and the use of *reflectors* to reflect the results of the analysis back to the UML level.

Other methodologies based on UML have been defined in order to specify security aspects of designs. UMLsec by Jan Jürjens [13, 14] is a versatile profile that includes a wide range of high-level security concepts like secrecy, integrity, no-down-flow, fair exchange etc. and allows the user to specify hardware platforms such as LAN, smart card, Internet and others. It is however not possible to specify correct authentication, which is the main security requirement on the key exchange protocols which are part of the case studies that we have considered. As in the UML content processed by the LySa extractor, UMLsec protocols are specified by sequence diagrams, and the constraints used in the sequence diagrams are similar. However, the UML use supported by the LySa extractor provides a means to specify cryptopoints in sequence diagrams, which is an essential prerequisite for analysing correct authentication with LySa.

8 Conclusions

We have presented a novel method for analysing security and performance questions about UML-described systems which follow a modern, open design pattern. The classes of behaviours understood within the system are described by class and state diagrams. The interactions between object instances of these classes are described using collaboration diagrams and sequence diagrams. The Choreographer design platform automatically processes descriptions of systems structured in this way, and packaged as a UML project. Process algebra representations of the formal content of the diagrams are extracted and passed to efficient analysers which check performance and security properties. The results of these analysers can be inspected directly or reflected back through the Choreographer design platform in order to present all of the analysis at the UML level.

Through the use of the UML as an interface to the security and performance analysis process we hope that we have an accessible framework which could attract developers facing difficulties in engineering secure systems with high performance to consider formal analysis as a beneficial complement to their current design practices. There are many benefits to the use of formal modelling and analysis methods, not the least of which is the ability to display that due care and attention has been taken in the development of secure services which are to be used in business-to-business contexts.

Acknowledgements. The work described in the present paper was undertaken while the authors were supported by the DEGAS (Design Environments for Global ApplicationS) project IST-2001-32072 funded by the FET Proactive Initiative on Global Computing. The Choreographer design platform is a Java application which has been successfully tested on Windows and Red Hat Linux systems. It is available for download from `http://www.lfcs.ed.ac.uk/choreographer`.

References

[1] Gentleware AG systems. Poseidon for UML web site, November 2004. `http://www.gentleware.com/`.

[2] C. Bodei, M. Buchholtz, P. Degano, F. Nielson, and H.R. Nielson. Automatic validation of protocol narration. In *Proc. of the 16th Computer Security Foundations Workshop (CSFW 2003)*, pages 126–140. IEEE Computer Security Press, 2003.

[3] J. Hillston. *A Compositional Approach to Performance Modelling*. Cambridge University Press, 1996.

[4] M. Buchholtz, C. Montangero, L. Perrone, and S. Semprini. For-LySa: UML for authentication analysis. In C. Priami and P. Quaglia, editors, *Proceedings of the second workshop on Global Computing*, volume 3267 of *Lecture Notes in Computer Science*, pages 92–105, Rovereto, Italy, 2004. Springer Verlag.

[5] Dieter Gollmann. *Computer Security*. Wiley, 1999.

[6] D. Dolev and A.C. Yao. On the security of public key protocols. *IEEE Transactions on Information Theory*, 22(6):198–208, 1983.

[7] F. Nielson, H.R. Nielson, H. Sun, M. Buchholtz, R.R. Hansen, H. Pilegaard, and H. Seidl. The Succinct Solver suite. In *Proceedings of Tools and Algorithms for the Construction and Analysis of Systems (TACAS 2004)*, volume 2988 of *LNCS*, pages 251–265. Springer-Verlag, 2004.

[8] J.P. López-Grao, J. Merseguer, and J. Campos. From UML activity diagrams to stochastic Petri nets: Application to software performance analysis. In *Proceedings of the Seventeenth International Symposium on Computer and Information Sciences*, pages 405–409, Orlando, Florida, October 2002. CRC Press.

[9] Juan Pablo López-Grao, José Merseguer, and Javier Campos. From UML activity diagrams to Stochastic Petri nets: application to software performance engineering. In *Proceedings of the fourth international Workshop on Software and Performance*, pages 25–36. ACM Press, 2004.

[10] D.C. Petriu and H. Shen. Applying the UML performance profile: Graph grammar-based derivation of LQN models from UML specifications. In *Proceedings of Tools'02*, number 2324 in LNCS, pages 159–177. Springer-Verlag, April 2002.

[11] C. Lindemann, A. Thümmler, A. Klemm, M. Lohmann, and O. P. Waldhorst. Performance analysis of time-enhanced UML diagrams based on stochastic processes. In Tucci [15], pages 25–34.

[12] S. Bernardi, S. Donatelli, and J. Merseguer. From UML sequence diagrams and statecharts to analysable Petri net models. In Tucci [15], pages 35–45.

[13] Jan Jürjens. UMLsec: Extending UML for secure systems development. In *5th Intl. Conference on the Unified Modeling Language (UML) 2000*, LNCS 2460, 2002.

[14] Jan Jürjens. *Secure Systems Development with UML*. Springer, 2004.

[15] Salvatore Tucci, editor. *Proceedings of the Third International Workshop on Software and Performance (WOSP 2002)*. ACM Press, Rome, Italy, July 2002.

Application of Formal Methods to the Analysis of Web Services Security*

Llanos Tobarra, Diego Cazorla, Fernando Cuartero, and Gregorio Díaz

Escuela Politécnica Superior de Albacete,
Universidad de Castilla-La Mancha. 02071 Albacete, Spain
{mtobarra, dcazorla, fernando, gregorio}@info-ab.uclm.es

Abstract. Web Services technologies have introduced a new challenge for security protocols. Traditional security protocols cannot handle intermediaries and the flexibility of Web Services bindings. Thus, several proposals for introducing security in Web Services have been presented. One of these is *Web Services Security*. In this paper we illustrate how this protocol works, with an example, and analyse whether it is a good option guaranteeing the security of Web Services.

Keywords: Protocols and standards for WS, Security of WS, Secure Electronic Commerce.

1 Introduction

The rapid development of the World Wide Web in recent years has dramatically increased the exchange of information between clients and companies, and has also boosted electronic commerce transactions. Traditionally, the environment where electronic transactions occur consists of a web server that offers 'services' to human clients who use a web browser to select the information or products they wish to obtain. Nowadays this view is changing; companies wish to offer and use services automatically, i.e., they want to 'live' in a world where interoperability between various software applications running on separate platforms is possible, and, for example, Java can talk with Perl, and Windows applications can talk to UNIX applications.

A technology that has emerged recently and offers these kinds of transactions is Web Services [27]. Web Services implements a new Service Oriented Architecture (SOA), which is based on loosely coupled services. In a Web Services environment we find the following components:

- *Service providers*: they implement the web service and, in most cases, publish the service interface and the service registry information.

* This work has been partially supported by the MCyT project "Description and Performance of Distributed Systems and Application to Multimedia Systems" (Ref. TIC2003-07848-c02-02) and the JCCM project "Design and Implementation of Efficient Multimedia Systems by using Formal Techniques" (Ref. PAC-03001)

M. Bravetti et al. (Eds.): EPEW 2005 and WS-FM 2005, LNCS 3670, pp. 215–229, 2005.

- *Service brokers*: they allow clients to access the service interface and the implementation information.
- *Service clients*: they look for a service in a broker registry and then connect to the service provider in order to use it.

One of the most important issues in Web Services development is that each functional block should be platform or programming language-independent, and accessible for everybody. Thus, each block has to be described using an internet standard. The most important internet standards related to web services are the following:

- *XML* (eXtensible Markup Language)[26] is a markup language which underlies most of the specifications related to Web Services. XML is actually a metalanguage (a language for describing other languages) which lets you design your own customised markup languages for unlimited different types of documents
- *SOAP* (Simple Object Access Protocol)[22] is an XML-based messaging protocol used to encode the information in Web Services request and response messages before sending them over a network. SOAP messages are independent of any operating system or protocol and may be transported using a variety of Internet protocols, including SMTP, MIME and HTTP.
- *WSDL* (Web Services Description Language)[23] is an XML format for describing network services as a set of endpoints operating on messages containing either document-oriented or procedure-oriented information. Service providers use a WSDL document to specify available services. It also contains service access information.
- *UDDI* (Universal Description, Discovery and Integration)[19] is the client-side API and a server implementation based on SOAP. It stores and retrieves information about service providers and web services.

In order to use a web service, a client obtains a WSDL file in which a particular web service is described. If the client knows where the web service is located, they can retrieve it directly. Otherwise they can search for it using the UDDI protocol. Then, they prepare a SOAP request, which is an XML document that follows an XML schema. Each SOAP message is composed of a main element called an *envelope*. Each envelope has two main parts: payload data, included into the body, and one or more headers that contain control data such as addressing data, security items or quality options. The client sends the request through a transport protocol, usually HTTP. When a web service receives a request, it executes the requested actions and responds to the client with a SOAP response message. This message includes the result of the actions.

One of the main problems in using web services is that they are exposed to security attacks. Traditional security protocols, such as SSL [7], TLS [1] and IPsec[13], are used to protect communication between two agents in a network. Nevertheless, these are point-to-point technologies, whereas web services need end-to-end level security because the information does not travel straight to the endpoint; usually information needs to pass through several intermediate agents that may need to use or alter some parts of the information. Moreover, traditional security protocols secure communication at transport rather than message level. Therefore, messages are protected only while in transit on the wire.

In order to introduce security in web services, we can consider (among others) the following protocols: Web Services Security [11], Security Assertions Markup Language (SAML) [21], Identity Federation [18] and Extensible Access Control Markup Language (XACML) [20].

In this paper we will focus on Web Services Security (WS-Security), a protocol that extends SOAP in order to implement *message integrity* and *confidentiality*. While SOAP provides a flexible technique for structuring messages, it does not directly address how to secure these messages. WS-Security builds on the SOAP specification, structuring the use of essential security capabilities. WS-Security uses binary tokens for authentication, digital signatures for integrity and content-level encryption for confidentiality. It is based on XML Encryption [24] and XML Signature [25] and guarantees the integrity and confidentiality of information. Several companies such as IBM, Microsoft and Sun have adapted its development tools for Web Services in order to support this security protocol.

In line with the development of e-commerce and security protocols, some techniques have also been developed to model a system and check its properties on it. One of the most promising techniques of this type is *model checking*. Model checking [5] is a formal methods based technique for verifying finite-state-concurrent systems, and has been implemented in several tools. One of the main advantages of this technique is that it is automatic and allows us to see if a system works properly or not. In case the system does not work as expected, the model checking tool provides a trace that leads to the source of the error.

In this paper we present a formal verification of WS-Security using the Casper/FDR2 toolbox [15,6]. Casper is a compiler that accepts a syntax very similar to the syntax used to specify protocols, and translates a model into CSP [9] code which is verified using the model checker FDR2. Although Casper uses a general purpose model checker, the translation to CSP code is done automatically and transparently to the user, and the results of the verification are presented in terms of the Casper model.

We have modelled and analysed a web service application (license server) previously developed by using Microsoft .NET 2003 and Microsoft Web Services Enhancement (WSE) [16]. We have abstracted the application code in order to build a simple Casper model which deals with the exchange of sensitive (encrypted and signed) information (SOAP messages) between client and server.

Several papers [12,8,17] can be found which use formal methods to analyse Web Services, and in which formal methods are used to analyse the behaviour and the performance of web services standards; these analyses help designers to correct any errors. More related to our work, however, are [14] and [4]. The first maps out of SOAP messages (including WS-Security information) to Casper input is presented. The second one presents a scripting language called *TulaFale* for specifying SOAP security protocols and verifying attacks. TulaFale is based on Pi-Calculus and some extensions for symbolic cryptographic operations. They verified the WS-Security protocol family in [2] with this tool. These same group of researchers have developed an implementation of an automatic tool, described in [3], that translates security policy files into a TulaFale script and verifies some properties by invoking a theorem prover.

The paper is organised as follows. In Section 2 we describe our web service application (software license server) and the SOAP messages that client and server exchange. In Section 3 we build the Casper specification that models the system, describe the security requirements that the system should achieve, and verify the model against these requirements. Finally, in Section 4 we give our conclusions and some outlines for future work.

2 A Web Services Example: A Software License Server

In this section we illustrate how WS-Security works, through an example. A software company offers on its web site a set of applications for its clients. When a client wants to use one of these programs they register through a web service and pay for several licenses through a payment service. Then, they can download the programmes and get several product keys using another web service (the license server). If they do not register they will not be able to install the application because during the installation process they will be asked for the product key. A general overview of the system is depicted in fig. 1.

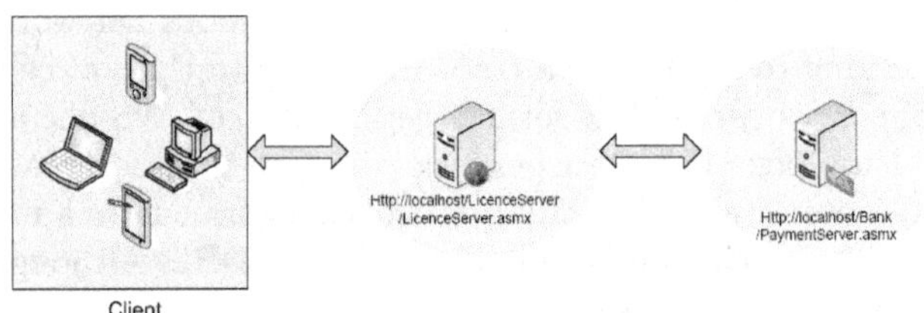

Fig. 1. General overview of the system

We shall look at two web services:

1. A web service for registering clients, where a client gives their financial data, a set of selected applications and a number of licenses for each application.
2. A web service for obtaining product keys. This web service generates a new product key if the client is registered. The web service accepts as parameters a username, password and product identifier.

First, a client who wants to use several software products must be registered in the system. In order to register, the client connects to the register web service and send their data. Then, the license server processes the information and generates an invoice that is sent to the payment service that carries out the purchase order. When the payment service responds to the server with a payment authorisation code, the server sends this back to the client together with information on the result of the transaction.

Afterwards, a registered client will need a product key in order to install the application. So, the client sends a request to the license server. The server checks if the client is allowed to use that program and the status of the client subscription. If everything is right, the server generates a new product key for the request and sends it to the client.

Although we have described two web services, in the rest of the paper we will focus on the second, i.e., the license server.

A registered client calls on the web service, which allows it to get a new product key for an application (see fig. 2). The client gets the keys through a small program that asks for the username, the corresponding password and an application code. This program generates a request, which is a SOAP message that follows the specification of the WSDL protocol. If the client has been registered and has the corresponding permissions, the server sends a SOAP message response that includes the newly generated product key. An overview of the system and the two exchanged SOAP messages is depicted in fig. 2.

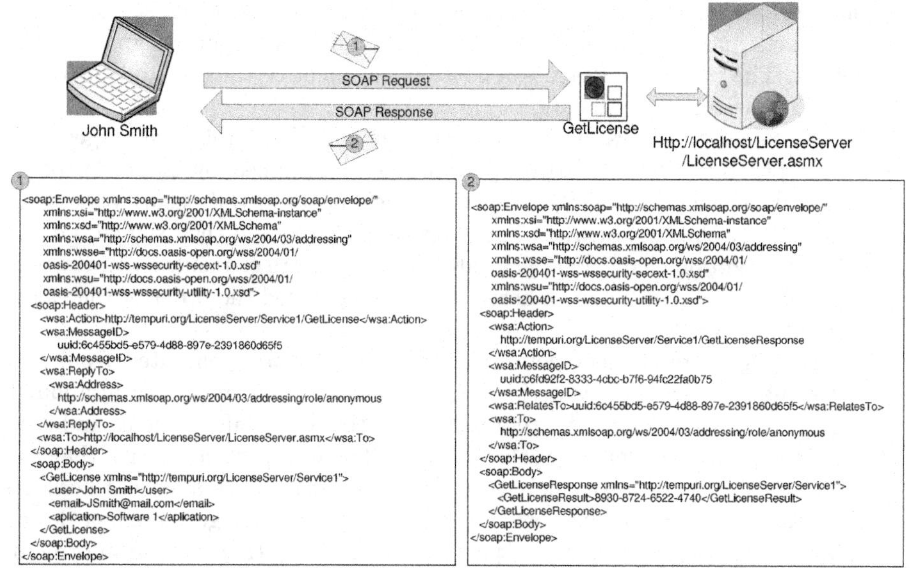

Fig. 2. SOAP messages

It is clear that this web service needs to guarantee several security properties, such as the confidentiality of the client authorisation data items. First, a registered client proves that they can be trusted, with their username and password. If an intruder guesses these variables they will be able to access the product keys. We must be sure that the username and passwords are secrets shared between server and client. WS-Security also allows us to cipher data to guarantee its confidentiality, thus, we must encrypt the request message body.

We must cipher the response body too. In it, the server sends the product key. If an intruder can guess it, they will be able to install the program without paying for it. It is the client who pays instead of the intruder in this case. The server must guarantee the confidentiality of the product key, which must be a secret shared with the client.

When the server generates a product key, this key is valid for only one kind of application. If the client asks for a key to a program and tries to install a different one, they will not be able to use the received key in the installation. An intruder can alter the request message and change the selected application code, meaning the client receives an incorrect key and that, therefore, they cannot install the program. Thus, the integrity of the message must be checked in order to avoid these kinds of attacks. WS-Security offers the possibility of signing a message; this way, both agents, server and client, can verify the integrity of the signed parts.

WS-Security adds a new header element called *Security* to each SOAP message (see fig. 3). In it, we include the necessary security tokens for the message. The first XML element is usually a BinarySecurityToken, which represents a binary token as a X.509 certificate, or a Kerberos ticket. It is used to sign message parts and to cipher symmetric keys. In this case we only sign the message with it. The request message will contain the client certificate, and the response message the server certificate.

WS-Security allows clients to first sign and then cipher messages or vice versa. The order of these two operations is determined by the order of XML Signature elements and XML Encryption elements in the Security header. We will consider the case of when a message is ciphered and then signed, i.e., when XML Encryption elements appear after the Signature element, as represented in fig. 3. If the message were ciphered *after* being signed the order of the elements would be different.

The Signature element contains a digital signature computed from several parts of the message. It is divided into two main parts: information about how the signature was computed, represented by the SignedInfo element, and the signature value in the SignatureValue element. The first part deals with the canonicalisation method and the signature algorithm. It includes a list of references in the References element. For each signed part in the message there is a Reference element that points to a signed part of the message, that in turn informs us of the digest algorithm and the digest result. There is also a KeyInfo element that refers to the certificate used in the signature.

The EncryptedKey element represents a symmetric key that is ciphered with the other public agent key. The EncryptionMethod element indicates which algorithm is used to cipher the key. Then, there is a KeyInfo element that makes a reference to the certificate used to secure the key. If the certificate is unknown to the receiver, the producer must include it in a BinarySecurityToken. After the KeyInfo item there is a CipherValue element which includes the ciphered value of

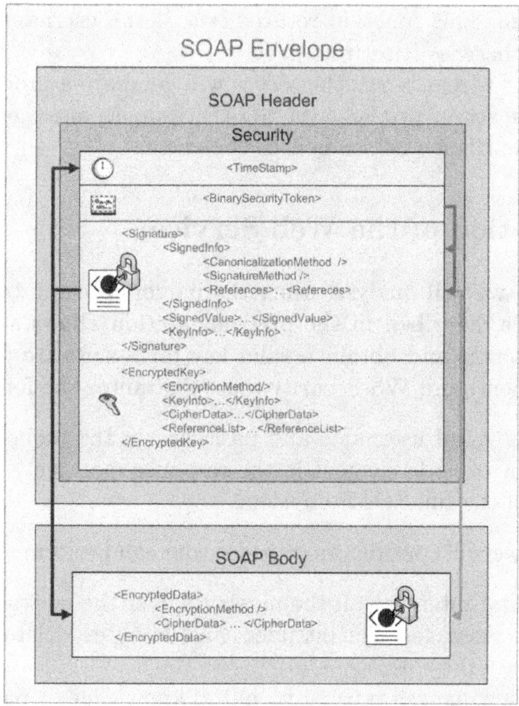

Fig. 3. Abstract structure of a SOAP Message with WS-Security

the key. If the shared key has been exchanged before, it will contain a reference to that key instead of its ciphered value. In the last subelement of EncryptedKey, the ReferenceList element, is a list of references in which each reference points to a ciphered message part. When a message part is encrypted, it is replaced by a EncryptedData, where there is a reference to the key, and the result of the cipher process.

If we look at encryption *before* signature, the protocol works as follows:

- First, the client creates a SOAP request message without any security measures.
- Then, they include a security header and generate a symmetric key that ciphers the message with the server public key. The key is added to the message.
- The client ciphers their username, their password and the selected application code with the newly generated symmetric key. The body element is replaced by an EncryptedData element as a result of this step.
- The client computes a digital signature from the ciphered body of the message. The client adds all the security elements corresponding to the digital signature and sends the message to the server.
- The server receives the message and verifies the digital signature, it then decrypts the message body and checks the client data with the function

registered. This function returns *true* if the username and password are correct. Otherwise it returns *false*.
- If the client is registered, the server will generate a product key.
- Finally, the server prepares the SOAP response message following the same steps as the client and sends it to the client.

3 Verification of the Web Service

In this section we will analyse, using the model checking tool Casper, whether the web service described in the previous section allows a registered client to connect to a server and obtain a valid key for a software product. In order to achieve this client aim, WS-Security must guarantee the following results:

- Confidentiality of username and password in the request message, and the product key or code element in the response message.
- Integrity of the full SOAP envelope.

In our model, we will consider an intruder who can perform the following actions:

- Overhear and intercept all the messages over the network.
- Modify the messages. The intruder can add bytes, delete bytes or change the value of several bytes.
- Generate new messages using its initial knowledge or parts of the overheard messages.
- Send a new or captured message to another entity in the system.

We will assume that the intruder cannot perform any cryptanalysis.

We use Casper syntax to represent a SOAP message (see fig. 4). First, we suppose that all digest functions, encryption methods and signature algorithms are secure. In WS-Security there is only one hash function, SHA-1, which is represented by the hash type function `sha` in our protocol description. Computation of the digest of several variables is represented as `sha(v1,...,vn)`. If we wish to represent a message `m` that is ciphered with the key `K`, we do so with the expression $\{\texttt{m}\}_{\texttt{K}}$.

We will suppose that the clients and the web service server know each other's certificates. We represent certificates by means of two functions: *PK(A)*, which returns the public key of the agent A, and *SK(A)*, which returns the private key of the agent A. This allows us to represent binary tokens as X.509 certificates and Kerberos tickets.

We described WS-Security messages in the previous section. Firstly, there is a certificate that, as we have just explained is replaced by two functions. Then, there is an EncryptedKey element, a symmetric key ciphered with the receiver public key, represented by $\{\texttt{Key}\}_{\texttt{PK(Receiver)}}$. Only the owner of the private key partnering the public one can decipher it and find out the symmetric key. After the symmetric key there is a digital signature. A digital signature is a digest value ciphered with the signer's private key. The sender signs the message body after it has been encrypted, so we have $\{\texttt{sha(}\{\texttt{Body}\}_{\texttt{Key}}\texttt{)}\}_{\texttt{SK(Agent)}}$.

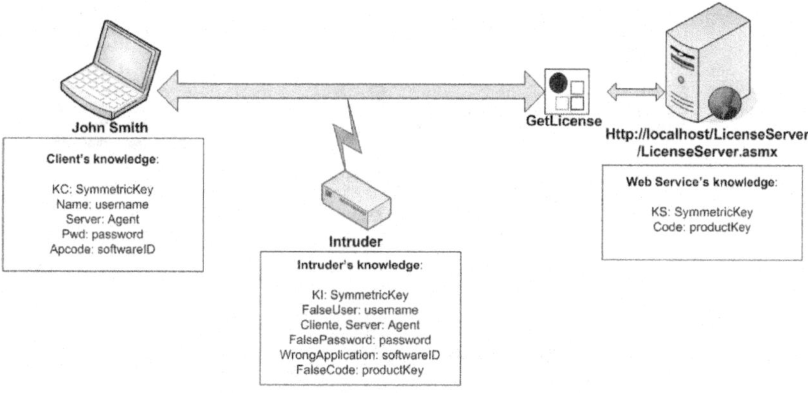

PROTOCOL:

1. Client -> Server : $\{KC\}_{PK(Server)}$, $\{sha(\{name,pwd,apcode\}_{KC})\}_{SK(Client)}$, $\{name,pwd,apcode\}_{KC}$ [registered(name,pwd)]
2. Server -> Client : $\{KS\}_{PK(Client)}$, $\{sha(\{code\}_{KS})\}_{SK(Server)}$, $\{code\}_{KS}$

Fig. 4. Representation of the analysed system and the resulting protocol

In the request message we represent the body with three important variables: username, password and application code. In the response message we represent the body with the variable *code* which represents the product key. The body of each message is ciphered with the corresponding symmetric key, included in the EncryptedKey.

We now check the following properties:

1. Aliveness(Client,Server) and Aliveness(Server,Client). Both properties check that the client executes the protocol with the server, and vice versa. So, the intruder cannot take the place of the client nor the server.
2. StrongSecret(Client,name,[server]) and StrongSecret(Client, pwd,[server]). These search a trace where the intruder can guess the value of the username *name* and the password *pwd*.
3. Secret(Client, KC, [Server]). This verifies that the client only shares a symmetric key, KC, with the server and that the intruder cannot guess it. So, if the intruder does not know it, they will not be able to decrypt the message body. The difference between Secret and StrongSecret is that the latter checks all traces, even though the protocol has not been executed completely.
4. Agreement(Client,Server,[KC, name, pwd, apcode]). This verifies that the client executes a complete run of the protocol with the server and that both share the same value for the variables username, password and application code.
5. StrongSecret(Server, code, [Client]). This confirms that the protocol guarantees the confidentiality of the variable code, which represents the product key.
6. Secret(Server, KS, [Client]). This checks that the server only shares a symmetric key, KS, with the client and that the intruder cannot guess it. So, if

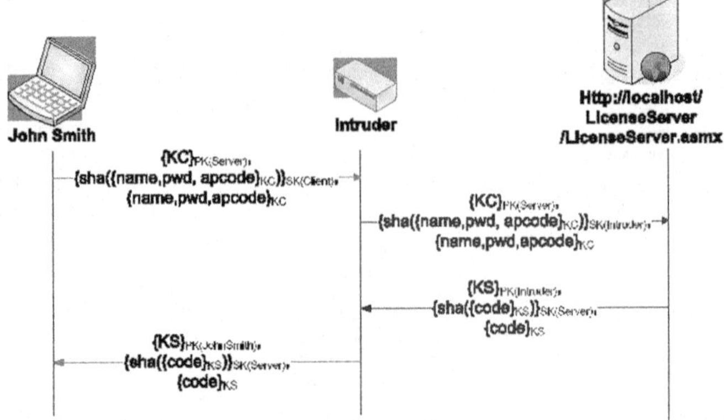

Fig. 5. Attack on the protocol for obtaining a license

the intruder does not know it, they will not be able to decrypt the message body.

7. Agreement(Server,Client,[KS,name,pwd,apcode,KC,code]). This checks that the server executes a complete run of the protocol with the client, and that they share the same value for the following variables: KS, name, pwd, apcode, KC and code. Thus, it verifies the integrity of the two messages.

We check all these properties with Casper and our system specification. We look at two different situations. In the first, a client only wants a product key for a single program and runs the protocol once. In the second, the client runs the protocol twice because they want to install two different software programs, *sw1* and *sw2*.

In the first case, Casper finds an attack (see fig. 5). The intruder knows the client public key, so can find out the value of $\text{sha}(\{\text{name,pwd,apcode}\}_{KC})$. From this information, the intruder can generate a correct request message and is then able to take the place of the client. The intruder executes the protocol, with the server as an intermediary. The problem is that the username and the password are not associated with the agent identifier. Therefore we must include the agent identifier in the message. A possible option is to use WS-Addressing, which allows us to include *sender identifier* and *receiver identifier* amongst other information. We include these identifiers and we sign them. The resulting protocol is

1. Client → Server: $\{KC\}_{PK(Server)}$,
   $\{sha(\{name, pwd, apcode\}_{KC}, \mathit{Server}, \mathit{Client})\}_{SK(Client)}$,
   $\{name, pwd, apcode\}_{KC}$
   [registered(name,pwd)]
2. Server→ Client: $\{KS\}_{PK(Client)}$,
   $\{sha(\{code\}_{KC}, \mathit{Server}, \mathit{Client})\}_{SK(Server)}$,
   $\{code\}_{KS}$

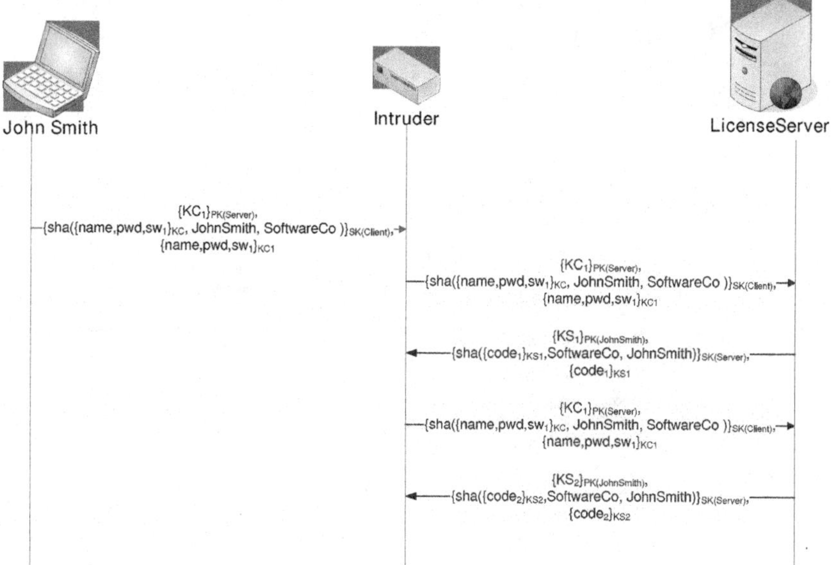

Fig. 6. First attack on the protocol for obtaining a license with two executions

We check all the properties again with this version; Casper does not find any attack. Then, we check what happens if a client gets a product key and then tries to get another. If we have a variable v that is used in both executions of the protocol, we will use v_i to denote the value of v in every run of the protocol. For example, KC_1 is the client symmetric key for the first execution of the protocol, and KC_2 is the same value but for the second. We suppose these variables are refreshed in each execution.

We find two new attacks as result of our verification of the two-executions version of the protocol. As we can see in figures 6 and 7, the intruder behaves as a intermediate and records all the messages. After one execution, they can replace one of the honest agents and cheat the other. In the first attack, the intruder takes the place of the client and gets a product key. A client can request a fixed number of product keys, thus, the intruder reduces the number of requests by the client and so the client loses money. In the second attack, the client is deceived by the intruder and gets a wrong product key for the selected application. Both attacks share the feature that the intruder uses previously recorded messages (known as *replay attack*).

To avoid replay attacks, as in the both cases explained above, we need to introduce some information to each message to make it unique, e.g., a time-stamp or a message identifier.

WS-Security allows us to include time-stamps in a message. A `timestamp` consist of a creation time and an expiry time. Clients should select a short time validity period, because otherwise, an intruder could use the message in a replay attack before it expires. WS-Security time-stamps may be modelled in Casper by

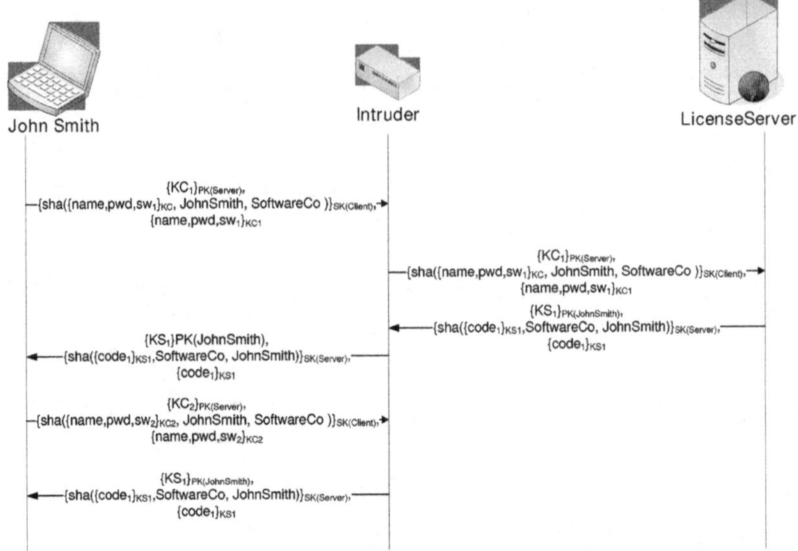

Fig. 7. Second attack on the protocol for obtaining a license with two executions

using a special kind of variable. With this variable we can represent the creation time but not the expiry time; thus, we have to include a condition in the time-stamp which checks how many time units have passed since the message was sent. Taking time-stamps into account, the protocol specification is as follows:

1. Client → Server:
   Clock, $\{\mathrm{KC}\}_{\mathrm{PK(Server)}}$,
   $\{\mathrm{sha}(\{\text{name, pwd, apcode }\}_{\mathrm{KC}}, \mathit{Server}, \mathit{Client}, \mathit{Clock})\}_{\mathrm{SK(Client)}}$,
   $\{\text{name, pwd, apcode}\}_{\mathrm{KC}}$
   [registered(name,pwd) and (Clock==now or Clock==now-1)]
2. Server → Client:
   Clock, $\{\mathrm{KS}\}_{\mathrm{PK(Client)}}$, $\{\mathrm{sha}(\{\text{code}\}_{\mathrm{KC}}, \mathit{Server}, \mathit{Client}, \mathit{Clock})\}_{\mathrm{SK(Server)}}$,
   $\{\text{code}\}_{\mathrm{KS}}$
   [Clock==now or Clock==now-1]

Casper time-stamps and protocol time-stamps nevertheless have a different semantics. While Casper only gives consideration to local clocks, i.e., each agent (process) has an internal clock, represented by an integer, which starts from zero when the agent sends the first message, WS-Security time-stamps are obtained from global clock, i.e., each time-stamp is a date includes the day, month, year, hour, minutes and seconds. Thus, in Casper it is possible for two different messages to have the same time-stamp because they were sent by different agents, while in WS-Security it is very difficult for two messages to have the same time-stamp.

Although we have found an attack on the Casper model including time-stamps, we cannot conclude that WS-Security suffers from this attack, because in fact, the model is not representing the protocol.

The second solution considered above to avoid replay attacks was to introduce a unique message identifier. In this case, the server can store every message identifier and check whether a new message is actually new or is being replayed. The message identifier should be signed in order to guarantee its integrity. The protocol model could be as follows:

1. Client → Server:
   MessageID1,$\{KC\}_{PK(Server)}$,
   $\{sha(\{name, pwd, apcode\}_{KC}, Server, Client, MessageID1)\}_{SK(Client)}$,
   $\{name, pwd, apcode\}_{KC}$
   [registered(name,pwd)]
2. Server → Client:
   MessageID2,$\{KS\}_{PK(Client)}$,
   $\{sha(\{code\}_{KC}, Server, Client, MessageID2)\}_{SK(Server)}$, $\{code\}_{KS}$

Despite this, in Casper we cannot represent the server cache of message identifiers, so we cannot check if this version guarantees all the security properties.

4 Conclusions and Future Work

In this paper we have presented a web service application (a software license server) that studies security issues by means of WS-Security. In order to analyse whether this web service is secure, we have built the SOAP messages exchanged by the client and the server, and then translated these messages into Casper syntax in order to verify some security properties. We have looked at two scenarios: in the first, a client wishes to obtain a single product key, whereas in the second the client wishes to obtain two different product keys.

Taking into account the results of the verification, we can put forward the following conclusions:

- Even in the most simple case, an intruder could supplant the client and obtain a product key. This means that, besides WS-Security another mechanism is needed which allows agents to identify themselves. One possibility is to use WS-Addressing which allows us to insert in a SOAP message information about the participants.
- Even if we use WS-Addressing, it is possible that an intruder could obtain a product key if we consider a more sophisticated environment (the two run version). In this case, the problem is which the intruder can record messages that can be used to perform a replay attack.

The problem in the second case is that a message can be stored and replayed as many times as the intruder needs. As mentioned before, a unique message identifier, or a time-stamp with a short validity period, could be a solution to this attack. Unfortunately, Casper failed to model SOAP messages that include timestamps and/or messages identifiers, so we cannot say whether this model is secure or not. We could use another feature of WS-Security in order to avoid replay attacks. We could add a *UsernameToken* element to a SOAP message signed by the client. This element contains a username, the corresponding password and a nonce (a fresh random value), which guarantees the uniqueness of the message. The username and password are secrets shared between the client and the server. Thus, we should only have to add the nonce to our representation of the protocol.

Another solution could be to identify each message as part of a flow or a conversation. Some protocols, such as WS-ReliableMessaging, include in each message a unique identifier for each sequence of messages. It also includes the number of the message in the sequence. Each time a client starts a new sequence the identifier is renewed. When an agent wants to establish a sequence it sends a request for a new sequence identifier to the other end. Then it can send its message. The other end should send an acknowledgement of the received message. When an agent does not want to send more messages, it must send a finished sequence message. All these control messages are an overhead for a simple protocol, as with the one we have analysed.

Our future work is concerned with building a model of the system which allows us to prove that WS-Security (working together with other protocols such as WS-Addressing and/or WS-ReliableMessaging) is a good option in guaranteeing the security of Web Services (including replay attacks).

Finally, it is worth pointing out that WS-Security does not provide a full security solution by itself. It should be used with other protocols. In a request/response conversation a client and a server do not negotiate any security options. So it is recommended that developers use WS-Policy to establish the security requirements of clients and servers. Currently, a set of complementary protocols is being developed to complement the security level of WS-Security. These include WS-Trust and WS-Secure Language [10].

References

1. T. Dierks; C. Allen. *"The TLS Protocol. Version 1.0 ". RFC 2246.* Standards track, Network Working Group, January 1999.
2. K. Bhargavan, C. Fournet, A.D. Gordon, and R.Corin. *"Secure Sessions for Web Services"*. August 2004. At `http://research.microsoft.com/projects/samoa/secure-sessions-with-scripts.pdf`.
3. K. Bhargavan, C. Fournet, and A.D. Gordon. Verifying policy-based security for web services. In *CCS '04: Proceedings of the 11th ACM conference on Computer and communications security*, pages 268–277, New York, NY, USA, 2004. ACM Press.
4. K. Bhargavan, C. Fournet, and A.D. Gordon, and R. Pucella. Tulafale: A security tool for web services. In *Formal Methods for Components and Objects: Second International Symposium, FMCO 2003*, volume 3188 of *Lecture Notes in Computer Science*, pages 197 – 222. Springer, November 2003.

5. E. M. Clarke, O. Grumberg, and D. A. Peled. *Model Checking.* The MIT Press, 1999.
6. Formal Systems (Europe) Limited. FDR Manual. `http://www.fsel.com/fdr2_manual.html`.
7. O. Alan Freier, Philip Karlton, and Paul C. Kocher. *"The SSL Protocol Version 3.0"*. Internet draft, Netscape, March 1996.
8. G.Díaz, J. Pardo, E. Cambronero, V. Valero, and F. Cuartero. *"Verification of Web Services with Timed Automata". 1st Int'l Workshop on Automated Specification and Verification of Web Sites*, 2005.
9. C.A.R. Hoare. *Communicating Sequential Processes.* Prentice Hall, 1985.
10. IBM and Microsoft. *"Security in a Web Services World: a proposed architecture and roadmap". http://www.-106.ibm.com/developerworks/library/ws-secmap/*, April 2002.
11. IBM, Microsoft, and VeriSign. *"Web Services Security (WS-Security). Version 1.0"*. April 2002.
12. J.E. Johnson, D.E. Langworthy, L. Lamport, and F.H.Vogt. *"Formal Specification of a Web Services Protocol". Electronic Notes in Theoretical Computer Science 105 (2004) 147-158*, February 2004.
13. S. Kent and K. Seo. Security architecture for the internet protocol. Internet Draft, october 2004.
14. E. Kleiner and A.W.Roscoe. *"Web Services Security: a preliminary study using Casper and FDR". Proceedings of the Workshop on Automated Reasoning for Security Protocol Analysis (ARSPA 2004)*, June 2004.
15. G. Lowe. Casper: A Compiler for the Analysis of Security Protocols. *Journal of Computer Security*, 6:53–84, 1998.
16. Microsoft. Microsoft Web Services Enhacements (WSE) 2.0. `http://http://msdn.microsoft.com/webservices/building/wse/`.
17. S. Nakijima. *"On verifying Web Services Flows". Proc. SAINT 2002 Workshop*, pages 223–224, January 2002.
18. OASIS. *"Identity Federation. Liberty Alliance Project "*, 2004.
19. OASIS. *"UDDI Version 3.0.2". http://www.oasis-open.org/committees/uddi-spec/doc/tcspecs.htm#uddiv3*, October 2004.
20. OASIS. *"eXtensible Access Control Markup Language (XACML) v2.0"*, February 2005.
21. OASIS. *"Security Assertion Markup Language (SAML) v2.0 "*, April 2005.
22. W3C. *"Simple Object Access Protocol (SOAP) 1.1". http://www.w3c.org/TR/2000/NOTE-SOAP-20000508*, May 2000.
23. W3C. *"Web Services Description Language (WSDL) 1.1 ". http://www.w3.org/TR/wsdl*, March 2001.
24. W3C. *"XML Encryption Syntax and Processing". http://www.w3c.org/TR/2002/REC-xmldend-core-20021210*, December 2002.
25. W3C. *"XML Signature Syntax and Processing". http://www.w3c.org/TR/2002/REC-xmldsig-core-20020212*, February 2002.
26. W3C. *"Extensible Markup Language (XML)1.1". http://www.w3.org/TR/2004/REC-xml11-20040204/*, April 2004.
27. W3C. *"Web Services Architecture". http://www.w3c.org/TR/2004/NOTE-ws-arch-20040211*, February 2004.

Automatic Translation of WS-CDL Choreographies to Timed Automata*

Gregorio Diaz, Juan-José Pardo, María-Emilia Cambronero, Valentín Valero, and Fernando Cuartero

Departamento de Informática,
Universidad de Castilla-La Mancha,
Escuela Politécnica Superior de Albacete. 02071 - Spain
{gregorio, jpardo, emicp, valentin, fernando}@info-ab.uclm.es

Abstract. In this paper we show how we can translate Web Services described by WS-CDL into a timed automata orchestration, and more specifically we are interested in Web services with time restrictions. Our starting point are Web Services descriptions written in WSBPEL-WSCDL (XML-based description languages). These descriptions are then automatically translated into timed automata, and then, we use a well known tool that supports this formalism (UPPAAL) to simulate and analyse the system behaviour. As illustration we take a particular case study, an airline ticket reservation system.

1 Introduction

In the last years some new techniques and languages for developing distributed application have appeared, such as the Extensible Markup Language, XML, and some new Web Services frameworks [7,13,18] for describing interoperable data and platform neutral business interfaces, enabling more open business transactions to be developed.

Web Services are a key component of the emerging, loosely coupled, Web-based computing architecture. A Web Service is an autonomous, standards-based component whose public interfaces are defined and described using XML [15]. Other systems may interact with a Web Service in a manner prescribed by its definition, using XML based messages conveyed by Internet protocols.

The Web Services specifications offer a communication bridge between the heterogeneous computational environments used to develop and host applications. The future of E-Business applications requires the ability to perform long-lived, peer-to-peer collaborations between the participating services, within or across the trusted domains of an organization.

The Web Service architecture stack targeted for integrating interacting applications consists of the following components [15]:

* This work has been supported by the CICYT project "Description and Evaluation of Distributed Systems and Application to Multimedia Systems",TIC2003-07848-C02-02 and the UCLM project "Aplicación de Métodos Formales al Desarrollo y Verificación de Web Services"

M. Bravetti et al. (Eds.): EPEW 2005 and WS-FM 2005, LNCS 3670, pp. 230–242, 2005.

- **SOAP[13]:** It defines the basic formatting of a message and the basic delivery options independent of programming language, operating system, or platform.
- **WSDL[18]:** It describes the static interface of a Web Service. Then, at this point the message set and the message characteristics of end points are here defined. Data types are defined by XML Schema specifications.
- **Registry[7]:** It makes visible an available Web Service, and it also describes the concrete capabilities of a Web Service.
- **Security layer:** It ensures that exchanged informations are not modified or forged in a verifiable manner and that parties can be authenticated.
- **Reliable Messaging layer:** It provides a reliable layer for the exchange of information between parties.
- **Context, Coordination and Transaction layer:** It defines interoperable mechanisms for propagating context of long-lived business transactions and enables parties to meet correctness requirements by following a global agreement protocol.
- **Business Process Languages layer[2,8]:** It describes the execution logic of Web Services based applications by defining their control flows (such as conditional, sequential, parallel and exceptional execution) and prescribing the rules for consistently managing their non-observable data.
- **Choreography layer[15]:** It describes collaborations of parties by defining from a global viewpoint their common and complementary observable behavior, where information exchanges occur, when the jointly agreed ordering rules are satisfied.

The Web Services Choreography specification is aimed at the composition of interoperable collaborations between any type of party regardless of the supporting platform or programming model used by the implementation of the hosting environment.

Web Services cover a wide range of systems, which in many cases have strong time constraints (for instance, peer-to-peer collaborations may have time limits to be completed). Then, in many Web Services descriptions these time aspects can become very important. Actually, they are currently covered by the top level layers in Web Services architectures with elements such as time-outs and alignments. Time-outs allow each party to fix the available time for an action to occur, while alignments are synchronizations between two peer-to-peer parties.

Thus, it becomes important for Web Services frameworks to ensure the correctness of systems with time constraints. For instance, we can think in a failure of a bank to receive a large electronic funds transfer on time, which may result in huge financial losses. Then, there is growing consensus that the use of formal methods, development methods based on some formalism, could have significant benefits in developing E-business systems due to the enhanced rigor these methods bring [14]. Furthermore, these formalisms allow us to reason with the constructed models, analysing and verifying some properties of interest of the described systems. One of these formalisms are timed automata [1], which are very used in model checking [6], and there are some well-known tools supporting them, like UPPAAL [9,10,16] and KHRONOS [3].

Then, our goal with this paper is to describe how we can translate Web Services with time constraints into a formalism using automatic techniques in order to verify it. This verification process starts from the top level layers of Web Services architectures (Business Process Language Layer and Choreography layer). The particular Business Process Language layer that we use here is the Web Service Business Process Execution Language (WS-BPEL) [2], and the concrete Choreography Layer that we use is the Web Service Choreography Description Language (WS-CDL) [15]. Therefore, the starting point are specification documents written in WS-CDL and WS-BPEL. However, these description languages are not very useful for the verification process. Thus, these descriptions are automatically translated into timed automata, and the UPPAAL tool is used to simulate and verify the system correctness.

As illustration of this methodology, we use a particular case study, an airline ticket reservation system, whose description contains some time constraints.

The paper is structured as follows. In Section 2 we describe the main features of WSBPEL - WSCDL. The translation of WSCDL documents into timed automata is presented in Section 3. In Section 4 we apply this methodology to the case study, and the UPPAAL tool is used to describe, simulate and analyze the obtained timed automata. Finally, the conclusions and the future work are presented in Section 5.

2 WSBPEL - WSCDL Description

The Web Services Choreography specification is aimed at being able to precisely describe collaborations between any type of party regardless of the supporting platform or programming model used by the implementation of the hosting environment. Using the Web Services Choreography specification, a contract containing a "global" definition of the common ordering conditions and constraints under which messages are exchanged, is produced that describes, from a global viewpoint, the common and complementary observable behavior of all the parties involved. Each party can then use the global definition to build and test solutions that conform to it. The global specification is in turn realized by combination of the resulting local systems, on the basis of appropriate infrastructure support.

In real-world scenarios, corporate entities are often unwilling to delegate control of their business processes to their integration partners. Choreography offers a means by which the rules of participation within a collaboration can be clearly defined and agreed to, jointly. Each entity may then implement its portion of the Choreography as determined by the common or global view. It is the intent of WS-CDL that the conformance of each implementation to the common view expressed in WS-CDL is easy to determine. Figure 1 demonstrates a possible usage of the Choreography Description Language, where we see that we use WS-BPEL as the Business Process Execution Layer (BPEL for short).

WS-CDL describes interoperable, collaborations between parties. In order to facilitate these collaborations, services commit to mutual responsibilities by

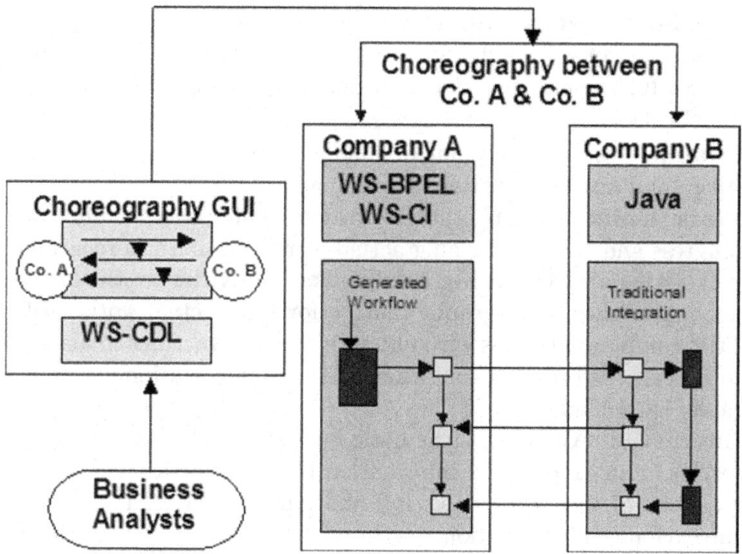

Fig. 1. WS-CDL and WS-BPEL usage

establishing Relationships. Their collaboration takes place in a jointly agreed set of ordering and constraint rules, whereby information is exchanged between the parties. The WS-CDL model consists of the following entities:

- **Participant Types, Role Types and Relationship Types** within a Choreography. Information is always exchanged between parties within or across trust boundaries. A Role Type enumerates the observable behavior a party exhibits in order to collaborate with other parties. A Relationship Type identifies the mutual commitments that must be made between two parties for them to collaborate successfully. A Participant Type is grouping together those parts of the observable behavior that must be implemented by the same logical entity or organization.
- **Information Types, Variables and Tokens.** Variables contain information about commonly observable objects in a collaboration, such as the information exchanged or the observable information of the Roles involved. Tokens are aliases that can be used to reference parts of a Variable. Both Variables and Tokens have Types that define the structure of what the Variable contains or the Token references.
- **Choreographies** define collaborations between interacting parties:
  - **Choreography Life-line**: It shows the progression of a collaboration. Initially, the collaboration is established between the parties; then, some work is performed within it, and finally it completes either normally or abnormally.
  - **Choreography Exception Block**: It specifies the additional interactions that should occur when a Choreography behaves in an abnormal way.

  • **Choreography Finalizer Block**: It describes how to specify additional interactions that should occur to modify the effect of an earlier successfully completed Choreography (for example to confirm or undo the effect).
- **Channels** establish a point of collaboration between parties by specifying where and how information is exchanged.
- **Work Units** prescribe the constraints that must be fulfilled for making progress and thus performing actual work within a Choreography.
- **Activities and Ordering Structures.** Activities are the lowest level components of the Choreography that perform the actual work. Ordering Structures combine activities with other Ordering Structures in a nested structure to express the ordering conditions in which information within the Choreography is exchanged.
- **Interaction Activity** is the basic building block of a Choreography, which results in an exchange of information between parties and possible synchronizations of their observable information changes, and the actual values of the exchanged information.

2.1 WS-BPEL

WS-BPEL is an interface description language. It describes the observable behaviour of a service by defining business processes consisting of stateful long-running interactions in which each interaction has a beginning, a defined behaviour and an end, all of this being modelled by a flow, which consists of a sequence of activities. The behaviour context of each activity is defined by a scope, which provides fault handlers, event handlers, compensation handlers, a set of data variables and correlation sets.

Let us now see a brief description of these components:

- **Events**, which describe the flow execution in an event driven manner.
- **Variables**, which are defined by using WSDL schemes, for internal or external purposes, and are used in the message flow.
- **Correlations**, which identify processes interacting by means of messages.
- **Fault handling**, defining the behaviour when an exception has been thrown.
- **Event handling**, defining the behaviour when an event occurs.
- **Activities**, which represent the basic unit of behaviour of a Web Service. In essence, WS-BPEL describes the behaviour of a Web Service in terms of choreographed activities.

3 Translation

Figure 2 illustrates the relationship between WS-CDL, the choreography layer and the orchestration level (WS-BPEL), taking an orchestra as a metaphor of this relation. The key document is the director score, which corresponds to the WS-CDL document, in which each participant is represented as well as the time

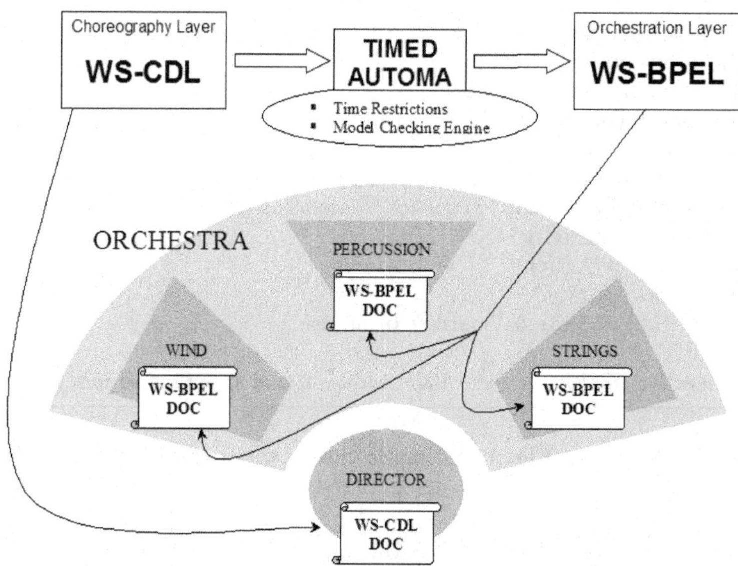

Fig. 2. From the Choreography layer to the Orchestration layer

it enters into action. Furthermore, the wind, percussion and strings scores correspond to the WS-BPEL documents, which show the behaviour of each particular group.

From this Figure we can also see that WS-CDL documents are translated into timed automata in a first step, which is the main goal covered with this paper, and in a second step we intend to translate the timed automata thus obtained into WS-BPEL documents. Therefore, we now present the automatic translation from WS-CDL documents into timed automata. For this purpose, we must first analyse the WS-CDL documents in order to identify the common shared points between them. The first stage is to obtain the general structure describing the system that we are analyzing. In timed automata, this structure is defined by the so-called *System*, which consists of the individual processes that must be executed in parallel. Each one of these processes is defined by using a template. Templates are used to describe the different behaviors that are available in the system.

Then, for each component of a WS-CDL description we have the following correspondence in timed automata (see Fig. 3 for a schematic presentation of this correspondence):

Role: They are used to describe the behaviour of each class of party that we are using in the choreography. Thus, this definition matches with the definition of a *template* in timed automata terminology.

Relation type: They are used to define the communications between two roles, and the needed channels for these communications. In timed automata we just need to assign a new channel for each one of these channels, which are the parameters of the templates that take part in the communication.

Role = Template
Relation Type = Channel^+
Participant Type = Process^+
Channel Type = Channel
Variables = Variables
Choreography = Choreography^+ | Activity
Activity = Work Unit | Sequence | Paralelism | Choice
Sequence = Activity^+
Paralelism = Activity^+
Choice = Activity^+
Work Unit = State & Guard & Invariant

where the symbols +, | are BNF notation, and & is used to join information

Fig. 3. Schematic view of the translation

Participant type: They define the different parties that participate in the choreography. In timed automata they are processes participating in the system.

Channel types: A channel is a point of collaboration between parties, together with the specification of how the information is exchanged. As said before, channels of WS-CDL correspond with channels of timed automata.

Variables: They are easily translated, as timed automata in UPPAAL support variables, which are used to represent some information.

Now the problem is to define the behaviour of each template. This behaviour is defined by using the information provided by the flow of choreographies. Choreographies are sets of workunits or sets of activities. Thus, activities and workunits are the basic components of the choreographies, and they capture the behavior of each component. Activities can be obtained as result of a composition of other activities, by using sequential composition, parallelism and choice. In terms of timed automata these operators can be easily translated:

- The sequential composition of activities is translated by concatenating the corresponding timed automata.
- Parallel activities are translated by the cartesian product of the corresponding timed automata.
- Choices are translated by adding a node into the automata which is connected with the initial nodes of the alternatives.

Finally, time restrictions are associated in WS-CDL with workunits and interaction activities. These time restrictions are introduced in timed automata by means of guards and invariants. Therefore, in case a workunit of an activity has a time restriction we associate a guard to the edge that correspond to the initial point of this workunit in the corresponding timed automaton.

4 Case Study: Travel Reservation System

Some examples of the use of WS-CDL can be found in [4,5,11]. The case study that we are going to use to illustrate how the translation works is inspired from the work [11], where this particular case study was used to illustrate how timed automata can be used for the formal verification of properties.

This system consists of three participants: a Traveller, a Travel Agent and an Airline Reservation System, whose behaviour is as follows:

A Traveller is planning on taking a trip. Once he has decided the concrete trip he wants to make he submits it to a Travel Agent by means of his local Web Service software (*Order Trip*). The Travel Agent selects the best itinerary according to the criteria established by the Traveller. For each leg of this itinerary, the Travel Agent asks the Airline Reservation System to verify the availability of seats (*Verify Seats Availability*). Thus, the Traveller has the choice of accepting or rejecting the proposed itinerary, and he can also decide not to take the trip at all.

- In case he rejects the proposed itinerary, he may submit the modifications (*Change Itinerary*), and wait for a new proposal from the Travel Agent.
- In case he decides not to take the trip, he informs the Travel Agent (*Cancel Itinerary*) and the process ends.
- In case he decides to accept the proposed itinerary (*Reserve Tickets*), he will provide the Travel Agent with his Credit Card information in order to properly book the itinerary.

Once the Traveller has accepted the proposed itinerary, the Travel Agent connects with the Airline Reservation System in order to reserve the seats (*Re-*

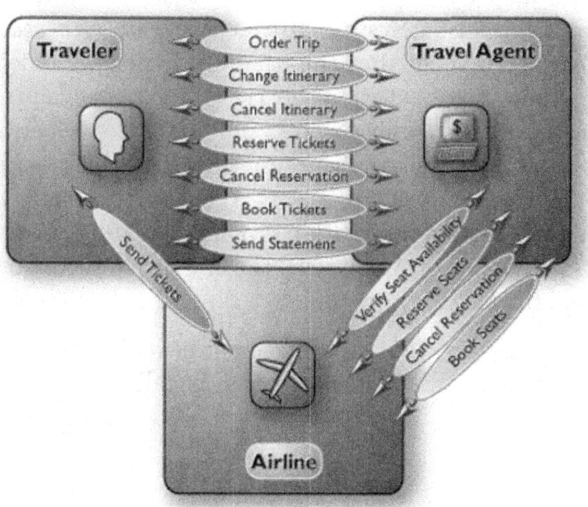

Fig. 4. Flow of the messages exchanged

```
<interaction  name="reservation&booking"
              channelVariable="travelAgentAirlineChannel"
              operation="reservation&booking"
              align="true"
              initiate="true" >
   <participate  relationshipType="TravelAgentAirline"
                 fromRole="TravelAgent" toRole="Airline" />
   <exchange  name="reservation"
              informationType="reservation" action="request" >
     <send    variable="tns:reservationOrderID" causeException="true" />
     <receive   variable="tns:reservationAckID" causeException="true" />
   </exchange>
   <exchange  name="booking" informationType="booking" action="respond">
     <send      variable="tns:bookingRequestID" causeException="true"/>
     <receive   variable="bookingAckID" causeException="true" />
   </exchange>
   <timeout  time-to-complete="24:00" />
   <record  name="bookingTimeout" when="timeout" causeException="true"/>
     <source
       variable="AL:getVariable('tns:reservationOrderCancel', '', '')"/>
     <target
       variable="TA:getVariable('tns:reservationOrderCancel', '', '')"/>
   </record>
</interaction>
```

Fig. 5. Part of WS-CDL especification

serve Seats). However, it may occur that at that moment no seat is available for a particular leg of the trip, because some time has elapsed from the moment in which the availability check was made. In that case the Travel Agent is informed by the Airline Reservation System of that situation (*No seats*), and the Travel Agent informs the Traveller that the itinerary is not possible (*Notify of Cancellation*). Once made the reservation the Travel Agent informs the Traveller (*Seats Reserved*). However, this reservation is only valid for a period of just one day, which means that if a final confirmation has not been received in that period, the seats are unreserved and the Travel Agent is informed. Thus, the Traveller can now either finalize the reservation or cancel it. If he confirms the reservation (*Book Tickets*), the Travel Agent asks the Airline Reservation System to finally book the seats (*Book Seats*).

According to the previous description, the high level flow of the messages exchanged within the global process (which is called *PlanAndBookTrip*) is that shown in Fig. 4.

4.1 Translation of the Case Study

Figure 5 presents a detailed piece of the WS-CDL document describing our example. It describes part of the relationship between the Airline and the Travel

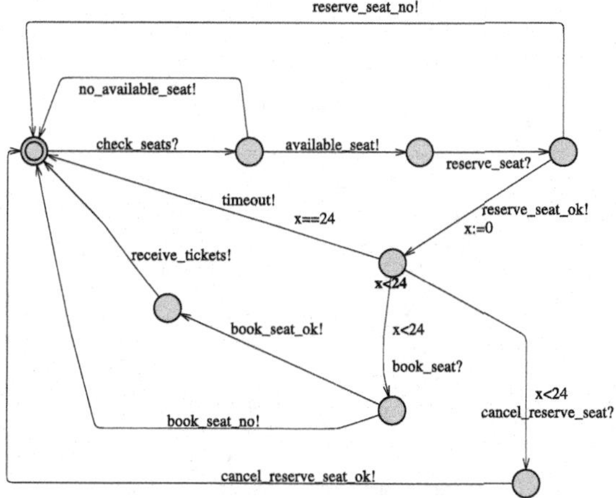

Fig. 6. Timed automata for airline Reservation System

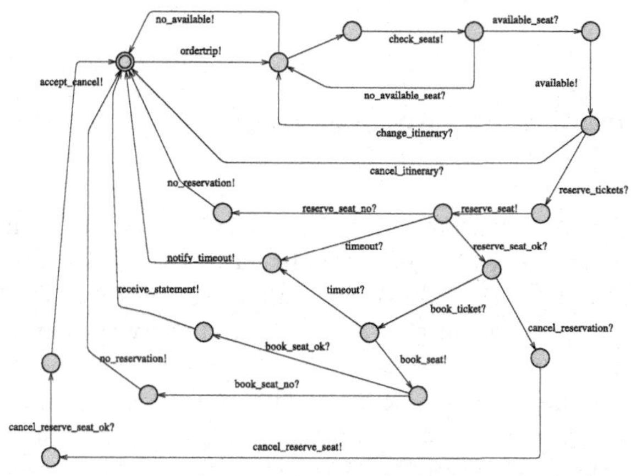

Fig. 7. Timed automata for Travel agent web service

Agent. This interaction establishes the time in which the reservation is available, in this case one day.

We have used this WSCDL document to obtain the translation into timed automata. Following the guidelines described above we have obtained in this case three timed automata: the traveler, the travel agent and the airline company. These automata are shown in Figures 6, 7 and 8.

Notice the use of the clock x in the timed automaton corresponding to the airline reservation system, which is used to control when the reservation expires. This clock is initialized when the action *reserved_seat* is done.

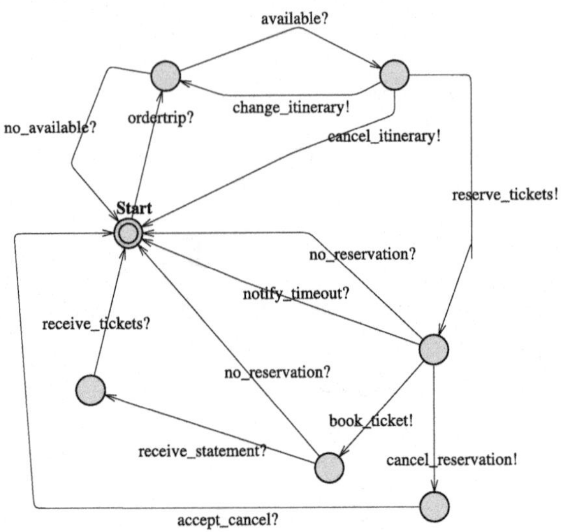

Fig. 8. Timed automata for traveler

5 Conclusions and Future Work

Nowdays Web Services are becoming a powerful tool for the implementation of distributed applications over Internet. In many cases these services have associated time restrictions, as we have seen in the case study that we have presented. Therefore, the specification and design of Web Services can be made by using some well known formalisms, as timed automata, and tools supporting them (UPPAAL) in order to verify and validate the system behavior. Consequently, it becomes of interest to obtain a translation of the specifications written in a Choreography language (WS-CDL) into timed automata in order to exploit these capabilities that timed automata can provide us. Thus, in this paper we have seen how this translation can be made, and it has been applied to a particular case study. We are currently implementing this translation in a tool that uses UPPAAL as the engine for the simulation and verification.

Our future work will focus on the second step of this methodology of traduction, in which our intention is the generation of WS-BPEL documents from WS-CDL documents, using as intermediary objects the timed automata obtained with the translation presented in this paper. Notice that these timed automata will have some internal information, which will not be used by UPPAAL, but that will be necessary in order to obtain the corresponding WS-BPEL documents.

Once this second step has been completed we will have a complete methodology for obtaining correct orchestration descriptions of Web Services from choreography descriptions.

References

1. R. Alur and D. Dill, *Automata for modeling real–time systems*, In Proceedings of the 17th International Colloquium on Automata, Languages and Programming, volume 443, Editors. Springer–Verlag, 1990.
2. Assaf Arkin, Sid Askary, Ben Bloch, et. al., *Web Services Business Process Execution Language Version 2.0*, Editors. OASIS Open, December 2004. In http://www.oasis-open.org/committees/download.php/10347/wsbpel-specification-draft-120204.htm
3. M. Bozga, C. Daws, O. Maler, A. Olivero, S. Tripakis and S. Yovine, *Kronos: A model-checking tool for real-time systems*, In Proc. 1998 Computer-Aided Verification, CAV'98, Vancouver, Canada, June 1998. Lecture Notes in Computer Science 1427, Springer-Verlag.
4. Mario Bravetti, Roberto Lucchi, Gianluigi Zavattaro and Roberto Gorrieri , *Web Services for E-commerce: guaranteeing security access and quality of service*, In Proc. of the 19th ACM Symposium on Applied Computing (SAC'04), special track on E-Commerce Technologies , ACM Press, 2004.
5. Mario Bravetti, Claudio Guidi, Roberto Lucchi and Gianluigi Zavattaro , *Supporting E-commerce system formalization with Choreography Languages*, In Proc. of the 20th ACM Symposium on Applied Computing (SAC'05), special track on E-Commerce Technologies , ACM Press, 2005.
6. Edmund M. Clarke and Jr. and Orna Grumberg and Doron A. Peled, *Model Checking*, MIT Press, 1999.
7. Luc Clement, Andrew Hately, Claus von Riegen and Tony Rogers, *UDDI Version 3.0.2*, Editors. OASIS Open, 19 October 2004. In http://uddi.org/pubs/uddi_v3.htm.
8. Francisco Curbera et al. *Business Process Execution Language for Web Services, Version 1.0.* In http://xml.coverpages.org/WS-BPELv10.pdf.
9. G. Diaz, F. Cuartero, V. Valero and F. Pelayo, *Automatic Verification of the TLS Handshake Protocol*, In proceedings of the 2004 ACM Symposium on Applied Computing.
10. G. Diaz, K.G. Larsen, J. Pardo, F. Cuartero and V. Valero, *An approach to handle Real Time and Probabilistic behaviors in e-commerce: Validating the SET Protocol*, In proceedings of the 2005 ACM Symposium on Applied Computing.
11. G. Diaz, J. J. Pardo, M. E. Cambronero, V. Valero and F. Cuartero, *Verification of Web Services with Timed Autoamata*, In proceedings of First International Workshop on Automated Specification and Verification of Web Sites, Valencia, March 2005.
12. Eurostat yearbook 2004. *The statistical guide to Europe. Data 1992-2002.* European Commission: EUROSTAT, Office for Official Publications of the European Communities, 2004
13. Marc Hadley, Noah Mendelsohn, Jean-Jacques Moreau, et. al., *SOAP Version 1.2 Part 1: Messaging Framework* , Editors. World Wide Web Consortium, 24 June 2003. In http://www.w3.org/TR/soap12-part1.
14. Constance Heitmeyer and Dino Mandrioli. *Formal Methods for Real-Time Computing.* John Wiley & Sons. 1996.
15. Nickolas Kavantzas et al. *Web Service Choreography Description Language (WSCDL) 1.0.* In http://www.w3.org/TR/ws-cdl-10/.
16. K. Larsen and P. Pettersson and Wang Yi, UPPAAL *in a Nutshell*, Int. Journal on Software Tools for Technology Transfer, Editors. Springer–Verlag vol.1, 1997.

17. Jean Paoli, Eve Maler, Tim Bray, et. al.,*Extensible Markup Language (XML) 1.0 (Third Edition)*, Editors. World Wide Web Consortium, 04 February 2004. In http://www.w3.org/TR/2004/REC-xml-20040204.
18. Sanjiva Weerawarana, Roberto Chinnici, Martin Gudgin, et. al., *Web Services Description Language (WSDL) Version 2.0 Part 1: Core Language*, Editors. World Wide Web Consortium, 03 August 2004. In http://www.w3.org/2002/ws/desc/.
19. Simon Woodman, et al., *Specification and Verification of Composite Web Services*, In proocedings of The 8th Enterprise Distributed Object Computing Conference 2004.

Executable Semantics for Compensating CSP

Michael Butler and Shamim Ripon

School of Electronics and Computer Science,
University of Southampton, UK
{mjb, sr03r}@ecs.soton.ac.uk

Abstract. Compensation is an error recovery mechanism for long-running transactions. Compensating CSP is a variant of the CSP process algebra with constructs for orchestration of compensations. We present a simple operational semantics for Compensating CSP and outline an encoding of this semantics in Prolog. This provides a basis for implementation and model checking of the language.

1 Introduction

Web services technology provides a platform on which to develop distributed services. In order to define web service composition, that is, the definition of complex services out of simple ones, *web services choreography* has been introduced. There have been several proposals for describing web services for business processes presented in the recent years including BPML [3] by BPMI, XLANG [20] and BizTalk [16] by Microsoft, WSFL [15] by IBM, BPEL4WS [10] by OASIS (draft standard).

Business transactions involve interaction and coordination between several services. Business transactions need to deal with faults that can arise in any stage of such an environment and this is both difficult and critical. In a long running transaction the usual database approaches, e.g., rollback, are not possible to handle faults. Usually, a long-running transaction interacts with the real world which makes it difficult to undo the transaction. In order to recover from faults in long-running transactions, the concept of compensation was introduced [11]. Compensation is the act of making amendments or making up of a previously completed task. If a long-running transaction fails, appropriate compensations are run to compensate for completed parts of the transaction.

Operational semantics is given by a set of rules which specify how the states of a program change during execution. The overall states of the program are divided into a number of components. Each rule specifies certain precondition on the content of some component and their new content after application of the rule.

The Compensating CSP (cCSP) language was introduced by Butler et al [9] as a language to model long running transactions in the framework of CSP process algebra [12]. The semantics of the cCSP language was described by using denotational semantics (trace semantics). This paper presents the operational semantics of standard as well as compensable processes of compensating CSP

M. Bravetti et al. (Eds.): EPEW 2005 and WS-FM 2005, LNCS 3670, pp. 243–256, 2005.

using the approach of Plotkin [18]. The operational semantics gives a precise understanding of the execution of the language. Roscoe [19] describes the operational semantics of standard CSP and our work builds on that.

We make the operational semantics executable by directly encoding the rules in Prolog. Our hope is that this can serve as a useful basis for model checking cCSP processes. XTL [1] is a model checker which allows a wide range of system specification. It accepts specifications written by using high level Prolog predicates describing the transition between different states of the system. Given a Prolog encoding of the operational semantics, the XTL package provides us with an experimental animator and model checker for cCSP.

This paper is organized as follows. Section 2 gives a brief introduction of the cCSP language. Followed by the introduction of the language, Section 3 presents the operational semantics of cCSP. An executable semantics of the operational semantics is presented in Section 4. Section 5 presents the related work and motivates our contribution with respect to them. Concluding remarks are drawn up in Section 6 and some future directions of the present work are mentioned.

2 Compensating CSP

In this section we briefly introduce the cCSP language. The language was inspired by two main ideas: transaction processing features and process algebra, especially CSP. As in CSP, processes in compensating CSP are modelled in terms of atomic events they can engage in and the operators provided by the language support sequencing, choice, parallel composition of processes. In order to support failed transactions, compensation operators are introduced and processes are categorized into standard and compensable processes. We use P, Q to identify standard processes and PP, QQ to identify compensable processes.

The syntax of compensating CSP is summarised in Figure 1. The basic unit of a standard process is an atomic event. Standard process are constructed with the usual CSP operators for choice, sequencing and parallel composition. The process $SKIP$ terminates immediately successfully. The language also provides interrupts and interrupt handling. The primitive process $THROW$ throws an interrupt immediately. In a purely sequential process, the exception causes an immediate disruption to the flow of control. An interrupt handler may be used to catch interrupts: in $P \rhd Q$, an interrupt raised by P triggers execution of the handler Q. In parallel processes, the whole group of parallel processes may fail when one of the processes throws an exception and all the other processes are willing to disrupt their flow of control and yield to the exception. A process that is ready to terminate is also willing to yield to an interrupt. A process may also yield at mid points in its execution. Yield points are inserted in a process though the primitive $YIELD$ process. For example, $P; YIELD; Q$ is willing to yield to an interrupt in between execution of P and Q. Parallel composition is defined so that throwing of an interrupt in one process synchronises with yielding in another process. The current version of cCSP does not support synchronised

Standard processes:

$$
\begin{array}{rll}
P, Q ::= & A & \text{(atomic action)} \\
& \mid P \; ; \; Q & \text{(sequential composition)} \\
& \mid P \; \Box \; Q & \text{(choice)} \\
& \mid P \parallel Q & \text{(parallel composition)} \\
& \mid SKIP & \text{(normal termination)} \\
& \mid THROW & \text{(throw an interrupt)} \\
& \mid YIELD & \text{(yield to an interrupt)} \\
& \mid P \rhd Q & \text{(interrupt handler)} \\
& \mid [PP] & \text{(transaction block)}
\end{array}
$$

Compensable processes:

$$
\begin{array}{rll}
PP, QQ ::= & P \div Q & \text{(compensation pair)} \\
& \mid PP \; ; \; QQ & \\
& \mid PP \; \Box \; QQ & \\
& \mid PP \parallel QQ & \\
& \mid SKIPP & \\
& \mid THROWW & \\
& \mid YIELDD &
\end{array}
$$

Fig. 1. Syntax of compensating CSP

communication between parallel processes. Parallel process groups synchronise only on joint execution of compensation, joint termination and joint interruption.

A compensable process is one which has compensation actions attached to it. A compensable process consists of a forward behaviour and a compensation behaviour. In the case of an exception, compensation will be executed to compensate the forward behaviour. Both the forward and compensation behaviour are standard processes. The basic way of constructing a compensable process is through the compensation pair construct $P \div Q$, where P is the forward behaviour and Q is its associated compensation. Q should be designed to compensate for the effect of P and may be run long after P has completed.

The parallel and sequential composition operators for compensable processes are designed in a way which ensures that after the failure of a transaction the necessary atomic transactions are performed in an appropriate order to compensate the effect of already performed actions. Sequential composition of compensable processes is defined so that the compensations for all performed actions will be accumulated in the reverse order to their original performance. Parallel composition of compensable processes is defined so that compensations for performed actions will be accumulated in parallel.

By enclosing a compensable process PP in a transaction block $[PP]$ we get a complete transaction which converts the compensable process PP into a standard process. The behaviours of the transaction block are defined in terms of the behaviour of PP. Successfully completed PP represents successful completion of the whole transaction block and compensations are no longer needed. When the forward behaviour of PP throws an interrupt, the compensations are executed in the appropriate order and the interrupt is not observable outside the block.

A standard process can be transformed onto a compensable process by adding to it a compensation process, which actually does nothing (SKIP). The compensable basic processes, which we get from standard basic processes, are as follows:

$$SKIPP = SKIP \div SKIP$$
$$THROWW = THROW \div SKIP$$
$$YIELDD = YIELD \div SKIP$$

An example of a transaction for processing customer orders in a warehouse is presented in Figure 2 in the cCSP language. The first step in the transaction is a compensation pair. The primary action of this pair is to accept the order and deduct the order quantity from the inventory database. The compensation action simply adds the order quantity back to the total in the inventory database. After an order is received from a customer, the order is packed for shipment, and a courier is booked to deliver the goods to the customer. The *PackOrder* process packs each of the items in the order in parallel. Each *PackItem* activity can be compensated by a corresponding *UnpackItem*. Simultaneously with the packing of the order, a credit check is performed on the customer. The credit check is performed in parallel because it normally succeeds, and in this normal case the company does not wish to delay the order unnecessarily. In the case that a credit check fails, an interrupt is thrown causing the transaction to stop its execution, with the courier possibly having been booked and possibly some of the items having being packed. In case of failure, the semantics of the transaction block will ensure that the appropriate compensation activities will be invoked for those activities that did take place.

$$\begin{aligned}
OrderTransaction &= [ProcessOrder] \\
ProcessOrder &= (AcceptOrder \div RestockOrder) \; ; FulfillOrder \\
FulfillOrder &= BookCourier \div CancelCourier \; \| \\
&\quad\; PackOrder \; \| \\
&\quad\; CreditCheck \; ; (\; Ok ; SKIPP \\
&\qquad\qquad\qquad\quad \Box \; NotOk \; ; THROWW \;) \\
PackOrder &= \| \, i \in Items \; \bullet \; (PackItem(i) \div UnpackItem(i))
\end{aligned}$$

Fig. 2. Order transaction example

3 Operational Semantics

The operational semantics is a way of defining the behaviour of processes by specifying atomic transitions on process terms. We will write labelled transition

$$P \xrightarrow{A} P'$$
$$PP \xrightarrow{A} PP'$$

to denote that execution of event A causes the transition from term P or PP to term P' or PP' respectively.

The set of events that a process can perform is called its alphabet. We differentiate between observable and terminal events. The set of observable events is represented by Σ. The terminal events $\Omega = \{\checkmark, !, ?\}$ represent the different ways in which a process may terminate: successful termination is represented by the $\surd$ event, throwing of an interrupt is represented by the ! event and yielding is represented by the ? event. In order to define the semantics we extend the syntax with the null process 0 that cannot perform any events. The terminal events effect standard and compensable processes differently. When a standard process performs a terminal event ω ($\omega \in \Omega$) then the process is finished either normally or abnormally and no further operation occurs.

$$P \xrightarrow{\omega} 0 \qquad (\omega \in \Omega)$$

When a compensable process PP executes a terminal event, instead of evolving to the null process (0), it evolves to a standard process P representing its compensation.

$$PP \xrightarrow{\omega} P \qquad (\omega \in \Omega)$$

In Section 3.2 we will see how these resulting compensations are treated by the various operators for compensable processes.

3.1 Semantics of Standard Processes

This section presents the operational semantics of standard processes of compensating CSP. A process A performs the atomic event and then terminates successfully:

$$A \xrightarrow{A} SKIP \qquad (A \in \Sigma)$$

$SKIP$, $THROW$ and $YIELD$ are primitive processes of cCSP. The effect of terminal events on the special processes are presented here:

$$SKIP \xrightarrow{\surd} 0$$

$$THROW \xrightarrow{!} 0$$

$$YIELD \xrightarrow{\surd} 0$$

$$YIELD \xrightarrow{?} 0$$

In a sequential composition $P;Q$, P may perform non-terminal events while Q is preserved:

$$\frac{P \xrightarrow{\alpha} P'}{P;Q \xrightarrow{\alpha} P';Q} \qquad (\alpha \in \Sigma)$$

If the first process P terminates normally, then Q starts and the $\surd$ action is hidden from outside:

$$\frac{P \xrightarrow{\surd} 0 \wedge Q \xrightarrow{\alpha} Q'}{P;Q \xrightarrow{\alpha} Q'} \qquad (\alpha \in \Sigma \cup \Omega)$$

When the first process P performs a throw or a yield then the whole sequential composition is terminated:

$$\frac{P \xrightarrow{\omega} 0}{P;Q \xrightarrow{\omega} 0} \quad (\omega \in \{!,?\})$$

The interrupt handler is similar to sequential composition, except that the flow of control from the first to the second process is caused by the throw event rather than the $\surd$ event:

$$\frac{P \xrightarrow{\alpha} P'}{P \rhd Q \xrightarrow{\alpha} P' \rhd Q} \quad (\alpha \in \Sigma)$$

$$\frac{P \xrightarrow{!} 0 \wedge Q \xrightarrow{\alpha} Q'}{P \rhd Q \xrightarrow{\alpha} Q'} \quad (\alpha \in \Sigma \cup \Omega)$$

$$\frac{P \xrightarrow{\omega} 0}{P \rhd Q \xrightarrow{\omega} 0} \quad (\omega \in \Omega \wedge \omega \neq !)$$

In choice operation occurrence of an event in either of the processes resolves the choice:

$$\frac{P \xrightarrow{\alpha} P'}{P \,\square\, Q \xrightarrow{\alpha} P'} \qquad \frac{Q \xrightarrow{\alpha} Q'}{P \,\square\, Q \xrightarrow{\alpha} Q'} \quad (\alpha \in \Sigma \cup \Omega)$$

We are only considering the parallel processes synchronising on terminal events. In a parallel composition, either process may progress independently by performing a non-terminal event:

$$\frac{P \xrightarrow{\alpha} P'}{P \parallel Q \xrightarrow{\alpha} P' \parallel Q} \qquad \frac{Q \xrightarrow{\alpha} Q'}{P \parallel Q \xrightarrow{\alpha} P \parallel Q'} \quad (\alpha \in \Sigma)$$

Processes placed in parallel will synchronise on joint termination or joint interruption. If we consider ω and ω' are the terminal events of two distinct parallel processes then their joint event will be $\omega \& \omega'$. The definition of this operator is shown in Table 1. Synchronisation of standard processes is defined as follows:

$$\frac{P \xrightarrow{\omega} 0 \ \wedge \ Q \xrightarrow{\omega'} 0}{P \parallel Q \xrightarrow{\omega \& \omega'} 0}$$

3.2 Semantics of Compensable Processes

In this section we present the semantics of the operators for compensable processes. Recall that a compensable process consists of forward behaviour and compensation behaviour.

The compensation pair $(P \div Q)$ is constructed from two standard processes. The first one is called forward process which is executed during normal execution

Table 1. Synchronization of terminal events

ω	ω'	$\omega \& \omega'$
!	!	!
!	?	!
!	$\surd$	!
?	?	?
?	$\surd$	?
$\surd$	$\surd$	$\surd$

and the second one is called the compensation of the forward process which is stored for future use when it is required for compensation. If the forward process can perform a non-terminal event, then so can the pair:

$$\frac{P \xrightarrow{\alpha} P'}{P \div Q \xrightarrow{\alpha} P' \div Q} \quad (\alpha \in \Sigma)$$

If the forward process terminates normally, then the pair terminates with Q as the resulting compensation.

$$\frac{P \xrightarrow{\surd} 0}{P \div Q \xrightarrow{\surd} Q}$$

If the forward process terminates abnormally, then so does the pair, resulting in an empty compensation process:

$$\frac{P \xrightarrow{\omega} 0}{P \div Q \xrightarrow{\omega} SKIP} \quad (\omega \in \{!, ?\})$$

The definition of the compensation pair defined in the traces model of cCSP [9] has a subtle difference to that presented here. An extra behaviour for the compensation pair was included in the traces model definition which allows the compensation pair to yield immediately with an empty compensation. This forces an automatic yield at the beginning of the compensation pair. The same behaviour can be obtained using the definition presented here by adding a yield sequentially followed by the forward process.

$$P \div' Q \mathrel{\hat{=}} (YIELD; P) \div Q$$

As for the standard case, in a sequential composition $PP; QQ$, PP may perform non-terminal events while QQ is preserved:

$$\frac{PP \xrightarrow{\alpha} PP'}{PP; QQ \xrightarrow{\alpha} PP'; QQ} \quad (\alpha \in \Sigma)$$

If PP throws or yields to an interrupt, the whole process terminates and the compensation from PP is returned:

$$\frac{PP \xrightarrow{\omega} P}{PP; QQ \xrightarrow{\omega} P} \quad (\omega \in \Omega \wedge \omega \neq \surd)$$

If PP terminates normally, QQ commences and the compensation from PP should be maintained to be composed with the compensation from QQ at a later stage. In order to deal with this we introduce a new auxiliary construct to the language of the form $\langle QQ, P\rangle$. The effect of $\langle QQ, P\rangle$ is to execute the forward behaviour of QQ and then compose the compensation from QQ with P. This is used to define the transfer of control in a sequential composition:

$$\frac{PP \xrightarrow{\checkmark} P \wedge QQ \xrightarrow{\alpha} QQ'}{PP; QQ \xrightarrow{\alpha} \langle QQ', P\rangle} \qquad (\alpha \in \Sigma)$$

However, if QQ involves in a terminal event after PP terminates normally, then instead of introducing the new auxiliary construct, the maintained compensations of both processes are accumulated.

$$\frac{PP \xrightarrow{\checkmark} P \wedge QQ \xrightarrow{\omega} Q}{PP; QQ \xrightarrow{\omega} Q\ ;\ P} \qquad (\omega \in \Omega)$$

The process QQ in the construct $\langle QQ, P\rangle$ can perform non-terminating events:

$$\frac{QQ \xrightarrow{\alpha} QQ'}{\langle QQ, P\rangle \xrightarrow{\alpha} \langle QQ', P\rangle} \qquad (\alpha \in \Sigma)$$

When QQ terminates then its compensation is composed in front of the existing compensation, which ensures that the compensations are accumulated in reverse order to their original sequential operation:

$$\frac{QQ \xrightarrow{\omega} Q}{\langle QQ, P\rangle \xrightarrow{\omega} Q; P} \qquad (\omega \in \Omega)$$

An event in PP or QQ resolves the choice in a choice composition.

$$\frac{PP \xrightarrow{\alpha} PP'}{PP \,\Box\, QQ \xrightarrow{\alpha} PP'} \qquad \frac{QQ \xrightarrow{\alpha} QQ'}{PP \,\Box\, QQ \xrightarrow{\alpha} QQ'} \qquad (\alpha \in \Sigma)$$

The terminal events ($\checkmark$,!,?) also resolve the choice resulting in the corresponding compensations:

$$\frac{PP \xrightarrow{\omega} P}{PP \,\Box\, QQ \xrightarrow{\omega} P} \qquad \frac{QQ \xrightarrow{\omega} Q}{PP \,\Box\, QQ \xrightarrow{\omega} Q} \qquad (\omega \in \Omega)$$

Parallel processes evolve independently through non-terminal events:

$$\frac{PP \xrightarrow{\alpha} PP'}{PP \parallel QQ \xrightarrow{\alpha} PP' \parallel QQ} \qquad \frac{QQ \xrightarrow{\alpha} QQ'}{PP \parallel QQ \xrightarrow{\alpha} PP \parallel QQ'} \qquad (\alpha \in \Sigma\})$$

As the processes are compensable, when they synchronise over any terminal events, the forward processes are terminated and the corresponding compensation processes will be accumulated in parallel:

$$\frac{PP \xrightarrow{\omega} P \ \wedge \ QQ \xrightarrow{\omega'} Q}{PP \parallel QQ \xrightarrow{\omega \& \omega'} P \parallel Q}$$

Although a transaction block is a standard process rather than a compensable process, we describe its semantics in this section rather than the previous one since it requires an understanding of the semantics of compensable processes. A transaction block is formed from a compensable process PP by enclosing PP in a transaction block $[PP]$. A transaction block converts a compensable process into a standard process. A non-terminal event changes the state of the process inside the block:

$$\frac{PP \xrightarrow{\alpha} PP'}{[PP] \xrightarrow{\alpha} [PP']} \quad (\alpha \in \Sigma)$$

Successful completion of the forward behaviour of the compensable process of a transaction block represents successful completion of the whole block and compensation is no longer needed and it is discarded:

$$\frac{PP \xrightarrow{\checkmark} P}{[PP] \xrightarrow{\checkmark} 0}$$

When the forward behaviour throws an exception, then the resulting compensation is run:

$$\frac{PP \xrightarrow{!} P \wedge P \xrightarrow{\alpha} P'}{[PP] \xrightarrow{\alpha} P'} \qquad (\alpha \in \Sigma \cup \Omega)$$

Since a transaction block is a standard process, P' in this rule is not a compensation that is stored for later execution, rather it describes the behaviour of $[PP]$ after execution of event α.

Note that there is no rule for a yield transition (?) in a transaction block. This is because a transaction block does not yield to interrupts from the outside. Yields by a sub-process of PP will synchronise with interrupts from some other sub-process resulting in the ! event making yields within PP non-observable.

3.3 Correspondence with Trace Semantics

When both an operational and denotational semantics are defined for a particular language, a natural question is how these are related. In this section, we briefly describe the way in which we are attempting to show the correspondence between the operational semantics presented in this paper and the denotational semantics presented in traces model shown in [9].

Given our operational rules for cCSP which defines a labelled transition relation between process terms, we can define a lifted transition relation labelled by sequences of events in the usual way:

$$P \xrightarrow{s} Q$$

Roscoe [19] describes how to extract the traces from operational rules as follows:

$$traces(P) = \{s \in \Sigma^{*\checkmark} \mid \exists Q.P \xrightarrow{s} Q\}$$

We derive traces from the operational rules in a similar way. In the standard traces model for CSP, process are modelled as prefixed-closed sets of traces. However, in the traces model for cCSP, processes are modelled as sets of completed traces, where a completed trace ends in one of the terminal symbols $\Omega = \{\checkmark, ?, !\}$. The traces model for cCSP is not closed under trace prefixes.

Standard traces are defined as set of traces of the form $p\langle\omega\rangle$ where $p \in \Sigma^*$ and $\omega \in \Omega$. The derived traces of a standard cCSP process P are denoted by $DT(P)$ which is defined as follows:

$$DT(P) = \{\ p\langle\omega\rangle \mid P \xrightarrow{p\langle\omega\rangle} 0\ \}$$

As compensable processes contain forward behaviour and compensation behaviour, they are modelled as pairs of traces of the form $(p\langle\omega\rangle, p'\langle\omega'\rangle)$ where $p\langle\omega\rangle$ represents forward behaviour and $p'\langle\omega'\rangle$ represents the corresponding compensation behaviour. The derived traces of a compensable cCSP process PP are denoted by $DT(PP)$ which is defined as follows:

$$DT(PP) = \{\ (p\langle\omega\rangle, p'\langle\omega'\rangle) \mid \exists P \cdot\ PP \xrightarrow{p\langle\omega\rangle} P \wedge P \xrightarrow{p'\langle\omega'\rangle} 0\ \}$$

Let $T(P)$ be the traces of a standard term P as defined in [9]. Similarly for $T(PP)$. By structural induction over process terms P and PP, it should be possible to prove the following correspondence:

$$DT(P) = T(P)$$
$$DT(PP) = T(PP)$$

4 Prolog Implementation

In this section we outline a prolog implementation of the operational semantics presented in Section 3. We encode the operational rules as Prolog clauses and we use a tool which can animate this encoded semantics and support model checking and refinement of the specification. XTL [1] is a model checker which allows a wide range of system specification. It accepts specifications written by using high level Prolog predicates describing the transition between different states of the system. The XTL animator supports step by step animation showing transition between different states of specification and also support backtracking.

The input language for XTL is very simple. There are two key predicates that can be entered into XTL: `trans/3` and `prop/2` where:

`trans(A,S1,S2)`: A transition from state S1 to state S2 by the action A.
`prop(S,P)`: property P holds in state S.

Consider the following simple system specified in this way:

```
trans(a1,p,q). trans(a2,q,p). trans(a3,r,r).
prop(p,safe). prop(q,safe). prop(r,unsafe).
```

These lines specify that by the action `a1`, there is a transition from `p` to `q`, that action `a2` causes the reverse transition and action *a3* causes `r` to `r`. The property clauses specify that state `p` and `q` are safe and that `r` is unsafe. The XTL model checker supports checking of temporal properties written in CTL (Computation Tree Logic) of systems specified in this way.

As the operational semantics of compensating CSP are described by using operational rules, they are easily transferable to corresponding `trans/3` predicates. We reproduce some operational rules and their corresponding Prolog predicates. For example, consider one of the rules for sequential composition of standard processes:

$$\frac{P \xrightarrow{\alpha} P'}{P;Q \xrightarrow{\alpha} P';Q} \qquad (\alpha \in \Sigma)$$

The Prolog representation of this is:

```
trans(seq(P,Q),A,seq(P1,Q)):-
        member(A,sigma),
        trans(P,A,P1).
```

Compensable processes are encoded in a similar way with the compensable operators being differentiated from the standard ones. For example, consider the following rule for compensable sequential composition:

$$\frac{PP \xrightarrow{\alpha} PP'}{PP;QQ \xrightarrow{\alpha} PP';QQ} \qquad (\alpha \in \Sigma)$$

This is represented in prolog as:

```
trans(cseq(PP,QQ),A,cseq(PP1,QQ)):-
        member(A,sigma),
        trans(PP,A,PP1).
```

The XTL package provides us with an experimental animator and model checker for cCSP. We are currently investigating the use of this further. We are also investigating the use of the prolog encoding as a basis for a refinement checking tool. Refinement checking is currently supported by the ProB model checker [14] using similar prolog techniques to XTL.

5 Related Work

Bocchi et al [2] define a language πt-calculus for modelling long-running transactions based on Milner's π-calculus [17]. The πt-calculus includes a transaction construct that contains a compensation handler and a fault manager. In this approach a transaction process remains active as long as its compensation might be required. This doesn't allow for the sequential composition of compensable transactions in which compensations are composed in reverse order.

Recently, Laneve and Zavattaro [13] defined a calculus for web transactions called webπ which is an extension of asynchronous π-calculus with timed transaction construct. The major aspects considered in webπ are that the processes are interruptible, failure handlers are activated when main processes are interrupted and time which is considered in order to deal with latency of web activities or with message losses. A transaction executes either until its termination or until it fails and upon failure the compensation is activated. However, it has the similar problem as πt-calculus where compensations of sequentially composed transactions are not preserved in reverse order and it is not possible to get the compensation of a successfully completed process after the failure of a process composed sequentially with the previous one.

One of the authors (Butler) was involved in the development of the StAC (Structured Activity Compensation) language [6,7] for modelling long-running business transactions which includes compensation constructs. An important difference between StAC and cCSP is that instead of the execution of compensations being part of the definition of a transaction block, StAC has explicit primitives for running or discarding installed compensations (*reverse* and *accept* respectively). This separation of the *accept* and *reverse* operators from compensation scoping prevents the definition of a simple compositional semantics: the semantics of the reverse operator cannot be defined on its own as its behaviour depends on the context in which it is called. This necessitated the use of configurations involving installed compensation contexts in the operational semantics for StAC. Note that BPEL also has an operator for explicit invocation of compensation. A mapping from BPEL to StAC may be found in [8].

Bruni et al [5] have developed an operational semantics for a language with similar operators to cCSP, including compensation pairs and transaction blocks (or sagas as they call them). As in cCSP, and unlike StAC, the invocation of compensation in a saga is automatic depending on failure or success which leads to a neater operational semantics. However, unlike the work presented here, the operational semantics in [5] is defined by using big-step semantics. Big-step semantics describe how the overall results of the execution are obtained. The big step semantics are closer to the trace semantics while our small-step semantics describes how compensating processes should be executed. A comparison of the operators of cCSP and the language described in [5] may be found in [4].

6 Conclusions and Future Work

Compensating CSP has evolved from the development of the StAC language. StAC has a somewhat complicated operational semantics because of the need to maintain compensation contexts in process configurations. Compensating CSP was developed through a trace semantics which forces a compositional semantic definition. This leads to a more structured treatment of compensation which in turn has lead to a much simpler operational semantics than that of StAC. We are currently working on proving the corespondence between the trace and operational semantic models of cCSP.

Our operational semantics provides the basis for a prototype model checker for cCSP as well as a basis for an implementation strategy for a language with compensations.

Acknowledgements

Thanks to Hernan Melgratti and to the anonymous WS-FM05 referees for useful comments on an earlier version of the paper. Thanks for Michael Leuschel for help with XTL.

References

1. Juan C. Augusto, Michael Leuschel, Michael Butler, and Carla Ferreira. Using the extensible model checker XTL to verify StAC business specifications. In *3rd Workshop on Automated Verification of Critical Systems (AVoCS 2003)*, pages 253–266, Southampton, UK, 2003.
2. Laura Bocchi, Cosimo Laneve, and Gianluigi Zavattaro. A calulus for long-running transactions. In *FMOODS'03*, volume 2884 of *LNCS*, pages 124–138. Springer-Verlag, 2003.
3. Business Process Modeling Language (BPML). [www.bpmi.org].
4. Roberto Bruni, Michael Butler, Carla Ferreira, Tony Hoare, Hernan Melgratti, and Ugo Montanari. Reconciling two approaches to compensable flow composition. Technical report, 2005.
5. Roberto Bruni, Hernán Melgratti, and Ugo Montanari. Theoretical foundations for compensations in flow composition languages. In *POPL*, pages 209–220, 2005.
6. Michael Butler and Carla Ferreira. A process compensation language. In *Integrated Formal Methods(IFM'2000)*, volume 1945 of *LNCS*, pages 61 – 76. Springer-Verlag, 2000.
7. Michael Butler and Carla Ferreira. An operational semantics for StAC, a language for modelling long-running business transactions. In *Coordination 2004*, volume 2949 of *LNCS*. Springer-Verlag, 2004.
8. Michael Butler, Carla Ferreira, and M.Y. Ng. Precise modelling of compensating business transactions and its application to BPEL. *Journal of Universal Computer Science, to appear*, 2005.
9. Michael Butler, Tony Hoare, and Carla Ferreira. A trace sematics for long-running transaction. In A.E. Abdallah, C.B. Jones, and J.E. Sanders, editors, *Proceedings of 25 Years of CSP*, volume 3525 of *Springer LNCS*, London, 2004.

10. F. Curbera, Y. Goland, J. Klein, F. Leymann, D. Roller, S. Thatte, and S. Weerawarana. *Business process execution language for web services, version 1.1.*, 2003. [http://www-106.ibm.com/developerworks/library/ws-bpel/].
11. H. Garcia-Molina and K. Salem. Sagas. In *ACM SIGMOD*, pages 249–259. ACM Press, 1987.
12. C.A.R. Hoare. *Communicating Sequential Process.* Prentice Hall, 1985.
13. Cosimo Laneve and Gianluigi Zavattaro. Foundations of web transactions. In *FoSSaCS*, volume 3441 of *LNCS*, pages 282–298, 2005.
14. Michael Leuschel and Michael Butler. ProB: A model checker for B. In Keijiro Araki, Stefania Gnesi, and Dino Mandrioli, editors, *FME 2003: Formal Methods*, LNCS 2805, pages 855–874. Springer-Verlag, September 2003.
15. Frank Leymann. The web services flow language (WSFL 1.0). Technical report, Member IBM Academy of Technology, IBM Software Group, 2001. [http://www-4.ibm.com/software/solutions/webservices/pdf/WSFL.pdf].
16. B. Metha, M. Levy, G. Meredith, T. Andrews, B. Beckman, J. Klein, and A. Mital. Biztalk server 2000 business process orchestration. *IEEE Data Engineering Bulletin,*, 24(1):35–39, 2001.
17. Robin Milner. A calculus of mobile processes. *Journal of Information and computing*, 100(1):1–77, 1992.
18. G. Plotkin. A structural approach to operational semantics. Technical Report DAIMI FN-19, Aarhus University, Computer Science Department, September 1981.
19. A.W. Roscoe. *The Theory and Practice of Concurrency.* Prentice Hall, pearson edition, 1998.
20. S.Thatte. *XLANG: Web Services for Business Process Design.* Microsoft Corporation, 2001. [www.gotdotnet.com/team/xml/wsspace/xlang-c].

Verifying the Conformance of Web Services to Global Interaction Protocols: A First Step*

M. Baldoni, C. Baroglio, A. Martelli, V. Patti, and and C. Schifanella

Dipartimento di Informatica — Università degli Studi di Torino,
C.so Svizzera, 185 — I-10149 Torino (Italy)
{baldoni, baroglio, mrt, patti, schi}@di.unito.it

Abstract. Global choreographies define the rules that peers should respect in their interaction, with the aim of guaranteeing interoperability. An abstract choreography can be seen as a protocol specification; it does not refer to specific peers and, especially in an open application domain, it might be necessary to retrieve a set of web services that fit in it. A crucial issue, that is raising attention, is verifying whether the business process of some peers, in particular the parts that encode the communicative behavior, will produce interactions which are conformant to the agreed protocol (legality issue). Such issue is tackled by the so called *conformance test*, which is a means for certifying the capability of interacting of the involved parts: two peers that are proved conformant to a same protocol will actually *interoperate* by producing a legal conversation. This work proposes an approach to the verification of a priori conformance of a business process to a protocol, which is based on the theory of formal languages and guarantees the interoperability of peers that are individually proved conformant.

Keywords: web service interaction protocols, conformance test, formal verification, finite state automata.

1 Introduction

In this work we propose a formal framework for verifying the conformance and the interoperability of web services with respect to a high-level specification of the global protocol. This proposal builds upon experience of protocol conformance problems in the research area of Multi-agent systems (MASs).

Web services are heterogeneous devices that can be "composed" (in a broad meaning) so as to accomplish complex tasks. Even though web services are not necessarily agents, the two share some similarities. For instance, they are usually supposed to bear an executable description of their business process, that,

* This research is partially supported by MIUR Cofin 2003 "Logic-based development and verification of multi-agent systems" national project and by the European Commission and by the Swiss Federal Office for Education and Science within the 6th Framework Programme project REWERSE number 506779.

M. Bravetti et al. (Eds.): EPEW 2005 and WS-FM 2005, LNCS 3670, pp. 257–271, 2005.

in particular, accounts for their interactive behavior. Similarly, agents are commonly supposed to make their communicative behavior (the agent's interaction policy) public. In both cases this description can be used to *take decisions* about the entity, such as deciding if it can take part to a system of cooperating parties.

According to Agent-Oriented Software Engineering [14], a distinction is made between the global and the individual points of view of the interaction between the various parties. The *global* viewpoint is captured by an *abstract protocol*, expressed by formalisms like AUML, automata or Petri Nets. The *local* viewpoint of one of the parties, instead, is captured by the agent's policy. Being part of the agent implementation, policies are usually written in some executable language. Having these two descriptions it is possible to decide if an agent can take a role in an interaction. In fact, this problem can be read as the problem of proving if the agent's policy *conforms* to the abstract protocol specification.

A similar need of distinguishing a global and a local view of the interaction is recently emerging also in the area of Service Oriented Architectures. In this case there is a distinction between the *choreography* of a set of peers, i.e. a global specification of the way a group of peers interact, and the concept of *behavioral interface*, seen as the specification of the interaction from the point of view of an individual peer: "The fundamental difference between the concept of choreography on the one hand, and the concept of behavioral interface (i.e., BPEL abstract process) on the other, is that a choreography focuses on interactions seen from a global viewpoint, while behavioral interfaces focus on communication actions seen from the viewpoint of one of the participants" [4]. A third concept is that of *orchestration* (e.g. BPEL executable process) which, intuitively, describes the whole service, i.e. both its communicative and its non-communicative behavior, allowing execution. The recent W3C proposal of the choreography language WS-CDL [15] is emblematic. In fact the idea behind it is to introduce specific *choreography languages* as languages for a high-level specification, captured from a global perspective, distinguishing this representation from the other two, that will be based upon ad hoc languages (like BPEL or ebXML).

Taking this perspective, choreographies and agent interaction protocols undoubtedly share a common purpose. In fact, they both aim at expressing *global interaction protocols*, i.e. rules that define the global behavior of a system of cooperating parties. The respect of these rules guarantees the interoperability of the parties (i.e. the capability of *actually* producing an interaction), and that the interactions will satisfy given requirements.

One problem that becomes crucial is the development of formal methods for verifying if the behavior of a peer respects a choreography. The applications would be various. A choreography could be used *at design time* (a priori) for verifying that the internal processes of a service enable it to participate appropriately in the interaction. At *run-time*, choreographies could be used to verify that everything is proceeding according to the agreements. A choreography could also be used unilaterally to detect exceptions (e.g. a message was expected but not received) or help a participant in sending messages in the right order and at the right time. Moreover, choreographies allow the implementation of a top-down methodology in the design of web services. The work in [7] already takes this approach by using WS-CDL and BPEL4WS as complementary design tools: the first design step of an interaction protocol (for the peers of an e-commerce system) consists in the development of a WS-CDL description; this is followed by an implementation step, where BPEL4WS is exploited for representing the behavior of the single peers [7]. A further step could be exploiting formal methods for synthesizing behavioral interfaces (e.g. abstract BPEL) from the choreography definition, on the line of the work in [8].

In the literature the problem of verifying conformance of the behavior of an individual to a general interaction protocol is known as *conformance* testing. A conformance test can be considered as a tool that, by verifying the respect of a protocol, *certifies* the interoperability of a set of parties: we expect that two parties which are proved conformant to a same protocol *will produce* an interaction, that is legal w.r.t. the encoded rules, when they will interact. In the last years two kinds of conformance have been studied w.r.t. MASs [12]: *a priori* conformance (checked at design time) [9,10], and *run-time* conformance [3,1]. If we call a *conversation* a specific interaction between two agents, consisting only of communicative acts, the former is a property of the *implementation as a whole* –intuitively it checks if an agent will never produce conversations that violate the abstract interaction protocol specification–, while the latter is a property of the *on-going conversation*, aimed at verifying if *that* conversation is legal. Notice that the *same tests* are envisioned for choreographies and for the individual peers that should play a role defined in them.

In this work we focus on testing *a priori conformance* and develop a framework based on the use of formal languages. In our framework a global interaction protocol (a choreography), is represented as a finite state automaton, whose alphabet is the set of messages exchanged among peers. It specifies permitted conversations. Atomic services (peers), that have to be composed according to the choreography, are described as finite state automata as well. Given such a representation we capture a concept of conformance that answers positively to all these questions: *is it possible to verify that a peer, playing a role in a given global protocol, produces at least those conversations which guarantee interoperability with other conformant peers? Will such a peer always follow one of these conversations when interacting with the other parties in the context of the protocol? Will it always be able to conclude the legal conversations it is involved in?* Technically, the conformance test is based on the acceptance of both the peer's behavior and the global protocol by a special finite state automaton. The interesting characteristic of this test is that it guarantees the interoperability of peers that are proved conformant *individually* and *independently* from one another.

This approach can be applied to a wide variety of cases with the proviso that both the protocol specification and the behavioral interface can be specified by regular expressions. Besides simplicity and readability, the reason for adopting regular expressions is that they guarantee *decidability*. Of course, in this way it is not possible to represent *concurrency*. We are aware of this limit but this is just a first step of a wider research, and we mean to extend the approach in the near future. Focussing on finite state automata is not too much restrictive, anyway, because many protocols used in MASs can be expressed in this way and we believe that the same holds for many web services. So far, the framework only deals with 2-party global protocols. This is also, of course, a limitation that we aim to relax in future work by extending the framework (see the conclusions for further discussion). To make this proposal more concrete in Section 4 we explain these ideas with the help of an example, in which we consider a choreography and a web service; we show that the latter conforms to the former and, thus, it will be able to interoperate with any other service that is as well conformant and that plays another role.

2 Conformant and Interoperable Peers

A business process is a program that defines the behavior of a specific peer, implemented in some programming language. We focus on the interactive behavior of the peer and we will denote it by the term *conversation policy* of the peer. A choreography specifies the overall behavior of a group of interacting peers; many proposals of languages (e.g. WSCI and WS-CDL) for representing choreographies can be found in the literature. Also in this case we will focus only on that part of the choreography that denotes the message exchange among the parties. For this reason, hereafter the term *choreography* and the term (conversation) *protocol* will be used as synonims.

We face the problem of conformance verification by interpreting "a priori conformance" as a property that relates two *formal languages*: the language of the conversations allowed by the conversation policy of a peer, and the language of the conversations allowed by a choreography. They will respectively be denoted by $L(p^{ws}_{lang})$ and $L(p_{spec})$, where *spec* is the choreography specification language, *lang* is the language in which the policy, executed by the peer ws, is written, and p is the name of the policy or of the protocol at issue. The assumption that we do throughout this paper is that the two languages are *regular sets.* This choice restricts the kinds of protocols to which our proposal can be applied, because finite state automata cannot represent concurrent operations, however, it is still significant because a wide family of protocols (and policies) of practical use can be expressed in a way that can be mapped onto such automata. Moreover, the use of regular sets ensures decidability. Another assumption is that the conversation protocol encompasses only *two peers.* The extension to a greater number of peers will be tackled as future work. Notice that the peers might be implemented in *different languages.*

A conversation protocol specifies the sequences of messages that can possibly be exchanged by the involved peers, and that we consider as legal. In agent languages that account for communication, messages (named "speech acts") often have the form $m(ag_s, ag_r, l)$, where m is the performative, ag_s (sender) and ag_r (receiver) are two agents and l is the message content. It is not restrictive to assume that messages have this form also in the case of web services and to assume that conversations are sequences of messages of this form [2]. In the following analysis it is important to distinguish the incoming messages, w.r.t. a specific peer ws, from the messages sent by it. We respectively denote the former, where ws plays the role of the receiver, by $\mathsf{m}(\overleftarrow{ws})$, and the latter, where ws is the sender, by and $\mathsf{m}(\overrightarrow{ws})$. We will also simply write $\overleftarrow{\mathsf{m}}$ (*incoming message*) and $\overrightarrow{\mathsf{m}}$ (*outgoing message*) when the peer that receives or sends the message is clear from the context. Notice that these are just short notations, that underline the *role* of a given peer from the *individual perspective* of *that* peer. This view is consistent with the unilateral view typical of languages like BPEL [6], used to represent behavioral interfaces from the point of view of a peer. So, for instance, $m(ws_s, ws_r, l)$ is written as $\mathsf{m}(\overleftarrow{ws_r})$ from the point of view of ws_r, and $\mathsf{m}(\overrightarrow{ws_s})$ from the point of view of the sender but the three notions denote the same object.

A *conversation*, denoted by σ, is a sequence of messages that represents a dialogue of a set of peers. We say that a conversation is legal w.r.t. a protocol if it respects the specifications given by the protocol. Since $L(p_{spec})$ is the set of all the legal conversations according to p, the definition is as follows.

Definition 1 (Legal conversation). *We say that a conversation σ is legal w.r.t. a protocol specification p_{spec} when $\sigma \in L(p_{spec})$.*

We can now explain, with the help of simple examples, the intuition behind the terms "conformance" and "interoperability", that we will then formalize.

> *Interoperability is the capability of a peer of actually producing a conversation when interacting with another.*

A new peer can be introduced in an execution context provided that it satisfies the rules of the system. As long as this happens, it will not be necessary to verify interoperability with the single components of the system. This can be done by checking the interactive behavior of the peer against the rules of the group, i.e. against its *interaction protocol.* Such a proof is known as *conformance test* and must, intuitively, guarantee the following expectations.

> *We expect that two peers, that conform to a protocol, will produce a legal conversation, when interacting with one another.*

Let us begin with considering the following case: suppose that the communicative behavior of the peer ws is defined by a policy that accounts for two conversations $\{\mathsf{m}_1(\overrightarrow{ws})\mathsf{m}_2(\overleftarrow{ws}), \mathsf{m}_1(\overrightarrow{ws})\mathsf{m}_3(\overleftarrow{ws})\}$. This means that after sending a message m_1, the peer expects one of the two messages m_2 or m_3. Let us also suppose that the protocol specification only allows the first conversation, i.e. that the only possible incoming message is m_2. Is the policy conformant? According to Def. 1 the answer should be no, because the policy allows an illegal conversation. Nevertheless, when the peer will interact with another peer that is conformant to the protocol, the message m_3 will never be received because the partner will never send it. So, in this case, we would like the a priori conformance test to accept the policy as *conformant* to the specification.

Talking about incoming messages, let us now consider the symmetric case, in which the *protocol specification* states that after the peer ws has sent m_1, the other peer can alternatively answer m_2 or m_4 (ws's policy, instead, is the same as above). In this case, the expectation is that ws's policy is *not conformant* because, according to the protocol, there is a possible legal conversation (the one with answer m_4) that can be enacted by the *interlocutor* (which is not under the control of ws), which ws cannot handle. So it does not comply to the specifications.

> *As a first observation we expect the policy to be able to handle any incoming message, foreseen by the protocol, and we ignore those cases in which the policy foresees an incoming message that is not supposed to be received at that point of the conversation, according to the protocol specification.*

Let us, now, suppose that peer ws's policy can produce the following conversations $\{\mathsf{m}_1(\overleftarrow{ws})\mathsf{m}_2(\overrightarrow{ws}),\ \mathsf{m}_1(\overleftarrow{ws})\mathsf{m}_3(\overrightarrow{ws})\}$ and that the set of conversations allowed by the protocol specification is $\{\mathsf{m}_1(\overleftarrow{ws})\mathsf{m}_2(\overrightarrow{ws})\}$. Trivially, this policy is *not conformant* to the protocol because ws can send a message (m_3) that cannot be handled by any interlocutor that is conformant to the protocol.

> *The second observation is that we expect a policy to never send a message that, according to the specification, is not supposed to be sent at that point of the conversation.*

Instead, in the symmetric case in which the policy contains only the conversation $\{\mathsf{m}_1(\overleftarrow{ws})\mathsf{m}_2(\overrightarrow{ws})\}$ while the protocol states that ws can answer to m_1 alternatively by sending m_2 or m_3, *conformance holds.* The reason is that at any point of its conversations the peer will always send legal messages. The restriction of the set of possible alternatives (w.r.t. the protocol) depends on the peer implementor's own criteria. However, the peer must foresee *at least one* of such alternatives otherwise the conversation will be interrupted. Trivially, the case in which the policy contains only the conversation $\{\mathsf{m}_1(\overleftarrow{ws})\}$ is *not conformant.*

> *The third observation is that we expect that a policy always allows the peer to send one of the messages foreseen by the protocol at every point of the possible conversations. However, it is not necessary that a policy envisions all the possible alternatives.*

To summarize, at every point of a conversation, we expect that a conformant policy never sends messages that are not expected, according to the protocol, and we also expect it to be able to handle any message that can possibly be received, once again according to the protocol. However, the policy is not obliged to foresee (at every point of conversation) an outgoing message for every alternative included in the protocol (but it must foresee at least one of them). Incoming and outgoing messages are, therefore, *not handled in the same way.*

These expectations are motivated by the desire to define a minimal set of conditions which assure the construction of a conformance test that guarantees the *interoperability* of peers. We claim –and we will show– that two peers that respect this minimal set of conditions (w.r.t. an agreed protocol) will *actually* be able to interact, respecting the protocol. The relevant point is that this certification is *a property that can be checked on each single single peer, rather than on the choreographed system as a whole.*

3 Conformance Test

In order to decide if a policy is conformant to a protocol specification, it is not sufficient to perform an inclusion test; instead, as we have intuitively shown by means of the above examples, it is necessary to prove mutual properties of both $L(p^{ws}_{lang})$ and $L(p_{spec})$. The method that we propose, for proving such properties, consists in verifying that both languages are recognized by a special finite state automaton, whose construction we are now going to explain. Such an automaton is based on the automaton that accepts the *intersection* of the two languages. This, however, is not sufficient, because there are further conditions to consider, for instance there are conversations that we mean to allow but that do not belong to the intersection.

3.1 The Automaton M_{conf}

If $L(p^{ws}_{lang})$ and $L(p_{spec})$ are regular, they are accepted by two (deterministic) *finite automata*, that we respectively denote by $M(p^{ws}_{lang})$ and $M(p_{spec})$, that we can assume as having the *same alphabet* (see [13]). An automaton is a five-tuple $(Q, \Sigma, \delta, q_0, F)$, where Q is a finite set of states, Σ is a finite input alphabet, $q_0 \in Q$ is the initial state, $F \subseteq Q$ is the set of final states, and δ is a transition function mapping $Q \times \Sigma$ to Q. In a finite automaton we can always classify states in two categories: *alive states*, that lie on a path from the initial state to a final state, and *dead states*, the other ones. Intuitively, alive states accept the language of the prefixes of the strings accepted by the automaton.

For reasons that will be made clear shortly, we request the two automata to show the following property: the edges that lead to a same state must *all* be labelled either by incoming messages or by outgoing messages w.r.t. *ws*.

Definition 2 (IO-automaton). *Given an automaton $M = (Q, \Sigma, \delta, q_0, F)$, let $E_q = \{m \mid \delta(p, m) = q\}$ for $q \in Q$. We say that M is an IO-automaton iff for every $q \in Q$, E_q alternatively consists only of incoming or only of outgoing messages w.r.t. a peer ws.*

Notice that an automaton that does not show this property can always be transformed so as to satisfy it, in linear time w.r.t. the number of states, by splitting those states that do not satisfy the property. We will denote a state q that is reached only by incoming messages by the notation $\overleftarrow{q}$ (we will call it an I-state), and a state q that is reached only by outgoing messages by $\overrightarrow{q}$ (an O-state).

Finally, let us denote by $M^{\times}(p^{ws}_{lang}, p_{spec})$ the deterministic finite automaton that accepts the language $L(p^{ws}_{lang}) \cap L(p_{spec})$. It is defined as follows. Let $M(p^{ws}_{lang})$ be the automaton $(Q^P, \Sigma, \delta^P, q^P_0, F^P)$ and $M(p_{spec})$ the automaton $(Q^S, \Sigma, \delta^S, q^S_0, F^S)$:

$$M^{\times}(p^{ws}_{lang}, p_{spec}) = (Q^P \times Q^S, \Sigma, \delta, [q^P_0, q^S_0], F^P \times F^S)$$

where for all q^P in Q^P, q^S in Q^S, and m in Σ, $\delta([q^P, q^S], m) = [\delta^P(q^P, m), \delta^S(q^S, m)]$. We will briefly denote this automaton by $M^{\times}$.

Notice that all the *conversations* that are accepted by $M^{\times}$ are surely *conformant* (Def. 1). For the so built automaton, it is easy to prove the following property.

Proposition 1. *$M^{\times}(p^{ws}_{lang}, p_{spec})$ is an IO-automaton if $M(p^{ws}_{lang})$ and $M(p_{spec})$ are two IO-automata.*

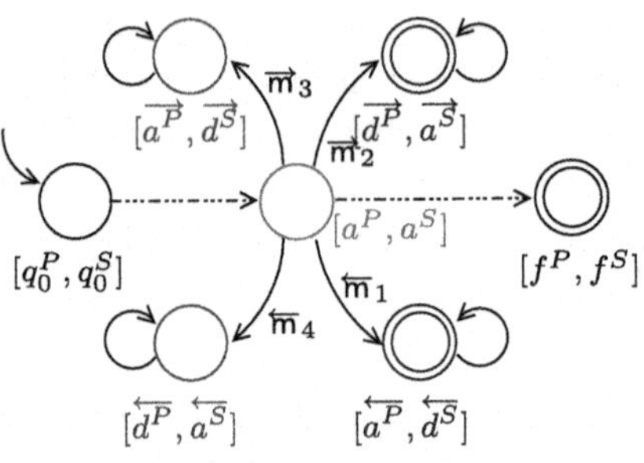

Fig. 1. A general schema of the M_{conf} automaton. From bottom-right clockwise cases (a), (b), (c), and (d).

Definition 3 (Automaton M_{conf}). *The finite state automaton $M_{conf}(p^{ag}_{lang}, p_{spec})$ is built by applying the following steps to $M^{\times}(p^{ag}_{lang}, p_{spec})$ until none is applicable:*

(a) if $\overleftarrow{q} = [\overleftarrow{a}^P, \overleftarrow{d}^S]$ in Q is an I-state, such that $\overleftarrow{a}^P$ is an alive state and $\overleftarrow{d}^S$ is a dead state, we set $\delta(\overleftarrow{q}, m) = \overleftarrow{q}$ for every m in Σ, and we put $\overleftarrow{q}$ in F;
(b) if $\overleftarrow{q} = [\overleftarrow{d}^P, \overleftarrow{a}^S]$ in Q is an I-state, such that $\overleftarrow{d}^P$ is dead and $\overleftarrow{a}^S$ is alive, we set $\delta(\overleftarrow{q}, m) = \overleftarrow{q}$ for every m in Σ, without modifying F;
(c) if $\overrightarrow{q} = [\overrightarrow{a}^P, \overrightarrow{d}^S]$ in Q is an O-state, such that $\overrightarrow{a}^P$ is alive and $\overrightarrow{d}^S$ is dead, we set $\delta(\overrightarrow{q}, m) = \overrightarrow{q}$ for every m in Σ (without modifying F);
(d) if $\overrightarrow{q} = [\overrightarrow{d}^P, \overrightarrow{a}^S]$ in Q is an O-state, such that $\overrightarrow{d}^P$ is dead and $\overrightarrow{a}^S$ is alive, we set $\delta(\overrightarrow{q}, m) = \overrightarrow{q}$ for every m in Σ, and we put $\overrightarrow{q}$ in F.

These four transformation rules can, intuitively, be explained as follows. Rule (a) handles the case in which, at a certain point of the conversation, according to the policy it is possible to receive a message that, instead, cannot be received according to the specification (it is the case of message $\overleftarrow{m}_1$ in Figure 1). Actually, if the peer will interact with another peer that respects the protocol, this message can never be received, so we can ignore the paths generated by the policy from the message at issue onwards. Since this case does not compromise conformance, we want our automaton to accept all these strings. For this reason we set the state as final. Rule (b) handles the symmetric case (Figure 1, message $\overleftarrow{m}_4$), in which at a certain point of the conversation it is possible, according to the specification, to receive a message, that is not accounted for by the implementation. In this case the state at issue is turned into a trap state (a state that is not final and that has no transition to a different state); by doing so, all the conversations that are foreseen by the specification from that point onwards will not be accepted by M_{conf}. Rule (c) handles the cases in which a message can possibly be sent by the peer, according to the policy, but it is not possible according to the specification (Figure 1, message $\overrightarrow{m}_3$). In this case, the policy is not conformant, so we transform the current state in a trap state. By doing so, part of the conversations possibly generated by the policy will not be accepted by the automaton. The symmetric case (Figure 1, message $\overrightarrow{m}_2$), instead, does not prevent conformance, in fact, a peer is free not to send a message foreseen by the protocol. However, the conversations that can be generated from that point, according to the latter, are to be accepted as well. For this reason the state is turned into an accepting looping state.

One may wonder if the application of rules (b) and (c) could prevent the *reachability of states*, that have been set as accepting states by the other two rules. Notice that their application cannot prevent the reachability of *alive-alive* accepting states, i.e. those that accept the strings belonging to the intersection of the two languages, because all the four rules only work on dead states. If a state has been set as a trap state (either by rule (b) or (c)), whatever conversation is possibly generated after it by the policy is illegal w.r.t. the specification. So it is correct that the automaton is modified in such a way that the policy language is not accepted by it and that the final state cannot be reached any more.

3.2 Conformance and Interoperability

We can now discuss how to check that a peer conforms to a given protocol. The following is a first definition of conformance, that guarantees the expectations that we have explained by examples in Section 2. That is: the peer will always send, at any point of conversation, messages that are legal according to p_{spec} (though it is not necessary that it foresees all the alternatives), and it will be able to handle at least every incoming message, expected by the protocol. A first attempt of defining conformance is the following.

Definition 4. *A policy p^{ws}_{lang} is conformant to a protocol specification p_{spec} iff the automaton $M_{conf}(p^{ws}_{lang}, p_{spec})$ accepts both languages $L(p^{ws}_{lang})$ and $L(p_{spec})$.*

The following proposition underlines the *role of the public protocol* of representing the set of *all the possible interlocutors*.

Proposition 2. *All the conversations that a policy p^{ws}_{lang}, that is conformant according to Def. 4 to a protocol specification p_{spec}, will produce when it interacts with any peer that is equally conformant to p_{spec}, are always legal w.r.t. this protocol, according to Def. 1.*

Proof. Let us consider the general schema of M_{conf} in Figure 1. If p^{ws}_{lang} is conformant, $L(p^{ws}_{lang})$ is accepted by M_{conf}. Then, by construction M_{conf} does not contain any state $[\overrightarrow{a^P}, \overrightarrow{d^S}]$ due to illegal messages sent by the peer nor it contains any state $[\overleftarrow{d^P}, \overleftarrow{a^S}]$ due to incoming messages that are not accounted for by the policy. Obviously, no conversation σ in $L(p^{ws}_{lang})$ can be accepted by states of the kind $[\overrightarrow{d^P}, \overrightarrow{a^S}]$ because the peer does not send the messages required to reach such states. Finally, no conversation produced by the send will be accepted by states of the kind $[\overleftarrow{a^P}, \overleftarrow{d^S}]$ if the interlocutor is also conformant to the protocol, because the latter cannot send illegal messages. **q.e.d.**

In other words, whatever conversation is in the intersection $\bigcap_{ws_i}^{i=1,2} L(p^{ws_i}_{lang_i})$, where $p^{ws_i}_{lang_i}$, $i = 1, 2$ are the conversation policies of two peers that conform to p_{spec}, it is legal. However, we would like conformance to have a *stronger implication*: if two peers, playing the two roles of a same protocol, are proved conformant to it, we would like *each of them* to be able to lead to an end all the conversations *it is involved in* by the other peer (which will respect the protocol). Def. 4 guarantees the satisfaction of the first two expectations reported in Section 2, however, it is *not enough to guarantee* the above statement (third expectation), which requires that, at every state of the conversation, if a role is supposed to send a message out of a set of possibilities, the peer's policy envisions *at least one* of them.

Given $L(p_{spec})$ and $L(p^{ws}_{lang})$, let us consider $M(p_{spec}) = (Q^S, \Sigma, \delta^S, q^S_0, F^S)$ and $M_{conf}(p^{ws}_{lang}, p_{spec}) = (Q^P \times Q^S, \Sigma, \delta, [q^P_0, q^S_0], F_{conf})$. Let us consider those states $q^S \in Q^S$, that emit edges labelled with outgoing messages, w.r.t. ws, which are part of strings accepted by $M(p_{spec})$ (legal conversations according to the protocol specification). More formally, for each such state q^S there is at least one $\mathsf{m}(\overrightarrow{ws})$ such that $\delta^S(q^S, \mathsf{m}(\overrightarrow{ws})) = p^S$ and p^S is an *alive state*. We will denote by $Mess_{q^S}$ the set of all such messages.

Definition 5 (Complete automaton). *We say that the automaton M_{conf} is complete iff for all states of form $[q^P, q^S]$ of M_{conf}, such that $Mess_{q^S} \neq \emptyset$, there is a message $\mathsf{m}(\overrightarrow{ws})' \in Mess_{q^S}$ such that $\delta([q^P, q^S], \mathsf{m}(\overrightarrow{ws})')$ is a state of M_{conf} composed of two alive states.*

Definition 6 (Policy conformance test). *A policy p^{ws}_{lang} is conformant to a protocol specification p_{spec} iff the automaton $M_{conf}(p^{ws}_{lang}, p_{spec})$ is complete and it accepts both languages $L(p^{ws}_{lang})$ and $L(p_{spec})$.*

We are now in condition to state that a policy that passes the above test can carry on *any* conformant conversation it is involved in.

Theorem 1. *Given a policy p^{ws}_{lang} that is conformant to a protocol specification p_{spec}, according to the test in Def. 6, for every prefix σ' that is common to the two languages $L(p_{spec})$ and $L(p^{ws}_{lang})$, there is a conversation $\sigma = \sigma'\sigma''$ such that σ is in the intersection of $L(p^{ws}_{lang})$ and $L(p_{spec})$.*

Proof. (*sketch*) If σ' is a common prefix, then it leads to a state of the automaton M_{conf} of the kind $[a^P, a^S]$ (see Figure 1). By the same reasons on which the proof of Prop. 2 is based, *if* there is a conversation $\sigma = \sigma'\sigma''$ in $L(p^{ws}_{lang})$, then this must be a legal conversation. Now, at every step after the state $[a^P, a^S]$ mentioned above, due to *policy conformance* all the incoming messages (w.r.t. the peer) must be foreseen by the policy. Moreover, due to the *completeness* of M_{conf}, in the case of outgoing messages, the policy must foresee at least one of them. Therefore, from $[a^P, a^S]$ it is possible to perform one more common step. **q.e.d.**

Notice that the *intersection* of $L(p^{ws}_{lang})$ and $L(p_{spec})$ cannot be empty because of policy conformance, and also that Theorem 1 does not entail that the two languages coincide (i.e. the policy is not necessarily a full implementation of the protocol). As a consequence, given that the conversation policies of two peers ws_1 and ws_2, playing the different roles of an interaction protocol p_{spec}, are *conformant* to the protocol, according to Def. 6, and denoting by I the intersection $\cap^{i=1,2}_{ws_i} L(p^{ws_i}_{lang_i})$, we can prove ws_1 and ws_2 *interoperability*. The demonstration is similar to the previous one. Roughly, it is immediate to prove that every prefix that is common to the two policies also belongs to the protocol, then, by a reasoning process that is close to the previous demonstration, it is possible to prove that a common legal conversation must exist

Proposition 3 (Interoperability). *For every prefix σ' that is common to the two languages $L(p^{ws_1}_{lang_1})$ and $L(p^{ws_2}_{lang_2})$, there is a conversation $\sigma = \sigma'\sigma''$ such that $\sigma \in I$.*

Starting from regular languages, all the steps that we have described that lead to the construction of M_{conf} and allow the verification of policy conformance, are decidable and the following theorem holds.

Theorem 2. *Policy conformance is decidable when $L(p^{ws}_{lang})$ and $L(p_{spec})$ are regular languages.*

4 An Example

Let us, now, show by means of an example how the proposed conformance test works. Given an interaction protocol (a choreography) and the interaction policy of a specific web service, we mean to verify (a priori, at design time) if the web service fits the interaction schema encoded by the choreography, from the point of view of one of the roles (the role that the peer should play). We will, then, verify its a priori conformance. Given that conformance holds, we are guaranteed that the service will be able to interoperate with any other service, equally proved conformant to the protocol, that will play the other foreseen role. The protocol is reported in a graphical notation in Fig. 2. It is very simple: the peer that plays the role "cinema" waits for a request from another peer (the request is whether a certain movie is played); then, it can alternatively send the requested information (yes or no) or refuse to supply information; the protocol is ended by an acknowledgement from the customer to the cinema.

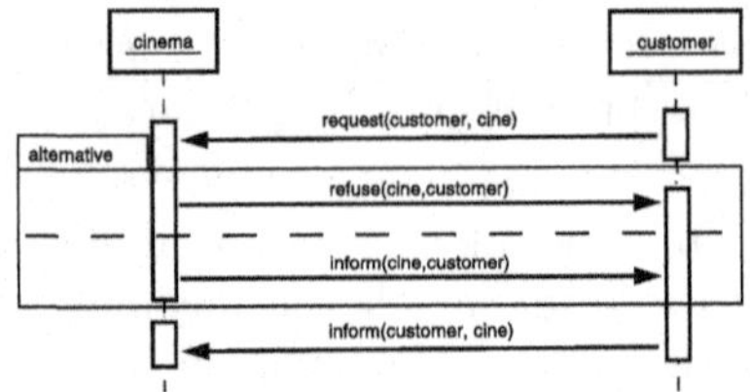

Fig. 2. The interaction protocol as an AUML sequence diagram [17]

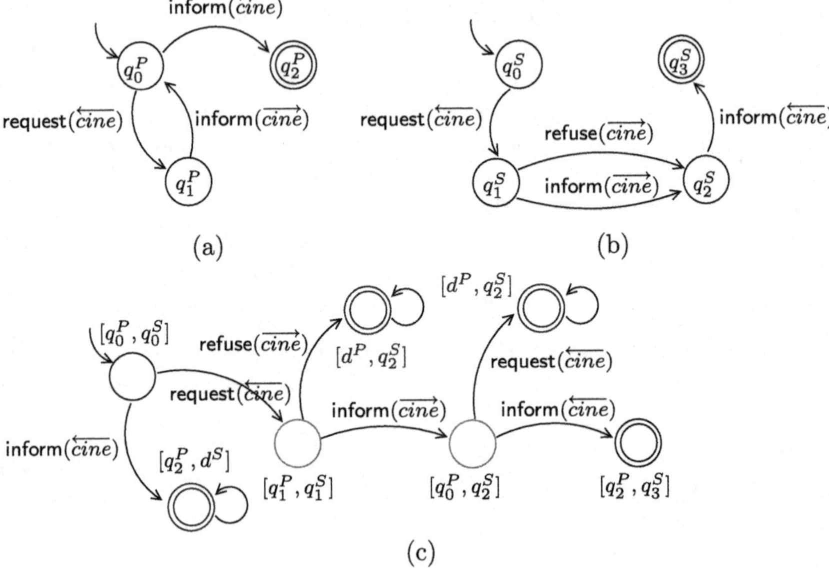

Fig. 3. (a) Policy of agent *cine*; (b) global protocol specification; (c) M_{conf} automaton. Only the part relevant to the discussion is shown.

The peer's policy could, for instance, be described in an executable business process language, such as BPEL4WS. Actually, in the literature other authors have already proposed algorithms for extracting a formal representation from a BPEL representation. For instance, Viroli [18] proposes a formal semantics for this language, focussing right on the message exchange and correlation sets. It is not difficult to see that, disregarding the operator that concerns concurrency (*flow*), the exception and fault handlers, and correlation sets, it is possible to turn a BPEL description in a regular language (i.e. a finite state automaton). Fig. 3 (a) reports a finite state automaton that represents the interactive behavior of our cinema service, [1] Briefly, the web service has a *reactive behavior* and it is not trivial to see that it conforms to the protocol: it waits for a message; if it is

[1] The program of the customer is not given: we will suppose that it adheres to the public and global choreography, against which we check the peer's conformance.

a request from a customer, then it (always) supplies the requested information; if it is an acknowledgement it stops. In the remainder of the paper we will refer to this web service by the name *cine*. For what concerns the choreography, we can say something similar, at least for what concerns the current proposal for WS-CDL. If we ignore the constructs for dealing with concurrency it is possible to turn a choreography in an automaton. The automaton reported in Fig. 3(b), for instance, is obtained straightforwardly from the WS-CDL representation reported in the Appendix.

The question that we want to answer is whether *cine*'s policy is *conformant* to the given protocol, and we will discuss whether another agent that plays as a customer and that is proved conformant to the protocol will actually be able to *interoperate* with this particular player of the cinema role. [2] The protocol allows only two conversations between *cine* and *customer* (the content of the message is not relevant in this example, so we skip it): $\mathsf{request}(customer, cine)$ $\mathsf{inform}(cine, customer)$ $\mathsf{inform}(customer, cine)$ and $\mathsf{request}(customer, cine)$ $\mathsf{refuse}(cine, customer)$ $\mathsf{inform}(customer, cine)$. Let us denote this protocol by $\mathsf{get\_info\_movie}_{WSCDL}$ (WS-CDL is the specification language). Let us now consider the web service *cine*. The service's behavior depends on the message that it receives, and its policy allows an infinite number of conversations of any length. Let us denote this language by $\mathsf{get\_info\_movie}^{cine}_{BPEL}$ (BPEL should be the implementation language). In general, it allows all the conversations that begin with a (possibly empty) series of exchanges of kind $\mathsf{request}(\overleftarrow{cine})$ followed by $\mathsf{inform}(\overrightarrow{cine})$, concluded by a message of kind $\mathsf{inform}(\overleftarrow{cine})$.

To verify its conformance to the protocol, and then state its interoperability with other peers that respect such protocol, we need to build the M_{conf} automaton for its policy and the protocol specification. For brevity, we skip its construction steps and directly report M_{conf} in Fig. 3(c). Let us now analyze M_{conf} for answering our queries. Trivially, the automaton is *complete* and it *accepts both languages* (of the policy and of the protocol), therefore, $\mathsf{get\_info\_movie}^{cine}_{BPEL}$ is policy conformant to $\mathsf{get\_info\_movie}_{WSCDL}$. Moreover, when the service interacts with another service *customer* whose policy is conformant to $\mathsf{get\_info\_movie}_{WSCDL}$, the messages $\mathsf{request}(\overleftarrow{cine})$ and $\mathsf{inform}(\overleftarrow{cine})$ will not be received by *cine* in all the possible states it expects them. The reason is simple: for receiving them it is necessary that the interlocutor utters them, but by definition (it is conformant) it will not. The fact that $\mathsf{refuse}(\overrightarrow{cine})$ is never uttered by *cine* does not compromise conformance and interoperability.

5 Conclusions and Future Work

In this work we propose a formal framework that can be applied for verifying the conformance and the interoperability of web services with respect to a global protocol definition which is meant to be provided at the choreography level. The idea is that a choreography definition can be exploited *at design time*

[2] Notice that in Fig. 3 all the short notations for the messages are to be interpreted as incoming or outgoing messages w.r.t. the cinema service.

for verifying that the internal processes of a web service will enable it to participate appropriately in the choreography. For achieving this goal we need a formal framework for specifying both general interaction protocols and web services' local interaction policies. We proposed a framework based on the theory of *formal languages*, where both the global protocol and the web service behavior are expressed by using finite state automata. Finite-state automata have been adopted also by Berardi et al. [5] but for web service composition.

Within this framework we formalize a notion of *a priori* conformance (see Def. 6), having some important property. First, it guarantees that the service, at any point of its conversations, can only send messages which are legal w.r.t. the global interaction protocol, because of the M_{conf} construction step, given by rule (c). Moreover it guarantees that the service will be able to handle any incoming message, foreseen by the protocol. Notice that the service may also expect incoming messages, that are not expected by the protocol specification, for this does not prevent the correct interaction with another conformant service. Finally, it guarantees that the service will always send at least one of the messages foreseen by the protocol, although it is not necessary that its policy envisions all the possible alternatives (e.g. the designer can restrict the set of the possible answers). All these properties define a minimal set of conditions which, on the one hand, ensure the preservation of the *interoperability* of the peers, while, on the other hand, they give some flexibility in designing service policies.

As we explained from the very beginning the current choice of finite state automata bears some serious limitation: the impossibility of tackling concurrency. Moreover, the framework so far can only check conformance of a service, whose behavioral interface contains interactions with only another service. Multi-party interaction is not tackled. These limitations were, in a way, necessary to allow the identification of a set of concepts and of conditions that characterize interoperability and its verification: the first step of the work. As future directions of research, however, it is mandatory to study, on the one hand, the possible extensions to policies that encode the interaction with many parties, and on the other to study whether it is possible to decide conformance in presence of concurrency, by adopting more expressive kinds of automata. For what concerns the first problem we think (but still have to prove) that the test as it is now could quite easily be extended so as to tackle unilateral interactions with many parties which do not interact with one another. For what concerns the latter problem, instead, it will be necessary to identify alternative representations. For instance, process algebras are formal tools that are commonly used for verifying properties of interacting processes, we could study whether and how to apply them to prove a property like conformance. Also concurrent regular expressions [11] should be investigated. Last but not least, a crucial point is the semantics of the languages used for representing choreographies and behavioral interfaces (or orchestrations), e.g. BPEL4WS and WS-CDL, which is not precisely defined yet. The absence of a formal semantics is, indeed, an obstacle to the automation of property check in service oriented applications. Concerning BPEL4WS, some proposal of a formal semantics exists and the proposed formal methods derive from formal models for concurrency and coordination of distributed systems (e.g. process algebras) [18,16].

References

1. M. Alberti, M. Gavanelli, E. Lamma, P. Mello, and P. Torroni. Specification and verification of agent interactions using social integrity constraints. In *Proc. of the Workshop on Logic and Communication in Multi-Agent Systems, LCMAS 2003*, volume 85(2), Eindhoven, the Netherlands, 2003. Elsevier.
2. G. Alonso, F. Casati, H. Kuno, and V. Machiraju. *Web Services.* Springer, 2004.
3. M. Baldoni, C. Baroglio, A. Martelli, V. Patti, and C. Schifanella. Verifying protocol conformance for logic-based communicating agents. In *Proc. of CLIMA V*, LNCS series 2005. To appear.
4. A. Barros, M. Dumas, and P. Oaks. A critical overview of the web services choreography description language(ws-cdl). *Business Process Trends*, 2005. http://www.bptrends.com.
5. D. Berardi, D. Calvanese, G. G. De Giacomo, M. Lenzerini, and M. Mecella. Automatic composition of e-services that export their behavior. In *Proc. of ICSOC 2003, LNCS* 2910, pages 43–58. Springer, 2003.
6. BPEL4WS. http://www-106.ibm.com/developerworks/library/ws-bpel. 2003.
7. M. Bravetti, C. Guidi, R. Lucchi, and G. Zavattaro. Supporting e.commerce systems formalization with choreography languages. In *Proc. of SAC'05.* ACM Press, 2005.
8. T. Bultan, X. Fu, R. Hull, and J. Su. Conversation specification: A new approach to design and analysis of e-service composition. In *Proc. of WWW'03*, 2003.
9. U. Endriss, N. Maudet, F. Sadri, and F. Toni. Protocol conformance for logic-based agents. In *Proc. of IJCAI-2003*, pages 679–684. 2003.
10. U. Endriss, N. Maudet, F. Sadri, and F. Toni. Logic-based agent communication protocols. In *Advances in agent communication languages, LNAI* 2922, pages 91–107. Springer-Verlag, 2004.
11. V. Garg and M.T. Ragunath. Concurrent regular expressions and their relationship to Petri nets. *Theoretical Computer Science*, 96:285–304, 1992.
12. F. Guerin and J. Pitt. Verification and Compliance Testing. In *Communication in Multiagent Systems, LNAI* 2650, pages 98–112. Springer, 2003.
13. J. E. Hopcroft and J. D. Ullman. *Introduction to automata theory, languages, and computation.* Addison-Wesley Publishing Company, 1979.
14. M. P. Huget and J.L. Koning. Interaction Protocol Engineering. In *Communication in Multiagent Systems, LNAI* 2650, pages 179–193. Springer, 2003.
15. N. Kavantzas, D. Burdett, G. Ritzinger, and Y. Lafon. Web services choreography description language version 1.0. Available at http://www.w3.org/TR/ws-cdl-10, 2004.
16. M. Mazzara and R. Lucchi. A framework for generic error handling in business processes. In *Proc. of WS-FM 2004*, volume 105 of *ENTCS*. Elsevier, 2004.
17. J. Odell, H. V. D. Parunak, and B. Bauer. Extending UML for agents. In *Proc. of the Agent-Oriented Information System Workshop at AAAI'00.* 2000.
18. M. Viroli. Towards a formal foundation to orchestration languages. In *Proc. of WS-FM 2004*, volume 105 of *ENTCS*, pages 51–71, Eindhoven, the Netherlands, 2004. Elsevier.

From Theory to Practice in Transactional Composition of Web Services*

Roberto Bruni[1], Gianluigi Ferrari[1], Hernán Melgratti[1], Ugo Montanari[1], Daniele Strollo[2], and Emilio Tuosto[1]

[1] Dipartimento di Informatica, Università degli Studi di Pisa, Italy
{bruni, giangi, melgratt, ugo, etuosto}@di.unipi.it
[2] Istituto Alti Studi IMT Lucca, Italy
daniele.strollo@imtlucca.it

Abstract. We address the problem of composing Web Services in long-running transactional business processes, where compensations must be dealt with appropriately. The framework presented in this paper is a Java API called *Java Transactional Web Services* (JTWS), which provides suitable primitives for wrapping and invoking Web Services as activities in long-running transactions. JTWS adheres to a process calculi formalisation of long-running transactions, called Naïve Sagas, which fixes unambiguously the implemented compensation policy. In particular, the primitives provided by JTWS are in one-to-one correspondence with the primitives of Sagas, and they are abstract enough to hide the complex details of their realization, thus favouring usability. Moreover, JTWS orchestrates business processes in a distributed way.

1 Introduction

One of the emerging issues when aggregating *Web Services* (WS) is constituted by the so-called *long-running transactions* (LRTs), i.e., the possibility of requiring a set of WS interactions to be executed atomically. Note that the problem is not just to coordinate the updates of a distributed repository (e.g., a database), since components are independent and any of them is responsible for maintaining the consistency on local data. In order to achieve atomicity, LRTs may use *compensations*, namely, ad-hoc activities that are responsible for undoing the effects of partial executions when the overall orchestration cannot be completed. In fact, most of the languages proposed in recent years for orchestrating WS (e.g., WSCL [30], BPML [6], WSFL [23], XLANG [31], BPEL4WS [4]) include primitives for handling LRTs. Noteworthy, all those proposals formalise the orchestration syntax but not the semantics, whose informal description can make the intended behaviour of constructs ambiguous and can lead to different implementations of the same language. (As an example, see the large list of open issues for BPEL4WS [5].) Moreover, those proposals mix together many different concepts and programming constructs. Hence, it is difficult to establish a clear semantics for them because of the mutual interactions of such different constructs.

* Research supported by the Project FET-GC II SENSORIA and by the Project HPRN-CT-2002-00275 SEGRAVIS.

M. Bravetti et al. (Eds.): EPEW 2005 and WS-FM 2005, LNCS 3670, pp. 272–286, 2005.

In this paper, we first take advantage of a formal framework for isolating and studying LRTs and then we use an experimental framework for implementing and exercising the theoretical choices in a WS scenario. We are aimed at building a framework for coordinating transactional compositions of WS over a solid formal basis. The main goal of our work is two-fold. Firstly, we provide application designers with a formally specified language for defining transactional aggregations at a high level of abstraction, i.e., in terms of the involved WS and the control flow among them regardless of low level details, e.g. distribution, asynchrony. Secondly, after selecting a coordination infrastructure, we map high level transactional primitives into concrete orchestration patterns. One of the main advantages of our approach lies in the reciprocal benefits that theory and practice can gain in this case. For instance, several alternative semantics can be given when composing parallel transactional flows [7]. The possibility of giving prototype implementations of those semantics and apply them to realistic scenarios (like WS applications) can help in evaluating and refining the theoretical models. Moreover, applications deployed with the aid of formal methods are more robust.

The high level language we choose is Naïve Sagas [9], a process calculus for compensable transactions, while the orchestration infrastructure we propose is *Java Transactional Web Services* (JTWS) [27], an execution platform that supports the transactional capabilities of Naïve Sagas. Indeed, JTWS embeds the transactional policies of Naïve Sagas into a framework for programming WS.

From the existing calculi for LRTs [13,12,14,16,9,3,22,8,15,18,25,24], we have chosen Naïve Sagas because it exposes the orchestration mechanism behind LTRs In fact, activities in a saga are described at the high level of abstraction, where the elementary actions are not interpreted. Transactional flows are processes built by composing with the standard parallel and sequential composition plus the *compensation pair* construct. Given two actions A and B, the compensation pair $A \div B$ corresponds to a process that uses B as compensation for A. Intuitively, $A \div B$ yields two flows of execution: the *forward flow* and the *backward flow*. During the forward flow, $A \div B$ starts its execution by running A and then, when A finishes: (i) B is "installed" as compensation for A, and (ii) the control is forwardly propagated to the other stages of the transactions. In case of a failure in the rest of the transaction, the backward flow starts so that the effects of executing A must be rolled back. This is achieved by activating the installed compensation B and afterward by propagating the rollback to the activities that were executed before A. Note that B is not installed if A is not executed.

The execution platform JTWS is a Java implementation of the APIs defined in [27,21]. JTWS is based on a signal passing style of programming. Conceptually, JTWS is divided in two levels: *Java Signal Core Layer* (JSCL) and *Java Transactional Layer* (JTL). The former provides a set of primitives for defining and handling the flow of signals among components. The latter, uses the primitives of JSCL to define the behaviour of transactional constructs according to Naïve Sagas. Basically, WS are wrapped into JTWS components that exchange a fixed set of suitable signals. Similarly, JTWS fixes a precise flow of signals for composed services. It is worth remarking that the JSCL layer provides a general framework for implementing different transactional policies. Indeed, one can easily change the behaviours of transactions by replacing the JTL layer. Therefore, we can prototype and experiment with different semantics for transactional flows without changing the code of the application.

Related Works. Several process calculi have been proposed to deal with different flavours of transactions. Notably, models for ACID (i.e., usual database transactions) transactions in Linda [17] have been proposed in [1,11,20,10]. Unlike Sagas, ACID transactions are regarded as not suitable for computations that may elapse for a long period of time. Similarly, our work differs in scope from [18], which is aimed at extending an object oriented programming language with primitives for handling ACID transactions.

Another mainstream in transactional process calculi takes as starting point well-known name passing calculi, like π and Join, and adds to them transactional features like compensable nested contexts [3], timed transactions [22,24], interacting compensable transactions [8] and event scopes [25]. We prefer Sagas to those approaches because Sagas naturally abstracts away from low level computations and communication patterns, while it highlights the composition structure of transactional processes. Similarly, we prefer Sagas to approaches like [15], where the coordination mechanism relies on the operations performs over a centralised log.

Sagas is much more in the spirit of StAC [12,13] and cCSP [14]. (We refer to [7] for a detailed comparison.) We prefer Sagas to those proposals because it is more compact.

As far as the execution platform is concerned, our approach is different from the existing implementations of orchestration languages such as Biztalk [2], Oracle BPEL Process Manager [26] and WebSphere [28], because JTWS does not rely on an engine that rules the execution of a composed process. Instead, JTWS translate transactional primitives as suitable interaction patterns among services over a middleware. It is worth noting that the coordination logic in JTWS is kept distributed (i.e., JTWS establishes a kind of choreography [29] among involved services). In some sense, JTWS is similar in spirit to [19]. Noteworthy, the work in [19] is aimed at specifying a middleware able to implement several transactional models, while our work is main concerned at showing how transactional models can be mapped into a concrete middleware.

2 Background: Sagas Calculus

In this section we introduce the formal basis for the implementation of the JTL package. In particular, we exploit a process algebra for compensable flow composition that is essentially the algebra of Naïve Sagas in [9], but whose semantics is here presented in the simpler style of compensating CSP (cCSP) [14].

2.1 Syntax

Sagas are built over a set of atomic activities $\Sigma \cup \{0, THROW\}$, where 0 (the nil activity) and $THROW$ (the interrupting activity) are two distinguished elements. Atomic activities are ranged over by A, B, ... The set of processes is defined as follows:

$$\text{(NAÏVE SAGAS)} \quad S,T ::= A \mid [P] \mid S;T \mid S|T$$

$$\text{(COMPENSABLE PROCESSES)} \quad P,Q ::= A \div B \mid P;Q \mid P|Q$$

COMPOSITION OF STANDARD TRACES

Sequential $\begin{cases} p\langle\checkmark\rangle; s = ps \\ p\langle\omega\rangle; s = p\langle\omega\rangle \text{ when } \omega \neq \checkmark \end{cases}$

Parallel $p\langle\omega\rangle||q\langle\omega'\rangle = \{r\langle\omega\&\omega'\rangle \mid r \in int(p,q)\}$, where

ω	!	!	!	?	?	✓
ω'	!	?	✓	?	✓	✓
$\omega\&\omega'$	!	!	!	?	?	✓

and $\begin{cases} int(p,\langle\rangle) = \{p\} \\ int(\langle\rangle,q) = \{q\} \\ int(\langle x\rangle p, \langle y\rangle q) = \{\langle x\rangle r \mid r \in int(p,\langle y\rangle q)\} \cup \{\langle y\rangle r \mid r \in int(\langle x\rangle p, q)\} \end{cases}$

TRACES OF Naïve Sagas

$\Gamma \vdash \ 0 = \{\langle\checkmark\rangle\}$

$\Gamma \vdash \ A = \{\langle A, \checkmark\rangle\}$ when $A \in \Sigma \wedge \Gamma(A) = \checkmark$

$\Gamma \vdash \ A = \{\langle !\rangle\}$ when $A = THROW \vee (A \in \Sigma \wedge \Gamma(A) = !)$

$\Gamma \vdash S;T = \{s;t \mid \Gamma \vdash s \in S \wedge \Gamma \vdash t \in T\}$

$\Gamma \vdash S|T = \{s' \mid s' \in (s||t) \wedge \Gamma \vdash s \in S \wedge \Gamma \vdash t \in T\}$

$\Gamma \vdash [P] = \{p\langle\checkmark\rangle \mid \Gamma \vdash (p\langle\checkmark\rangle, s) \in P\} \cup \{ps \mid \Gamma \vdash (p\langle !\rangle, s) \in P\}$

Fig. 1. Trace semantics of Naïve Sagas

A Naïve Sagas is either a basic activity A, a transaction block enclosing a compensable process $[P]$, the sequential composition $S;T$ of sagas, or the parallel composition $S|T$ of sagas. A basic compensable process is a compensation pair $A \div B$ where A is a basic activity and B is its compensation. We write A as an abbreviation for $A \div 0$. Compensable processes can be composed either in sequence $P;Q$ or in parallel $P|Q$. Without loss of generality, we assume that any activity in Σ appears at most once in any saga (resp. process), i.e. that different instances of the same action are named differently.

2.2 Semantics

The semantics is defined in terms of admissible execution traces. A trace for a saga is a string $s\langle\omega\rangle$, where $s \in \Sigma^*$ is said the *observable flow* and $\omega \in \Omega$ is the *final event*, with $\Omega = \{\checkmark, !, ?\}$ (✓ stands for success, ! for fail, and ? for yielding to a concurrent interrupt and it is assumed that $\Sigma \cap \Omega = \emptyset$). Hereafter, we let p,q,r range over Σ^* and s,t range over the set of traces $\Sigma^*\Omega$. The sequential composition $s;t$ concatenates the observable flows of s and t only when s terminates with success, otherwise it is s. The composition of two concurrent traces $p\langle\omega\rangle||q\langle\omega'\rangle$ corresponds to the set $int(p,q)$ of all possible interleavings of the observable flows p and q followed by the final event $\omega\&\omega'$, where the associative and commutative operator & defines the final event corresponding to the parallel composition of traces. The set of traces is evaluated according to a scenario $\Gamma : \Sigma \to \{\checkmark, !\}$ decreeing the success or failure of each basic activity. We write $\Gamma \vdash S = S'$ if S and S' represent the same set of traces under the scenario Γ. We write $\Gamma \vdash s \in S$ if the set of traces associated to S under the scenario Γ includes s.

Figure 1 summarises the trace semantics of Naïve Sagas. The definition for the traces of sagas is straightforward. The most interesting definition is for a transaction

COMPOSITION OF COMPENSABLE TRACES

$$\textbf{Comp. pair}\ \begin{cases} p\langle\checkmark\rangle \div s = (p\langle\checkmark\rangle, s) \\ p\langle\omega\rangle \div s = (p\langle\omega\rangle, \langle\checkmark\rangle) \text{ when } \omega \neq \checkmark \end{cases}$$

$$\textbf{Sequential}\ \begin{cases} (p\langle\checkmark\rangle, s);(t,t') = (pt, t';s) \\ (p\langle\omega\rangle, s);(t,t') = (p\langle\omega\rangle, s) \text{ when } \omega \neq \checkmark \end{cases}$$

$$\textbf{Parallel}\ \begin{cases} (p\langle\checkmark\rangle, s)||(q\langle\checkmark\rangle, t) = \{(r\langle\checkmark\rangle, s') \mid r \in int(p,q) \wedge s' \in (s||t)\} \\ \qquad\qquad \cup \{(r\langle ?\rangle, \langle\omega\rangle) \mid r\langle\omega\rangle \in (ps||qt)\} \\ (p\langle\omega\rangle, s)||(q\langle\omega'\rangle, t) = \{(r\langle\omega\&\omega'\rangle, \langle\omega''\rangle) \mid r\langle\omega''\rangle \in (ps||qt)\} \\ \qquad\qquad \text{when } \omega\&\omega' \in \{!, ?\} \end{cases}$$

TRACES OF COMPENSABLE PROCESSES

$$\Gamma \vdash A \div B = \{s \div t \mid \Gamma \vdash s \in A \wedge \Gamma \vdash t \in B\}$$
$$\Gamma \vdash P;Q = \{s;t \mid \Gamma \vdash s \in P \wedge \Gamma \vdash t \in Q\}$$
$$\Gamma \vdash P|Q = \{s' \mid \Gamma \vdash s' \in (s||t) \wedge \Gamma \vdash s \in P \wedge \Gamma \vdash t \in Q\}$$

Fig. 2. Trace semantics of compensable processes

block $[P]$. Note that any trace of a compensable process P is a pair $(p\langle\omega\rangle, s)$, where $p\langle\omega\rangle$ is the forward trace and s is the corresponding compensation trace. Then, the definition for $[P]$ selects all successful traces of P (i.e., $p\langle\checkmark\rangle$), and the traces corresponding to the failed forward flows followed by their compensations, i.e., ps. A compensated trace ps ending with ✓ corresponds to an aborted execution that has been compensated successfully. Instead, if the compensated trace finishes with !, then the execution of some compensation failed. We refer to the latter case as to an execution that raises an exception. Moreover, note that a trace that finishes with ✓ has not enough information to distinguishing whether it corresponds to the successful execution of the forward flow (i.e., a commit) or to a successfully compensated flow (i.e., an abort with a complete compensation). Note that all pairs whose forward traces end with ? are just discarded.

Figure 2 gives the semantics of compensable processes. The traces of a compensation pair are just given by the pairs of traces for the forward and backward flows, but the compensation is installed only if the forward activity ends with success. When composing compensable traces in series, the forward trace corresponds to the sequential composition of the original forward traces, while compensations are executed in the reverse order w.r.t. the associated forward activities. The parallel composition is defined as suitable interleavings of the forward and the backward flows. The parallel composition of two successful traces contains all the interleavings of the forward flows compensated with the interleavings of the original compensations, and a set of yielding traces. Yielding traces stand for the behaviours of processes $P|Q$ in case they are composed in parallel with a process that fails, for instance $P|Q|THROW$. Note that this is the only case where yielding behaviours are generated in the semantics (in particular, neither backward traces, nor standard traces can ever contain the final event ?). Finally, the parallel composition when at least one trace ends with ? or ! is defined as the interleavings of the original compensated flows.

The trace semantics can be used to prove interesting laws which hold under every scenario. We write $S \equiv T$ if for all Γ we have $\Gamma \vdash S = T$. For example, it can be readily

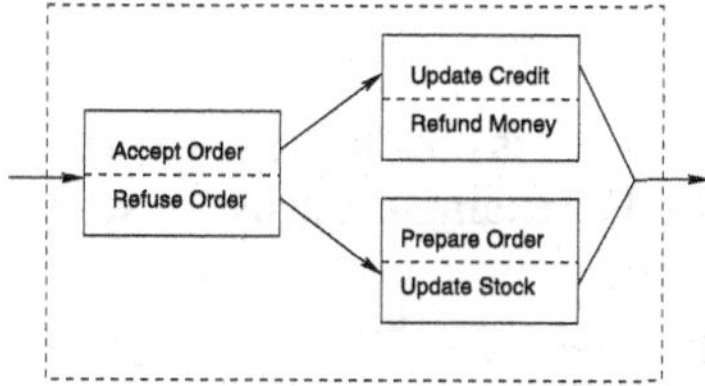

Fig. 3. A parallel saga for handling orders

proved that sequential and parallel compositions of sagas (resp. compensable processes) are associative and commutative under any scenario Γ. Other easy equivalences are:

$$
\begin{array}{rclcrcl}
0;P \equiv P;0 & \equiv & P & \quad & THROW;P & \equiv & THROW \\
0;S \equiv S;0 & \equiv & S|0 \equiv S & & THROW;S & \equiv & THROW \\
THROW \div A & \equiv & THROW \div 0 & & [A \div A'|B \div B'|THROW] & \equiv & (A;A')|(B;B')
\end{array}
$$

We describe here a small example illustrating the features of Naïve Sagas.

Example 1 (Handling Purchase Orders). Consider the simple business process for handling purchase orders depicted in Figure 3. The first activity Accept Order handles a request from a client and it is compensated by Refuse Order, which will contact the client to notify her/him that the order was cancelled. After that, both the balance of the client's account is updated and the order is prepared. The step Update Credit charges the amount of the order to the balance of the client. This activity could fail, for instance when the client has not enough credit to proceed, which will activate the compensation installed so far (i.e., Refuse Order). Instead, if it succeeds, then the compensation Refund Money is also installed. Refund Money is responsible for updating the balance with the amount detracted previously. Finally, Prepare Order handles the packaging of the order and updates the stock. Its compensation Update Stock will increment the stock with the proper values. Using the obvious acronyms in place of activities, the saga for handling purchase orders can be written as

$$\textsf{HPO-saga} \stackrel{\text{def}}{=} [\textsf{A.O.} \div \textsf{R.O.}; (\textsf{U.C.} \div \textsf{R.M.} | \textsf{P.O.} \div \textsf{U.S.})]$$

In a scenario Γ in which all activities are successful, the set of traces will be

$$\Gamma \vdash \textsf{HPO-saga} = \{\langle \textsf{A.O.}, \textsf{U.C.}, \textsf{P.O.}, \checkmark \rangle, \langle \textsf{A.O.}, \textsf{P.O.}, \textsf{U.C.}, \checkmark \rangle\}$$

Instead, in a scenario Γ' like Γ but where the client has not enough credit to proceed, the activity Update Credit fails and thus

$$\Gamma' \vdash \textsf{HPO-saga} = \{\langle \textsf{A.O.}, \textsf{P.O.}, \textsf{U.S.}, \textsf{R.O.}, \checkmark \rangle\}$$

As a last scenario, consider Γ'' like Γ' but where upon failure of Update Credit the compensation Update Stock of the activity Prepare Order fails because the goods cannot be unpackaged without damage. Then, the saga will raise an exception:

$$\Gamma'' \vdash \textsf{HPO-saga} = \{\langle \textsf{A.O.}, \textsf{P.O.}, ! \rangle\}$$

2.3 Discussion

The calculus we have presented is obtained by mixing the ingredients coming from two different proposals [9,14]. For example, the use of scenarios comes from [9], while the interleaving trace semantics is more in the style of [14]. For the sake of presentation, we focus here just on parallel sagas by leaving out several other features considered in [9,14], like exception handling, choices, and nesting.

The integration the two approaches is sustained by the detailed comparison carried out in [7], where Sagas [9] and cCSP [14] are reconciled. In particular, it is shown that for the sequential composition both approaches coincide in the way in which compensations are installed and activated, while different compensation policies are used for parallel composition. In fact, [9] proposes already two different semantics for parallel compensations, called *naïve* and *revised*. Nevertheless, none of them coincides with the one in [14]. The key difference lies in the activation of sibling compensations in parallel branches of a transaction when one of the branches compensates. In fact there are several policies for notifying the abort to sibling processes. Roughly, such policies can be characterised in terms of two orthogonal strategies: (i) whether the forward flow can be interrupted to activate the compensation procedure as soon as possible or not; and (ii) whether the compensation procedure is activated in a centralised or in a distributed way. The combination of these strategies gives the following four different policies

No Interrupt & Centralized (emerged in [7])	$\subseteq$	No Interrupt & Distrib. (Naïve Sagas [9])
$\subseteq$		$\subseteq$
Interrupt & Centralized (cCSP [14])	$\subseteq$	Interrupt & Distrib. (Revised Sagas [9])

The main result in [7] is to relate the different semantics arising in the four cases, which justifies the inclusion relations depicted above. Suitable counterexamples for proving that Naïve Sagas $\not\subseteq$ cCSP and cCSP $\not\subseteq$ Naïve Sagas are given in [7].

The four strategies mentioned above correspond to alternative implementations for the compensation mechanism. The policy adopted by the semantics in Figures 1 and 2 is *no interruption and distributed compensation*, a distributed procedure for compensating parallel branches that may allow the execution of activities of the backward flow even when parts of siblings forward flow are still in execution. As an example, the aforementioned law $[A \div A' \mid B \div B' \mid THROW] \equiv A;A'|B;B'$ illustrates this policy. Note that the forward flow is executed completely (i.e., A and B) but parallel branches are independently compensated for, e.g. A' can be executed even before B completes.

We conclude this section by remarking that our calculus is tailored to Naïve Sagas, and hence some syntactic assumptions and the semantics in Figures 1 and 2 are slightly different w.r.t. the presentation in [7], where a uniform style of description for the four policies has been preferred.

3 Java Transactional Web Services

In this section we describe `JTWS`, a Java-implementation of Naïve Sagas based on the APIs introduced in [27,21]. The programming pattern adopted in `JTWS` is based on

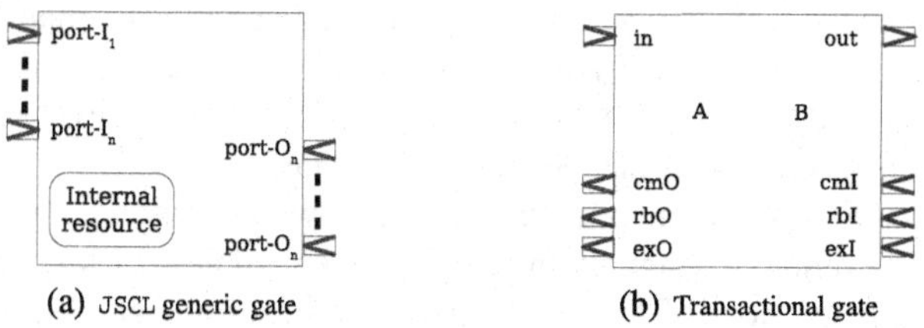

(a) JSCL generic gate (b) Transactional gate

Fig. 4. Gates

signal passing. Basically, WS become JTWS components that interact by exchanging suitable signals. It is possible to divide JTWS in two conceptual levels, JSCL and JTL: the former provides the signal handling primitives that the latter uses to define the transactional ones. Hereafter, JTWS components are called *gates*.

Signal Core Layer. The signal layer JSCL abstracts the primitive mechanisms for defining and exchanging signals among gates. A signal represents an event that occurs on a given gate, for instance, a service may notify a successful execution by emitting a suitable signal. Like in the event-notification pattern, "handlers" are associated to signals. Handlers must subscribe in order to be notified and are not necessarily unique, i.e., a signal may have several associated handlers. Unlike the event-notification pattern, JSCL gates behave as handlers and emitters for different signals at the same time.

The class SIGNAL defines the JSCL signals that carry some *internal information* (e.g., sender/receiver identifiers, synchronous/asynchronous, timestamp...) and *session data*. The session data can be accessed by invoking the methods for getting/setting the session attributes (e.g., GETPARAM, SETPARAMVALUE, ID). (For a detailed presentation of the whole session and internal data APIs, the reader is referred to [27] . Details therein are not necessary to understand the rest of the paper.)

Conceptually, a generic JTWS gate, graphically represented in Figure 4(a), controls its internal resources and communicates with other gates by means of I/O ports where signals of a specified type can be received/sent. Ports are an idealisation, indeed in JTWS they are not effectively implemented as objects, but are characterised by the signal types. Therefore, signals having different types corresponds to signals sent on different ports. All the types of the input (or output) ports of a gate are pairwise distinct.

Ports are connected through *links* that carry signals from emitters to handlers. The links in JSCL are typed, unidirectional and unicast (namely, links connect a single emitter to a single handler). More complex scenarios (e.g., multi-casting, bi-directionality) can be obtained by opportunely connecting links. For instance, multi-casting is achieved by connecting the same emitter to several handlers (with as many links as the handlers). As for the ports, links are not explicitly implemented in JTWS; links are effectively represented by writing the information about the handlers in the internal data of the signal. The emitter e can create a link toward the handler h by executing e.CREATELINK(t,h) that also specifies the type t of the link. Afterward, e can emit signals toward h with the EMITSIGNAL method provided by the API. If many links exist between e and h, the type of the emitted signal is used to determine which is the actual link to be used.

Transactional Layer. JTL represents a specialisation of JSCL focused on describing the transactional aspects related to the forward and backward flows across gates. This level fixes the set of the signals that gates may exchange and their semantics. According to Naïve Sagas, JTL gates must handle four flows of execution, which are represented by the signals FORWARD, COMMIT, ROLLBACK and EXCEPTION. All of them are exchanged on specific ports (see Section 4 for details).

The signal FORWARD encodes the forward flow of sagas and implements the normal execution. The remaining signals encode the backward flows. More precisely, COMMIT corresponds to the flow of the correct termination of a saga, while ROLLBACK and EXCEPTION detect the failures of the saga. Indeed, ROLLBACK encodes the flow of execution that starts when a normal execution fails and EXCEPTION encodes the flow starting when a rollback flow fails.

A *transactional gate* (shortly TG) can be defined by specialising the class TRANSACTIONALCOMPONENT and implementing the methods ONFORWARD, ONCOMMIT, ONROLLBACK and ONEXCEPTION that handle the corresponding signals. The mechanism to emit a signal is inherited from JSCL. The classes TRANSACTIONALSEQUENCE and TRANSACTIONALPARALLEL provide the methods for creating transactional gates by sequential and parallel composition of TGs. Their public interfaces remain the same as the one of TG so that they can be inductively composed, as shown in Sections 4.1 and 4.2. Moreover, they are equipped with the method `addInternalComponent` that allows to add a new gate to an existing sequential or parallel gate.

4 Sagas in JTWS

The main ingredients of the translation from Naïve Sagas to JTWS are: (1) the signals representing the states of the transactions, (2) the atomic tasks representing the atomic actions of Naïve Sagas and (3) the transactional generic gates corresponding to sagas.

The signal EXCEPTION implements the final event '!' while ROLLBACK and COMMIT are the counterpart of '✓', the final event decorating the traces that successfully terminate either their forward or backward flows. Furthermore, ROLLBACK is used as the (internal) signal for starting the compensation of a saga, while COMMIT represents the normal termination. Hereafter, we assume that signal emissions do not fail.

At the JSCL level, the method `onHandleSignal` is overridden so that the appropriate method is invoked when a signal is received. For instance, when a ROLLBACK is emitted, the `onHandleSignal` of all the registered handlers are called so that the method associated to it (i.e., `onRollback`) is invoked.

4.1 Gates for Compensation Pairs and Sequential Composition

Transactional gates are objects of the class `TG` and are the building blocks of sagas, which are obtained by gluing together transactional gates. Basically, a transactional gate is a generalisation of the elementary step $A \div B$, graphically represented in Figure 4(b). The atomic actions A and B are implemented as objects `A` and `B`, respectively, in a class implementing the interface `AtomicTask`:

```
public interface AtomicTask {
  public abstract Object execute (Signal signal) throws AtomicActionException;
}
```

```
public class Step extends
  GenericTransactionalGate {
  private AtomicTask A = null;
  private AtomicTask B = null;

  public comp(AtomicTask A, AtomicTask B)
    {this.A = A; this.B = B }

  public int onForward(Signal signal) {
    try {
      if (A != null) then A.execute(signal);
      signal.setType(SignalType.FORWARD);
      emitSignal(signal);
    } catch (AtomicActionException e) {
      signal.setType(SignalType.ROLLBACK);
      emitSignal(signal);
    }
}
 public int onCommit(Signal signal) {
   signal.setType(SignalType.COMMIT);
   emitSignal(signal);
 }
  public int onRollback(Signal signal) {
    try {
      if (B != null) then B.execute(signal);
      signal.setType(SignalType.ROLLBACK);
      emitSignal(signal);
    } catch (AtomicActionException e) {
      signal.setType(SignalType.EXCEPTION);
      emitSignal(signal);
    }
  }
  public int onException(Signal signal) {
    try {
      signal.setType(SignalType.EXCEPTION);
      emitSignal(signal);
    } catch (Object e) {
      emitSignal(signal);
    }
  }
}
```

Fig. 5. The class `GenericTransactionalGate`

where we assume that an `AtomicTask` object starts its execution when its `execute` method is invoked on a signal and throws an exception if a failure occurs.

The function `comp(A,B)` records `A` and `B` into a transactional gate as illustrated in Figure 4(b). Intuitively, `A` starts its execution when a FORWARD signal is received on the `in` port. Commenting on Figure 5, when the `onForward` method is executed, the gate tries to run `A`; whenever the execution of `A` normally terminates, the FORWARD signal is propagated. On the contrary, if `A` throws an exception, a ROLLBACK is emitted. The other methods act similarly.

If `A` normally terminates its execution, `comp(A,B)` forwards on the `out` port the signal for invoking the next gates in the saga. When a COMMIT signal is received on the `cmI` port, the gate `comp(A,B)` forwards it on the `cmO` port.

If an exception occurs during the execution of `A`, then `comp(A,B)` emits a ROLLBACK on port `rbO` so that the gates waiting for the result of the saga can compensate. Differently, A signal received on port `exI` informs that a previously executed compensation have raises an exception. For instance, if `B` catches an exception, it emits on its `exO` port the signal EXCEPTION. Hence, the gate that receives it will backwardly propagate EXCEPTION to the previous gates in the saga.

Transactional gates can be sequentially composed in an easy manner as illustrated in Figure 6(a). An arrow from a port to another represents a link for a specific type of signals from the emitter to the handlers. Hence, all the target gates of the arrow have been registered as handlers for that signal. For instance, in Figure 6(a), the signals emitted from `Q` on its `cmO` are handled by `P`, which receives them on the `cmI` port. As explained in Section 3, the ports are associated with the proper methods that should be executed when a signal is received on them; for instance, signals received on `rbI` are associated with the `onRollback` method that activates the compensation of the gate.

Given two transactional gates `P` and `Q`, `seq(P,Q)` yields the transactional gate having as `in`, `cmO`, `rbO` and `exO` ports those of `P`, while the ports `out`, `cmI`, `rbI` and `exI` are those of `Q`. The behaviour of `seq(P,Q)` is as follows: any FORWARD signal received from the

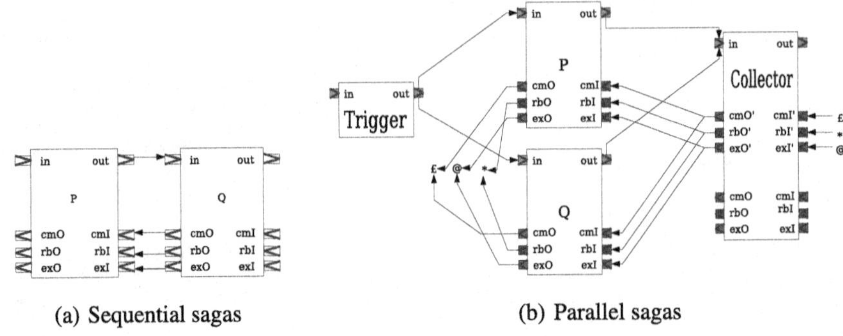

(a) Sequential sagas

(b) Parallel sagas

Fig. 6. Composition of sagas

`in` port of `P` is sent on the `out` port of `P` if it terminates normally, otherwise a ROLLBACK is sent on the `cmO` port of `P`. Gate `Q` after receiving the FORWARD (i.e., `P` has executed correctly) executes as any other gate. Notice that, in case `Q` fails its normal execution, the ROLLBACK is handled by `P`, which starts its compensation and either backwardly propagates the ROLLBACK (if the compensation succeeds) on the port `rbO` of `P` or emits an EXCEPTION signal on the port `exO` of `P` (if the compensation of `P` fails).

Signals received from `Q` on its `cmI` and `exI` ports are simply propagated (on the corresponding ports) to `P`, which backwardly propagates them to the rest of the saga.

4.2 Gates for Parallel Composition and Sagas

The behaviour of a parallel saga is the most complex among the coordination constructs of Naïve Sagas. The function `par` yields the transactional gate obtained by composing in parallel a (finite) number of transactional gates. For simplicity, we illustrate `par` in the case of the parallel composition of two gates `P` and `Q`, as illustrated in Figure 6(b) (for simplicity we connect some ports by using reference symbols £, @ and * instead of drawing a line). The case where more than two gates are composed in parallel is analogous and equivalent to compose `P | Q` with `R`.

Function `par` uses two auxiliary gates: the `Trigger` and the `Collector`. These gates are transparent to the users. Note that the `Trigger` and the `Collector` are not transactional gates themselves. On the invocation signal, the `Trigger` simply triggers all the gates of the parallel saga. The `Collector` manages the result of the parallel saga and interfaces the intermediate results of `P` and `Q` with the transactional gates outside the saga. As shown in Figure 6(b), `Collector` has the ports for receiving/sending signals to `P` and `Q` and those for external gates `cmI`, `cmO`, `rbI`, `rbO`, etc.

The parallel saga is activated when `Trigger` sends the FORWARD received from its `in` port to its `out` port. According to our assumption, `P` and `Q` start their executions. At this point several cases are possible depending on the results from `P`, `Q` and the signals from the gates external to the parallel saga. In order to forward the invocation signal, the `Collector` waits for the invoke signals from `P` and `Q`. When those signals are received, `Collector` waits for the rest of the saga to communicate the result.

1. If a COMMIT is received on port `cmI`, then it is forwarded on `cmO'` to `P` and `Q` which forward it on their `cmO` ports to `Collector`. Once all the commit signals are collected, a COMMIT is emitted on the port `cmO` of `Collector`.
2. If a ROLLBACK is received on port `rbI`, then it is forwarded on `rbO'` to `P` and `Q` which activate their compensations. At this point, either `P` and `Q` signal a ROLLBACK on their `rbO` ports or one of them emits a `exception` on `exO`. In the former case, analogously to the previous case, the rollback is propagated on the `rbO` port of `Collector`. If one of `P` or `Q` (or both of them) emits an exception, then `Collector` propagates an exception signal on `exO` instead of a rollback one on `cmO`.
3. If an EXCEPTION is received on port `exI`, then it is forwarded on `rbO'` to `P` and `Q` (which activate their compensations). At this point, the signals from `P` and `Q` are ignored and `Collector` emits an exception signal on `exO`.

Either `P` or `Q` might fail their normal execution and emits a ROLLBACK signal. Consider that `P` emits a ROLLBACK signal. In this case, the simplest scenario is when also `Q` emits a ROLLBACK: `Collector` will simply emit a ROLLBACK of its `rbO` port. If `Q` sends an FORWARD signal, as soon as `Collector` receives it replies with a ROLLBACK for `Q`. Afterward, if `Q` sends the second ROLLBACK, `Collector` proceeds as in the previous case; on the contrary, `Q` might reply with an EXCEPTION signal. In this case, `Collector` signals an exception on its `exO` port.

By `closure(P)`, any saga can be seen as a method invocation. This is obtained by simply connecting the `out` port of the gate `P` with its `cmI` port. The saga is invoked by sending a signal on the `in` port of `P`. The control is returned when `P` emits a signal either on port `cmO` or on `rbO`. An exception is raised if `P` emits a signal on port `exO`.

Finally, we summarise the mapping from Naïve Sagas to `JTWS` as follows:

$$[\![A \div B]\!] = \texttt{comp(A,B)} \qquad [\![P;Q]\!] = \texttt{seq}([\![P]\!],[\![Q]\!])$$
$$[\![P|Q]\!] = \texttt{par}([\![P]\!],[\![Q]\!]) \qquad [\![[P]]\!] = \texttt{closure}([\![P]\!])$$

5 A Case Study

In this section, we exemplify the use of `JTWS` to accomplish the task of providing transactional behaviour to WS composition. Our case study scenario will focus on the development of an application combining two overlay networks, namely the Internet and a telecommunication network. The application provides a SMS Taxi Booking facility. The basic idea of the application is that registered customers can book a taxi by sending a SMS text message to the Taxi call-centre. The customer gets a SMS reply back from the taxi company confirming the booking along with the estimated arrival time, place, fare and vehicle details. Moreover, the full amount of the fare at the end of the journey will be payed on-line by exploiting the registered information about customer credit card. This application has been designed, deployed, and executed within a framework that integrates WS, a rich set of telecommunication services (including call/session control, messaging features, presence and location features) and WS for telecommunications (Parlay X WS) [27]. Our aim is to show the adequacy of `JTWS` (and the underlying process calculus Naïve Sagas) for designing LRTs. Indeed, our case study offers a test-bed for the programming features of `JTWS`.

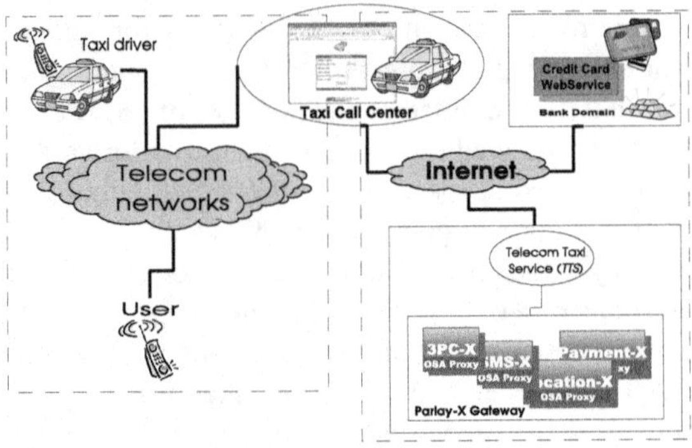

Fig. 7. SMS Taxi Booking Service

```
seq (
  comp (UserProfile, null),
  comp (RetrieveReservation, LogFailure),
  par (
    comp (Bank, RestoreAmount),
    comp (CreditCardMgr, RestoreAmount)
  ),
  comp(SendSMS, null)
)
```

Fig. 8. Stage3: The On-line Payment

Figure 7 illustrates the overall structure of the application. The SMS Taxi Booking service is structured into three stages. The first stage treats the taxi booking activities. The second stage manages the communications for the confirmation of the booking. Finally, the last stage handles the taxi payment service. We focus on the implementation of the first and third stages, which involve non-trivial transactional facets. The saga implementing the first stage is just the sequential composition of several services:

$$[\texttt{ReceivedSMS} \div \texttt{SendSMSErr};\ \texttt{UserProfile};\ \texttt{LocateUser};\ \texttt{SearchTC};\ \texttt{MakeCall}]$$

The `ReceiveSMS` service is the access gateway of the application and it is activated upon receipt of the SMS message. Its main activity consists in generating the activation signal for all the other services, which check whether the customer is authorised to access the service (`UserProfile`), determine the location of the user (`LocateUser`), select the Taxi Company (`SearchTC`) and finally set up a call between the taxi company and the customer (`MakeCall`). Note that the `ReceiveSMS` compensation (`sendSMSErr`) is indeed the only compensation of the whole sequence: it will be executed in case of the failure of the booking (an appropriate error message will be sent to the user). The compensations of the other services are all empty, indeed none of them modifies the local state and their failures just activate the emission of the ROLLBACK signal.

The saga in Figure 8 describes the more interesting implementation of the third stage of the application. Intuitively, after having retrieved the reservation data, the services for the payment of the fare are activated. This is done by the parallel execution of two activities: one performs the money transfer to the taxi company account (`Bank`), the other charges the fare on the customer credit card (`CrediCard`). In both cases, the compensations of failures restore the data on the corresponding account.

Our experimentation has shown that Naïve Sagas and `JTWS` provide a natural setting to design and deploy transactional business processes at a high level of abstraction. Indeed, the coordination details are hidden inside the `JSCL` implementation.

6 Concluding Remarks

Starting from a formal specification of parallel sagas we have presented `JTWS`, a Java API that provides the basic primitives for composing WS in (compensable, parallel) LRTs. The implementation is conceptually separated in two layers: `JSCL` and `JTL`. The former is a general framework for building networks of gates connected by typed signals. The latter is a specialised variant of `JSCL` where gates come equipped with few carefully selected signals that are tailored to the treatment of WS transactions. The underlying `JSCL` layer makes the implementation fully distributed. The overall contribution is a setting for designing business process transactions where three level are reconciled: (1) a visual/graphical representation of parallel sagas, (2) a process calculus description in bijective correspondence with sagas diagrams, and (3) an executable, distributed translation of symbolic processes.

One interesting result of our experimentation is that level 2 is crucial for linking business analyst designs (level 1) to their actual implementations (level 3). Indeed, as already observed in [7], the process calculus formalisation forces us to deal with design choices that are not so evident at level 1 (e.g. centralised vs. distributed interrupt and compensation). Furthermore, level 3 can test and ensure that the design choices made at level 2 are really implementable / feasible.

As future work, we intend to exploit the flexibility of `JSCL` to implement and experiment with the alternative design choices identified in [7], including advanced features like nesting, speculative choice and alternative activities to provide a full-fledged transactional framework.

References

1. B. Anderson and D. Shasha. Persistent linda: Linda + transactions + query processing. *Research Directions in High-Level Parallel Programming Languages*, vol. 574 of *Lect. Notes in Comput. Sci.*, pp. 93–109. Springer, 1992.
2. BizTalk Server Web site. `http://www.microsoft.com/biztalkserver`.
3. L. Bocchi, C. Laneve, and G. Zavattaro. A calculus for long-running transactions. *Proc. of FMOODS'03*, vol. 2884 of *Lect. Notes in Comput. Sci.*, pp. 124–138. Springer, 2003.
4. BPEL Specification (v.1.1). `http://www.ibm.com/developerworks/library/ws-bpel`.
5. BPEL and BTP issues list. `http://www.choreology.com/external`.
6. Business Process Modeling Language. `http://www.bpmi.org/BPML.htm`.
7. R. Bruni, M. Butler, C. Ferreira, T. Hoare, H. Melgratti, and U. Montanari. Comparing two approaches to compensable flow composition. To appear in *Proc.* of CONCUR 2005.

8. R. Bruni, H. Melgratti, and U. Montanari. Nested commits for mobile calculi: extending Join. *Proc. of IFIP-TCS 2004*, pp. 569–582. Kluwer, 2004.
9. R. Bruni, H. Melgratti, and U. Montanari. Theoretical foundations for compensations in flow composition languages. *Proc. of POPL 2005*, pp. 209–220. ACM Press, 2005.
10. R. Bruni and U. Montanari. Concurrent models for Linda with Transactions. *Mathematical Structure in Computer Science*, 14(3):421–468, Cambridge University Press, 2004.
11. N. Busi and G. Zavattaro. On the serializability of transactions in javaspaces. *Elect. Notes in Th. Comput. Sci.*, vol. 54. Elsevier, 2001.
12. M. Butler, M. Chessell, C. Ferreira, C. Griffin, P. Henderson, and D. Vines. Extending the concept of transaction compensation. *IBM Systems Journal*, 41(4):743–758, 2002.
13. M. Butler and C. Ferreira. An operational semantics for StAC, a language for modelling long-running business transactions. *Proc. of Coordination 2004*, vol. 2949 of *Lect. Notes in Comput. Sci.*, pp. 87–104. Springer, 2004.
14. M. Butler, T. Hoare, and C. Ferreira. A trace semantics for long-running transactions. *Proc. of 25 Years of CSP*, vol. 3525 of *Lect. Notes in Comput. Sci.*, pp. 133–150. Springer, 2005.
15. T. Chothia and D. Duggan. An architecture for secure fault-tolerant global applications. *Theor. Comput. Sci.*, 322(3):567–613, 2004.
16. V. Danos and J. Krivine. Reversible communicating systems. *Proc. of CONCUR 2004*, vol. 3170 of *Lect. Notes in Comput. Sci.*, pp. 293–307. Springer, 2005.
17. D. Gelernter. Generative communication in Linda. *ACM Transactions on Programming Languages and Systems*, 7(1):80–112, 1985.
18. A. Hosking, S. Jagannathan, J. Vitek, and A. Welc. A semantic framework for designer transactions. *Proc. of ESOP 2004*, vol. 2986 of *Lect. Notes in Comput. Sci.*, pp. 249–263. Springer, 2004.
19. I. Houston, M. Little, I. Robinson, S. Shrivastava, and S. Wheater. The corba activity service framework for supporting extended transactions. *Softw. Pract. Exper.*, 33(4):351–373, 2003.
20. S. Jagannathan and J. Vitek. Optimistic concurrency semantics for transactions in coordination languages. *Proc. of Coordination 2004*, vol. 2949 of *Lect. Notes in Comp. Sci.*, pp. 183–198. Springer, 2004.
21. Java Transactional Web Services. `http://www.di.unipi.it/~etuosto/jtws.html`.
22. C. Laneve and G. Zavattaro. Foundations of web transactions. *Proc. of FoSSaCS 2005*, vol. 3441 of *Lect. Notes in Comp. Sci.*, pp. 282–298. Springer, 2005.
23. F. Leymann. Web Services Flow Language (v.1.0). http://www-306.ibm.com/software/webservices/pdf/WSFL.pdf.
24. M. Mazzara and S. Govoni. A case study of web services orchestration. Proc. of Coordination 2005, vol. 3454 of *Lect. Notes in Comput. Sci.*, pp. 1–16. Springer, 2005.
25. M. Mazzara and R. Lucchi. A framework for generic error handling in business processes. *Proc. of WS-FM 2004, Elect. Notes in Th. Comput. Sci.*, vol. 105, pp. 133–145. Elsevier, 2004.
26. Oracle BPEL Process Manager. `http://www.oracle.com/technology/bpel`.
27. D. Strollo. Composizionalità di transazioni e Web Services nell'ambito della telefonia mobile. Master's thesis, Dipartimento di Informatica, Pisa, 2005. In Italian.
28. WebSphere. `http://www-306.ibm.com/software/info1/websphere/index.jsp`.
29. Web Services Choreography Description Language (v.1.0). http://www.w3.org/TR/ws-cdl-10
30. Web Services Conversation Language (v.1.0). `http://www.w3.org/TR/wscl10/`.
31. Web Services for Business Process Design (XLANG). `http://www.gotdotnet.com/team/xml_wsspecs/xlang-c/default.htm`.

Timing Issues in Web Services Composition

Manuel Mazzara

Department of Computer Science, University of Bologna, Italy
mazzara@cs.unibo.it

Abstract. webπ is a recent process calculus introduced to formally specify Web Services composition. It extends the π-calculus with timed workunits, namely an asynchronous and temporized mechanism for events raising and catching. In this paper we encode Berger-Honda Timed-π in webπ timed workunits and we prove a simulation theorem. The overall perspective of this work is to make webπ comparable with both real composition languages and well established models for distributed components.

1 Introduction

Service Oriented Computing (SOC) is an emerging paradigm for distributed computing and e-business processing that finds its origin in object-oriented and component computing. Web services technology is a widespread accepted instantiation of SOC which should facilitate integration of newly built and legacy applications both within and across organizational boundaries avoiding difficulties due to different platform, heterogeneous programming languages, security firewall, etc... Exploiting this kind of ubiquitous network fabric would result in an increase of productivity and in a reduction of costs in B2B processes [17]. The idea behind this approach is to allow independently developed applications to be exposed as services and interconnected exploiting the already set up Web infrastructure with relative standards (HTTP [31], XML [12], SOAP [7] and WSDL [11]). These technologies, related to develop basic services and interconnect them on a point-to point basis, can be considered well established but B2B processing requires managing complex interactions involving a large number of participants and none of the above standards are able to meet this need. The way to build complex services out of simpler ones is called *composition* and it is still an open challenge [28].

Different organizations are presently working on composition proposals. The most important in the past have been IBM's WSFL [21] and Microsoft's XLANG [29]. These two have then converged in Web Services Business Process Execution Language [3] (WS-BPEL or BPEL for short) which is presently a working draft by OASIS. Another recent proposal in phase of standardization by the World Wide Web Consortium (W3C) is WS-CDL [18]. Both allow the definition of workflow-based composition of services with some similarities and some differences. Describing in details a synopsis between these two proposals is beyond the scope of this paper, however in section 2 some points will be sketched.

M. Bravetti et al. (Eds.): EPEW 2005 and WS-FM 2005, LNCS 3670, pp. 287–302, 2005.

1.1 Need for Foundations

XLANG, WS-BPEL and WS-CDL are claimed to be based on formal models (the π-calculus or its variant) to allow rigorous mathematical reasoning. For example, WS-CDL authors explicitly state to be in some relation with fusions and solos. In particular, WS-CDL is built atop the Global Model formalism (as presented in [17]) which refers to a precise π-calculus variant: the Explicit Solos Calculus [13], the theory underlying the Fusion Machine (a virtual machine implementing in a distributed manner the π-calculus). However, despite all this hype, no interesting relations with process algebras have been so far emphasized (no conceptual tools for analysis and reasoning, no software verification). In this way any mathematical rigor becomes pointless.

$\mathtt{web}\pi_\infty$ [24] has been introduced to fill this gap. It is a simple and conservative extension of the π-calculus where the original algebra is augmented with an operator for asynchronous events raising and catching in order to enable the programming of widely accepted error handling techniques (such as long running transactions and compensations) with a reasonable simplicity. The ability to handle time is also considered a very appropriate feature when programming transactions where business services cannot wait forever for the reply of other parties. For this reason, $\mathtt{web}\pi_\infty$ has a timed counterpart, $\mathtt{web}\pi$ [19], which allows events to be temporized, i.e. to happen not only when processes explicitly raise them but also when timers expire. We address the problem of composing services starting directly from the π-calculus and considering our proposals as foundational models for composition simply to verify statements regarding any mathematical foundations of composition languages and not to say that the π-calculus is more suitable than other models (such as Petri nets) for these purposes. For an ongoing discussion about these foundational aspects refer to [30].

1.2 Error Handling and Web Transactions

Loosely coupled components like Web services, being autonomous in their decisions, may refuse requests and suspend their functionality without notice, thus making their behavior unreliable to other activities. Henceforth, most of the web languages also include the notion of loosely coupled transaction – called *web transaction* [22] in the following – as a unit of work involving loosely coupled activities that may last long periods of time. These transactions, being orthogonal to administrative domains, have the typical atomicity and isolation properties relaxed, and instead of assuming a perfect roll-back in case of failure, support the explicit programming of compensation activities. Web transactions usually contain the description of three processes; the body, the failure handler, and the compensation.

The failure handler is responsible for reacting to events that occur during the execution of the body; when these events occur, the body is blocked and the failure handler is activated. The compensation, on the contrary, is installed when the body commits; it remains available for outer transactions to require some undo of previously performed actions. BPEL and WS-CDL both use this approach. However, in [25,23] we showed that different mechanisms for error handling are not necessary and we presented the BPEL semantics in terms of $\texttt{web}\pi_\infty$ which is based on the idea of event notification as the unique error handling mechanism. The same is feasible considering WS-CDL. This result allows us to extend any semantic considerations about $\texttt{web}\pi_\infty$ and $\texttt{web}\pi$ to BPEL and WS-CDL.

1.3 Contribution of the Paper

In [24] we used $\texttt{web}\pi_\infty$ as a theoretical and foundational model for web services composition and we proved its usefulness formalizing an e-commerce transactional scenario experimented in our preliminary work [14]. In those papers we did not address timing issues at all. We recognized the limits of those works and the usefulness of time handling when programming business transactions. For this reason, in this paper we consider *timed transactions*, i.e. transactions that can be interrupted by a timeout. Real workflow languages presently provide this feature: XLANG, for instance, includes a notion of timed transaction as a special case of long running activity. BPEL also allows similar behaviors by means of alarm clocks.

To meet the challenge of time in composition, $\texttt{web}\pi$ has been equipped with an explicit mechanism for time elapsing and timeout handling. Adding time we are able to express more meaningful and realistic scenarios in composition. The $\texttt{web}\pi$ model of time is inspired by Berger-Honda Timed-π skipping the idle rule plus some minor variations. In this paper we present a synopsis of the two approaches underlying differences and similarities. We show the ability of $\texttt{web}\pi$ to cope with timing issues in a context of B2B web transactions proving that skipping the idle rule is not source of expressiveness loss. To do this we encode their time construct, called timer, in our timed workunit and we prove in detail a simulation theorem. This is intended as a major result of the paper and convinces us of the great flexibility of $\texttt{web}\pi$.

Another contribution stands in section 2 where we clarify some semantical aspects of composition languages and where we modify some terminology of $\texttt{web}\pi$ presenting detailed motivations. The overall perspective of this work is to make $\texttt{web}\pi$ comparable with both real composition languages and well established model for distributed components.

1.4 Related Work

Other papers discussing the formal semantics of compensable activities in this context are: the work by Hoare [15] which is mainly inspired by XLANG, the calculus of Butler and Ferreira [10] which is inspired by BPBeans, the πt-calculus [6] considering BizTalk and the work [8] dealing with short-lived transactions in BizTalk. The work in [9] also presents the formal semantics for a hierarchy of transactional calculi with increasing expressiveness.

1.5 Outline of the Paper

The paper is structured as follows: after the above introduction, section 2 tries to clarify some semantical aspects of composition languages and of our model. Section 3 presents webπ with its syntax and semantics while section 4 is devoted to an analogous description of the counterpart, π_t. The encoding of timers is showed and explained in section 5 where the correctness proof is also detailed and described. Finally, section 6 reports some conclusive considerations.

2 WS-BPEL, WS-CDL and webπ

It is worth noting that in this paper we are changing some terminology with respect to previous works presenting webπ [19,20] or webπ_∞ [24,23]. In particular we are replacing the term *transaction* or *timed transaction* with the term *timed workunit* and the term *compensation* with the term *event handler*. This is because we believe that, using the old terminology and continuously associating webπ with real composition languages like WS-BPEL or WS-CDL, confusion and ambiguity can raise.

As explained in detail in [23], the WS-BPEL Recovery Framework has two different mechanisms for coping with abnormal situations: fault handler and compensation handler. Also WS-CDL provides mechanisms with a similar semantics called exceptions and finalizers. The basic wrapper containing operations and associated handlers is `scope` for WS-BPEL and `choreography` for WS-CDL. These mechanisms are thought to be used at different stages of computation: fault handling during the execution of an activity while compensation handling after its successful completion. While fault/exception handlers are typically provided by classical concurrent programming languages, compensation handlers or finalizers are peculiar to composition languages. Compensations are related with long running web transactions and the relative semantic deserves some attention.

It is important to remind that scopes and choreographies can be structured in a tree of nesting. Both WS-BPEL and WS-CDL allow compensations (or finalizer) to be available for a scope (or choreography) after its successful termination. BPEL has a constraint which forces a compensation to be triggered only by an enclosing scope which failed for some reason. WS-CDL, instead, allows a finalizer to be simply activated by a parent choreography which failed or not, without imposing particular constraints (motivation for this decision are related to speculative parallelism and can be found at [1,2]).

Anyway, compensation semantics is strictly about "partially reversing" of successful activities included in a "larger work" which failed. Differently, fault handling is a mechanism thought to interrupt "immediately" an activity when some abnormal situation happens. At that point, the normal execution is broken and no way to access the compensation handler is still available. After these considerations it is easy to see how webπ semantics is very far from the compensation semantics of composition languages. Indeed, webπ mechanism is more similar to fault handling. Anyway, we want to avoid to call it fault handler because we want to provide a foundational mechanism which is able, as already showed, to encode both the presented mechanisms. In some sense, our work is close to the CORBA Activity Service Framework [16] which uses a similar event signalling mechanism. Both these approaches result more flexible with respect to WS-BPEL and WS-CDL semantics. For this reason we call it *event handler*. In fact, it is simply a generic framework for event handling and catching.

A last remark deserves to be made to clarify completely any possible objections. While WS-CDL does not support additional mechanisms except the two described above, WS-BPEL provides also a third mechanism called *event handler*, as in webπ. Its semantics, however, is different: a BPEL event handler listens to messages or alarm clock concurrently to the scope execution and handles all the events concurrently, even when multiple instances occur. If the scope terminates but some of these occurrences are still alive, they are allowed to normally terminate their execution. We showed that also this semantic can be encoded in webπ, so the presence of this additional machinery is not harmful. Anyway, it is important to underline that, although the names are equal, the behaviors are different.

We decided to adopt what we intend to be the more foundational mechanism to encode all the others and we gave it a name which was as general as possible. As a consequence of all these considerations, we changed also the term *transaction* in *workunit*, because, in general, a transaction is the composed effect of many workunits, not just a single one.

3 The Calculus webπ

webπ is a timed extension of the asynchronous π-calculus with an explicit wrapping constructor for activities and an associated event handler, developed in order to provide mathematical foundation for composition languages. Composition essentially describes workflow, with a particular emphasis on the communication aspects of loosely coupled activities, i.e. activities executed by remote, heterogeneous and independent services that could belong to different administrative domains, such as different companies.

3.1 webπ Syntax

The syntax of webπ relies on a countable set of *names*, ranged over by $x, y, z, u, w, s, s' \cdots$. Tuples of names are written $\widetilde{u}$. Natural numbers $\{0, 1, 2, 3, \cdots\}$ or ∞ are ranged over by $n, m, \cdots$. The set of *processes* is defined by the following syntax:

$$
\begin{array}{lll}
P ::= & & \textbf{(processes)} \\
& \mathbf{0} & \text{(nil)} \\
& \mid \overline{x}\,\langle \widetilde{u} \rangle & \text{(message)} \\
& \mid x(\widetilde{u}).P & \text{(input)} \\
& \mid (x)P & \text{(restriction)} \\
& \mid P \mid P & \text{(parallel composition)} \\
& \mid\ !x(\widetilde{u}).P & \text{(lazy replication)} \\
& \mid \langle\!| P \,;\, P |\!\rangle_s^n & \text{(timed workunit)}
\end{array}
$$

A process can be the inert process $\mathbf{0}$, a message $\overline{x}\langle\widetilde{u}\rangle$ sent on a name x that carries a tuple of names $\widetilde{u}$, an input $x(\widetilde{u}).P$ that consumes a message $\overline{x}\langle\widetilde{w}\rangle$ and behaves like $P\{\widetilde{w}/\widetilde{u}\}$, a restriction $(u)P$ that behaves as P except that inputs and messages on u are prohibited, a parallel composition of processes, a replicated input $!x(\widetilde{u}).P$ that consumes a message $\overline{x}\langle\widetilde{w}\rangle$ and behaves like $P\{\widetilde{w}/\widetilde{u}\} \,|\, !x(\widetilde{u}).P$ or a timed workunit $\langle\!| P \;;\; R |\!\rangle^n_s$ that behaves as the *body* P except that the *event handler* R is triggered after n steps or because the opportune abort signal $\overline{s}\langle\rangle$ is received. The label n is called the *time stamp*. We remark that workunit names should be used with output capability only. For instance, it is not possible to write $s().P$. Our intuition is that workunit names are process identifiers, therefore two different workunits should never have the same name. Even if we conform with such intuition in this paper, we purposely do not enforce in webπ a discipline for the use of these names.

The calculus accounts for time by using positive natural numbers or ∞. The *timeless workunit* $\langle\!| P \;;\; R |\!\rangle_s$ is an abbreviation for $\langle\!| P \;;\; R |\!\rangle^\infty_s$, and we assume that $\infty + 1 = \infty$. Input $x(\widetilde{u}).P$, restriction $(x)P$ and lazy replication $!x(\widetilde{u}).P$ are binders of names $\widetilde{u}$, x, and $\widetilde{u}$, respectively. The scope of these binders is the process P. We use the standard notions of alpha-equivalence, *free* and *bound names* of processes, noted $\mathtt{fn}(P)$ and $\mathtt{bn}(P)$, respectively. In particular, $\mathtt{fn}(\langle\!| P \;;\; R |\!\rangle^n_x) = \mathtt{fn}(P) \cup \mathtt{fn}(R) \cup \{x\}$ and alpha-equivalence equates $(x)(\langle\!| P \;;\; Q |\!\rangle^n_x)$ with $(s)(\langle\!| P\{s/x\} \;;\; Q\{s/x\} |\!\rangle^n_s)$.

3.2 The Reduction Semantics

We are now ready to introduce the formal specification of the semantics of webπ. Following the tradition of π-calculus [26,27], we first define a structural congruence which equates all agents we will never want to distinguish for any semantic reason, and then use this when giving the operational semantics.

Definition 1. *The* structural congruence $\equiv$ *is the least congruence closed with respect to alpha-renaming, satisfying the abelian monoid laws for parallel (associativity, commutativity and* $\mathbf{0}$ *as identity), and the following axioms:*

1. *the scope laws:*

$$
\begin{array}{rl}
(u)\mathbf{0} \equiv \mathbf{0}, \qquad (u)(v)P \equiv (v)(u)P, & \\
P \,|\, (u)Q \equiv (u)(P \,|\, Q)\,, & \textit{if } u \notin \mathtt{fn}(P) \\
\langle\!| (z)P \;;\; Q |\!\rangle^n_s \equiv (z)\langle\!| P \;;\; Q |\!\rangle^n_s\,, & \textit{if } z \notin \{s\} \cup \mathtt{fn}(Q) \\
\langle\!| P \;;\; (z)Q |\!\rangle^0_s \equiv (z)\langle\!| P \;;\; Q |\!\rangle^0_s\,, & \textit{if } z \notin \{s\} \cup \mathtt{fn}(P)
\end{array}
$$

2. *the repetition law:*

$$!x(\widetilde{u}).P \equiv x(\widetilde{u}).P \,|\, !x(\widetilde{u}).P$$

3. *the workunit laws:*

$$
\begin{array}{c}
\langle\!| \mathbf{0} \;;\; Q |\!\rangle^s_x \equiv \mathbf{0} \\
\langle\!| \langle\!| P \;;\; Q |\!\rangle^n_{s'} \,|\, R \;;\; R' |\!\rangle^m_s \equiv \langle\!| P \;;\; Q |\!\rangle^n_{s'} \,|\, \langle\!| R \;;\; R' |\!\rangle^m_s
\end{array}
$$

4. the floating laws:

$$\langle\!| \overline{z}\,\langle \widetilde{u} \rangle \,|\, P \;;\; Q |\!\rangle^{n}_{s} \equiv \overline{z}\,\langle \widetilde{u} \rangle \,|\, \langle\!| P \;;\; Q |\!\rangle^{n}_{s}$$
$$\langle\!| y(\widetilde{v}).P \,|\, P' \;;\; \overline{z}\,\langle \widetilde{u} \rangle \,|\, Q |\!\rangle^{0}_{s} \equiv \overline{z}\,\langle \widetilde{u} \rangle \,|\, \langle\!| y(\widetilde{v}).P \,|\, P' \;;\; Q |\!\rangle^{0}_{s}$$

The scope and repetition laws are almost standard: let us discuss workunit and floating laws. The law $\langle\!| \mathbf{0} \;;\; Q |\!\rangle^{n}_{s} \equiv \mathbf{0}$ defines committed workunits, namely those with $\mathbf{0}$ as body. These workunits, being committed, are equivalent to $\mathbf{0}$ and, therefore, cannot fail anymore. The law $\langle\!| \langle\!| P \;;\; Q |\!\rangle^{n}_{s'} \,|\, R \;;\; R' |\!\rangle^{m}_{s} \equiv \langle\!| P \;;\; Q |\!\rangle^{n}_{s'} \,|\, \langle\!| R \;;\; R' |\!\rangle^{m}_{s}$ moves workunits outside the parent, thus flattening the nesting. Notwithstanding this flattening, the parent can still affect the children by means of workunit names. The law $\langle\!| \overline{z}\,\langle \widetilde{u} \rangle \,|\, P \;;\; R |\!\rangle^{n}_{s} \equiv \overline{z}\,\langle \widetilde{u} \rangle \,|\, \langle\!| P \;;\; R |\!\rangle^{n}_{s}$ floats messages outside workunits, thus modelling the fact that messages are particles uploaded on the network as soon as they are emitted. The intended semantics is the following: if a process emits a message, this message traverses the surrounding boundaries, until it reaches the corresponding input. In case an outer workunit fails, recoveries for this message may be detailed inside the relative handler.

The main technical difficulty is time elapsing. In this model all the processes run on the same orchestrator, thus competing for the same processor time. We assume that every reduction costs one time slot. When a subprocess performs a reduction, the flow of time is communicated to all the running processes. This amounts to decrease the time stamps of the running timed workunits by 1, thus triggering handler processes of those that become dead. This operation is modelled by the *time stepper function* below, which is an accommodation to $\texttt{web}\pi$ of the corresponding function in [4]. The definition of this function and two other auxiliary functions are in order:

the input predicate $\texttt{inp}(P)$: this predicate verifies whether a process contains an input that is not underneath a workunit. Formally:

$$\begin{array}{ll}
\texttt{inp}(x(\widetilde{u}).P) & \\
\texttt{inp}((x)P) & \text{if } \texttt{inp}(P) \\
\texttt{inp}(P \,|\, Q) & \text{if } \texttt{inp}(P) \text{ or } \texttt{inp}(Q) \\
\texttt{inp}(!x(\widetilde{u}).P) &
\end{array}$$

the time stepper function $\phi(P)$: this function decreases the time stamp by 1 and is defined inductively in the following way:

$$\begin{array}{rl}
\phi((x)P) = & (x)\phi(P) \\
\phi(P \,|\, Q) = & \phi(P) \,|\, \phi(Q) \\
\phi(\langle\!| P \;;\; R |\!\rangle^{0}_{s}) = & \begin{cases} \langle\!| \phi(P) \;;\; \phi(R) |\!\rangle^{0}_{s} & \text{if } \texttt{inp}(P) \\ \langle\!| \phi(P) \;;\; R |\!\rangle^{0}_{s} & \text{otherwise} \end{cases} \\
\phi(\langle\!| P \;;\; R |\!\rangle^{n+1}_{s}) = & \langle\!| \phi(P) \;;\; R |\!\rangle^{n}_{s} \\
\phi(P) = & P \quad \text{otherwise}
\end{array}$$

All the preliminaries are in place for the definition of the reduction relation.

Definition 2. *The reduction relation $\rightarrow$ is the least relation satisfying the following reductions:*

$$\text{(COM)} \qquad \overline{x}\,\langle\widetilde{v}\rangle \mid x(\widetilde{u}).Q \rightarrow Q\{\widetilde{v}/\widetilde{u}\}$$

$$\text{(FAIL)} \quad \overline{s}\,\langle\rangle \mid \langle\!| z(\widetilde{u}).P \mid Q \; ; \; R |\!\rangle_s^{n+1} \rightarrow \langle\!| z(\widetilde{u}).P \mid \phi(Q) \; ; \; R |\!\rangle_s^{0}$$

and closed under $\equiv$, $(x)\_$, and the rules:

$$\frac{P \rightarrow Q}{P \mid R \rightarrow Q \mid \phi(R)} \qquad \frac{P \rightarrow Q}{\langle\!| P \; ; \; R |\!\rangle_s^{n+1} \rightarrow \langle\!| Q \; ; \; R |\!\rangle_s^{n}}$$

$$\frac{P \rightarrow Q}{\langle\!| y(\widetilde{v}).R \mid R' \; ; \; P |\!\rangle_s^{0} \rightarrow \langle\!| y(\widetilde{v}).R \mid \phi(R') \; ; \; Q |\!\rangle_s^{0}}$$

Rule (COM) is standard in process calculi and models the input-output interaction. Rule (FAIL) models workunits failure: when an abort is emitted, the corresponding workunit is terminated by setting the time stamp to 0, thus activating the event handler (last rule). On the contrary, aborts are not possible if the workunit is already terminated, namely every thread in the body has completed its own work. The inference rules lift reductions to parallel contexts and workunit contexts, updating them because a time slot is elapsed.

We say that P has a barb x, and write $P \downarrow x$, if P manifests an output on the free name x.

Definition 3. *Let $P \downarrow x$ be the least relation satisfying the rules and closed for $\equiv$:*

$$\begin{array}{ll} \overline{x}\,\langle\widetilde{u}\rangle \downarrow x & \\ (z)P \downarrow x & \textit{if } P \downarrow x \textit{ and } x \neq z \\ (P \mid Q) \downarrow x & \textit{if } P \downarrow x \textit{ or } Q \downarrow x \\ \langle\!| P \; ; \; R |\!\rangle_s^{0} \downarrow x & \textit{if } P \downarrow x \textit{ or } (\mathtt{inp}(P) \textit{ and } R \downarrow x) \\ \langle\!| P \; ; \; R |\!\rangle_s^{n+1} \downarrow x & \textit{if } P \downarrow x \end{array}$$

4 The Calculus π_t

The advent of π-calculus has shown how diverse computational structures in both sequential and concurrent computing are uniformly representable as interacting processes. This allows the application of standard syntactic reasoning methods developed for process calculi to a wide variety of computational phenomena. However, in spite of its high expressive power and its interaction-based computing model, the π-calculus does not suffice for a complete and satisfactory description of basic elements of distributed computing systems. This is due to the difficult in decomposing some operations and phenomena in terms of message-passing, because they represent computational mechanisms left implicit or not treated in the π-calculus. For example, loss of message in transit, timers, process failure and recovery are not taken into account by the π-calculus. The work by Berger — his PhD thesis [5] and other papers (for example [4])— is concerned on the study of an extension for the original π-calculus in order to provide a reasonable framework able to represent more realistic distributed systems. He tried to give extensions that can be basic and incremental, i.e. that combinations of a few simple extensions can represent a wide range of phenomena essentials to distributed systems.

4.1 Core Syntax

In this section we will illustrate the core syntax of the calculus presented by Berger.

$$
\begin{array}{lll}
P ::= & & \textbf{(processes)} \\
 & \mathbf{0} & \text{(nil)} \\
 & \mid \overline{x}\,\langle \widetilde{y} \rangle & \text{(message)} \\
 & \mid x(\widetilde{y}).P & \text{(input)} \\
 & \mid (x)P & \text{(restriction)} \\
 & \mid P \,|\, P & \text{(parallel composition)} \\
 & \mid\, !x(\widetilde{y}).P & \text{(lazy replication)} \\
 & \mid \mathtt{timer}^n(x(\widetilde{v}).P, Q) & \text{(timer)}
\end{array}
$$

A timer is a pair of processes, say P and Q, and a deadline n, which represents the amount of disposed time. The semantic of timers is quite simple: a timer $\mathtt{timer}^n(\mu.P, Q)$ waits for a μ action until the total amount of time n elapses. If the action μ is performed, the timer reduces to the continuation P, and the timeout continuation Q is discarded. Contrariwise, if the time n elapses without any action μ, the timer reduces to the continuation Q, and the time-in continuation P is discarded. The introduction of timers requires some extensions to the original π-calculus, which is not able to manage time. In particular, Berger and Honda introduce the *time-stepper function* ϕ_t , which indicates how the time passing influences the various constructs:

$$
\phi_t(P) = \begin{cases}
\mathtt{timer}^{n-1}(Q, R) & \text{if } P = \mathtt{timer}^n(Q, R),\ t > 1 \\
R & \text{if } P = \mathtt{timer}^n(Q, R),\ t \leqslant 1 \\
\phi_t(Q) \,|\, \phi_t(R) & \text{if } P = Q \,|\, R \\
(x)\phi_t(Q) & \text{if } P = (x)Q \\
P & \text{else}
\end{cases}
$$

Thus $\phi(P)_t$ ticks each timer in P by one discrete degree: this can be thought of as the passing of, say, one second. Now we can introduce the reduction semantics, $\equiv_t$ is as usual.

Definition 4. *The* reduction relation $\rightarrow_t$ *is the least relation satisfying the following axioms and rules, and closed with respect to* $\equiv_t$ *and* $(x)\_$*:*

$$\text{(REP)}\quad \overline{x}\,\langle\widetilde{v}\rangle \,|\, !x(\widetilde{y}).P \;\rightarrow_t\; P\{\widetilde{v}/\widetilde{y}\} \,|\, !x(\widetilde{u}).P$$

$$\text{(STOP)}\quad \mathtt{timer}^{n+1}(x(\widetilde{v}).P, Q) \,|\, \overline{x}\,\langle\widetilde{y}\rangle \;\rightarrow_t\; P\{\widetilde{y}/\widetilde{v}\}$$

$$\text{(IDLE)}\quad P \rightarrow_t \phi_t(P) \qquad \text{(PAR)}\quad \frac{P \rightarrow_t P'}{P \,|\, Q \rightarrow_t P' \,|\, \phi_t(Q)}$$

Rules (STOP) and (PAR) are quite simple; they model the execution of timers and parallel processes. The rule (IDLE), instead, is a little more subtle: it allows the computation to pause or *idle* at arbitrary moments and, through repeated applications, for an unlimited period of time.

Now, we are ready to introduce the concept of *barb*, which will be used to prove the correctness of timers encoding. Informally, we say that P has a barb x, and write $P \downarrow_t x$, if P manifests an output on the free name x.

Definition 5. *Let $P \downarrow_t x$ be the least relation satisfying the rules and closed for $\equiv_t$:*

$$\begin{array}{c} \overline{x}\,\langle\widetilde{y}\rangle \downarrow_t x \\ (P \,|\, Q) \downarrow_t x \text{ if } P \downarrow_t x \text{ or } Q \downarrow_t x \\ (x)P \downarrow_t y \text{ if } P \downarrow_t y \text{ and } y \neq x \end{array}$$

5 Encoding Timers

In this section we show how to implement timers using workunits, then we will prove the correctness of this encoding. To this end we define the recursive function $[\![P]\!] : \pi_t \rightarrow \mathtt{web}\pi$ which maps π_t in $\mathtt{web}\pi$ processes:

Definition 6 (π_t encoding in $\mathtt{web}\pi$). *Timers are defined by induction on n, for the missing cases it holds $[\![P]\!] = P$.*

$$[\![\mathtt{timer}^1(y(\widetilde{u}).P, Q)]\!] = (x)(s)(\langle\!|\, y(\widetilde{u}).\overline{x}\,\langle\widetilde{u}\rangle \;;\; [\![Q]\!] \,|\!\rangle^1_s \,|\, x(\widetilde{u}).[\![P]\!])$$

$$[\![\mathtt{timer}^n(y(\widetilde{u}).P, Q)]\!] = (x)(s)(\langle\!|\, y(\widetilde{u}).\overline{x}\,\langle\widetilde{u}\rangle \;;\; [\![\mathtt{timer}^{n-1}(y(\widetilde{u}).P, Q)]\!] \,|\!\rangle^1_s \,|\, x(\widetilde{u}).[\![P]\!])$$

It is worth noting that this is not the only function satisfying our goals. We decided to adopt it after several investigations in order to achieve a tradeoff between mathematical elegance and quick understandability.

The encoding of a timer set to 1 behaves as follows: if the input-prefix $y(\widetilde{u})$ can react, the workunit emits the output message $\overline{x}\,\langle\widetilde{u}\rangle$, which triggers the continuation P. In this case, the workunit becomes the null process $\mathbf{0}$, and commits. Otherwise, if the input-prefix cannot react, it triggers the handler, reducing to the time-out continuation Q. It is easy to see that this is the expected behavior. The inductive case is quite similar, because it uses the same workunit set to 1. In this case, however, the event handling process is the recursive encoding of a timer, in which the deadline has approached of one unit. If the input-prefix

$y(\widetilde{u})$ can react, the workunit triggers the time-in continuation P, and commits; otherwise, the workunit runs the handler, and the timer encoding is called recursively.

The proposed encoding has obviously the required behavior, but it is *weak*, i.e. it requires an additional computational step, with respect to the native timer construct. In particular, when the input-prefix reacts, we must trigger the time-in continuation, while the timers in π_t reduce directly. Let us illustrate this issue with an example. The π_t program

$$\mathtt{timer}^n(x(\widetilde{u}).\overline{y}\,\langle\widetilde{z}\rangle, Q) \,|\, \overline{x}\,\langle\widetilde{v}\rangle \,|\, \mathtt{timer}^2(y(\widetilde{w}).R, S)$$

reduces, in one step, in the program

$$\overline{y}\,\langle\widetilde{z}\rangle \,|\, \mathtt{timer}^1(y(\widetilde{w}).R, S)$$

for the rules (STOP) and (PAR). Moreover, this evolves in $R\{\widetilde{z}/\widetilde{w}\}$. The correspondent encoding in $\mathtt{web}\pi$, instead, reduces, with an adjunctive τ step, in the program

$$\overline{y}\,\langle\widetilde{z}\rangle \,|\, (x)(s)(\langle\!|y(\widetilde{w}).\overline{x}\,\langle\widetilde{w}\rangle\ ;\ [\![S]\!]|\!\rangle_s^0 \,|\, x(\widetilde{w}).[\![R]\!])$$

for (COM) and the rules for parallel and time elapsing. The point is that, while in the π_t program the second timer had still a possibility to trigger, in its correspondent encoding the timer has elapsed and the time-out continuation is executed. Fortunately, this issue is harmless, because in π_t we could execute idle steps, applying the rule (IDLE), in order to synchronize with the correspondent encoding in $\mathtt{web}\pi$. In particular, after triggering a timer, we execute an idle step:

$$\overline{y}\,\langle\widetilde{z}\rangle \,|\, \mathtt{timer}^1(y(\widetilde{w}).R, S)$$

reduces with the rule (IDLE) to

$$\overline{y}\,\langle\widetilde{z}\rangle \,|\, \mathtt{timer}^0(y(\widetilde{w}).R, S)$$

and finally to the time-out continuation S.

This example stress out an important difference between π_t and $\mathtt{web}\pi$, i.e. the former is divergent, because it is possible to *idle* the computation for an unlimited period of time, while the latter does not allow to delay reductions to favor idle steps. So, what we are doing is encoding *one* of the many possible computations.

Now we will prove that a simulation exists between π_t processes encodings and the processes themselves. Although it is possible to prove the existence of a simulation avoiding any particular constraints, for the sake of brevity we will show just a restricted proof. We will not allow a process P in a parallel context $\mathsf{C}[\cdot]|P$ to be or to contain *time sensitive* operators (timers or timed workunits) and we use the notation P^-. As a consequence, we will avoid nested timed workunits because it is always possible to extrude by structural congruence and run them in parallel.

Definition 7 (Contexts). Process contexts, *noted* $\mathsf{C}[\cdot]$, *are defined by the following grammar:*

$$\mathsf{C}[\cdot] ::= [\cdot] \mid \mathsf{C}[\cdot]|P^- \mid (x)\mathsf{C}[\cdot]$$

We always assume that when we write $\mathsf{C}[P]$ *the resulting process is well-formed.*

The result can be easily extended to the general case but we got a longer proof. The basic idea behind the extended proof stands in the explanation above. When we introduce time sensitive operators in the context we have to force π_t processes to synchronize with the correspondent encoding in `webπ` applying the rule (IDLE). The inductive case for parallel in the second part of the proof has to be extended with the relative sub-cases for time sensitive operators. This require some space and does not give additional hints about the result. For this reason we do not present here that part.

In order to present the proof we must introduce some preliminary definitions. If $\rightarrow$ is a binary relation, $\rightarrow_n$ is a shorthand for $\underbrace{\rightarrow \dots \rightarrow}_{n}$. We write $\rightarrow^+$ if $\rightarrow_n$ for some $n > 0$. The Barbed Simulation is the basic machinery we use to provide the correctness proof:

Definition 8 (Barbed Simulation). *A barbed simulation* $\mathcal{S}$ *is a binary relation between processes such that* $P\,\mathcal{S}\,Q$ *implies*

1. *if* $P \downarrow x$ *then* $Q \downarrow x$
2. *if* $P \rightarrow P'$ *then* $Q \rightarrow^+ Q'$ *and* $P'\,\mathcal{S}\,Q'$

Barbed similarity is the largest barbed simulation that is closed under contexts. P and Q are barbed similar and we write $P \lesssim Q$ if $P\,\mathcal{S}\,Q$ for some barbed simulation $\mathcal{S}$.

Since we are simulating processes over different systems we need a particular adaptation of the above definition:

Proposition 1 (Barbed Simulation over Different Systems). *Given two different systems* $(\mathbf{P}, \rightarrow_P, \downarrow_P, \equiv_P)$ *and* $(\mathbf{Q}, \rightarrow_Q, \downarrow_Q, \equiv_Q)$, *let us define* $\mathcal{S} = \{(P, Q) \mid P \in \mathbf{P}, Q \in \mathbf{Q}\}$ *such that* $(P, Q) \in \mathcal{S}$ *implies:*

1. *if* $P \downarrow_P x$ *then* $Q \downarrow_Q x$
2. *if* $P \rightarrow_P P'$ *and* $Q \rightarrow_Q^+ Q'$ *then* $P' \equiv_P P''$ *and* $(P'', Q'') \in \mathcal{S}$ *with* $Q'' \equiv_Q Q'$

In the following we consider the two systems $(\mathbf{P}, \rightarrow, \downarrow, \equiv)$ and $(\mathbf{Q}, \rightarrow_t, \downarrow_t, \equiv_t)$ where $\mathbf{P}$ are `webπ` processes and $\mathbf{Q}$ are π_t processes. The following theorem proves that, if a timer encoded by the timed workunit behaves in a certain way, also π_t timers can behave in the same way.

Theorem 1 (Barbed Similarity between $[\![P]\!]$ and P).

$$\forall\, P \in \pi_t,\ \mathsf{C}[[\![P]\!]] \lesssim \mathsf{C}[P]$$

Proof. The relation $\mathcal{S}$ defined as follows is a barbed simulation:

$$\begin{aligned}\mathcal{S} = &\{(\llbracket P\rrbracket, P) \mid P \in \pi_t\} \\ &\cup \{((x)(s)(\langle\!| \overline{x}\langle\widetilde{v}\rangle \,;\, \llbracket Q\rrbracket |\!\rangle_s^0 \mid x(\widetilde{u}).\llbracket P\rrbracket), P\{\widetilde{v}/\widetilde{u}\}) \mid P, Q \in \pi_t\} \\ &\cup \{((x)(s)(\langle\!| y(\widetilde{u}).\overline{x}\langle\widetilde{v}\rangle \,;\, \llbracket Q\rrbracket |\!\rangle_s^0 \mid x(\widetilde{u}).\llbracket P\rrbracket), Q) \mid P, Q \in \pi_t\} \\ &\cup \equiv_t\end{aligned}$$

Let us prove the two conditions required to have a simulation.

1. Firstly, if $\mathsf{C}[\llbracket P\rrbracket] \downarrow x$ then $\mathsf{C}[P] \downarrow_t x$. By induction over contexts:
   (a) **Base Case:** if $\mathsf{C}[\cdot]$ is $[\cdot]$: By induction on the structure of P:
      i. P is not a timer: the statement is obvious, because the encoding in this case is the identity function;
      ii. P is a timer: its encoding does not show any barb, so the statement is banally true;

   (b) **Inductive Case for Restriction**: we have to prove that if $(y)\mathsf{C}[\llbracket P\rrbracket] \downarrow x$ then $(y)\mathsf{C}[P] \downarrow_t x$. If $\mathsf{C}[\llbracket P\rrbracket] \downarrow x$, there are two possible cases:
      i. we restrict the actual name x: $(x)\mathsf{C}[\llbracket P\rrbracket] \downarrow$, so the statement is banally true.
      ii. we restrict the name y, $y \neq x$: if $(y)\mathsf{C}[\llbracket P\rrbracket] \downarrow x$, $(y)\mathsf{C}[P] \downarrow_t x$, so the statement is true.

   (c) **Inductive Case for Parallel**: we have to prove that if $\mathsf{C}[\llbracket P\rrbracket] \mid Q \downarrow x$ then $\mathsf{C}[P] \mid Q \downarrow_t x$:
   if $\mathsf{C}[\llbracket P\rrbracket] \mid Q \downarrow x$, then $\mathsf{C}[\llbracket P\rrbracket] \downarrow x$ or $Q \downarrow x$; moreover, $\mathsf{C}[P] \downarrow_t x$ or $Q \downarrow_t x$ by inductive hypothesis. This means that $\mathsf{C}[P] \mid Q \downarrow_t x$.

2. The second part of the proof consists in showing that if $\mathsf{C}[\llbracket P\rrbracket] \to P'$ then $\mathsf{C}[P] \to_t^+ P''$ and $P' \,\mathcal{S}\, P''$. By induction over contexts:
   (a) **Base Case:** if $\mathsf{C}[\cdot]$ is $[\cdot]$: By induction on the structure of P:
      i. P is not a timer: the encoding of P is the identity function, and this preserves the relation:

      $$\llbracket P\rrbracket{=}P \text{ and } \llbracket P\rrbracket \to P',\ \text{then } \exists\, P'' \text{ such that } P \to_t P'' \text{ and } P'{=}P''$$

      ii. P is a timer of the shape $\mathtt{timer}^1(y(\widetilde{u}).A, B)$:

      $$\llbracket\mathtt{timer}^1(y(\widetilde{u}).A, B)\rrbracket = (x)(s)(\langle\!| y(\widetilde{u}).\overline{x}\langle\widetilde{u}\rangle \,;\, \llbracket B\rrbracket |\!\rangle_s^1 \mid x(\widetilde{u}).\llbracket A\rrbracket)$$

      This object cannot reduce by itself, it would require some other process running in parallel to trigger $y(\widetilde{u})$ or to make possible for the time to pass. Thus, the statement is obviously true.

      iii. P is a timer of the shape $\mathtt{timer}^n(y(\widetilde{u}).A, B)$:

      $$\llbracket\mathtt{timer}^n(y(\widetilde{u}).A, B)\rrbracket = (x)(s)(\langle\!| y(\widetilde{u}).\overline{x}\langle\widetilde{u}\rangle \,;\, \llbracket\mathtt{timer}^{n-1}(y(\widetilde{u}).A, B)\rrbracket |\!\rangle_s^1 \mid x(\widetilde{u}).\llbracket A\rrbracket)$$

      this object cannot reduce. The same considerations of above holds.

(b) **Inductive case for restriction:** if $\mathsf{C}[\cdot]$ is $(x)\mathsf{C}[\cdot]$, we have to prove that if $(x)\mathsf{C}[\llbracket P \rrbracket] \rightarrow P'$, then $(x)\mathsf{C}[P] \rightarrow_t P''$ and $P' \mathcal{S} P''$. If $(x)\mathsf{C}[\llbracket P \rrbracket] \rightarrow (x)Q$, then $\mathsf{C}[\llbracket P \rrbracket] \rightarrow Q$. By inductive hypothesis, $\mathsf{C}[P] \rightarrow_t Q'$ such that $Q \mathcal{S} Q'$. By structural congruence, $(x)Q \mathcal{S} (x)Q'$.

(c) **Inductive case for parallel:** if $\mathsf{C}[\cdot]$ is $\mathsf{C}[\cdot]|P^-$, we have to prove that if $\mathsf{C}[\llbracket P \rrbracket] \,|\, Q \rightarrow P'$, then $\mathsf{C}[P] \,|\, Q \rightarrow_t P''$ and $P' \mathcal{S} P''$. $\mathsf{C}[\llbracket P \rrbracket] \,|\, Q$ can reduce for three reasons:

i. $\mathsf{C}[\llbracket P \rrbracket] \,|\, Q \rightarrow \mathsf{C}[\llbracket P \rrbracket]' \,|\, Q$: we can say that $\mathsf{C}[\llbracket P \rrbracket] \rightarrow \mathsf{C}[\llbracket P \rrbracket]'$ and, applying the inductive hypothesis, $\mathsf{C}[P] \rightarrow_t \mathsf{C}[P]'$ and $\mathsf{C}[\llbracket P \rrbracket]' \mathcal{S} \mathsf{C}[P]'$. Now, $\llbracket \mathsf{C}[P] \rrbracket' \,|\, Q \,\mathcal{S}\, \mathsf{C}[P]' \,|\, Q$.

ii. $\mathsf{C}[\llbracket P \rrbracket] \,|\, Q \rightarrow \mathsf{C}[\llbracket P \rrbracket] \,|\, Q'$: This case is symmetric with respect to the previous one.

iii. $\mathsf{C}[\llbracket P \rrbracket] \,|\, Q \rightarrow \mathsf{C}[\llbracket P \rrbracket]' \,|\, Q'$: since Q is not time sensitive, we must consider only the following sub-cases:

A. P does not contain a timer: $\llbracket \cdot \rrbracket$ is the identity function, and the statement is obvious.

B. Q triggers a timer in P receiving the message $\overline{y}\,\langle \widetilde{v} \rangle$: the process has the shape $\llbracket \mathtt{timer}^n(y(\widetilde{u}).A, B) \rrbracket \,|\, \overline{y}\,\langle \widetilde{v} \rangle \,|\, Q''$ and reduces to $(x)(s)(\langle\!| \overline{x}\,\langle \widetilde{v} \rangle \,;\, \llbracket \mathtt{timer}^{n-1}(y(\widetilde{u}).A, B) \rrbracket |\!\rangle^0_s \,|\, x(\widetilde{u}).\llbracket A \rrbracket) \,|\, Q''$. On the other side, $\mathtt{timer}^n(y(\widetilde{u}).A, B) \,|\, \overline{y}\,\langle \widetilde{v} \rangle \,|\, Q''$ in one step reduces to $A\{^{\widetilde{v}}/_{\widetilde{u}}\} \,|\, Q''$.
Now, $(x)(s)(\langle\!| \overline{x}\,\langle \widetilde{v} \rangle \,;\, \llbracket \mathtt{timer}^{n-1}(y(\widetilde{u}).A, B) \rrbracket |\!\rangle^0_s \,|\, x(\widetilde{u}).\llbracket A \rrbracket) \,|\, Q''$ is in relation $\mathcal{S}$ with $A\{^{\widetilde{v}}/_{\widetilde{u}}\} \,|\, Q''$ by definition of $\mathcal{S}$ and inductive hypothesis.

C. P contains a timer and Q makes it possible for the time to pass and for the workunit to trigger the handler. The timer can have two possible forms:

– P is a timer of the shape $\mathtt{timer}^1(y(\widetilde{u}).A, B)$:
$\llbracket \mathtt{timer}^1(y(\widetilde{u}).A, B) \rrbracket = (x)(s)(\langle\!| y(\widetilde{u}).\overline{x}\,\langle \widetilde{u} \rangle \,;\, \llbracket B \rrbracket |\!\rangle^1_s \,|\, x(\widetilde{u}).\llbracket A \rrbracket)$
This process reduces to $(x)(s)(\langle\!| y(\widetilde{u}).\overline{x}\,\langle \widetilde{v} \rangle \,;\, \llbracket B \rrbracket |\!\rangle^0_s \,|\, x(\widetilde{u}).\llbracket A \rrbracket)$.
On the other hand, $\mathtt{timer}^1(y(\widetilde{u}).A, B) \rightarrow_t B$ and, by definition of $\mathcal{S}$: $(x)(s)(\langle\!| y(\widetilde{u}).\overline{x}\,\langle \widetilde{v} \rangle \,;\, \llbracket B \rrbracket |\!\rangle^0_s \,|\, x(\widetilde{u}).\llbracket A \rrbracket) \,\mathcal{S}\, B$.

– P is a timer of the shape $\mathtt{timer}^n(y(\widetilde{u}).A, B)$:

$$\llbracket \mathtt{timer}^n(y(\widetilde{u}).A, B) \rrbracket = (x)(s)(\langle\!| y(\widetilde{u}).\overline{x}\,\langle \widetilde{u} \rangle \,;\, \llbracket \mathtt{timer}^{n-1}(y(\widetilde{u}).A, B) \rrbracket |\!\rangle^1_s \,|\, x(\widetilde{u}).\llbracket A \rrbracket)$$

This process reduces to:
$(x)(s)(\langle\!| y(\widetilde{u}).\overline{x}\,\langle \widetilde{v} \rangle \,;\, \llbracket \mathtt{timer}^{n-1}(y(\widetilde{u}).A, B) \rrbracket |\!\rangle^0_s \,|\, x(\widetilde{u}).\llbracket A \rrbracket)$.
On the other hand, $\mathtt{timer}^n(y(\widetilde{u}).A, B) \rightarrow_t \mathtt{timer}^{n-1}(y(\widetilde{u}).A, B)$ by the rule (IDLE) and, by definition of $\mathcal{S}$:

$$(x)(s)(\langle\!| y(\widetilde{u}).\overline{x}\,\langle \widetilde{v} \rangle \,;\, \llbracket \mathtt{timer}^{n-1}(y(\widetilde{u}).A, B) \rrbracket |\!\rangle^0_s \,|\, x(\widetilde{u}).\llbracket A \rrbracket) \,\mathcal{S}\, \mathtt{timer}^{n-1}(y(\widetilde{u}).A, B)$$

6 Conclusions

In this paper we showed how $\mathtt{web}\pi$ is able to cope with timing issues in the same way as Berger-Honda did. To show this we encoded their time construct, called timer, in our timed workunit and we proved a simulation theorem. The proof has some limitations. Firstly, we did not show the proof including time sensitive operators in parallel. As explained this was just for the sake of brevity and we gave some hints about the extension of the proof. A second point, instead, deserves more attention. Unfortunately, the result we presented is not symmetric, in the sense that we proved simply a simulation and not a bisimulation. For this reason our result could be considered too limited. However, we are working on extended results and we are quite confident about related theorems. We strongly rely on the fact that an analogous result can be proved for the viceversa. In particular $\mathsf{C}[P] \lesssim \mathsf{C}[\llbracket P \rrbracket \mid \tau^*]$ should hold. Another interesting result to verify is whether $P \lesssim Q \Leftrightarrow \llbracket P \rrbracket \lesssim \llbracket Q \rrbracket$. Presently, we are also showing how timed constructs of composition languages (e.g. BPEL alarm clocks) can be formalized in this timed calculus. This work can be intended as an extension of we did in [23] for the untimed ones but presenting here this kind of formalization goes beyond the scope of the paper.

Finally, we want to remark the fact that any mathematical rigor becomes pointless without the ability to provide conceptual tools for analysis and reasoning or software tools for verification. In this sense contracts conformance verification between different services should be investigated in the future.

References

1. Business Process Execution Language open issues list. http://www.oasis-open.org/apps/group_public/download.php/11285/wsbpel_issues34.html.
2. Questions on Choreology's coordinated choreographies proposals. http://lists.w3.org/Archives/Public/public-ws-chor/2004Nov/0016.html.
3. Assaf Arkin et al. *Web Service Business Process Execution Language.* OASIS, February 2005.
4. Martin Berger. *Towards Abstractions for Distributed Systems.* PhD thesis, Imperial College, London, 2002.
5. Martin Berger and Kohei Honda. The Two-Phase Commit Protocol in an Extended π-Calculus. In *Proc. EXPRESS'00*, volume 39 of *ENTCS*, 2000.
6. Laura Bocchi, Cosimo Laneve and Gianluigi Zavattaro. A calculus for long running transactions. In *Proc. FMOODS '03*, volume 2884 of *LNCS*. Springer-Verlag, 2003.
7. D. Box, D. Ehnebuske, G. Kakivaya, A. Layman, N. Mendelsohn, H.F. Nielsen, S. Thatte and D. Winer. Simple Object Access Protocol (SOAP) 1.1. [http://www.w3.org/TR/SOAP/], W3C, Note 08, May 2000.
8. Roberto Bruni, Cosimo Laneve and Ugo Montanari. Orchestrating transactions in the join calculus. In *CONCUR 2002*, volume 2421 of *LNCS*. Springer-Verlag, 2002.
9. Roberto Bruni, Hernán Melgratti and Ugo Montanari. Theoretical foundations for compensations in flow composition languages. In *POPL*. ACM, 2005. To appear.
10. Michael Butler and Carla Ferreira. An operational semantics for stac, a langage for modelling long-running businness transactions. In *COORDINATION 2004*, volume 2949 of *LNCS*. Springer-Verlag, 2004.

11. Erik Christensen, Francisco Curbera, Greg Meredith and Sanjiva Weerawarana. *Web Services Description Language (WSDL 1.1)*. W3C, 2001.
12. World Wide Web Consortium. Extensible Markup Language (XML) 1.0. W3C Recommendation, 1998. http://www.w3.org/TR/REC-XML.
13. Philippa Gardner, Cosimo Laneve and Lucian Wischik. The fusion machine (extended abstract). In *CONCUR 2002*, volume 2421 of *LNCS*. Springer-Verlag, 2002.
14. Claudio Guidi, Roberto Lucchi and Manuel Mazzara. A formal framework for web services coordination. In *FOCLASA 2004*. To appear in ENTCS, Elsevier. To appear.
15. Tony Hoare. Long-running transactions. http://research.microsoft.com.
16. Iain Houston, Mark C. Little, Ian Robinson, Santosh K. Shrivastava and Stuart M. Wheater. The CORBA activity service framework for supporting extended transactions. Softw. Pract. Exper. 33(4): 351-373 (2003).
17. Nickolas Kavantzas. Aggregating web services: Choreography and ws-cdl. http://lists.w3.org/Archives/Public/www-archive/2004Jun/att-0008/WS-CDL-April200 4.pdf.
18. Nickolas Kavantzas, David Burdett, Gregory Ritzinger and Yves Lafon. *Web Services Choreography Description Language Version 1.0*. OASIS, October 2004.
19. Cosimo Laneve and Gianluigi Zavattaro. Foundations of web transactions. In *Fossacs'05*, volume 3441 of *LNCS*. Springer-Verlag, 2005.
20. Cosimo Laneve and Gianluigi Zavattaro. Webπ at work. In *In Proc. of Symposium on Trustworthy Global Computing (TGC'05)*, LNCS. Springer-Verlag, 2005. To appear.
21. Frank Leymann. Web Services Flow Language (WSFL 1.0). [http://www-4.ibm.com/software/solutions/webservices/pdf/WSFL.pdf], Member IBM Academy of Technology, IBM Software Group, 2001.
22. Mark Little. Web services transactions: Past, present and future. http://www.idealliance.org/papers/dx_xml03/ html/abstract/05-02-02.html.
23. Roberto Lucchi and Manuel Mazzara. A π-calculus based semantics for ws-bpel. *Journal of Logic and Algebraic Programming (JLAP)*. To appear.
24. Manuel Mazzara and Sergio Govoni. A case study of web services orchestration. In *COORDINATION 2005*, volume 3454 of *LNCS*. Springer-Verlag, 2005.
25. Manuel Mazzara and Roberto Lucchi. A framework for generic error handling in business processes. In *First International Workshop on Web Services and Formal Methods (WS-FM)*, volume 105 of *ENTCS*. Elsevier, 2004.
26. Robin Milner. *Communicating and Mobile Systems: the π-Calculus*. Cambridge University Press, 1999.
27. Robin Milner, Joachim Parrow and David Walker. A Calculus for Mobile Processes. *Journal of Information and Computation*, 100:1–77, 1992.
28. Chris Peltz. Web services orchestration and choreography. *IEEE Computer*, 36(10):46–52, 2003.
29. S. Thatte. XLANG: Web Services for Business Process Design. Microsoft Corporation, 2001.
30. Wil van der Aalst. Pi-calculus versus petri nets: Let us eat 'humble pie' rather than further inflate the.
31. W3C. *HTTP - HyperText Transfer Protocol Specification*. www.w3.org/protocols.

A Compositional Operational Semantics for OWL-S

Barry Norton, Simon Foster, and Andrew Hughes

Department of Computer Science, University of Sheffield, UK
b.norton@dcs.shef.ac.uk

Abstract. Software composition via workflow specifications has received a great deal of attention recently. One reason is the high degree of fit with the encapsulation of software modules in service-oriented fashion. In the Industry, existing workflow languages have been merged to form WS-BPEL, the Business Process Execution Language for Web Services. In the Research community OWL-S, a ontology for web services, has been submitted for standardisation alongside OWL, the Web Ontology Language in which it is expressed. The OWL-S Process Model is based on an abstraction of the common features of industrial workflow languages. On the one hand, WS-BPEL has only informal semantics; on the other, the type of semantics given to ontology-based work tends to be structural rather than computationally oriented. As a result the semantics developed for DAML-S, which led to OWL-S, are still deficient in some regards. In this paper we shall survey the existing semantics and introduce a novel semantics for the latest version of OWL-S that is focussed on the principle of compositionality, so far not tackled.

1 Introduction

A recent article in the inaugural editorial of the *International Journal on Semantic Web and Information Systems* [12] reviewed the properties necessary for work on semantics for the Semantic Web. One fundamental proposed explained was that of *compositionality.* While well understood by the formal methods community as a property that should apply to *behavioural* semantics, the time is right to make this point, and present means to achieve it, to the semantic web (services) community. Generally stated, this principal means that where semantics are given to a formal language, any respective members of the equivalence classes of two terms should semantically compose into the same equivalence class as the semantics given to the composite expressed in the target language.

There are two important *practical* consequences that we should like to draw out in the context of behavioural semantics for service composition. The first is the ability to form a semantic model for an orchestration, step by step matching the workflow by which it is syntactically expressed, as this is built via interaction with an editor. The point is to avoid rebuilding the semantic model from scratch at each step. By rather extending the model *incrementally*, we can hope to represent semantic properties to the user in real time.

M. Bravetti et al. (Eds.): EPEW 2005 and WS-FM 2005, LNCS 3670, pp. 303–317, 2005.

The second consequence relates to the principal of *substitutability*, to which compositionality leads. Practically this allows us to take any member of the equivalence class of the semantics for a term to represent that term as further composition takes place. This allows us to somewhat avoid the state explosion problem, fundamental to concurrent systems, by abstracting from internal states at each point encapsulation takes place, having shown that a so-called *observational equivalence* that we shall review later, is a congruence in our intermediate syntax for semantic translation. Such an observational theory, allowing this abstraction, is the basis of the process calculus CCS [5] which is extended with mobility to form the Pi-Calculus [6], the inspiration for much work in workflow-oriented service composition.

Our previous work [8] has demonstrated the compositional modelling of dataflow-oriented software composition using a novel process calculus CaSE, a conservative extension of CCS. This calculus develops on the tradition of encoding the progress of time qualitatively via abstract ticks of a clock related to communication behaviour via the principle of maximal progress [4], *i.e.* where silent actions are preemptive over clock transitions. CaSE introduced the concept of setting scopes under which behaviour is measured by a specific clock, running at a different rate from other such, via an operator that at once 'hides' that clock, *i.e.* makes it both immune from the preemptive effects of outsiders' silent actions and unobservable to outsiders, and makes it preemptive over the clocks that are still open in the outside.

Our previous model was for systems where scheduling is governed in a data-driven fashion according to generalised dataflow graphs and in a serialised fashion, *i.e.* with course-grained interleavings so that the execution of each actor is atomic. In OWL-S this execution model is just one (specifically the *AnyOrder* process type) of several in an algebraic definition of workflow-oriented *processes* — analogous to 'components' in our previous work — defined hierarchically in terms of *performances* — analogous to our previous 'component instances' [3].

Rather than defining a compositional model for a grammar directly based on the Process Model part of the OWL-S ontology, we define a derived formal language, which we called CASheW-S (named for our project on the *Composition And Semantic Enhancement of Web Services*) that has a greater degree of 'composability' than this. In particular we seperate a first class notion of *connection* from the definition of performance. In OWL-S, performances have to be declared with their complete inbound dataflow attached. In CASheW-S, performances and connections between them can be seperately composed in the same way as they are in a graphical editor.

In the following section we will complete and explain our adapted syntax and review its informal semantics. In Section 3 we will present our syntax and operational semantics for a conservative extension to CaSE, which we name *CaSHew-NUtS* for *Calculus for Synchronous Hierarchies extended with Non-deterministic and Un-timed Synchronisations*. With this in place we can present a translation from our CASheW-S syntax into CaSHew-NUtS in Section 4. We compare this to existing approaches in Section 5 and conlude in Section 6.

2 CASheW-S Syntax

As shown in Table 1, processes in CASheW-S are either atomic or composite. Both are named from a set we chose, for the purposes of the semantics, to range over with m. Composite processes are defined in terms of performances of other processes each of which is given a name that, for our purposes, we allow to be ranged over by n and o and, like process names, must be guaranteed unique.

When it comes to the declaration of dataflow, there are two differences from OWL-S, but each allows a direct and compositional translation from the constructs there. We consider first the *Connection* syntax, introduced with the keyword **Connect**. This is a *first class* equivalent to the more restrictive **ValueSource** construct, as well as providing part of the role of the **ValueFunction** construct, in OWL-S. This also allows us to clarify the role of the **Produce** construct, which we cast as a specialisation to these connections rather than a specialisation of performance as in OWL-S, and to introduce the dual **Consume** construct.

Table 1. The CASheW-S Process Type

$$
\begin{array}{rcl}
Process & ::= & \textbf{AtomicProcess}\ m\ AProcess\ |\\
& & \textbf{CompositeProcess}\ m\ CProcess\\
& & \quad ConsumeList\ ProduceList\\
CProcess & ::= & \textbf{Any-Order}\ PerformanceList\ |\\
& & \textbf{Sequence}\ PerformanceList\ |\\
& & \textbf{Split}\ PerformanceList\ |\\
& & \textbf{SplitJoin}\ PerformanceList\ |\\
& & \textbf{ChooseOne}\ PerformanceList\ |\\
& & \textbf{IfThenElse}\ Performance\ Performance\ |\\
& & \textbf{RepeatWhile}\ Performance\ |\\
& & \textbf{RepeatUntil}\ Performance\\
Performance & ::= & \textbf{Perform}\ n\ Process\ DataAggregation\\
Connection & ::= & \textbf{Connect}\ n\ c\ o\ a\ j\\
PerformanceList & ::= & Performance\ |\\
& & (PerformanceList); Performance\ |\\
& & (PerformanceList); Connection\\
DataAggregation & ::= & ValueDataList\\
& & ValueCollectorList\\
ValueData & ::= & \textbf{ValueData}\ a\\
ValueDataList & ::= & \epsilon\ |\ ValueData\ ValueDataTail\\
ValueDataTail & ::= & \epsilon\ |\ ;\ ValueData\ ValueDataTail\\
ValueCollector & ::= & \textbf{ValueCollector}\ a\ k\\
ValueCollectorList & ::= & \epsilon\ |\ ValueCollector\ ValueCollectorTail\\
ValueCollectorTail & ::= & \epsilon\ |\ ;\ ValueCollector\ ValueCollectorTail\\
Consume & ::= & \textbf{Consume}\ a\ n\ b\ j\\
ConsumeList & ::= & \epsilon\ |\ Consume\ ConsumeTail\\
ConsumeTail & ::= & \epsilon\ |\ ;\ Consume\ ConsumeTail\\
Produce & ::= & \textbf{Produce}\ c\ n\ d\\
ProduceList & ::= & \epsilon\ |\ Produce\ ProduceTail\\
ProduceTail & ::= & \epsilon\ |\ ;\ Produce\ ProduceTail
\end{array}
$$

ValueSource and ValueFunction declarations in OWL-S are strictly tied to performances, in particular their implicit destinations, meaning that a performance must declare explicitly its complete in-coming dataflow when composed into a system, and can not be the subject (in the role of destination) to any further dataflow. In CASheW-S we should like to represent the degree of composition appropriate to an interactive editor and so allow connections to be composed as first class entities between any existing performances. As such they must identify two performances, n and o, and respectively the output c of the destination, and the input a of the source. It also declares a (numbered) component of the input, which is to be supplied, j.

Performances can split the inputs of the process being performed into components via the *ValueCollector* construct. This allows the second function of OWL-S *ValueFunctions* to be represented (the actual definition of the associated function is elided, just as it is as an XML literal in OWL-S, but we must know how many communications are needed). Whereas OWL-S performances contain *ValueData*, *ValueFunction* and *ValueSource* declarations, their associated *DataAggregation* construct in CASheW-S contain only *ValueData* and *ValueCollector* declarations. The dataflow that provides the input components of the value collectors, as well as the other inputs not provided as constants via value data declarations (implicitly having only a singleton component, numbered 0), is defined via connections. In our semantics these will become atomic names for channels c^n and a^n_j respectively. OWL-S performances can be compositionally translated since the implicit connections can be immediately composed with the CASheW-S performance.

In order to define a composite process two different type of connections are needed. To define a prototypical input, a, this must be associated with a component, b^n_j, of a performance input (associated with the prototypical input, b, defined by the process performed) of some component performance, n. This type of connection is introduced with the keyword **Consume**. The keyword **Produce**, unlike the one in OWL-S, is the direct dual to this, connecting a performance output, d^n, to the prototypical output, c, of the enclosing composite process. Neither of these constructs requires the use of the poorly named so-called dummy variable 'theParentPerform' used in OWL-S, but can be translated directly from such OWL-S *Produce* and *ValueSource* declarations.

3 CaSHew-NUtS

To provide an operational semantics for the CASheW-S language, we translate each term into the process calculus CaSHew-NUtS, for which the core syntax is defined in Table 2.

This depends on the labels defined in Table 3, which are divided into actions (α, β), on the left, and clocks (ρ, σ), on the right, and gives rise to an operational semantics in terms of a labelled transition system where terms are nodes and the edges represent behaviours labelled from the union of actions and clocks (γ), the latter being indexed from the set $0, 1$ to represent whether they respect maximal

Table 2. Core CaSHew-NUtS Syntax

$$\mathcal{E} ::= \mathbf{0} \mid \Delta \mid \Delta_\sigma \mid \alpha.\mathcal{E} \mid \lfloor\!\lfloor \mathcal{E} \rfloor\!\rfloor \sigma(\mathcal{E}) \mid \lceil\!\lceil \mathcal{E} \rceil\!\rceil \sigma(\mathcal{E}) \mid \mathcal{E} + \mathcal{E} \mid \mathcal{E}|\mathcal{E} \mid \\ \mathcal{E}[a \mapsto b] \mid \mathcal{E} \setminus a \mid \mathcal{E}/\sigma \mid \mathcal{E}/\!\!/\sigma \mid \mu X.\mathcal{E} \mid X$$

Table 3. CaSHew-NUtS Labels

$a, \bar{a}, b, \bar{b}, \cdots \in \Lambda \cup \overline{\Lambda}$		$\rho, \sigma, \cdots \in \mathcal{T}$
$L \subseteq \Lambda$		$T \subseteq \mathcal{T}$
$\mathcal{A} = \Lambda \cup \overline{\Lambda} \cup \{\tau\}$	$\mathcal{L} = \mathcal{A} \cup \mathcal{C}$	$\mathcal{C} = \mathcal{T} \times \{0, 1\}$
$\alpha, \beta, \cdots \in \mathcal{A}$	$\gamma, \delta, \cdots \in \mathcal{L}$	$\rho_i, \sigma_j \cdots \in \mathcal{C}$

Table 4. Derived CaSEew-NUtS Syntax

$$\begin{array}{rll}
\underline{a}.E = a.E + \Delta & \lfloor E \rfloor \sigma(F) = \lfloor\!\lfloor E + \Delta_\sigma \rfloor\!\rfloor \sigma(F) & \Delta_T = \Sigma_{\sigma \in T} \Delta_\sigma \\
\underline{a}_T.E = a.E + \Delta_T & \lceil E \rceil \sigma(F) = \lceil\!\lceil E + \Delta_\sigma \rceil\!\rceil \sigma(F) & \\
\sigma.E = \lceil \mathbf{0} \rceil \sigma(E) & \boldsymbol{a}.E = \Sigma_{i<|\boldsymbol{a}|}\, a_i.\langle a_1 \cdots a_{(i-1)} \cdot a_{(i+1)} \cdots a_{|\boldsymbol{a}|}\rangle.E & \\
\underline{\sigma}_T.E = \lceil \Delta_T \rceil \sigma(E) & \quad \text{where } |\boldsymbol{a}| > 1;\ \langle a \rangle.E = a.E &
\end{array}$$

progress or not. The transition relation is of type $\mathcal{E} \times \mathcal{L} \times \mathcal{E}$, and is the greatest such relation that satisfies the rules in Table 5.

As in CaSE [8], we ensure the well-definedness of the semantics by making the negative definitions in the latter side conditions depend only on auxiliary well-formed sets (so-called initial actions, $\mathcal{IA}$, and initial clocks, $\mathcal{IC}$), rather than the transition relation itself. The main difference is in the effect of maximal progress on, and determinism of, clocks. Whereas the latter principle has an immediate preemptive effect in CaSE, *i.e.* the presence of a τ-transition removes all σ-transitions from the semantics, in CaSHew-NUtS we simply note the effect in the index to the label (*cf.* rule Com4). In particular a σ_1-labelled transition is respectful of maximal progress and deterministic, a σ_0-labelled transition is not.

Regarding determinism, whereas in CaSE the so-called 'time-out' operators $\lfloor E \rfloor \sigma(F)$ and $\lceil E \rceil \sigma(F)$, by which clocks are introduced, overrides previous transitions on that clock, CaSHew-NUtS has variant operators $\lfloor\!\lfloor E \rfloor\!\rfloor \sigma(F)$ and $\lceil\!\lceil E \rceil\!\rceil \sigma(F)$ where the index of the previous clock is simply decremented so that there is at most one deterministic transition, labelled σ_1, per clock σ.

We take advantage of these changes in the semantics by having two hiding operators in CaSHew-NUtS. The first, E/σ, brings hidden clocks back in line with CaSE by only turning into silent actions deterministic, maximal progress-respectful clocks, σ_1. As in CaSE, this both closes the scope of a clock, so that it is neither synchronised, nor open to preemption by, the environment, but is capable of preempting open clocks (a kind of hierarchical scoping, as explained in [8]). In order to exploit the new semantics we have a second hiding operator, $E/\!\!/\sigma$, which allows non-deterministic and non-maximal-progress-respecting clocks to be hidden as well. This allows us to synchronise agents that still have internal work to do, as we shall later consider in giving semantics to the 'Split' operator.

Table 5. Operational Semantics for CaSHew-NUtS

$$\textsf{Idle}\quad \frac{}{\mathbf{0} \xrightarrow{\sigma_1} \mathbf{0}} \qquad\qquad \textsf{Stall}\quad \frac{}{\Delta_\sigma \xrightarrow{\rho_1} \Delta_\sigma}\,1$$

$$\textsf{Act}\quad \frac{}{\alpha.E \xrightarrow{\alpha} E} \qquad\qquad \textsf{Patient}\quad \frac{}{a.E \xrightarrow{\sigma_1} a.E}$$

$$\textsf{Sum1}\quad \frac{E \xrightarrow{\alpha} E'}{E + F \xrightarrow{\alpha} E'} \qquad\qquad \textsf{Sum2}\quad \frac{F \xrightarrow{\alpha} F'}{E + F \xrightarrow{\alpha} F'}$$

$$\textsf{Sum3}\quad \frac{E \xrightarrow{\sigma_i} E' \quad F \xrightarrow{\sigma_j} F'}{E + F \xrightarrow{\sigma_{i \cdot j}} E' + F'}$$

$$\textsf{Com1}\quad \frac{E \xrightarrow{\alpha} E'}{E \mid F \xrightarrow{\alpha} E' \mid F} \qquad\qquad \textsf{Com2}\quad \frac{F \xrightarrow{\alpha} F'}{E \mid F \xrightarrow{\alpha} E \mid F'}$$

$$\textsf{Com3}\quad \frac{E \xrightarrow{a} E', F \xrightarrow{\overline{a}} F'}{E \mid F \xrightarrow{\tau} E' \mid F'} \qquad\qquad \textsf{Com4}\quad \frac{E \xrightarrow{\sigma_i} E' \quad F \xrightarrow{\sigma_j} F'}{E \mid F \xrightarrow{\sigma_{i \cdot j \cdot k}} E' \mid F'}\,b$$

$$\textsf{TO1}\quad \frac{}{\lfloor E \rfloor \sigma(F) \xrightarrow{\sigma_i} F}\,a \qquad\qquad \textsf{TO2}\quad \frac{E \xrightarrow{\sigma_i} E'}{\lfloor E \rfloor \sigma(F) \xrightarrow{\sigma_0} E'}$$

$$\textsf{TO3}\quad \frac{E \xrightarrow{\gamma} E'}{\lfloor E \rfloor \sigma(F) \xrightarrow{\gamma} E'}\,2$$

$$\textsf{STO1}\quad \frac{}{\lceil E \rceil \sigma(F) \xrightarrow{\sigma_i} F}\,a \qquad\qquad \textsf{STO2}\quad \frac{E \xrightarrow{\sigma_i} E'}{\lceil E \rceil \sigma(F) \xrightarrow{\sigma_0} E'}$$

$$\textsf{STO3a}\quad \frac{E \xrightarrow{\alpha} E'}{\lceil E \rceil \sigma(F) \xrightarrow{\alpha} E'}\,2 \qquad\qquad \textsf{STO3b}\quad \frac{E \xrightarrow{\rho_i} E'}{\lceil E \rceil \sigma(F) \xrightarrow{\rho_i} \lceil E' \rceil \sigma(F)}\,1$$

$$\textsf{Hid1}\quad \frac{E \xrightarrow{\sigma_1} E'}{E/\sigma \xrightarrow{\tau} E'/\sigma} \qquad\qquad \textsf{Hid2}\quad \frac{E \xrightarrow{\alpha} E'}{E/\sigma \xrightarrow{\alpha} E'/\sigma}$$

$$\textsf{Hid3}\quad \frac{E \xrightarrow{\rho_i} E'}{E/\sigma \xrightarrow{\rho_i} E'/\sigma}\,1, c$$

$$\textsf{UHid1}\quad \frac{E \xrightarrow{\sigma_i} E'}{E /\!\!/ \sigma \xrightarrow{\tau} E' /\!\!/ \sigma} \qquad\qquad \textsf{UHid2}\quad \frac{E \xrightarrow{\alpha} E'}{E /\!\!/ \sigma \xrightarrow{\alpha} E' /\!\!/ \sigma}$$

$$\textsf{UHid3}\quad \frac{E \xrightarrow{\rho_i} E'}{E /\!\!/ \sigma \xrightarrow{\rho_i} E' /\!\!/ \sigma}\,1, d$$

$$\textsf{Res}\quad \frac{E \xrightarrow{\gamma} E'}{E \setminus a \xrightarrow{\gamma} E' \setminus a}\,\gamma \notin \{a, \overline{a}\} \qquad\qquad \textsf{Rel}\quad \frac{E \xrightarrow{\gamma} E'}{E[f] \xrightarrow{f(\gamma)} E'[f]}$$

$$\textsf{Rec}\quad \frac{E \xrightarrow{\gamma} E'}{\mu X.E \xrightarrow{\gamma} E'\{\mu X.E/X\}}$$

where: 1) $\rho \neq \sigma$
2) $\nexists i \cdot \gamma = \sigma_i$

and: a) $i = 0$ if $\tau \in \mathcal{IA}(E)$, 1 otherwise
b) $k = 0$ if $\tau \in \mathcal{IA}(E \mid F)$, 1 otherwise
c) $\sigma_1 \notin \mathcal{IA}(E)$
d) $\nexists i \cdot \sigma_i \in \mathcal{IA}(E)$

Table 6. Initial Action Set

$$\mathcal{IA}(\mathbf{0}) = \emptyset \qquad \mathcal{IA}(E+F) = \mathcal{IA}(E) \cup \mathcal{IA}(F)$$
$$\mathcal{IA}(\Delta) = \emptyset \qquad \mathcal{IA}(E \mid F) = \mathcal{IA}(E) \cup \mathcal{IA}(F) \cup \{\tau \mid a \in \mathcal{IA}(E) \wedge \overline{a} \in \mathcal{IA}(F)\}$$
$$\mathcal{IA}(\Delta_\sigma) = \emptyset \qquad \mathcal{IA}(\mu X.E) = \mathcal{IA}(E)$$
$$\mathcal{IA}(a.E) = \{a\} \qquad \mathcal{IA}(X) = \emptyset$$
$$\mathcal{IA}(\tau.E) = \{\tau\} \qquad \mathcal{IA}(E \setminus L) = \mathcal{IA}(E) \setminus (L \cup \overline{L})$$
$$\mathcal{IA}(\lfloor E \rfloor \sigma(F)) = \mathcal{IA}(E) \qquad \mathcal{IA}(E/\sigma) = \mathcal{IA}(E) \cup \{\tau \mid \sigma_1 \in \mathcal{IC}(E)\}$$
$$\mathcal{IA}(\lceil E \rceil \sigma(F)) = \mathcal{IA}(E) \qquad \mathcal{IA}(E /\!\!/ \sigma) = \mathcal{IA}(E) \cup \{\tau \mid \sigma_i \in \mathcal{IC}(E)\}$$

Table 7. Initial Clock Set

$$\mathcal{IC}(\mathbf{0}) = \{\sigma_1 \mid \sigma \in \mathcal{T}\}$$
$$\mathcal{IC}(\Delta) = \emptyset$$
$$\mathcal{IC}(\Delta_\sigma) = \{\rho_1 \mid \rho \in \mathcal{T} \wedge \rho \neq \sigma\}$$
$$\mathcal{IC}(a.E) = \{\sigma_1 \mid \sigma \in \mathcal{T}\}$$
$$\mathcal{IC}(\tau.E) = \emptyset$$
$$\mathcal{IC}(\lfloor E \rfloor \sigma(F)) = \mathcal{IC}(E) \cup \{\sigma_1 \mid \tau \notin \mathcal{IA}(E)\} \cup \{\sigma_0 \mid \tau \in \mathcal{IA}(E)\}$$
$$\mathcal{IC}(\lceil E \rceil \sigma(F)) = \mathcal{IC}(E) \cup \{\sigma_1 \mid \tau \notin \mathcal{IA}(E)\} \cup \{\sigma_0 \mid \tau \in \mathcal{IA}(E)\}$$
$$\mathcal{IC}(E+F) = \{\sigma_{i \cdot j} \mid \sigma_i \in \mathcal{IC}(E) \wedge \sigma_j \in \mathcal{IC}(F)\}$$
$$\mathcal{IC}(E \mid F) = \{\sigma_{i \cdot j \cdot (1 - |\{\tau\} \cap \mathcal{IA}(E \mid F)|)} \mid \sigma_i \in \mathcal{IC}(E) \wedge \sigma_j \in \mathcal{IC}(F)\}$$
$$\mathcal{IC}(\mu X.E) = \mathcal{IC}(E)$$
$$\mathcal{IC}(X) = \emptyset$$
$$\mathcal{IC}(E \setminus L) = \mathcal{IC}(E)$$
$$\mathcal{IC}(E/\sigma) = \begin{cases} \emptyset & \text{(if } \sigma_1 \in \mathcal{IC}(E)) \\ \mathcal{IC}(E) & \text{(otherwise)} \end{cases}$$
$$\mathcal{IC}(E /\!\!/ \sigma) = \begin{cases} \emptyset & \text{(if } \exists i \cdot \sigma_i \in \mathcal{IC}(E)) \\ \mathcal{IC}(E) & \text{(otherwise)} \end{cases}$$

In this work we shall consider only deterministic clocks so we derive the CaSE timeout operator, and several other derived operators used in that system, as follows:
A symmetric relation $\mathcal{R} \subseteq \mathcal{P} \times \mathcal{P}$ is a *weak bisimulation* if whenever$\langle P, Q \rangle \in \mathcal{R}$:

- If $P \xrightarrow{\gamma} P'$, $\gamma \neq \tau$, then $\exists Q' \cdot Q \xrightarrow{\tau}^* \xrightarrow{\gamma} \xrightarrow{\tau}^* Q'$ and $\langle P', Q' \rangle \in \mathcal{R}$
- If $P \xrightarrow{\tau} P'$ then $\exists Q' \cdot Q \xrightarrow{\tau}^* Q'$ and $\langle P', Q' \rangle \in \mathcal{R}$

We say that P is *weakly equivalent* to Q and write $P \approx Q$, if $\langle P, Q \rangle \in \mathcal{R}$ for some weak bisimulation $\mathcal{R}$.

A symmetric relation $\mathcal{R} \subseteq \mathcal{P} \times \mathcal{P}$ is a *temporal observation congruence* if whenever $\langle P, Q \rangle \in \mathcal{R}$:

1. $P \xrightarrow{\alpha} P'$ implies $\exists Q'. Q \xrightarrow{\tau}^* \xrightarrow{\alpha} \xrightarrow{\tau}^* Q'$ and $P' \approx Q'$.
2. $P \xrightarrow{\sigma} P'$ implies $\exists Q'. Q \xrightarrow{\sigma} Q'$ and $\langle P', Q' \rangle \in \mathcal{R}$.

Proposition 1. *Compositionality*
Temporal observation congruence is compositional through all operators.

Proposition 2. *Full Abstraction*
Temporal observation congruence is the coarsest congruence contained in temporal weak bisimulation.

4 CASheW-S Semantics in CaSHew-NUtS

In the semantic translation from the CASheW-S to the CaSHew-NUtS language we will use the variables in Table 8.

When we want to represent a collection we will use the corresponding capital, for instance A is a set of inputs; we abuse this syntax slightly by allowing lists to be represented the same way so that G represents, for instance, a consume list as defined in the CASheW-S syntax. Finally Q stretches the notation further by representing a CASheW-S performance list which has connections, as well as performances, as members and strictly has a performance at the head (and is expanded by '*snoc*ing', *i.e.* adding new members to the tail, and decomposed by reverse tail recursion).

At the top level we look at the semantics of processes. Our main semantic function $[\![]\!]$ is of type p -> m -> A -> C -> $\mathcal{E}$ (which then composes with the CaSHew-NUtS semantic function to derive a labelled transition system). There are two possibilities matched by this function: the atomic process and the composite process.

For an atomic process the process name must match the one declared syntactically, the inputs and outputs must match those semantically associated with the AProcess, the syntactic nature of which we have left open. One possibility is to consider all services as grounded in WSDL and having 'functional' behaviour, *i.e.* with all inputs required, and all outputs produced, at every execution. In this case all AProcess semantics will take the form shown in Figure 1, generalised

Table 8. Variables

p	: Process	q	: Performance
m	: Process Name	n, o	: Performance Name
a, b	: (Process) Input	a_j^n, b_j^o	: (Performance) Input Component
c, d	: (Process) Output	c^n, d^o	: (Performance) Broadcast Output
g	: Consume	u	: Value Data
h	: Produce	v	: Value Collector
w	: AProcess	z	: CProcess

Table 9. Process Semantics

$$
\begin{aligned}
&{}^m[\![\mathbf{AtomicProcess}\ m\ w]\!]_C^A = {}^m[\![w]\!]_C^A \\
&{}^m[\![\mathbf{CompositeProcess}\ m\ z\ G\ H]\!]_C^A \\
&\qquad = ({}^m[\![z]\!]_{C^m}^{A^m} \mid [\![G]\!]_\emptyset^A \mid [\![H]\!]_C^\emptyset) \setminus A^m \cup C^m \,/\, \{\sigma^{c^n} \mid c^n \in C^m\}
\end{aligned}
$$

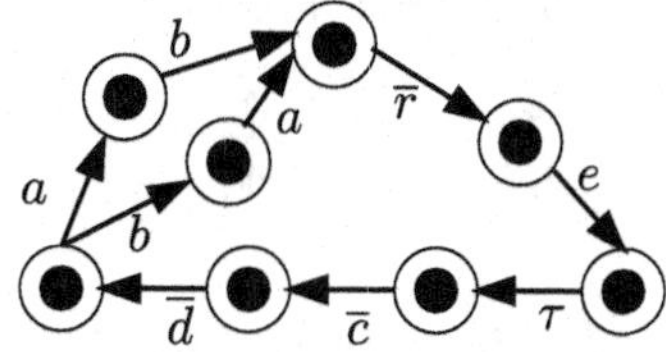

Fig. 1. Example AProcess Semantics

for different numbers of inputs and outputs, and the match will be syntactically based on a representation of WSDL. Our aim in the wider context, however, is to plug in a semantic translation of a choreography language at this point.

WSMO has proposed that two process models should be associated with a service to be properly described [11]. One, which we concentrate on in this paper, is named the *orchestration* and focuses on how the behaviour of a composite process is formed from the behaviour of its component services. The *choreography*, on the other hand establishes, in terms of interaction, how a client should interact with the service. There are many forms that this could take, and as yet little agreement, but our own previous work [9] has generalised on the ideas of *interface automata* [2].

We previously concentrated on data-driven scheduling of generalised dataflow-oriented systems, and showed how to accommodate statefulness, optional inputs and non-determinism in semantics such a scheme. In particular, automata allow us to easily mix statefulness and non-determinism, by representing the internal behaviour with an explicit silent action τ or choice between these. To these transition labels for inputs and outputs (we overline outputs as is usual in CCS) we add *'scheduling signals'* that allow us to be explicit about *'readiness'* for execution. The signal r signifies readiness (and can be non-deterministically offered alongside further inputs to show that these are optional), and is followed by signal e, which signifies permission to execute.

All of these features are widely claimed necessary in the composition of semantic web services, where the notion of service is as much based on work in agents as on SOAP/WSDL web services. The Any-Order composite process is given informal semantics as interleaving execution of the components explicitly according to their readiness to execute (based on inputs as well as non-data preconditions, from which we abstract).

The guiding principle for our semantics will therefore be drawn from our existing model scheme [8], where the prototypical level (here called processes, there components) are described in terms of such automata, and where compositions at the instance level (here called performances, there component instances) will be given a compositional semantics by means of a 'token passing game', synchronised by clocks. The ability to turn such clocks into silent actions, away from which we can abstract away in our equivalence theory in temporal observation congruence, gives us a means to form such an interface automaton (with no explicit clocks) for a composite process. As shown, the inputs and outputs for such are based on the Produces and Consumes contained, the other inputs and

Table 10. Produce and Consume Semantics

$$[\![\textbf{Consume}\ a\ n\ b\ j]\!]^{\{a\}}_{\emptyset} = \mu X.a.\overline{b^n_j}.X$$
$$[\![\textbf{Produce}\ c\ n\ d]\!]^{\emptyset}_{\{c\}} = \mu X.\underline{d^n}.\overline{c}.X$$

outputs of the composite CProcess being restricted away. At the same time, the clocks that coordinate the outputs, as described later, are hidden according to maximal progress.

Table 10 shows the semantics that are given to Consume and Produce declarations. In basic terms, these cyclically convert from process inputs to performance inputs, and from performance outputs to process outputs, respectively. The underlining in the syntax, as defined in the derived syntax, represents the timing of the two communications involved: the initial input is *'patient'*, meaning that an unspecified amount of time can pass on all clocks (*cf.* rule Patient) while the agent waits for the input; the subsequent output is *'insistent'* meaning that this communication is instantaneous, *i.e.* can be measured on no clock. This is represented in transition diagrams for these two agents shown in Figures 2 and 3 respectively. The double circle means that any clock not explicitly shown *'idles'*, *i.e.* has a self-transition at the state; the single circle means that any clock not explicitly shown cannot tick, *i.e.* has no transitions.

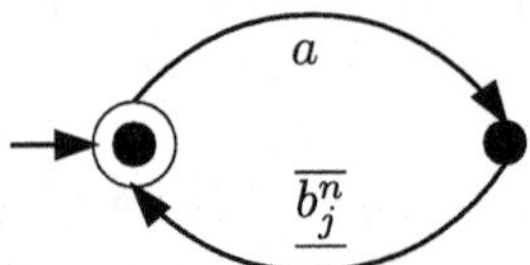

Fig. 2. Consume Semantics

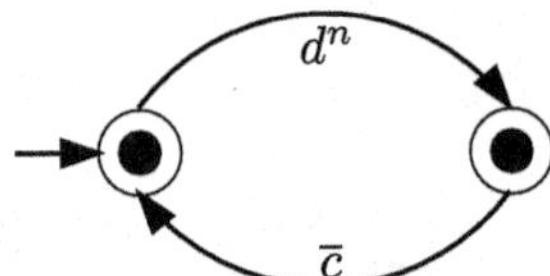

Fig. 3. Produce Semantics

Table 11. Data Aggregation Semantics

$$^{x}[\![K;L]\!]^{A^L \cup A^K}_{C^K \cup C^L} = {}^{x}[\![K]\!]^{A^K}_{C^K} \mid {}^{x}[\![L]\!]^{A^L}_{C^L}$$

Table 12. General Composition Semantics

$$[\![\textbf{ValueData}\ a]\!]_{\{a\}} = \mu X.\overline{a}.X$$
$$^{n}[\![\textbf{ValueCollector}\ a\ k]\!]^{\{a^n_j \mid j<k\}}_{a} = \mu X.\langle a^n_j \mid j<k\rangle.\tau.\underline{\overline{a}}.X$$

These agents are composed, to make a ConsumeList and ProduceList respectively, according to the general composition semantics shown in Table 12 (where x can stand for any symbol, including the absence of any such, and K and L any non-bracketed list, *i.e.* any list in the CASheW-S syntax except the PerformanceList). This is based directly on parallel composition and the accumulation of inputs and outputs.

Table 13. Performance Semantics

$$^{(m,n)}[\![\textbf{Perform}\ n\ p\ U\ V]\!]^{\{a_0^n \mid a\in A^m \wedge a\notin C^U \wedge a\notin C^V\}\cup A^V}_{\{c^n \mid c\in C^m\}}$$
$$= ([\![U]\!]_{C^U} \mid [\![V]\!]^{A^V}_{C^V} \mid {}^m[\![p]\!]^{A^m}_{C^m}[\{a \mapsto a_0^n \mid a \in A^m \wedge a \notin C^U \wedge a \notin C^V\}]$$
$$\mid \Pi_{c\in C^m}\mu X.\underline{c}_{\sigma^{c^n}}.\lceil \mu Y.\underline{\overline{c^n}}_{\sigma^m}.Y\rceil\sigma^{c^n}(X)) \setminus C^U \cup C^V \cup C^m$$

Table 14. Connection Semantics

$$^m[\![\textbf{Connect}\ n\ c\ o\ a\ j]\!] = \mu X.\, c^n.\,\underline{\overline{a_j^o}}.\sigma^{c^n}.\,X$$

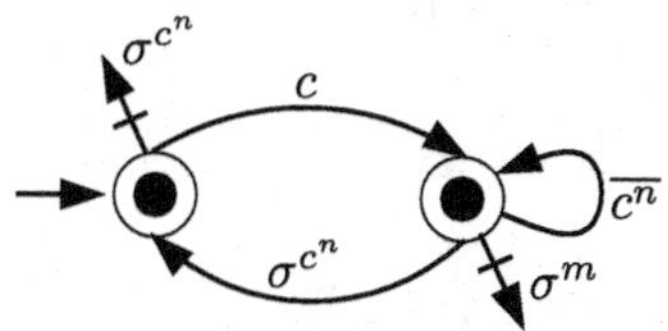

Fig. 4. Broadcast Semantics

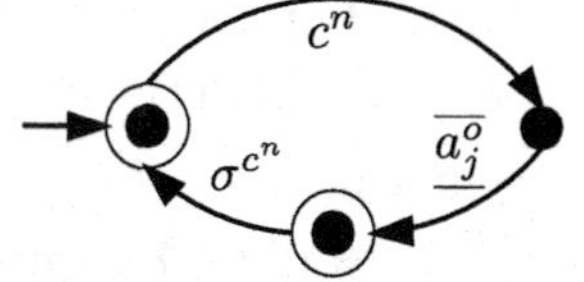

Fig. 5. Connection Semantics

This composition is also used in forming ValueDataLists and ValueCollectorLists from the individual semantics shown in Table 11.

Using this we are able to form semantics for performances as shown in Table 13.

Table 15. CProcess Semantics

$$^m[\![\textbf{AnyOrder}\ Q]\!]^A_C = {}^m_{an}[\![Q]\!]^A_C \setminus t \,/\, \sigma^m$$
$$^m[\![\textbf{Sequence}\ Q]\!]^A_C = {}^m_{se}[\![Q]\!]^A_C \setminus t \,/\, \sigma^m$$
$$^m[\![\textbf{Split}\ Q]\!]^A_C = ({}^m_{sp}[\![Q]\!]^A_C \mid \mu X.\sigma^m.\overline{r}.e.\sigma^m.\sigma^m.X) /\!\!/ \sigma^m$$
$$^m[\![\textbf{SplitJoin}\ Q]\!]^A_C = ({}^m_{sj}[\![Q]\!]^A_C \mid \mu X.\sigma^m.\overline{r}.e.\sigma^m.\sigma^m.X) /\!\!/ \sigma^m$$
$$^m[\![\textbf{ChooseOne}\ Q]\!]^A_C = ({}^m_{co}[\![Q]\!]^A_C \mid \mu X.\underline{r^i.\overline{r}.e.\overline{e^i}}_{\sigma^m}.\sigma^m.X) \setminus \{e^i, r^i\} \,/\, \sigma^m$$
$$^m[\![\textbf{IfThenElse}\ \ \textbf{Perform}\ n\ p^n\ U^n\ V^n\ \ \textbf{Perform}\ o\ p^o\ U^o\ V^o]\!]^{A^n\cup A^o}_{C^n\cup D^o}$$
$$= ({}^{(m,n)}[\![\textbf{Perform}\ n\ p^n\ U^n\ V^n]\!]^{A^n}_{C^n}[e \mapsto e^n, r \mapsto r^n] \mid$$
$$^{(m,o)}[\![\textbf{Perform}\ o\ p^o\ U^o\ V^o]\!]^{A^o}_{C^o}[e \mapsto e^o, r \mapsto r^o] \mid$$
$$\mu X.(\tau.\underline{r^n.\overline{r}.e.\overline{e^n}}_{\sigma^n}.\sigma^n.X\ + \tau.\underline{r^o.\overline{r}.e.\overline{e^o}}_{\sigma^o}.\sigma^o.X))$$
$$\setminus \{e^n, e^o, r^n, r^o\} \,/\, \sigma^n \,/\, \sigma^o$$
$$^m[\![\textbf{RepeatWhile}\ \textbf{Perform}\ n\ p\ U\ V]\!]^A_C$$
$$= ({}^{(m,n)}[\![\textbf{Perform}\ n\ p\ U\ V]\!]^A_C[e \mapsto e^i, r \mapsto r^i] \mid$$
$$\mu X.(\tau.\underline{r^i.\overline{r}.e.\overline{e^i}}_{\sigma^n}.\sigma^n.\mu Y.(\tau.X + \tau.\underline{r^i.\overline{e^i}}_{\sigma^n}.\sigma^n.Y)$$
$$+\tau.\overline{r}.e.X)) \setminus \{e^i, r^i\} \,/\, \sigma^n$$
$$^m[\![\textbf{RepeatUntil}\ \textbf{Perform}\ n\ p\ U\ V]\!]^A_C$$
$$= ({}^{(m,n)}[\![\textbf{Perform}\ n\ p\ U\ V]\!]^A_C[e \mapsto e^i, r \mapsto r^i] \mid$$
$$\mu X.\underline{r^i.\overline{r}.e.\overline{e^i}}_{\sigma^n}.\sigma^n.\mu Y.(\tau.X+$$
$$\tau.\underline{r^i.\overline{e^i}}_{\sigma^n}.\sigma^n.Y)) \setminus \{e^i, r^i\} \,/\, \sigma^n$$

Table 16. Connection Composition Semantics

$$ {}^{m}_{x}[\![(Q);\mathbf{Connect}\ n\ c\ o\ a\ j]\!]^{A}_{C} = {}^{m}[\![\mathbf{Connect}\ n\ c\ o\ a\ j]\!]^{A}_{C} \mid {}^{m}_{x}[\![Q]\!]^{A}_{C} $$

Table 17. Performance Composition Semantics

$$
\begin{aligned}
&{}^{m}_{an}[\![\mathbf{Perform}\ n\ p\ U\ V]\!]^{A}_{C}\\
&\quad = ({}^{(m,n)}[\![\mathbf{Perform}\ n\ p\ U\ V]\!]^{A}_{C}[e \mapsto e^{i}, r \mapsto r^{i}] \mid\\
&\quad\ \mu X.\underline{r^{i}}_{\{\sigma^{m},\sigma^{n}\}}.(\underline{\overline{r}.e.\overline{e^{i}}}_{\{\sigma^{m},\sigma^{n}\}}.\underline{\sigma^{n}}_{\sigma^{m}}.\lfloor \underline{\overline{t}}.\underline{\sigma^{m}}_{\sigma^{n}}.X \rfloor \sigma^{m}(X) +\\
&\quad\ \underline{t.\overline{e^{i}}.\sigma^{n}}_{\sigma^{m}}.\lfloor \underline{\overline{t}}.\underline{\sigma^{m}}_{\sigma^{n}}.X \rfloor \sigma^{m}(X))) \setminus \{e^{i}, r^{i}\}/\sigma^{n}\\
&{}^{m}_{an}[\![(Q);\mathbf{Perform}\ n\ p\ U\ V]\!]^{A^{Q}\cup A^{n}}_{C^{Q}\cup C^{n}}\\
&\quad = {}^{m}_{an}[\![\mathbf{Perform}\ n\ p\ U\ V]\!]^{A^{n}}_{C^{n}} \mid {}^{m}_{an}[\![Q]\!]^{A^{Q}}_{C^{Q}}
\end{aligned}
$$

$$
\begin{aligned}
&{}^{m}_{se}[\![\mathbf{Perform}\ n\ p\ U\ V]\!]^{A}_{C}\\
&\quad = ({}^{(m,n)}[\![\mathbf{Perform}\ n\ p\ U\ V]\!]^{A^{n}}_{C^{n}}[e \mapsto e^{i}, r \mapsto r^{i}] \mid\\
&\quad\ \mu X.\underline{r^{i}.\overline{r}.e.\overline{e^{i}}}_{\{\sigma^{m},\sigma^{n}\}}.\underline{\sigma^{n}}_{\sigma^{m}} \lfloor \underline{\overline{t}}.\underline{\sigma^{m}}_{\sigma^{n}}.X \rfloor \sigma^{m}(X))/\sigma^{n} \setminus \{r^{i}, e^{i}\}\\
&{}^{m}_{se}[\![(Q);\mathbf{Perform}\ n\ p\ U\ V]\!]^{A^{Q}\cup A^{n}}_{C^{Q}\cup C^{n}}\\
&\quad = ({}^{n}[\![\mathbf{Perform}\ n\ p\ U\ V]\!]^{A^{n}}_{C^{n}}[e \mapsto e^{i}, r \mapsto r^{i}] \mid {}^{m}_{se}[\![Q]\!]^{A^{Q}}_{C^{Q}}[t \mapsto t^{i}] \mid\\
&\quad\ \mu X.\underline{t^{i}}_{\sigma^{n}}.\underline{r^{i}.\overline{e^{i}}}_{\{\sigma^{m},\sigma^{n}\}}.\underline{\sigma^{n}}_{\sigma^{m}} \lfloor \underline{\overline{t}}.\underline{\sigma^{m}}_{\sigma^{n}}.X \rfloor \sigma^{m}(X))/\sigma^{n} \setminus \{r^{i}, e^{i}\}
\end{aligned}
$$

$$
\begin{aligned}
&{}^{m}_{sp}[\![\mathbf{Perform}\ n\ p\ U\ V]\!]^{A}_{C}\\
&\quad = ({}^{(m,n)}[\![\mathbf{Perform}\ n\ p\ U\ V]\!]^{A}_{C}[e \mapsto e^{i}, r \mapsto r^{i}] \mid\\
&\quad\ \mu X.\underline{r^{i}}_{\{\sigma^{m},\sigma^{n}\}}.\underline{\sigma^{m}.\sigma^{m}}_{\sigma^{n}}.\underline{\overline{e^{i}}}_{\{\sigma^{m},\sigma^{n}\}}.\underline{\sigma^{m}}_{\sigma^{n}}.X) \setminus \{e^{i}, r^{i}\}/\sigma^{n}\\
&{}^{m}_{sp}[\![(Q);\mathbf{Perform}\ n\ p\ U\ V]\!]^{A^{Q}\cup A^{n}}_{C^{Q}\cup C^{n}}\\
&\quad = {}^{m}_{sp}[\![\mathbf{Perform}\ n\ p\ U\ V]\!]^{A^{n}}_{C^{n}} \mid {}^{m}_{sp}[\![Q]\!]^{A^{Q}}_{C^{Q}}
\end{aligned}
$$

$$
\begin{aligned}
&{}^{m}_{sj}[\![\mathbf{Perform}\ n\ p\ U\ V]\!]^{A}_{C}\\
&\quad = ({}^{(m,n)}[\![\mathbf{Perform}\ n\ p\ U\ V]\!]^{A}_{C}[e \mapsto e^{i}, r \mapsto r^{i}] \mid\\
&\quad\ \mu X.\underline{r^{i}}_{\{\sigma^{m},\sigma^{n}\}}.\underline{\sigma^{m}.\sigma^{m}}_{\sigma^{n}}.\underline{\overline{e^{i}}}_{\{\sigma^{m},\sigma^{n}\}}.\underline{\sigma^{n}}_{\sigma^{m}}.\underline{\sigma^{m}}_{\sigma^{n}}.X) \setminus \{e^{i}, r^{i}\}/\sigma^{n}\\
&{}^{m}_{sj}[\![(Q);\mathbf{Perform}\ n\ p\ U\ V]\!]^{A^{Q}\cup A^{n}}_{C^{Q}\cup C^{n}}\\
&\quad = {}^{m}_{sj}[\![\mathbf{Perform}\ n\ p\ U\ V]\!]^{A^{n}}_{C^{n}} \mid {}^{m}_{sj}[\![Q]\!]^{A^{Q}}_{C^{Q}}
\end{aligned}
$$

$$
\begin{aligned}
&{}^{m}_{co}[\![\mathbf{Perform}\ n\ p\ U\ V]\!]^{A}_{C}\\
&\quad = {}^{(m,n)}[\![\mathbf{Perform}\ n\ p\ U\ V]\!]^{A}_{C}[e \mapsto e^{i}, r \mapsto r^{i}]/\sigma^{n}\\
&{}^{m}_{co}[\![(Q);\mathbf{Perform}\ n\ p\ U\ V]\!]^{A^{Q}\cup A^{n}}_{C^{Q}\cup C^{n}}\\
&\quad = {}^{m}_{co}[\![\mathbf{Perform}\ n\ p\ U\ V]\!]^{A^{n}}_{C^{n}} \mid {}^{m}_{co}[\![Q]\!]^{A^{Q}}_{C^{Q}}
\end{aligned}
$$

This composes the semantics of the ValueDataList and ValueCollectorList with the process being performed, having renamed those inputs not removed by a ValueData or componentised by a ValueCollector to form a single-component performance input (a_0^n), with one agent per process output (Π represents distributed parallel composition) that turns these into broadcast outputs. This broadcast agent is illustrated with the transition diagram in Figure 4. While waiting for a value this is patient in all clocks but is instantaneous in the unique associated clock σ^{c^n}. Once the process output c is received, it will be broadcast as c^n until the associated clock ticks. As we know from the semantics for composite processes, each such clock will be hidden under the conditions of maximal progress. This means that whenever there is an agent that can receive the broadcast, the subsequent silent action will prevent the clock. In this way the instant measured by the clock will necessarily contain each such communication.

We arrange for this communication by giving connections the semantics detailed in Table 14 and illustrated in Figure 5.

This agent patiently waits for the broadcast but then insistently relays this to the recipient performance. Only the value has been passed on will the agent synchronise on the associated clock to signal the end of the broadcast instant. It must wait for this clock before picking up a new value to avoid duplicates.

Having shown the semantics for performances we are now able to continue the semantics for composite processes. At the top level the semantics for CProcess are as shown in Table 15.

The first five types of composite process — Any-Order, Sequence, Split, Split-Join and ChooseOne — are defined over a list of performances and connections and we should therefore like to form a semantics for the list which is open to further composition under the clock σ^m. Since the exact form of composition depends on the process context, we define a family of semantic functions where this is a parameter. These functions are detailed in Table 17. Since the list may also include connections, we include a generic rule for composing these in Table 16.

The other types of composition are expressed directly in terms of their components and we similarly give them direct semantics, using silent transitions to encode the non-deterministic choice that is implicit.

5 Related Work

The original semantics for DAML-S were provided via translation to Petri Nets [7]. As well as problems with providing compositionality for a mathematical semantics for these, the translation was fundamentally non-compositional. Synchronisations were built for the fixed number of performances involved, for each form of composite behaviour, that are not open to the composition of further performances. Furthermore, the semantics was provided for a very early version of DAML-S, the fore-runner to OWL-S, where only control flow and no data flow was described. The question of the effect of data on control flow, which we have modelled as an explicit 'readiness to execute' signal, was therefore not considered at all. This would very much restrict the ability to use that model for analysis.

A more developed operational semantics have been provided in process calculus-like style derived from Concurrent Haskell/Erlang semantics [1]. In this work an intermediate language called *'Core DAML-S'* is treated to structured operational semantics like shown here for CaSHew-NUtS. Unfortunately no compositionality result is provided, or provable, for the Core DAML-S semantics since no equivalence theory is nominated. Furthermore, again the translation from the full process model is non-compositional since fixed size 'spawn' processes are created, as are agents which wait for fixed numbers of synchronisations signalling completion, not open to further composition once formed. Finally, since the dataflow for loop-type processes were not fixed, no semantics were given for these. In our formalism it is feasible nevertheless to offer semantics for the control-flow part of these processes.

6 Conclusions and Future Work

Our intention in establishing compositional operational semantics for OWL-S is twofold. First we should like to implement the semantics to provide an orchestration engine, which we are developing as an open source project in Haskell. The previous semantics have inspired the so-called *DAML-S Virtual Machine* [10], though this has not been made widely available. An informal argument about correctness of the DAML-S Virtual Machine is indirect, based on re-interpretation of the semantics as logical predicates. Our implementation will be more direct, with an inductive datatype directly representing the CaSHew-NUtS syntax and a step function directly representing its operational semantics.

Our second aim is to extend the verification results we have for our previous model [8]. In particular we should like to check the consistency of dataflows in an automatic fashion. In the same way as this has been cast as a system of behavioural types in our previous work [9], we should like to establish a formal link between orchestration and choreography. Whereas these are seperate models in current approaches, our belief is that application developers using service-oriented architectures should assign choreography models at each level of composition and a formal check that this choreography is consistent with the orchestration defined should implicitly check the internal consistency of the orchestration.

References

1. Anupriya Ankolekar, Frank Huch, and Katia Sycara. Concurrent execution semantics of DAML-S with subtypes. In *Proc. 1st Intl. Semantic Web Conference (ISWC2002)*, volume 2342 of *LNCS*, pages 308–332. Springer Verlag, May 2002.
2. L. de Alfaro and T.A. Henzinger. Interface automata. In *Proc. 8th European Soft. Eng. Conference and 9th ACM SIGSOFT International Symposium on Foundations of Soft. Eng. (ESEC/FSE 2001)*, volume 26, 5 of *Software Engineering Notes*, pages 109–120. ACM Press, 2001.
3. David Martin *et al.* OWL-S: Semantic markup for web services. http://www.daml.org/services/owl-s/1.1/overview/, 2004.
4. M. Hennessy and T. Regan. A process algebra for timed systems. *Information and Computation*, 117(2):221–239, March 1995.
5. A. J. R. G. Milner. *Communication and Concurrency.* Prentice Hall, 1989.
6. A. J. R. G. Milner. *Communicating and Mobile Systems: The Pi-Calculus.* Cambrudge University Press, 1999.

7. Srini Narayanan and Sheila A. McIlraith. Simulation, verification and automated composition of web services. In *Proc. 11th Intl. World Wide Web Conference (WWW2002)*, May 7-10 2002.
8. B. Norton, G. Lüttgen, and M. Mendler. A compositional semantic theory for synchronous component-based design. In *14th Intl. Conference on Concurreny Theory (CONCUR '03)*, number 2761 in LNCS. Springer-Verlag, 2003.
9. Barry Norton and Matt Fairtlough. Reactive types for dataflow-oriented software architectures. In Danielle C. Martin, editor, *Proceedings of 4th IEEE/IFIP Conference on Software Architecture (WICSA2004)*, volume P2172, pages 211–220. IEEE Computer Society Press, 2004.
10. Massimo Paolucci, Anupriya Ankolekar, Naveen Srinivasan, and Katia Sycara. The DAML-S virtual machine. In *Proc. 2nd Intl. Semantic Web Conference (ISWC2002)*, volume 2870 of *LNCS*, pages 290–305. Springer Verlag, 2003.
11. Dumitru Roman, Holger Lausen, and Uwe Keller. WSMO final draft. http://www.wsmo.org/TR/d2/v1.1/, February 2005.
12. A. Sheth, C. Ramakrishnan, and C. Thomas. Semantics for the Semantic Web: The implicit, the formal and the powerful. *Intl. Journal on Semantic Web and Information Systems*, 1(1):1–18, 2005.

A Parametric Communication Model for the Verification of BPEL4WS Compositions*

Raman Kazhamiakin and Marco Pistore

DIT, University of Trento,
via Sommarive 14, 38050, Trento, Italy
{raman, pistore}@dit.unitn.it

Abstract. In this paper we describe an approach for the verification of Web service compositions defined by a set of BPEL4WS processes. The key aspect of such a verification task is the model adopted for representing the communications among the services participating to the composition. Indeed, these communications are asynchronous and buffered in the existing execution frameworks, while most verification approaches adopt a synchronous communication model for efficiency reasons. In our approach, we model the asynchronous nature of Web service interactions without introducing buffers, by allowing a reordering of the messages exchanged during these interactions. This way, we can provide an accurate model of a wider class of service composition scenarios, while preserving an efficient performance in verification.

1 Introduction

Web services provide the basis for the development and execution of business processes that are distributed over the network and available via standard interfaces and protocols [9]. Service composition [10] is one of the most promising ideas underlying Web services: new functionalities can be defined and implemented by combining and interacting with pre-existing services. Different standards and languages have been proposed to develop Web service compositions. BPEL4WS (Business Process Execution Language for Web Services, BPEL for short) [3] is one of the emerging standards for describing a key aspect for the composition of Web services: the behavior of the service. It provides a core of process description concepts that allow for the definition of business processes interactions. This core of concepts is used both for defining the internal *business processes* of a participant to a business interaction and for describing and publishing the external *business protocol* that defines the interaction behavior of a participant without revealing its internal behavior.

BPEL opens up the possibility of applying a range of formal techniques to the verification of the behavior of Web services, and different approaches have

* This work is partially funded by the MIUR-FIRB project RBNE0195K5, "Knowledge Level Automated Software Engineering", and by the MIUR-PRIN 2004 project "Advanced Artificial Intelligence Systems for Web Services".

M. Bravetti et al. (Eds.): EPEW 2005 and WS-FM 2005, LNCS 3670, pp. 318–332, 2005.

been defined for verifying BPEL [7,11,13,12,8,15]. We are interested in particular in those techniques that are applied to the verification of BPEL compositions: in this case, we have to verify the behaviors generated by the interactions of a set of BPEL processes, each specifying the workflow and the protocol of one of the services participating to the composition.

A key aspect for this kind of verification is the model adopted for representing the communications among the Web services. Indeed, the actual mechanism implemented in the existing BPEL execution engines is both very complex and implementation dependent. More precisely, BPEL processes exchange messages in an asynchronous way; incoming messages go through different layers of software, and hence through multiple queues, before they are actually consumed in the BPEL activity; and overpasses are possible among the exchanged messages.

On the other hand, most of the approaches proposed for a formal verification of BPEL compositions are based on a synchronous model of communications, which does not require message queues and hence allows for a better performance in verification. This synchronous mechanism relies on some strong hypotheses on the interactions allowed in the composition: at a given moment in time, only one of the components can emit a message, and the receiver of that message is ready to accept it (see e.g., [8]).

In our experience, these hypotheses are not satisfied by many Web service composition scenarios of practical relevance, where critical runs can happen among messages emitted by different Web services. This is the case, for instance, when a Web service can receive inputs concurrently from two different sources, or when a service which is executing a time consuming task can receive a cancellation message before the task is completed.

Our goal is to provide extended composition mechanisms, where the hypotheses on synchronous communications are weakened, but an explicit introduction of message queues is still not required. This way, an accurate modelling is possible for a wider class of service composition scenarios, while an efficient performance is still possible.

In this paper, we propose a parametric model of composition, which is based on synchronous communications, but which allows for a reordering of the exchanged messages in order to model critical runs and message overpasses that may occur in the execution of BPEL processes. More precisely, we define three variants of this mechanism, depending on the degree of reordering allowed in the messages. The first variant, where no reordering is possible, corresponds to the synchronous model of [8]. The second variant permits to reorder only messages sent or received by different partners, that is, it takes into account that a difference between the order of emission and the order of reception of the messages due to the distributed nature of Web services. The third variant, finally, allows for reordering messages also between the same two partners, thus considering message overpasses that can occur in the message queues of the BPEL engines.

For each of the three composition models, we define a validity check, that determines whether the model is adequate for a given composition scenario. Moreover, we define a composition and verification algorithm that is correct and complete for those scenarios that pass the validity check. We have implemented the proposed approach and we report our preliminary experiments in its application to a case study based on a Virtual Travel Agency domain.

The paper is structured as follows. In Sect. 2 we introduce several instances of the case study that motivate the necessity to consider different variants of communication mechanism. Section 3 explains how BPEL processes can be translated into state transition systems. We give the formal definition of the extended composition and the notion of composition validity in Sect. 4, and describe different models basing on these notions in Sect. 5. Section 6 explains the architecture of the described analysis framework and reports the results of its experimental evaluation. Conclusions and future work are presented in Sect. 7.

2 Modelling BPEL Compositions

In order to illustrate the problem of modelling BPEL compositions we consider several variants of the Virtual Travel Agency domain. The goal of the Virtual Travel Agency is to provide a combined flight and hotel booking service by integrating separate, independent existing services: a Flight booking service, and a Hotel booking service. Thus, the composition describes the interactions of four partners: User, Virtual Travel Agency (VTA), Hotel and Flight services (see Fig. 1.a). We model the composition using BPEL specifications that describe the workflows and the interactions of the four partners.

Example 1: Tickets Reservation Scenario. The case study describes the behavior exposed by VTA that allows the user to book a flight to the specified place and reserve a room in the hotel at that place for a given period of time. Provided a reservation offer, the user can accept or reject it, sending a corresponding message to the VTA service (Fig. 1.b).

The Flight booking service becomes active upon a request for a given location (e.g., Paris) and a given period of time (e.g., August, 15-20). In the case the booking is not possible, this is signaled to the requestor, and the protocol terminates. Otherwise, the requestor is notified with an offer information and the protocol stops waiting for either a positive or negative acknowledgment. In case of positive answer the flight is successfully booked and the reservation ticket is sent, otherwise the interaction terminates with failure. Figure 1.c represents the protocol provided by the Flight booking service. The protocol of the Hotel service is similar.

The behavior of the VTA is as follows. Having received a reservation request from the user, VTA interacts with Flight and Hotel services to obtain ticket offers and expects either a negative answer if this is not possible (in which case the user is notified and the protocol terminates failing), or provides the user with an offer indicating hotel, flights and cost of the trip. After that the user may either accept or refuse the offer, and in the first case VTA provides the user with the tickets obtained from Hotel and Flight. The diagram corresponding to the BPEL protocol of VTA is represented in Fig. 1.d.

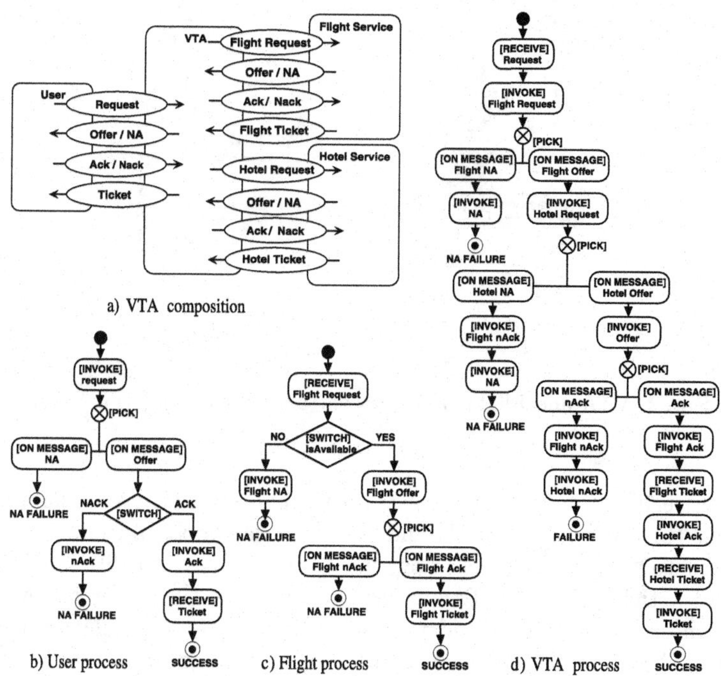

Fig. 1. Composition participants

The scenario exhibits an important property that allows for a very simple communication mechanism. At any moment of time only one message can be emitted by one of the partners. Moreover, such a message is acceptable by the corresponding receiver. Using the terminology of [8], the composition model satisfies the *synchronous compatibility*, *autonomy* and *lossless composition* properties. As a consequence, a synchronous communication model can be used to define the composition without loosing completeness of behaviors.

Example 2: Reservation with Cancellation. Unfortunately, the simplified communication model of the previous example is not applicable to all kinds of interactions. An indicative example is the business process with event handlers. Let us consider an extension of the above case study, such that the User, after having acknowledged the provided offer, can decide to cancel booking operation. In this case the User sends a `Cancel` message to the VTA process and waits for an outcome of the cancellation. The cancellation is forwarded to the Flight process (and similarly to the Hotel process, we omit this for the sake of simplicity). The latter waits a certain time for a cancellation message and if it is received, sends the notification about successful cancellation. Or, if time runs out, sends a ticket to the VTA thus forcing the failure of cancellation; then it consumes the cancellation sent by the VTA and ignores it. The excerpts of the corresponding process specifications are represented in Fig. 2.

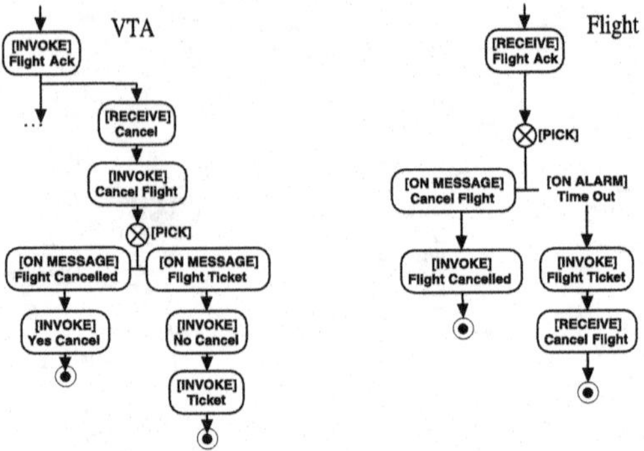

Fig. 2. VTA and Flight processes parts for the cancellation management

The verification under the synchronous communication model is not able to manage this example correctly and reports a deadlock. Indeed, if the Flight service fails to wait for a cancellation, the `onAlarm` activity is fired and it then tries to send a ticket to the VTA process. Meanwhile, the latter receives a cancellation message from User and then tries to send the cancellation to the Flight service. Therefore both services will try to send messages to each other and the composition is in a deadlock, since this is not acceptable by the synchronous semantics.

This deadlock is not real, in the sense it does not occur in real BPEL engines; since the Web services communications are asynchronous, and the message emission is not blocking, both processes will emit messages to each other. Both messages will be consumed then and the composition terminates correctly.

The problem we are facing here is that the synchronous model is too strict. The message delivery and processing may require a certain time, thus leading to situations where concurrent message emissions take place. These situations, however, are not allowed in the synchronous communication model. In order to verify correctly the considered example, a relaxed model is needed that allows to consider these concurrent message emissions.

Example 3: Extended Cancellation Scenario Let us consider a further modification of the case study. Now the fact that the cancellation is not possible is signalled with the special messages: `NoCancel` for the User and `NoFlightCancel` for the VTA process. Having sent the cancellation to the Flight service, the VTA waits for the message indicating that the cancellation is possible or not. In the latter case it waits for the ticket and sends a ticket to the User. The Flight service on the other side behaves as before with the only difference that, after emitting the ticket and receiving the cancellation, it sends a notification about cancellation rejection (i.e. `NoFlightCancel` message). The corresponding diagrams are represented in Fig. 3.

Even if one verifies the example allowing for concurrent message emission the following incorrect scenario will result. The Flight service sends a ticket and

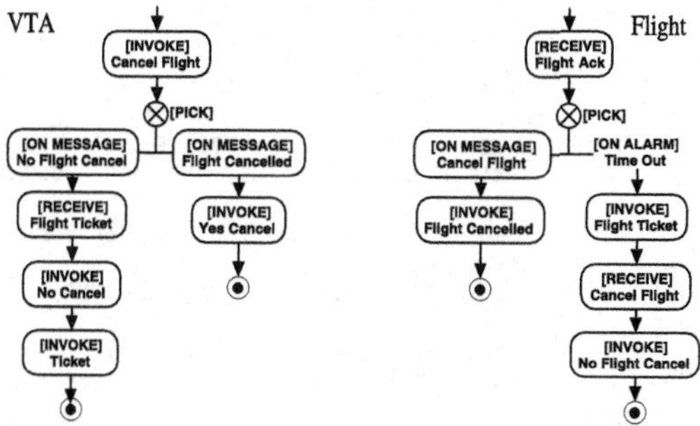

Fig. 3. VTA and Flight processes parts for the complex cancellation management

waits for a cancellation, the VTA process sends a cancellation, the Flight service in turn rejects a cancellation and finishes. The VTA has received a ticket and then a cancellation rejection, but it is not able to process the messages in this order. Only if the execution of processes in the run-time environment allows for reordering of messages (which is the case for existing implementations) the deadlock disappears, since the cancellation rejection can be processed before the ticket message.

This example shows a necessity not only to consider systems which do not follow the synchronous communication semantics, but also to accept less restrictive models where message reordering is allowed.

This chain can be further prolonged, leading to more complex communication models. One can think of lossy channels, complex ordering conditions, complex queue models etc. Notice, however, that each model requires additional assumptions on the environment where the analyzed system is supposed to execute. These conditions are not always possible to be enforced, or verified. Moreover, the complexity of the verification problem being applied to a certain model significantly varies up to undecidability.

In the following we will introduce the generalized model of the composition, suitable for the analysis of certain classes of communication models.

3 BPEL Processes as State Transition Systems

BPEL provides an operational description of the (stateful) behavior of Web services on top of the service interfaces defined in their WSDL specifications. An abstract BPEL description identifies the partners of a service, its internal variables, and the operations that are triggered upon the invocation of the service by some of the partners. Operations include assigning variables, invoking other services and receiving responses, forking parallel threads of execution, and nondeterministically picking one amongst different courses of actions. Standard imperative constructs such as if-then-else, case choices, and loops, are also supported.

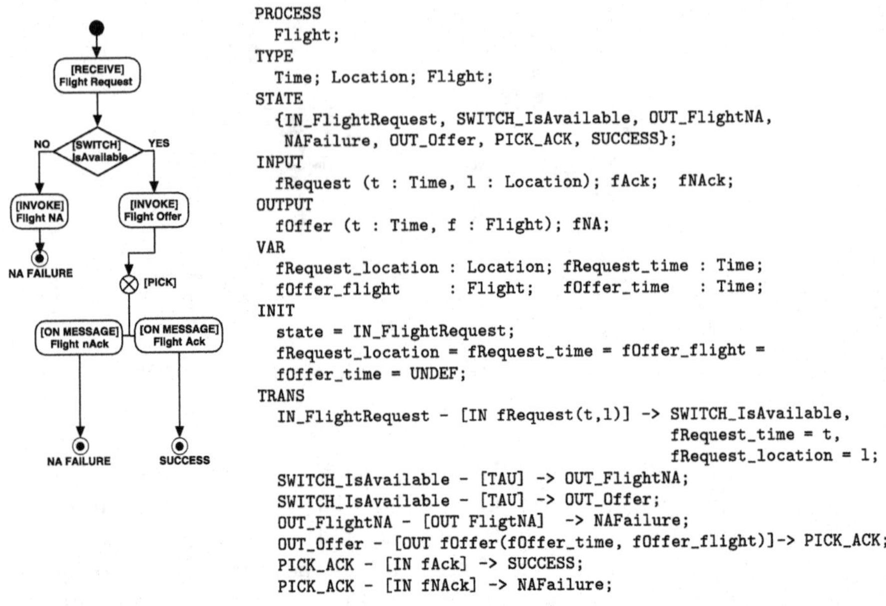


```
PROCESS
  Flight;
TYPE
  Time; Location; Flight;
STATE
  {IN_FlightRequest, SWITCH_IsAvailable, OUT_FlightNA,
   NAFailure, OUT_Offer, PICK_ACK, SUCCESS};
INPUT
  fRequest (t : Time, l : Location); fAck;  fNAck;
OUTPUT
  fOffer (t : Time, f : Flight); fNA;
VAR
  fRequest_location : Location; fRequest_time : Time;
  fOffer_flight     : Flight;   fOffer_time   : Time;
INIT
  state = IN_FlightRequest;
  fRequest_location = fRequest_time = fOffer_flight =
  fOffer_time = UNDEF;
TRANS
  IN_FlightRequest - [IN fRequest(t,l)] -> SWITCH_IsAvailable,
                                           fRequest_time = t,
                                           fRequest_location = l;
  SWITCH_IsAvailable - [TAU] -> OUT_FlightNA;
  SWITCH_IsAvailable - [TAU] -> OUT_Offer;
  OUT_FlightNA - [OUT FligtNA]  -> NAFailure;
  OUT_Offer - [OUT fOffer(fOffer_time, fOffer_flight)]-> PICK_ACK;
  PICK_ACK - [IN fAck] -> SUCCESS;
  PICK_ACK - [IN fNAck] -> NAFailure;
```

Fig. 4. The Flight BPEL process and the corresponding STS

We encode BPEL processes as *state transition systems* which describe dynamic systems that can be in one of their possible *states* (some of which are marked as *initial states*) and can evolve to new states as a result of performing some *actions*. Following the standard approach in process algebras, actions are distinguished in *input actions*, which represent the reception of messages, *output actions*, which represent messages sent to external services, and a special action τ, called *internal action*. The action τ is used to represent internal evolutions that are not visible to external services, i.e., the fact that the state of the system can evolve without producing any output, and independently from the reception of inputs. A *transition relation* describes how the state can evolve on the basis of inputs, outputs, or of the internal action τ.

Definition 1 (State transition system). *A* state transition system Σ *is a tuple* $\langle \mathcal{S}, \mathcal{S}_0, \mathcal{I}, \mathcal{O}, \mathcal{R} \rangle$ *where:*

- $\mathcal{S}$ *is the finite set of states and* $\mathcal{S}_0 \subseteq \mathcal{S}$ *is the set of initial states;*
- $\mathcal{I}$ *is a finite set of input actions and* $\mathcal{O}$ *is a finite set of output actions;*
- $\mathcal{R} \subseteq \mathcal{S} \times (\mathcal{I} \cup \mathcal{O} \cup \{\tau\}) \times \mathcal{S}$ *is the transition relation.*

Figure 4 shows the abstract BPEL process of the Flight service and the corresponding state transition system. The set of states $\mathcal{S}$ models the steps of the evolution of the process and the values of its variables. The special internal variable `state` tracks the information about the current execution step. The other variables (e.g., `fOffer_flight`, `fOffer_time`) correspond to those used by the process to store significant information. In the initial states $\mathcal{S}_0$ all the variables are undefined but `state` that is set to `IN_FlightRequest`.

The evolution of the process is modeled through a set of possible transitions. Each transition defines its applicability conditions on the source state, its firing action, and the destination state. For instance, "`SWITCH_IsAvailable - [TAU] -> OUT_FlightNA`" states that an action τ can be executed in state `SWITCH_IsAvailable` and leads to the state `OUT_FlightNA`.

According to the formal model, we distinguish among three different kinds of actions. The input actions $\mathcal{I}$ model all the incoming requests to the process and the information they bring (i.e., `fRequest` is used for the receiving of the initial request, while `fAck` models the confirmation of the order and `fNAck` its cancellation). The output actions $\mathcal{O}$ represent the outgoing messages (i.e., `FlightNA` is used when there are no tickets for the required date and location, while `fOffer` is used to bid the particular flight for the request). The action τ is used to model internal evolutions of the process, as for instance assignments and decision making (e.g., when the Flight process is in the state `SWITCH_IsAvailable` and performs internal activities to decide whether there are tickets available).

We remark that the definition of the state transition system provided in Fig. 4 is parametric w.r.t. the types `Time`, `Location`, and `Flight` used in the messages. In order to obtain a concrete state transition system, finite ranges have to be assigned to these types.

4 Extended Composition Model

A parallel product with synchronous communications is widely used as a composition model for Web services [7]. As shown in Sect. 2, this model is however not adequate for the description of scenarios where more complicated interactions are essential. We now define an extended composition model that is applicable to those scenarios. We start with some preliminary definitions.

Let $\Sigma = \langle \mathcal{S}, \mathcal{S}_0, \mathcal{I}, \mathcal{O}, \mathcal{R} \rangle$ be an STS. Let $s = s_0, \alpha_0, s_1, \alpha_1, \ldots, \alpha_{n-1}, s_n$ be a trace from s_0 to s_n and $\sigma = \alpha_0, \alpha_1, \ldots, \alpha_{n-1}$, where $\alpha_i \in \mathcal{I} \cup \mathcal{O} \cup \{\tau\}$, be a sequence of actions executed on the trace. We write $s_0 \xrightarrow{\sigma} s_n$, if there is such a trace, and call $Act(\sigma) \subseteq (\mathcal{I} \cup \mathcal{O})^*$ an *action word* that consists of the sequence of actions $\alpha_i \neq \tau$ executed in trace σ. We use ϵ to denote $Act(\tau^*)$. In the next definition transitions on action words are used to define extended STSs.

Definition 2 (Extended STS). *Given STS $\Sigma = \langle \mathcal{S}, \mathcal{S}_0, \mathcal{I}, \mathcal{O}, \mathcal{R} \rangle$ its extended STS, written as $\hat{\Sigma} = \langle \mathcal{S}, \mathcal{S}_0, \mathcal{I}, \mathcal{O}, \hat{\mathcal{R}} \rangle$, $\hat{\mathcal{R}} \subseteq \mathcal{S} \times (\mathcal{I} \cup \mathcal{O})^* \times \mathcal{S}$ is defined as follows: for each pair of states s, s', s.t. $s \xrightarrow{\sigma} s'$, $(s, Act(\sigma), s') \in \hat{\mathcal{R}}$.*

We say that a transition t of extended STS is *included by* some bigger transition t', written as $t \preceq t'$, if a trace described by the transition t' contains a trace described by t as a subsequence. For instance, the transition (s_1, ab, s_3) describing the trace s_1, a, s_2, b, s_3 is included by the transition (s_0, abc, s_4) describing the trace $s_0, \tau, s_1, a, s_2, b, s_3, c, s_4$.

The key idea underlying the introduced composition model is to provide an extended parallel product, where the synchronization is performed on *compatible* extended transitions.

Intuitively, two extended transitions $t_1 \in \hat{\mathcal{R}}^1$ and $t_2 \in \hat{\mathcal{R}}^2$ are *compatible*, written as $t_1 \approx t_2$, whenever they contain the same actions, even if we allow the order of actions in transitions to be different. The definition of compatibility relation depends on the particular communication model. It may require, for instance, that the matched symbols should appear in the same order, in the same places in words, etc. We will see the examples of this in the following section.

We define the product of extended state transition systems only for closed systems, that is all the communication actions of them should be shared. For the sake of simplicity we will introduce the definition of the product only for two STSs. The definition can be easily extended to the case with arbitrary numbers of components.

Definition 3 (Extended parallel product). *Let $\hat{\Sigma}^1$ and $\hat{\Sigma}^2$ be two extended STSs with $\mathcal{I}^1 = \mathcal{O}^2$ and $\mathcal{I}^2 = \mathcal{O}^1$. Their* extended product, *written $\hat{\Sigma}^1 \hat{\|} \hat{\Sigma}^2$ is an extended STS defined as follows:*

- $\mathcal{S} = \mathcal{S}^1 \times \mathcal{S}^2$;
- $\mathcal{S}_0 = \mathcal{S}_0^1 \times \mathcal{S}_0^2$;
- $\mathcal{I} = \mathcal{O} = \emptyset$;
- $t = ((s_1, s_2), \epsilon, (s_1', s_2')) \in \hat{\mathcal{R}}$ *if*
  - $(s_1, \epsilon, s_1') \in \hat{\mathcal{R}}^1 \wedge s_2 = s_2'$, *or* $(s_2, \epsilon, s_2') \in \hat{\mathcal{R}}^2 \wedge s_1 = s_1'$;
  - $\exists\ t_1 = (s_1, \sigma_1, s_1') \in \hat{\mathcal{R}}^1$, $t_2 = (s_2, \sigma_2, s_2') \in \hat{\mathcal{R}}^2$, $t_1 \approx t_2$;

The transition relation in the definition includes two types of transitions. The first type describe actions where no communications appear (internal transitions). In transitions of second type each communication operation takes place at both sides (synchronized communication).

We remark that, due to the fact that the output actions are non-blocking in Web service interaction, the extended composition may represent an unfaithful model of the execution. Consider for instance the following modification of the cancellation mechanism (Fig. 5). VTA sends a cancellation to the Flight service and either receives a ticket from it, concluding that the cancellation is rejected, or a time-out occurs and it concludes that the cancellation can be performed. On the other side, the Flight service simply sends a ticket accepting then the cancellation. In this example there is a possibility for the VTA service to send a cancellation confirmation to the user even if the Flight service sends a ticket. It is easy to see that this scenario, which occurs in real executions, will not be present in the extended composition model. Therefore, verification results obtained on such model may be wrong as they do not consider all scenarios that can occur in real executions. In order to be able to figure out such situations we introduce the definition of *valid* extended parallel product. If the product is shown to be valid then it describes all possible scenarios and therefore is a faithful model of execution and can be safely used for further verification.

Intuitively, the situation where some messages can be emitted without being ever consumed should not occur in valid composition. We say that two extended transitions $t_1 \in \hat{\mathcal{R}}^1$ and $t_2 \in \hat{\mathcal{R}}^2$ are *partially compatible*, written as $t_1 \sim t_2$, if some output actions in one trace can be unmatched in the other trace.

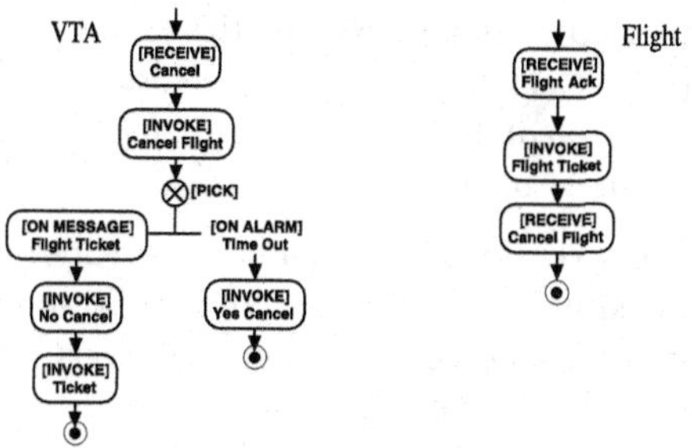

Fig. 5. Incorrect cancellation management

Definition 4 (Valid Composition). *Given two extended STSs $\hat{\Sigma}_1$ and $\hat{\Sigma}_2$, we say that their composition $\Sigma_1 \hat{\|} \Sigma_2$ is* valid *if for any state (s_1, s_2) reachable in the composition and any two transitions $t_1 = (s_1, \sigma_1, s_1')$ and $t_2 = (s_2, \sigma_2, s_2')$, such that $t_1 \sim t_2$, there are transitions $t_1' \succeq t_1$ and $t_2' \succeq t_2$, such that $t_1' \approx t_2'$.*

That is, the problem of checking the validity of the composition consists of finding reachable partially compatible extended transitions where some outputs can not be matched in any longer transitions.

5 Interpretation of Communication Models

We consider three instantiations of the general communication model introduced in the previous section. They correspond to the different cases of interactions introduced in Sect. 2. Formally, these models differ only in the way the actions in traces are matched when the compatibility is determined.

We remark that the extended composition model we introduce in this work relies on certain assumptions on the run-time environment. The following assumptions are common for any model we consider below:

- an output transition of the STS is non-blocking, i.e. the message can be emitted regardless a possibility to be ever consumed;
- the channels are perfect, i.e. the messages are not lost;
- the execution is fair, i.e. the enabled action can not be continuously ignored.

As we will show later, a particular model may additionally introduce certain specific assumptions.

5.1 Synchronous Communications

In this model the total order of all communication actions is relevant. That is, transitions are compatible if their sequences of communication actions are equivalent.

Definition 5 (Synchronous Compatibility). *Let $\hat{\Sigma}^1$ and $\hat{\Sigma}^2$ be two extended STSs, $t_1 = (s_1, \sigma_1, s'_1) \in \hat{\mathcal{R}}^1$ and $t_2 = (s_2, \sigma_2, s'_2) \in \hat{\mathcal{R}}^2$ extended transitions. Transitions t_1 and t_2 are compatible under synchronous communications model, written as $t_1 \approx_s t_2$ if $\sigma_1 = \sigma_2$.*

The validity of the system under this model coincides with the synchronizability property introduced in [8], i.e. the system is valid under this model whenever it does not allow for any concurrent message emissions. The example represented in Fig. 1 fits in this model. The composition of processes does not introduce any concurrent emissions, while the example in the Fig. 2 does. Therefore, the former can be faithfully verified under synchronous communication semantics, while the latter requires different semantic model, where the discovered kinds of executions might be considered as correct.

Due to the strong validity condition there is no need to put additional restrictions on the underlying middleware. Whenever the composition appears to be valid under this semantics, it can be executed independently of the BPEL engine implementation.

5.2 Ordered Asynchronous Communications

In the example of Fig. 2 there is a situation where the Flight and the VTA processes can send messages to each other simultaneously, thus violating the synchronous semantics. However, these messages are then consumed. Moreover, the mutual order of message emissions/consumptions is preserved in the composition. We position the systems of such kind as systems with ordered asynchronous communication semantics.

The compatibility relation for this class of systems has the following features. First, it handles each pair of partners separately. Second it distinguishes between the ordering of inputs from the ordering of outputs.

Definition 6 (Ordered Asynchronous Compatibility). *Let $\hat{\Sigma}^1$ and $\hat{\Sigma}^2$ be two extended STS, $t_1 = (s_1, \sigma_1, s'_1) \in \hat{\mathcal{R}}^1$ and $t_2 = (s_2, \sigma_2, s'_2) \in \hat{\mathcal{R}}^2$.*

Let $\omega_1^{\mathcal{I}}$ be the subsequence of σ_1, obtained by removing all actions symbols that are not input actions received from $\hat{\Sigma}^2$. Analogously, $\omega_1^{\mathcal{O}}$ is the subseqeunce of σ_1 with only outputs to $\hat{\Sigma}^2$.

Transitions t_1 and t_2 are compatible under ordered asynchronous communication model, written as $t_1 \approx_o t_2$, if $\omega_1^{\mathcal{I}} = \omega_2^{\mathcal{O}} \wedge \omega_2^{\mathcal{I}} = \omega_1^{\mathcal{O}}$.

This model is able to describe important scenarios, such as cancellation, that violate the synchronous communication semantics. It has to be noticed that the validity of the system under this model relies on the fact that the order in which messages are emitted has to be the same as the order in which they are consumed by the service. This, however, may be violated by real execution engines thus leading to incorrect behaviors. In order to avoid them, one should either verify that the system does not introduce incorrect behaviors under unordered communication model (see below), or enforce the order correctness explicitly in run-time. This can be done by introducing special monitors that will signal if the reordering has actually appeared.

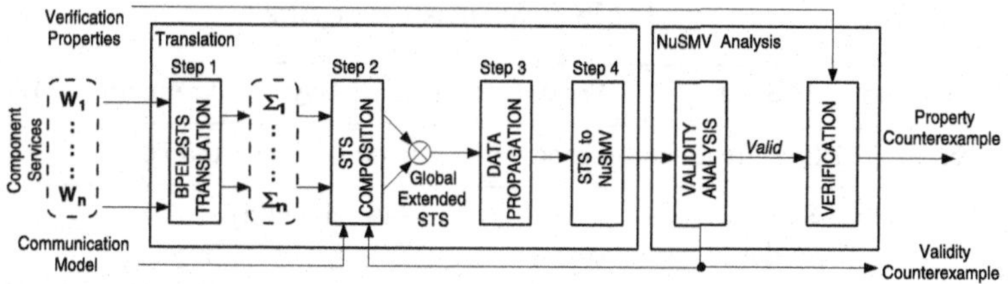

Fig. 6. The approach

5.3 Unordered Asynchronous Communications

While the previous model correctly describes the example in Fig. 2, it shows problems with the example in Fig. 3. The reason is that the latter will work correctly only if the order of messages is not relevant for consideration.

Such a model describes the systems where the order in which the messages are sent and received is irrelevant.

Definition 7 (Unordered Asynchronous Compatibility). *Let $\hat{\Sigma}^1$ and $\hat{\Sigma}^2$ be two extended STSs, $t_1 = (s_1, \sigma_1, s_1') \in \hat{\mathcal{R}}^1$ and $t_2 = (s_2, \sigma_2, s_2') \in \hat{\mathcal{R}}^2$.*

Transitions t_1 and t_2 are compatible under unordered asynchronous communication model, written as $t_1 \approx_u t_2$, if for any action symbol α appeared in σ_1 there is distinct corresponding action symbol appearing in σ_2.

This communication model is more liberal with respect to the previous in the sense that it permits more behaviors in the analyzed system. However, this requires a sophisticated queueing mechanism to be implemented in the BPEL engine.

6 Implementing the Approach

A preliminary prototype of a verification tool based on the parameric commuincation model presented in this paper has been implemented within the Astro toolkit and is available as part of the project (`http://www.astroproject.org`). Figure 6 represents the underlying architecture.

The tool consists of two modules. The first module, namely Translation module, is used to transform the initial set of BPEL process specifications into a specification accepted by the NuSMVmodel checker [6] for further analysis. There the input processes are transformed to the STS form; the extended product of their skeletons is built; the product is completed by adding the data manipulation operations and the result is emitted as NuSMVspecification. The specification is then passed to the analysis module, which verifies the specification. There the validity of the specification with respect to the given communication model is checked and the properties verification is then performed.

The algorithm that translates BPEL into NuSMVspecification relies on the following key consideration: in the extended composition it is not necessary to

Table 1. Verification results

Instance	Model	Translation	Validity	Deadlock	LTL
Example 1	Synchronous	0.5sec	1sec (valid)	0.5 sec	0.5sec
Example 2	Synchronous	2sec	4sec (invalid)	–	–
	Ordered	4sec	3sec (valid)	3sec	3sec
Example 3	Synchronous	4sec	5sec (invalid)	–	–
	Ordered	8sec	5sec (invalid)	–	–
	Unordered	9sec	5sec (valid)	5sec	4sec

consider all those extended transitions which contain as a prefix shorter transitions. I.e., if t_1 and t_2 are transitions of the extended composition, and $t_1 \preceq t_2$, then t_2 can be removed from the model without loosing behaviors. In the algorithm, we generate extended transitions incrementally, detect the compatibility as soon as it appears, and ignore longer transitions. This permits a finite system representation of the composed system and allows for efficient verification techniques to be applied. The only case when this approach may not work is when the composition contains cycles. In this case, we force a termination in the algorithm whenever an "incomplete" transition (in the sense of unmatched outputs) tries to traverse a cycle more than once. This condition may lead to consider invalid some scenarios that are actually valid. However, this problem does not appear in a wide range of interaction scenarios and models, including all non-cyclic protocols (such as those considered in Sect. 2), and all verifications based on the synchronous communication model. Currently we are working on a general solution for this problem.

We tested our approach on the different instantiations of VTA case study introduced in Sect. 2. The ranges of the domain types used in the messages (e.g. Flight, Time) were set to three values for each type. Although the examples described in the paper are relatively simple, they still are considerably more complex with respect to the set of samples presented in other tools (e.g. [8,7]). The size of the (reachable) state space ranges in the examples from 500 to 2200 states. The results of the verification are summarized in the Table 1. For the valid systems also property verification was tested. Besides checking the models for deadlocks, we checked also a property, specified as a Linear-time Temporal Logic formula, that states that the User eventually finishes the process with success if and only if both the Flight and Hotel processes eventually succeed.

7 Related Work and Conclusions

In this paper we presented a unified framework for the analysis and verification of Web service compositions provided as BPEL specifications. The framework is based on the special form of composition, namely extended parallel product, that allows one to analyze whether the given system is valid under particular communication model. We have shown how different examples of composed systems require increasingly sophisticated communication models, which can be expressed in terms of out framework. The presented analysis approach allows one to iteratively check the validity of the given system against different communication models. Whenever the model is valid the actual verification of the system can be performed where different properties of interest can be checked.

The problem of analysis of communication systems with (potentially infinite) channels is widely studied in literature. Although the problem is undecidable in general [4], there are a lot of works on restricted subclasses of such systems for which certain problems were shown to be decidable (see e.g. [2]). In particular, an interesting class of systems that can be represented using Petri Nets formalism is widely used for analysis of asynchronous systems and workflows [14,1]. Opposite to these works we investigate different cases of bounded models and make an attempt to prove the validity of the considered system under these models.

With respect to Web service analysis approaches, in particular BPEL processes, several works were described. The closest to our approach are the tools presented in [7] and [8]. The first one, namely LTSA-BPEL4WS, is based on the process algebra formalisms and allows for the analysis of basic properties of BPEL specifications, such as safety and progress checks. The tool currently does not support the analysis of composition of several BPEL specifications and was unable to handle complex specifications as those of the VTA case study. Moreover, it is based on the synchronous communications model thus being restrictive with respect to the set of systems it is able to correctly analyze. On the contrary, the WSAT tool [8] is equipped with the synchronizability analysis techniques that allow to check whether the behavior of the system is valid under synchronous communications semantics. However, the techniques currently provided allow only for partial analysis. That is, if the analyzed system does not pass the check it is not necessarily the case that the system is not synchronizable. The reason is that the synchronizability analysis is based on sufficient but not necessary conditions and that it ignores the information appearing in transitions conditions thus leading to spurious violations of the synchronizability. Also the provided techniques do not exceed the limits of the synchronizability analysis, and therefore do not allow for the reasoning about more sophisticated communication models.

One can also refer to works of [16], where the analysis is performed basing on Timed Automata, and of [5], inspired by process algebra notations. All these approaches exploit only the synchronous communication semantics, thus ruling out a certain class of systems (e.g. systems with cancellation), which are important in practice and can be managed in the proposed framework. On the contrary the aim of our approach is to attempt to find an appropriate communication model for the given system, under which it behaves correctly.

There are several directions for further research. We currently work on the extension of the translation from BPEL to STS for better coverage of constructs represented in the language. We also work on the optimizations of the validity analysis algorithm and enrichment of the approach with the possibility to reason about wider scope of communication models. Furthermore, we are interested in application of "knowledge level" reasoning techniques in order to perform the analysis of possibly infinite ranges of values and improve the verification performance shown in the previous section.

References

1. W. M. P. van der Aalst. Challenges in Business Process Management: Verification of Business Processing Using Petri Nets. *Bulletin of the EATCS 80: 174-199*, 2003.
2. P.A. Abdulla and B. Jonsson. Channel Representations in Protocol Verification (Preliminary Version). In *Proc. CONCUR'01*, August 2001.
3. T. Andrews, F. Curbera, H. Dolakia, J. Goland, J. Klein, F. Leymann, K. Liu, D. Roller, D. Smith, S. Thatte, I. Trickovic, and S. Weeravarana. Business Process Execution Language for Web Services (version 1.1), 2003.
4. D. Brand and P. Zafiropulo. On communicating finite-state machines. *Journal of the ACM, 2(5):323–342*, April 1983.
5. M. Koshkina and F. Breugel. Modelling and Verifying Web Service Orchestration by means of the Concurrency Workbench. *Proceedings of the Workshop on Testing, Analysis and Verification of Web Services (TAV-WEB), ACM SIGSOFT Software Engineering Notes*, 29(5), September 2004.
6. A. Cimatti, E. M. Clarke, F. Giunchiglia, and M. Roveri. NuSMV: a new symbolic model checker. *International Journal on Software Tools for Technology Transfer (STTT)*, 2(4), 2000.
7. H. Foster, S. Uchitel, J. Magee, and J. Kramer. Model-based verification of Web Service Compositions. In *Proc. ASE'03*, 2003.
8. X. Fu, T. Bultan, and J. Su. Analysis of Interacting BPEL Web Services. In *Proc. WWW'04*, 2004.
9. S. Graham, S. Simenov, T. Boubez, G. Daniels, D. Davis, Y. Nakamura, and R. Neyama. *Building Web Services with Java: Making Sense of XML, SOAP, WSDL and UDDI.* Sams, 2001.
10. R. Khalaf, N. Mukhi, and S. Weerawarana. Service Oriented Composition in BPEL4WS. In *Proc. WWW'03*, 2003.
11. J. Koehler and B. Srivastava. Web Service Composition: Current Solutions and Open Problems. In *Proc. of ICAPS'03 Workshop on Planning for Web Services*, 2003.
12. S. Narayanan and S. McIlraith. Simulation, Verification and Automated Composition of Web Services. In *Proc. WWW'02*, 2002.
13. S. Nakajima. Model-checking verification for reliable web service. In *Proc. OOPSLA'02 Workshop on OOWS*, 2002.
14. J.L. Peterson. Petri Net Theory and the Modelling of Systems. *Prentice-Hall*, 1981.
15. M. Pistore, M. Roveri, P. Busetta. Requirements-Driven Verification of Web Services. In *Proc. WS-FM'04, ENTCS*, 2004.
16. P. Geguang, Z. Xiangpeng, W. Shuling, and Q. Zongyan. Towards the Semantics and Verification of BPEL4WS. In *Proc. WS-FM'04, ENTCS*, 2004.

Reasoning About Interaction Patterns in Choreography

Roberto Gorrieri, Claudio Guidi, and Roberto Lucchi

Dipartimento di Scienze dell'Informazione, Università degli Studi di Bologna,
Mura Anteo Zamboni 7, I-40127 Bologna, Italy
{gorrieri, cguidi, lucchi}@cs.unibo.it

Abstract. Choreography languages provide a top-view design way for describing complex systems composed of services distributed over the network. The basic building block of such languages is the interaction between two peers which are of two kinds: request and request-respond. WS-CDL, which is the most representative choreography language, supports a pattern for programming the request interaction and two patterns for the request-respond one. Furthermore, it allows to specify if an interaction is aligned or not whose meaning is related to the possibility to control when the interaction completes. In this paper we reason about interaction patterns by analyzing their adequacy when considering the fact that they have to support the alignment property. We show the inadequacy of the two patterns supporting the request-respond interaction; one of them because it does not permit to reason on alignment at the right granularity level and the other one for some expressiveness lacks.

1 Introduction

Service Oriented Computing (SOC) paradigm provides a mean to design complex systems by exploiting and composing services available over the network. Web services technology, which is one of the most prominent technologies for SOC, provides several languages for composing services, the so-called orchestration (e.g., WSFL [4], XLANG [6], WS-BPEL [5]) and choreography (e.g. WS-CDL [7], WSCI [10]) languages. Althought there is not a common agreement on the meaning of orchestration and choreography, in [1] we have shown how orchestration and choreography work at different levels. On the one hand orchestration describes how to compose services from the point of view of a single entity, the so-called orchestrator, which coordinates the entire system, while on the other hand, choreography describes all the interdependencies among the different interactions between participants in a top-view way.

The most interesting proposal for choreography is Web Services Choreography Description Language (WS-CDL) which is an XML-based language. In a few words, choreography is composed of a static part describing the system (i.e. participants, variables and channels) and another one describing the behavior, that is the conversation rules of the system. The basic building block of WS-CDL for describing the conversational part is the interaction that can be composed

M. Bravetti et al. (Eds.): EPEW 2005 and WS-FM 2005, LNCS 3670, pp. 333–348, 2005.

by using sequential, parallel and alternative operators. An interaction describes a messages exchange between two participants and can be of two kinds: *request* and *request-respond*. A request interaction consists of a message exchanged by a participant to another one, while a request-respond is composed of a message transmitted by a participant to another one followed by a response message in the opposite direction.

Since the request-respond is a complex interaction containing two message exchanges, it is possible to define it in different ways. Indeed, it is possible to program separately the request and the response or programming them with a construct dealing with the entire request-respond interaction in an atomic way. Here we talk about interaction patterns referring to the language mechanisms which allow to express the request and the request-respond interaction types.

WS-CDL supports three different interaction patterns: the *request*, the *atomic request-respond* and the *splitted request-respond*. The request pattern simply maps the request interactions type. The splitted request-respond pattern allows to manage separately the request and the respond message exchanges, thus allowing for example to describe that a certain activity have to be performed after the request and before the respond. The atomic request-respond pattern allows to express the entire request-respond interaction as an atomic construct; in this case it is not possible to associate an activity that is to be performed "within" that interaction. An interesting property which can be associated to interactions is the *alignment*, that is the possibility to control when an interaction completes. WS-CDL permits to set alignment property at the level of both single message exchange (request and respond), by using the splitted request-respond pattern, and at the level of entire request-respond interaction by using the atomic one.

In this paper we reason about the interaction patterns analyzing their adequacy considering the fact that they have to support the alignment property. To this end we present a core sublanguage of WS-CDL, equipped with a formal semantics, supporting the three interaction patterns above. We show that for the request-respond interaction the splitted pattern does not capture the essence of the alignment property and it allows to program not valid conversations, while the atomic one allows to reason at the right granularity level but it lacks in expressiveness w.r.t. the splitted one. Furthermore, by using some examples we show that the atomic request-respond pattern has less expressive power than the splitted one. The investigation described above have one meaningful implication: the formal semantics of a significant fragment of WS-CDL has been defined. Indeed, to the best of our knowledge, this work represents the first attempt towards the formalization of WS-CDL semantics.

Finally, in light of the results obtained in this paper we show how our formal language CL presented in [3] deals with the right granularity level for the request-respond interaction, concluding that it can be considered a good starting point towards the definition of a formal framework for choreography.

The paper is structured as follows. Section 2 presents a core language of WS-CDL and its semantics. Section 3 is devoted to formally reason on the request-respond interaction patterns provided by WS-CDL. Section 4 concludes the paper with some final remarks.

2 The $WSCDL_{core}$ Language

As previously mentioned WS-CDL is composed of a static part describing the system (i.e. participants, variables and channels) and another one describing the conversation rules the participants have to follow.

In [3] we have presented a formal language proposal for representing choreography where we have extracted its essence following the same description approach of WS-CDL. Our proposal indeed, is composed by two parts: a *declarative* part and a *conversational* one. The former deals with the formalization of the participants involved in the choreography whereas the latter deals with the conversation rules they have to follow in order to interact each other.

In this paper choreographies are defined by exploiting the declarative part of our formal model, while the conversation rules are expressed by introducing a formal language which accounts for a significant fragment of WS-CDL. It is worth noting that the declarative part is not a faithful representation of the WS-CDL contructs which deal with participants, variables and channels but it just addresses their basic concepts. However, since we are interested on reasoning about interaction patterns, we can abstract from these details.

As far as the conversational part is concerned, here we present the language $WSCDL_{core}$ which formally represents the WS-CDL patterns we are interested in. The semantics of this language will be presented in terms of another language CL_P. Although that there are few differences between them, this choice is due to the fact that it simplifies the comparison with our conversation language CL whose semantics is defined in terms of the same language CL_P. In the following indeed, we are interested to test and verify the suitability of CL considering the issues raised by this paper.

In the following we explain the declarative part and we present $WSCDL_{core}$ syntax and semantics.

2.1 Declarative Part

Here we explain the declarative part of our choreography formal model which is based on the concept of *role*. A role represents the behaviour that a participant has to exhibit in order to fulfill the activity defined by the choreography. Each role can store variables and exhibit operations.

As far as variables are concerned, we associate to each role a set of variables which represent the information managed by the role and which will be used in the interactions between roles. In our proposal variables are only names without any values and they are exploited in order to represent the data flow among the roles.

As far as operations are concerned, each role is equipped with a set of operations it has to exhibit which essentially represent the access points that will be used by the other roles to interact with the owner one. Operations can have one of the following interaction modalities: *One-Way* or *Request-Response*.

In particular we remind that operations are defined in WSDL specifications [9] and they are the only mechanism for interacting with a Web Service. Briefly, an operation contains the definition of an incoming message for a service and, when used, the definition of the response message. Two different kinds of operation exist:

- *One-Way*: only the incoming message is defined.
- *Request-Response*: both the incoming message and the response one are defined.

When a Web service is invoked by using a *One-Way* operation, it receives the incoming message and starts its activities. On the other hand, when a Web Service is invoked by using a *Request-Response* operation, the service receives the message, starts its activities and, at the end, replies to the invoker with a response message.

Let us now introduce the formalization of *roles*, *variables* and *operations*.

Let Var be the set of variables ranged over by x, y, z, k. We denote with $\widetilde{x}$ tuples of variables, for instance, we may have $\widetilde{x} = \langle x_1, x_2, ..., x_n \rangle$.

Let $OpName$ be the set of operation names, ranged over by o, and $OpType = \{ow, rr\}$ be the set of operation types where ow denotes a One-Way operation whereas rr denotes the Request-Response one.

An operation is described by its operation name and operation type. Namely, let Op be the set of operations defined as follows:

$$Op = \{(o, t) \mid o \in OpName,\ t \in OpType\}$$

A role is described by a role name, the set of operations it exhibits and by a set of variables. Namely, let $RName$ be the set of the role names, ranged over by ρ. The set $Role$, containing all the possible roles, is defined as follows:[1]

$$Role = \{(\rho, \omega, V) \mid \rho \in RName,\ \omega \in \wp(Op), V \in \mathbf{P}(Var)\}$$

Exploiting this formalization, in the following we present the $WSCDL_{core}$ language.

2.2 Conversational Part

Before presenting the syntax of the $WSCDL_{core}$ language, we intend to spend some words in order to highlight some WS-CDL basics. In particular we focus on the basic building block `<interaction>` which can be composed exploiting the tags `<sequence>`, `<parallel>` and `<choice>` representing, respectively, the sequential, parallel and alternative composition. Now, we remind some basics of the WS-CDL `<interaction>` tag in order to explain its functioning.

---

[1] Given a set S, with $\wp(S)$ we denote the powerset of S.

The tag `<interaction>` is used for defining interactions and it has some enclosed elements and attributes. For the sake of this paper we are interested in discussing the inner tags `<participate>` and `<exchange>` and the attributes `channelVariables`, `operation` and `align`. We refer to WS-CDL specifications for more details.
The description of the inner tags follows:

- `<participate>`: this tag defines the participants involved in the interactions exploiting the attributes `relationshipType`, `fromRole` and `toRole`. In WS-CDL specification the participants involved in a choreography are described exploiting a complex hierarchical structure. Briefly, the roles express the observable behaviours of a participant and the relationships express the peer-to-peer links between participants.
- `<exchange>`: this tag defines the variables exchanged by the sender and the receiver. It contains two elements `<send>` and `<receive>` where the former defines the information sent by the sender whereas the latter defines the information received by the receiver. The attribute `action` defines the direction of the interaction and has two possible values: `request` or `respond`. In the first case the interaction is performed from the role `fromRole`, which is the sender, to the role `toRole` which is the receiver. In the second case the `toRole` is the sender and the `fromRole` is the receiver.
  One or two exchange tags can be defined within the tag interaction. If there are two exchange elements one must have action equal to request and the other must assume the value respond. The former defines the information exchange during the request interaction and the latter during the response one.

The description of the main attributes of the `<interaction>` tag follows:

- The attributes `channelVariable` and `operation` define the WS-CDL channel and the WSDL operation on which the interaction is performed and which has to belong to the interaction target.
- The attribute `align` defines if the interaction must be aligned or not. In the following we quote from the specification[7] the definition of the align attribute:

  > If the align attribute is set to "false" for the Interaction, then it means that the:
  > - Request exchange completes successfully for the requesting Role once it has successfully sent the information of the Variable specified within the send element and the Request exchange completes successfully for the accepting Role once it has successfully received the information of the Variable specified within the receive element
  > - Response exchange completes successfully for the accepting Role once it has successfully sent the information of the Variable specified within the send elementand the Response exchange com-

pletes successfully for the requesting Role once it has successfully received the information of the Variable specified within the receive element

If the align attribute is set to "true" for the Interaction, then it means that the Interaction completes successfully if its Request and Response exchanges complete successfully[...]:

- A Request exchange completes successfully once both the requesting Role has successfully sent the information of the Variable specified within the send element and the accepting Role has successfully received the information of the Variable specified within the receive element
- A Response exchange completes successfully once both the accepting Role has successfully sent the information of the Variable specified within the send element and the requesting Role has successfully received the information of the Variable specified within the receive element

This definition is far to be formal and deserves to be commented. An interaction is aligned when both the roles are aware of its state. On the contrary, it must be considered not aligned when the sender and the receiver act without a common knowledge about the interaction state. From the choreography point of view, that is a system top view, a common knowlegde about the interaction state is linked to the fact that it is possible to verify its termination or not. For this reason here we discriminate between aligned interaction and the not aligned one considering the fact that it is possible to control their termination or not.

Considering the meaning of the WS-CDL `<interaction>` tag, we extract three kinds of interaction patterns:

- *request*
- *splitted request-respond*
- *atomic request-respond*

The three type of interactions patterns *request*, *splitted request-respond* and *atomic request-respond* directly follow from the `<exchange>` elements within the `<interaction>` tag.

The *request* pattern is characterized by an interaction defined with only one exchange element and the action set to request. The operation through which the interaction is performed must be a One-Way operation.

In the following we present the WS-CDL code for a request interaction pattern where `opAB` is a One-Way operation:

```
<interaction name="interactionAB" channelVariable="tns:ABchan"
      operation="tns:opAB" align="true" >
      <participate relationshipType="tns:relationshipAB"
```

```
                fromRole="tns:roleA" toRole="tns:roleB"/>
      <exchange name="requestAB" action="request">
          <send variable="cdl:getVariable("tns:x", "", "")" />
          <receive variable="cdl:getVariable("tns:y", "", "")"/>
      </exchange>
</interaction>
```

The *splitted request-respond* pattern is characterized by two different interactions defined on the same Request-Response operation: one for expressing the request interaction and the other one for expressing the respond one. This pattern allows to program the request-response interaction in a low level manner where the two single interactions can be managed separately. In the following we present the WS-CDL code for a splitted request-respond pattern where a choreography `C` is performed between the request and the respond interactions:

```
<sequence>
   <interaction name="interactionCD"  channelVariable="tns:CDchan"
      operation="tns:opCD" align="true" >
      <participate relationshipType="tns:relationshipCD"
               fromRole="tns:roleC" toRole="tns:roleD"/>
      <exchange name="requestCD" action="request">
            <send variable="cdl:getVariable("tns:z", "", "")" />
            <receive variable="cdl:getVariable("tns:k", "", "")"/>
      </exchange>
   </interaction>
   <perform>
        <!--  Choreography C -->
   </perform>
   <interaction name="interactionCD2"  channelVariable="tns:CDchan"
      operation="tns:opCD" align="true" >
      <participate relationshipType="tns:relationshipCD"
            fromRole="tns:roleC" toRole="tns:roleD"/>
      <exchange name="responseCD" action="respond">
          <send variable="cdl:getVariable("tns:w", "", "")" />
          <receive variable="cdl:getVariable("tns:q", "", "")"/>
      </exchange>
   </interaction>
</sequence>
```

The *atomic request-respond* pattern is characterized by two exchange elements defined within the interaction tag. One represents the request exchange and the other represents the respond. The operation through which the interaction is performed must be a Request-Response one. In the following we present the WS-CDL code for an atomic request-respond pattern where `opCD` is a Request-Response operation:

```
<interaction name="interactionCD"  channelVariable="tns:CDchan"
      operation="tns:opCD" align="true" >
      <participate relationshipType="tns:relationshipCD"
            fromRole="tns:roleC" toRole="tns:roleD"/>
      <exchange name="requestCD" action="request">
        <send variable="cdl:getVariable("tns:z", "", "")" />
        <receive variable="cdl:getVariable("tns:k", "", "")"/>
      </exchange>
      <exchange name="responseCD" action="respond">
        <send variable="cdl:getVariable("tns:w", "", "")" />
        <receive variable="cdl:getVariable("tns:q", "", "")"/>
      </exchange>
</interaction>
```

Moreover, each interaction can be enriched with the alignment property setting the align attribute of the tag interaction. In the examples above we have considered all aligned interactions.

Now we are ready to present the syntax of $WSCDL_{core}$ which deals with such a kind of patterns. We start by modeling only the request and splitted request-respond patterns without considering the atomic request-respond one. Such a kind of pattern will be separately discussed in section 3 where we show that it is a special case of the splitted request-respond pattern.

Let us now present the syntax of $WSCDL_{core}$:

$$C_{core} ::= \mathbf{0} \mid \mu \mid \mu^A \mid C_{core}; C_{core} \mid C_{core} \parallel C_{core} \mid C_{core} + C_{core}$$

$$\mu ::= \mathtt{request}(\rho_A, \rho_B, o, \widetilde{x}, \widetilde{y}) \mid \mathtt{respond}(\rho_A, \rho_B, o, \widetilde{x}, \widetilde{y})$$

A conversation can be a terminated conversation $\mathbf{0}$, a not aligned interaction μ, an aligned interaction [2] μ^A or the sequential, parallel and alternative composition of conversations.

The interactions can be a `request` interaction or a `respond` one. Considering their arguments we have that:

- ρ_A and ρ_B represent the invoker role and the invoked one, respectively.
- o is the operation through which the interaction is performed and which has to be exhibited by the invoked role ρ_B.
- $\widetilde{x}$ and $\widetilde{y}$ are respectively the variables of ρ_A and ρ_B.

When a request interaction completes, the direction of the interaction is from role ρ_A to role ρ_B and $\widetilde{x}$ will populate[3] $\widetilde{y}$ whereas when a respond interaction

[2] Even if the correct notation is $\mathtt{request}(\rho_A, \rho_B, o, \widetilde{x}, \widetilde{y})^A$ and $\mathtt{respond}(\rho_A, \rho_B, o, \widetilde{x}, \widetilde{y})^A$, for the sake of clarity, we will use the notation $\mathtt{request}^A(\rho_A, \rho_B, o, \widetilde{x}, \widetilde{y})$ and $\mathtt{respond}^A(\rho_A, \rho_B, o, \widetilde{x}, \widetilde{y})$.

[3] In WS-CDL slang the term populate means that the values instantiated by the variables $\widetilde{x}$ will be stored within the variables $\widetilde{y}$. Since we use variables as names, in the following we will exploit the term populate in order to express the fact that an interaction represents an information flow from variables $\widetilde{x}$ to variables $\widetilde{y}$.

completes the direction is from role ρ_B to role ρ_A and $\widetilde{y}$ will populate $\widetilde{x}$. Depending on the type of the operation o the respond interaction is allowed or not. If o is a One-Way operation only a request interaction is allowed on that operation whereas if o is a Request-Response operation the two interactions are allowed and the respond one must logically follow the request. When an interaction is not aligned it is not possible to control when it completes whereas for the aligned one this is possible.

Finally, conversations can be: i) the sequential composition of two conversations $C_{core}; C'_{core}$ whose meaning is that C'_{core} can be performed after C_{core} completes, ii) the parallel composition of two conversations $C_{core} \parallel C'_{core}$ which represents the concurrent execution of conversations C_{core} and C'_{core}, and iii) the alternative composition of two conversations $C_{core} + C'_{core}$ whose meaning is that the conversation to be performed is non-deterministically selected between C_{core} and C'_{core}.

Now we define a choreography. A choreography, denoted by CH_{CDL}, is defined by a pair (C_{core}, Σ) where $C_{core} \in WSCDL_{core}$ and $\Sigma \subseteq Role$. Here we consider only well-formed choreographies whose definition follows:

Definition 1 (Well-formed set of roles). *Let $\Sigma \subseteq Role$. The set of roles Σ is well-formed if the following conditions hold:*

1. *Σ is finite;*
2. *if $(\rho_i, \omega_i, \sigma_i) \in \Sigma$ and $(\rho_j, \omega_j, \sigma_j) \in \Sigma$ and $\rho_i = \rho_j$ then $i = j$.*

Definition 2 (Well-formed choreography). *Let (C_{core}, Σ) be a choreography; C_{core} is well-formed if:*

1. *for any operation* $\texttt{request}(\rho_A, \rho_B, o, \widetilde{x}, \widetilde{y})$ *and* $\texttt{request}^A(\rho_A, \rho_B, o, \widetilde{x}, \widetilde{y})$ *it contains, the following conditions hold:*
   (a) $(\rho_A, \omega_A, V_A), (\rho_B, \omega_B, V_B) \in \Sigma$ *for some* ω_A, V_A *and* ω_B, V_B;
   (b) $(o, ow) \in \omega_B \vee (o, rr) \in \omega_B$;
   (c) $\widetilde{x}$ *and* $\widetilde{y}$ *have the same arity;*
   (d) $\widetilde{x} \subseteq V_A$ *and* $\widetilde{y} \subseteq V_B$
2. *for any operation* $\texttt{respond}(\rho_A, \rho_B, o, \widetilde{x}, \widetilde{y})$ *and* $\texttt{respond}^A(\rho_A, \rho_B, o, \widetilde{x}, \widetilde{y})$:
   (a) $(\rho_A, \omega_A, V_A), (\rho_B, \omega_B, V_B) \in \Sigma$ *for some* ω_A, V_A *and* ω_B, V_B;
   (b) $(o, rr) \in \omega_B$;
   (c) $\widetilde{x}$ *and* $\widetilde{y}$ *have the same arity;*
   (d) $\widetilde{x} \subseteq V_A$, $\widetilde{y} \subseteq V_B$

Definition 1 states that a set of roles Σ is well-formed if it is finite and the set of role names are all distinct.

Definition 2 states constraints for the interactions. Conditions *(a)* require that the roles involved are contained in the system, conditions *(b)* guarantee that the role which receives the interaction exhibits the operation used to interact (in the case of a respond interaction the type of the operation must be Request-Response), conditions *(c)* ensure that the sender and the receiver use the same number of variables and, finally, conditions *(d)* ensure that the specified variables belong to the corresponding role.

2.3 The Semantics

The semantics of $WSCDL_{core}$ is presented in terms of the semantics of an auxiliary language CL_P which has been already used to define the semantics of our conversation language CL.

Syntax of CL_P. The auxiliary language is defined by the following grammar:

$$C_P ::= \mathbf{0} \mid \mu \mid C_P; C_P \mid C_P \parallel C_P \mid C_P + C_P$$
$$\mu ::= (\rho_A, \rho_B, o, \widetilde{x}, \widetilde{y}, dir)$$

In the following we use CL_P, ranged over by C_P, to denote the set of conversations of such a language. We limit the description to the interaction μ since the composition operators ;,+,|| have the same meaning of those of $WSCDL_{core}$.

$(\rho_A, \rho_B, o, \widetilde{x}, \widetilde{y}, dir)$ means that an interaction from role ρ_A to role ρ_B is performed. In particular, o is the name of the operation $(o, t) \in Operation$ on which the message exchange is performed. Variables $\widetilde{x}$ and $\widetilde{y}$ are those used by the sender and the receiver, respectively. When the interaction completes, it is assumed that the information represented by the variables $\widetilde{x}$ will populate the variables $\widetilde{y}$. Finally, $dir \in \{\uparrow, \downarrow\}$ indicates whether the interaction is a request ($\uparrow$) or a response ($\downarrow$) of o. Thus the dir parameter is needed for allowing us to reason on simple interaction and at the same time for preserving information about the type of the operation on which the message exchange is performed.

Semantics of CL_P. $C_P \to C'_P$ means that the conversation C_P evolves in one step in a conversation C'_P. We define $\to$ as the least relation which satisfies the axioms and rules of Table 1 and closed w.r.t. $\equiv$.

Table 1. Semantics of CL_P conversations

(INTERACTION)
$$(\rho_A, \rho_B, o, \widetilde{x}, \widetilde{y}, dir) \to \mathbf{0}$$

(SEQUENCE)
$$\frac{C_P \to C'_P}{C_P; D_P \to C'_P; D_P}$$

(PARALLEL)
$$\frac{C_P \to C'_P}{C_P \mid D_P \to C'_P \mid D_P}$$

(CHOICE)
$$\frac{C_P \to C'_P}{C_P + D_P \to C'_P}$$

(STRUCTURAL CONGRUENGE)
$$\mathbf{0}; C_P \equiv C_P \qquad C_P \mid \mathbf{0} \equiv C_P \qquad C_P + \mathbf{0} = C_P$$
$$C_P + D_P \equiv D_P + C_P \quad C_P \mid D_P \equiv D_P \mid C_P$$
$$(C_P + D_P) + E_P \equiv C_P + (D_P + E_P)$$
$$(C_P \mid D_P) \mid E_P \equiv C_P \mid (D_P \mid E_P)$$

The structural congruence $\equiv$ is the least congruence closed w.r.t. the axioms of Table 1 which express the fact that abelian monoid laws for parallel and choice operators hold (associativity, commutativity and **0** as identity) and the sequence operator $C_P; D_P$ enables D_P only when C_P completes.

The description of axioms and rules follows. The axiom INTERACTION describes the behavior of an interaction. ρ_A is the name of the sender role whereas ρ_B is the name of the receiver one, while o is the operation name used to interact and $\widetilde{x}$, $\widetilde{y}$ are the variables used by the sender and the receiver to exchange data, respectively. The rules SEQUENCE, PARALLEL and CHOICE are standard.

Mapping of $WSCDL_{core}$. We define a mapping from $WSCDL_{core}$ conversations into terms of CL_P. Definition 3 defines the mapping function. Request and respond interactions are mapped in an interaction of CL_P where in the first case the direction parameter is $\uparrow$ and in the second is $\downarrow$. The rule 4 stands that either the aligned and the not aligned interactions are implemented in the same way. Their different behaviour is strictly related to the fact that it is not possible to control when the not aligned one completes. Such a difference is expressed in rules 5 and 6 where the sequence is preserved only in the case of the aligned interaction. In the opposite case, the sequence operator is replaced by the parallel one. Indeed, the sequence of a not aligned interaction with another conversation is implicitly a parallel composition of them because, since it is not possible to control when the not aligned interaction completes, it is impossible to express the fact that a certain conversation have to be performed after its completion. Thus, it is impossible to support sequencing of not aligned interaction.

For example, let $C = \texttt{request}(\rho_A, \rho_B, o, \widetilde{x}, \widetilde{y}); \texttt{request}^A(\rho_C, \rho_D, o', \widetilde{z}, \widetilde{k})$ be a conversation. The fact that the first `request` is not aligned implies that it is not possible to control when it completes. On the other hand, the sequence operator guarantees that the conversation which follows can be executed only when the previous one has completed. However, in this case such a condition cannot be tested. This means that it is not possible to control the sequential execution of not aligned interactions, therefore we map not aligned interactions composed in sequence by replacing the operator with the parallel one. Consequently, exploiting the rule 6 of the mapping function, the conversation C behaves as:

$$[\![C]\!] = [\![\texttt{request}(\rho_A, \rho_B, o, \widetilde{x}, \widetilde{y})]\!] \parallel [\![\texttt{request}^A(\rho_C, \rho_D, o', \widetilde{z}, \widetilde{k})]\!]$$

Finally the mapping preserves the parallel and the alternative composition.

Definition 3 (The mapping function). *The function* $[\![\ ]\!] : WSCDL_{core} \rightarrow CL_P$ *is defined inductively as follows:*

1. $[\![\mathit{0}]\!] = \mathit{0}$
2. $[\![\mathit{request}^A(\rho_A, \rho_B, o, \widetilde{x}, \widetilde{y})]\!] = (\rho_A, \rho_B, o, \widetilde{x}, \widetilde{y}, \uparrow)$
3. $[\![\mathit{respond}^A(\rho_A, \rho_B, o, \widetilde{x}, \widetilde{y})]\!] = (\rho_A, \rho_B, o, \widetilde{x}, \widetilde{y}, \downarrow)$

4. $[\![\mu]\!] = [\![\mu^A]\!]$

5. $[\![\mu^A; C_{core}]\!] = [\![\mu^A]\!]; [\![C_{core}]\!]$

6. $[\![\mu; C_{core}]\!] = [\![\mu]\!] \mid\mid [\![C_{core}]\!]$

7. $[\![C_{core} \mid\mid C'_{core}]\!] = [\![C_{core}]\!] \mid\mid [\![C'_{core}]\!]$

8. $[\![C_{core} + C'_{core}]\!] = [\![C_{core}]\!] + [\![C'_{core}]\!]$

3 The Request-Respond Patterns

This section is devoted to reason about the two request-respond interaction patterns supported by WS-CDL and represents the main contribute of this paper. In the first part we criticize the splitted request-respond pattern because it is not reasonable to specify separately the alignment property for the request and the respond. In the second part we model the atomic request-respond pattern where the alignment property is referred to the entire interaction showing that this is the right granularity level where alignment property has to be defined. Furthermore, we show that the atomic request-respond interaction has some lacks of expressiveness w.r.t. the splitted one.

3.1 Splitted Request-Respond Pattern

As confirmed by the choreography working group in the official mailing list [8], *a splitted request-respond pattern programmed in a conversation, say C, is considered* valid *when, for all the possible computation paths of C, the request is executed before the respond, and in the case the request is performed the corresponding respond is executed.* This directly follows by the fact that it is strictly related with the Request-Response operations where the response is subordinate to the request. Thus we can express splitted request-respond interactions in the following ways:

$$
\begin{array}{l}
\text{a) } \mathtt{request}(\rho_A, \rho_B, o, \widetilde{x}, \widetilde{y}); C[\mathtt{respond}^A(\rho_A, \rho_B, o, \widetilde{z}, \widetilde{k})] \\
\text{b) } \mathtt{request}(\rho_A, \rho_B, o, \widetilde{x}, \widetilde{y}); C[\mathtt{respond}(\rho_A, \rho_B, o, \widetilde{z}, \widetilde{k})] \\
\text{c) } \mathtt{request}^A(\rho_A, \rho_B, o, \widetilde{x}, \widetilde{y}); C[\mathtt{respond}^A(\rho_A, \rho_B, o, \widetilde{z}, \widetilde{k})] \\
\text{d) } \mathtt{request}^A(\rho_A, \rho_B, o, \widetilde{x}, \widetilde{y}); C[\mathtt{respond}(\rho_A, \rho_B, o, \widetilde{z}, \widetilde{k})]
\end{array}
$$

where $C[\,]$ is any conversation context. Here we intend to reason on the meaning of the alignment property for a splitted request-respond pattern, referring in particular on cases a) and b) where the request is not aligned. The following proposition expresses that any interaction with a not aligned request on a Request-Response operation is not valid. The idea directly follows from the semantics of the not aligned interaction. Indeed, in the cases a) and b) we cannot guarantee that a not aligned request is performed before the corresponding respond. Consequently, in a request-respond interaction we always have to use aligned requests.

Proposition 1. *Let* $(o, rr) \in Op$ *be an operation. For any conversation context* $C[\,]$*, for any* ρ_A *and* ρ_B*, for any* $\widetilde{x}$ *and* $\widetilde{y}$*, the conversations*

- $\mathtt{request}(\rho_A, \rho_B, o, \widetilde{x}, \widetilde{y}); C[\mathtt{respond}^A(\rho_A, \rho_B, o, \widetilde{z}, \widetilde{k})]$
- $\mathtt{request}(\rho_A, \rho_B, o, \widetilde{x}, \widetilde{y}); C[\mathtt{respond}(\rho_A, \rho_B, o, \widetilde{z}, \widetilde{k})]$

are not valid.

Let us consider the following example where C is the following conversation in order to clarify the meaning of the notion above:

$$C = \mathtt{request}(\rho_A, \rho_B, o, \widetilde{x}, \widetilde{y}); \mathtt{respond}^A(\rho_A, \rho_B, o, \widetilde{z}, \widetilde{k})$$

C behaves as follows:

$$[\![C]\!] = [\![\mathtt{request}(\rho_A, \rho_B, o, \widetilde{x}, \widetilde{y})]\!] \parallel [\![\mathtt{respond}^A(\rho_A, \rho_B, o, \widetilde{z}, \widetilde{k})]\!]$$

It is easy to observe that such an interaction is not valid because it is trivial to prove that there exist a computation path where the respond is performed before the request.

Thus, in a splitted request-respond interaction the request must be always aligned. Now we can assume that the aligned property shifts always on the respond interaction. The cases c) and d) above express this concept.

The case c) represents the aligned interaction whereas the case d) the not aligned one. Let us now consider the case d), does it make sense? Although it is syntactically correct, in our opinion, it represents a wrong interpretation of the request-respond interaction. The alignment property indeed means that we cannot control when an interaction completes. In the case d) we can control that the first part of a request-respond interaction completes leaving the not aligned behaviour only on the second one. Here we cannot state if WS-CDL authors were willing to allow such a behaviour but, in our opinion, the case d) does not address the nature of the alignment because we interpret a request-respond interaction, even splitted, as a unique concept where a property must hold on the entire interaction.

We conclude that, in our opinion, it is not reasonable to express alignment property at the level of single message exchange. For these reasons the splitted request-respond pattern is inadequate for expressing the alignment property.

3.2 Atomic Request-Respond Pattern

In this section we introduce the atomic request-respond pattern showing that it defines only valid conversations and allows to express the alignment property at the granularity level of the entire request-respond interaction which seems to be the right approach.

Here we extend the core language of Section 2.2 with the atomic request-respond pattern where the interactions μ are defined as it follows:

$$\mu ::= \texttt{request}(\rho_A, \rho_B, o, \widetilde{x}, \widetilde{y}) \mid \texttt{respond}(\rho_A, \rho_B, o, \widetilde{x}, \widetilde{y}) \mid \texttt{rr}(\rho_A, \rho_B, o, \widetilde{x}, \widetilde{y}, \widetilde{z}, \widetilde{k})$$

The atomic request-respond, denoted with $\texttt{rr}(\rho_A, \rho_B, o, \widetilde{x}, \widetilde{y}, \widetilde{z}, \widetilde{k})$, means that ρ_A performs a request-respond with ρ_B by using variables $\widetilde{x}$ (of ρ_A) and $\widetilde{y}$ (of ρ_B) for the request message and variables $\widetilde{z}$ (of ρ_A) and $\widetilde{k}$ (of ρ_B) for the response.

The semantics of the extended language is obtained by adding the following encoding rule to the ones of Definition 3:

$$\begin{aligned}&[\![\texttt{rr}^A(\rho_A, \rho_B, o, \widetilde{x}, \widetilde{y}, \widetilde{z}, \widetilde{k})]\!] = \\ &\qquad [\![\texttt{request}^A(\rho_A, \rho_B, o, \widetilde{x}, \widetilde{y})]\!]; [\![\texttt{respond}^A(\rho_A, \rho_B, o, \widetilde{z}, \widetilde{k})]\!]\end{aligned}$$

The atomic request-respond pattern is expressed in terms of the splitted one; it is trivial to verify that such kind of interactions are all valid accordinlgy with the notion given in section 3.1. Indeed, the request is aligned as well as the respond thus the sequential operator guarantees that the request is always performed before the respond.

So far, we have only presented the semantics of $\texttt{rr}^A$ without discussing that of $\texttt{rr}$. This is due to the fact that it is implicitly linked to the semantics of the alignment property. What does it mean performing a not aligned atomic request-respond? In this case we cannot control when the entire request-respond interaction completes. The semantics of such a condition follows from rules 4, 5 and 6 of the mapping function:

$$\begin{aligned}[\![\texttt{rr}(\rho_A, \rho_B, o, \widetilde{x}, \widetilde{y}, \widetilde{z}, \widetilde{k}); C]\!] &= ([\![\texttt{rr}(\rho_A, \rho_B, o, \widetilde{x}, \widetilde{y}, \widetilde{z}, \widetilde{k})]\!]) \parallel [\![C]\!] \\ [\![\texttt{rr}^A(\rho_A, \rho_B, o, \widetilde{x}, \widetilde{y}, \widetilde{z}, \widetilde{k}); C]\!] &= [\![\texttt{rr}(\rho_A, \rho_B, o, \widetilde{x}, \widetilde{y}, \widetilde{z}, \widetilde{k})]\!]; [\![C]\!]\end{aligned}$$

Here the alignment property is expressed at the level of the entire request-respond interaction contrarily to the case of the splitted one. Considering the two request-respond patterns, we conclude that the right granularity level for expressing the alignment property is represented by the atomic request-respond pattern.

Let us now consider the expressiveness of this construct w.r.t. the splitted one. Considering the semantics of the atomic request-respond pattern it is trivial to observe that it is less expressive than the splitted one. The following examples prove that there exist an expressiveness gap because they cannot be programmed by using the atomic pattern.

1. $\texttt{request}^A(\rho_A, \rho_B, o, \widetilde{x}, \widetilde{y}); C; \texttt{respond}^A(\rho_A, \rho_B, o, \widetilde{z}, \widetilde{k})$
2. $\texttt{request}^A(\rho_A, \rho_B, o, \widetilde{x}, \widetilde{y}); (\texttt{respond}^A(\rho_A, \rho_B, o, \widetilde{z}, \widetilde{k}) \parallel D)$
3. $\texttt{request}^A(\rho_A, \rho_B, o, \widetilde{x}, \widetilde{y}); C; (\texttt{respond}^A(\rho_A, \rho_B, o, \widetilde{z}, \widetilde{k}) \parallel D)$

where C is a choreography which is performed between the request and the respond interactions and D is a choreography which is executed in parallel with the respond interaction and after the request interaction accordingly with the semantics.

Summarizing, the atomic request-respond interaction pattern on the one hand has the right granularity level for expressing the alignment property and on the other hand it lacks expressiveness.

4 Conclusions

In this paper we have presented the formal semantics of a significant fragment of WS-CDL which provides a mean to deal with interactions. We have analysed the adequacy of such interaction patterns when the alignment property is considered by showing that the request-respond patterns do not represent the best choice. Indeed, the splitted one permits to align the single message exchange which, on the one hand allows to express not valid conversations and, on the other hand implements the not aligned property in a way which, in our opinion, does not address the nature of the alignment property. The atomic request-respond pattern on the contrary, provides the right level to reason about alignment but presents significant lacks of expressiveness (e.g. it is not possible to express that a certain conversation must be performed during the execution of a request-respond).

To the best of our knowledge, this is the first attempt towards the definition of interaction patterns in choreography when aligned property is considered. The only works which deal with choreography languages are [2] and [7]. In the former Web Service Choreography Interface (WSCI) [10] language is modeled whereas in the latter our formal language CL is presented.

CL, whose semantics is expressed in terms of CL_P, supports two interaction patterns where one is exactly the request of $WSCDL_{core}$ while the other one, used to program the request-respond, has a semantics which sounds like:

$$\mathtt{request}^A(\rho_A, \rho_B, o, \widetilde{x}, \widetilde{y}); C; \mathtt{respond}^A(\rho_A, \rho_B, o, \widetilde{z}, \widetilde{k})$$

such a pattern has the same granularity level of the atomic one of $WSCDL_{core}$ and covers some of its lacks of expressiveness. Indeed, it is trivial to verify that with this pattern it is possible to express an inner conversation between the request and the respond (example 1 of section 3.2). In light of these observations CL can be considered a good starting point for representing choreography.

As future works we intend to reason on other aspects of WS-CDL and at the same time to improve our formal language CL. Furthermore, we are interested to investigate the relationships which exist between the choreography approach and the orchestration one by introducing a notion of conformance between the two models starting by studying how the choreography alignment property affects a related orchestration.

References

1. Mario Bravetti, Claudio Guidi, Roberto Lucchi, and Gianluigi Zavattaro. Supporting e-commerce systems formalization with choreography languages. In *SAC*, pages 831–835, 2005.

2. A. Brogi, C. Canal, E. Pimentel, and A. Vallecillo. Formalizing web services choreographies. In M. Bravetti and G. Zavattaro, editors, *Proc. of 1st International Workshop on Web Services and Formal Methods (WS-FM 2004)*, volume 105 of *ENTCS*. Elsevier, 2004.
3. N. Busi, R. Gorrieri, C. Guidi, R. Lucchi, and G. Zavattaro. Towards a formal framework for Choreography. In *Proc. of 3rd International Workshop on Distributed and Mobile Collaboration (DMC 2005)*. IEEE Computer Society Press. To appear.
4. F. Leymann. Web Services Flow Language (WSFL 1.0). [http://www-4.ibm.com/software/solutions/webservices/pdf/WSFL.pdf], Member IBM Academy of Technology, IBM Software Group, 2001.
5. Microsoft,IBM, Siebel Systems, BEA. *Business Process Execution Language for Web Services Version 1.1.* [http://www-106.ibm.com/developerworks/library/ws-bpel/].
6. S. Thatte. XLANG: Web Services for Business Process Design. [http://www.gotdotnet.com/team/xml_wsspecs/xlang-c/default.htm], Microsoft Corporation, 2001.
7. W3C. *Web Services Choreography Description Language Version 1.0. Working draft 17 December 2004.* [http://www.w3.org/TR/2004/WD-ws-cdl-10-20041217/].
8. W3C. *Web Services Choreography Working Group, public mailing list.* public-ws-chor@w3.org.
9. W3C. *Web Services Description Language (WSDL) 1.1.* `http://www.w3.org/TR/wsdl`.
10. World Wide Web Consortium (W3C). Web service choreography interface (wsci) 1.0. [http://www.w3.org/TR/wsci], 2002.

Author Index

Lecture Notes in Computer Science

For information about Vols. 1–3564

please contact your bookseller or Springer

Vol. 3687: S. Singh, M. Singh, C. Apte, P. Perner (Eds.), Pattern Recognition and Image Analysis, Part II. XXV, 809 pages. 2005.

Vol. 3686: S. Singh, M. Singh, C. Apte, P. Perner (Eds.), Pattern Recognition and Data Mining, Part I. XXVI, 689 pages. 2005.

Vol. 3674: W. Jonker, M. Petković (Eds.), Secure Data Management. X, 241 pages. 2005.

Vol. 3672: C. Hankin, I. Siveroni (Eds.), Static Analysis. X, 369 pages. 2005.

Vol. 3671: S. Bressan, S. Ceri, E. Hunt, Z.G. Ives, Z. Bellahsène, M. Rys, R. Unland (Eds.), Database and XML Technologies. X, 239 pages. 2005.

Vol. 3670: M. Bravetti, L. Kloul, G. Zavattaro (Eds.), Formal Techniques for Computer Systems and Business Processes. XIII, 349 pages. 2005.

Vol. 3664: C. Türker, M. Agosti, H.-J. Schek (Eds.), Peer-to-Peer, Grid, and Service-Orientation in Digital Library Architectures. X, 261 pages. 2005.

Vol. 3663: W. Kropatsch, R. Sablatnig, A. Hanbury (Eds.), Pattern Recognition. XIV, 512 pages. 2005.

Vol. 3662: C. Baral, G. Greco, N. Leone, G. Terracina (Eds.), Logic Programming and Nonmonotonic Reasoning. XIII, 454 pages. 2005. (Subseries LNAI).

Vol. 3660: M. Beigl, S. Intille, J. Rekimoto, H. Tokuda (Eds.), UbiComp 2005: Ubiquitous Computing. XVII, 394 pages. 2005.

Vol. 3659: J.R. Rao, B. Sunar (Eds.), Cryptographic Hardware and Embedded Systems – CHES 2005. XIV, 458 pages. 2005.

Vol. 3654: S. Jajodia, D. Wijesekera (Eds.), Data and Applications Security XIX. X, 353 pages. 2005.

Vol. 3653: M. Abadi, L.d. Alfaro (Eds.), CONCUR 2005 – Concurrency Theory. XIV, 578 pages. 2005.

Vol. 3649: W.M.P. van der Aalst, B. Benatallah, F. Casati, F. Curbera (Eds.), Business Process Management. XII, 472 pages. 2005.

Vol. 3648: J.C. Cunha, P.D. Medeiros (Eds.), Euro-Par 2005 Parallel Processing. XXXVI, 1299 pages. 2005.

Vol. 3645: D.-S. Huang, X.-P. Zhang, G.-B. Huang (Eds.), Advances in Intelligent Computing, Part II. XIII, 1010 pages. 2005.

Vol. 3644: D.-S. Huang, X.-P. Zhang, G.-B. Huang (Eds.), Advances in Intelligent Computing, Part I. XXVII, 1101 pages. 2005.

Vol. 3642: D. Ślezak, J. Yao, J.F. Peters, W. Ziarko, X. Hu (Eds.), Rough Sets, Fuzzy Sets, Data Mining, and Granular Computing, Part II. XXIV, 738 pages. 2005. (Subseries LNAI).

Vol. 3641: D. Ślezak, G. Wang, M.S. Szczuka, I. Düntsch, Y. Yao (Eds.), Rough Sets, Fuzzy Sets, Data Mining, and Granular Computing, Part I. XXIV, 742 pages. 2005. (Subseries LNAI).

Vol. 3639: P. Godefroid (Ed.), Model Checking Software. XI, 289 pages. 2005.

Vol. 3638: A. Butz, B. Fisher, A. Krüger, P. Olivier (Eds.), Smart Graphics. XI, 269 pages. 2005.

Vol. 3637: J. M. Moreno, J. Madrenas, J. Cosp (Eds.), Evolvable Systems: From Biology to Hardware. XI, 227 pages. 2005.

Vol. 3636: M.J. Blesa, C. Blum, A. Roli, M. Sampels (Eds.), Hybrid Metaheuristics. XII, 155 pages. 2005.

Vol. 3634: L. Ong (Ed.), Computer Science Logic. XI, 567 pages. 2005.

Vol. 3633: C. Bauzer Medeiros, M. Egenhofer, E. Bertino (Eds.), Advances in Spatial and Temporal Databases. XIII, 433 pages. 2005.

Vol. 3632: R. Nieuwenhuis (Ed.), Automated Deduction – CADE-20. XIII, 459 pages. 2005. (Subseries LNAI).

Vol. 3629: J.L. Fiadeiro, N. Harman, M. Roggenbach, J. Rutten (Eds.), Algebra and Coalgebra in Computer Science. XI, 457 pages. 2005.

Vol. 3628: T. Gschwind, U. Aßmann, O. Nierstrasz (Eds.), Software Composition. X, 199 pages. 2005.

Vol. 3627: C. Jacob, M.L. Pilat, P.J. Bentley, J. Timmis (Eds.), Artificial Immune Systems. XII, 500 pages. 2005.

Vol. 3626: B. Ganter, G. Stumme, R. Wille (Eds.), Formal Concept Analysis. X, 349 pages. 2005. (Subseries LNAI).

Vol. 3625: S. Kramer, B. Pfahringer (Eds.), Inductive Logic Programming. XIII, 427 pages. 2005. (Subseries LNAI).

Vol. 3624: C. Chekuri, K. Jansen, J.D.P. Rolim, L. Trevisan (Eds.), Approximation, Randomization and Combinatorial Optimization. XI, 495 pages. 2005.

Vol. 3623: M. Liśkiewicz, R. Reischuk (Eds.), Fundamentals of Computation Theory. XV, 576 pages. 2005.

Vol. 3621: V. Shoup (Ed.), Advances in Cryptology – CRYPTO 2005. XI, 568 pages. 2005.

Vol. 3620: H. Muñoz-Avila, F. Ricci (Eds.), Case-Based Reasoning Research and Development. XV, 654 pages. 2005. (Subseries LNAI).

Vol. 3619: X. Lu, W. Zhao (Eds.), Networking and Mobile Computing. XXIV, 1299 pages. 2005.

Vol. 3618: J. Jedrzejowicz, A. Szepietowski (Eds.), Mathematical Foundations of Computer Science 2005. XVI, 814 pages. 2005.

Vol. 3617: F. Roli, S. Vitulano (Eds.), Image Analysis and Processing – ICIAP 2005. XXIV, 1219 pages. 2005.

Vol. 3615: B. Ludäscher, L. Raschid (Eds.), Data Integration in the Life Sciences. XII, 344 pages. 2005. (Subseries LNBI).

Vol. 3614: L. Wang, Y. Jin (Eds.), Fuzzy Systems and Knowledge Discovery, Part II. XLI, 1314 pages. 2005. (Subseries LNAI).

Vol. 3613: L. Wang, Y. Jin (Eds.), Fuzzy Systems and Knowledge Discovery, Part I. XLI, 1334 pages. 2005. (Subseries LNAI).

Vol. 3612: L. Wang, K. Chen, Y. S. Ong (Eds.), Advances in Natural Computation, Part III. LXI, 1326 pages. 2005.

Vol. 3611: L. Wang, K. Chen, Y. S. Ong (Eds.), Advances in Natural Computation, Part II. LXI, 1292 pages. 2005.

Vol. 3610: L. Wang, K. Chen, Y. S. Ong (Eds.), Advances in Natural Computation, Part I. LXI, 1302 pages. 2005.

Vol. 3608: F. Dehne, A. López-Ortiz, J.-R. Sack (Eds.), Algorithms and Data Structures. XIV, 446 pages. 2005.

Vol. 3607: J.-D. Zucker, L. Saitta (Eds.), Abstraction, Reformulation and Approximation. XII, 376 pages. 2005. (Subseries LNAI).

Vol. 3606: V. Malyshkin (Ed.), Parallel Computing Technologies. XII, 470 pages. 2005.

Vol. 3604: R. Martin, H. Bez, M. Sabin (Eds.), Mathematics of Surfaces XI. IX, 473 pages. 2005.

Vol. 3603: J. Hurd, T. Melham (Eds.), Theorem Proving in Higher Order Logics. IX, 409 pages. 2005.

Vol. 3602: R. Eigenmann, Z. Li, S.P. Midkiff (Eds.), Languages and Compilers for High Performance Computing. IX, 486 pages. 2005.

Vol. 3599: U. Aßmann, M. Aksit, A. Rensink (Eds.), Model Driven Architecture. X, 235 pages. 2005.

Vol. 3598: H. Murakami, H. Nakashima, H. Tokuda, M. Yasumura, Ubiquitous Computing Systems. XIII, 275 pages. 2005.

Vol. 3597: S. Shimojo, S. Ichii, T.W. Ling, K.-H. Song (Eds.), Web and Communication Technologies and Internet-Related Social Issues - HSI 2005. XIX, 368 pages. 2005.

Vol. 3596: F. Dau, M.-L. Mugnier, G. Stumme (Eds.), Conceptual Structures: Common Semantics for Sharing Knowledge. XI, 467 pages. 2005. (Subseries LNAI).

Vol. 3595: L. Wang (Ed.), Computing and Combinatorics. XVI, 995 pages. 2005.

Vol. 3594: J.C. Setubal, S. Verjovski-Almeida (Eds.), Advances in Bioinformatics and Computational Biology. XIV, 258 pages. 2005. (Subseries LNBI).

Vol. 3593: V. Mařík, R. W. Brennan, M. Pěchouček (Eds.), Holonic and Multi-Agent Systems for Manufacturing. XI, 269 pages. 2005. (Subseries LNAI).

Vol. 3592: S. Katsikas, J. Lopez, G. Pernul (Eds.), Trust, Privacy and Security in Digital Business. XII, 332 pages. 2005.

Vol. 3591: M.A. Wimmer, R. Traunmüller, Å. Grönlund, K.V. Andersen (Eds.), Electronic Government. XIII, 317 pages. 2005.

Vol. 3590: K. Bauknecht, B. Pröll, H. Werthner (Eds.), E-Commerce and Web Technologies. XIV, 380 pages. 2005.

Vol. 3589: A M. Tjoa, J. Trujillo (Eds.), Data Warehousing and Knowledge Discovery. XVI, 538 pages. 2005.

Vol. 3588: K.V. Andersen, J. Debenham, R. Wagner (Eds.), Database and Expert Systems Applications. XX, 955 pages. 2005.

Vol. 3587: P. Perner, A. Imiya (Eds.), Machine Learning and Data Mining in Pattern Recognition. XVII, 695 pages. 2005. (Subseries LNAI).

Vol. 3586: A.P. Black (Ed.), ECOOP 2005 - Object-Oriented Programming. XVII, 631 pages. 2005.

Vol. 3584: X. Li, S. Wang, Z.Y. Dong (Eds.), Advanced Data Mining and Applications. XIX, 835 pages. 2005. (Subseries LNAI).

Vol. 3583: R.W. H. Lau, Q. Li, R. Cheung, W. Liu (Eds.), Advances in Web-Based Learning – ICWL 2005. XIV, 420 pages. 2005.

Vol. 3582: J. Fitzgerald, I.J. Hayes, A. Tarlecki (Eds.), FM 2005: Formal Methods. XIV, 558 pages. 2005.

Vol. 3581: S. Miksch, J. Hunter, E. Keravnou (Eds.), Artificial Intelligence in Medicine. XVII, 547 pages. 2005. (Subseries LNAI).

Vol. 3580: L. Caires, G.F. Italiano, L. Monteiro, C. Palamidessi, M. Yung (Eds.), Automata, Languages and Programming. XXV, 1477 pages. 2005.

Vol. 3579: D. Lowe, M. Gaedke (Eds.), Web Engineering. XXII, 633 pages. 2005.

Vol. 3578: M. Gallagher, J. Hogan, F. Maire (Eds.), Intelligent Data Engineering and Automated Learning - IDEAL 2005. XVI, 599 pages. 2005.

Vol. 3577: R. Falcone, S. Barber, J. Sabater-Mir, M.P. Singh (Eds.), Trusting Agents for Trusting Electronic Societies. VIII, 235 pages. 2005. (Subseries LNAI).

Vol. 3576: K. Etessami, S.K. Rajamani (Eds.), Computer Aided Verification. XV, 564 pages. 2005.

Vol. 3575: S. Wermter, G. Palm, M. Elshaw (Eds.), Biomimetic Neural Learning for Intelligent Robots. IX, 383 pages. 2005. (Subseries LNAI).

Vol. 3574: C. Boyd, J.M. González Nieto (Eds.), Information Security and Privacy. XIII, 586 pages. 2005.

Vol. 3573: S. Etalle (Ed.), Logic Based Program Synthesis and Transformation. VIII, 279 pages. 2005.

Vol. 3572: C. De Felice, A. Restivo (Eds.), Developments in Language Theory. XI, 409 pages. 2005.

Vol. 3571: L. Godo (Ed.), Symbolic and Quantitative Approaches to Reasoning with Uncertainty. XVI, 1028 pages. 2005. (Subseries LNAI).

Vol. 3570: A. S. Patrick, M. Yung (Eds.), Financial Cryptography and Data Security. XII, 376 pages. 2005.

Vol. 3569: F. Bacchus, T. Walsh (Eds.), Theory and Applications of Satisfiability Testing. XII, 492 pages. 2005.

Vol. 3568: W.-K. Leow, M.S. Lew, T.-S. Chua, W.-Y. Ma, L. Chaisorn, E.M. Bakker (Eds.), Image and Video Retrieval. XVII, 672 pages. 2005.

Vol. 3567: M. Jackson, D. Nelson, S. Stirk (Eds.), Database: Enterprise, Skills and Innovation. XII, 185 pages. 2005.

Vol. 3566: J.-P. Banâtre, P. Fradet, J.-L. Giavitto, O. Michel (Eds.), Unconventional Programming Paradigms. XI, 367 pages. 2005.

Vol. 3565: G.E. Christensen, M. Sonka (Eds.), Information Processing in Medical Imaging. XXI, 777 pages. 2005.